AND THE Spurs GO MARCHING ON...

Glory, Glory, Hallelujah
Glory, Glory, Hallelujah
Glory, Glory, Hallelujah
And the Spurs go marching on

(to the tune of The Battle Hymn
of the Republic, *1865)*

AND THE Spurs GO MARCHING ON....

by Phil Soar

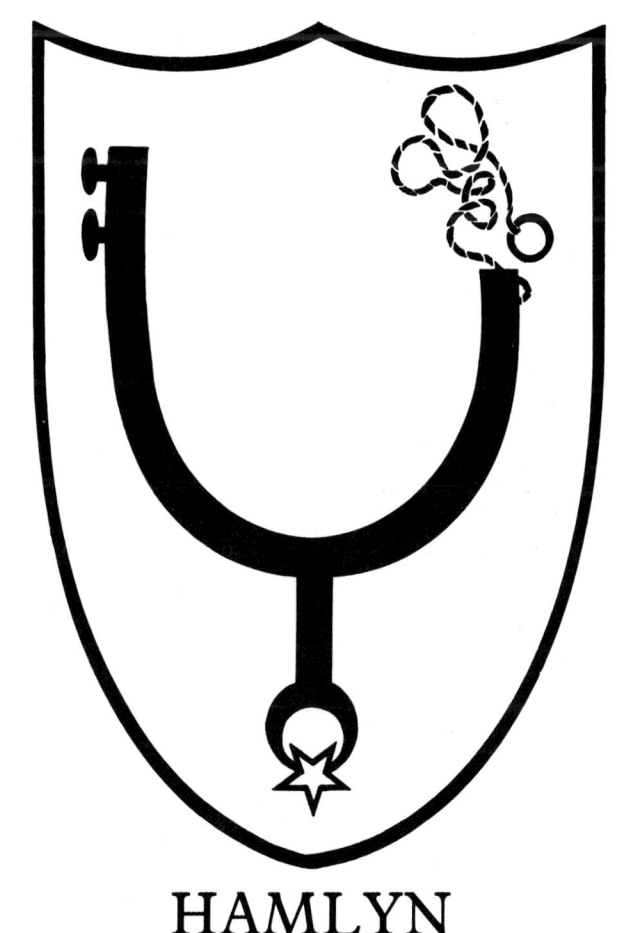

HAMLYN

The statistics were prepared by Ray Spiller, Chairman of the Association of Football Statisticians, with the assistance of the late Morley Farror, Alex Wilson, A. Porter and editorial back-up from Richard Widdows and Simon Moore.

Designed by Brian Thomas.

Additional text and contributions from Danny Blanchflower, Pat Collins, Jonathan Culverhouse and Martin Tyler.

Artwork by Paul Buckle.

Typesetting and reproduction by Erik Pordes of Imago Publishing, Thame High Street, Thame, Oxon.

Published 1982 by
Hamlyn Publishing
a division of The Hamlyn Publishing Group Limited
Bridge House, London Road, Twickenham, Middlesex

Revised edition 1985

ISBN 0 600 50175 2

Printed in Canary Islands

Larsa – D. L. TF.: 742 – 1985

It is sometimes said in Fleet Street that there are only four important football clubs in England – Arsenal, Liverpool, Manchester United and Spurs. Report on them, and worry about the rest later. True or false, it is certainly not a view that could have been expressed during the first seventy years of Tottenham Hotspur's existence. For not until the great days of push-and-run, of Ron Burgess, Alf Ramsey, Bill Nicholson, Eddie Baily and Arthur Rowe, did White Hart Lane really host a first rate club. Admittedly, Tottenham had already won the FA Cup twice (then so had Bury and Old Etonians) but it may come as a surprise to learn that, up to that time, Spurs had spent a mere fifteen seasons in the First Division.

It is the concentrated success of the past three decades that has made Tottenham Hotspur the name that is celebrated throughout the world today and, of course, those successes are almost all associated in one way or another with one man – Bill Nicholson. To call him the most significant figure in Spurs' history is pure understatement. It is surely doubtful whether, without him, Spurs would now boast their magnificent new stand or their place at the very pinnacle of the British game, and it is fruitless to speculate on what would have happened to the club had Ben Ives not sent his fateful letter to Mr and Mrs Nicholson on Leap Year's Day, 1936.

And yet, if it is ever possible to isolate a single occasion which changed and made a club's history, then for Spurs that moment probably came well before Bill Nicholson was even born.

On Saturday 27 April 1901, at Burnden Park and before the smallest Cup final crowd this century, Tottenham Hotspur became the only non-League club ever to win the FA Cup. This feat seems even more remarkable now than it did then for, at the time, the League had been in existence for just a dozen years and only retrospectively can we see that Tottenham were never a very good Southern League side anyway, not even passing the Cup quarter-final stage again until after the Great War.

When they applied for membership of the Football League in 1908 they were resoundingly rejected, coming fifth out of six in the ballot. And yet, by chance, an extra place appeared in the Second Division a month later when Stoke suddenly resigned. After three tied ballots, Spurs succeeded in taking Stoke's place, basically because of the kudos that the FA Cup win gave an otherwise mediocre side. Without it they would have remained a Southern League club at least until the Third Division was formed in 1920.

Hence they would almost certainly have been unable to build the side which won the 1921 FA Cup and, much more important, would have been less able to resist Arsenal's claim on North London support after the Gunners' move in 1913. If Highbury had had those extra seven years to establish itself as the home of the senior club in the area, then Spurs would quite possibly never have been able to rise above the level of a

Introduction
and acknowledgements

Fulham, Brentford or Orient.

This is, of course, all conjecture, though none the less interesting for that. There are moments in the histories of all football clubs when the hopes and the fears, the dreams and the ambitions must surely come together in a single match. In modern times, Spurs' most critical game, possibly excluding Cup finals, was at Molineux on 23 April 1960. Wolves were right on the verge of the Double and, had they beaten Spurs, would have become the first side this century to achieve it. But it was to be the scene of one of Tottenham's best-ever League performances. They held a team talk on the pitch before the game began and goals by Smith, Mackay and Jones led to a 3-1 victory. Wolves, like Manchester United in 1957, thus missed the Double by a single game. Danny Blanchflower says of that match at Molineux: "We had beaten the best of the rest, and done it in style; it was difficult to see who would stop us the following season." Had Wolves beaten Spurs that day, then Tottenham's Double would have meant so much less, because it would have duplicated Wolves' success of a year before. Such is the way history is made, with most of us no more than unwitting observers.

It is, of course, the Double and the unforgettable side of 1960–61 which have ensured Tottenham's position in British football history and legend. Even through the successes and style of the last three seasons, it is the Double that most of us instinctively think of when we hear the name Tottenham Hotspur. It is such a central part of the story that, to add to the chapter on 1961, we have decided to start the whole tale with those glorious days. Happily, it is a story told directly by one of the major participants – Danny Blanchflower.

It is virtually impossible for a single author to absorb everything in the hundred year history of a football club which, at time of writing, has won the FA Cup seven times, the Championship twice, European trophies three times, reached thirteen cup finals and fielded probably the greatest club side this country has ever seen. I make no apologies, therefore, for admitting that this history is a joint effort.

I should like to thank Danny Blanchflower for his introduction and his insights into the Double side and its era, Pat Collins for much of the material in the 1951 and 1961 chapters, Jonathan Culverhouse for the story of the club in the 1970s, Martin Tyler for his impressions of the club's victorious 1981 semi-final and FA Cup final and Ray Spiller for preparing the statistical appendix at the end of the book.

From the very beginning, everyone concerned with 'And the Spurs go marching on' was determined that it would be unlike any previously published club history. Never before has there been a complete chronological record of a first-class club's playing history. Nor has there ever been a year-by-year record of appearances, goalscorers, and league tables for a single club, allowing every fan to trace Spurs' complete story not only season-by-season but literally week-by-week. This massive undertaking was carried out by Ray Spiller, chairman of the Association of Football Statisticians and a Tottenham follower, with the help of the late Morley Farror, A. Porter, Alex. Wilson and Simon Moore. I must also mention Brian Thomas, art editor of the book, Peter Arnold, Tony Bagley and Linda Middleton at Hamlyn, and yet again offer my thanks to Jean Otway-Norwood and Angela Edwards-Jones for their continued support and patience.

'And the Spurs go marching on' has been written and produced on behalf of Tottenham Hotspur as their official Centenary publication and much of the inspiration and encouragement has come from the club. Many people concerned with Spurs assisted in its preparation. Club chairmen Sidney Wale and Arthur Richardson were always extremely helpful and willing to devote their time and energies to the project, as was commercial manager Mike Lewis. Keith Burkinshaw and Terry Neill both spoke freely of their time at White Hart Lane, though Mr Neill has asked us to say that the parts of the book concerning the 1970s are published without his agreement and approval. Bill Nicholson not only contributed memories and details of his time with the club, but also spent countless hours reading and correcting the manuscript so that it gives an accurate and thorough impression of those magnificent days. I must also mention Bob Gardam of TVS television, who originally proposed the idea of a fully illustrated, statistical work, and, in particular, Geoffrey Richardson, who originated the project when vice-chairman in 1979 and was the main source of encouragement at the club.

I feel I should add here that this is by no means the only history of Tottenham Hotspur, and that two earlier books, in particular, are invaluable. The club's then vice-chairman, G. Wagstaffe Simmons, wrote the first official history to celebrate 75 years of Spurs in 1946, and Julian Holland wrote by far the best history of the club ('Spurs') in 1954. Both contain a wealth of information on the early years and, because they were not illustrated and were written well before the great days of the early 1960s, 1970s and 1980s, both authors were able to devote more space to that earlier period.

The single largest problem the author of a club history faces is that he cannot tell everyone's story. This is a weakness but, I fear, an unavoidable one. Of necessity, the recollections here are largely those of the club's major actors – of Arthur Rowe, of Eddie Baily, of Danny Blanchflower, of Keith Burkinshaw, of Steve Perryman and, of course, of the most important of them all, Bill Nicholson. These are, however, the men who have made Tottenham the great club it has become since the Second World War. It is to them, and to all who have played for Spurs, that this book is dedicated. May the club they inspired go marching on. . . .

Phil Soar

Contents

FRONT ENDPAPER: *Focus on centre-forward Dave Dunmore as Bill Nicholson and Terry Medwin engage in a half-time debate in 1958.* BACK ENDPAPER: *The focus switches to manager and winger.*

ON PAGE 1: *The only picture known to exist of a Tottenham team in their old strip of chocolate and gold stripes. This was taken immediately after the club had turned professional at the end of 1895. Standing fifth from the left is club captain Stanley Briggs, while seated on the far right is Ernie Payne, whose problems with boots eventually led to the club being suspended by the London FA and, as a result, turning professional. These were the only two members of the first team who retained their places when the club began to pay players. Standing second from left is Ham (nicknamed Sam) Casey, one of the founders of the club and its secretary for most of the first twenty years. The strip was changed to the Preston colours of navy blue and white after an FA Cup tie at Deepdale on 27 January 1900.*

ON PAGE 3 (TITLE PAGE): *The first official club badge, a spur. After flirting briefly with both a large letter H and a Maltese cross, the spur was understandably adopted by the club, probably in 1887. In various forms it remained the symbol until 1909, when it was finally replaced by the cockerel (an association with cockspur) and the original bird and ball were placed on the old Main Stand. The spur design seen here is taken from an original blue and white shirt worn by first team member Hedley Bull in the late 1880s.*

PICTURES SUPPLIED BY:

Mick Alexander/Sportsimage 153, 155, 159, 167, 173, 177, 202; David Allen 37, 46; Danny Blanchflower 91, 94, 95, 96, 97, 100, 101, 104, 105, 120, 121, Endpiece; Hedley Bull 22, 26; Central Press 77, 88, 89, 109, 112, 113, 156, 197; Colorsport Jacket 54, 55, 139, 150, 179, 182, 183; Fox Photos 79, 80, 81, 93, 118; Ray Green 86, 87, 143, 147, 178; Hulton Picture Library Back Jacket 32, 39, 48, 49, 51, 52, 53, 56, 57, 59, 62, 63, 69, 70, 72, 73, 74, 189, 200; Keystone 83, 112; Marshall Cavendish 190; Popperfoto 85, 102, 103, 116, 117, 122, 124, 125, 126, 127; Press Association 126, 127, 141; Sport & General 9, 98, 127, 136, 137; Syndication International Jacket, Back Jacket 107, 114, 115, 122, 125, 130, 132, 133, 134, 138, 144, 148, 156, 157, 158; Bob Thomas 177, 180, 184; Hugh Wrampling 71; STW Jacket, Back Jacket, Title 21, 22, 23, 24, 25, 27, 28, 29, 30, 31, 32, 33, 34, 35, 36, 38, 40, 41, 42, 43, 44, 45, 47, 50, 51, 57, 59, 60, 61, 64, 65, 66, 67, 75, 76, 82, 98, 109, 110, 111, 113, 114, 115, 129, 160, 162, 163, 165, 166, 168, 169, 170, 171, 173, 174, 175, 186, 187, 189, 199, 200.

The Double and the Glory
by Danny Blanchflower

'*Football is not really about winning, or goals, or saves, or supporters . . . it's about glory. It's about doing things in style, doing them with a flourish; it's about going out to beat the other lot, not waiting for them to die of boredom; it's about dreaming of the glory that the Double brought.*'

The first time I heard their name was from a crystal radio set, back in the 1930s, when I was a kid growing up in Belfast...'TOTTEN-HAM HOTSPURS'. There was something special about them. They were not just City, United or Rovers. They were one of a small bunch with more appealing names like Forest, Villa, North End and Argyle. They were like far-away planets to me – out there somewhere, where distance lends enchantment.

In April 1949 I drifted nearer Hotspurs' orbit although that did not occur to me at the time. I had been transferred from Glentoran to Second Division Barnsley for £6,000. 'You'll not be sorry to join our club,' the Barnsley manager, Angus Seed, had told me.

Danny Blanchflower slots home Spurs' third and final goal in the 1962 FA Cup final as Spurs beat Burnley 3-1. Wembley the year before was the scene of Blanchflower's most celebrated bon mot. The Duchess of Kent noticed that the Leicester players had their names on the tracksuits and asked why Spurs did not: 'Ah well, mam,' replied the captain, 'you see we all know one another.'

I thought he was joking when I sat alone in a train compartment, trundling down through the slag heaps from Leeds to Barnsley, trying to resist the feeling that I was tumbling down a coal mine into some football oblivion. But hindsight was to prove Angus right. Barnsley was the start of 'The Yellow Brick Road' that led me to White Hart Lane.

If my dreams, before Barnsley, had come true then Glentoran would have transferred me to Wolves, or Arsenal, or another of the top English teams of the day, and I might never have made it. I had to learn the tricks of the trade and my nature demanded that I learn them thoroughly. I needed time and opportunity because, first, you must find the right questions before you find the right answers. And opportunity leads you to mistakes and mistakes hurt and hustle you to find the right way to do it. Then more time and opportunity will help you to do it right. They call it trial and error. The top teams of the day might not have suffered me through all this and might have brushed me aside. I could hold my own at Barnsley for a few years. They wanted me no more than I needed them.

In that 1949–50 season, in the Second Division, fate denied me something special. Injury and international duty kept me out of Barnsley's two league matches with stylish Spurs. I missed seeing the champions of our division that year. Some of my Barnsley teammates talked about the Spurs style but they had not recognised its details; it was a mystery to them. And even more so to me. I wondered what it was like as Spurs soared up into the First Division, up into a higher orbit again.

Some of the mysterious clouds evaporated the following season when Spurs won the League Championship. They were the big stars of radio and the words push-and-run were introduced to football. The commentators tried to explain it but they were talking through their hats. With television, a young pro might have been able to see the magic ingredients, but in a way radio was better than TV. Radio did not show you just the camera's angle to reduce the argument. It left a touch of mystery about the style and television does not know that all style must have a sense of mystery. Push-and-run was magic to me, although I had not yet seen it, and it had a distant influence on me while I was learning the trade at Barnsley.

In March 1951 I was transferred from Barnsley to Aston Villa in the First Division. And the following season, 1951–52, I came face to face with Spurs at White Hart Lane and Villa Park. They were very good indeed and they appealed to me more than any other team I had seen at the time. They beat us 2-0 in London and 3-0 in Birmingham. The next season, when I played against them again, they had lost their edge. Other teams were learning how to stop them and some of the vital links in the team were ageing. It is easier to stop something good than to create it. The rise and decline of push-and-run, the lesson that good things come to an end, was part of my education of football at the time.

I had polished up my individual ball skills at Barnsley and learned old tricks of the game from Raich Carter, Peter Doherty and Jimmy Hagen, who were all around Yorkshire at the time. Then I had been transferred into a long

ball game at Villa Park, learning its strengths and weaknesses in a team which always preferred to play long. And playing against Tottenham's shorter push-and-run game had given me something else to think about.

All these parts were playing upon my instincts during the 1953–54 season. How could I mix them up and apply them successfully? I tried to persuade some Villa players to co-operate in training with me but they could feel no urge to change. Why should they? They were regular first team players, comfortable with their own familiar habits. And Villa were one of the all time greats, a big club with famous traditions. Just being at Villa was a privilege itself. I was a banana case, wanting to change things, a round peg in a square hole.

Was I out of order or were they lacking ambition? I sat in the huge Villa dressing-rooms thinking about that and wondering what the old Villa giants of the past had been like. Then I wandered down the corridors at Villa Park, peering at the old framed pictures on the walls, sniffing the ghosts of yesterday. And then, reluctantly, I realised I was living in the past – somebody else's past...In September 1954 I wrote a transfer request and put it in an envelope. No one would take it from me. The manager, the secretary, the assistant secretary kept their hands behind their backs. They knew what was in the envelope and nobody wanted to be the bearer of bad news. I had to post it.

The Villa board tried to persuade me to stay, and then put a £40,000 fee on my head. It was front page news, twenty per cent up on the previous record. Everybody seemed to be talking about it, except me. The newspapers revealed that Arsenal and Spurs had both bid £28,000. The Midland opinion was that the Londoners had ganged up to deny Villa the proper price. One morning I was summoned to the Villa offices. 'Come with me,' said the secretary, 'Mr Whittaker, the Arsenal manager, wants to see you.'

A taxi took us out to the home of the Villa chairman where Mr Whittaker was waiting. He told me he wanted me to come to Arsenal and I agreed. 'The transfer fee is crazy,' he said, 'but they will come to their senses and we'll outbid any other club.'

The next morning I was summoned to the Villa offices again. 'What's going on?' the Villa secretary, Billy Smith, asked me with narrow eyes. 'Are you looking for extra money?'

'No,' I answered firmly.

'Oh, well...' he dismissed it, 'I was just going to tell you how to go about it.' And as he turned and headed for his own office he told me that Arthur Rowe was waiting for me in the snooker room.

Arthur Rowe had said hello to me the previous season after an international match at Swansea where Ron Burgess had been playing for Wales. Nothing more. I hardly knew him but, of course, I knew about him. It was a distant respect. And I wondered why the Villa secretary had called him Arthur Rowe while he had called the Arsenal manager Mr Whittaker? I, myself, had done the same. Arsenal and Villa were the old noble clubs of the game, with similar traditions. Spurs, though they had won honours long before

Arsenal, were sort of upstarts with that fancy push-and-run business. Mr Whittaker had met me at the chairman's home. Arthur Rowe was waiting for me in the snooker room.

Arthur Rowe won me over by talking more about football than transfer details. He was such a down to earth man, sincere and honest, too modest to expect anyone to call him anything but Arthur. 'You will like it at Spurs,' he told me, 'where it's still football for football's sake.' I told him I had promised Mr Whittaker that I would go to Highbury and they would outbid everyone. 'That's alright,' he said, 'but we are not out of it yet. I just want to know if you will come to Spurs if we beat Arsenal to a deal with Villa?'

I said I would and forgot about it. A couple of weeks later a damaged knee, which had delayed the negotiations, seemed better and I played for Villa against Cardiff City. That was early in December 1954 and the following Wednesday I travelled to London to have lunch with the Northern Ireland team who were playing a friendly with The Army at Highbury. I never reached Highbury. When I arrived at the London hotel for lunch my younger brother Jackie greeted me with a smile.

'Hey, kid,' he said, 'you've just been transferred to Tottenham.' He had answered a phone call for a "Mr Blanchflower".

'Eric here,' a voice had told him, 'you've been transferred to Spurs.' Jackie realised it was Eric Houghton, the Villa manager, at the other end of the phone.

'I'm sorry, Eric,' he said, 'you've got the wrong one.' (meaning brother).

'Oh, no,' Eric argued, 'Arsenal would not meet our price,' misunderstanding him.

A few minutes later Arthur Rowe phoned me at the hotel and told me Arsenal would not go beyond £28,000. Spurs had agreed to pay £30,000. Arthur had persuaded his directors that a future captain was worth another £2,000. And he asked me to be ready to jump into his taxi to avoid press interference when it arrived at the hotel.

It did not give me much time to think about my transfer. Mr Whittaker had not kept his promise to outbid any opposition. Nor had he explained it to me. Arthur Rowe had been right. Spurs were not out of it. But I had heard stories that Spurs were a mean club. I would have to ask Arthur about that. The stories were rumours, he told me, and perhaps there was some truth in them. But he thought they were no worse than the usual rumours about every club. It was just that Spurs somehow, probably unluckily, became more public victims of their own silly deeds than most. Most clubs were silly at times. He thought he was fairly well established as manager but would not like to make false promises about that. If I joined him at Spurs perhaps that would strengthen his hand. He hoped we could build another good team together.

Then he was a bit hesitant. 'Would you mind having that injured knee examined by our specialist?' he asked. 'No,' I said, and we went to have it examined. We finished up in Newman Street, W1, in the offices of Headlam & Sims, a boot and shoe manufacturer which had made a popular football boot with Arthur Rowe's name on it. That is where I signed the forms to become a Spur.

TO WHITE HART LANE

The Championship team of 1951 was falling apart and Arthur was trying to rebuild at the time. Ron Reynolds was becoming a regular in goal, Mel Hopkins was at left-back, Harry Clarke at centre-half, Tony Marchi at left-half; Johnny Gavin at outside-right, Duquemin at centre-forward, Baily and George Robb on the left wing and Johnny Brooks at inside-right, with Alf Ramsey behind me at right-back. Alf was the captain and we struck a good patch just after I arrived. We battled through the early rounds of the FA Cup with some style; and hopes were rising when we were drawn away to York City in the fifth round.

A tricky day lay in wait for us at York. The icy pitch was unpredictable and suited the less cultured style of the home team. They beat us 3-1 and the atmosphere was thick with remorse on the way back to London, the worst atmosphere I had ever known in a football club. It was a bitter blow for Arthur Rowe and it did me no good. I had lived long in the aftermath of success at Villa Park and now it was clear I had missed it again at Spurs. But this time I had moved in nearer the glory. I was rubbing shoulders with some of the players who had shared it – Ditchburn, Ramsey, Clarke, Duquemin and Baily. I could still see the shadow of the glory and I could sense it retreating. I followed in its wake, trying to understand it as it drifted off, leaving broken hearts behind.

Arthur Rowe took ill. The news of his breakdown surprised me because I was still travelling down from Birmingham on match days only. Arthur was a genuinely decent man with a deep understanding of the game and its players and I wondered what conflicts undermined him. He had been the main agent in Spurs push-and-run success and their first ever League Championship. Now, under pressure, he retired quietly and almost invisibly like the glory itself. And I was left in a sort of no-man's-land because he had been the main reason for my joining Spurs. And I heard that some of the directors had said that he had made a mistake in buying me. I had not, it seemed, strengthened his hand.

I moved down from Birmingham and became more familiar with White Hart Lane. At first sight it was not as impressive as Villa Park. It was surrounded by houses, shops, pubs and factories. The front office looked medieval and there was not the same sense of space in the stadium as at Villa Park. Then gradually I learned that familiarity with it bred respect. On match days, with the crowd all around, it was the most lively and exhilarating stadium I have ever known.

The fans were hard to please. But so was I, and I hoped I could find a style that would please us both. But after Arthur Rowe left the climate turned again at White Hart Lane. Jimmy Anderson became the manager and the responsibilities were a burden for him. He had given the club years of loyal service on the scouting side and had earned the reward. He had run the show during the war when circumstances were entirely different but his appointment now was too late. One of the first things Jimmy did was to drop Alf Ramsey and make me the captain. I was embarrassed because I thought Ramsey had at least another year to go. He was left out of the summer tour to Hungary and when we returned for training in July 1955 he had gone off to Ipswich as manager.

We started the new season badly with three points from seven matches. It was a time of change and uncertainty. Maurice Norman joined the club from Norwich in November, playing at full-back, and Eddie Baily moved out to Port Vale. Then Bobby Smith joined us from Chelsea. Jimmy Anderson was doing what he did best, bringing new talent to the club. But he had no great instinct or experience for handling that talent.

These days were not great ones for Spurs but they were better days than for most other clubs. Arthur Rowe had left some valuable footprints behind him, good standards and modern habits with a sense of style. Push-and-run was still around, although familiarity had bred some contempt for it. The new players coming to the club could not change the team's traditional style. They came in ones or twos and had to fit in with the habits of the majority. That is how clubs maintain a discernable style over decades. They picked up the habits of push-and-run and adapted them to suit their own ability. And sometimes I used to think that our style flattered some of the average players at the club, that it made them look better than they might have looked somewhere else.

After Maurice Norman and Bobby Smith settled in at White Hart Lane the team looked more settled too. The Double side was assembling – now we were gradually moving towards our own moments of glory. But as we approached the FA Cup in the early months of 1956 we had a problem at outside-right. In the third round we beat Boston United 4-0 with Micky Dulin there. In the fourth round Dave Dunmore was at outside-right when we beat Middlesbrough 3-1. In the fifth round at Doncaster Tommy Harmer was on the right wing. This looked the best bet to me. Tommy played deep on the wing, dragging the full-back into deep waters while Johnny Brooks, at inside-right, advanced into space behind the full-back. This confused our opponents' defence and helped us to a 4-0 win at Chelsea before our sixth round tie with West Ham at White Hart Lane.

The quarter-final with West Ham was to prove one of the most critical days in my ten years with Spurs. In a tense derby atmosphere they were leading 3-1 when I sent Maurice Norman up from right-back to centre-forward in the last twenty minutes. I had noticed he was making their defence anxious when he had been going up for corner-kicks with big Harry Clarke. A big centre-forward can make most defences shake and Maurice helped us to come back and draw 3-3.

The newspapers said I was a genius, the hero of the revival, Jimmy Anderson looked relieved, and the directors had nothing to complain about when we won the replay 2-1, thanks to Tommy Harmer on the right-wing. We were on our way to a semi-final of the FA Cup. We hedged around a bit in a couple of unimportant league matches and on the Tuesday before the semi-final Tommy Harmer was chewing his finger nails with anxiety when I arrived in the dressing-room.

'I've been dropped for the semi-final,' he said.

'How do you know that?' I asked.

'Jimmy Anderson didn't speak to me this morning when I said hello to him,' he said sadly.

I dismissed this as fantasy but later in the morning I began to believe it. Bill Nicholson was coaching Alfie Stokes through some right-wing manouvres. Then Jimmy Anderson called me off the field to tell me he was thinking of playing Alfie Stokes at outside-right in the semi-final.

'What about Tommy?' I asked.

'He's not strong enough to resist tough tackling and semi-finals are rough matches,' he said. I kept my thoughts to myself. Johnny Brooks and I had reached an understanding with Tommy on the right wing. Now we were going to forsake that for something tough looking.

I felt sorry for Tommy. His football skills were magic. He had grown up in the street games of London's East End, without speed or strength or stamina worth talking about. He had survived by his skills alone. Now he was an outcast again. It was almost as if he had been born in a foreign land, like a Brazilian or a Hungarian with all the super skills we liked to talk about. But if those skills belong to one of our lads it's funny how suspicious we become of their true merit. The Barbarians of Europe, they call us.

Tommy was a beloved outcast – to be given some consideration when we needed him and then too easily dismissed. How perceptive he had been about being dropped for the semi-final. The manager had not spoken to him. Perhaps Tommy had the same doubts in his own mind. He had lived with it all his football days. A magician with beautiful and unpredictable skills that could lead him into a disappearing act.

What sort of team was it that could not carry Tommy Harmer, and who could predict the day when his skills would not work? The doubts were coming to the surface – although we had to believe there were none. We wanted to hide them. You do not go to a semi-final talking about your doubts when fate has already been kind to you. It is the hopes you express and want to happen.

On Wednesday night Alfie Stokes played at outside-right in the reserve team, and, on Thursday morning, Jimmy Anderson told me he had decided to play Dave Dunmore at outside-right for the semi-final. I led the Spurs out onto the Villa pitch that I knew so well on 17 March 1956; St Patrick's Day, not to be a lucky day for this Irishman. It was a dull, tense semi-final and Dave Dunmore looked completely lost on the right-wing. He was a centre-forward by habit and desire with an excellent right-foot, but he could be terribly erratic and completely lose confidence. Manchester City, our opponents, had scored in the first half but they looked as bad as we did. With fifteen minutes to go I sent Maurice up front again and played with six forwards and no full-back. What had we to lose except my scalp?

George Robb had a chance when he dummied Bert Trautmann on the edge of City's box. All he had to do was kick the ball into the empty goal but Trautmann grabbed both of George's legs and the officials turned a blind eye to it all. Jimmy Anderson charged into our gloomy dressing-room and turned on me: 'You shouldn't have done that,' he complained. 'My directors are asking what is going on and who gave you the authority to change the team.' I was old enough to know that bad losers always look for a scapegoat. 'Why didn't they ask you that when we drew with West Ham?' I said, 'All I was doing was trying to win.'

Jimmy understood my point but he could not agree with it. Irate fans and directors had humiliated him. If you want to be smart you have to win. The media climbed all over me. They said I had lost the match by changing the team. Nobody seemed to consider that I had changed the team because we were losing the match.

Five weeks later I was in more trouble. We were trying to escape relegation. At half-time we were a goal in front of Huddersfield Town, who were also in trouble. Half way through the second-half Ron Reynolds came out for a harmless cross which Maurice Norman headed back into the empty net. Then their centre-forward, Dave Hickson, miskicked the ball so badly it swerved into the net from an almost impossible angle. Tony Marchi pleaded with me to let him go up front and how could I deny my own beliefs? Jimmy Anderson dashed into the dressing-room again.

'I've told you not to change the team,' he snapped.

'It was my fault, Jimmy,' Ron Reynolds intervened.

'Don't tell me who's fault it was,' Jimmy argued. I apologised to him and persuaded Ron not to interfere. 'We'll talk about it later,' Jimmy said and then rushed off.

When the other results came through, we needed one point from two matches – away to Cardiff City and at home to Sheffield United – to escape the drop. 'When we get that point,' I told Ron Reynolds, 'I'll hand in the captaincy.' The conflict continued. Jimmy left me out of the next game – probably to stop me changing the team. He said I was injured, I said I didn't know I was injured because he hadn't told me. The Press got hold of it inadvertently and, in the end, I asked him to appoint someone else as captain.

The world of football is a conflict between the individual and the team. And the road to glory is littered with sacrificial lambs. First you develop your own natural skills, like Tommy Harmer. Then you have to compromise by fitting them in, in some way, with the team. But the team changes as players get old and others drift away. Now you have to adjust some more to suit different players. Then, if you learn all that business, you might become a captain. But you cannot become a good captain if you do not learn some more. And you cannot do that without the authority to match your responsibility, without doing something, trial and error, and all that.

It was never my idea to muck about with the team. That was the manager's job. But in FA Cup matches, and certain relegation games, the immediate result is more important than these sort of principles. Here was the dilemma. Did you sit tight and go down, waiting for a distant command that rarely came; or did you get up and try something? Most of the captains of my day did nothing. I was lucky. I was captain of the Northern Ireland team when Peter Doherty was manager, the most positive man I've ever met. He encouraged me to take responsibility and chances on the field when we had nothing to lose.

This conflict was not Jimmy Anderson's fault, nor was it Spurs. Conformity has a compelling hold on its people. They like it. It suits them. They don't like to change until they can see that it works for somebody else. They do not understand change and therefore conformity is right for them.

I tell these stories not because I regard my career as central to what happened in the 1960–61 season, but because they illustrate a point that has to be made about a successful football club. I'm sure the other members of the Double team could tell of their own ups and downs. Great teams and great victories don't come out of nothing. They have to be worked for. I had been playing first class football for 15 years when we won the Double, Bill Nick had been at Tottenham a quarter of a century. It can take that long to get it right. You learn from experience, from good experiences and success, yes, but basically from failure, because that makes you think. Everything that happened to me at Glentoran, Barnsley, Villa and Tottenham contributed to that Double, as did all Bill Nick's years coaching in the army, playing under Arthur Rowe and gradually building his team. It took us a long time to become an overnight sensation.

We were not a bad side in the mid-1950s, but we didn't win anything. The seasons came and went and I was happy to serve under Harry Clarke, John Ryden and Tony Marchi. I was a bit tired after the 1958 World Cup campaign in Sweden, when Northern Ireland got to the quarter-finals, and Spurs started the 1958–59 season badly with three points from seven games again. We had finished second and third in the two previous seasons and hoped to go to the top. Now we were being revealed. Finishing second had been our peak. Now we were sliding down again.

Jimmy Anderson took ill, like Arthur Rowe had done, and suddenly he had gone. The way both of them had left bothered me; they suddenly disappeared out of the back door. Bill Nicholson became the manager. We scored ten goals against Everton at White Hart Lane on his first match as the Boss. 'Well done,' I said to him, 'it can only get worse.' Bill tried everything to stop the rot. I had been playing below standard and I was banished to the stiffs (the reserves) and new experiences like the day we played at Tunbridge Wells. 'I suppose it'll be all ticket' I was reported (not entirely accurately) as saying when I heard.

Bill Nick told me he wanted to tighten up the defence, with a defensive wing-half to balance Jim Iley's attacking style. I could not argue about that. I was thirty three and Jim was younger. Then Nick said he might use me as an inside-forward. I told him I had all that experience at wing-half and if I was not better than Jim Iley it was too late to change position. I suggested he might want to transfer me. He did not hesitate. He was definitely against that and would not agree to it if I put in a request. That helped me to realise that he knew I was better than Iley.

I did play a couple of matches at inside-forward for the first team but the service I got from behind was a joke to an old pro. If Nick did not see that quickly he was not the quality half-back he used to be. He was just horsing around with that trial and error business to find his own way of shaping a team and, all the time, it was coming closer.

On 2 March 1959 we travelled up to Wolverhampton; we were on the brink of relegation and Wolves needed the points for the Championship. Bill Nicholson had not come up with us for some reason. Bobby Smith had been the captain, taking over from John Ryden, who had fallen into the reserve team for a while. But Bobby was hurt and not likely to play that night. The doubts were coming to the surface again and we had a vital match.

Bill arrived about 6pm and hustled us into a private room in the hotel to announce the team and give us a talk. It was Hollowbread, Baker and Hopkins; myself, Norman and Ryden; Harmer, Brooks, Medwin, Dunmore and Jones. Then he said he was making me the permanent club captain and that the players should all respect my position. 'We'll talk about your authority later,' he said, in front of them all.

Obviously Bill had spent the day thinking things over and now he had made a positive decision. He had recognised my experience as an attacking wing-half and an international captain. We were as good as the champions that night and took home a valuable point. And the following Saturday we thrashed Leicester City, another relegation contender, 6-0 and chased away all thoughts of going down.

Bill Nick had decided to build around me. By doing that he had cleared the undergrowth to see what we really needed to make a great team. And he went out to look for a wing-half to partner me. There was talk about Mel Charles choosing Arsenal instead of Spurs. Just the opposite of what fate had done for me all those years ago. Then Nick came back with Dave Mackay and surprised us all. No one thought Hearts would ever let him go. Dave played in one of the Easter fixtures for the first time at White Hart Lane. I could see right away that we would suit one another. Even though he was still suffering the healing pains of a broken foot.

'I'm not fit,' he apologised, 'but wait until next season.'

We finished that season six points clear of relegation and went East to Russia on a close season tour in the summer of 1959. It was my fifth year at the club, and I recalled how I had come in at the wrong end of the glory, and how I had tried to analyse the back side of success as it had drifted away from White Hart Lane, leaving the broken hearts behind.

Of course I had seen the other side of it, with the Irish team in the World Cup finals. But that was a smaller rainbow, with lesser expectations, its glory a lesser carat. Now I could sense it coming again, with more variety and a stronger mix. Dave Mackay would bring the best out of Cliff Jones on the left wing. Cliff had been signed by Jimmy Anderson in February 1958 while still in the army. Then he had broken a leg at the start of the following season and had come back into a struggling team. We had not seen the best of him before but now he was looking great.

Mel Hopkins was injured during the same season as Jonesy and Ron Henry had taken his chance at full-back with some style. Ron Reynolds, our keeper, had been very reliable but kicks around the head had hindered his eyes and he was wearing contact lenses. Games under floodlights could be a nightmare for him; occasionally we'd find him groping in completely the wrong place for a long shot coming out of the lights. Bill Nicholson decided it was time to sign another keeper and he bought Bill Brown from Dundee in June 1959. After that he bought Tony Marchi back from Italy and sold Jim Iley to Nottingham Forest. Now we had a formidable squad with cover in vital positions and competition for places. It was possible we could do great things.

We started the 1959–60 season with a 5-1 win at Newcastle and had an unbeaten run of twelve matches. The names in the team were beginning to rhyme...Brown, Baker and Henry; Blanchflower, Norman, Mackay; Medwin, Harmer, Smith, Brooks and Jones. Tony Marchi was twelfth man and Dave Dunmore moved in and out of the forward line. The team was holding up, more stable than it had been before in my time with the club. A winning team picks itself.

On the first Saturday of October, Mackay, Brown and myself went to Belfast for the Northern Ireland v Scotland match. Scotland won comfortably with some new faces in their team. John White was the one that impressed me most. On Monday morning, when I returned to White Hart Lane, Bill Nick was waiting for me.

'What about John White?' he asked.

'First class,' I said, 'good positional sense and smooth ball control.'

'I can get him for £20,000,' he said.

'Don't miss the first plane,' I said.

Bill had it all arranged. He just wanted confirmation. John White was signed before the day was out. John and Tommy Harmer became the regular inside-forwards. We played some dazzling football but we were still a bit goal-shy. The fabric was not yet complete. In December 1959 Bill Nicholson exchanged Johnny Brooks for Les Allen from Chelsea. Les was a second centre-forward for us with an unobtrusive style for scoring goals, a silent killer who was always better than he appeared to be. Though his name is always remembered as one of the great Double side, in fact he played in the first team for only two seasons. With Les in the team, John White moved to outside-right.

For a spell I had John and Tommy Harmer on my flank and we revelled in combinations of collective skills. Sometimes we indulged too much but the crowd loved it. But Peter Baker, our right back, didn't – he was the one who had to solve the problems if it all broke down. 'You're giving me nightmares,' he used to complain.

At this time I began to believe we could do the Double. It was a judgement of instinct and experience. I had seen Manchester United just miss it in the 1957 Cup final when Ray Wood, their keeper, had been clobbered in the early stages of the match by Peter McParland. They had won the League by eight clear points. I remembered that well because we were second, with a frankly mediocre Spurs team.

I told some of our players that I thought we could do it. 'Oh yes,' they said, as if they did not disbelieve it, or maybe they didn't know what I was talking about. Then I mentioned it to Bill Nick. He looked at me cautiously, as if it were another of my fancy ideas. Then he surprised me. 'I was thinking about that myself,' he said.

We agreed that we all had to believe in it to do it. We must create the right atmosphere. Bernard Joy, then with the *Evening Standard*, heard about it.

'You really think it can be done?' he asked me.

'Yes,' I said, 'and you can quote me.'

After beating Newport County in the third round we were drawn against Crewe Alexandra in the fourth. When we arrived there the town was buzzing with excitement. People packed the pavements and hung out of windows. It was like raiding a bee-hive. The pitch was frosty and I had an old uneasy feeling. It reminded me of York in my first Cup tie for Spurs back in 1955. We played too cautiously and were glad to come away with a 2-2 draw. We beat them 13-2 in the replay at White Hart Lane, Tottenham's record win. Then the Double bubble burst.

Blackburn Rovers beat us in the next round at White Hart Lane. They deserved the win. They caught us on a bad day. But we were still top of the League. We could concentrate on that. Wolves and Burnley were chasing us. It was touch and go. Then we lost at Bolton and Luton took a point from us, and a touch of thoughtlessness showed itself again. The club refused to release our Scottish players for the match against England at Hampden. The League clubs had to release their English players but not the Scots. The Scottish press went mad and Tottenham were the Mr Nasties of football. They had even declined the use of a new League rule that permitted the club to rearrange the fixture with two players called up for international duty.

I was angry about it at the time. If they had refused me permission to play for Northern Ireland then I would not have played on that same day for the club. These thoughts were in our minds when we went up to Goodison Park and lost to Everton, a useful team at the time. We restored our championship chances with a win at Chelsea in the first of our three Easter fixtures. But we threw it away again by losing the other two to Manchester City and Chelsea, both at White Hart Lane. These were a couple of flukey results which I put down to bad luck at the time.

Later I realised they had some significance. It was fate that was testing us to prove we were good champions, rather than lucky ones. I was already in my sixth year at Spurs, in search of glory. They had been six years of ups and downs, comings and goings, captain and non captain, and sometimes an outcast. We had been climbing a mountain to reach the peak. The higher you climb the harder it gets to keep your foothold. We had lost our foothold again by losing those two Easter home games. Perhaps because we had not been so close before as a team. The air was a little too rare for us; but it would help us to become acclimatised if we could learn something from it.

Wolves were leading the table when we travelled up there the following Saturday. They had also won through to the Cup final. Was the Double to be theirs and not ours? We dominated the match at Molineux with a comfortable 3-1 win. It was the confidence and style of our play that reassured me that we could do the Double first. We had made Wolves look old fashioned that day and taught them that we were the new masters of the British style. Looking back it was a vital game for us to win. Had we lost Wolves would have done the Double and the glory that came to White Hart Lane would have been so much the less for being a repeat of Wolves' success.

We beat Blackpool at White Hart Lane in our last match of that season and then listened for the other results, just in case. Wolves had won and they were a point ahead of us and Burnley – but Burnley had a game in hand. They won it on the Monday night, Wolves went to Wembley for the Cup final knowing their Double was no longer possible. It was still open for grabs.

'I am sure we can do the Double this season,' I told Mr Bearman, the chairman, on the first day of training in July 1960. In our last match at Wolverhampton we had been clearly better than the best of the competition and this was the base of my confidence. Now we had to prove it. Mr Bearman said he thought we would too. 'That's it,' I answered him, 'if we all keep crying "Wolf" then one day it'll happen.'

GLORY, GLORY SEASON

I was 34 years of age, the years of reckoning for most players. But I felt fitter and stronger and more mature than ever. I had been chosen by the press after the 1958 World Cup finals for a selected World team. I had improved since then and I was ready to show it. Of course there were the usual doubts of luck and injury and bad days at the wrong time. There always are. You only have to lose once in the Cup. But experience helps you to handle them. And I was impressed with the growing ability of the players in our squad and how the challenge from one another in practice was urging us all on and all the time improving our teamwork.

The players were obsessed with football for football's sake, as Arthur Rowe had told me when he signed me for Spurs. Jones and White and Mackay and Harmer and Dyson were constantly competing with one another, throwing small coins up in the air, catching them on their foot, flicking them up onto their forehead and then nodding the coin back into their pocket. They would do the same at hotels with oranges, sometimes standing on restaurant tables even, and they continued to improvise and improve with these games.

Jonesy would sometimes challenge me to do it. 'Look son,' I would tell him, 'when you can do that with a coin and a ball at the same time then come and see the old pro.' He loved that.

So we talked about the Double. Even the fates seemed in our favour. Spurs had won the Cup in 1901 and 1921. They had won the Championship in 1951. It helped us to believe we could win them both. Everybody welcomes a prediction of fate in their favour. It can influence the thoughts of a whole neighbourhood and when people believe something can happen they can make it happen. A little encouragement can go a long way.

We won our first eleven matches to break the record. Then we dropped a home point to Manchester City and won the next four games. Sixteen matches, one lost point, and all exciting affairs with a high degree of attacking skills. Then we lost 2-1 in a dull match at Sheffield Wednesday, the defenders of the day. And the critics said we were about to crack. We cracked alright. We lost a point at home to Burnley and then won our next seven games. Then we slept through a narrow 3-2 win against Charlton in the third round of the Cup. And on the following Monday night we lost a tough, physical match against Manchester United at Old Trafford by 2-0. It was our second defeat in 27 matches.

'SPURS LOSE AGAIN,' one newspaper headline summed it up. We won another couple of League and Cup matches before Leicester City beat us at home. 'They'll never win the Double,' some Leicester players told the Press. They were such a mediocre team they had the right to believe that; after they had beaten us, we deserved to win nothing. If they had known that we would meet them in the Cup final, and that they would be the last hurdle, perhaps they would have been more circumspect.

As coincidence would have it, we had a League match at Villa Park the week before our fifth round Cup tie there with Villa. And the media wondered if Villa could get a psychological advantage to knock us out of the Cup by first winning the League match.

They tried very hard. Joe Mercer, the Villa manager, had decided to put me out of the game. One of his players shadowed me the whole match and showed me no mercy. And some of our players would not pass the ball to me because I was tightly marked. I took my shadow back into his own defence and advised John White to exploit the space I had left. At half time we could talk about it more.

'You're not giving me the ball,' I said. 'But you're marked,' the defenders protested. 'That's what Villa want! You're doing their job for them,' I argued. 'The solution is push-and-run isn't it? We're supposed to be good at that aren't we? Give it to me and run forward, and I'll knock it straight to you and then you go on with it.'

Even a shadow cannot stop a quick wall pass. My marker was frustrated and their whole plan fell apart. We beat them 2-1 in that tough, tense atmosphere and it was us who had the psychological advantage for the Cup tie. We won that comfortably 2-0 but the Press turned against us. Because there was not the same tension as in the first match they blamed us for disappointing the Villa crowd. You can win them all sometimes, but you can't please them all.

The *Daily Mail* accused us of going to play Sunderland in the sixth round with defensive tactics. A journalist, who had not spoken to me, quoted me liberally in revealing our defensive tricks. I suppose an attacking team today would cause the same suspicions. Sunderland, the old greats, had been lost in the Second Division for some years. Now they had a young team going twenty matches without defeat. They had roused their tremendous fans and national opinion was that Spurs would tumble at Roker Park.

We controlled the match with positive play in the first half. We scored a good goal and missed some easy chances. The crowd were very quiet. They had nothing to shout about. In the second-half Sunderland forced a corner. Suddenly the great Roker crowd awakened. All hell broke loose behind our goal. They shouted and whistled and screamed. The noise was unbearable. It penetrated my concentration. It was destroying the invisible links of understanding in our defence. Eighteen players were packed in our goal mouth. The ball flew in. There was a wild scramble and then the ball was scrambled over the bye line for another corner. The same again, and then yet another corner. The tension grew and the noise from the terracing was like a gale force wind. They scored from the fourth corner-kick and then the crowd invaded the pitch.

'Let them work it off,' I said to the ref, 'we don't mind.'

'Let's keep the ball up in their end of the pitch,' I told our players, 'It'll be another Wednesday night job.'

We had played the crowd at Roker Park. When we played the team at White Hart Lane we beat them 5-0. No single game stands out in the Double season, it wasn't that kind of triumph. But if you pushed me to name two matches that were significant I think I'd remember those two – Villa because of the tactics, and the fact that Joe Mercer revealed his hand a week too early, and Sunderland because of the crowd.

We lost at Cardiff the week before the semi-final of the Cup against Burnley at Villa Park. Despite press criticism I was not unhappy with a defeat at Cardiff. We were due to lose a match somewhere. Better at Cardiff than at Villa Park. Spurs had lost three semi-finals at Villa Park since the War. But this time we had the home dressing room, and Burnley had not won at Villa Park when I was a Villa player. I kidded Jimmy McIlroy of that. 'Maybe,' he replied, 'but we've never lost here in these shirts.' Burnley, of course, had to change when they went to Villa.

It was a good game and Burnley were a bit unlucky but, in the end, we deserved to win an exhausting match. After that we lost a home match to Newcastle and dropped a point at Fulham. Sheffield Wednesday, in second place, had closed the gap from ten points to four. At Easter we drew away again with three comfortable victories, learning the lesson of the previous season. Then we won at Birmingham and beat Sheffield Wednesday at White Hart Lane to clinch the League Championship with three matches still to play.

We eased up after the winning post, losing two of the three matches, and finishing with 66 points to equal Arsenal's record in 1931. We were 8 points clear at the top. Another win or two and it would probably have been an all-time record, but we were not thinking about records then. Our eyes were only on the Cup final.

I had played in all 42 League matches and all the Cup games, as well as International matches, and I had taken some stick in most of these. Every ambitious hatchet man was after me. I had a bruised foot and strained knee ligament as Cup final day approached.

All sorts of deals sprang out of the woodwork like worms. All sorts of people with wonderful schemes wanted to help the players. Most of them were like Sergeant Bilko. They wanted to help themselves, not the players, and their deals fell apart in the end. On top of all this my father was in hospital, very ill, fading away. I wondered what he would think of these activities and then I wondered whether he had the strength to care. On the Friday before the final we retreated to our north London hotel to escape all intrusions. That night, a bus took us into the West End for the late showing of 'The Guns of Navarone'. The idea was to help release the tension and return late enough to be tired enough to sleep soundly.

On Saturday morning I read in the *Daily Express* that I had spent the previous night telling the players jokes to keep their minds off the match. The *Daily Mail* said I looked tense and strained. In the TV build up for the final, the late Wally Barnes, Wales and Arsenal full-back and a commentator for the BBC, stood out on the pitch at the spot where he had been injured and carried off in the 1952 final.

There were still no substitutions in 1961 and Wally predicted another injury that could rob Spurs of the Double. At 5 minutes past 2pm we hung our coats in the Wembley dressing-room. It was quieter than White Hart Lane. But the time passed quickly and we walked up the tunnel and out onto the field. Whatever the fans thought, the Double wasn't yet in the bag. Leicester certainly stood far more chance of beating us than Aston Villa had been given of stopping United's Double four years before. The Duchess of Kent was first introduced to the Leicester players. Her handshake was frail as we shuffled along our team. Near the end of the line she turned to me and asked: 'The other team have their names on their suits?'

'Yes, mam,' I answered, 'but we all know one another.'

The talk was better than the match. It was a day that Spurs will be remembered for, but one I would rather forget. We played just well enough to beat Leicester City, and that was not all that good.

Wally Barnes' instincts had been right. He had just read them slightly wrong. Len Chalmers, the Leicester full-back, was carried off and Leicester's chances with him. It might have been the worst match the 1961 team played for Spurs but it was good enough to clinch the Double. Bad matches teach you more than good ones. This one confirmed that our team could play well below par, disappoint all our expectations, and still beat average teams like Leicester. Some people might call that 'coasting' or 'idling' or maybe 'rubbish'. But it is a part of a good professional's make-up that he can have a below average or plain bad day and still beat the average teams. The trick is to know your own capabilities, and to recognise a bad day when you see one, to ride along with it, taking less chances and minimising the errors. When you can do that you are a real pro.

At 2pm on Sunday we met at Tottenham Town Hall to meet the Mayor. 'There will be policemen every ten yards along the way,' he said. He was referring to the lap of honour we were due to ride down the Tottenham High Road from Edmonton Town Hall to Tottenham Town Hall.

'In that case,' one of us said, 'there'll be nothing but policemen.'

The High Road seemed empty when we travelled up it to Edmonton. We really didn't expect the sort of crowd that the big provincial clubs get. There was a queue at The Royal Dance Hall, but that was for the bingo. There was a small crowd to meet us at the Edmonton Town Hall, perhaps 2,000, but we thought that would be the lot.

We were surprised. At 3.30pm, when the open top, double decker bus left Edmonton Town Hall, all the roads were packed from one Town Hall to the other. I have never seen so many people crowding pavements, clinging to trees and hanging out of windows down the three mile route. What I particularly remember, funnily, was a small, round man in a white suit, heavily made up with what looked like actors' powder. He got on our bus and waved to the crowd the whole way. None of us knew who he was, and I don't think anyone ever asked.

At The Royal Dance Hall the band was out on the balcony, adding to the jazz. It was a day that summed up the whole season for me. Here was the real glory. The trust and respect of the fans in their team, for a season of skill and style and crowds, and the triumph of the first Double this century...

EUROPEAN CHALLENGE

In the 1961–62 pre-season training we discussed the European Cup. What new demands might it bring? How could we prepare for them? On reflection it seems presumptious. How can you prepare for the unexpected? If you could it would hardly be the unexpected.

The first round draw against Gornik surprised us. Who were they? Some Polish team we had never heard of. We took it with a mixture of ignorance and complacency, while Bill Nick travelled out there to weigh them up. When he returned he looked puzzled. He gave the impression he could not make up his mind about them. And I began to understand his dilemma on the bus ride across Warsaw to catch the train south to Katowice. I felt alone in a strange land, confused by its values.

The hotel in Katowice was primitive. I was not alone there. A local character sought me out, knocking on my bedroom door. I gave him razor blades and biscuits and traded information about the match. He showed me a picture of himself and two other men in uniform and said he had served in the U.S. Marines. He seemed to know all about me, offering me his guidance and hospitality while I was in Poland.

Here was the unexpected. A fascinating stranger who knows you well. He could have been an ex-marine, or a secret policeman, or just a lonely local guy down on his luck. He did me no harm and I shall always remember him. He symbolised the whole Gornik experience for me.

On the bus ride to the stadium armed guards watched over prisoners working on the cobbled streets. Outside the dreary town we turned suddenly into a sporting paradise. Up a winding road, through lush green fields and sparkling ponds, to a castle on the hill-top. Cardboard spaceships lined the road, pointing to the moon, reminding us the Russians had been there first. And the castle turned into a magnificent stadium, with a score of women, on their knees, apparently cutting the grass with scissors.

The Gornik players filed out through a back door to warm up. I saw them through the dressing-room window. They had thick legs and wore old fashioned boots. They could have been a team of farmers and I felt sympathy for them. I had never done that before.

My sympathy turned to sorrow when they scored two goals. I could not believe they were beating us. I tried to make an effort but found it difficult, as if I had been drugged with what I had seen.

And my sorrow deepened when they scored another two goals. I thought our European Cup dreams were over. In the last twenty minutes they collapsed and we managed two easy goals by way of reply. On the journey home it all seemed like a bad dream. When I got home I felt different. The worst was over. How would they feel when they came to our strange land?

It was the greatest match in all my years at White Hart Lane. The atmosphere was full of hope and expectancy. Even when Gornik scored a goal nobody believed they had a chance. The fans began to sing *Glory, Glory, Hallelujah*. It was the first time I had ever heard it. Yet it had been hanging in the air for some time and now this was their spontaneous contribution. It was virtually a religious feeling. They were showing their faith and they were not denied. Gornik were swept aside with eight emotional goals. Defeat had been transformed into glorious victory.

And twenty years later the doubts about Gornik still linger. How good were they? I still can't make up my mind.

The next round against Dukla Prague was easier to rationalise. I had played against some of their players in the 1958 World Cup finals in Sweden. Northern Ireland had beaten the Czechs twice and I knew we were better than Northern Ireland. I respected Dukla and the quality of their football but there were no mysteries about them. We beat them comfortably and it was the Tottenham fans who again stood out in this particular round. At least that is what I remember about it.

Most football clubs have a cosmopolitan range of fans from the high and low to the tough and the tame. We had One Arm Lou, Johnny the Stick, Julian Holland, Lord Ted Willis, Professor Freddy Ayer and Hans Keller, the last from the world of music but with a football intelligence as bright as that of anyone I've met. I was on speaking terms with all these football lovers.

Johnny the Stick was a legend at Spurs. He had a number of season tickets at both Spurs and Arsenal. They say he hated Arsenal but business is business. I never did business with Johnny, though some of my friends did. They trusted him. They said his word was his bond. If he promised a ticket for £3 he would keep his word even if the market price soared.

Sometimes he wanted to argue with me and I would listen. My fondest memory of him was flogging tickets in Prague, along the road to the stadium. He was doing it for pride because in those days you could not take Czech money out of the country.

Professor Freddy Ayer told me a story at around that time. My memory may distort the details, but it's still worth telling. Freddy is a highly intellectual man who loved to stand in the queue at White Hart Lane on Sunday mornings for his tickets for big matches. He loved the banter in the queue.

He was also welcome at highbrow political parties. And the weekend before the Dukla match at White Hart Lane he received a telephone call from Washington. It was the US Secretary of State who was visiting London and requesting Freddy's company at a dinner party on Wednesday night.

'But we are playing Dukla,' Freddy apologised.

The frustrated phone caller could not understand. Freddy explained about the European Cup and how important it was to beat the Czechs and why he couldn't miss it. The Secretary of State was bewildered by Freddy's enthusiasm.

'Are you playing?' he gasped . . .

Of course he was. So was One Arm Lou and Johnny the Stick, Julian Holland and probably Lord Ted Willis and Hans Keller. United we stood.

BENFICA AND BELA

We had an old Irish trainer in the national squad who would answer complaints with a joke. 'Never mind,' he would say, 'you'll forget about it in twenty years.' It's twenty years since we lost that European Cup semi-final and I have not forgotten it. It is too late to moan but it deserves some explanation.

We had two goals disallowed in Lisbon at critical moments in the match. One of them might have won, or at least drawn, the game for us. There was a question mark about one, although I felt we deserved the benefit of the doubt. The other was a good goal and the referee gave it. But the linesman put up his flag and the ref changed his mind without consultation. The linesman might have had reason for waving his flag although I could not think of one that could cancel the goal, unless it was pure incompetence.

Like anyone else he had made a mistake. Then why did the ref condone it? Probably to avoid argument with the linesman which could have angered the home crowd. Nobody escapes this kind of injustice in sport. If you don't grin you bear it. What made it worse was that it happened again at White Hart Lane. Jimmy Greaves scored a good goal which the ref accepted and then the linesman changed his mind again.

The story that Bela Guttmann hypnotised the ref is partially true. Bela was somebody special. He was a domineering, attacking centre-half for the Austrian club Hakoah (meaning strength and power) when Austrian football was at a peak that hardly anyone in Europe could match. You can read about his travels as a coach and manager elsewhere in this book.

I first met Bela after our 3-1 defeat in Lisbon. I told him we could get the two goals back at White Hart Lane. (We would have if the ref had not denied Greavesy's goal). Bela thought they would just sneak through. He was more worried about us than Real Madrid.

When Benfica came to London some pressmen went up to talk with Bela. He said he was worried about the aggression of Bobby Smith and Dave Mackay. The journalists misconstrued his meaning of 'worried'. Maybe deliberately, although I do not think they were that smart. The result was a rousing story about 'brutality' with Bela pleading for a fair deal from the ref.

Did the referee read the newspapers and respond to it? Nobody asked the ref. When I tried to speak English to him at the toss he did not respond. How could he read the English newspapers? Perhaps somebody translated them for him, though there was nothing brutal about the goal Jimmy scored. But I honestly think it is simpler than all that, there was nothing underhand about it all. The linesman was incompetent and nervous about the nearness of the crowd. He could have given any decision that night. We were more than unlucky to have three goals denied – two of them genuinely good ones – in the two legs of the tie. I believe we were just a little better than Benfica as a team. What would losing three good goals have done to them?

At the top of the heap or at the bottom these injustices become more significant in analysing why you won and why you lost. I think Bela knew he was lucky. Two Benfica players I met later that night at a party at Julian Holland's were generous enough to make that point. I did not begrudge Bela that luck. Maybe he deserved it as payment for all his travels and experience that Nick or I could not match. Rubbing shoulders with the likes of Bela Guttmann can help an open mind to get smarter.

Who can change their luck? Some think they can with effort. You cannot practise luck. If you could you might be sorry. Spurs were not as unlucky as Manchester United in the European Cup. Spurs lost a semi-final but United had already lost a team that might have won the prize.

CUP WINNERS AND CUPS

I believed we could win the Cup Winners Cup. I did not know I would be maimed in the first round at Ibrox against Rangers. Their floodlights, perched low along the stand roof, cast shadows of the players across the pitch. I could read the match from the shadows. And, when volleying a ball out from our six yard box, I could see two shadows closing in to mug me. They left me struggling on the ground with a wobbly knee, their only satisfaction from the match. Cecil Poynton said Nick wanted me to carry on in case my absence might inspire them. My knee wobbled more with every minute until the end.

Six weeks later I was wheeled into an operating theatre before the anaesthetic knocked me out. 'That lamp,' the specialist said, trying chatting me to sleep, 'casts no shadow.'

'Then I will not see the knife approach,' I thought, as I drifted into the shadows. When I awakened the specialist showed me my cartilage in a little glass bottle. 'There is nothing wrong with it, I'm sorry to say,' he said. Another incompetent linesman, I remember thinking. It was supposed to be an exploratory operation. Another doctor later told me you could only tell whether a cartilage is good or not by experience – there was no other way.

Four weeks after the operation I played outside right in the third team. I was thirty-seven years old and had no time to waste. I was assistant to the manager and helping handle training with the first team.

When the side went off to Belgrade to play

OFK I stayed with the reserves at home. I had to be ready for the second leg at White Hart Lane. If I could not play in that one Tony Marchi would have more right to a place in the final than I did.

On the morning of the OFK home match I played five-a-side in the gymnasium. One of the younger players with bandy legs closed me into a corner. He twisted his leg round mine to contact the ball and twisted my wobbly knee. A pain shot through it for some minutes. But as I hobbled along the pain wore off. It felt more extreme than the manipulation doctors were giving me at the time. I went in to see Nick at lunchtime and told him I would decide at 5pm. 'Why?' he asked. 'I'll try it out on the track,' I explained. Then I ran around the pitch for three hours and told him I wanted to play.

I was lucky. Two excellent passes in the early stages lead to two goals. That deceived the critics. They said I was back to form, but really I was a passenger who had not been challenged. I just kept out of the way as the knee grew weak again.

Each time my knee was stretched, the torn ligament was bleeding. If I stopped soldiering on to nurse it, it would sleep and the muscles in my leg would get out of condition. So I limped through the rest of the season, learning new tricks. How could I make it more difficult for opponents without tackling? By quicker anticipation. When you move slower you must think quicker.

The blood in my knee gathered and on the Monday before the Cup Winners Cup final I had some of it extracted. Bill Nick was worried whether it would improve enough as we approached the final. And Dave Mackay was not fit. Some players think Bill lost his confidence before the final. That is not fair. Players do not worry about the manager's problems, nor understand them. It's better that they don't.

Nick asked me to take them training that morning. I could not see the point but he insisted. By doing it a purpose was realised. On the bus to the training ground the players were moaning. It sounded like they were bottling it. 'What's the team?' some asked. 'And what about the bonus?'

I locked the door at the training ground to keep out the Press. And I gave the players a bollocking. 'What's all the moans about?' I challenged them. 'I think you are afraid. Leave the bonus to me. Have I ever let you down? And what's this about the team? It's been the same team for five years. If Dave's out Tony Marchi comes in. If I'm out John Smith is in. If you want to train follow me. If not, please yourself.'

They all trained and when we returned I cornered Bill Nick. 'Pick the team now,' I explained. 'And let them know.'

'Dave's not fit,' he said. 'What about you?'

'I want to play,' I said. 'You can have me on one leg or John Smith on two.'

He picked the team and made the right decision whatever the result. If Dave had been fit Tony would have replaced me. Tony Marchi had a lot more experience at the club than John Smith. John was unlucky that day. He could have been a hero. But two regulars out of the final might have been dodgy.

Bill did not bottle it. At the team meeting

he was his usual self, worrying about the opposition. Some of it was useful and some negative. But there had been doubts about the whole team at the end of the League season. We had been in a slump and the Press were giving us a hard time.

Desmond Hackett wrote some fiction about it that morning. He blew Atletico up into monsters. Their Argentinian goalkeeper and thug of a centre-half would be sent home to South America if they lost the match, or some such story.

'What do you think?' Nick asked me.

'What about the bonus?' I said. I could see their faces brighten up when he told them – it was more than they expected.

'Well,' I said, 'it's not bad but let's talk more about it after the match.' I knew if we won they would grab the bonus in their delight. If we lost what was there to talk about?

'Who are we going to send home if we lose?' I asked the team. 'We had a lot of trouble and expense getting this side, so did Atletico getting theirs. Only journalists would send them home. So they have this big black fellow at inside-left. Who has ever heard of him? Leave him to me. And they have this fast outside-left called Jones. I'll bet he's not as fast as our Jonesy. What are they going to be thinking? Bobby Smith will frighten the life out of them. Greavesy has cost a fortune. That will worry them. And what about Big Maurice Norman when he takes his teeth out to play?'

Bill had kept faith in all of us through the slump and for five years before. Now all he wanted was for us to repay that faith. And we did. Nobody said a word about the bonus after the match. It was a good match. We had all played well and Terry Dyson was the hero. 'When are we going to have a team meeting which assumes Terry will play like that?' I asked Nick after the match.

The challenge had roused us. We won without Dave Mackay and we would have won better with him. I had a good match. It's a myth about Blanchflower winning the match without playing. It was the last really good match I did play.

Everybody loves fancy talk and myths. They make us humans seem less fallible, and gives us something to crow about. We had a special team back in the 1960s. Everywhere we went people appreciated our style and methods. Bill Nick was in the middle of all that. He took the blame and we grabbed the credit. It is impossible for players to share with the manager. They have to be a little worried and suspicious about him. He sits in that office on his own while they listen to each other's troubles in the dressing-room.

Bill knew about our problems. We knew little about his. He proved his worth with other teams when we were gone, only to find disappointment when he resigned. But I suppose he was lucky, like the rest of us, just to belong to that special team. When people talk about Bill's bottle, the only one that comes to mind is champagne.

FINALE AT OLD TRAFFORD

My knee improved a little the following season. Other people had doubts about it. To erase those doubts I would have to look better than I had done before the injury. That is tricky when you are 38 with a wobbly knee. On the Thursday before a league match at Old Trafford they manipulated my knee again. The anaesthetic made me dizzy and I was told not to drive a car for at least 24 hours. I had a bad cold and did not feel right at Old Trafford. When I put my foot out for the ball it was not there. Did the effect of the anaesthetic still linger? Cecil Poynton and the club doctor dismissed that. The Press gave me a slating and agreed I was finished.

The next Tuesday morning Nick came down to see me in the dressing-room: 'I'm thinking of leaving you out,' he said with a tear in his eye.

'You've decided you mean,' I answered.

'The others have not been helping you,' he began...

'Then you're right to leave me out,' I agreed. 'If I need help I am a passenger.'

We had gone a long way since he first left me out. When they said I was a luxury a bad team could not afford. I thought that was funny. Some people say the same about Glenn Hoddle. It is fancy talk. A popular phrase to explain something people don't understand. A smart contradiction. The poorest of families need some luxury. It gives them hope. It is the bad players who are the luxuries in a bad team. The good player shows them up. It is easier to take him out than take out six or seven.

But now I was left out for the last time. I was a luxury player without a future. If I could no longer lead the team somewhere it would take me nowhere. It was time to go and Nick had helped me do it at the right time and in the right way.

In November 1980 a good surgeon operated on one of the disfigured toes on my left foot. The next evening I awoke still dizzy from the anaesthetic. 'Could that affect me for another day?' I asked. 'Different people, different times,' he said. 'It could.'

Perhaps I could have gone on. But where to? The anaesthetic probably helped me to make a good decision. I don't regret it. I was real lucky. I worked hard for the glory and I had all my medals at the end of my career. It could not have been better.

I was born in Belfast in a district called Bloomfield. I played youth football at a place called Orangefield. I finished at White Hart Lane with the Lillywhites. Blanchflower is Whiteflower. John White was my partner. He was struck by lightning the year I retired. Neither of us started the new season. Bloomfield led to a lot of white flowers. What does that mean? Maybe...the soul goes marching on...Glory, Glory, Hallelujah...

Early Days

If you have been watching Tottenham Hotspur play some sunny September afternoon and are leaving White Hart Lane, pause a while. Instead of heading for your car, or for White Hart Lane railway station, turn left outside the ground and walk south down the High Road towards the City. Not far, just until the second lamp-post on the right-hand side of the road. Stop there, and try to imagine that scene as it was one hundred years ago. Imagine, if you can, a group of perhaps a dozen or so boys in their early teens gathered there. Of course, in those days it would have been a delicate gas-lit lamp and not the headless green pole that we see today. Underneath it were not badly dressed boys, for they all came from relatively good homes around Northumberland Park. Not poorly educated boys either, for nearly all of them attended either St John's School (a local Scottish Presbyterian institution run by a Mr Cameron) or Tottenham Grammar School, now part of The Somerset Comprehensive School on White Hart Lane.

In the way of boys of all ages and nationalities, they would have answered to two nicknames – the 'Northumberland Pups' or the 'Saints' (after their school). The local rivals, who were soon to resent their pretensions in running a formal football club, were the 'High Road Cads', sons of shopkeepers on the main street, and 'Barkers' Bulldogs', from a rival school apparently run by a Mr Barker.

The Pups had probably been playing cricket down by the River Lea on Captain Delano's farm. He was the uncle of two of the boys under that lamp-post – the Thompson brothers – and he didn't mind them and their friends playing cricket on his land. If he, or any of their parents, were aware of the name they

The earliest picture of a Spurs team, probably taken before the club's first ever competitive match, a London Cup tie against St Albans on Saturday 17 October 1885. The team was (back row 1 to r) W. C. Tyrell, F. Lovis, Jack Jull, John Ripsher (President), Hedley Bull (who kept this print), Sam Casey and (front row 1 to r) T. W. Bumberry, R. Amos, Bobby Buckle, Billy Mason, Billy Harston and Frank Cottrell. The team is wearing its new blue and white quartered strip, after Blackburn Rovers.

TOTTENHAM HOTSPUR FOOTBALL CLUB.

(ESTABLISHED 1880.)

PROGRAMME

OF FIRST GRAND

ANNUAL ATHLETIC MEETING

(Under A. A. A. Laws), held in the Grounds of

BRUCE CASTLE, TOTTENHAM,

ON SATURDAY, JUNE 13, 1891,

During Loan and Industrial Exhibition,

Commencing at 3.30 p.m.

OFFICIALS.

Referee (Pink Rosette)—HARRY LOOMAN, Esq. (Hon. Sec. S.C.C.C.A.)

Judges (Blue & White)—A. E. MARTIN, Esq., H. W. MILES, Esq. (Finchley Harriers), H. V. STARBUCK, Esq., J. TURNBULL, Esq., and S. A. MORRIS, Esq. (Tower A.C.)

Clerks of the Course (Red)—Messrs. A. E. BROADBERRY, R. BUCKLE, T. W. BUMBERRY, H. D. CASEY, J. M. DEXTER, F. DEXTER, H. GODDARD, J. C. JULL, W. MASON, A. S. PETTER, E. RUDSTON, H. R. STEPHENS, and F. S. WALFORD.

Starter (White)—F. J. MACKIE, Esq. (Tower A.C.)

Timekeeper (Yellow)—H. H. COOPER, Esq. (Tower A.C.)

Handicappers—Open Events—HARRY LOOMAN, Esq. (S.C.C.C.A.)
Members Events—Messrs. H. GODDARD (Tower A.C.) and F. G. HATTON.

Sports Committee—Messrs. R. BUCKLE, T. W. BUMBERRY, H. D. CASEY, J. C. JULL, F. J. MACKIE, H. R. STEPHENS.

Hon. Sec. Club (Badge)—Mr. R. BUCKLE, White Cottage, White Hart Lane, Tottenham.

Hon. Sec. Sports (Shield)—Mr. F. G. HATTON, 3, Richmond Villas, Park Lane, Tottenham.

PRICE TWOPENCE.

PRINTED BY E. H. CRUSHA, "HERALD" OFFICE, TOTTENHAM.

ABOVE: The first programme known to have been issued by the club, for an athletic meeting in 1891. Note that the date of establishment is given as 1880, almost certainly when the cricket club came into being but two years before soccer was adopted.
RIGHT: Hedley Bull's membership card, dated 17 September 1887. Note that the annual subscription was 7s 6d (37p) and that the club gave its ground as the Marshes. The cards were coloured navy blue and this is thought to be the oldest existing memento of the club.

gave themselves, the Hotspur Cricket Club, no doubt they were amused by such airs and graces. September is the time the cricket season comes to an end, so discussion no doubt turned to what they would do during the winter. And in such simple fashion was born one of Britain and the world's greatest soccer clubs.

The boys decided to form a football club to be called, naturally enough, the Hotspur Football Club, and to play to association rather than rugby rules. Despite the fact that the Football Association had been in existence for nearly 20 years, there was still no single set of soccer rules, though this was to be rectified within months at the first formal meeting of the four national associations. The date of formation of the Hotspur Football Club is usually given as 5 September 1882, the day that subscriptions to the new club were first

This is to certify that Mr. H. Ball. has been admitted and duly enrolled a Member of the Tottenham-Hotspur Football Club.

this 17 September 1887.

Hon. Sec.

INITIALS.

SEASON:
1887-88
1888-89
1889-90

NOT TRANSFERABLE.

GROUND—
TOTTENHAM MARSHES

Tottenham-Hotspur
FOOTBALL CLUB.
L.F.A.

received. That day was actually a Tuesday.

There were, appropriately, just 11 founder members – E. Beaven, Bobby Buckle (the club's first captain), Fred Dexter, Stuart Leaman (the first goalkeeper), E. Wall, the brothers Anderson (J. and T.), the brothers Casey (L. and Ham who was sometimes nicknamed Sam) and the brothers Thompson (Jack and Peter), whose uncle loaned them that cricket pitch. Another eight members were to join during the year and, as all wanted to play, this was thought more than enough for the time being.

How exact are the date and details of the club's foundation cannot now be determined, but the basic facts were related as late as the mid-twentieth century by Charlie Denyer, who joined the club soon afterwards, and by L. R. Casey, the club's first treasurer. Casey's father had provided the first goalposts, symbolically painted blue and white, and it was an older Casey brother who had given the club its first ball and had, apparently, been responsible for suggesting the name Hotspur for the cricket club.

Harry Hotspur, immortalized in numerous history books and by Shakespeare in Richard II and Henry IV part 1, was the teenage son of the Earl of Northumberland. Sir Henry Percy, to give Hotspur his correct title, died leading rebel forces against the usurper King Henry IV at the battle of Shrewsbury in 1403. Henry IV had come to power just four years before by deposing Richard II, whom he later had murdered in Pontefract Castle. The Northumberland family are better known as the Percys, the lords of the Scottish border who dominated north-east England for centuries as if it were a personal kingdom. From their great castles at Alnwick and Warkworth they controlled the main route to Scotland and were arguably the most powerful family in the land after the crown. They came to own lands in North London and part of that area later became known as Northumberland Park.

One of the football club's earliest bases,

the YMCA, was called Percy House and they were to use the Northumberland Arms intermittently as a changing room for several years. The lives of the club's founders, then, were regularly touched by the history of the Percys, so what better name for their creation than Hotspur, a name so redolent of youth and glory. We have cause to be grateful to brother Casey for his suggestion. Along with the likes of Sheffield Wednesday and Nottingham Forest, Tottenham Hotspur is one of those romantic names which breaks up the dull litany of Citys, Towns and Uniteds on a Saturday evening.

EARLY MATCHES

The Hotspurs' first serious game was apparently against neighbours Latymer, but it was not until the following season, 1883–84, that their fixtures became at all formal. By this time they had asked a John Ripsher to place the club on a more permanent footing. Mr Ripsher was a prominent local figure both at All Hallows Parish Church and at the YMCA. Several of the team attended his bible classes and he had helped earlier with the cricket club. Such church connections

ABOVE LEFT: *The site of what was once Captain Delano's farm, where the young Hotspurs started playing cricket in 1880. The ground is still marshy and the River Lea is beyond the tree-lined bank in the right distance.*
ABOVE: *The lamp-post on the corner of the High Road and Park Lane under which the Hotspurs are reputed to have decided to form a soccer club. In the distance are the Red House, their headquarters from 1886 to 1891 and now adorned with a cockerel, and the White Hart pub, from which the ground draws its name.*

23

were not rare at the time; Everton and Southampton sprang from similar origins. Ripsher used the YMCA as the team's first base and, at what could be called the club's first Annual General Meeting in August 1883, 21 boys turned up.

Among the first rules were that all members should attend scripture classes at All Hallows Church on Wednesdays, and that a rota should be established to determine which boys should carry the goalposts on Saturdays.

They had carried on playing soccer close to where they played cricket, on some marshy ground between the Great Eastern Railway and the River Lea, and the stationmaster at Northumberland Park allowed them to keep the posts in the station during the week. No doubt the players of the time were pleased that there was no crossbar to carry, only a tape. The Marshes (as the area has always been called locally) were already the home of two other clubs; University College Hospital played rugby there, while Park FC (later to be absorbed by Hotspur) played soccer.

The organiser of that first AGM was a clerk in Edmonton County Court named Jim Randall. He had joined the Hotspurs from local rivals the Radicals and was elected the new captain with Billy Harston as his deputy. Harston had an amazing career with the club. He partnered Bobby Buckle on the left wing for ten years, remained behind the scenes afterwards as assistant secretary and, over sixty years after being elected vice-captain, was still to be seen at home games as press box steward.

The Hotspurs did not stay at the YMCA long. During one scratch game in the basement of the building, a YMCA councillor investigating the noise was hit in the face by a ball, while other minutes mention the propensity of some boys to 'play cards and sample the mulberries at the end of the garden'. Having been ejected from Percy House, the club moved briefly to Dorset Villas and then on to the Red House in the High Road, which was used as headquarters for six years (1886–91). By remarkable chance this building, adjacent to the present ground, was later purchased by the club and is now used as their administrative offices with the address 748 High Road; truly a return to their roots. They did not actually get changed at the Red House, which was nearly a mile away from their pitch, but hired rooms in pubs closer to the Marshes, usually the Milford, the Park, or the Northumberland Arms.

The first game the club completed which was actually recorded anywhere was that match against Latymer. Playing on Saturday 6 January 1883, our young heroes lost 8-1! Matters improved and, over the next two seasons, 1883–84 and 1884–85, the Hotspurs were reported to have played 47 games, of which they won 27 and drew 4. One must treat these reports with caution, however, for it is impossible to gauge the quality of the opposition or even if they were playing first elevens. By this time it appears that only four of the founding fathers, Bobby Buckle, Fred Dexter, Sam Casey and Stuart Leaman, were still regular members of the first team.

Particular interest was always taken in that local derby against Latymer. It was the Spurs v Arsenal clash of its day and the history of

TOP: A picture of the whole club, also taken before the game with the City business house club St Albans in 1885. Back row, left to right L. Brown, T. Wood, T. W. Bumberry, John Anderson, John Ripsher, Ham, known as Sam, Casey (the first secretary); middle row, left to right R. Amos, W. Tyrell, Frank Lovis, Jack Jull, H. E. Goshawk, H. Hillyer, Stuart Leaman (the club's first goalkeeper) A. Bayne, Jim Randall, organizer of the first AGM and club captain; bottom row, left to right: Jack Thompson Jnr, Billy Randall (Jim's brother), Bobby Buckle (the first captain), G. Burt, G. Bush, P. J. Moss, Billy Mason, Billy Harston, the deputy captain and still press box steward as late as 1946, Frank Cottrell and Hedley Bull. Though the club's badge was supposed to be a large 'H', close examination shows that, at this stage, it was a Maltese Cross. This photograph was taken on the banks of the River Lea and, if the photographer had turned round, he would have seen the view BOTTOM LEFT displaced in time by a century. There is nothing remaining to suggest that football was ever organized on the Marshes, but it is probable that the Hotspurs played where the allotments are today. White Hart Lane can be seen about a mile off in the distance and Alexandra Palace, where a joint ground with Arsenal was proposed in the mid-1970s, can just be picked out on the far left.

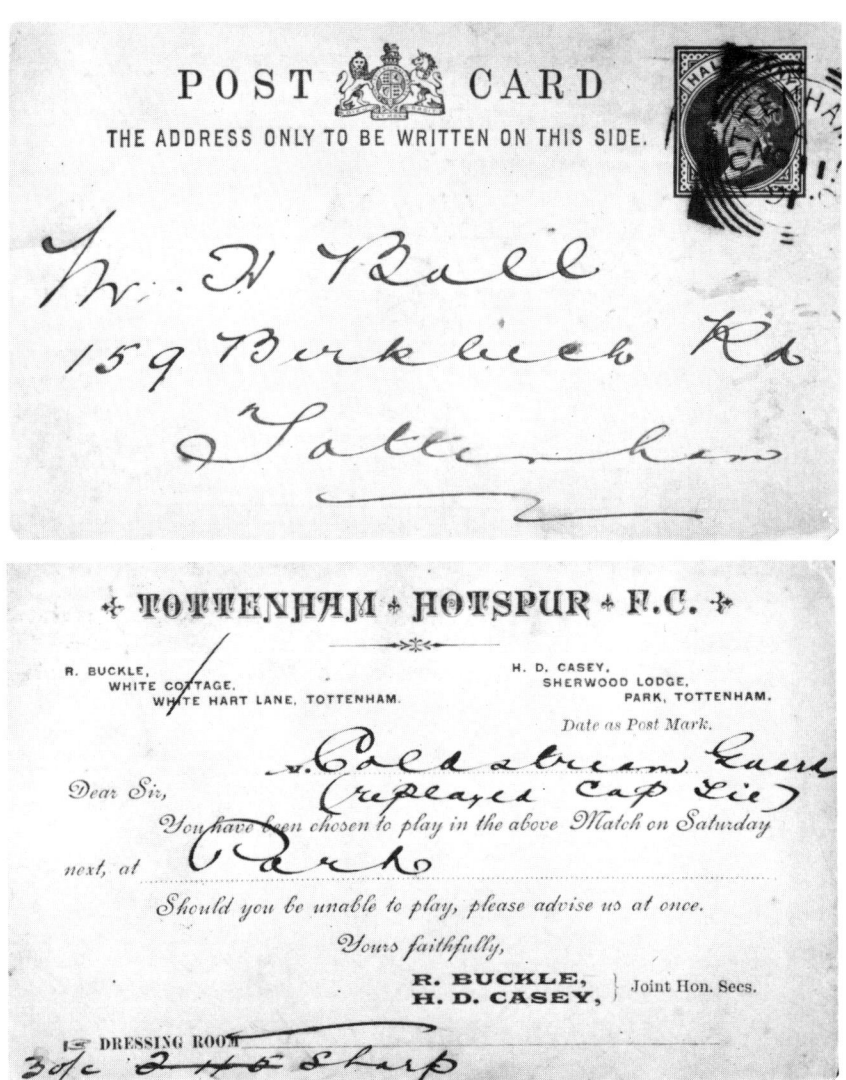

THE ADDRESS ONLY TO BE WRITTEN ON THIS SIDE.

Mr. H Ball
159 Birkbeck Rd
Tottenham

✠ TOTTENHAM ✠ HOTSPUR ✠ F.C. ✠

R. BUCKLE,
WHITE COTTAGE.
WHITE HART LANE, TOTTENHAM.

H. D. CASEY,
SHERWOOD LODGE,
PARK, TOTTENHAM.

Date as Post Mark.

Dear Sir,
v Coldstream Guards
(replayed Cap tie)
You have been chosen to play in the above Match on Saturday
next, at *Park*

Should you be unable to play, please advise us at once.

Yours faithfully,

R. BUCKLE,
H. D. CASEY,
} Joint Hon. Secs.

DRESSING ROOM
30/c 2·45 Sharp

In the club's early days, players were informed that they had been selected by postcard. This one was sent to Hedley Bull on 11 November 1891 and asked him to turn out at Park (meaning the Northumberland Park ground) at 3pm on the following Saturday, 14 November. Their opponents were Coldstream Guards in a replayed Luton Charity Cup match, which Spurs went on to win 7-2. As can be seen from the printed card, Bobby Buckle and Sam Casey were still running the club, nearly 10 years after they had founded it.

contests between the two clubs makes delightful reading. On 27 December 1883, Latymer turned up with only five players, though two arrived later. At the end of the match the teams could not agree on the score (Hotspur said it was 2-0 in their favour) and it remained unprinted in the *Tottenham Weekly Herald*, though that paper did remark that Latymer had suffered much verbal abuse from Hotspur supporters. Next time round the *Herald* got even more irate, pointing out that the club captains had submitted completely contradictory reports and that the paper would not print any more until they sorted things out. Then, as now, local papers relied on the clubs to give accurate reports of what transpired. Latymer attempted to overcome these various hurdles the next season by playing with twelve men, until the ruse was discovered at half-time. They tried the same thing in a reserve match soon afterwards but the Hotspurs had got wise to such ungentlemanly conduct by their neighbours and the fixture with the Edmonton club was dropped.

At the end of the 1884–85 season came another significant change. Sam Casey, the secretary, had been receiving mail addressed to another club called London Hotspur. As a result the Hotspurs decided to change their name to Tottenham Hotspur and distinguish themselves from this other side – which presumably soon passed out of existence after its brief appearance on the stage of football history. At the same time the club decided

to change its strip from all blue to blue and white quarters. This was the result of a visit to Kennington Oval to see the 1885 Cup final. Blackburn Rovers, in their familiar blue and white, won the Cup for the second consecutive year by beating Glasgow's Queen's Park 2-0, and so impressed the Tottenham lads that the latter paid their own tribute. In case anyone should mistake them for the Rovers, the Tottenham shirts had a large 'H' near the left shoulder, though on the very first team picture, taken in October 1885, the badge appears to be a Maltese cross. For a few seasons in the 1890s the team bedecked itself in red shirts and navy blue shorts, even changing for a time to the then Wolves strip of chocolate and gold. It was not until 1900, after playing Preston North End in the Cup, that the Preston colours of white shirts and navy blue shorts were adopted and they have remained the same to this day.

A CHANGE OF HOME

Despite their relative success, life for the the club was nothing if not impermanent. The marshland between the River Lea and the railway was public ground and the club had no more right to play there than a dozen kids who happened to turn up with a ball made from old rags. Fights over who could use a marked out pitch were not uncommon. The club had no control over any spectators who turned up, nor could it charge them anything. As the side became more established things did become a little easier – they were recognised as the best in the district and no longer had to fight for their pitch – but matters could not be said to be satisfactory.

P. J. Moss, who played for the club around this period, wrote about the last season on the Marshes in *The Football News* in 1900: 'In some of the games, with absolutely no gate money, it is no exaggeration to say that 4,000 spectators surrounded the field. They were not always considerate of the feelings of visiting teams and I well remember some East End Cup ties in which the visitors were pelted with mud, rotten turnips and other vegetable refuse.'

In 1888 Bobby Buckle, Sam Casey and Jack Jull (the club's best player, who had appeared whenever he was home from school right from the earliest days) found a pitch for hire just off Northumberland Park (which is actually a street running off the High Road, not a patch of open ground.) It was an area shared by Foxes FC and was used for tennis in summer. The rent was £17 per annum. The first match there was reported to be a reserve game versus Stratford St John's early in September 1888 and the takings were a heady 17 shillings (85 pence). At the time there was much muttering locally about the the club overreaching itself and getting 'too big for its boots' and it must be remembered that this really still was a group of ex-schoolfriends, few out of their teens, playing friendly matches every Saturday. In essence it was not so different from thousands of weekend pub teams around the country today.

In their later years on the Marshes, Spurs had begun to entertain some not undistinguished guests. In October 1885 they played their first ever competitive match in the first round of the London Cup. A crowd estimated

LEFT: *The Herald's report of the club's first annual dinner, held at the Milford Tavern on Tuesday 20 April 1886.*

FAR LEFT: *The Milford Tavern on the corner of Park Lane and Somerford Grove as it appears today. The annual dinner would have been held in the upstairs rooms, which were also often hired by the club as changing facilities before their games on the Marshes in the 1880s.*

The Tottenham that we know today was not the Tottenham of the club's founders. As late as the 1870s a traveller wrote: 'Tottenham has many outlying farms and much of the land is under plough ... flowers are grown for the London market in the numerous nurseries.' It was, indeed, one of those nurseries (Beckwith's) which was to become White Hart Lane. The population of the area was much smaller. In 1881 there were only 23,000 people living in Edmonton, but the next twenty years saw new housing throughout North London and Edmonton had grown to 62,000 by the time Spurs won the Cup in 1901.

at 400 saw them beat St Albans (not the current side of that name but a club based in the City of London) though the second round was something of a let-down as they crashed 8-0 to mighty Casuals at Wandsworth. Still, even to play the Casuals was something – in 1894 that club was to reach the final of the first ever Amateur Cup. The following season Spurs also entered the East End Cup and reached their first final, where they played another side to scale the heights of amateur football in later years, the Caledonians. The final was decided on the Marshes on Saturday 16 April 1887, but Tottenham were to lose by the only goal of the game, a low shot which skidded through their goalkeeper's legs. Hotspur were to find Cup finals rather easier in years to come.

THE ARRIVAL OF ARSENAL

One last game on the Marshes must be mentioned, Spurs first ever against Royal Arsenal. The game took place on 19 November 1887 and Spurs were leading 2-1 when the game was abandoned 15 minutes from time. Apparently Arsenal had turned up late, scored an early goal, defended for the rest of the match and were saved by the fall of darkness. Nonetheless, it was an auspicious start for Spurs in one of the greatest of all derby fixtures.

The first season at Northumberland Park proved a great success and the club even made a profit of £6. On Saturday 13 October 1888 the Old Etonians had come to Tottenham in the first round of the London Senior Cup, winning 8-2 with five of their goals scored by Arthur Dunn, a great Corinthian who was to give his name to the annual Public Schools Cup. The significance of the fixture could only be seen retrospectively. Just six years earlier Old Etonians had won the FA Cup. For nearly two decades it was felt that they may have been the last Southern side ever to do so – but who could then have believed that

Spurs would emulate them within a dozen seasons?

In 1889 the club joined the Football Association as a full member. Crowds were increasing (reaching 3,000 for another appearance by the Casuals in the London Senior Cup in 1893) and the team was taking on more and more of what we would today call a professional appearance. Bobby Buckle resigned as secretary in the same year, leaving only Jack Jull of the early club members still playing. Jull had been a fixture at right-back from 1883 and was club captain for many years, also becoming the first Spurs player to win representative honours when he was selected for Middlesex in 1889. He died aged only 53 on 22 December 1920 and the *Weekly Herald* carried a glowing obituary, by chance alongside the first installment of their 'History of Tottenham Hotspur'. Sam Casey remained as assistant secretary, and Bobby Buckle and Jack Thompson Jnr (his father, Jack Snr, had helped the club in its early days) were still on the committee.

PROFESSIONALISM ARRIVES

Obviously by this stage the club was looking for something better. It could continue arranging friendlies for ever, but the players were more ambitious. There were, nonetheless, obstacles. Soundings had already been made by the same Royal Arsenal who had come to the Marshes in 1887 about setting up a Southern League, with the implication that at least some of the teams would be professional. In 1892 a meeting of interested clubs had been held and 12 sides were provisionally elected. Spurs had tried to join but came bottom of the poll with only one vote, presumably their own. As it happened, nothing came of this meeting anyway. Most of the senior sides had been scared away by the intransigent attitude of the London FA, which made it quite clear that it would suspend any member club which embraced professionalism in any form.

This was a problem which was to continue for some years, finally reaching a bitter conclusion with the founding of the Amateur Football Alliance by the London, Middlesex and Surrey FAs in 1907. Arsenal had decided to ignore the threats and joined the Football League in 1893. Other senior clubs (and Spurs were, at the time, only in the second rather than first rank of these) faced worsening problems. They were experiencing the same difficulties as had the major Northern and Midland clubs before the formation of the Football League – namely that repetitive friendlies were not very attractive to crowds and that games had to be cancelled or rearranged at short notice when opponents found themselves engaged in the later stages of numerous cup competitions. At the same time, lack of organised fixture lists and unpredictable crowds meant that they were unable to sign the very best players, who went to Football League clubs. Spurs solved this problem, albeit temporarily, by joining the newly founded Southern Alliance with Erith, Slough, Windsor and Eton, Polytechnic, Old St Stephen's and Upton Park (not the current West Ham). They lost only three games in this league in its only season, and reached the fourth round of the London Senior Cup before losing again to old rivals Casuals. All in all, a satisfactory season, if one which consisted largely of marking time.

The same year saw the rather comical incident which eventually led to the club becoming professional. It became known, melodramatically, as 'The Affair of Payne's Boots'. The gentleman in question was one Ernie Payne, a left-winger who had not played for Fulham's first team for some time when, at the beginning of the 1893–94 season, Spurs offered him a game. At the time both clubs were amateur and, if a player could not get a game with one club, he was perfectly free to move where he could. For some reason, however, Payne's move to Spurs was not appreciated by some at the Half Moon (where Fulham then played) and, on the morning of his first game for Spurs (21 October 1893), he found his kit had disappeared. Spurs thus had to kit him out. As they had no spare boots which fitted he was given ten shillings to buy a pair. Fulham heard about this and, presumably still annoyed by the incident, complained to the London FA that Spurs were guilty of poaching and professionalism. A week later Spurs were found guilty of paying inducements to Payne, though not guilty of poaching.

Payne returned the ten shillings to the club and it was argued, not unconvincingly, that if a club official, rather than Payne himself, had run out to buy the boots then the charge would not have held water. At the end of the day Spurs were suspended for a fortnight, and Payne for one week – actually rather a light

THE WEEKLY HERALD, FRIDAY, October 19, 1894.

The 'Spurs have got through the first round of the qualifying stage of the English Cup, but victory was only achieved after a very hard struggle. The attendance was the largest the 'Spurs have had this season, over 2,000 persons being present.

The local team was the same that beat the Casuals with the exception that Julian played instead of Dickie. Jull, contrary to anticipations filled his old position at back, and Monk kept goal. Elliott and Burrows were absent, the former thinking it better to go over to Notts Forest, whilst the latter aided the Arsenal Reserves. Elliott's re-instatement apparently, was of little good. Stanley Briggs looked like an old warrior with his head bound up.

West Herts were handicapped by the absence of two or three of their prominent men, including Weeler, but their eleven included footers of considerable ability. Their team was as follows: S. King (goal); L. S. Lidderdale and J. R. Paul (backs); J. Penney, F. C. Robins and G. E. Green (halfbacks); H. R. L. Wright, S. C. Hobbs, J. O. Anderson, S. S. Taylor and R. M. Strout (forwards).

Play was commenced very punctually, Mr Bisiker tootling the whistle at half past three exactly. West Herts forwards showed pretty combination. Julian having fouled, the ball was sent into the net without touching any body and directly after Monk was called upon to save, which he did, although at the expense of a corner. Goodall cleared and in turn either goal was visited. The locals attacked, and Payne was conspicuous for tricky play. After the Herts forwards had again been stopped, Hunter gave to Cubberley who put in a clinker but Lidderdale nullified. Jull brought up the visiting forwards and Payne had a chance of scoring. Instead, he shot yards over.

'Spurs were pressing. Archie Cubberley was tricking the Herts defence again and again, and sending in some fine shots. Taylor, by a splendid effort put the home citadel in danger but his shot was too feeble to get past Monk. Anderson also kicked over. Eccles transfered play to the other end. Payne secured and passed to Hunter who headed the ball into the net amidst great cheers.

'Spurs attacked almost continuously from now to half time. It was only occasionally that the Herts forwards could get away. King was a tower of strength to his side. Frequently had he to use his fists in expelling the sphere from the goal mouth, and right well did he acquit himself. Eccles, Payne, Cubberley and Goodall each shot but they found King invulnerable. At last the latter got the ball by the custodian and so was able to place his team two on.

Upon the sphere being set in motion, Welham had to repulse an attack of West Herts, and then the 'Spurs again gave their opponents defence a warm time of it. There was only one team in it now, the locals doing pretty well as they liked, except that they could not get the pilule past King. At half-time no more goals had been scored.

Having had four-fifths of the game with the slope against them it was naturally expected that the 'Spurs would be the superior lot in the second half. But how often does the unexpected happen. Whether they had been dosed with some wonderful physic during the interval, I can't say, but, West Herts now played with the utmost vigour. A corner was obtained directly after the restart, and Wright directed the ball into the net, cheers from the visitors supporters—of whom, by the bye, there were several—greeting such a successful re-commencement. Herts again looked dangerous but the home defence interposed with success. Julian shot across to Payne, who sent in a clinker, King stopped and fell to the ground with the ball. A general scuttle ensued at the goal mouth, the poor custodian remaining on the ground; at last he got the sphere away, being loudly cheered. It was more like a bit of Rugby.

West Herts again pressed. Strout passed to the right wing, and Hobbs headed a second goal for his side, thus making the scores equal. All was now suspense, and excitement ran very high. The visitors still hung round the home goal, and Monk and Jull in turn saved. Then Cubberley relieved, and Hunter tried King without effect. Roused by the cheers of their supporters the home forwards showed better combination. The sphere reaching Goodall from Cubberley, he balked the West Herts defence. King ran out to meet him, but was not in time and Donald was able to score a third point with an easy shot.

Thundering were the cheers that followed. Directly after the locals all but scored again. West Herts were not dismayed and getting up placed Monk's charge in jeopardy. Shephard just managed to clear. Hands against 'Spurs was followed by Payne sending in a splendid centre which Goodall should have—but did not—converted into a goal. Eccles tried his luck, and it appeared that the ball went under the cross-bar, but the referee ruled otherwise. The visitors, although trying hard, failed to equalise and so the 'Spurs won by 3 goals to 2.

OPPOSITE TOP: *The Park Hotel beside Northumberland Park station, another of the local pubs which the players used as changing rooms during the 1880s. They would then use the level crossing on the left to reach their pitch, which was just a piece of common ground open to the public. The stationmaster at Northumberland Park allowed the club to keep its blue and white striped posts in the station during the week, thus saving the mile-long walk back to the High Road.*

OPPOSITE BOTTOM: *The Northumberland Arms on Northumberland Park; the club's first official ground was on playing fields behind this pub. When League Champions Aston Villa came to play a friendly on Saturday 11 April 1896, they refused to get changed at the ground and hired the Northumberland Arms instead.*

LEFT: **The Herald's** *report on Spurs first FA Cup match, against West Herts on 13 October 1894. Spurs won 3-2, but note the reference to the ball going under the crossbar but the referee disagreeing. Clearly Spurs were not using nets at the time. They reached the fourth qualifying round that year before being knocked out by Luton Town – a highly creditable performance. West Herts were the forerunners of Watford FC.*

RIGHT: *White Hart Lane was ready for use in September 1899 and the opening first team match was a friendly against Notts County on the evening of Monday 4 September. County, fifth in the First Division the previous season, were well beaten 4-1. The ground had no official name at the time and the report carefully avoids mentioning a title. The substitute goalkeeper who so impressed everyone, Walter Bull, was later to join Spurs.*

OPPOSITE: *The critical decision to go professional, made on Monday 16 December 1895. The committee obviously tried to stage-manage the meeting and push the proposal through. Several of the players opposed the move, largely because they expected to find themselves without a first team place if it succeeded. They were quite right; within three months only Stanley Briggs (the club captain and its best player, who refused to come to the meeting) and Ernie Payne remained in the side. The other nine were all new professionals.*

A Knock for Notts.
THE LAMBS LOSE.

Fresh from their splendid victory over Derby County in the League, Notts County came South to give the Spurs their first game on the new ground on Monday evening. They altered their team in one or two respects, the most interesting of the changes being to substitute Montgomery, the old Spurs' back, for Prescott. The Spurs gave Morris a run in place of Stormont, but otherwise the eleven was the same as against Millwall. To add some semblance of dignity to the opening proceedings, Mr. C. D. Roberts, the chairman of directors (in the absence of Col. H. F. Bowles, M.P., who had been invited to perform the function) set the ball rolling.

In spite of the warmth, the first half was very spiritedly contested, and the play was decidedly interesting. In former days it used to be reckoned that League clubs, when playing exhibition matches in the South, always kept a bit up their sleeves. Other times have brought other methods, and, now if League teams want to win they have to go their hardest—and then are frequently unsuccessful. Notts were in no mood to be beaten. They went at it hammer and tongs until the interval, and so did the Spurs. The visiting forwards were very smart with the ball, and they had a hard and vigorous style. The Spurs played a somewhat closer game, and exhibited an excellent understanding, with the result that they also were frequently on the offensive. In fact the play was of a very spicy character, the ball travelling backwards and forwards with great rapidity, and oft-times either goal was in danger.

A sharp bit of play by the Notts' left wing afforded McCairns a chance to score, but he aimed too wide. Almost directly after, Smith and Pratt initiated an attack from which Kirwan nearly scored. The ex-Everton man was conspicuous in these early stages, and one shot from him was only stopped by Suter throwing himself on to the ground. In the mere matter of exchanges the teams could, perhaps, cry quits, but some twenty minutes from the start Notts obtained a goal, the shot going off Tait into the net. With a little luck they would have quickly scored again. Fletcher—or was it McCairns—seemed to have the goal at his mercy, but Clawley rushed out and interrupted his kick. Smith got a chance to equalise, and lifted the ball too high. However, the Spurs had not very long to wait before drawing level. Smith and Pratt worked the ball prettily into the Notts' quarters, and the former shot it across the goal-mouth. Kirwan sent it back again into the centre, and Pratt rushing in kicked it through. Thus, at half-time the scores were one all.

Notts County had the misfortune to lose the services of Suter, their goalkeeper, when the second half was fifteen minutes old. Copeland, in trying to head the ball through, caught him with his foot under the heart, and he was led off. In the first half also he was stretched out, but this was a mere temporary matter. Bull fell back into goal, and a right good custodian he made. But the enforced change threw the team out of shape, and the Spurs had by far the most of the subsequent play. Before

Suter left the Spurs succeeded in taking the lead. The goal was first jeopardised by Cameron, who, after running past the opposition, kicked the ball a trifle too far from him so that the goalkeeper reached it first, and Copeland, who struck the post, but the latter made no mistake when he was left with another opening, after Suter had cleared from Pratt.

The Notts defence, as deranged, failed to hold the Spurs' forwards, who played in brilliant style. Copeland registered a third goal from a pass by Cameron, and before the finish he also converted a centre from Kirwan. In addition to these successes Cameron twice put the ball through from offside positions. These reverses could not be put down to the account of Bull. He saved any number of shots, difficult ones, too, and was just the man for the place in such an emergency. The Notts' forwards did their best to make headway, but four men cannot do so much as five, and the home backs were able to save Clawley from any serious trouble. The final score was were:—

SPURS 4, NOTTS 1.

The hour and a half's play at Millwall apparently had an excellent effect in knitting the Spurs together. The combination of the forwards was greatly improved, and they seemed to have got into thorough working order.

The front line was sound in every part. Pratt is not a showy player, but we are thinking the Spurs will have a warm right wing. His weight is an important factor, and in this game it was respected. Tom Smith was very speedy, and he could easily leave Lowe behind. One run of his in the second half roused the spectators to a high pitch of excitement. Copeland was a capital pivot, and was in amongst the goals. Cameron and Kirwan's play was all that could be desired. The Spurs' manager is a footballer of the first rank.

Of the half-backs, Morris was continually to the front, both in the matter of tackling and feeding. McNaught and Jones were likewise up to the mark, and the backs and goalkeeper performed satisfactorily, without doing anything exceptional. By the way, Mr. Brettell considers that Tait was the best left back in the League last season. We do not suppose Notts would have been so badly beaten but for the mishap to Suter, who is a goalkeeper of ability. Bull played a clever game at half-back, and when he fell back the line was considerably weakened. Our old friend Montgomery, with his partner, performed well in the first half, but we did not seem to see so much of them afterwards.

The turf had a greatly improved appearance, and except for one or two places where it was loose, played well. The Notts team, we are told, had a flattering opinion of the ground. There were about 5,000 people present, and the takings at the gate amounted to £115.

Tottenham Hotspur:—Clawley; Erentz and Tait; Jones, McNaught and Morris; Smith, Pratt, Copeland, Cameron and Kirwan.

Notts County:—Suter; Lewis and Montgomery; Ball, Bull and Lowe; Hadley, Macconachie, McCairns, Fletcher and Chalmers. Referee: C. D. Crisp.

---

punishment. G. Wagstaffe Simmons, later vice-chairman of the club, was to write that: '...the London FA issued a series of findings that staggered the football world...in their naked absurdity...' Bobby Buckle was rather more relaxed about it. He told Julian Holland some sixty years later that the committee of the time never had any doubts that the club would be suspended and were just unlucky to be caught breaking the extremely strict rules of the time.

But out of disaster can come strength, and so it was with Tottenham Hotspur. The Payne affair had drawn attention to the club and they were popular opponents everywhere – for instance over 6,000 turned up to see them at Southampton St Mary's a month or so later. The committee had also begun to seriously doubt the wisdom of remaining within the control of the London FA, given its almost fanatic obsession about professionalism. This attitude is a difficult one to convey today, perhaps the only comparable modern example being the Rugby Union's censure on anyone who has ever played rugby league. It might also be recalled that Corinthians, the premier amateur club of the day who were twice chosen en-bloc (in 1894 and 1895) to represent the *senior* England side in a full international, had an article in their constitution stating that they could not enter any organised competition of any kind.

Spurs, though without any conspicuous competitive success, had clearly exhausted the possibilities open to them as an amateur club. The move towards change was helped by the election of a new president in 1894. John Oliver, a carpet manufacturer in the City who was able to offer his players jobs, had been responsible for founding the Southern Alliance. He must have seen the potential that Spurs presented and was soon dragging them, some kicking and screaming, towards professionalism. It was a course that had already been adopted in the south by Woolwich Arsenal, Millwall Athletic and Luton Town.

He quickly erected the first stand at Northumberland Park and though it fell down in a gale soon afterwards it was a move in the right direction. By autumn 1895 the critical decision had been made and the club voted to go professional on Monday 16 December 1895. Only one member, a Mr Roynan, voted against, though there was considerable dissension at the meeting and a fair number of fans apparently transferred their allegiance to the still amateur London Caledonians over in Tufnell Park. Stanley Briggs, probably the club's best player at the time, was also against and refused to attend the meeting at The Eagle. He was the only amateur to continue playing for the side on a regular basis after professionals had been added to the staff.

AMATEUR CUP FROLICS

Tottenham had been having a successful time on the field. The previous season they reached the fourth qualifying round (the rough equivalent of the last 64) of the FA Cup and the second round of the Amateur Cup. Spurs career in the Amateur Cup was short but not without incident. They had been invited, along with 80 other sides, to institute the competition in 1893 and their first game was in the second round (having got a bye in the first). That was on 11 November 1893, when Vampires were beaten 3-1 at Northumberland Park. Unfortunately Spurs were unable to play Clapham Rovers, 1880 FA Cup winners, in the next round because of their suspension after the Payne's Boots affair.

The following season saw a strange juxtaposition of events. On 13 October 1894 Spurs played West Herts in their first ever FA Cup match, winning 3-2. A week later, they were contesting the Amateur Cup and crushed Old Harrovians 7-0. One Peter Hunter scored in both games. The next two rounds of the Amateur Cup saw equally impressive results – 6-1 against City Ramblers and 8-0 away at Romford. The fourth qualifying round was tougher – 1-1 and 3-3 draws against London Welsh (not the rugby club) followed by a 4-2 win at the Spotted Dog, at the time the home of the Upton Park club. By this time Peter Hunter had scored nine goals in the competition. Nottingham club Beeston were the next to go down, 2-0 at home, in the first round proper. The second goal, the last ever scored by Spurs in the Amateur Cup, was Hunter's tenth.

On 16 March 1895 Spurs entertained Amateur Cup holders Old Carthusians at Northumberland Park in the next round and crashed 5-0 before a massive 5,000 crowd. The Carthusians had five England internationals on display, including the immortal centre-forward G. O. Smith and the Walters brothers, A.M. and P.M. Full-back partners for many years, they were inevitably nicknamed Morning and Afternoon. Carthusians remain one of only two clubs ever to win both the FA and Amateur Cups. Spurs also progressed well that year in the FA Cup, reaching the fourth qualifying round before losing a replay to Luton Town.

The next season, 1895–96, Spurs were allowed to go through to the first round proper of the Amateur Cup, where they were drawn against Chesham. The game was never played for, as the *Weekly Herald* plaintively remarked on 20 December 1895: 'Had not the Spurs adopted professionalism last week they would have had to play Chesham after Christmas. The Spurs are now drawn against Stoke in the first round of the English Cup (the then commonly used name for the FA Cup) on 1 February. The Spurs have certainly had no luck in the draws this season...it is not likely any effort will be made to induce Stoke to come to Tottenham to play their tie.' How different from 1981, when Spurs had to leave London just once in nine FA Cup matches.

Tottenham's first game as a professional club was actually against the old enemy, the Casuals, on 21 December and they won 3-1. No declared professionals were allowed to play against amateur teams like the Casuals

THE WEEKLY HERALD,
FRIDAY December 20, 1895.

The team selected by the North Middlesex League against West Norwood, on Boxing Day, is as follows:—Hale, (Barnet); Searle, (Noel Park), Toon (Barnet); Hilton (Highgate Town), Vanderpump (Enfield), McLeod (Hornsey United); Shepherd (St. James), Hollyman (Noel Park), Crickmer (Wood Green), Stokes (Edmonton Minerva), and Speedy (Novocastrians.)

Edmonton Minerva (R) journeyed to Walthamstow to fulfill their league engagement with St. Gabriel's. Minerva sustained defeat by 3 goals to nil. [The report was received mid-day yesterday, which compelled us to cut it down. All reports should be sent in EARLY in the week.]

THE 'SPURS AND PROFESSIONALISM.

Every other matter, locally, so far as football is concerned, pales before the adoption of professionalism by the 'Spurs. For some weeks past the necessity of adopting this course has become more and more apparent, and for two or three reasons. One reason is in regard to the quality of the team. Those who have been present at the last two or three matches must have been struck with the fact that the 'Spurs have no good men to fall back on in case of accident to the ordinary players, and the result is that we have had bad displays, which are a source of much grumbling on the part of the spectators. I am not altogether an advocate of professionalism, as I think it tends to make sport a business; but under existing circumstances and conditions, I don't know that the 'Spurs had any option if they wished to maintain the prestige of the club.

The question was decided on Monday night. The club room at the Eagle was crowded with an excited gathering. Mr J. Oliver, the president, occupied the chair, and among those present were most of the committee, and several of the players, namely Pryor, Jull, Collins, Shepherd, Hunter, and Almond. Stanley Briggs was not there. The meeting quickly came to business, Mr Buckle proposing the adoption of a recommendation by the committee that the time had now arrived when professionalism should be adopted. The committee, it appeared, had met on Tuesday, and after full consideration of the matter, unanimously resolved to make the recommendation. Mr Buckle pointed out the difficulty that was now experienced in raising a good team when men were injured, and declared that unless the course suggested by the committee were agreed upon, their gates would dwindle down to one-half of what they were at present. Ralph Bullock seconded, and the Chairman and Mr J. H. Thompson, Senr., and others spoke in favour, all of them agreeing that the club could not ascend any higher in the ladder of fame if it remained an amateur organization. The Chairman said that unless the resolution were carried, he should at once resign the presidency of the club.

A considerable number of questions were asked, and once or twice the meeting became very excited. An opinion was expressed by one member, Mr Roynan, that the matter should not have been sprung upon them as it had been, and he proceeded to allude to the secrecy that had been observed. Despite of this, he said, he had it from one of those " in the know" what the meeting was to be about. This statement was the cause of considerable uproar, as the Chairman demanded to know the name of the person divulging the secret, a demand in which he was supported by a majority of the gathering. Mr Roynan, however, refused to give the name, and the Chairman then went so far as to order him to leave the room, but Mr Roynan did not obey.

One person wanted to know if a company were to be formed, and the reply was in the negative. Other questions put were as to the club's financial position, and whether the books had been called for. It appears that the club is in debt to the extent of £65, including £60 due upon the grand stand, but it was mentioned that hitherto a large number of matches had been played away. Regarding the other matter, the club's books had been called for, but not until after the notices for the meeting were issued. Another point was as to whether the players were favourable to the change. Mr Buckle said most of them were supporting the proposal.

At last the question was put to the vote, and the resolution was heartily carried, only one hand being held up against. Several abstained from voting.

ARCHIE CUBBERLEY'S BENEFIT.

The proposal to play a benefit match for Archie Cubberley has taken practical effect, and all the preliminary arrangements have been decided, as will be seen from the following letter from Mr F. J. Golding, who is interesting himself a great deal in the matter :—

Sir,—A meeting of local junior football club secretaries was held at the Spotted Dog, Church-road, Tottenham, on Monday evening last, when the ......

the leading clubs in the land in friendlies (Notts County beat them 5-1, mighty Aston Villa, unarguably the best of them all, won 3-1 on 11 April 1896) but Spurs clearly needed the stimulus of competition. In July 1896 they applied to join the Southern League, set up by Millwall Athletic's persistence two years earlier, and were elected straight to the First Division. A month earlier they had applied to join the Football League, where they were resoundingly rejected, coming bottom in a poll of ten clubs with just two votes. The actual voting was Blackpool 19, Walsall 16, Gainsborough 15, Burslem Port Vale 10, Luton 10, Crewe 4, Fairfield 3, Glossop 3, Macclesfield 2 and Tottenham 2.

THE SOUTHERN LEAGUE

Because of Spurs' dramatic rise to fame at the turn of the century, it is often assumed that the club was a great success in the Southern League days. It is true that they never finished lower than seventh during their twelve year stint, but generally there were no more than half a dozen good sides in the League at any one time (usually Southampton, Portsmouth, Fulham, Millwall, the two Bristols and Tottenham themselves). Apart from their Championship season of 1899–1900, with virtually the same team that won the Cup a year later, Spurs never looked like winning the Southern League. When they applied for membership of the Football League in 1908 they had finished only seventh in the Southern League, behind QPR, Plymouth, Millwall, Crystal Palace, Swindon and Bristol Rovers and could thus count themselves fortunate to be elected. None of the sides above them applied and, even then, Spurs finished fifth out of six in the first ballot.

During their Southern League career Spurs regularly fielded senior sides in other competitions – notably the Western League – and their first team fixture list was invariably crowded. An important Western League match one week might see most first team players involved, whereas the following Saturday might throw up a Cup tie and either a Southern League or a rearranged Western League match. In this case the Western League side would effectively be the second team. Other leagues, such as the United or Thames and Medway, were clearly less important and, although they were always recorded as first class fixtures, the reserve side must often have deputised. For this reason it is very difficult to chart the exact record of the Spurs senior team in these years. In 1899–1900 they supposedly played 67 senior fixtures, winning 49 and scoring over 200 goals (thought to be a record in a single season by a genuinely senior club) but it is simply not possible that Spurs were represented in all of these games by their best side. The League tables from these years are all included in the appendices, as are all games which could have been senior matches, but readers should beware of interpreting their standard absolutely literally.

ABOVE: *The two men who ran Tottenham Hotspur for almost half a century; secretary Arthur Turner (left), whose arrival spelt the end of the Cameron era, and Charles Roberts, who was chairman from 1898 until his death in 1943. It was Roberts who decided in 1898 that the club must become a limited company and needed a better ground.*
RIGHT: *Roberts proposed the formation of a company at a meeting in the Red Lion on the High Road on 2 March 1898. This picture, taken 83 years later before the 1981 FA Cup final, is a good indication of how close the club has always been to its locality and how its roots have remained on the High Road throughout its history.*

and the first competitive game as a professional club was that tie at Stoke on 1 February. It was not a memorable start – Stoke won 5-0.

The new professionals were paid between 15 and 25 shillings per week (75p to £1.25) and, amazingly enough, three months into 1896 only two of the side which had represented the club in December 1895 remained in the team. They were Ernie Payne, of boots fame, and Stanley Briggs, the tough centre-half who had joined the club in 1890. The founding fathers by now had virtually no influence on the club's direction, despite it being only thirteen years old. John Ripsher had become the patron and even John Oliver remained on the committee only until 1898 before fading from the scene.

Having turned professional Spurs had no formal fixture list and they took to entertaining

1901

John Cameron • Southern League champions •
Percy Park or White Hart Lane • Charles Roberts •
The First FA Cup • Joining the League •
Promotion and Relegation • Sick as a Parrot

There have been, perhaps, no more than a dozen great sides in English soccer history. Tottenham has produced at least two of these – the 1960–61 Double team, arguably the greatest of them all, and the 1901 Cup winners, who so astounded their contemporaries. For the origins of that earlier side, one has to go back a couple of years into the nineteenth century. Like 1908 and 1958, the year from mid-1898 is one of the most critical in Tottenham's proud history. The team performed only moderately on the pitch and at the next AGM the club declared a loss of over £500 but, firstly, the club turned itself into a limited company, secondly it moved to White Hart Lane and thirdly, and most importantly, it began its first, brief, flowering with the appointment of John Cameron as manager. It was, incidentally, also the season in which the club won its first ever trophy – the reserves heading the London League.

The first of these key events was formalised on Wednesday 2 March 1898 at the Red Lion in the High Road. Though the team was moderately successful on the field, attendances were not really up to expectations and the club was sliding slowly into the red. The club had plenty of time to consider off-the-field matters at the time as the ground had been closed and several players censured on 21 February after a mini-riot during a game against Luton. Spectators had invaded the pitch and assaulted three of the Luton team!

One Charles D. Roberts was a figure known in the northern home counties for fund raising via events like military tattoos. He had also, apparently, once been a baseball pitcher with the Brooklyn Dodgers in New York. He was

Sandy Brown (shaking hands on edge of goal area) has just equalized from a John Kirwan (on far side of field) free-kick in the 1901 Cup final against Sheffield United at Crystal Palace. Brown's 25th minute header was his 13th goal of the competition that season and he went on to make it a record 15 in all. Sheffield United goalkeeper Billy Foulke, about to pick the ball out of the net, was the largest man ever to play first-class football. At this time he weighed around 21 stone.

Part of the massive 114,815 crowd which gathered at Crystal Palace on 20 April 1901; it was the first football crowd ever to top six figures and remains the third biggest (after the 1913 and 1923 finals) at any game played in England. The Crystal Palace ground has no connection with the club of that name, but was part of a massive amusement park.

An advertisement appearing in The Weekly Herald *on 26 April 1901 proclaiming the first moving pictures of a Cup final. The event was a great success, particularly as it showed that Mr Kingscott, the referee at the Palace, had been wrong in awarding Sheffield United their second goal.*

approached by Spurs, probably with a view to organising a fund raising event at Northumberland Park. Once he got involved, however, it became apparent to him that the club needed far more cash than a mere tattoo could raise and he recommended turning Tottenham Hotspur into a limited company as a means of both raising money and protecting the committee from taking personal risks. It was around this time that the major clubs in the land were doing the same thing. The major advantage of the step was that it encouraged clubs to take risks and invest in the game, without the individuals in charge having to fear that they would become personally responsible for the club's debts and failures.

Roberts' proposal was accepted by the members, 8,000 shares of £1 apiece were issued and subscriptions were invited. A new board of directors was appointed – consisting of Charles Roberts (who remained a director until his death in July 1943), John Oliver (who resigned in November 1898), Bobby Buckle (who remained on the board until 1900, the last link with the original Spurs), Jack Thompson (another original Hotspur, nephew

of Captain Delano, who resigned in 1899) and Ralph Bullock (who resigned on leaving the country in 1902). One can only speculate as to why four of the five original directors resigned so quickly – but Charles Roberts was apparently not noted for having a shy and retiring personality. To the evident surprise of the directors, the share issue did not go well. Twelve months later a mere 296 applications had been received for only 1558 of the shares. Over three-quarters remained unsold.

But while money may not have been coming in through shareholdings, it was beginning to accumulate through the gate. On 29 April 1899 Northumberland Park saw its greatest ever attendance – 14,000 for the game against Woolwich Arsenal. That was at least twice as many as could see the game in comfort (there were still very few banked terraces on English football grounds) and dozens of people climbed onto the roof of the refreshment bar. It couldn't stand the weight, collapsed and there were some minor injuries.

That accident, fortunately not serious, persuaded the directors that they should find better accommodation. They struck lucky, for just a few yards from where the club had been founded, and where the heart of its support had always been, was an undeveloped plot called Beckwith's Nursery. The only buildings on it were greenhouses and nursery sheds used for growing plants. The land had been bought by Charrington's Brewery as it was adjacent to their White Hart public house on the High Road. They were thinking of building some rows of terraces on the site, partially to provide custom for the pub.

The landlord of the pub had spread around a rumour that there was a football club interested in taking the land, because his previous pub had been near the Millwall ground and had been worth a fortune to him. He was therefore very keen to attract another club to the open space behind his premises. Having heard the rumour, and discovered the landlord was basically flying a kite, Charles Roberts and Bobby Buckle then approached Charringtons. After some debate the brewers agreed to Spurs leasing the ground – asking only that the club guarantee 1000 spectators at first team matches and 500 at reserve games.

In return, Tottenham have served only Charrington beers ever since. The stands (being rather flimsy structures) were moved from Northumberland Park and the new stadium had undercover accommodation for 2,500 seated ticket holders. The ground was formally opened on Monday 4 September 1899 when Spurs beat the country's oldest professional club, Notts County, 4-1 in a friendly and 5,000 people paid £115 to watch.

This was not actually the first game on the pitch. There had already been three 'Whites versus Stripes' trials and a game for schoolboy hopefuls. All four matches had been open for the public. Though before the First World War it was generally referred to as 'The High Road Ground', it has been known as White Hart Lane ever since – despite the fact that its address is 748 High Road and it is some distance from White Hart Lane itself. The White Hart Ground would no doubt be a better name but the club, having initially preferred Percy Park, were happy to accept any name popularly bestowed upon their new 30,000 capacity stadium. Within a decade improvements had taken the capacity up to

ABOVE: *The crowd at Crystal Palace surrounds the grandstand as the Tottenham players go up to be presented to Sir Redvers Buller at the end of the game. The Cup was not, of course, being presented. Note the packed banks behind the stand.*

LEFT: *More of the hemmed-in crowd, no doubt all hoping to see Spurs become the first non-League club to lift the FA Cup. Although the Cup final was held at Crystal Palace between 1895 and 1914, the ground had no terracing in the sense it is understood today. Spectators gathered on the slopes of what was effectively a natural amphitheatre and, needless to say, few got a good view of proceedings.*

BELOW LEFT: *Fans from the banked seats invade the pitch at the end of the game. The old pitch markings with a penalty line and semi-circles drawn 6-yards from the goal-posts were changed a year later.*

40,000, easily large enough for all but FA Cup semi-finals.

In 1901, Roberts bought the freehold of the ground from Charringtons for £8,900 and, at the same time, purchased land and houses behind the northern end (then called the Edmonton goal) for another £2,600. To finance this he organised another share issue, but this proved no more successful than the last, raising only £2,000. Roberts borrowed the balance of the money and Charringtons helped him out by turning £6,500 of the purchase price into a long-term mortgage to be paid back over several years.

The game against Notts County was the first of the 1899–1900 season, the year that John Cameron's great team gelled. Cameron had joined the club in that critical autumn of 1898. A native of Ayr, he had played for his home town club and then for mighty Queen's Park, where he had won a Scottish cap against Ireland. He had moved to Liverpool, where he worked for Cunard and played for Everton as an amateur. It was not until Spurs asked him to come to London that he had ever been paid for playing football. He was a classic Scottish inside-forward in all except build, being a slim six-footer. As well as playing, he soon became secretary-manager and this remarkable man also took on the administration of the newly formed and ill-fated Players' Union. Within two years of his, and the club's, arrival at White Hart Lane together they had won both the Southern League and the FA Cup.

THE FIRST GREAT SIDE

What was truly remarkable about the 1901 Cup winning side was that none of the eleven had played for the club for more than four seasons and only four could recall playing at Northumberland Park just two seasons before the FA Cup win. How John Cameron got them to play as a team so quickly remains something of a mystery, if a massive compliment to his footballing genius.

The old timer of the side was Jack Jones, who had joined the club in 1897, was captain of the Cup winning team and won 16 Welsh caps in all. A strong left-half, he formed the critical left-wing triangle with Kirwan and Copeland which was to create so many of Spurs' vital goals in the Cup run. Spurs were his sixth club – he had already played for Rhuddlan, Bootle, Stockton, Grimsby and Sheffield United. Harry 'Tiger' Erentz had been signed from Newton Heath (later Manchester United) at the same time as Cameron in 1898. A Scotsman, born in Dundee, he was the heaviest (13 stone) and toughest member of the side, a fierce tackling right-back who followed an elder brother on to Spurs' books. The fourth player from the pre-1899 era was Thomas Smith, who had also joined the club in 1898. Born in Maryport, he had played for Preston before moving south. Essentially a simple right-winger, his great strengths were his pace (he was a cup winning sprinter) and the accuracy of his crosses.

In 1899 Cameron was to add six more of his great side. George Clawley, born in the Potteries, came from Southampton to keep goal and he was to feature in a quite remarkable incident in the 1901 final itself. He broke a leg during his first season at White Hart Lane, but recovered in time to regain his place for the Cup run. Sandy Tait, the left-back, was perhaps the best of all Cameron's signings. He hailed from the famous village of Glenbuck, bordering Ayrshire and Lanarkshire and later noted for its junior team, the Glenbuck Cherrypickers, which brought on such names as Bill Shankly. Tait originally played for Motherwell, moving to Spurs via Preston.

Tom Morris, the right-half, had the distinction of being born in Grantham, which made him special in being born further south than any of the other ten and hence closest to Tottenham itself. The hard man of the team, he was signed from the Lincolnshire club Gainsborough Trinity, which had a brief spell in the League between 1896 and 1912. Edward Hughes was the surprise member. Standing only 5 ft 6 in, he took over the centre-half spot when team captain Jim McNaught was injured in the 1900–01 first round tie against Preston. He played so well that McNaught never regained his place. Another Welshman, he had been a colleague of Cameron at Everton and eventually won 14 Welsh caps, the last in 1907.

Cameron showed a distinct liking for players with a similar background to himself and his inside-left, Davie Copeland, was even born in the same town, Ayr. He was the quiet one of the team, having had a relatively undistinguished career with Ayr Parkhouse and Walsall Town Swifts. Outside Copeland, Cameron added John Kirwan, a genuinely tricky winger who had also played with his new manager at Everton. Copeland and Kirwan, who won 16 Irish caps, developed a critical understanding on the left wing, often aided by Cameron holding back behind them to play as a scheming midfield man.

There was only one gap in this remarkable team, and this was not to be filled until the beginning of the 1900–01 season when Alexander 'Sandy' Brown joined the team as centre-forward from Portsmouth. Like the other 'Sandy', Alexander Tait, Brown was born in Glenbuck. He had played for St Bernard's in

Winner's Medal   *Reverse*

A Series, No 44.

PACKETS OF

OGDEN'S TAB CIGARETTES

Contain Photos of

GENERAL INTEREST.

Jas. R. McNaught – Tottenham Hotspur Association Football Club, Winners of English Cup, 1900-1901. Also Winners of Southern League, 1899-1900.

This Series contains 150 Photographs.

Edinburgh before joining Preston, like Tait and Smith. He had gone to Portsmouth the season before and, so far in his career, had done little to suggest that he was suddenly to become one of the most talked about centre-forwards of all time and one whose record of 15 goals in one season's FA Cup competition still stands. His career with Spurs was quite astonishing. Despite his fame he played for the club for just twelve months – moving on to Middlesbrough in the autumn of 1901 before winning his one Scottish cap.

He was an excellent header of the ball and Cameron had clearly decided that he needed a target for the accurate crosses of Smith and Kirwan. Despite being a great trier Brown was never really skilful enough (a fact fully appreciated by the newspapers of the time, if not by opposition defences) and Cameron was either remarkably perspicacious or remarkably lucky to fit him in at that particular time. Brown's brief flowering was astounding, he was to score in every round of the competition, the first man known to do so, and netted four in the semi-final. Given the run of the ball and the confidence of success, he had an excellent shot and was a fine header of the ball. And yet he was a relatively easy player to 'find out' and hence to stop. He did not have the all-round range of skills that a great centre-forward needs, nor the genuine speed. Spurs' relative decline after 1901 was in large part because Cameron never again had a player on song like Brown to convert the team's build-up into goals. Vivian Woodward, Brown's successor, was indeed a great

37

player, but was arguably not a great centre-forward, as Brown certainly had been for that one amazing year.

The coincidences in the team Cameron built are too glaring to be ignored. Five were Scots, four of them coming from Ayrshire and its Lanarkshire borders. Two were Welsh, one Irish and, of the three Englishmen, none was born within 100 miles of White Hart Lane. Three had played for Preston, three for Everton. Despite being brought together quickly, then, the team members did find much that was familiar at Tottenham and John Cameron was there, on the field and off, to build a remarkable side.

The club had already had its first taste of real Cup success in 1898–99, although only four of the 1901 team were playing at the time. In all Tottenham played 10 games in the competition that year, eventually defeating Wolverton, Clapton (after a replay), Luton (after two replays), Newton Heath (1-1 at home then a 5-3 win in Manchester) and mighty Sunderland (League Champions in 1892, 1893 and 1895) 2-1 at home before 12,371

fans. In the quarter-finals, however, they had to travel to Stoke and the Potters, just as they did in Spurs' first professional game, had little trouble eliminating them – this time 4-1.

The following season Spurs were allowed to go straight through to the competition proper without contesting the qualifying rounds, but had the misfortune to be drawn away at Deepdale and went out 1-0 at their first hurdle. Imagine their concern, then, when in 1900–01 they were yet again drawn against Preston in the first round, albeit at home.

By that time, at least, Spurs did have the confidence of having won a major competition. In the 1899–1900 Southern League they won 20 and drew 4 of their 28 games, scoring 67 goals and finishing three points clear of Portsmouth. All in all they won 49 of their 67 first team matches, losing only 10. After the financial loss of the previous year the club made a profit – if only £71 18s 8p (£71.94). Even the reserves did well, finishing second in the London League and the club was dubbed 'The Flower of the South' by the London newspapers. Support was beginning to grow

fast, and the mood of the district is well summed up by a verse originally printed in the *Tottenham Herald* and repeated by Julian Holland in his book 'Spurs':

> What care I of things South African,
> Or whether the Boers will fight,
> Or that France has ceased to know the way,
> Between what is wrong and right?
> I care not for things political,
> Or which party's out or in,
> The only thing I trouble about,
> Is will Tottenham Hotspurs win?

Note that the club was still popularly referred to as Hotspurs at the time.

The references to South Africa related to the Boer War, then at its height. The local ardour cooled a little as the 1900–01 season got under way. By November Tottenham were well down the field, quite unable to reproduce the understanding of the previous season. But from then onwards things began to improve, too late to assist in the League, where they finished a mediocre fifth out of fifteen, but just in time for the Cup, which started as late as Saturday 9 February that year, delayed because of Queen Victoria's death. Like many sides before and since, Spurs were unquestionably helped by having only the Cup to think about for the second half of the season.

THE 1901 CUP RUN

Spurs did not start well either in their Cup tie against Preston. Perhaps it was the blue and white stripes they had agreed to wear because of the colour clash (it was not until 1924–25 that the away side changed automatically). After 28 minutes a long shot by the Lancastrian full-back McMahon left Clawley unsighted and Preston, 1-0 up, retreated back into defence for the rest of the game. The tactic almost paid off. Peter McBride in the Preston goal was excellent while Sandy Brown, in his first Cup tie for Spurs, could barely do a thing right. The man Brown had replaced, Tom Pratt, had been transferred to Preston and was having by far the better game. Who could have guessed then what was to happen in the next three months? In the 82nd minute Kirwan broke clear and centred for Brown to throw himself at the ball and thus score what was, by all accounts, a remarkable goal. No doubt the 18,000 crowd would, by that time, have regarded any goal as remarkable. So the final score was 1-1 and the tie had to be replayed at Deepdale on Wednesday 13 February, where the home side were clear favourites. Surprisingly, large numbers of fans travelled from London, paying 21/9 (£1.09) return for the privilege. Spurs made two changes. Hughes came in at centre-half for the injured McNaught and Jack Jones returned at left-half in place of Stormont, taking over as captain from McNaught. The team was to remain unchanged throughout the rest of the Cup run.

The Lancastrian home crowd of 6,000 was soon disappointed. In quick succession Cameron and Brown (twice) scored for Spurs and the game was effectively over by half-time. In the second half Brown completed his hat-trick and Preston's two goals from Becton and Pratt, against his old club, were academic.

The Tottenham team with the Sheriff of London's Charity Shield, which they won by beating Corinthians 5-2 on Saturday 1 March 1902. The Sheriff of London's Shield was the forerunner of the present Charity Shield and was contested annually between 1898 and 1907 by the teams judged to be the best amateur and best professional sides in the country. Tottenham contested the annual charity showpiece for the eighth time in 1981, having lost only once – 2-0 to West Bromwich in 1920. The Shield below is held by Jack Jones, the Welsh club captain.

ABOVE: *The Cup itself was photographed at the King's Hall in Holborn during the celebration banquet. This was the first time that a club had been known to put coloured ribbons on the trophy. At the end of the banquet they were taken home by Mrs Morton Cadman, wife of one of the directors, and she took them with her to the 1921 Cup final and placed the very same ribbons on the new FA Cup two decades later.*

ABOVE RIGHT: *The 1901 board with their first national trophy; (back row) J. Hawley, T. Deacock, Morton Cadman, Ralph Bullock; (seated) John Cameron and Charles Roberts. Cameron was the club's second secretary-manager, taking over from Frank Brettell in 1898. Brettell had taken on the job when the club went professional.*

Tottenham's reward for beating Proud Preston was an even tougher tie – against Cup holders Bury. The Lancashire club, known as The Shakers, were proof that, even in football, every dog has its day. Bury's day was around the turn of the century. At Crystal Palace in 1900 they had beaten Southern League Southampton 4-0 and, in the 1903 final, were to go two better by beating Derby County 6-0 for what remains the record Cup final victory. Bury had been drawn away in every round of their 1900 Cup run and had won their first round tie in 1901 away again, 1-0 at The Wednesday. No wonder, then, that 21,000 people turned up at White Hart Lane on Saturday 23 February. As they had against Preston, Tottenham started nervously and, within just two minutes, they were a goal down. For half an hour it looked as if Bury would overrun the home side but then a cross from Smith reached Brown and his shot beat keeper Thompson easily; 1-1 at half-time and Spurs had a chance. The second half saw just one goal, a rerun of the first with Smith centring for Brown to score his sixth goal of the competition so far. Spurs were through to the quarter-finals of the FA Cup for only the second time in their history.

Tottenham were relatively lucky in the next draw – away to Southern League Reading on 23 March 1901. All the other six sides in the quarter-finals – including the West Midlands quartet of Small Heath (Birmingham), Villa, Wolves and West Brom – were in the Football League. Reading were a modest Southern League side, at the time ninth in the table, but they had home advantage and were known as a tough, hard-tackling team.

It is usually the case that the team which wins the FA Cup has one critical moment which can be ascribed to good fortune rather than skill – an incident on which their success is later seen to turn. In Spurs' case, this occurred in the last few minutes of their match at Reading. The score at the time was 1-1. For the third consecutive tie, Spurs had gone behind in the first half – this time to a 20-yard shot by Evans – and John Kirwan had

equalised in the second half. Then, in the dying minutes, a Reading shot dropped over Clawley's head and Sandy Tait dashed in to fist it behind just before it crossed the line. There does not seem to have been much doubt in the minds of anyone who saw the incident that it was a penalty. But the referee was unsighted and the linesman, who was consulted, had apparently not seen anything and a goal-kick was given. The 14,417 crowd, then the largest Elm Park had ever seen, was not well pleased and the officials were abused right up to the final whistle. Spurs fans, who had paid 3 shillings (15p) for a cheap-day return, were no doubt mightily relieved. It was an incident which, in retrospect, might not only have altered the course of 1901 for Spurs, but could have changed the club's whole history.

The teams met again at White Hart Lane on Thursday 28 March before a crowd of 12,000. This time things were completely different. Copeland and Brown (from another Smith cross) had scored by half-time and Brown got another (his eighth of the competition) early in the second half; 3-0 to Spurs and they were in the semi-finals for the first time ever.

The draw for the semi-final had already been made and Spurs were to meet West Bromwich. The West Brom directors had been at the replay and immediately approached the Tottenham board to suggest Villa Park as a semi-final venue, despite it being only three miles down the road from The Hawthorns. Surprisingly Tottenham had no objections, perhaps because they would be guaranteed the receipts from a massive crowd there, and the match was set for Easter Monday. At the time clubs could make their own arrangements with the FA's approval, which was forthcoming.

Spurs could not play on the Saturday as their Southern League opponents, Bristol City, refused to let them cancel that day's match, nor would the Southern League let Spurs put out a reserve team. City were annoyed because Spurs had sent a reserve team for the Western League fixture at Bristol on 27 March, before the first team played Reading, and the West

Countrymen stood to lose part of a second large gate within two weeks if they again faced the reserves. As a result, the first team played against City, won 1-0, and went up to Birmingham for what is, as far as is known, the only semi-final initially scheduled for a Monday.

The game itself, on Monday 8 April, proved a massive anti-climax. Albion, though bottom of the First Division of the Football League, were favourites but Spurs, playing as well as the club had ever done in its history, were to win easily 4-0. As *The Sporting Life* said at the time, with considerable understatement: '. . . it is very difficult to single out any particular Spurs player for praise, but possibly Tottenham will regard Brown as the hero of the match. It really must be said that the centre-forward made the most of his opportunities...' In fact Sandy Brown scored all four goals, two with his head and two with his feet, one from 30 yards. This is an astonishing semi-final performance by any standards – and as far as can be ascertained from the records Brown remained the only man to score four goals at this stage until Fred Tilson did so for Manchester City in 1934.

Oddly all the goals came in the second half. Yet again it was the service Brown received from wingers Kirwan and Smith that broke Albion – the pattern of the previous games was sustained and Cameron's tactical planning had proved itself against yet another major side.

Because of the delayed start to the competition, the final followed just twelve days later, on Saturday 20 April at Crystal Palace. The enthusiasm and excitement were probably unprecedented before a Cup final. The reasons are not hard to find. Tottenham stood on the verge of a threefold triumph – that of becoming the first southern club since 1882, the first London professional side, and the first non-Football League club since that body was created to win the FA Cup. It is certainly true that clubs like Wanderers, Old Etonians and Clapham Rovers were London, or at least Home Counties, based, but their organization and support were as far removed from those of Spurs as the Isle of Man League is from the German Bundesliga.

Tottenham were the first London club with a widespread support and with working-class origins to reach an FA Cup final, then unquestionably *the* event in the football calendar. They were not, incidentally, the first professional southern club to reach the final – Southampton had done that the year before only to lose 4-0 to Bury. After knocking out Preston, Bury and West Bromwich, London really believed that this could be Tottenham's year, and turned up in their tens of thousands to see it happen. Estimates on the size of the crowd vary, but the papers the following day gave it as 114,815 and this is not likely to be an overestimate.

This was the first game in football history which attracted a crowd of over 100,000 and it remains the third largest crowd ever for a football match in England – the two higher attendances being for the 1913 and 1923 Cup finals. The press of bodies was so great that the Spurs team could not get in through the players' gate, so director Ralph Bullock took them round to the official entrance. Here, in an incident so beautifully symbolic of its era and of many of the attitudes behind the Football Association, the team were told they couldn't come in because they hadn't got the right tickets. Bullock, to his credit, did manage

The 1921 Cup winners banquet was also held at the King's Hall in Holborn and the 1901 side was invited. All attended except goalkeeper George Clawley, who had died the year before, and the two sides were photographed together.

BELOW: *After Spurs' Cup win John Cameron became something of a celebrity; among other writing assignments he was commissioned to produce one of the first, if not the first, guide on how to play the game. Not all of the illustrations were entirely convincing; the two featured here are entitled 'Centring from the left wing' and 'Shooting with the instep'.*

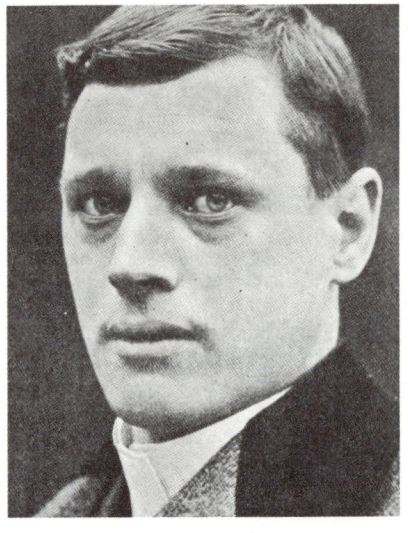

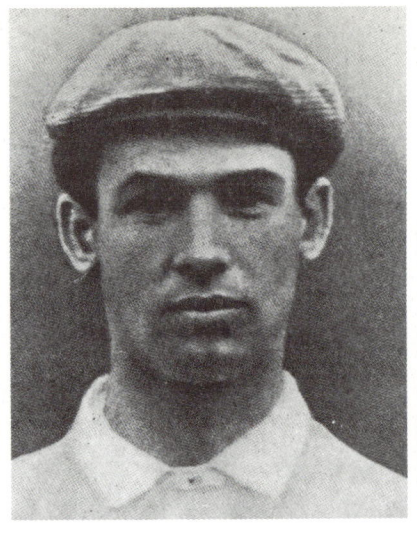

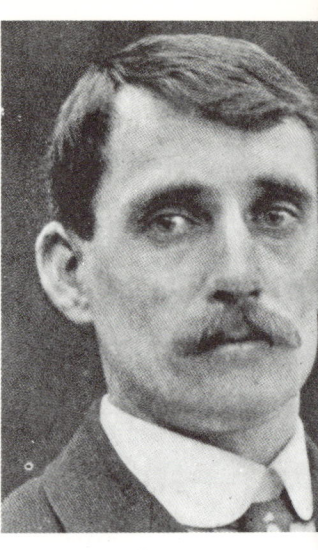

to persuade the officials concerned that their attitude was a little short-sighted, but one wonders what significance was put on the incident by the Spurs players or quite what those officials thought 114,815 people had turned up to see.

Their opponents were Sheffield United, though most of the crowd would have turned up just the same if it had been Penzance United. The Blades had won the League Championship in 1898, the FA Cup in 1899 and had beaten Sunderland, Everton, Wolves and Villa (all First Division clubs) on their way to the final. It was their semi-final defeat of the great Aston Villa which had made United favourites for the Cup, though they were only 14th in the League. They had a remarkably talented team. In goal was Billy Foulke, 6 ft 2 in and even then weighing 21 stone, the biggest man ever to play professional football. In the centre were Tom Morren, one of only two men to win both FA and Amateur Cup winners medals, and the incomparable Ernest 'Nudger' Needham. The forward line was equally famed – Bennett, Field (the only one of the 22 players born in London or anywhere near it), Headley, Lipsham and Fred Priest, who became one of only half a dozen men to score three goals in FA Cup finals and the first to score two in a final and still finish on the losing side.

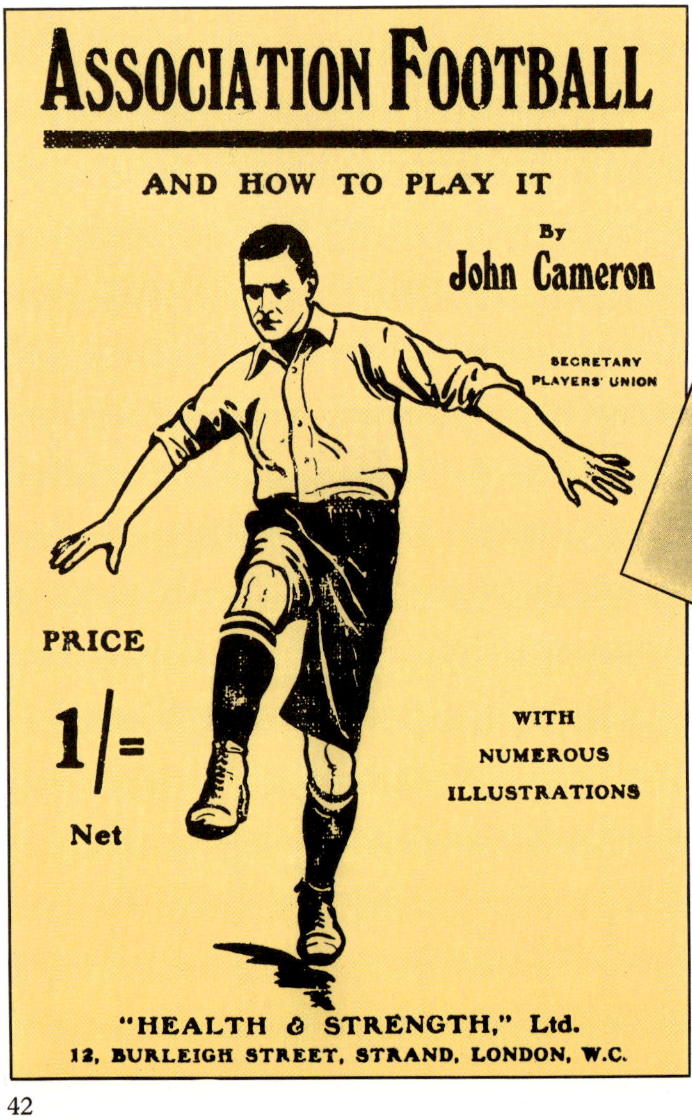

ASSOCIATION FOOTBALL
AND HOW TO PLAY IT
By
John Cameron
SECRETARY
PLAYERS' UNION
PRICE
1/=
Net
WITH
NUMEROUS
ILLUSTRATIONS
"HEALTH & STRENGTH," Ltd.
12, BURLEIGH STREET, STRAND, LONDON, W.C.

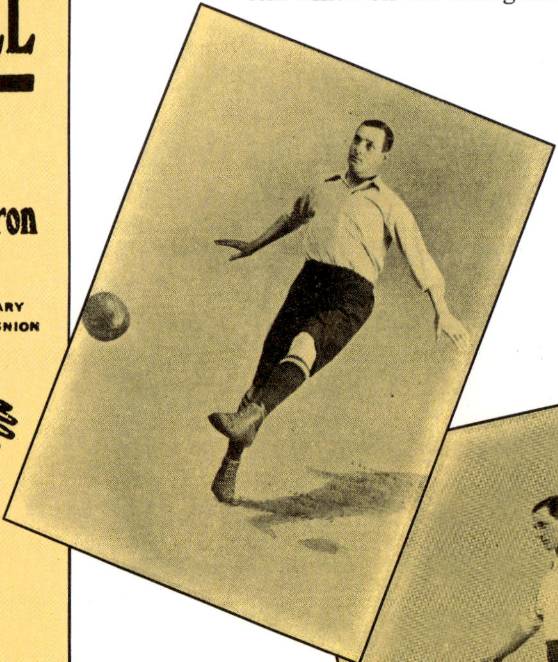

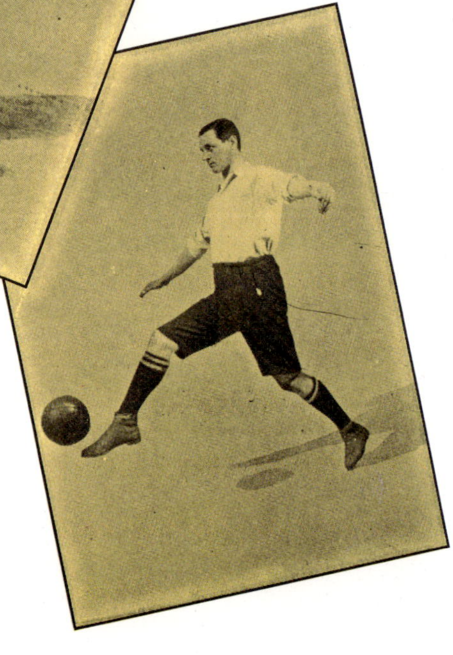

Six of the major actors in Spurs 1901 Cup success. From left to right: John Cameron, Scottish international, manager and secretary of the club, secretary of the first Players' Union and inside-right in the Cup winning team; George Clawley, the goalkeeper who recovered from a broken leg just in time for the Cup run and who was wrongly penalized for supposedly carrying the ball across his own line in the final; Tom Morris, the right-half and the team member born closest to Tottenham – in Grantham; John Kirwan, the left-winger who made a goal for Brown in each of the finals and kept the ball with which Spurs won the Cup until he died; Alexander 'Sandy' Tait, left-back, the first in a long line of 'thinking' Spurs full-backs and future club captain; and Mr Kingscott, the referee whose error in awarding Sheffield United their second goal was captured on film to haunt him for years afterwards.

On form, history and individual flair United certainly deserved to be favourites. Jack Jones and Nudger Needham tossed just as the guest of honour, Redvers Buller, took his seat to, according to the papers, great public enthusiasm. Buller has found lasting fame in the history books by failing to win a single Boer War battle but could do little harm at Crystal Palace. Needham won the toss and, sensibly enough, chose to play with the sun and wind at his back. Kicking off at 3.30 p.m. Spurs again started nervously, and after 12 minutes Fred Priest shot past Clawley from 20 yards. This was not so disheartening for the Londoners crowded on the shallow banks – Spurs had now conceded the first goal in four of their five ties, in each case early on in the game.

It took the inevitable Sandy Brown only 13 minutes to equalise. John Kirwan took a free-kick on the left, up went Brown for the header and Foulke could only pick the ball out of the net. The game was following the script of Tottenham's well rehearsed earlier ties. There was no further score at half-time but, six minutes after the restart, Brown popped up again for his 14th goal of the competition. Jones to Kirwan, Kirwan to Brown, an interchange of passes with John Cameron and Brown was away to finish the move with a rasping, high shot off the crossbar – 2-1 to the Londoners and the crowd went berserk.

Those who saw Jack Allen score the 'over-the-line' goal for Newcastle against Arsenal in the 1932 final will argue that it was the most contentious ever conceded in an FA Cup final. They are wrong. One minute after Spurs had gone ahead thirty one years before, Sheffield United 'scored' the goal that never was. So certain was everyone concerned, and everyone watching, that the ball had never gone over the line, that it has never been decided to whom the goal should be credited. And the ultimate irony was that the referee, Derby based Mr Kingscott, became the first (but by no means the last) official ever to be caught out by the camera; the game was the first ever to be filmed and the producers, realising they were sitting on a gold mine, rushed out prints of the incident the following week. The moving pictures, which still survive, support the view that the ball never went over the line, or even went within a foot of it.

What happened was that Bert Lipsham, on the United left, got in a shot that Clawley could not hold. As the ball bounced in front of the goalkeeper, William Bennett rushed in but could only force it off Clawley behind the goal-line. Clawley appealed for a goal-kick, Bennett for a corner (a view which the linesman supported) and the referee gave a goal. For a time no-one could understand why, but Mr Kingscott eventually explained that he thought the ball had gone over the line when Clawley fumbled Lipsham's shot. The referee refused to consult his linesman, who clearly disagreed with the decision, and the goal stood. If it was any consolation to Tottenham, the fates were perhaps only taking back what they had so generously given earlier at Reading. After this the game was played in a slightly unreal atmosphere, Sheffield having the better of the play but neither side coming near to scoring, and the game ended at 5.12 p.m. as a 2-2 draw. It was not until 1913 that extra-time was allowed if the scores were level after 90 minutes, so the teams shook hands and left the pitch contemplating a replay.

THE EMPTY REPLAY

The teams met again the following Saturday, 27 April 1901, at Burnden Park, Bolton. Yet again, the officials of the Football Association had failed to distinguish themselves with the arrangements for the replay, the first in a Cup final for fifteen years. They had originally proposed Goodison Park as the venue (the scene of the 1894 final) but Liverpool had protested as they were playing Nottingham Forest at Anfield, just a mile away, on the same day. Quite why the FA could not have chosen one of the Birmingham (Villa were away) or Nottingham grounds, quite convenient for both clubs, remains something of a mystery. Bolton was also patently a bad choice as the main railway station was being rebuilt and the Lancashire and Yorkshire Railway did not want hordes of soccer supporters invading the town. As a result they refused to offer cheap-day return tickets and the paying gate was only 20,740, easily the smallest at a Cup final this century (though pre-paid tickets and some Bolton season ticket holders probably pushed the figure over 30,000). Sad and sorry tales were told for years afterwards of pie salesmen having to throw away their uneaten wares, the expected exodus from London and Sheffield never having materialised. Spurs own receipts from the match were only £400. Eighty years later

the final and its replay grossed over £1,500,000 to be shared between the FA, the FA pool, Spurs and Manchester City.

It was a cold day, with occasional showers and a strong wind. This, combined with what one newspaperman called '...a peculiar ground, sloping from the centre to the touch lines...' made for a rather scrappy game. The teams were unchanged, Sheffield again displaying their nine internationals opposed to Tottenham's four. Five minutes before the interval Tottenham yet again went behind, for the fifth time in their Cup run, when an unchallenged Fred Priest banged the ball home. Only Mick Jones in 1970 has since scored two goals in a Cup final and ended with a losers medal as reward.

It took Tottenham until the 55th minute to equalise, via a John Cameron snap shot, and from this point onwards the Spurs midfield took control. Tom Smith scored a clever second after another Cameron shot had been blocked and the inevitable Sandy Brown back-headed a third from either a Cameron or Kirwan (the newspaper reports differ) corner with ten minutes left. It was his 15th goal in the 1900–01 FA Cup, scored in only five rounds (rather than the six today) and established a record that will surely never be beaten. It was also the last Cup goal he was to score for Spurs. Kirwan, for his part, grabbed the ball at the end of the game, took it home and kept it until his death.

The trophy was presented to Jack Jones by Lord Arthur Fitzgerald Kinnaird, the President of the FA. Appropriately for it was he, as captain of Old Etonians in 1882, who had been the last man to receive the Cup on behalf of a southern side. When he did so, standing on his head in front of the pavilion at The Oval

in celebration, Tottenham Hotspur FC had not even been formed.

Back in North London, the reserves were deputising for the first team in a Southern League fixture against Gravesend United (they won 5-0). Again, the Southern League had not allowed the game to be postponed. Needless to say, no-one was much interested in the result of that game, but the reaction of the crowd to the score from Bolton was a sight to behold. The team did not get back from Lancashire until 1 a.m. the following morning, but there was a massive reception on the High Road, with a band playing 'Hail the Conquering Heroes Come' and a firework display.

'Arbee', who had followed the Spurs faithfully in the *Tottenham Weekly Herald* for a decade and a half, quite lost control of himself in the following Friday's report. His piece, which ran to a full page, began: 'There are times in a man's life when he thinks a lot of things he can't give expression to, and that's just how I feel about last Saturday's magnificent accomplishment at Bolton. It really seems a hopeless task to adequately paint the picture in the way I would wish the Spurs supporters to read, mark, and learn. Our whole aim and ambition has been to bring that coveted trophy, the English Cup, to Tottenham, and yet their names are few who have ever thoroughly believed such would be the case. I know Bob Buckle was always very keen on seeing this happy state of affairs before he renounced active association with the team, and I can understand the feelings of the same Bob, Jack Jull, Sam Casey, Jack Thompson, and Billy Mason must have had last Saturday evening. And again, one's mind turns to that little mound in Tottenham Cemetery, whereunder poor Frank Hatton (secretary of the club in the 1890s) sleeps, and deplores the fact that he wasn't spared to see the fruit blossom on the tree he did a deal to nourish and train. There are a whole flood of recollections come to one's mind in this hour of triumph. The early enthusiasm of our amateurs when men like Sykes, Briggs, Burrows, Jull, Cubberley, and Payne did their bit to push the club along, the subsequent advent of Jack Oliver with a wonderful wave of prosperity, and then the drastic change in our constitution by that big leap into professionalism. And after that! Well, dark days, but always a silver lining. We've had rare friends and staunch 'all weather' supporters like Mr Jull Senior, Mr Roberts, Harry Burton, T. Barlow, J. T. Thompson, and always the aforesaid Jack Oliver, and, to go further back, Johnny Ripsher – a name immortal to old Spurs. Yes, the management have been in tight corners financially. But that's a detail. Begone dull care! Let us live in the sunshine of the present and talk about what is more seasonable.'

The club held a celebration banquet a week later at the King's Hall in Holborn, where Bobby Buckle proposed the toast to the Cup winners and spoke of the club's history. No doubt he, like his listeners, found it astonishing that the boys' team he and ten others had founded a mere nineteen years before had just won the single biggest prize in the game. Charles Crump, a vice-president of the FA, responded by saying that he hoped the Cup would remain in the south. It didn't, indeed it was twenty years before it returned, and the

team that was to bring it back was none other than Tottenham Hotspur.

THE JOINING OF THE LEAGUE

It seemed after the 1901 Cup success that Tottenham Hotspur must go from strength to strength and become one of the country's great sides. But, just as mysteriously as it had risen, so the Tottenham side declined. It was by no means a spectacular decline, rather a dull meandering without peaks or excitement. Cameron's failure to repeat his successes of 1900 and 1901 remains an enigma. Somehow it seems bound up with the departure of that remarkable talisman Sandy Brown. As has been mentioned before, the Southern League performances were acceptable, but in no way outstanding – second, fourth, second, fifth, fifth, sixth, seventh. The first team won the Western League (something of a misnomer as none of the premier division sides then came from further west than Bristol) in 1903–04 and the reserves had a particularly good season the year before, winning the top two divisions of the London League as well as the South Eastern League.

The Cup was unsatisfactory for the first eleven. In 1901–02 the holders, as many holders before and since, went out at the first attempt. It took three games for Southampton to dismiss them – the last one ending 2-1 in a snowstorm with the lines being continually re-marked as the game went on. Southampton were to go on to their second final, where they were beaten by Sheffield United. In the next six seasons Spurs reached the quarter-finals four times, but were to go no further until after the First World War.

Tottenham did figure in one interesting tie in that dull period, a second round match against Aston Villa at White Hart Lane. Spurs had won away at Goodison in the first round and, as a result, there was a feeling that this might again be Tottenham's year. The crowd for the Villa game was massive and the club put benches around the edge of the pitch to accommodate more people. Villa scored in the first half and, at half-time, a large part of the crowd invaded the pitch and refused to leave. It remains unclear quite what the purpose of the invasion was, but it seems likely that this was the first example of a crowd deliberately invading a pitch in the hope of getting a game

abandoned because their team was losing. It has happened several times in recent years of course, notably at Newcastle. In this case the fans were remarkably successful. Referee Jack Howcroft could not get the pitch cleared and the game was abandoned. The FA ordered the match to be replayed at Villa Park the following Thursday (25 February) and fined Tottenham £350. To everyone's surprise Spurs won the replay 1-0, the goal being scored by Bristol Jones who was tragically to die of typhoid a few years later while still an active player. Having been transferred from Bristol Rovers, he was called Bristol to distinguish him from Jack Jones. Nowadays, no doubt, the FA would have awarded the game to Villa and fined Spurs much more severely.

At the time Spurs could afford the £350. They made a good profit every year between their first as a professional club (1898–99) and the First World War, when the finances of many clubs collapsed. The first six seasons in the League, 1908–14, were particularly profitable, the club making over £22,000 in all.

Money was, of course, a major reason for Tottenham's desire to join the footballing elite, but there was a stronger driving force. This

was sheer frustration with the attitudes of the Southern League. Conservative would probably be far too kind a term for its approach to twentieth-century football. Matters had come to a head between 1905 and 1907. Chelsea in 1905, and then Clapton Orient in 1906, had applied for membership, been refused, and had gone on to join the far more powerful Football League, which was happy to have members from the capital. In 1907 Fulham, champions of the Southern League the two previous seasons, joined them.

All of this was very worrying for the remaining major London clubs – Spurs, QPR, Millwall, Crystal Palace and West Ham. Leading Football League clubs were much bigger draws than their regular Southern League opposition (sides such as Leyton, Reading, Bristol Rovers etc) and Spurs were beginning to suspect a movement of their support to the Football League clubs in the metropolis. It might be added that the club's relatively poor playing record in recent years hardly helped crowds either. Spurs did try to overcome any financial problems a little by organising a baseball league at White Hart Lane in the summer. In the 1906–07 handbook they comment: 'Many supporters have got quite enthusiastic over the game...anyone who is desirous of playing should apply for a trial next spring.' To the regret of their baseball pitching chairman the scheme was a failure.

THIS PAGE: *The programme from a London Challenge Cup tie against Chelsea on 10 October 1910, which Spurs won 3-0. This was the year in which the cockerel symbol became firmly established with the placing of bird and ball on the roof of the Main Stand, and this style of programme and newspaper illustration was common until after the Second World War. The caption 'I've got a terrible left!' presumably refers to the wing pair of Bert Middlemiss and Billy Minter which represented Spurs' major scoring threat at the time. Tottenham went on to win the London Challenge Cup (sometimes known as the London Charity Cup) this season, defeating Fulham 2-1 in the final at Stamford Bridge. It was, however, to be their last success in the competition until 1929.*
OPPOSITE TOP & CENTRE: *Two views of the players' social club, situated on the corner of the High Road and White Hart Lane, taken in 1904. Note the bar and the picture of the 1901 Cup winning team over the mantelpiece.*
OPPOSITE BOTTOM: *The home team changing room at around the same time; nearest the camera is Tom Morris, the most durable of the Cup winning team, who received two hefty benefits and was still playing for the first eleven at the start of the 1911–12 season.*

46

The Southern League refused to concern itself with the financial fears of its members and would not streamline its organisation or look to closer links with the Football League. It was a policy which was eventually to bring the Southern to a previously unimaginable low-ebb in the 1920s. Spurs became so frustrated by all this that they decided to resign from the Southern in 1908. Queen's Park Rangers did the same. Unfortunately neither club had anywhere to go. QPR, then Southern League champions, changed their mind and asked to be readmitted, which they were but only on the financially crippling terms that they had to play all their home games in midweek. Tottenham were rejected for Football League membership at the annual general meeting in summer 1908 (the voting was Grimsby 32, Chesterfield 23, Bradford Park Avenue 20, Lincoln 18, Spurs 14 and Burton United 1) but refused to go back cap in hand to the Southern. The result was that, as August approached, they had no fixtures except for friendlies and the FA Cup.

Fate smiled on them in a surprising way. Stoke (they did not become Stoke City until 1925) had been relegated to the Second Division in 1907 but found, after a season there, that crowds were not big enough to support the club. They decided on 17 June 1908 to resign from the League, a hasty move that the people of the Potteries were soon to regret. But, before doing so, the Stoke chairman got in touch with Charles Roberts to tell him of the decision. Some deal was struck between the clubs, possibly financial, and Stoke supported Spurs behind the scenes. By the time of the election, however, the Stoke board had changed its mind and decided to enter the new ballot. Nonetheless, a place had been created in the Second Division and Tottenham applied for it, as did Lincoln City. City's claim was good. They were founder members of the Division in 1892, had temporarily fallen on hard times being voted out in favour of Bradford PA in 1908, and were much closer geographically to most of the other clubs. Tottenham had only two advantages – they offered the potential of large crowds in London and they still had the mystique of that astonishing Cup win.

From a playing point of view Spurs had little or no claim – fifth, sixth and seventh in the last three Southern League seasons impressed no-one and they had lost in the first round of the Cup (1-0 at Goodison) the previous season. The voting could not have been closer: Tottenham and Lincoln tied twice (17 and 20 each) before the League Management Committee gave Tottenham their vote, 5-3. It was said later that it was the unspecified deal with Stoke which had swung the balance, but the reality is that nothing could ever compete with the lustre 1901 had added to Tottenham's name.

EARLY LEAGUE YEARS

Before the First World War, the football season began on the first day of September. On occasions the League treated that quite literally so, in 1908, Tottenham found themselves playing their first ever Football League game on a Tuesday afternoon, that day being September 1st. Their opponents could not have been more attractive, FA Cup holders

Wolverhampton Wanderers, and a crowd of 20,000 turned out despite the pouring rain. The Midlanders, whose old strip Spurs had once worn, had just become only the second Division 2 side to win the FA Cup, and they had beaten hot favourites Newcastle United 3-1 to do so.

But Wolves were to find Spurs far trickier opposition, and the Londoners recorded their first League victory, 3-0, at the first attempt, Vivian Woodward scoring their first ever League goal after just six minutes. The side was interesting in that it contained only one member of the 1901 Cup-winning team; it was Hewitson, Coquet, Burton, Morris, Dan Steel, Darnell, Walton, Vivian Woodward, Macfarlane, Bob Steel and Middlemiss. Tom Morris was the sole survivor, though Sandy Tait, the club captain, had played on until the previous season aged 34. A fierce tackler, deadly serious on the field but apparently charming off it, Tait was an Edwardian Nobby Stiles and, by all accounts, the favourite of the crowd. Dan and Bob Steel were brothers, both from Glasgow, and Bobby Steel eventually took over his brother's key centre-half role. In those days this was not solely a defensive position, instead rather the link between attack and defence. The star of the 1908 side was, of course, Vivian Woodward.

Among Woodward's other accomplishments, and apart from scoring Spurs' very first League goal, he was, at the time, on the board of directors of the club – a remarkable combination. He was capped 23 times for the full England international side, 67 times for the England and United Kingdom amateur international teams, and captained the United Kingdom Olympic gold medal winning teams of 1908 and 1912. In his 23 full internationals he scored 29 goals, a record not bettered until Tom Finney scored his 30th in 1958. Tall and slim, he was a great dribbler, his style as well as his attitudes in some way belonging to the 1870s rather than the 1900s. It was said that he was never paid even the cost of a tram ride to the ground – an admirable amateur position, though one he could afford to adopt.

It was a great disappointment to the club

when he decided to turn out for Chelsea in the 1909–10 season. Woodward remained on the Chelsea playing staff until the First World War, by which time he had scored 50 goals in 133 League games. There cannot have been many directors of League clubs who have played, even after their resignations, for another League club. Woodward, arguably the greatest centre-forward the club ever had, was to die on 31 January 1954, the same day as his friend and fellow director G. Wagstaffe Simmons, the club's first biographer and a journalist on *The Sporting Life*. How strange

Blackburn goalkeeper Arthur Robinson gathers the ball from Sandy Young during the FA Cup second round replay at White Hart Lane on Thursday 9 February 1911. Bob Steel, brother of centre-half Dan, looks on anxiously. Blackburn won the game 2-0. Note the unusual method reserve forward Young is using to hold up his shorts.

that these two central figures in Tottenham's history should pass away on exactly the same day.

Wagstaffe Simmons' views about the game coincided closely with those one assumes Vivian Woodward held. In his 1946 *History of Tottenham Hotspur FC*, the first serious biography of the club since the *Tottenham Weekly Herald* had produced a series of articles in 1921, Simmons ranges far and wide over his own experiences as a referee and covers at great length the minutae of various political debates over entertainment tax and shareholder problems. It is interesting that in his section of 'Red Letter Events' he records such moments as '1924: First Annual Concert. Visit of T. R. H. Prince and Princess Arthur of Connaught' and '1926: Visit of H. R. H. Prince Feisal'.

With the deaths of Charles Roberts in July 1943, Arthur Turner in 1949 and Wagstaffe Simmons in 1954 it is clear that a whole era was put to rest. Between the First World War and the death of Charles Roberts in 1943 there was only one boardroom change, and that was caused by the death of one of the directors.

ABOVE: *The Spurs side lines up at the Park Lane End before their first game of the 1912–13 season, versus Everton on 2 September. From left to right: Middlemiss, Darnell, Bliss, Tattersall, Rance, Collins, Lunn, Grimsdell, Lightfoot, Minter, Brittan. They lost the game 2-0 and did not win a League match until 23 November, after nine defeats and three draws. This remains Spurs' worst start to a League season, though they somehow ended it seven points clear of relegation.*

LEFT: *West Brom goalkeeper Pearson punches away a Spurs corner from the head of Billy Minter on 9 September 1911. Spurs won the game 1-0.*

49

More than a whole generation of key Spurs figures was to be swept away soon after the Second World War.

Back in 1908–09, the first League season was a good one for Tottenham. They were unbeaten at home until 13 March, when West Bromwich won 3-1. With a week left Bolton, West Brom and Tottenham were neck and neck at the top of the division with just one game left each. By chance all three had to play Derby County! West Brom went first and lost; Spurs went second and drew 1-1 at the Baseball Ground; Bolton went third and won. So Spurs went up on goal average ahead of West Bromwich, who had led the table for most of the season, and Bolton were champions. But if Spurs had drawn 2-2 with Derby, rather than 1-1, they would not have been promoted, such was the closeness of the race and the idiosyncracies of the goal average system.

Promotion was a long awaited follow-up for the club, which was progressing in other ways. The old Main Stand, pulled down in 1980, took five years to build in all and was opened at the start of the 1909–10 season. It was on that stand that the cockerel and ball were first placed. These were transferred to the massive East Stand five decades later.

The origin of the cockerel symbol has never been satisfactorily explained. The Duke of Northumberland believes that Henry Percy became known as Hotspur because of the enthusiasm with which he led his troops into battle, digging his spurs deep into his horse's flanks to gain maximum speed. The spurs that were attached to the legs of fighting cocks (until the sport was outlawed) were very similar and the club's badge in the nineteenth century was actually a simple spur. It must be assumed that a link was made between the fighting cock and cockspur and the cockerel took over as the symbol. Certainly by the turn of the century newspaper cartoons were featuring Tottenham as a cock and this continued through to the early 1950s, when that kind of illustration began to die out.

SICK AS A PARROT

Winged symbols are not unique in football and Spurs might also lay claim to being the originators of the most ubiquitous of them all – the sickly parrot. This story begins at the same time as the cockerel and ball were put on the roof, and was told by G. Wagstaffe Simmons in his 1946 history. The club's first tour was to the Argentine in 1908. On the field things went successfully, the team losing only one game in seven, and that to fellow tourists Everton. Off the field things were less cosy. Several people were shot during a riot in a town where the team were attending a music hall, and during one game a troop of cavalry took to the pitch to beat back spectators with the flats of their swords. Apparently the gates had been broken down and the promoters wanted to drive the spectators out so that they would have to pay to get back in.

In those days, of course, journeys were by boat and it took weeks to reach South America. On the way home, one of the amusements the ship laid on for passengers was a fancy dress contest, which was eventually won by two of the Tottenham squad dressed as Robinson Crusoe and Man Friday. Suffering some

LEFT: *Bert Middlemiss and Chelsea's Taylor appear indifferent to the ball during a First Division fixture at White Hart Lane on 27 December 1913. Chelsea won 2-1.*
BELOW: *Before that season's other fixture between the clubs (at Stamford Bridge on 6 September 1913) Spurs captain Tom Collins, his Chelsea equivalent and the referee appear to be asking a passing bird whether they can have their penny back. Spurs won this one 3-1.*

understandable confusion with the story of Long John Silver, they borrowed the ship's pet parrot to make their efforts more authentic and, in recognition of their success, the talisman bird was presented to the club by the ship's captain.

It apparently survived happily on the High Road for ten years, dying, according to Wagstaffe Simmons, on the day Arsenal were given Spurs' First Division place in 1919. Is it just possible that, in this incident, we find the roots of British soccer's most mysterious incantation: 'Sick as a parrot, Brian.'

Twelve months after promotion in 1909, Spurs were engaged in another tense battle, this time at the foot of the table. Again their fate was not resolved until the last match of the season, against neighbours Chelsea. Chelsea had 29 points, Spurs had 30 and, when the teams met at White Hart Lane one or other had to go down with bottom club Bolton. The unlucky ones were Chelsea, with Tottenham scraping home 2-1.

In some senses Tottenham's survival was of little significance. The club meandered along until the First World War, never rising above the halfway mark in the League, and it was honestly not a period which warrants much recalling. The Cup provides no more fertile ground for a historian, but there were a couple of games that deserve their place in the records. In the first round of the 1912–13 competition, Tottenham drew 1-1 with Blackpool at White Hart Lane. The Lancastrians, a Second Division club, were attracting poor crowds at the time, and agreed to sell their right to a home replay to Spurs. As a result the second game was played at Tottenham the following week and Blackpool, with two men off the field injured, went down 6-1.

The following year threw up a far more remarkable first round draw – away at Second Division Leicester Fosse's Filbert Street (they changed from Fosse to City after the First World War). That game resulted in Tottenham's highest scoring first-class draw, 5-5! Spurs won the replay 2-0 but went out to Manchester City at that club's old ground, Hyde Road, in the second round.

OPPOSITE PAGE: *The Red House was the club's headquarters from 1886 to 1891. For many years it was a hotel and dining room and advertised in the Spurs' handbook as 'adjoining the Spurs ground'. The club eventually bought the building (on the right of the lower picture), turned it into administrative offices and raised the cockerel and clock. The cockerel, perhaps distressed that the club was about to move into the new stand, fell off the clock in November 1981. The annual handbook was probably first issued in 1904–05 and did not change format until the 1940s. It was usually written by G. Wagstaffe Simmons, a referee, journalist and director of the club* (LEFT).

51

Despite the declaration of war in August 1914, the League and Cup were to continue for another season. This was, sadly, not to Tottenham's benefit. The club lost a disproportionate number of players who volunteered for the forces and this, added to the fact that the squad had never really got on top of First Division football anyway, meant that the club struggled from the start. The season's results make depressing reading: Sunderland won 6-0 at White Hart Lane and 5-0 at Roker, Liverpool won 7-2 at Anfield and Middlesbrough also scored 7. In the latter case Spurs did manage 5 by way of reply. The one bright spot was a Cup win over that same Sunderland side, a 2-1 victory being some consolation for all those League goals conceded. At the end of the season Tottenham finished bottom with 28 points, just one behind Chelsea and two behind Manchester United.

There was an interesting sequel to the season's final positions. Manchester United's last game of the season had been against Liverpool and it was later proved to have been fixed. When the League recommenced after the War this fact, plus Arsenal's intense ambition for First Division football, were to result in some very debatable manouvrings from which Spurs were clearly the losers. This story is told in full in the chapter on the North London rivalry, as is Arsenal's unwelcome arrival on Highbury Hill.

1921

Second Division records • Jimmy Seed • Peter McWilliam • Dimmock's goal • The Cup again • The Freak Season • Rise and Fall • Managerial merry-go-round • Northfleet nursery

Though it was not apparent at the time, Spurs' second great team was already largely built by the time British troops were fighting the first battle of the Great War, at Mons. Bert Bliss and Arthur Grimsdell had arrived in 1912, Jimmy Cantrell and Fanny Walden a year later, and John Banks, Bobby McDonald and Tommy Clay were signed before the outbreak of war. More important, Peter McWilliam, the Newcastle and Scotland half-back, became manager during the 1912–13 season. McWilliam had been left-half of that great Newcastle side which won three Championships and reached five Cup finals between 1905 and 1911. He was not a great tactical manager, but he was a good judge of men and of footballers. The story is told that, after the change in the offside law in 1925

(easily the most important alteration in the game this century), he held no team talks to work out new tactics. Rather he left Jimmy Seed, the team's key-man and scheming inside-forward, to drop back into midfield and work out the problem himself.

Interestingly, that first game under the offside law was against Arsenal at Highbury on 29 August 1925. Seed worked it out, and Spurs won 1-0. Given the direction the two North London clubs went in the next decade and a half (Arsenal won five Championships and two FA Cups, Spurs won nothing), plus Herbert Chapman's famed central role in developing the third-back tactic to counter the new offside rule, the result of the very first game under that revised system has a certain irony.

The Spurs team leaves Stamford Bridge with the Cup after the 1921 FA Cup final. The rain having finally stopped, the open topped charabanc drove through the West End and up the Seven Sisters Road to White Hart Lane.

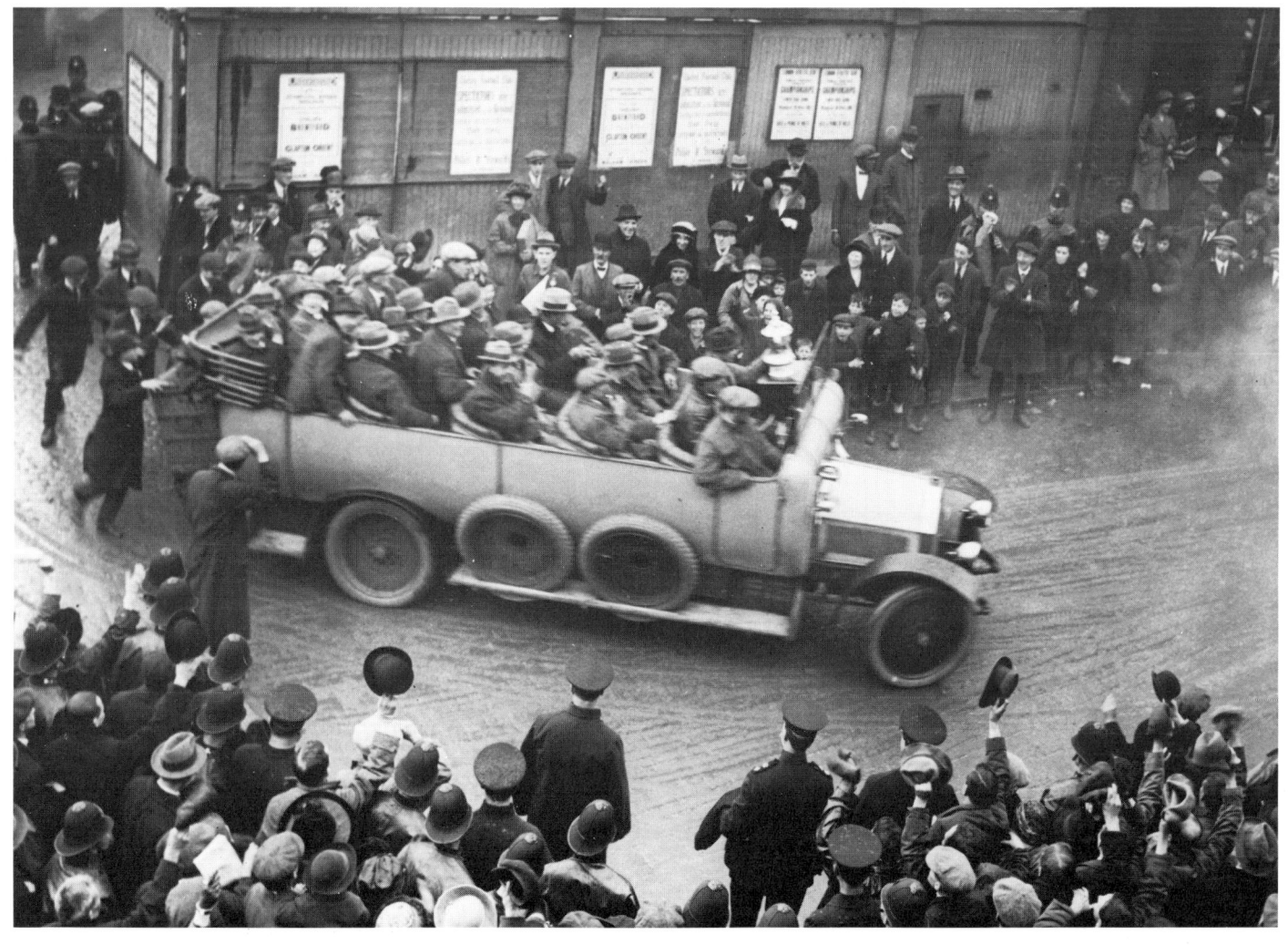

To today's ears McWilliam's lack of direction sounds vaguely unprofessional, but it was a structured era and one in which managers primarily picked men they thought could play and then let them get on with it. Managers were often also the secretary, though Tottenham had had a separate occupant of that position, Arthur Turner, since 1907. Turner had been one of the promoters of Rotherham Town FC and was a Yorkshire accountant. He remained at White Hart Lane for four decades, a critical influence behind the scenes.

The manager's skill was blending the right players into a particular pattern, as John Cameron did so successfully when he brought in Sandy Brown to complete his Southern League champions of 1900. Peter McWilliam was to do the same, only his key man was not a forward but a schemer, Jimmy Seed.

The parallels between Cameron's side and McWilliam's are uncanny. They both had a very brief flowering, spanning just three seasons. They both won a major League one season and the FA Cup the next. They both added a key member after winning the League but before embarking on their Cup run. But, on a less memorable note, neither really fulfilled their apparent promise and both sides faded, not spectacularly as some clubs do, but rather they gently subsided. Seed, always recognisable with his slicked-back, black hair

LEFT: A first team line-up from the record breaking Second Division season 1919–20. Standing (left to right); Archibald, Smith, Jacques, Grimsdell, Lowe, Brown; seated; McDonald, Banks, Seed, Cantrell, Bliss, Dimmock. Bert Bliss was the season's only ever present and scored 31 league goals. The team scored 102 goals and finished with a record 70 points.

ABOVE: Programmes from five of Tottenham's six Cup finals up to 1981. The only one missing is 1901, from which no copy is known to exist. Four of the 1921 Cup winning team, Smith, Grimsdell, Bliss and Dimmock, played for England against Scotland two weeks before the final.

was born in Durham but made his name with the Welsh club Mid-Rhondda. That unsung side was good enough to win the first ever Welsh League title after Seed had gone in February 1920, as well as one of the sections of the Southern League.

Jimmy Seed had been signed by his local club, Sunderland, at the start of the War but they released him after he had been gassed in France. Hence his arrival in Wales. After his playing career was over, he became manager of Clapton Orient, where he made headlines in his first managerial season. Arsenal were using Orient as something of a nursery club, guaranteeing debts and holding control over the player registrations. In 1931 the League ordered Herbert Chapman to stop this empire building and, as a result, Seed found himself managing a club without a single player on its books at the beginning of the next season.

Seed coped, and quickly moved on to humble Charlton Athletic. In 1935 Charlton were promoted as champions of Division 3 South. A year after that they were promoted straight through to Division 1, the first club ever to achieve this (only QPR have done it since). The following season Seed almost completed a spectacular treble when Charlton finished runners-up to Manchester City in Division 1. He took them to the FA Cup finals of 1946 and 1947 (when they beat Burnley 1-0) and, in all, he remained manager at The Valley for over 23 years, longer than any manager at any

other English League club.

But to return to Spurs. After McWilliam had signed Seed he never again went scouting in South Wales without a wig and false beard, so violent had been the scenes when Seed's transfer was announced. After his last game for Mid-Rhondda, Seed had to address a crowd outside the dressing room, promising them that he was not being forced to leave. After this the crowd allowed the directors and players to leave the ground, though they missed Peter McWilliam, who was to be thrown into a nearby bog.

Jimmy Seed was at his best combining with Fanny Walden on the right-wing. Walden, a tiny man who had first been signed by Herbert Chapman at Northampton, was capped in 1914 and 1922 but missed what should have been the most important game of his career through injury – the 1921 Cup final. He was also a county cricketer for Northamptonshire. Chapman, who unquestionably became the greatest manager in British football with Huddersfield in the 1920s and Arsenal in 1930s, had been on Spurs books (playing just 42 Southern League games) and his discovery joined Tottenham for £1,700 in 1913. Walden's place on the wing, after his injury in February against Arsenal, was taken by John Banks, a converted inside-forward, who took his chance well and ended with a Cup winners' medal to show for it.

Apart from Seed, the team's other thinker

Second Round—ENGLISH CUP.   Kick-off 3.0.

TOTTENHAM HOTSPUR.

RIGHT WING.   LEFT WING.

GOAL
Jacques
1

BACKS

Clay   McDonald
2   3

HALF-BACKS

Smith   Walters   Grimsdell
4   5   6

FORWARDS

Walden   Seed   Cantrell   Bliss   Dimmock
7   8   9   10   11

Referee—Mr. H. RYLANCE.
Linesmen—Messrs. H. Miller and A. E. Betts.

12   13   14   15   16
Cook   Howson   Hibbert   Marsh   Bonl
                            FORWARDS

17   18   19
McIlvenny   Storer   Duckett
                    HALF-BACKS

20   21
Boocock   Potts

BACKS
22
Ewart
GOAL

LEFT WING.   RIGHT WING.

BRADFORD CITY.

ANY ALTERATION WILL BE NOTED ON THE BOARD.

English League.—Division 1.
Made up to January 26th.

	P.	W.	D.	L.	For	Ag.	Pts.
Burnley ...	24	16	5	3	53	19	37
Newcastle United ...	24	13	5	6	47	26	31
Bolton Wanderers ...	25	11	9	5	46	29	31
Manchester City ...	24	13	4	7	49	30	30
Everton ...	26	10	10	6	41	36	30
Liverpool ...	24	11	7	6	41	23	29
Middlesbrough ...	24	11	7	9	37	33	29
Tottenham Hotspur ...	24	11	4	9	53	35	26
Arsenal ...	24	9	8	7	35	35	26
Manchester United ...	24	10	6	8	42	41	26
Aston Villa ...	25	10	5	10	41	43	25
Preston North End ...	24	9	5	10	37	35	23
West Bromwich Albion ...	23	7	9	7	31	36	23
Chelsea ...	24	8	7	9	26	36	23
Blackburn Rovers ...	21	7	8	9	35	36	22
Sunderland ...	24	7	8	9	29	38	22
Bradford City ...	23	7	7	9	32	34	21
Huddersfield Town ...	25	7	6	12	20	30	20
Sheffield United ...	27	4	10	13	24	48	18
Oldham Athletic ...	24	3	9	12	24	58	15
Derby County ...	24	2	10	12	18	34	14
Bradford ...	24	4	5	15	26	49	13

BEWARE!
The public is cautioned against buying "pirate" programmes. They are in no sense official. Our boys outside the Ground will in future wear caps labelled "Tottenham Hotspur Programme."

Seats may be reserved for any League Match on application to the Secretary, at 750, High Road, Lower Tottenham, enclosing P.O. for 5s. No seats can be booked by telephone.

London Combination.
Made up to January 26th.

	P.	W.	D.	L.	For	Ag.	Pts.
West Ham United ...	21	14	6	4	52	33	34
Tottenham Hotspur ...	24	12	5	7	61	32	29
Fulham ...	23	13	4	7	39	26	28
Queen's Park Rangers ...	19	10	6	3	47	25	26
Millwall ...	19	8	4	7	30	21	20
Crystal Palace ...	23	8	5	10	50	53	21
Chelsea ...	21	6	7	8	32	28	19
Arsenal ...	21	8	0	13	44	45	16
Clapton Orient ...	20	6	4	10	37	52	16
Brentford ...	22	2	4	16	21	72	8

THE BEST WAY HOME TO ALL PARTS OF LONDON — By Metropolitan Electric Trains from outside the ground to Finsbury Park Station and thence by

UNDERGROUND

LEFT: *The programme from what became known as Jimmy Seed's game – the second round tie in 1921 between Spurs and Bradford City on 29 January 1921. Seed got a hat-trick in the second half, a 45-minute spell which he later called the best display of his life. John Banks, who had replaced Fanny Walden on the right wing, got a fourth and Spurs won 4-0. Apart from Alex Hunter replacing Jacques in goal when the latter was injured, the side was the same as the one which won the Cup. The numbers beside the players' names were of little practical help. Despite the efforts of Spurs and Arsenal, numbering was not introduced in League games until 1939.*

FAR LEFT: *Spurs supporters parade the short distance between Fulham Broadway underground station (then called Walham Green) and Stamford Bridge on the morning of the 1921 Cup final.*

BELOW: *Jimmy Cantrell breaks through the Southend defence during the 1921 third round tie at the Essex club's old Kursaal Gardens ground (the funfair can be seen in the background). Cantrell scored Spurs' equaliser to make it 1-1, but Southend then missed a penalty before Tottenham pulled away to win 4-1 in the second half.*

BELOW : *Arthur Grimsdell holds the Cup outside Stamford Bridge; after the obligatory photo was taken Grimsdell handed the Cup to trainer Billy Minter and caught a train home to Watford, not taking part in any of the celebrations afterwards.*

OPPOSITE TOP : *Despite the quagmire of a pitch, both King George V and the future George VI (then Prince Albert, Duke of York) came out to meet the teams. Here King George is shaking hands with Jimmy Seed while full-backs Tommy Clay and Bobby McDonald wait their turn.*

OPPOSITE CENTRE : *An hour and three quarters later Arthur Grimsdell receives the FA Cup from the King.*

OPPOSITE BOTTOM : *A very wet Stamford Bridge during the final.*

was right-back Tommy Clay, who joined from Leicester Fosse in 1913. Not very quick, but extremely clever positionally, he was a great passer of the ball. Oddly, the abiding White Hart Lane memory of Clay was of a mistake. It was in the quarter-finals of the 1919–20 FA Cup, against old enemies Aston Villa. Spurs, running away with the Second Division title, were well fancied to achieve a rare double when Clay, faced with a harmless ball and in no particular danger, somehow sliced his clearance backwards into his own net. It was the only goal of the game and Spurs went out, 1-0. Nearly forty years later, Tommy Clay remembered it as the single most vivid moment of his career. The England Selection Committee obviously didn't consider it so important, for Clay was picked for his first international two days later and he won four caps in all.

No great side has eleven great players. Apart from Clay and Seed, the Spurs of 1921 had perhaps two other stars, the left side partnership of Arthur Grimsdell and Jimmy Dimmock. Grimsdell, club captain throughout the 1920s, was born in Watford and was the epitome of a scheming, attacking wing-half. Spurs' single, most basic, movement was a triangle formed by Grimsdell, Dimmock and Bert Bliss. Grimsdell would play the ball down the left wing to Dimmock, Dimmock would beat the back, reach the goal-line and pass it

inside for inside-left Bert Bliss, or centre-forward Jimmy Cantrell, to shoot home.

Julian Holland said of Arthur Grimsdell: 'When he was injured he was sorely missed. He inspired his men, and he stamped his personality on them...he was a players' player. Not only did he know what to do in any given situation, he could also do it. He impressed players and spectators alike with the *efficiency* of his play . . . it was utilitarian football with an emphasis on craftsmanship and it made him the greatest half-back of the decade, if not of all time.'

Seed, the counterbalance, was used not so much as the creator but as the organiser. It was Seed who had to drop back to cover the space left by Grimsdell's constant foragings down the left in support of Dimmock. And it was Seed who had to drop back to play the linkman after the offside law change. When Spurs were not seeing enough of the game (unlike Arsenal they have never been a side content to absorb pressure and defend for long spells; teams from White Hart Lane have always sought out the ball, not just the result) it was Seed who had to drop back to try and win the ball more often.

Dimmock was the idol of the fans, a local lad from Edmonton who was not yet 21 when he won his first England cap and his Cup winners' medal. A classic flying left-winger, he

was the fourth of the side to be first capped in the Cup winning year and there were seven caps in all – Clay, Grimsdell, Seed, Dimmock, Bliss, Walden and Bert Smith. It should be remembered that, at this time, the home countries played only three games a year, and to be capped was a far rarer achievement than it is today when international sides usually play four or five times as many fixtures.

Bert Bliss, at inside-left, was another great crowd-pleaser, the trigger man. He was small (5 ft 6 in) and balding, a West Midlander from Willenhall by birth. His 'glory' was really reflected glory. He succeeded because of the service he received from Dimmock and Grimsdell, a constant stream of passes which he converted to hammer-shots towards the goal or, more often, well wide or over it. One can see why he was such a crowd-pleaser. The other Bert, Smith, was actually signed on Bert Bliss's recommendation while the former was playing as a forward with Huddersfield. He was tried at right-half and succeeded well enough to play against Scotland in 1921 and against Wales a season later.

The four less well known members of the Cup winning side were goalkeeper Alex Hunter, signed from Queen's Park as an amateur, who took over from 26 February 1921 when regular keeper Jacques was injured against West Bromwich. Another Scot, Bobby

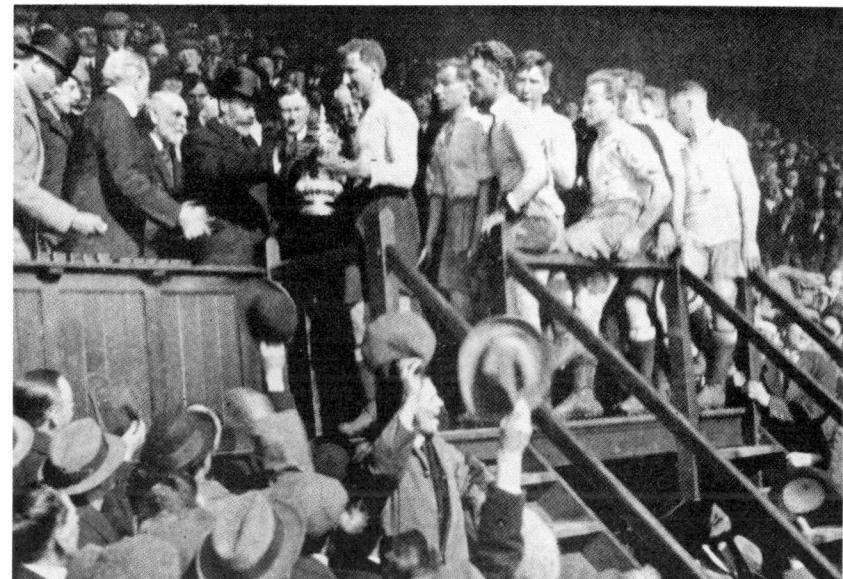

McDonald, was Clay's partner at left-back and, like Hunter, was an amateur when he signed from Inverness Caledonian. Centre-forward Jimmy Cantrell came from Notts County in 1913 and performed as something of a dual spearhead with Bert Bliss. Heaviest (12½ stone) and biggest (5 ft 11 in) was centre-half Charles Walters. Yet another amateur when he joined Spurs, Walters had made his name playing for Oxford City. With the exception of Seed (who replaced Banks in midfield) this was the team which walked away with the Second Division Championship in 1920.

THE 1921 FA CUP RUN

When Tottenham's lack of success in the pre-war First Division is considered, it is arguable that the Football League did the club something of a favour by refusing to elect it to that division in 1919. The injustice felt by club, players and fans was the perfect spur to show all concerned that a major mistake had been made. Tottenham ran away with the Second Division from the start. They won their first seven matches, scoring 28 goals and conceding just four. They dropped just two points at home (draws with Blackpool and Birmingham) all season and lost just four games away. All in all, they accumulated 70 points, easily the highest up to that time for any club in a season and not surpassed until Doncaster Rovers managed 72 in Division 3N in 1946–47. Tottenham's 70 points remained a record for the division until the end of the two points for a win system in 1981, and the club's 32 wins is still the highest number ever obtained in Division 2. Only one English club (Doncaster) has bettered it in a 42-match season. Of the club's 102 goals, 31 were scored by Bert Bliss, 19 by Cantrell, 14 by Grimsdell.

Hence Spurs had recorded their lowest ever League points total (28 in 1914–15) and their highest (70 in 1919–20) in consecutive League seasons.

The following season, 1920–21, the side settled down well in the First Division, eventually finishing sixth, but, as in 1900–01, it was the FA Cup that drew everyone's attention. This time Tottenham went right through the six rounds without a replay and the first two of these proved relatively easy. First round opponents on Saturday 8 January 1921 were Third Division Bristol Rovers (there was only one Third Division at the time). A crowd of 35,000 saw Spurs win easily 6-2, Rovers being further handicapped by having to play with ten men for virtually the whole game. Seed, Clay, Smith, Walden, Cantrell and Bliss got the goals.

Three weeks later First Division Bradford City should have proved tougher opposition at White Hart Lane in the second round, but a 39,000 crowd saw an equally one-sided match. This was Jimmy Seed's game for he scored a hat-trick (two within the space of 30 seconds) and ran the match. John Banks got the fourth from a Dimmock corner. Banks had come back into the side for Fanny Walden after the winger had been injured against Arsenal. All four goals came in the second half and Seed later said that it was probably the best 45 minutes he ever played. After the match Peter McWilliam ticked Seed off over his third goal – a 35-yard screamer – saying he should have dribbled it in and not shown off.

LEFT: *The sole picture known to exist of the only goal of the 1921 FA Cup final. Jimmy Dimmock (white shirt, directly in line with photographers) ran down the left wing almost from his own half, somewhat fortuitously beat two Wolves defenders on the way, cut into the penalty area and hit a half-powered shot from around 15 yards out. The ball skidded in the mud just in front of keeper George and slipped underneath his diving arms. The ball can be seen entering the net just beside the left hand post. The two well placed Spurs players in the area are John Banks and, beside the penalty spot, Jimmy Seed. The picture on page 59, which shows Dimmock attacking down the left, was taken from the block of flats in the centre distance. The winning team was: Hunter, Clay, McDonald, Smith, Walters, Grimsdell, Banks, Seed, Cantrell, Bliss and Dimmock. As can be seen from the two photographs, Stamford Bridge had virtually no cover from the elements at that time. The Chelsea ground, originally the home of the London Athletic Club, was opened for football in 1905 and was chosen for the first three post-war Cup finals because it had the largest capacity of all the London soccer grounds at that time. The crowd was 72,805 and the receipts (£13,414) were the highest then recorded for any football match.*

ABOVE: *The diminutive right-winger Fanny Walden, a five-foot-tall county cricketer with Northampton. A regular for five seasons after the War, he missed the 1921 Cup final through injury. Here he is flanked by keeper Jacques and Tommy Clay.*
ABOVE: *Bert Smith, Grimsdell and Jacques, plus a publicity conscious Midland Railway porter, pose before the team set off from St Pancras for the FA Cup semi-final against Preston at Hillsborough on 25 March 1922. It was an exact rerun of the previous year's round – same ground, score and opponents. The only difference was that Preston won this time.*

The third round should have been easier than it proved. The draw took them down the Thames to Southend, then playing on their old Kursaal Gardens ground. It was a classic David versus Goliath Cup-tie – Southend running, harrying, tackling and putting Spurs off their game. The Londoners did not respond too well to the problems Southend set, and were a goal down within 15 minutes, scored for the Third Division side by winger Nicholls. This at least provoked a response and Cantrell quickly headed home an equaliser from a Banks corner. A quarter of an hour before the break Southend should have gone ahead. Smith fouled Nuttall on the goal-line and skipper Fairclough prepared to take the kick. The referee, however, had noticed that the ball was not on the spot and moved it himself. Fairclough walked up to reposition it (a nervous habit rather than anything else) but the referee would not allow him to touch it. After some arguing Fairclough took the kick and shot wide. That was the turning point and Spurs did not allow Southend to regain the initiative in the

second half. Banks, Bliss (with a 25-yard free-kick) and Seed settled matters at 4-1 and Tottenham were through to the quarter-finals. But what would have happened if Fairclough *had* scored from that penalty did not bear thinking about.

By an odd quirk of fate, Tottenham's quarter-final opponents were Aston Villa, who had put them out at the same stage the season before. And, as in 1919–20 and in that famous replayed game in 1903–04, there was only to be one goal in it. 52,000 fans paid £6,992 to see the game at White Hart Lane, both figures easily records for the club at the time and the receipts were actually the highest ever recorded for any club game (other than a Cup final) in England. Villa had won the Cup the year before and were favourites to become the first club since Blackburn in 1890 and 1891 to do so in consecutive years. The goal came from a Dimmock move on the left; he centred for Seed but the schemer dummied and allowed the ball to run through to his right for Banks to side-foot it home from a narrow angle. For a reserve winger Banks was remarkably effective. Seed said afterwards that he hadn't dummied at all, but had frozen and that Banks had had to kick both Seed and the ball to take advantage of the sudden confusion in the Villa defence. The shot had lacked power only because most of the force had been absorbed by Seed's back!

The semi-final was against Preston North End. The game was played at Hillsborough before a crowd of 44,668. It was actually a poor contest, Spurs being by far the superior team. In the first half they had two seemingly good goals disallowed (one when the referee, a Mr Forshaw of Birkenhead, brought play back to give Spurs a free-kick) and Dimmock hit the bar when he should have scored. Bert Bliss did better with two goals in the 51st and 56th minutes, both from moves set up by the magical Arthur Grimsdell. Preston replied once later in the game – an own goal off Tommy Clay's knee. Unlike his own goal against Villa the year before, this one fortunately didn't matter.

THE 1921 CUP FINAL

Crystal Palace, home of the Cup final between 1895 and 1914, had been requisitioned by the Army during the war as a munitions dump. No one had restored the ground after the war ended and the Football Association had to turn elsewhere for a venue. Indeed, Crystal Palace was never again used as a football ground; Selhurst Park, home of the current Crystal Palace club, has no connection with its far more famous predecessor. The FA chose Stamford Bridge, essentially because it had a bigger capacity than any other London ground. It nearly proved a big mistake, for Chelsea reached the semi-finals in 1920 and would have played the final at home had Villa not defeated them. In 1921 Spurs clearly enjoyed the advantage any London club holds in a Cup final – a shorter distance to travel and an inevitably friendly crowd. Their opponents were Wolves, the first club Tottenham had ever played in the Football League and semi-final victors over Cardiff City. They were a Second Division club, but so had they been when they won the Cup in 1908. The crowd for the final was 72,805, easily the biggest at

the ground up to that time, and the receipts were the biggest for any football match in history (though they were easily surpassed at the first Wembley final two years later). The crowds were so great that they were let into the ground at 10.30 a.m., hours before the kick-off at 2.55 p.m. It was not until 1924 that the Cup final became all ticket.

The match is perhaps best remembered for the weather. It had rained all day and, apart from a brief spell of sunshine just before the kick-off, it continued that way. Pictures of the two Kings (George V and the future George VI) shaking hands with teams appear to show the Tottenham eleven lost somewhere in a paddy field. The weather also kept the photographers away. Only one picture survives of Jimmy Dimmock's goal, and that was taken from the terraces. In honesty, the conditions turned the game into something of a farce. Spurs were (and remained so throughout the next 40 or so years) a club which played the ball on the ground. A certain amount of rain was no disadvantage for them as favourites – it made defending harder – but a tropical downpour was a disaster. Strength would clearly tell over skill.

The game does not bear much recounting. The players slugged away, slipping and sliding in the mud, and, in general, Tottenham were the better side with Wolves creating hardly any chances. Tottenham took just one of the few good ones they created. Jimmy Dimmock was generally regarded by the following day's newspapers as having had a poor game, but

in the 54th minute, he took a pass near the halfway line from Bert Bliss. He ran the ball through the Wolves half, beat Gregory, but could not beat Woodward, who intercepted the ball. Unfortunately for the Wolves right-back, who had kept Dimmock quiet all afternoon, the ball bounced back off his legs before he could clear it and Dimmock was able to pick it up again. He cut into the penalty area and shot left-footed from about 15 yards. The ball skidded on the quagmire, kept artificially low, shot under the out-stretched arms of Wolves keeper George and just slipped inside the far post. Any goal that wins a Cup final is a good goal, but some are luckier than others and few can have been luckier than Dimmock's. It was also a selfish goal, for both Seed and Banks were well placed for a killing pass. On a good day Dimmock would probably not have beaten either Woodward or George, but then on a good day Spurs would probably have won in far more style and the fans would have been far better entertained into the bargain.

Wolves pressed but could achieve nothing, particularly with Charles Walters in inspired form at the centre of the Spurs defence. If it was anyone's match, it was his. In the very last minute, soon after Jimmy Dimmock had hit the crossbar, Wolves outside-left Brooks broke clear a few yards out. He should have equalised, but Walters got across fast enough to deflect the shot. Walters was never very creative, but he was very fast and that was his strength.

Keeper Herbert Blake and Bert Smith combine to clear a Cardiff attack during a third round FA Cup tie at White Hart Lane on 24 February 1923. Arthur Grimsdell (centre) looks unsure about Blake's punching abilities. Spurs won the game 3-2 but went out in the quarter-finals to Derby County.

Memorable Moments

1952 BAILY v HUDDERSFIELD

Great goals can only be scored in a great context. That is why it is impossible to pick the 'best' Tottenham goals of all time. A magnificent individual goal may be scored in a game which Spurs lost 4-1 and be of no relevance. Conversely, a goal like Jimmy Dimmock's in 1921 may not be the best he ever scored but it remains in the memory because it won the FA Cup and because it reflected the terrible weather conditions that day. This collection is simply of six moments that will always live in the memory; most are Cup-winning goals, but all will still be memorable when another hundred years have passed by.

BELOW : *Jimmy Dimmock scores the only goal of the 1921 Cup final. Edmonton born Dimmock, still not 21, picked up the ball just inside the Wolves half, beat Gregory and tried to slip it between the legs of right-back Woodward. The ball bounced back off Woodward's knee, Dimmock luckily picked up the rebound and shot left-footed from 15 yards. The ball skidded under George's body and Spurs had won the Cup.*

GEORGE

BANKS

SEED 1

WOODWARD 1

GREGORY

DIMMOCK 1

1921 DIMMOCK v WOLVES

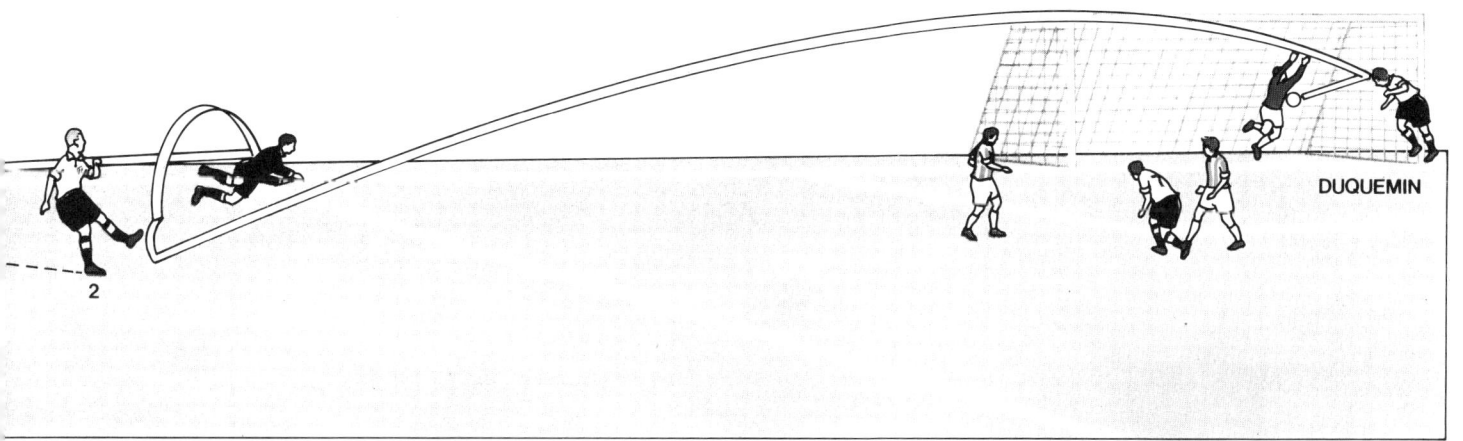

ABOVE : *Eddie Baily's illegal goal against Huddersfield on 2 April 1952. The referee had just ticked Baily off for arguing when Spurs won a corner in almost the last minute of the match. Baily took it, only to hit the referee in the back and knock him to the ground ('The crowd thought I did it deliberately,' said Baily afterwards). Baily played the ball a second time, illegally, and Len Duquemin headed the game's only goal. The referee, who had not seen what happened, let the score stand despite relegation-threatened Huddersfield's protests.*

BELOW : *Bobby Smith's magnificent goal in the 1962 FA Cup final against Burnley, his second in a Cup final in consecutive years. John White and Cliff Jones played a one-two on the left, White went down the wing, drawing defenders towards him, and centred. Bobby Smith controlled the ball left-footed with his back to the goal, swivelled round and beat keeper Adam Blacklaw with his right before the defence could intervene. It was a vital moment as Robson had equalised for Burnley and this goal made it 2-1 (see picture P126).*

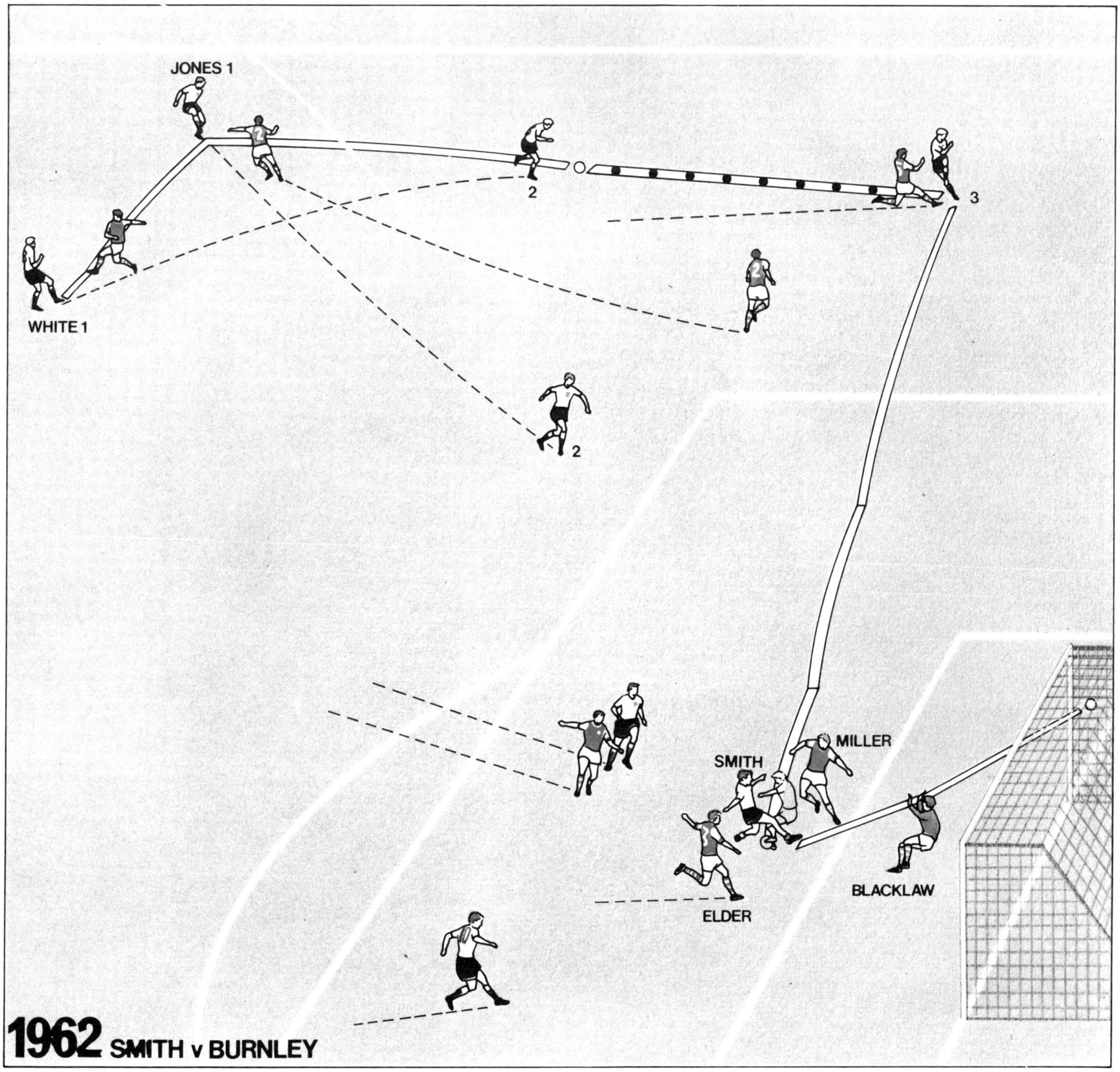

JONES 1

WHITE 1

MILLER

SMITH

ELDER

BLACKLAW

1962 SMITH v BURNLEY

1967 GREAVES v FOREST

ABOVE : *The Jimmy Greaves goal which changed the course of Tottenham's semi-final with Nottingham Forest at Hillsborough on 29 April 1967. Mike England sent a long clearance out of the penalty area, Alan Gilzean won the ball from Bobby McKinlay, and Greaves suddenly snapped at the chance from outside the penalty area. The half-volley went in off Peter Grummitt's post and Spurs were 1-0 up. They finally won the game 2-1 but it was this goal which demoralised a Forest side that had been on top for the first half hour.*

BELOW : *The last game Alan Mullery played for Spurs was the second leg of the UEFA Cup final against Wolves at White Hart Lane on 17 May 1972. Called back from Fulham, where he had been on loan, to captain Tottenham for the season's last nine matches, none of which were lost, Mullery got the home side's only goal of the second leg. Peters floated the ball from the left, Chivers drew defenders with a dummy run and Mullery got in front of McCalliog and Parkes to head home. Spurs thus won 3-2 on aggregate.*

1972 MULLERY v WOLVES

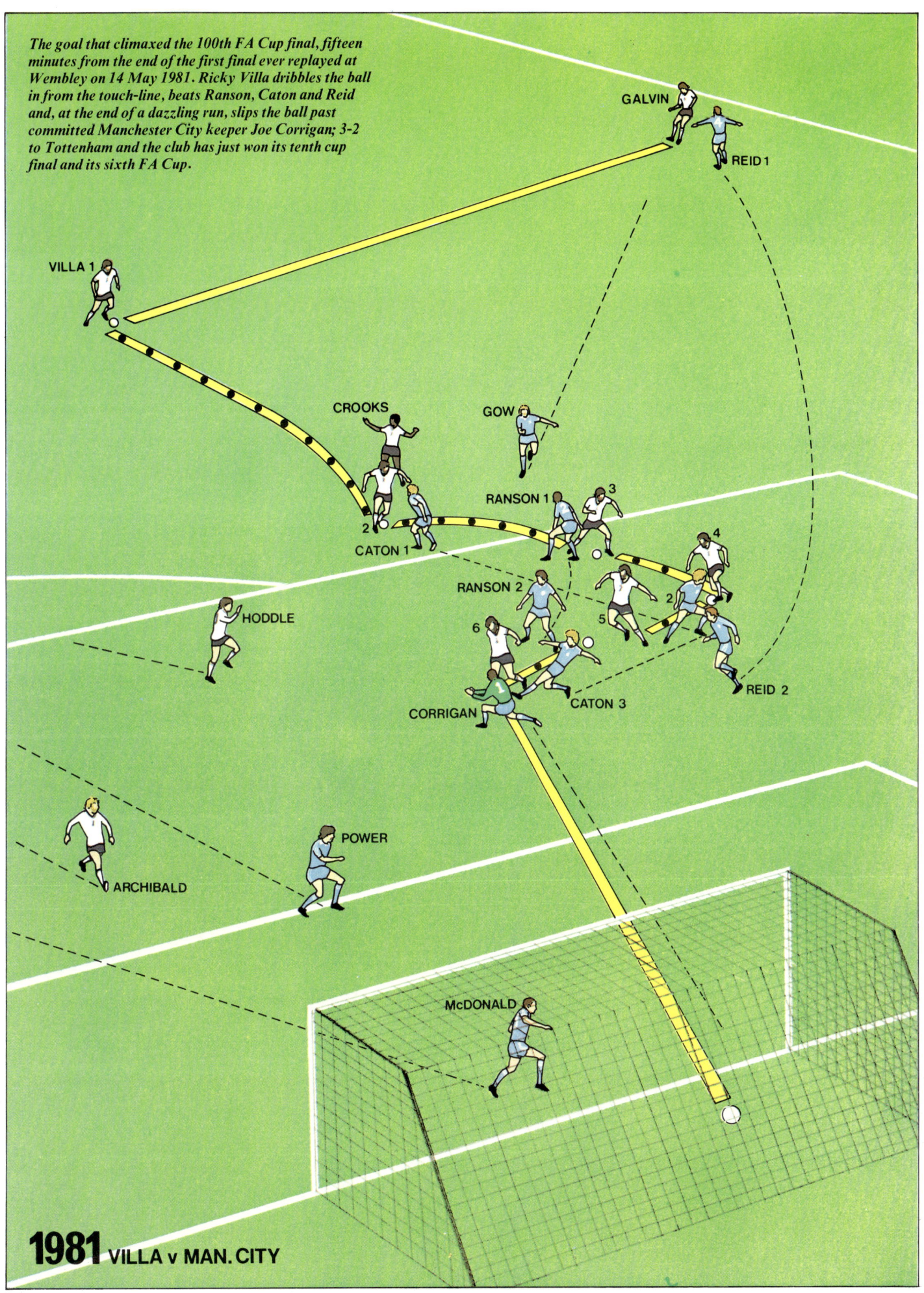

The goal that climaxed the 100th FA Cup final, fifteen minutes from the end of the first final ever replayed at Wembley on 14 May 1981. Ricky Villa dribbles the ball in from the touch-line, beats Ranson, Caton and Reid and, at the end of a dazzling run, slips the ball past committed Manchester City keeper Joe Corrigan; 3-2 to Tottenham and the club has just won its tenth cup final and its sixth FA Cup.

GALVIN

REID 1

VILLA 1

CROOKS

GOW

2

CATON 1

RANSON 1

3

RANSON 2

4

HODDLE

6

5

2

CATON 3

REID 2

CORRIGAN

POWER

ARCHIBALD

McDONALD

1981 VILLA v MAN. CITY

OPPOSITE TOP: *Eugene 'Taffy' O'Callaghan scores Spurs only goal of the ill-fated FA Cup quarter-final at Huddersfield on 3 March 1928. Town were 5-0 up at half-time and ran out 6-1 winners. Manager Billy Minter had taken the players out for walks on the snow covered Derbyshire moors from their hotel in Buxton and several later complained that they had caught colds before the match as a result.*

OPPOSITE BOTTOM: *Huddersfield was not the only club that could pack in massive crowds during the 1920s. On Thursday 9 March 1922 Spurs entertained Cardiff in an FA Cup quarter-final replay and won the game 2-1. The gates were closed before kick-off time, leaving a sight that was to become familiar in the 1950s and 1960s. When the new stand was being built in 1981 there was some talk of moving the famous gates, but sentiment in the club was firmly against.*

So Spurs had yet again brought the Cup back to London, still the only professional southern side to win the game's greatest honour. It was a record they were to maintain until Arsenal won the 1930 final, though Cardiff City in 1927 might claim to be included. Celebrations were certainly different then. Captain Arthur Grimsdell, having collected the Cup from the King, handed it over to trainer Billy Minter and went back home to Watford. It was carried back to Tottenham, via Hyde Park, Camden Town and the Seven Sisters Road, in an open charabanc. Attached were the original ribbons from the rather more glorious moment of twenty years before. There was, as in 1901, a celebration dinner at the Holborn Restaurant. The whole of the 1901 team attended with the sole exception of goalkeeper George Clawley, who had died on 16 July 1920.

The Cup was paraded around the ground the following week, carried by groundsman John Over. Four decades earlier Over had laid out the pitch at Kennington Oval for the first England v Australia test match and had joined Spurs from Edmonton Cricket Club. No one was allowed to set foot on the White Hart Lane pitch while he remained in charge of it. Even stars like Seed and Grimsdell would be disciplined if they ignored this rule; it was even rumoured that Over had doubts about them trespassing on his pitch on Saturday afternoons. When he died, his son Will took over as head groundsman.

THE INTER-WAR DECLINE

When a club is one hundred years old it may seem a little strange to concentrate only briefly on a quarter of that whole period. But compared with what had gone before and, more significantly, what has happened since, the period from the 1921 FA Cup win through to Arthur Rowe taking over after the Second World War can only be called disappointing. The club reached the semi-finals of the Cup in 1921–22, and finished second in the League, but from here onwards it was down all the way. They did not finish above the halfway mark for the next six seasons and were relegated to the Second Division in remarkable circumstances in 1928. It took five years to get back again but, after a brief flowering in third place in 1933–34, Spurs went straight back down again. And there they stayed for another decade and a half until Arthur Rowe's push-and-run team took football by storm.

If the predominant reflection on Spurs' League performances in this period is one of mediocrity, then at least the Cup provided more than a little interest. A good run in the 1921–22 competition took Spurs to a repeat semi-final, against Preston at Hillsborough. It was a game that Spurs should have won. They were one up at half-time but Preston equalised after the break having (according to the Press) drunk champagne during the interval. Towards the end Bert Bliss scored with a blistering drive but, at the moment it entered the net, the referee blew for attention to be given to a Preston player near the half-way line. It was an odd decision, to say the least, and, according to Wagstaffe Simmons, the player was not even injured anyway. The incident threw Spurs and Preston got the winner near the end. Preston's luck ran out in

the final; they lost to Huddersfield after the referee gave a penalty against them for a tackle which was clearly outside the area.

Between 1922 and the Second World War, Spurs got no further than the quarter-finals, though they did that in three consecutive seasons (1935–36, 1936–37, 1937–38) while in the Second Division. There were certainly some interesting performances in that three-year spell. In the 1935–36 third round draw, Southend were drawn at White Hart Lane. Memories were revived of the same round in 1920–21, though this time Spurs' job was expected to be easier. It wasn't: Tottenham scored four goals just as they did in 1921 but, amazingly enough, Third Division Southend did the same. Spurs won the replay 2-1, this time at Southend Stadium, but lost 3-1 away at Bramall Lane to Sheffield United in the quarter-final.

The following season, 1936–37, saw one of the most exciting games the club has ever taken part in. In fact it is difficult to think of a more exciting match from the great days of the 1960s. It came in the fifth round. Spurs had been drawn away at Goodison. It was a poor game, which sprang to life in the last five minutes after Everton had been awarded a penalty for a foul on William 'Dixie' Dean. Dean took the kick himself, but his shot was saved by ex-Manchester United goalkeeper John Hall. Dean followed up on the loose ball, but Hall saved again and cleared downfield. Jimmy McCormick picked up the ball and Spurs, right against the run of play, were suddenly ahead. But that wasn't the end of it. Coulter equalised for Everton and the game went to a replay at White Hart Lane on Monday 22 February 1937.

This was the game that Joe Mercer later wrote about as the most memorable match he ever played in. Everton were leading 3-1 with just seven minutes left. It should have been 4-1 after a strange incident revolving around a throw-in by Mercer himself. The linesman flagged for a foul throw but the referee did not notice. Everton attacked down the left, winger Gillick was fouled in the area and Everton were awarded a penalty. At this point the referee spoke to the linesman – and decided to award Spurs a throw-in back where Mercer had taken his. While the referee's judgement on facts is always correct, of course, having let play go on so long the usual response would have been to continue as if the foul throw had never occurred. At the time it did not seem to matter but, with just six minutes left, centre-forward Jack Morrison made it 3-2. Two minutes later Joe Meek ran through to equalise with a solo goal. The relief on the terraces was enormous, but they had yet to witness the finale for, with the last kick of the game, Morrison got a fourth and Spurs had won a game (4-3) which was as unwinnable as any they had ever played.

Joe Mercer said afterwards: 'I stood there hardly able to realise that we had lost ... Programmes were going up in the air, coming down and being thrown up again. Men and women and boys were dancing in circles, shaking hands and slapping one another on the back and throwing hats (which probably did not belong to them) in the air. I bet there were thousands of hats lost that day and I bet no-one cared. On the day it was played I hated

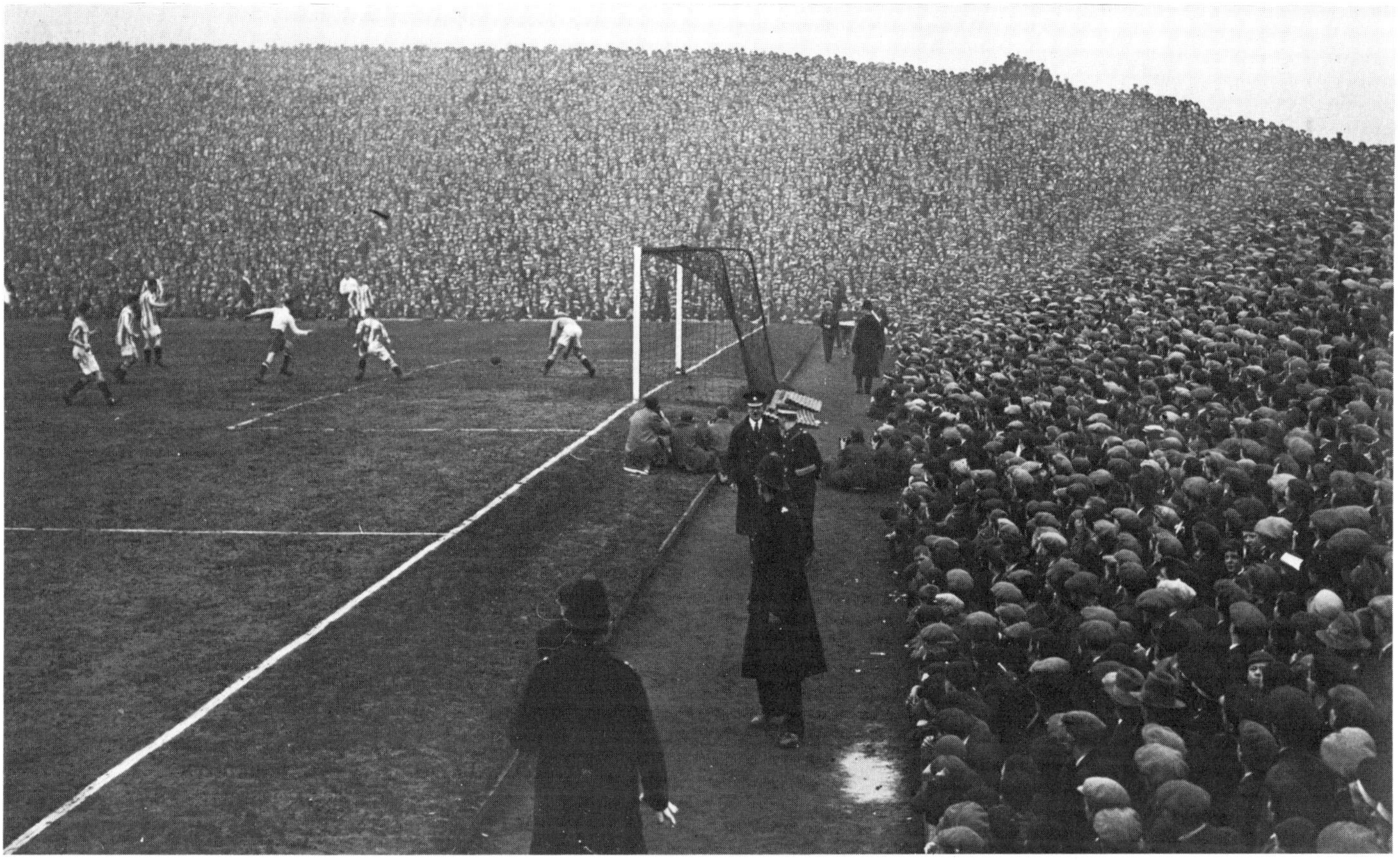

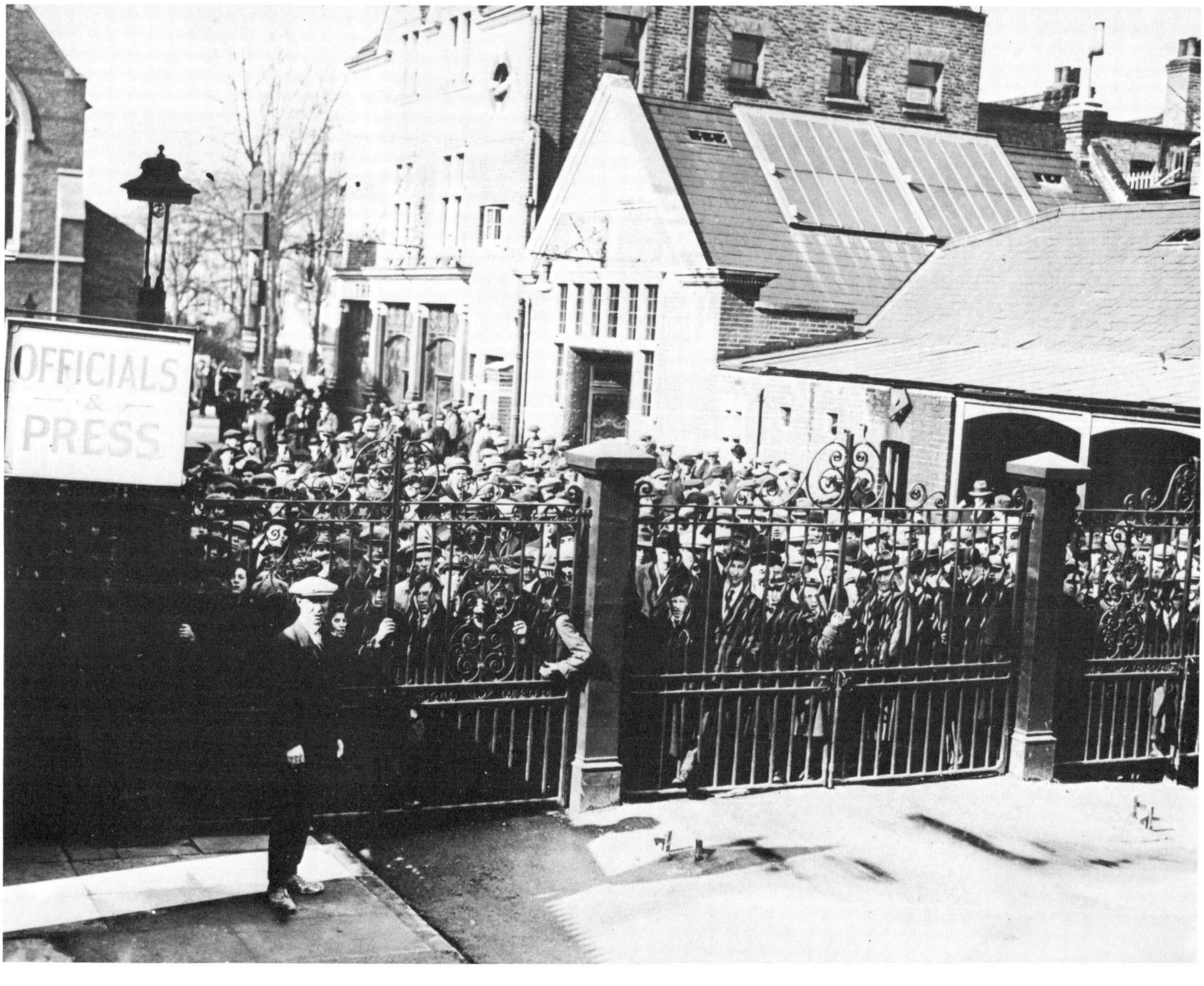
OFFICIALS
&
PRESS

BELOW RIGHT : *Taffy Day (left) and Eugene O'Callaghan leave White Hart Lane to join the Welsh team in Belfast before the home internation-al there on 4 November 1933. Welsh secretary and team manager Ted Robbins had rung Spurs secretary Arthur Turner a few hours before to ask whether he knew of anyone who could turn out for the much depleted Welsh national side. Turner had mentioned that Spurs had a promising reserve half-back called Day who, Turner thought, might be Welsh. He checked and thus Day found himself turning out for Wales before he had ever played for Tottenham or any other first class side. It also explains why photo-graphers were present to record this otherwise mundane event.*

that game. Today it stands out as the greatest in which I ever took part, a belief in which I must be joined by everyone who was there.'

As Spurs had won a remarkable third round game away at Fratton Park (home of then highly rated Portsmouth) by a startling 5-0, hopes were understandably high for further progress. Sadly, there was no fairy story to follow, for Preston won 3-1 at White Hart Lane in the quarter-finals. It was the fourth time Spurs and Preston had met in the Cup since the First World War, and laurels had remained equal, a 2-1 and a 3-1 win each. 1938 saw another quarter-final, this time with consider-ably less drama. Spurs had struggled to get there, having been taken to replays by undis-tinguished New Brighton and Chesterfield. They were drawn against Sunderland at White Hart Lane in the sixth round, and the game drew the largest attendance in the club's history, 75,038. The technical capacity was even higher (78,000) but this crowd will

surely remain the largest ever to see a game on the High Road.

They were to be sorely disappointed, Sunderland winning 1-0. There was one odd incident in the game, however. Colin Lyman shot home for Spurs from an acute angle on the left and Alec Gibbons, sure that the ball was over the line, celebrated by punching it into the back of the net. The referee gave a goal, but a linesman flagged that the ball had not crossed the line when Gibbons handled it, though it was clearly on its way. It was a very strange incident indeed, and it probably cost Spurs a semi-final place.

Not all inter-war Cup matches were wine and roses. Lowly Crystal Palace beat Spurs 2-0 at Selhurst Park in 1923–24, while unlikely Reading did exactly the same in Berkshire five years later. Neither of these humiliations compared with the quarter-final tie at Hudders-field on Saturday 3 March 1928 however. The home side, League Champions in 1924, 1925 and 1926, and runners-up in 1927 and 1928, scored five goals in the first half and presumably let up only out of pity after the break. They eventually ran out winners 6-1 in a game best glossed over. The players were later to complain that they had been made to go out on long walks across the snow covered Derbyshire moors from their Buxton hotel and had all contracted colds.

Peter McWilliam had remained as manager of the club until February 1927, when Middlesbrough offered him £1,500 per annum to take over at Ayresome Park. Spurs were reputedly paying him only £850, but he would have stayed for £1,000. The Spurs board refused, for whatever reason, to give Mc-William that small rise and he left, only to be asked to return nearly a dozen years later.

THE SEED AFFAIR

Billy Minter, an inside-forward with the club in the pre-war years, had been trainer of the 1920–21 Cup winning side and took over as manager from McWilliam. It was soon after-wards that the club perpetrated perhaps its

biggest ever mistake on the transfer market. In recent years only the sale of Pat Jennings to Arsenal can remotely compare with Jimmy Seed's departure for Sheffield Wednesday.

Seed had been injured and a Welsh lad from the Northfleet nursery, Taffy (Eugene) O'Callaghan, had been promoted to the first team. O'Callaghan and Spurs colleague Willie Evans were later to be key members in Wales' Home Championship winning sides of 1932–33, 1933–34, and 1936–37. He was playing so well on the left side of the field, combining magnificently with the ex-Fulham forward Frank Osborne, that Seed could not get his place back from 'Boy Wonder' O'Callaghan. Of course a place should have been found for both of them, for no club finds players of their quality more than once or twice a decade. But Seed was granted a transfer and went off to apparently doomed Sheffield Wednesday.

Arthur Grimsdell had broken a leg in 1926 and missed nearly a whole season, after which he was never quite the same player as in the early 1920s. The loss in such a short space of time of the two great orchestraters of the 1920–22 period (and remember that footballers' careers were much longer and slower to develop in those days), was too much for the club to bear. Seed, in his autobiography, said that he left Spurs basically because they reduced his wages from £8 per week to £7 while he played in the reserves.

It was unknown at the time, but Seed's departure was to have a far more immediate effect on Spurs' fortunes. He joined Wednesday during the 1927–28 season, when the Yorkshire side seemed certain of relegation from the First Division. With only ten matches left to play, they were five points behind the 21st club. But Seed's arrival rejuvenated them and, as Easter approached, they seemed to have a chance, if a faint one, of survival. Spurs, with just six games left to play, were in the top half of the table with 35 points. The League was so close that year that the players were thinking of perhaps just scraping into the 'talent money' places – the top four in the division where clubs were allowed to pay bonuses to their players over and above the maximum wage. It is doubtful that relegation had ever occurred to anyone at White Hart Lane, for in many ways the season had been an encouraging one. Their best result was at

Goodison where they had beaten League leaders Everton 5-2 and Taffy O'Callaghan had confirmed his continuing selection with four of the goals.

But Easter was to prove vital. Wednesday and Spurs had to play each other twice. On Good Friday, 6 April 1928, the Yorkshiremen won 3-1 at White Hart Lane. Seed scored. On Easter Tuesday, 10 April 1928, they also won, 4-2 at Hillsborough. Seed scored again. Wednesday could now save themselves. Spurs, still with no thought of relegation, finished their season earlier than most of the division (they were above the danger area) and went off to the Netherlands on a tour. They had drawn 2-2 at Burnley on 14 April, lost 4-1 at home to Bury on 21 April and lost again, 2-0 away at Anfield on 28 April. When they returned a few days later they were a Second Division club. The results had fallen in such a remarkable way that seven clubs had ended with 39 points. Tottenham had 38 and Middlesbrough 37, the highest points totals ever recorded by two relegated clubs from a 22-team division before the introduction of three points for a win.

The whole table was a complete statistical freak. Derby, who finished fourth, had just six more points than Spurs. A span of seven points covered all but three of the clubs in the division – and champions Everton managed only 53. Nothing like it had happened before nor has happened since.

But it made little difference to Spurs – they were a Second Division club again. Wednesday and Seed had not only saved themselves, they finished a respectable 14th. The following two seasons, 1928–29 and 1929–30, Seed led Wednesday to the Championship. Taffy O'Callaghan and Tottenham Hotspur had done him a quite remarkable favour.

RISE AND FALL
Billy Minter's reign as manager did not last long. On the two previous occasions the club had been in the Second Division they were promoted at their first attempt. But Spurs could finish only 10th in 1928–29 and 12th in 1929–30 (still the worst performance in the club's League history), and Minter, who remained as an assistant secretary until his death, was replaced by Bury manager Percy Smith. Smith rapidly remodelled the side – its most

notable members being centre-half Alf Messer from Reading, Taffy O'Callaghan at inside-forward, and Eddie Harper at centre-forward. Harper had been the First Division's leading scorer with Blackburn in 1925–26, and was capped against Scotland the same year. He had been bought from Sheffield Wednesday in 1929, and, though past his best, scored 36 goals in 1930–31. No Spurs player beat this in a single season until Jimmy Greaves got one more in 1962–63. Yet within 12 months Harper had been replaced by the 'Chesterfield Tough', George Hunt.

The last survivor from the great side of the early 1920s left the same season. That was Jimmy Dimmock, who now weighed 13½ stone and who had been having problems for some time. And while the older fans mourned his passing, they could not fail to be delighted by the very promising team that Percy Smith was building. George Greenfield, a local boy from Hackney, was really the greatest talent and the man who paved the way for promotion in 1933. But before that season was even halfway through he broke a leg at Fulham and his career never flourished again. Smith replaced him immediately with the remarkable Willie Hall, who was to find lasting fame with his five goals in 28 minutes for England against Northern Ireland at Old Trafford on 16 November 1938. Three of those goals came within 210 seconds and no other player has ever scored more than five for England in a single international.

He was playing inside-right for his country that day, and was obviously helped in no small way by Stanley Matthews' performance on the wing. Hall scored seven goals for England that season, only two less than he managed for his club! Hall, who came from Nottingham and had previously played for Notts County, was also remarkable for his build. The inside-right was only 5 ft 7 in tall but weighed 11½ stone. This rather rotund, muscular shape was easily distinguishable to crowds not yet assisted by numbers on the back of shirts. For that improvement, incidentally, they have Spurs to thank, for the club pushed the change through a previously reluctant League before the beginning of the ill-fated 1939–40 season. Hall, whose name has happily lived in the record books, had a less happy sequel to his distinguished career. He was afflicted by disease and eventually lost both his legs. The club gave him a testimonial in 1946 which raised a hefty sum for the times.

After their unhappy five-year sojourn in the Second Division, Percy Smith's Spurs eventually fought their way back up on 29 April 1933. Their elevation was not very impressive and, though the highlight of a 25-year period, was rather in keeping with the mood of that quarter century. Spurs lost 1–0 at Upton Park on that day while their only challengers, Fulham, went down by the same score at home to Grimsby. Stoke were champions, just one point ahead of Spurs, who at least had the distinction of being the only team in the top two divisions not to lose at home. Tottenham had started the season appallingly and were in the relegation zone in October. But they lost only three of their last 35 games, didn't once lose at home, and slowly pulled themselves up through the table. To celebrate both promotion and the club's

50th anniversary, the 1933–34 handbook tells us that '...a Grand Concert was held at the Municipal Hall.'

The club's successful spell continued into the following season. George Hunt, not at all cowed by the First Division, scored another 32 League goals to add to his 32 of the previous campaign, Willie Hall and half-back Arthur Rowe received their first caps, and the side finished an excellent third. They were ten points behind Arsenal and it must be admitted that they never really looked like actually winning the Championship after losing first place on 25 November. Nonetheless, portents were good for the future.

Portents may have been good, performance was anything but. The side fell apart almost from the start of the following season, 1934–35. In 1933–34 the goal record had been 79–56. In 1934–35 it was virtually the reverse, 54–93. The problem was in defence, where Cecil Poynton had gone (to Ramsgate), club captain Frank Felton had been released, and Arthur Rowe was injured so badly that his career never recovered. Suddenly the Spurs defence found itself without enough experience and took on the properties of a sieve. In all, 36 players were tried in the team during the season, but the problems were never really solved. Arsenal beat them 5-1 at Highbury and 6-0 at White Hart Lane, one of the most humiliating results in the club's history.

Taffy Day (left) and the 'Chesterfield Tough', George Hunt, on their way from Kings Cross to Bradford for a fifth round FA Cup tie against Park Avenue on 15 February 1936. Spurs drew the game 0-0 and won the Monday afternoon replay 2-1. They then travelled back to Bradford the following Saturday and won 5-2 in the League – a rare trio of games in one week for the same clubs. In the background is Fred Bearman, who was chairman of the club during the Double season. A director for half a century, he played just once for the first team – in a wartime London Combination match in 1917.

Between 26 December 1934, (when they beat Grimsby 2-1) and 19 April 1935 (when they beat Blackburn 1-0) Spurs did not win a League game. This run of 16 matches remains an unequalled spell of failure in the history of the club, though, oddly, they won two Cup games in January. The board and the manager had been squabbling all season, and Percy Smith's departure at the end of it was singly ungracious, considering that he had taken them to third place in the League but 12 months before. But then these things often are.

It was hardly a good time to open the new East Stand, then easily the most impressive structure on any English League ground. The cost was a staggering £60,000, largely financed through the support of Barclays Bank. As an illustration of just what an investment that was, £60,000 was almost exactly the same amount as the club's total aggregate profits (meaning annual profits minus losses) since the First World War. The most they had ever made in a single season was £17,417 in 1921–22 and in 1934–35 the club made only £8,777. Of the previous ten seasons, Tottenham had lost money in four.

Jack Tresadern, manager of Crystal Palace, took over for three seasons. He is best remembered for captaining West Ham United at the 1923 'White Horse' Cup final. He complained after that game that, when David Jack had scored Bolton's first goal, he was trapped in a section of the crowd which had prevented him getting back on the pitch after he had taken a throw-in. Sadly, his three years at White Hart Lane produced little to compare with that famed occasion. Tresadern's most memorable decisions were the sales of George Hunt to Arsenal, where he found a place in that all-conquering club's First Division line-up, and Taffy O'Callaghan to Leicester. O'Callaghan proved a critical factor in Leicester's

subsequent promotion to the First Division a season later in 1937 but he, like Willie Hall, did not survive to celebrate a comfortable middle-age for he was prematurely dead within a decade. The shades of Seed and Jennings did not go unnoticed by the fans, who never forgave Tresadern for seeming to blame these two great performers for Tottenham's troubles. Their later successes hardly assisted the manager's cause either, and his departure was inevitable.

Peter McWilliam came back to his old job for the last season before the Second World War, but time was obviously too short to work the miracles of 1920 and 1921. There were parallels with that period, however. Just as the post-Great War team had been emerging before it, so it was with Arthur Rowe's push-and-run side. McWilliam had sensibly decided that the team he inherited would not do the job, and he began to promote youngsters from the Northfleet nursery through the combination side. Les Bennett, Ted Ditchburn, Bill Nicholson and Ron Burgess all had their first taste of senior football before the War. Arthur Rowe had gone (to take a coaching job in Hungary) but he would be back.

THE WARTIME YEARS
The War was a bleak period for most clubs. Spurs had already been in relatively poor financial straights – by 1940 they had lost money in as many years as they had made it since their loss of permanent First Division status in 1928. Indeed, in 1929–30 they lost over £10,000 for the first time ever. Secretary Arthur Turner organised the side during the War and the club had some fleeting success in reaching the semi-finals of the London Cup in 1941 (they lost to Brentford). Later on in the War the club was clearly finding its feet, winning the Football League South in both 1943–44 and 1944–45. In the latter season, Spurs lost only one of their 30 games. All in all, these wartime results should not be taken too seriously. They obviously reflected the availability of players and the particular skills and positions of key individuals – some clubs had more players in the forces than others for instance. It is no coincidence that Aldershot, with so many army bases nearby, were the best side of the period. We have, nonetheless, included all first-team results from this period in the appendix for they do make interesting reading.

One other intriguing event in the war years was the expulsion of Spurs, among a dozen London clubs, from the Football League in 1941. These clubs had refused to travel long distances for some games arranged by the League (on the grounds that they could not get their players released from war duties for long journeys) and organised their own League instead. The breach was healed quickly enough, though it generated a remarkable amount of heat for a time.

1951

**Arthur Rowe • Push-and-run • Semi-final blues •
Eddie Baily • Second Division champions •
Make-it-simple, make-it-quick • Champions
at last • Danny Blanchflower**

In the annals of Tottenham Hotspur the immediate post-war era will always be associated with Arthur Rowe and 'push-and-run'. The phrase originated in Spurs style: push because it was a short, accurate passing game where the ball was pushed for exactness, run because the three-man triangle and 'wall pass' (often described as a 'one–two' or, in America, as 'give-and-go') were an integral part of the style and required the man passing the ball to run immediately into a new position to receive it back. As it happens, Rowe never liked the phrase 'push-and-run', thinking it descriptively inadequate.

The memory is often deceptive in football. It was, in fact, almost exactly four years after VE-Day that Arthur Rowe returned to Tottenham. Nor did he build that great team of the era; it was already there. He basically gave it confidence, moulded its talents, and directed its style of play. And within twelve months Spurs were back in the First Division.

The Second World War had brought changes to Tottenham. When first-class football emerged from the gloom in 1946, the club had a new chairman and a new manager. Chairmen can be remarkably important, equally they can be irrelevant. At White Hart Lane, Charles Roberts had been the dominant force for over four decades. He had taken over the club in the previous century, at a time when the balance sheet showed a deficit of £501 and there was great concern for its financial future. One wonders what he would make of the expenditure of £4,000,000 on a new stand.

His right-hand man for virtually the whole period had been secretary Arthur Turner, who was to die six years after Roberts in 1949. And while their era had begun so well, with the 1901 Cup win, the entry to the League and the excellent side of the post-Great War years, the subsequent quarter-century must have proved a great disappointment to them both.

The team that is always associated with push-and-run and the 1951 Championship; standing left to right: trainer Cecil Poynton, Bill Nicholson, Alf Ramsey, Harry Clarke, Ted Ditchburn, Arthur Willis, Ron Burgess and Arthur Rowe; seated left to right: Sonny Walters, Les Bennett, Len Duquemin, Eddie Baily and Les Medley. Missing from the picture is Peter Murphy, who made 25 appearances that season. No other players made more than seven.

Doubly so, one assumes, because of the astonishing success of neighbours Arsenal. The Gunners in the 1930s were the most successful team in soccer history and only Liverpool in the 1970s and 1980s can be said to have surpassed them domestically since.

And it was to Arsenal's memory that Spurs went for their first post-war manager – specifically to Joe Hulme. He had appeared in five Wembley Cup finals, for Arsenal and Huddersfield, a record only Pat Rice has equalled since. For Hulme, the club and football generally, the immediate post-war years were an unreal period. Though, unlike the Great War, few British players had actually died in the fighting, the disruptions to home life had been much greater, and the experienced, talented players of 1939 had lost their late twenties and early thirties to the war. The younger players had had no concentrated experience of first-class football, and in this context the younger players were now aged between 24 and 30.

Hulme never blended the old and the new quite well enough. Spurs were often in with a chance, but always flattered to deceive, finishing sixth, eighth and fifth in their first three post-war Division 2 seasons. The 1948 FA Cup semi-final was the bitterest moment. Spurs had fought their way past Bolton, West Bromwich, Leicester and Southampton to reach Villa Park for their first semi-final in nearly three decades. Blackpool were the opposition after a simpler trot past Leeds, Chester, Colchester and Fulham.

It was a semi-final Spurs seemed to have won in the 63rd minute when centre-forward Len Duquemin scored after a goalmouth melee. But with four minutes left that marvellous imp Stan Mortensen went past four defenders and goalkeeper Ted Ditchburn and squeezed the ball home from an impossible angle on the goal-line. In extra-time Mortensen scored twice more and Spurs' season collapsed. Mortensen scored in every round that year, though Blackpool lost the final to Manchester United, and then became the only man to score a Wembley FA Cup final hat-trick in 1953; Spurs were just one of the clubs whose dreams were shattered by the England centre-forward. In Julian Holland's beautiful metaphor: 'Their paws buttered, they slipped helplessly down the rungs of the League ladder...' They did not score in their next four games, and well founded hopes of promotion disappeared with the April winds.

That single moment was really the end of Joe Hulme's managership, though Arthur Rowe did not take over until the end of the following season, on 4 May 1949. To Hulme's credit, it must be pointed out that the great side of the early fifties was already playing for him. Eddie Baily, energetic, enthusiastic, perhaps the key man, and Les Bennett were at inside-forward, Les Medley and Sonny Walters were on the wings, Harry Clarke, at 6ft 3in, had joined as the solid stopper centre-half from Lovell's Athletic in the March (Spurs, despite their cultured traditions elsewhere, have no history of stylish centre-halves), Ted Ditchburn was in goal, Bill Nicholson and Ronnie Burgess firmly estab-

lished at half-back, and Channel Islander Len Duquemin was a brave, tough and willing, if not skilful, centre-forward.

At the end of Hulme's last season, after the transfer deadline, assistant manager Jimmy Anderson went down to Southampton and brought back the final link. He was the latest in a long line of thinking Spurs full-backs, following in the pattern of Sandy Tait and Tommy Clay and he was later to make something of a name for himself as a manager – Alf Ramsey. At age 29 Ramsey might reasonably have assumed that his brief first-class career was not far from an end, but he was to have five marvellous years with Spurs and England and it must have been a spell that taught him much that he was later to put into practice at Ipswich and at Wembley.

We are now entering a period when it is possible at last to let the actors speak for themselves. Before this date today's historian has only written memories, newspaper reports, second hand conversations; the principals of this post-war era are still, happily, with us and, wherever possible, it is best to let them tell their own stories.

ARTHUR ROWE – ONE MAN'S SOCCER VISION

It was a handful of sugar cubes spread round a table in the dining car of a London-bound express that originally brought the speaker's point home. That scene is recalled by neat, soft-spoken Arthur Rowe, folding back almost half a century as he tells you what happened: 'We were returning home from a match at Bradford Park Avenue and were all dead pleased at our £2 win bonus, talking over the game and the last minute goal which had done the trick for us. I spread the sugar around, trying to map out the moves leading up to our goal. It was one to savour because there were about seven passes starting out from our own penalty area. I argued that if we could plan moves like that instead of just hoping for it to happen we would score more often.'

So spoke a man with a vision, a man born just 10 minutes away from White Hart Lane. Fifty years ago push-and-run soccer was even then taking shape in the mind of the Tottenham centre-half, the club captain who was honoured once by his country, against France, and in time was destined to retrace his steps and manage his old club, his only club as a player. When he arrived at White Hart Lane the prodigal was firmly on trial as the manager of his first League club. Rowe had done things and won things as the secretary-manager of Chelmsford City, had been a big success. But that was the Southern League. It had brought him recognition and awards, but had it geared him sufficiently for a much greater challenge?

He spent the close season of 1949 planning the spreading of the soccer gospel according to Arthur Rowe. Modestly he now says: 'Our style was basically the method of Spurs football taught down the years...with variations. Tottenham had always tried to play football to entertain. When you can get both, entertainment with effectiveness, you are on the right road. Push-and-run, that was the label they came to pin on our style although, quite

OPPOSITE PAGE: *Referee Arthur Ellis signals for a free-kick against Les Bennett as he goes up for the ball with Preston North End goalkeeper Malcolm Newlands. Preston won the game, played at Deepdale on 4 October 1952, by the only goal. Spurs links with Preston have often been close. After the two played each other in the Cup in January 1900 (Preston winning 1-0) Spurs decided to adopt Preston's strip; fifty years later the club second strip was the reverse – blue shirts and white shorts. The two also met in the Cup in 1901, when Spurs gained revenge with three ex-Preston players in their side, and in two consecutive semi-finals, 1921 and 1922. Les Bennett was the one player in the push-and-run side to operate outside the mould. He might slow the whole game down, or try to dribble through the middle of a packed defence. He was the source of the side's unpredictability, essential to varying the flow and direction of attack.*

honestly, I was never very fond of it. You often saw something like our style happening in a match, any kind of match; a side suddenly stringing together short, quick passes and players moving intelligently to give and take them. It's as if the game suddenly got an electric shock. The thing about the Tottenham side I had was that we tried to make it happen all the time.'

He makes a surprising admission: 'I never told anybody how to play, I just made suggestions on playing patterns, put up ideas. I'd ask players if they had ever tried a certain move, talk it over with them, get them to discuss between themselves...then we'd try it out.'

'Make it simple, make it quick' was the maxim Rowe endlessly pumped into his men. That was the content of a famous telegram Rowe sent to ex-Spur Vic Buckingham on the eve of an Amateur Cup semi-final. Buckingham was managing Pegasus, the intellectual Corinthians of the mid-twentieth century. Pegasus beat Hendon in the semi-final and then went on to win the final against Bishop Auckland. As Rowe says: 'I took our style back to the streets, the way we played it as kids – off the kerb, off the wall, taking the ball at different angles, enlisting the kerb as a team-mate who let you have the ball back immediately after you had played it quickly...the quicker the better. And all the time you were tailoring your ideas, your hopes to the limits or the limitations of your players, not asking them to do the things they could not do.'

Arthur Rowe had stored admiring memories of an old rival, Clem Stephenson, the star of a Huddersfield Town which had won a hat-trick of League Championships in the 1920s. Said Rowe of Stephenson, whom the England selectors of the time also only remembered to honour once: 'He was great. I was enthralled when I played against him, he best illustrated the style I wanted my teams to play. He played everything off quickly, you didn't catch him in possession. He was like Alex James but did things faster. I saw how much trouble he caused and thought "What if you get them *all* playing it like that?"'

'So many players wanted to show their individual skills in those days, but it's a team game, everybody had to come into it. I tried to build a side who would play for each other because that's what the push-and-run style demanded if they were to get the most out of it. Some players had greater skills than others but you had to try and make all of them feel that they had a big part to play. For instance, I asked Sonny Walters if he was prepared to work harder by coming back more into our half...not something wingers reckoned to do in those days. I told him that he would have to defend more but he would also get more of the ball. I put it to Alf Ramsey that while I knew he was brought up on using long, measured passes, these tended to leave him out of the action once he had played them. But had he ever thought how much more accuracy was guaranteed, how much more progress could be made, if he pumped 15 or 20-yard passes to a withdrawn Walters?

'The opposing left-back would hesitate to follow Walters back into the Spurs half, which was definitely no-man's-land to the full-back then, thus giving Walters the vital gift of space. And Sonny could also now make an inside pass if Alf followed up and made himself available. We had one more option; with Ramsey's precision, once advanced he could drive the ball down the right for Les Bennett, coming to the near post, to turn the ball inside with his head. And Bennett created numerous chances doing just that. Ramsey's advances would throw a heavier load in defence on Bill Nicholson but he was the ideal cover at half-back – sound, solid and a rattling tackler.'

Ramsey at the back and Bill Nicholson in front of him patrolled the right-hand side of the field and remain the best known of that great side. But they were arguably not the stars. Captain was Ronnie Burgess, the successor to the great Arthur Grimsdell, and also left-half and captain for his country, Wales. While Nicholson kept back, protecting the flank and allowing Ramsey more freedom, Burgess played the roving half-back. He was always happier in attack, utilising a remarkable burst of speed for a nominal defender, and it took years of coaching, first from Peter McWilliam and then Arthur Rowe, to persuade him to curb this tendency when it was in the team's best interests.

INTERNATIONAL HONOURS

Eddie Baily, at inside-left, was the crowd's favourite. A local from Clapton he was the effervescent enthusiast – always running, always willing, always involved. A great dribbler, a great passer of the ball, possessor of an excellent shot, perhaps his one fault was confidence – he could so easily lose it, become unsure of himself. But it was around him that Rowe really built his team, for 'push-and-run', or whatever nomenclature one may wish to use, was virtually Baily's natural game. He was to win nine England caps, scoring five times. Nicholson, oddly, won only one, though he scored against Portugal in the opening seconds of that game. Ramsey won 31 caps while with Spurs, and scored three times from the penalty spot for England. They were not the only members of that side to be capped; Ted Ditchburn eventually appeared six times for England, Les Medley the same number, and full-back Arthur Willis, not an absolute regular in the side, picked up a cap against France in 1951. Ron Burgess appeared for Wales on 32 occasions, as well as for Great Britain against the Rest of Europe in 1947. Billy Rees, another reserve, won a Welsh cap in March 1950 – making eight internationals in all, a remarkably high number for a club gathered together in the middle of the Second Division and with virtually no outside purchases.

The team also had its unsung members – particularly inside-forward Peter Murphy, signed from Coventry, who played 25 times in the Championship season and yet whose name is rarely remembered. Arthur Rowe knew the way he wanted to play the game and he longed to try out his ideas with good players. That chance came, but he never believed it would be his old club which gave it to him or that any club could provide such talent: 'Not just good players, I took over some *marvellous* players. Eddie Baily, a natural one-touch player. I never saw a man who could play a moving ball either way and with either foot as quickly or as accurately.

Ted Ditchburn's successor, Ron Reynolds, gathers a high ball under the watchful eye of Alf Ramsey. The opposition that day, Saturday 12 February 1955, were Blackpool and a massive crowd had turned out because of Stanley Matthews, who can be seen in the left distance. The other Tottenham defenders are Mel Hopkins, Tony Marchi and Harry Clarke and Spurs won the game 3-2. It was, however, a poor season. Seven days later they were knocked out of the Cup at Third Division York City and finished the League in only 16th position. Note the new design in the middle of the Main Stand and Spurs' strange socks.

Where would you find an inside-forward like him now? Then there was the skipper, Ronnie Burgess, brilliant, a great player. And I don't use that word easily. I wanted the ball moved at speed from the midfield and that is what this priceless pair did for me. Then there was Alf Ramsey who gave us our momentum... from the back.

'There was no finer competitor than Ted Ditchburn in goal, nor did I think there was a better keeper to be found. Ditchburn, Baily, Ramsey and Burgess...they played as you wanted them all to play. They were the ones who most used their abilities to the full.'

Eddie Baily tells of the lead-up and the outcome of that first season under the new Spurs boss: 'There were a lot more instinctive players about then than now. That team just came together and you really didn't know why. When Arthur took us over he had players with a lot of natural ability. He was a kindly, amiable man who soon saw that they could play the way he wanted the game to be played, the way it ought to be played. So he gave us every encouragement.

'He would encourage the simple principles, on and off the ball and the urge to play this more exacting but much more exciting game took us along with the obvious enthusiasm of the man. There was no coaching to it, we improved and improvised as we went along. We just did things instinctively and being good players – and we were – we chose to do the right things

more often than not. Basically, we played our game in a series of triangles, moves involving three players at a time with each learning and getting to know each others' parts. The whole thing became very fluid, there were no attackers and defenders, in a given situation we all became defenders or attackers.'

This was most obvious with Ted Ditchburn. Today the tactic of retaining possession by having the goalkeeper throw the ball to a full-back is commonplace. When Ditchburn and Alf Ramsey did it consistently in the 1950s it was a remarkable departure in approach. Ditchburn would rather deflate the budding tactician Ramsey when he was asked how the ploy developed: 'Simply because I was such an awful kicker,' he would explain.

'We changed things,' says Baily today. 'We gave the ball to the man who *was* marked. But other players slipped into support positions to give the man with the ball more options. That in turn depended on how the ball had been given and we had to guarantee that our man received it. It was the kerb or the wall game with players in support to allow the man in possession a choice of angles. It drew defenders, it got our rivals chasing as well. Fine players like Joe Harvey of Newcastle and Pompey's Jimmy Scoular, always tough competitors, would have a few choice words to say as they tried to close you down. Joe used to call across to me at the start of a game: "We'll get you today, you little — " It wasn't

meant as a threat or any kind of intimidation, just part of the ribbing that went on in those days. But it also carried a note of respect for you and your side.'

SECOND DIVISION CHAMPS

Rowe's push-and-run stylists swept Spurs to the top. Nobody could have bargained for such a dramatic impact in the new manager's first season. There was a home stutter in a 2-3 defeat by Blackburn Rovers in their third match, after delighting supporters with 4-1 victories over both Brentford and Plymouth Argyle. Then Burgess and his boys powered away on an unstoppable run from the 2-0 return win at Plymouth on August 31 until Leeds United halted them with their 3-0 success at Elland Road on 14 January 1950, an unbeaten sequence of 22 League matches at the end of which was a Cup win over Stoke City to make it 23 games in a row.

It meant that from the beginning of September until the season closed for them on May 6, they stood astride the Second Division, a nine-month reign at the close of which their rivals only got within a distant nine points as the rampant Spurs eased down on the home straight. For over the regulation promotion course of 42 League matches from August to May, Spurs had jinked their way clear of all opposition to burst into the 1950s with a lead of ten points, and then went on to stretch it to a runaway thirteen as April brought its usual

clutter of games before the close down. And the crowds crammed into White Hart Lane as Rowe's side stormed on. Loyal fans were rewarded for their patience as Tottenham served out the end of the fifteen year exile in the Second Division.

Luke-warm followers saw a light rekindled, others came in from the fringes of North London and beyond for the first time as Spurs and their winning ways became the capital's leading attraction. North London indeed had become the mecca of football with the Tottenham home gates for that glorious season returning an average of 54,405, an incredible figure as you look at it now, and the next highest in the League having been established across at Highbury where Arsenal had totalled 51,381. White Hart Lane attendances topped 50,000 on no less than 15 occasions; the Southampton visit on February 25 brought the season's biggest gate...70,305; 66,880 came to the April match with Hull City and the meetings with Queen's Park Rangers, Chesterfield and Leicester City all passed the 60,000 mark. More than a million and a half customers passed through the Tottenham turnstiles that season, still a record for the club. The return to the First Division could not have been gained in more conclusive fashion. Spurs scored more goals (81) and conceded less (35) than any of their rivals in the Second Division. The fans' cheers were particularly sweet music for Arthur Rowe. Though injured for several

Confusion at the back as Ditchburn fails to gather the ball from West Brom right-winger Griffin and Nicholson and Ramsey prepare to clear the danger area. Spurs 3-1 win in this 9 October 1954 fixture was more than welcome; it was their first for ten matches and only their second at home since the season began. Ted Ditchburn and Ron Reynolds shared the goalkeeper's jersey, rather unsatisfactorily, for the next four seasons.

THE GOAL

TOTTENHAM HOTSPUR FOOTBALL CLUB

LEAGUE CHAMPIONSHIP

F.A. CUP

...WHILE THE SPURS GO MARCHING ON

ABOVE: *The rather premature cartoon which appeared in the club programme on Tuesday 26 December 1950, showing Arthur Rowe dreaming of Ron Burgess leading the side to the Double. The dreams and hopes were to be shattered just a week and a half later at Huddersfield, on 6 January 1951, when Spurs went out of the Cup 2-0 at the first hurdle. But perhaps it was really a premonition of ten years later.....*

OPPOSITE PAGE: *Ted Ditchburn at his best, diving to save a Burnley shot on 27 October 1956. He kept a clean sheet that day, Spurs winning 2-0 against a side which was to figure prominently in the dramas of the next few seasons. Ditchburn was the last survivor of the push-and-run side.*

months, he had played 18 games fifteen years before in that last season in Division 1.

Now they were back – and with a bang. In the Cup they had taken on First Division opposition in beating Stoke in the third round. For Sunderland in the fourth round there was an enormous crowd of 66,246, and Spurs turned the tap full on.

Sunderland, good enough to end the season third in the League, were simply swamped in a breath-taking home display, especially in the second half. Coming up after the interval with a 2-1 lead Tottenham then bewitched, bothered and bewildered a Sunderland defence which was laboriously slow and had the fact rubbed home by the speedy switchings up front and the rapid change of the points of attack by quick-silver Spurs forwards. Sunderland were run ragged as Tottenham piled up a 5-1 win, Sonny Walters and Les Bennett having helped themselves to two goals apiece and Les Medley getting the other. But Goodison Park in round five saw Everton in no mood to share a fate as bad or worse than Sunderland's. The Liverpudlians retained their Cup interest by the only goal scored, and a disputed penalty at that. Big Harry Clarke was ruled to have handled in the early minutes. Spurs protested at the penalty award but it made no difference. And they bade their Cup farewell when Wainwright rapped in the spot kick.

The return to the First Division lifted the spirits of everybody and everything connected with the club. Now there was an expectancy, a feeling of things about to happen. The lengthening queues for advance ticket sales heightened interest and hopes. Baily harks back to the players' mood at that time: 'You felt that you couldn't get started quickly enough. Remember, none of us had sampled the First Division before. We didn't fear it, we knew we were a very good side now. But we were impatient to find out just how good.'

All the time Arthur Rowe fed his players virtual 'Sunday school' tracts; 'Make it simple, make it quick'; 'A rolling ball gathers no moss'; 'He who stops is lost'. 'I said them so often the boys must have got sick of hearing them,' he admits. He even had them printed and scattered around wherever the players

might appear. Said Eddie Baily: 'It got so that we were making them up ourselves.'

But what could have sounded very much like children at school repeating parrot-wise after teacher was apparently very real to the Tottenham players. Baily readily admits to chanting them aloud as reminders in the hottest of practice matches. There were cartoons, too. Rowe had one printed which showed a burglar with customary swag-bag at the ready, hurling a brick through a jeweller's window. The inevitable policeman approaches and over the shattered window we read, 'If we make space'; down to the second cartoon and a judge proclaiming 'three years' over the burglar with caption, 'We get time', and the last strip shows our hero, arrowed suit and all, breaking stones in a vast wilderness which could only be Dartmoor and the final lesson: 'And time means space.'

Spurs had never been able to boast a League title when they set out in the 1950–51 season. Their best effort had been as runners-up to Liverpool in 1922, six points adrift. Rowe himself was in the 1932–33 team which won promotion to the First Division, a point behind Stoke City, and then the following season did well enough to take third place in the title race behind Arsenal and Huddersfield Town, the dominant teams of the era. Some thought that there might have been some cracks showing in the side after their finish to the 1949–50 campaign, given the fact that they lost four of their last five matches and drew the other. Were they too casual or too arrogant in believing they had already done their job, it was asked?

Arthur Rowe shrugs it off now: 'We had won the Second Division with six or seven games to go and if we had finished the job in the manner in which we had been playing up till then we must have ended up with a record points total. I don't think the players knew, or felt, that they were easing up. And I don't think that I was aware of it either. It happened, and that was it. It wasn't that we just didn't care once the title had been won. But there was a lesson there for us.'

The summer which intervened between Tottenham's Second and First Division Championships had seen what still has to be regarded as England's greatest humiliation – the 1-0 defeat by the United States in Belo Horizonte, Brazil. Ramsey, Baily, Ditchburn and Nicholson were all part of that discredited squad and they returned home to a still soccer obsessed nation which was asking just where English football went next. The answer was to White Hart Lane.

THE LEAGUE CHAMPIONSHIP
Spurs had marked the opening of the season with a 1-4 home deflation by Blackpool. It furrowed the brows of the faithful. Then things began to fall into a more fruitful pattern four days later with a similar score, this time in their favour at Burnden Park with Bolton as the victims. A 2-2 away draw with Arsenal, four more goals against the unfortunate Bolton side, another away point at Charlton and it left no doubts. Tottenham were well able to take care of themselves in this more rarefied football atmosphere and their slick, slippery soccer, their punchy pace, sent out danger signals to every team in the First Division.

Their hurricane broke with a run of eight straight victories between the very last kick of September and mid-November. It was devastating and deadly, nothing could stem its force. Everything came together at once in a sustained, co-ordinated spell unparalleled by even the best this now great side had shown up to then. At the end of it all 28 goals had humiliated such as Aston Villa, Burnley, Chelsea and Stoke City, West Bromwich Albion, Portsmouth, Everton and Newcastle United. Among all eight opponents they mustered a feeble six scoring efforts in reply. And felt as if they had been through a threshing machine.

Said Eddie Baily: 'I have been lucky to have been in the right place at the right time to give me a lifetime of football satisfaction, but this was something else again.' The centrepiece of it all was three consecutive home performances, virtuoso stuff which stunned Stoke City with six goals, then rattled home a further five past proud Portsmouth, League Champions in the two previous seasons, and finally flattened luckless Newcastle United, who were to win the FA Cup that season but

failed to raise a whisper of defiance when seven successful scoring attempts filled the net behind them.

Baily himself and left-wing partner Les Medley each helped themselves to hat-tricks from this harvest, and Eddie tries to keep the pride from his voice in remembering: 'Our style commanded a lot of respect from others because of its freshness, because of the way it was played and the men who played it. You felt that you were helping to lift the tone of the game and so you got that respect from crowds as well. Other players would quiz you on it, and discuss how they might combat a team which moved all the time and always seemed to have more men than they did...the true yardstick of a great team.'

Arthur Rowe, the quiet genius behind it all, swallows hard at the recollection: 'I never had more pleasure from the game than that team gave me,' he states. 'When it was flowing like that and all going right I would sit transfixed at some of the football they put on. I was jealous for them, anxious that they should do justice to themselves. That was the only pressure, the rest was sheer pleasure.'

Tottenham's programme for Boxing Day, 1950, and the home match with Derby County contained a cartoon of manager Rowe, surrounded by the seasonal festive drinks and eats and snoozing by the fire with his feet up. He's dreaming a dream which has Burgess and his men marching towards a twin goal of the League Championship and the FA Challenge Cup. Perhaps it was not a dream at all, but a premonition of ten years hence. Within a fortnight Huddersfield Town had brought a rude awakening to at least the Cup part of the dream. They tumbled Tottenham out with a 2-0 third round eclipse on their own Leeds Road pitch, seemingly always a bad ground for Tottenham.

The Town, in fact, paid scant respect to Tottenham's soaring reputation that season for they beat them in three straight sets, 3-2 in their first League meeting, 2-0 in the Cup (both at Leeds Road) then 2-0 at White Hart Lane to end another Spurs run of unbeaten games late in the season and so dilute and delay the Tottenham title hopes. Not that the Yorkshiremen were any great shakes themselves; they had all their work cut out to avoid relegation at season's end, finishing 19th in the table.

A look on the Tottenham line-ups of the time proves how successful was the youth policy of the club, begun in the old Northfleet nursery era and, it must be said, in the days when clubs appeared to be able to find the time to wait for youngsters to come through. The worth of such a policy together with a tight talent net spread locally by the club scouts meant that an astonishingly high proportion of seven first team players came from London, or within a few miles of the capital, and most of the others came up through the Spurs farm teams: keeper Ted Ditchburn came from Gillingham, Bill Nicholson was born in Yorkshire but at Northfleet from school, Charlie Withers (Edmonton), Alf Ramsey, bought from Southampton but hailing from Dagenham, Harry Clarke from Lovell's Athletic but first from Woodford, Ronnie Burgess, belonged to Cwm, Monmouth, but another nursery graduate, Les Bennett came from Wood Green, Sonny Walters from Edmonton, Eddie Baily was a native of Clapton and his wing twin Les Medley was another of the Edmonton crop.

And checking down the playing staff we find Vic Buckingham (Greenwich), striker Jack Gibbons (Charlton), dapper little Tommy Harmer (Hackney), George Ludford (Barnet), Tony Marchi – Edmonton once more, Sid McClelland, a Rowe buy from Poplar, reserve keeper Ron Reynolds, from Aldershot, and Sid Tickridge from Stepney in the East End. By any standards that was a tremendous haul of local and home-grown talent, both in quality and quantity, and said much for the alert coverage of the Tottenham scouts under the shrewd chief spotter, Ben Ives.

Baily talked of the great bond between the players fostered by Rowe which came to mean equally as much as any other part of the team's preparation. 'It meant so much to us all,' he said. 'We were always playing for each other, it was genuine team spirit. We gave and accepted criticism of our game, of ourselves that was honest and well-intended. You played with a pride in yourself and the team. And all

that for a win bonus of two pounds.'

He smiles wryly and adds: 'You know I never had a car until I was 34 years old; the only players I can recall owning one then were Ronnie Burgess and Ted Ditchburn. I believe it was Ted who had a big old thing that came straight out of the American bootlegging days...we called it 'Dillinger' because Ted looked for all the world like the gang leader Jack Dillinger when he set off in it...

'I lived in Clapton and on match days I used to walk up the road and queue with the fans waiting to catch a bus to our ground. On the journey you would have to settle playing queries, chat about football generally and then give an optimistic forecast of the afternoon's game, and often having to stand all the way. Then, because the crowds were so great, you would have to drop off some way down the High Road and try and thread your way along the jammed pavements. But, at the end of the day, you might be two pounds better off.'

ROWE THE PLAYER

Arthur Rowe himself came up through the ranks like most of his team. He went to, and through, the Northfleet nursery after joining Spurs as a teenager when Peter McWilliam was still manager. But with a young eye on security he kept up his apprenticeship as an upholsterer until he had passed out. At 20 he felt that his football career was not taking off fast enough and he asked the then manager, Billy Minter, about it. To which he was asked quickly: 'What do you mean, has somebody been getting at you?' Then thinking on, Minter added: 'Come and see me next week.' And that's how young Rowe forced through his ambition to become a Spur, which he did after signing on at White Hart Lane for £4 a week.

He got his League chance, and took it, in the 1931–32 season and Spurs won promotion in 1933, ascending to the First Division with their young, attacking centre-half now firmly established in a very good side. Rowe gained his one England cap on his native White Hart Lane pitch on 6 December 1933 against France, a match which the powerful English side won 4-1 with two goals coming from George Camsell, of Middlesbrough, one from dynamic Eric Brook, the Manchester City winger, and the other from Birmingham's strolling Tom Grosvenor at inside-right. Club-mate Willie Hall was in that same English side and the names of the rest of his colleagues that day sound like a roll of drums in soccer history...goalkeeper Harry Hibbs, uncommonly short of stature for a keeper, this Birmingham star, but rated by many as the greatest we have ever had; full-backs Roy Goodall, of Huddersfield, and Newcastle's Dave Fairhurst (Goodall, it transpired, was getting the last of his 25 caps that day while for Fairhurst, like Rowe, this was to be a once-in-a-lifetime appearance); Alf Strange, of Sheffield Wednesday and the fearsome Wilf Copping played either side of new boy Rowe at right and left-half respectively.

Rowe played adventurously at centre-half in accordance with Spurs wont to take the fight to opponents; he was never shackled by plans or areas of the playing pitch, the whole arena was his domain. So when England began to over-run the struggling French, Rowe was

in close support to a raid down the right-wing, much to the amazement of Strange, then gaining what was to be the last of his 20 caps. 'What are you doing, coming over to my side of the field?' he demanded of England's newcomer. 'I came over to see if you wanted any help,' was the cheeky answer Strange apparently received. The following season Rowe and Hall both suffered cartilage operations and Spurs went back to Division 2 and stayed there until Rowe regained the reins.

Rowe's playing career ended in 1938–39 when he lost his battle against injuries. He had played more than 200 League matches for Tottenham and took up a coaching appointment in Hungary, thus following in the footsteps of pioneer Jimmy Hogan some years earlier. He thoroughly enjoyed his stay at a Budapest college and was in the process of negotiating a three-year contract to become Hungary's national coach when the war clouds blew up even more menacingly. He said: 'I felt I was lucky to have got away before someone blew the whistle on me. I would liked to have stayed under different circumstances but it was obvious by then that something was going to happen.'

So instead of helping to loose a stream of future Hidegkutis, Puskases and Boszıks on unprepared Englishmen, Arthur Rowe went off instead to the Army to become one of the many sportsmen organising training, recreation and entertainment for the troops and travelling extensively. With the war over and football literally trying to find its feet again, he landed his job with Chelmsford City, to the great advancement of himself and the non-League club. The City, under Rowe, began in stirring fashion, winning both the Southern League title and the Southern League Cup in their first season together. And so it was that he was recalled to White Hart Lane and a team that was already waiting for him. 'Watching them was nothing short of uplifting,' said Rowe. 'I used to wish that all teams could have played like it for the benefit of the game. The fans at White Hart Lane loved us and that was a crowd that was well educated because they had seen good football through the years. Fathers watched it and brought up their sons on it; that was the Tottenham tradition. And it's so good to have seen it happening again in more modern times. There was no thuggery in our game, it had no part. You played football and you won the ball by positional sense. You played them out of the game. We did it in style, no jealousies, all pals together. It would have been great to have had all those wonderful games on tape so that you could take them down when you wanted and enjoy them all over again.'

CHAMPIONS AT LAST

Among those on the shelf above the video machine would surely have been the highlights from that last third of the season, while Spurs were still in the championship foothills. They had gone to the top of the First Division on 30 December 1950, the first time for 17 years. Tottenham held on to a one-point lead over Middlesbrough going into February of 1951 and Manchester United were lurking on the premises. But Spurs had given off the glint of champions and were to save themselves for a finishing burst in true Lester Piggott fashion.

With the Easter matches included, they had to play seven matches in March, which meant them rounding off the month with four games in nine days, a stiff programme. Altogether they then had twelve matches left to play.

Taking a leaf from Lewis Carroll, they became football's March Hares as they scudded ahead of their rivals with a powerful surge which saw them whip through the month's seven barriers with hardly a falter. Playing as confidently and as consistently as prospective champions should they gathered in twelve of the fourteen points the month had offered, a fitting tribute to their skill and dedication. First Chelsea were set aside 2-1 at White Hart Lane, next Stoke City held 0-0 in the Potteries. West Bromwich Albion were crushed in the capital, Len Duquemin notching a hat-trick in a 5-0 romp, and Fulham were 1-0 victims on Good Friday at Craven Cottage. On the Saturday, Portsmouth were held to a 1-1 draw at Fratton Park, Fulham seen off again, this time 2-1 in the Easter Monday return fixture, before the curtain came down on a prolific month's work with a 3-0 home beating of Everton.

Against that Tottenham run of success, the strength of Manchester United's challenge is clearly shown by the fact of their getting within three points of the leaders with just two games left to play. And this even though Tottenham had taken nineteen points from their last dozen matches – eight wins, three

RIGHT: *Another Cup tie against lowly Humberside opposition – at newly elected Scunthorpe's Old Show Ground in the third round on 12 January 1952. Captioned 'the optimist' by photographer Ray Green, a lone Scunthorpe forward confronts the might of the Tottenham side; from left to right the Spurs players are Ted Ditchburn, Tommy Harmer (partly obscured), Harry Clarke, Bill Nicholson, Charlie Withers, Ron Burgess, Len Duquemin, Les Medley and Alf Ramsey. The only ones missing are Sonny Walters and Eddie Baily. Spurs won the game 3-0.*

draws and one defeat against, of course, their bogey team, Huddersfield Town. That three-point gap left Tottenham in the fortunate position of having to play both their last two matches at home, against Sheffield Wednesday and Liverpool, the very last on 5 May.

But on Saturday 28 April 1951, it mattered little to visiting Wednesday that Spurs were at home with a crowd which had turned out solely to cheer them on to their first title success. Wednesday had their own worries – how to win so that they could stay in the First Division (they failed on goal difference). But they meant to sell the pass dearly. Duquemin ('Reliable Len we used to call him because when all the other forwards were off the mark it was usually old Len who saved our faces,' says Eddie Baily) looked to have set Tottenham on the right road when he gave them the lead in the first half. As the game went on, however, a one-goal lead seemed a none too safe anchorage as desperate Wednesday fought to save First Division football for Hillsborough.

Then, with a quarter of an hour to go, the Tottenham roar began to well up, slowly gaining in power and rising to a pitch as the crowd sent out an urgent 'Hold out' demand to their favourites. The roar was at its height when a massed case of heart failure was avoided with the final whistle. Seven decades after playing on the Marshes, the British game's ultimate prize had at long last found its way to White Hart Lane.

That defeat of Wednesday meant Tottenham still had three points more than Manchester United so there was nothing left to play for in the final game except the credit of a job well done. Ironically enough, as Spurs were making hard work of removing lowly Wednesday from their path, the United were ramming six goals past Huddersfield Town. Alas for Matt Busby's side, they were to finish as runners-up for the fourth time in five years, having previously had a hat-trick of near misses as they finished below Liverpool in 1947, Arsenal in 1948 and Portsmouth in 1949.

A week later, after Spurs had beaten Liverpool 3-1 to close the season, Arthur Drewry, President of the Football League, made the presentation to skipper Ronnie Burgess, as a year earlier he had done with the Second Division Championship Shield. And the most rewarding part of his short speech was again, as the year before, the President's reference to the manner of the title achievement. Said Mr Drewry: 'I not only congratulate them on having won it, but also on the manner in which they did so.'

SECOND AGAIN

Spurs were unable to maintain their momentum in the following season. They swapped places with Manchester United and finished second. There were those who were ready to make excuses and blame the very heavy pitches of the season's winter months for Spurs not

OVERLEAF: *Sonny Walters heads home Eddie Baily's cross to give Spurs their first goal against Hull City in an FA Cup fifth round replay on Wednesday 24 February 1954. Baily can be seen beyond the far post; Duquemin and George Robb run in to challenge goalkeeper Bill Bly. Spurs won the game 2-0. Edmonton born Walters was first choice right-winger for just five seasons from 1949, but was an integral part of the great side of the era.*

OPPOSITE PAGE: *At £30,000 Danny Blanchflower was the most expensive wing-half in Britain, a distinction he held until Dave Mackay joined Spurs four years later. Blanchflower's first game for Tottenham after his move from Villa was on a muddy day at Maine Road, 11 December 1954, which ended in a goalless draw. While the new signing guards keeper Ron Reynolds, left-back Mel Hopkins heads clear and Harry Clarke keeps an eye on proceedings. Blanchflower was purchased by Arthur Rowe as the central cog of what the manager hoped would become a team to rival the push-and-run side. But it was to be five often controversial years, and two changes of manager, before Blanchflower was to really fulfil that role for Tottenham Hotspur. Nonetheless, Arthur Rowe described this game against Manchester City as: 'The first I had been able to enjoy for weeks.'*

being able to produce one more League title. There was substance in it but in truth football clubs, like people, get the weather they get and have to make the best of it.

That being said, it could be argued that, of all the major teams, Spurs, geared to a moving style and a ball coming through quickly, would most likely suffer when the ground was stodgy, as it most surely was in the last quarter of 1951. And those who so believed were able to chide: 'What did I tell you?' when they received the news that the White Hart Lane pitch, because of the difficulty of proper drainage through a hard topsoil, was to be ripped up. It duly happened at the 1951–52 season's end and 3,500 tons of what had, in many eyes, prevented a second title was borne off and dumped on Hackney Marshes to make way for 2,000 tons of special new topsoil and nearly 25,000 turves.

Nor were there the happiest of auguries for the season when the stolid, dependable Harry Clarke was missing for the start after being injured in a practice match. Clarke had not missed a game in the two previous seasons; this time he was out of action for nine matches. 'Harry was a miss because he was such a great fellow to have around', said Eddie Baily. 'He was one of the blokes who did so much to make up the real spirit of the side. Funnily enough he never believed he should have been in the team. He didn't think he was good enough. On the pitch he was a hard, determined player, off it he was an old sentimentalist. He was a much better player than he realised.' Arthur Rowe agrees with that assessment of the towering pivot, who was bought by Jimmy Anderson just before Rowe took over. 'He was a determined old-time stopper and we all believed in him. He was very strong on his left side and this helped him a lot because most centre-forwards tend to swivel to the right and in doing so they ran into Harry's stronger side...and knew all about it.'

During that shaky start Newcastle United put seven September goals past Spurs at St James' Park...sweet revenge for the seven slammed past them a year earlier at White Hart Lane. Rowe's famed team talks probably had some positive effect, but from the end of November, in worsening weather, until the first League games of February the results were appalling...of twelve matches played they won four, drew one and lost seven. They rallied but by now it was too late and they fell four short of Manchester United's winning total and pipped Arsenal into second place by decimals.

The season's end saw one remarkable game which is worth recalling. This was Tottenham's 1-0 defeat of Huddersfield Town on 2 April, which helped send the Yorkshire club down to the Second Division. That solitary goal caused all the trouble. Tottenham had struggled against a Town side desperate to win points and keep themselves in the First Division. It had been a tough tussle, without a goal from either side to show for it, when Tottenham won a corner almost in the last minute. Eddie Baily took the kick.

The referee, who had just ticked Baily off, was along the bye-line, between the kicker and Huddersfield's near post. Baily, curling the ball in, struck the back of the referee and the ball rebounded into the path of the

Spurs' forward. So Baily moved to the ball, centred into the Town goalmouth and there was the alert Duquemin to head the ball home. That's when the storm broke...

Huddersfield players rightly claimed that the goal should not stand because the same Spurs player had touched the ball twice without another player intervening. The referee consulted the linesman nearest to the happening and maintained his ruling of a goal to Tottenham. The Huddersfield chairman, a gentleman of considerable proportions, hurried angrily down from the directors' box to the referee's dressing room and brushed all the waiting reporters aside as they lined up to get the referee's account of the incident. 'You can all wait, I'm seeing him first,' he stormed.

The air around was blue and the Town chairman announced that he would appeal to the League to have the match replayed. Which he did and everybody interested – and that meant every soccer fan in the country – took their different sides. Eventually the Football League Management Committee turned down Huddersfield's request for a replay and the Town then went to a Board of Appeal set up by the Football Association for an inquiry into all the evidence regarding that goal. But this was turned down too...and Huddersfield in due course went down as well. The conclusions were relatively simple. The referee said that he thought another player had touched the ball before Baily centred, though, as he was presumably face down on the pitch, no-one explained how he could have seen this. The fact that he was incorrect was irrelevant. If he said he thought another player had intervened, then his judgement was final.

By 1952–53 the great Spurs side was beginning to show the same signs of decline as had the League winning sides of 1900 and 1920. Despite a very successful close-season tour of North America, during which Spurs beat Manchester United 5-0 and 7-1 on successive evenings, they could finish only tenth in the First Division. Meanwhile the Cup was to revive memories of that melancholy semi-final in 1948. Tottenham began with two games against Tranmere Rovers, about halfway up the Third Division North at the time, then two very tough ties with Preston North End, due to lose the League title only by decimals; next came a softer touch in turfing out Halifax Town, also of the Third North, at their Shay Ground and then three encounters of the closest possible kind in the sixth round against Birmingham City, finally concluded by a late Sonny Walters goal at Molineux.

RAMSEY'S SLIP

Blackpool in the semi-final was supposed to be a revenge performance for the tragedy of 1948. Eddie Baily, a central figure in the terrible conclusion for Tottenham, still finds it difficult to talk about his greatest disappointment as a player – not getting to a Wembley final. 'I've been there seven or eight times with Spurs and West Ham since, but always to watch. Yet that was the time we should have made it, and we really thought we were going to...'

The story of this meeting, of course, was of the slip by the usually so immaculate Alf Ramsey when his pass back to Ted Ditchburn was too short. Jackie Mudie nipped in, fastened

onto the chance and put Blackpool into the final for the third time in five years. Baily takes it up: 'We knew there wasn't long to go and we began to think about extra-time. I don't think any of us were worried about that because we felt that we had been the better team and would still pull it off. Alf took all the stick for us not making it – on TV and the radio, in the papers all over the weekend and for years afterwards. Everybody blamed him, every headline reminded him – him, an England full-back, a man of his experience, and so on. The fans laid the defeat unquestionably at his door.

'But he took it all marvellously, and he needn't have done really. There was no better student of the game than Ramsey. He could go over a match and tell you everything that had happened in it. He often did so in our dressing-room. And he did just that at Villa Park, where we must have been the most miserable bunch of players in football history. Without any recrimination or attempt to shift the blame he told me where I had gone wrong on that goal. He went over every sickening moment...how I, having conceded a free-kick and stood there disputing it, argued with the referee that I had not handled the ball. Then how Blackpool rushed the kick to Bill Perry on their left wing who in turn was challenged by Ramsey...then that back pass.

'Alf made his point, telling me that if I had not stopped to dispute the referee's decision I would have been back deeper in our half and helping provide cover against the free-kick. As it was, I left a gap. And, as he always was, he was right this time. That might not have prevented Mudie's goal but we asked for trouble by not maintaining field discipline. I accepted Ramsey's findings, just as the rest did. Just as we always did when we criticised each other. None of it was made because of the sheer frustration of losing. It was a hard and bitter lesson and it was the first time I'd seen that team with their heads down. They were down because of the manner of our defeat and because we realised that it could well be the last real Cup throw for many of the side.'

Baily was right about the last throw of the dice for the great side of the 1950s. The second semi-final was to be their last flirtation with greatness. The records simply say that Perry's first half goal put Blackpool in front, that Les Bennett made the leveller for Duquemin in the second and that Spurs then lost Bennett as an effective unit for the last half hour after he had had to go off following a violent knock in the face. But the real story of that game was of Ramsey's back pass, and it will always be recalled as one of those matches that one side loses rather than the other wins. The team then broke up fast. Les Medley left to live in Canada, the appearances of the great names became fewer and fewer, the side struggled in a First Division dominated by the youthful Manchester United – 16th, 16th and 18th between 1953 and 1956.

Rowe took the gradual break-up of his ageing side to heart and suffered more than anybody realised for the men who had been through so much with and for him. The fifth round Cup defeat by Third Division York City in 1955 at Bootham Crescent was the final blow – he was a sick man and had to rest. It was his second breakdown. He never went back to White Hart Lane.

But just before Rowe handed over to long-serving Jimmy Anderson, with Bill Nicholson becoming club coach, Arthur Rowe completed the transfer of Robert Dennis Blanchflower from Aston Villa, his most inspiring, most successful transfer and a testimony to the historical continuity that has always been evident at White Hart Lane.

FROM ROWE TO ANDERSON

Blanchflower serves as the bridge between the fade out of the fifties squad and the re-found glories that the sixties were to bring. For now the push-and-run conquerors were moving out and moving on...after Medley's departure came that of the magnificent Burgess and that neat little left-back Arthur Willis, the pair joining Swansea; Bill Nicholson's role now was clearly to show others the way; Les Bennett went to West Ham. The two North London First Division clubs were the chief rivals for the signature of the slightly built Blanchflower and the late Tom Whittaker was favourite to bring him to Highbury and make amends for an earlier missed opportunity to sign the now 29-year-old Northern Ireland captain. This happened when a much younger Blanchflower was playing for his Irish club, Glentoran, but Highbury moved too slowly and he went to Barnsley instead.

Managers Rowe and Whittaker, firm friends for all the intense rivalry of their clubs' followers, also had a great professional respect for each other. Aston Villa were reportedly asking £40,000 for Blanchflower and the fee frightened off most clubs. But neither Rowe nor Whittaker had any intention of going so high and, because they wanted no part of an auction, the two came to a gentlemens' agreement that they would not go beyond £30,000 on any account. And if both clubs made the same offer then it would be left to the player to make his choice of a move. The managers agreed to keep in touch and to keep the fee at around £28,000. They had the field to themselves.

Rowe badly wanted to enrol the classic wing-half skills of the cultured Blanchflower. Equally he needed the leadership he was sure he would get if the lively, loquacious Irish star would take over the captaincy of a Spurs team struggling to regain an identity. Rowe had already realised that Blanchflower was a one-off, a midfield thinker probably without a parallel in the twentieth century. With this argument he won his case for increasing his club's bid by £2,000 to reach the £30,000 ceiling he and Whittaker had agreed. Then Rowe, incredibly by any standards today, rang the Arsenal manager and told him the position; that if Arsenal wanted to match Tottenham's bid of £30,000 then it would be up to the player himself. But Arsenal stuck on £28,000 and Blanchflower had to take what had originally appeared second best. He was the most expensive half-back in soccer history and he began his Spurs career on 11 December 1954, playing at Maine Road against Manchester City and helping his new club to gain a much needed point from the 0-0 draw.

'The first match I'd been able to enjoy for some weeks,' recalls Rowe. And the lift in Tottenham's form went on so that they lost only one of the first ten League matches in

OPPOSITE PAGE: *Tommy Harmer slots home a penalty against Chelsea keeper Bill Robertson with perfect economy of effort on Wednesday 20 February 1957. Spurs, who finished second in the League this season, lost the game 4-3. Possibly the most popular Tottenham player of the post-war era, Harmer played in every League game of this season and appeared to be developing an excellent relationship with Blanchflower. The hopes were not, however, to be fulfilled, Harmer ultimately being thought too frail to cope week after week with heavy grounds and more than his fair share of tough tackling. Nicholson eventually replaced him with John White, a Scottish waif for a Cockney wisp. Harmer later moved to Chelsea, where he scored the goal against Sunderland in 1963 that took the Pensioners back to the First Division.*

which the new man played. 'I got Danny because the team was running down. I knew that we had to change the pattern; other teams had been latching onto our game and getting to know it too well. Nor had we the players left to carry on as we were even if we had wanted to keep the pattern going. The team I had in mind was Blanchflower at right-half with little Tommy Harmer at inside-left as the axis of another, somewhat different, side. Those two had the combined skills to carry us forward. I was ready to throw the responsibility on them to pull us round.'

Rowe had been criticised over Tottenham's slump in form. He was found guilty of being too loyal for too long, that he did not make changes, or at least not quickly enough. He was accused of not playing Harmer early or often enough. Nothing or nobody split the fans as much as the abilities of the little genius who looked on field for all the world like some white-shirted scarecrow that had been left there by mistake. He was an impish football conjuror, a frail, pale wisp of a man who scaled 9st. when wet through and could see over a

five-barred gate if he stood on tiptoes. 'Harmer the Charmer' he was dubbed and he could be sheer soccer magic to his supporters. Quiet, shy and nervous off the field, he could bestride a match like some colossus with touches to illuminate the bleakest winter afternoon. But his detractors thought otherwise, that he was too small, lacked the stamina for heavy grounds and the strength to resist cynical and calculated tough tackling.

Rowe thought the world of him but looking back is as firm in his conviction as he had been then: 'With Blanchflower in the same side another pattern of play might have been created...that was my hope. But I couldn't see Tommy in the other (push-and-run) side. That was unfortunate for him. It also caused more argument than enough with those who wanted him in and could not see why he wasn't playing regularly. I told him, "You can rest assured that if any clubs come in for you and you wish to go, you can – with my blessing. And if you go somewhere and don't like it there, I'll gladly have you back." He was a most gifted player and it was quite sad because

he was such a lovely little fellow. In different circumstances he would have been your first choice. But, as it was, I never really got the Blanchflower-Harmer tie-up working before my health broke and I had to give up the Spurs altogether.'

Harmer had joined Tottenham as an amateur in 1945, turned professional in 1948 and made his League debut early in the 1951–52 season when he played 13 games; but over his first five seasons he averaged only ten League matches. Amid other disappointments his biggest was surely being dropped during the 1955–56 season and before the club's third post-war FA Cup semi-final, against Manchester City, a match which had fierce repercussions.

Manager Jimmy Anderson, a cheerful, popular man but perhaps now too old and too inexperienced tactically, was installed for his second and more prolonged term of office following Arthur Rowe's departure; Bill Nicholson was appointed his right-hand man. Alf Ramsey, who had been left out towards the end of the previous season made his move to fame, glory and Ipswich Town in the close season; Eddie Baily also went, to Port Vale, and Anderson bought Maurice Norman from Norwich City and Bobby Smith from Chelsea

as 1955 drew to its end. Only Duquemin and Clarke survived in the first team from the push-and-run days. Anderson had done virtually everything at Spurs except play. He had come to White Hart Lane before the club had even joined the League and, just before he left, a party was held to celebrate his 50 years service.

The situation with Ramsey was an odd one. Within the club it was known that he was keen to go into management, but Bill Nicholson, who had considerable coaching experience during his army days and had kept it up by looking after the Cambridge University side, was firmly established as coach. There could never be room at that level for both of them but, over a quarter of a century later, it is easy to see what a difficult choice it would have been. There were Spurs with the two greatest English managers of the next decade, both hoping to be asked to make Spurs a great club again. Not only were they contemporaries and team-mates, they had played together for so long, the one in front of the other. It was a situation that was to add poignancy to the tactical Spurs v Ipswich clashes of the early sixties, when Nicholson and Ramsey were fighting each other for the Championship.

The League performances were moderate enough for most of season 1955–56, but the Cup still stirred. Non-League Boston United were 4-0 home victims in the third round; Middlesbrough fell 3-1 at White Hart Lane in the fourth; Doncaster Rovers were beaten 2-0 on their Belle Vue ground and the short hop to Upton Park saw West Ham removed in the sixth after a 3-3 draw at White Hart Lane had seen Spurs pull two goals back in the dying minutes. So for Manchester City on 17 March, St Patrick's Day, and the semi-final at ill-omened Villa Park. After the West Ham triumph Spurs travelled with high hopes that they could reach their first final in nearly 40 years.

Micky Dulin was on the Spurs right wing for the Boston success, Dave Dunmore took over there when beating the Boro. Then Harmer was tried as a deep lying outside-right against Doncaster, proved a success, was there for a solid 4-0 League win over Chelsea and stayed for the victory over the Hammers. The tactic was to play Harmer in a withdrawn position, tempting the full-back forward. To have played him way up on the wing would have invited his disappearance from the game as well as some physical treatment from the era's backs. Blanchflower recalls how Ander-son, following the League game before the semi-final, had seen Harmer take enough tough tackling from Portsmouth to raise the manager's doubts about playing him against the likes of the Manchester City hard man, Roy Paul. He told his captain he was thinking of playing Alfie Stokes for his speed. But after a midweek reserve match in which both Dunmore and Stokes played, it was Dave Dunmore who got the vote, the dropping of Harmer clearly disrupting the team's rhythm. That semi-final provided a third defeat in eight years at Villa Park for the luckless Spurs, a Bobby Johnstone header deciding the game in City's favour. But there was no doubt in Tottenham ranks that they would have earned a draw if German goalkeeper Bert Trautmann had been penalised for holding the legs of George Robb as the left-winger was about to knock the ball into an empty City net. Blanch-flower has told his own story of that dejected Villa Park dressing-room...of the gamble which failed in the last twenty minutes when he pushed big Maurice Norman up in attack, dropping Johnny Brooks back...then, still hoping to drive Spurs level in the last minutes, he sent Brooks forward again...of how he had tried and failed. It seemed that Spurs could never hope to break the Cup hoodoo

A worm's eye view of the end of the Anderson era as Spurs entertain Burnley in the 1957–58 season. Spurs players in the picture include Peter Baker, Cliff Jones, Ron Reynolds, John Ryden, Terry Dyson and Maurice Norman. On top of the East Stand sit the cockerel and ball, which had been transferred from the Main Stand at the time the first floodlights were erected. Manager Jimmy Anderson had served the club for over 50 years in virtually every capacity except that of player. During this season a special presentation was made to him in recognition of this service, which began before Spurs had even entered the Football League.

Dreams of a Double...as 1960 approaches the hopes are real. Manchester United just failed to achieve it by a single game, in 1959–60 Wolves fail by the same margin. Blanchflower believes it will be done, Nicholson is prepared to admit it's possible. In 1959 Blanchflower, new goal-keeper Bill Brown, just signed from Dundee, and trainer Cecil Poynton discuss the club's prospects.

that appeared to have settled on the Tottenham High Road.

In the League, Tottenham now needed a point from Cardiff and their final home match against Sheffield United, who in due course were relegated with Huddersfield, to be safe. But Blanchflower did not take part in the 0–0 draw with Cardiff, the result which meant safety. Manager Anderson gave out that he was injured, Blanchflower, when asked, said that he was fit. Manager and player discussed the captaincy before that last game with the Yorkshire club. Blanchflower said he could not be captain if he wasn't trusted with authority on the field. So the captaincy was taken off him for the game with Sheffield United. Harry Clarke started as captain the following season. Then Marchi, Bobby Smith and John Ryden took turns. But Blanchflower was still in the wings, waiting for his time to come.

Jimmy Anderson did almost every job there was to do at Tottenham in his fifty splendid years with the club. Twice he stepped into the breach when Arthur Rowe was ill, the second time for some three and a half years when he had to see off the rear end of the miserable 1954–55 season, with Spurs taking a moderate 16th place in the table. Despite the captaincy problems, Anderson was actually fitting the pieces well; Harmer and Blanch-flower could work together and the pair of them turned in virtually a full complement of

League matches in 1956–57. This in itself was a great tribute to their staying powers, their skills having long been accepted and admired. But here they were, successful too as Spurs recovered and ended the season as runners-up again to Manchester United. Essentially Spurs were still an attacking side, and their century of goals was the first by any club in Division One for two decades.

And that welcome improvement by the team was maintained sufficiently for Spurs to finish in third place a year later behind Wolves and Preston North End. It was a good return for Anderson in his second term of office (he had been in charge at the end of the War) but it took its toll. As with Rowe, the strain of big-time managership, and the need for the 24 hours-a-day application it brings, laid him low only weeks into 1958–59 when a familiar early season slump had settled in and the Tottenham defence was having one of its most harrassing times anybody could remember. Second and third in the League was hardly a disgrace, but it is also necessary to remember Anderson's good stewardship down the years, the manner in which he fashioned a side to trouble the best in those two previous seasons; besides which there were his shrewd signings... Maurice Norman...Bobby Smith...Cliff Jones...Terry Dyson...Terry Medwin... Jim Iley...John Ryden. Already the best side Spurs, and perhaps the Football League, has ever had was in the making.

1961

Nicholson's ten-goal debut ● White, Mackay and Allen ● Dreams of the Double ● A Molineux close shave ● Team of the Century ● Benfica ● Glory, Glory, Hallelujah ● Dyson's match ● Sadness and sorrow

Remarkable though Bill Nicholson's managerial career at White Hart Lane was, nothing ever really matched his very first game in charge. At lunch-time on Saturday 11 October 1958, Nicholson was called to the Tottenham boardroom and appointed manager of the club in succession to Jimmy Anderson. In itself, this was no great surprise. He had been coaching the first team for three years and Spurs have ultimately always preferred to promote those they know (Minter, Rowe, Anderson, Burkinshaw to name other obvious examples).

The fixture that afternoon was not an attractive one. Spurs, with only nine points from eleven games, were sixteenth, a point clear of the bottom three. Everton were actually one of that bottom trio. What happened is history, for the game was to produce the biggest aggregate score of any ever played in the First Division – its 14 goals equalling a record set up when Aston Villa beat Accrington 12-2 a mere 66 years before. Spurs got ten of those goals and, as one paper reported: 'Tommy Harmer scored one and made nine.'

It was perhaps the peak of Tommy Harmer's amazing career, yet he had approached it with trepidation: 'All I can remember is feeling miserable that morning. I had been dropped for the previous four games and it was in the balance whether I'd get my place back.' Harmer's goal, Spurs' eighth, was as uncharacteristic as the day: 'The ball just bounced towards me and I hit it first time, on the half-volley, from 20 yards and it flew into the top corner of the net. I hardly ever scored from that range. It was just one of those days when everything goes in.'

A winning Spurs' side in the bath early in 1960. Clockwise from the top: Danny Blanchflower, Cliff Jones, Dave Mackay, Terry Medwin, Bobby Smith, Bill Brown and Mel Hopkins.

RIGHT : *Bobby Smith heads home a centre from Alfie Stokes for the third of his four goals against Everton on 11 October 1958. It was Bill Nicholson's first game in charge and Spurs won 10-4, easily a record managerial debut. It also equalled the record aggregate score for any First Division game. Spurs' other goals were scored by Alfie Stokes (2), George Robb, Terry Medwin, John Ryden and Tommy Harmer. As the teams left the pitch Harmer commented to his new manager: 'We don't score 10 every week you know.' Alfie Stokes was a fine goalscoring inside-forward, finding the net 40 times in only 65 League games.*

BELOW RIGHT : *More mudlarking at White Hart Lane for Bobby Smith, who has just beaten Preston keeper Fred Else to make an easy goal for right-winger Terry Medwin. The game, on 18 January 1958, ended 3-3. Smith finished 1957–58 with 36 goals, equalling the club record in a season of League games. He eventually broke the club aggregate record as well, ending with 176 goals from 271 League appearances. This season was also to be Preston's last as a truly great club – they finished second, eight points ahead of Spurs, but within four years were playing Second Division football and the nostalgic clashes between two sides which had shared the same strip and contested so many dramatic Cup ties were to be no more.*

Harmer's last comment probably sums the game up. For Spurs Bobby Smith got four, Alfie Stokes two, George Robb, Terry Medwin, the injured John Ryden and Harmer one each. For Everton Jimmy Harris joined the select band (possibly the only member) of those who have scored a hat-trick and still seen their team lose by six clear goals, and Bobby Collins got the fourth. Everton reserve keeper Albert Dunlop had let in four against a South African touring team in a friendly three days before; in one week he had thus picked the ball out of the net fourteen times. 'We must protect this man from lumbago,' wrote one witty Merseyside journalist on the Monday.

Harmer was nothing if not sanguine: 'We don't score ten every week you know,' he said to Nicholson as the sides left the field. Nicholson, as befitted his slightly pessimistic character, was equally cautious: 'I've been in this game long enough to know you can be in the clouds one minute and down to earth the next.' In this case, he was quite right. The next Saturday, Spurs did almost as well, winning 4-3 at Leicester, but Nicholson was more interested in his defence's porousness than his attack's magnificence. In his first four games, including these two, they let in 15 goals and, after the Leicester match, won only one of their next 11 League fixtures. The phrase 'false dawn' could almost have been invented for Nicholson's managerial career.

FOOTBALL CORNUCOPIA

Though matters improved, the 1958–59 season was to all intents and purposes a write-off. It was an odd interlude in a period of dramatic success – their League positions went 2nd, 3rd, 18th, 3rd, 1st, 3rd, 2nd between 1956 and 1963, when the great days were to come to an end. Blanchflower and Harmer were dropped in turn, and with both of them out of touch Spurs were a pallid shadow of the side which had, for instance, taken two points away from pre-Munich Manchester United in a 4-3 thriller at Old Trafford, the first time a London club had won there for 19 years. Blanchflower had been a delight that previous season. As well as leading Northern Ireland to a highly improbable quarter-final place in the World Cup finals in Sweden, he had become the first Spurs player to be elected Footballer of the Year (he was to win the award again in 1961 and thus become, with Stanley Matthews and Tom Finney, a near-immortal). It is possible that Blanchflower was playing even better than in the Double year at this time. Julian Holland said of his displays in the 1957–58 season that: 'The football poured out of him in a ceaseless irresistable profusion, as though his genie had been taking lessons from the sorceror's apprentice. He was a footballing cornucopia... at this stage in his career he was the unfaltering dynamo tirelessly feeding the striving attack.'

But Blanchflower and Harmer were not the only ones suffering a few months later. Cliff Jones, the wonderful, direct winger from Swansea was finding it difficult to carry the game's most expensive player (£35,000) tag. Like his uncle Bryn, who had moved to Arsenal twenty years before for £14,000, Jones was thoroughly uncomfortable with the expectations this distinction carried. The Spurs crowd was not noted for its generosity to new signings ('I wouldn't say they were impatient' said Terry Venables a decade later, 'they wait till the third game before they give you the bird.') It was almost Jones' good fortune that he collided with Peter Baker in an early season practice match and broke a leg. He returned half-way through the season, when the crowd had forgotten his earlier fumblings, and he was allowed to develop, with Dave Mackay behind him, to become almost the definitive flying, goalscoring winger. Certainly it is hard to think of a better one since the Second World War. And while, strangely, Jones is somehow remembered as a left-winger, he wore the number seven shirt far more often than the eleven and rarely played for long on either wing anyway. Rather he was the most mobile of the prompting second line – starting anywhere and finishing anywhere.

To add to Nicholson's early season problems in 1958–59 Ted Ditchburn's career had been finished with a bad injury and reserve keeper John Hollowbread was in goal. Things were so difficult that Nicholson decided to put Blanchflower in the reserves where, at 33, the Irishman was trying, and failing, to raise any enthusiasm as a late developing inside-right. It was Nicholson's idea that he should try this out while the club tried to find a more defensive right-half for the League team in order to put a few more mines in the ever open pathway to the Tottenham goal area. The transfer request which followed, and Nicholson's solemn declaration that he would have the board turn it down, was in fact the end and the beginning of the matter. Blanchflower decided that he could work with, and for, the new Tottenham manager. There is no record of any real differences between the pair from that day forward. Their respect for each other continues and they remain close friends.

It was on 2 March 1959, before a drawn game at Wolverhampton, that Nicholson publicly acknowledged he needed Blanchflower. Spurs had not won one of their last four home matches. With the Irishman restored as captain they crushed Leicester 6-0 at home five days later. It was the turning point. From here onwards the only way was up.

Mel Hopkins was then injured on duty for Wales and this provided a long sought chance for the tidy Ron Henry at left-back. Hopkins had given fine service to Tottenham but soon the Baker-Henry full back partnership took off and became one of the solid essentials in the Nicholson build-up.

Having squirmed through season 1958–59 the way ahead began to take on a more hopeful hue. Just before Easter Nicholson had set off on the sort of journey which was to become more frequent over the years, the kind of trip about which no-one knew anything but the closing of the door as Nicholson disappeared. This, one of his earliest, was supposed to have ended with him returning with Mel Charles. Instead of Charles, brother of the great John, the Nicholson capture came from over the other border, Dave Mackay from Hearts. At £32,000 he took over Blanchflower's mantle as Britain's most expensive half-back. It was the first of many transfers to be completed by Nicholson while others waited and wondered. Mackay and Blanchflower took to each other from the off.

Spurs headed for the sixties with higher

hopes than the previous season could substantiate. Eighteenth in the table was far from being the surest way of keeping the customers happy. Even less promising was a defence like a sieve which had 95 goals sunk past it, the worst defensive League offering anybody at White Hart Lane could remember. But Nicholson had begun to ring the changes. After Mackay he bought another Scot, another keeper to make a third along with Ron Reynolds and John Hollowbread, Scottish international Bill Brown of Dundee for £16,000. Tottenham had also bought back the commanding Tony Marchi from Italian football, where for two years he had effectively been on loan to Lanerossi Vicenza and Torino.

Outgoings there had to be to keep a balance and there was a warm, sentimental farewell to the last remaining players of the fabulous push-and-run team . . . Ted Ditchburn, twenty years with Spurs and with a club record of 418 League appearances, went to Romford . . . gangling Harry Clarke, who left to enter management, and the 'quiet man', Len Duquemin, leaving behind him a mark of 135 goals in League and Cup as he joined Bedford Town. These three left indelible memories and hard to follow standards. Other less significant actors were also to leave, Jim Iley to Nottingham Forest, Alfie Stokes to Fulham.

Blanchflower had been among the first to spot the new signs of hope in that past season, but few would have believed that the glory to be won would have much to thank for its lift-off to the playing fields of the USSR. Bill Nicholson himself was ever-grateful for the bond he was able to build in Russia between his players. Of that twelve-day close season tour he says: 'I was glad of the opportunity of getting the players together. I had said that we would go to see what it was like there. "It's a lot different," I had told the boys. There wasn't much chance for entertainment, so we had every day for training. We trained hard and we played three matches. I cannot overstate the value of that trip in terms of getting things together. And we still had a very enjoyable time, very enjoyable.'

Medwin scored the only goal against Moscow Torpedo, Johnny Brooks got two against Kiev (Spurs winning 2-1) and then he also got the only reply as the third game was lost 3-1 against a national squad in Leningrad. The full benefits of that Russian tour and of the understanding built up in advance of the new season came to fruition at the gateway to the sixties as Tottenham were caught up in a League title race with Burnley and the Wolves.

On 3 October 1959, Danny Blanchflower was in the Northern Ireland team which took a 4-0 home beating at Windsor Park, Belfast, from the Scots. In the Scottish side were his Spurs colleagues, Bill Brown and Dave Mackay. There was also a slim, pale youngster from Falkirk named John White, who scored one of those four Scottish goals. Blanchflower remembers his return from that debacle for the Irish and the greeting from Nicholson: 'What did you think about young John White?' Among the hints, the guesses and the crystal-bowl guidelines of the soccer gossip columns he had seen a vague reference connecting the youngster, unknown south of the border, and the Spurs.

When Nicholson filled in the gaps by telling

his skipper that he could get White for a bargain £20,000, Blanchflower told him to grab the next plane bound for Scotland. Mackay and Brown backed up the Irishman's high regard for their young countryman so that manager Nicholson was up and away and within the next 24 hours the signing was all but complete. All but, because ex-Scotland keeper Tommy Younger, the old Hibs and Liverpool favourite who was then managing Falkirk, having brought his player down to White Hart Lane to finalise the deal, saw that Nicholson was not happy with progress. He discovered the reason when he took White aside to ask him what was holding up the deal. He got the surprising answer: 'I'm not good enough for here, I'll never fit in with these players.' Younger said that he had never known a worse case of an inferiority complex: 'He

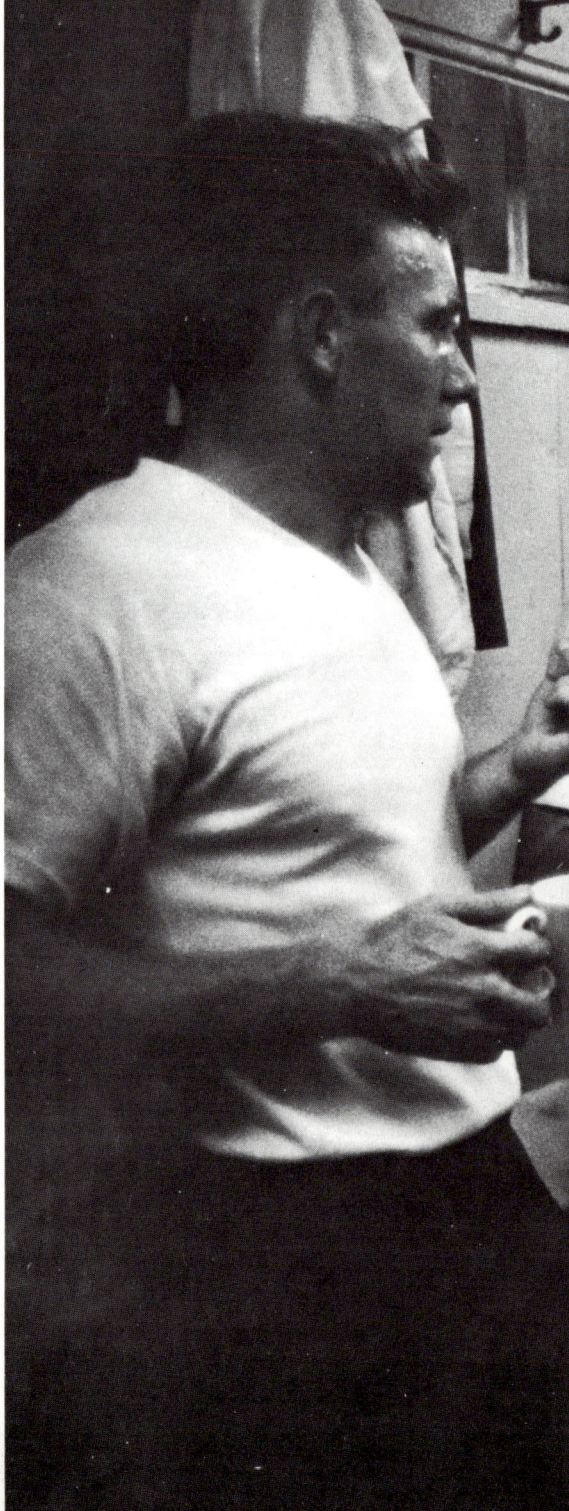

RIGHT: *Exchanges in the dressing-room during the 1959–60 season, when Spurs would have taken the Championship had they won either of their two home games over Easter. Here Medwin, Mackay, Smith, Jones and Baker listen to Bill Nicholson's plans for getting outside the opposing full-back. Walter Winterbottom, England team manager at the time, said of the side Nicholson was building: 'His system had individual expression, but it was based on teamwork. The great personalities had been harnessed to be unselfish and, above all else, the team effort made the lesser players look so good.'*

had become a luxury for us because he was thinking two and three moves ahead and his passes were not being picked up,' understood the Falkirk manager.

And exactly as if to prey on those early fears of John White came Tottenham's first defeat of that 1959–60 season. It was Tottenham's 13th League match and was also White's debut, at Hillsborough against a powerful Sheffield Wednesday side...and Spurs were missing three regulars in Hopkins, Jones and Medwin, all playing for Wales that afternoon. White did manage to score the solitary Tottenham goal in their 2-1 defeat, but did little more. Two months later Nicholson swooped again to add striker Les Allen to his squad as Johnny Brooks crossed to Chelsea in an exchange deal. Allen and Bobby Smith were essentially similar – they were both goalscorers. Both

could look clumsy out of the penalty area, but they were part of a necessary mixture. A team cannot be composed entirely of John Whites. Swiftly, shrewdly, Bill Nicholson had, did we but know it, put together a collection powerful enough to tackle the world. It had taken him just a year and the mixture was now formed. For three months of 1959–60 – from December to March – Spurs led the way at the top of the First Division, their elevation coinciding with Allen's two-goal debut in the 4-2 Boxing Day success at Elland Road. In the return two days later Leeds United hammered Spurs 4-1 at White Hart Lane; it didn't help the Yorkshiremen to avoid relegation, but it showed that Spurs did not yet have the consistency of a great side.

That was one shock result for Tottenham. Two more at Easter, just as big, ended any

title hopes. Spurs had three Easter fixtures, then two more to complete their programme. But just as their own 3-1 win at Molineux was to rob Wolves of an historic League and Cup Double in the last but one match of the season, so did two unaccountable home beatings in 48 hours – 0-1 to Manchester City on Easter Saturday, and another 0-1 to Chelsea on Easter Monday – end any Tottenham title chance.

Tottenham lost the Championship by just two points, and they should have had them both against Manchester City. Cliff Jones' penalty, at the end of the first half, was well saved by goalkeeper Bert Trautmann but the Welshman, following up, tapped home the rebound. Unfortunately for Spurs, the referee had added time on for the penalty to be taken and the goal did not stand. Had it done so, they might have approached the second half differently and not conceded City's vital single goal. That being said, no team which loses its last two home matches deserves to win anything very much.

WOLVES AND THE DOUBLE

The Championship is always a matter of ifs and buts, never more so than in 1960 when Burnley's success was unquestionably unique. The Lancastrians never led the League until *after* their, and the Division's, final game, which they won at Maine Road. Burnley had actually lost 6-1 at Molineux only weeks before and, with just three weeks left, were little more than hopeful outsiders behind Spurs and Wolves. Wolves themselves had thrown away

a Championship which seemed to be theirs for the taking when Spurs came to Molineux on Saturday 23 April 1960. This was one of the truly critical games of Spurs' great years – ranking alongside the Cup ties against Aston Villa and Sunderland, the European Cup semi-final with Benfica and the last gasp of the era, the European Cup Winners Cup final against Atletico.

Wolves were not only running strongly for the Double (and odds-on with the bookmakers to become the first team this century to achieve it) but were also on the verge of equalling Huddersfield's and Arsenal's record of a hat-trick of Championships. But even on the edge of such an achievement, it was clear to some that Molineux's great days were at an end – Wright, Swinbourne, Hancocks, Mullen and Wilshaw had all gone. Stan Cullis's long ball game remained, but the replacements were not as good as their predecessors. That being said, Wolves were now four points clear of Burnley and three clear of Spurs. If they beat Tottenham they had only Chelsea to overcome and the Championship was theirs. If Burnley did not get maximum points, then just beating Spurs would be enough. It did not seem too great a task for a team that was to walk over Blackburn Rovers in the Cup final two weeks later – particularly as opponents Spurs had lost their last two games, both at home.

But this was to be one of those moments when an observer can actually sense history turning. Spurs were relaxed, their chances of winning the League virtually gone. Blanch-flower held his team talk in the middle of the

pitch rather than in the dressing-room and, within two minutes, had created the first goal. Feinting to put Cliff Jones away on the right, he changed direction and centred for Bobby Smith. The centre-forward did the rest while the Wolves defence still covered the threat from Jones. Broadbent equalised but Mackay, with a rare header, put Spurs back in front. Their third, and final, goal was a classic: Terry Dyson flying down the left wing, a perfect cross and there was Jones with a full-length header.

Wolves did beat Chelsea at Stamford Bridge, 5-1, but Burnley pipped them anyway and the hat-trick and the Double had both gone. Wolves had been as baffled by Barcelona in the European Cup as they had by Spurs (who had also beaten them 5-1 at White Hart Lane). It was a decisive end to Wolves' great era. They have not won the League or Cup since.

Though everyone had hoped for better, third place behind champions Burnley and Wolves was still a boost for Bill Nicholson and Spurs. The rise from eighteenth in the table to third place a season later was improvement indeed. So was the performance of the defence, which had 45 less goals rattled past it this time. There was also proof that Tottenham were giving the fans what they wanted – they were the best supported home side in the country with an average of 47,948, a total only seriously challenged by Manchester United. It was also the season which brought the club's record victory...the 13-2 swamping of little Crewe Alexandra in an FA Cup fourth round replay in February 1960. Mighty Spurs had

stuttered and spluttered at Gresty Road. Blanchflower said that the Crewe supporters worked themselves up to a belief that they could provide a Cup shock and Spurs played so cautiously as to fumble over scraping a 2-2 draw in the first meeting. Only a shot which bounced back off a post saved Spurs from their fourth humiliation in six years – Third Division York, Bournemouth and Norwich already being in the record books.

The outcome of the Tottenham visit was a record 20,000 home gate for Fourth Division Alexandra, the reward for making Spurs play it again at White Hart Lane on the following Wednesday a massive 64,365 gate to share. But that and a rare look round the capital were all poor Crewe were allowed as Spurs turned cold killers under the arc lights to pile up the agony of a 10-1 half-time lead. Only a second-half easing down spared further torture for Crewe and unfortunate keeper David Evans, who had picked the ball out of his net 15 times (his only concession from fortune being two scores which were ruled out). Les Allen got five, Bobby Smith four, Cliff Jones three and Tommy Harmer the other goal. The story, perhaps apocryphal, is still told of how Crewe arrived on platform 2 at Euston and went home from platform 13. Poor Evans; he afterwards admitted to fearing seven or eight home efforts going past him, but 13! 'I don't know WHERE those other five goals came from,' he said, 'and I didn't feel too good about it.' But that was the end for Tottenham too, and on an off day in the next round Blackburn Rovers took away a 3-1 victory at the Lane.

ABOVE: *A flying Bill Brown fails to connect with a Blackburn centre at Ewood Park on 27 August 1960. While Maurice Norman, now restored to his rightful centre-half spot, heads away, captain Danny Blanchflower appears to look on amused. Spurs won the game easily, 4-1.*

OVERLEAF: *Half-time during Bill Nicholson's first, difficult, season in charge, when the side finished 18th in the First Division. Right-winger Terry Medwin discusses where he was standing, or perhaps should have been standing, while, in the foreground, centre-forward Dave Dunmore concentrates on his cup of tea. Medwin had already won 19 Welsh caps by the beginning of this season, and in the summer had scored the goal against Hungary which put Wales into the World Cup quarter-finals during their only appearance in that competition's later stages.*

DREAMS OF A DOUBLE

Blanchflower, looking back, remembers how the team's new-found power began to give him ideas, how the all-round strength of the squad had increased, the force of 5-1 victories gained against Newcastle United at St James' Park, at Old Trafford when meeting Manchester United and of similar home wins over Preston and Wolves...days when everyone and everything moved in harmony. He could see only the Double, the Double which both Manchester United and Wolves had missed so narrowly in the past four seasons.

The 'impossible' Double was a far more common topic of football conversation then than it had been, say, thirty years before or was twenty years later. That was largely because both Manchester United and Wolves had come so close to achieving it within the space of three years. Both had failed by a single match – United in a Cup final they couldn't possibly lose, Wolves by conceding a home game to a side which had just lost two consecutive home matches. These amazingly close-run attempts had apparently proved one of two things to soccer journalists – that the Double certainly was possible or, alternatively, that it obviously wasn't. The latter school of thought quoted the psychology of the four-minute mile; that the mental barriers became so great in the home stretch that few athletes could break through them. But, up in North London, sat football's own squad of Roger Bannisters.

Joe Mercer recalls coming back from Sweden after the World Cup in 1958. On the plane, says Joe, Blanchflower could talk of little else to himself and Stan Cullis. It went on in the taxi from Heathrow. 'He told us over and over again that it was going to be done. "And we'll be the ones to do it," he had promised.' The Spurs captain repeated the vow when the elderly club chairman, Mr Fred Bearman, asked him what 1960–61 might bring for Tottenham. 'We'll get the Double for you this time...the League and the Cup,' came the confident answer. In fact Blanchflower had originally been confident about the Double before 1959–60. Looking back he says: 'We could have done it then, but we hadn't been there before, hadn't had the experience. The following season we were able to pace ourselves better.'

'That third in the League table was a boost,' says Bill Nicholson. 'We were getting it together, getting the team working and playing for one another and getting to know each other. Ron Henry for Mel Hopkins at left-back was an important change. Then Terry Dyson came in for Terry Medwin. I felt that we would have a good shout in the League, but in the Cup...well, who knows about the Cup? One afternoon on a strange pitch, an awkward ground, one or two little things going the opposite way and bingo! You're gone. It's different again, the Cup.'

Then, very firmly, he adds: 'Anyway, I never did make predictions, it wasn't my job to. And it's not a thing I'd lend myself to, the game is so fickle. If Danny liked to say it... well, that was Danny. He should have known by then that teams often win games they don't deserve to win.'

Nicholson takes a deep breath after this, as if trying to summon memories, those magical moments from perhaps the greatest single season in any English club's history, to feel for an echo of a sustained season of soccer classics and maintained at a pitch of performance no year had ever previously seen. Smooth, soft skills...perfect patterns... tenacity of purpose laced with hard discipline ...still with a stylish swing to refresh their every game. And all the threads painstakingly pulled together by the stolid Nicholson, dependable as man and player, who had always performed within his own honest limitations, few as they were, forever pursuing excellence in his teams.

'I tried to keep our football as simple as possible,' he says. 'We had good players but I didn't want them to indulge themselves too much as individuals. "We've got to be effective, not exhibition players" I used to tell them. "You've got to involve other players like the 1950 side." You are always preaching involvement but the situations come on the field and the player has to do it himself. The good player will always know what it is best to do.

'In the 1950 side we played the short game. If you kick the ball any length there's a good chance the other side will intercept, and naturally you cannot be so accurate. It was so different from the long game favoured by the Wolves who lashed the ball from side to side and reckoned that long stuff to forwards, if not getting on the mark, did enough to unsettle defenders. Then they always had players coming through quickly, either to close down rivals or ready to snap up any half chances their assaults might have given them to feed on.

'In the sixty side we had the skill to play balls first time, like the Rowe side did, but also the skill to play the longer game.' It is a theme he has no doubt had to develop on many occasions, with him loyally insisting on including a salute for his old comrades in arms. 'Harry Evans, once the Aldershot manager, joined me as my assistant. He took a lot of work off to leave me free for the real job of preparing a team.' Unhappily, the popular Harry was to die in harness after a brief stay with the club, sorely missed by Nicholson.

GLORY, GLORY, HALLELUJAH

'I felt in 1960 that I had a side well prepared to do something. You cannot put it into words, it's a feeling you get. And I had this strong feeling around that time.' The result was that: Spurs became the first club to take the League and Cup Double this century; their 66 points total equalled the First Division record set up by Arsenal in 1930–31; their 33 away points also equalled Arsenal's of the same season; eleven consecutive victories from the start of the season bettered the record of Hull City, with their nine opening successes in 1948–49; the total of 31 winning matches was a First Division record, as was the 16 victorious away matches; Spurs achieved 11 doubles over their League rivals, which equalled the First Division performances of Manchester United (1956–57) and Wolves (1958–59); they attained 50 points in 29 games, faster than any club previously; and their 115 goals was a club scoring record for a season.

Statistics are a mundane wrap-around for a glorious season played out to the challenging background of 'Glory, Glory, Hallelujah', but they help us take in the picture more readily. Like the 31 points from the first 32 when only Manchester City's 1-1 draw at the Lane in October had temporarily stubbed a toe before sturdy Sheffield Wednesday ended that unbeaten run at Hillsborough on 12 November.

Spurs had opened up a seven-point lead over Wednesday, their nearest challengers, but the eight previous clubs that had journeyed to Hillsborough had not taken a single point away. Fittingly it was a giant of a match, tough, mean, abrasive with the 56,363 crowd stoking up a furnace-like atmosphere. Wednesday were nothing if not a defensive side. The strapping Peter Swan blocked the goalpath to Bobby Smith, who earlier in the season had hat-tricked his way against Blackpool into being Tottenham's best-ever goalscorer with 141 goals in his five years since joining from Chelsea. Alongside Swan, and soon to suffer with him in a bribery scandal, was red-headed firebrand Tony Kay. With burly Don Megson behind it was mainly these three who turned the tide against Spurs and their unbeaten record.

Billy Griffin's goal near half-time stilled the Tottenham roars. Maurice Norman set them off again when he equalised from a quickly taken Dave Mackay free-kick. But, with some 20 minutes to go, Megson attacked and crossed down the left for John Fantham to get the home winner. So Spurs had fallen at the 17th hurdle, after taking a record 31 points from the first 32. If anything, they were pleased. The tension of waiting for the inevitable defeat had been massive. It was a surprisingly cheerful team coach which left Hillsborough that evening, some of the players singing on the way to Sheffield Midland station. Long before this defeat they had earned a glowing tribute from that stern taskmaster Stan Cullis, manager of Wolves, after Spurs had buried them again, this time 4-0 on their own Molineux turf. 'They are the finest club side I've ever seen in the Football League – even better than the great Spurs of ten years ago.'

Three weeks later came the unforgettable meeting with Burnley, the reigning champions, an epic 4-4 clash which first established Tottenham as true heirs-apparent to the League throne and then fully proved that the crown

had been worn well, and not uneasily, by the Lancastrians.

Tottenham halted any early Burnley aggression on a miserable, rainy December afternoon, then struck three times in three minutes, first through Norman then with two breakaway efforts by Jones. And when Mackay came up with a fourth goal inside 40 minutes it was as certain as anything could be that Burnley were to be added to the list of Tottenham scalps. Even Bill Nicholson himself admits that he could not imagine soccer turning so fickle. But, before the interval, winger John Connelly strode through the home defence to pull one back and battle recommenced with Burnley drawing on pride and pedigree to push Blanchflower and company completely out of their stride. Next, Jimmy Robson, then the blond Ray Pointer, nipped in for Burnley goals and the noise was truly deafening when, with only a dozen minutes left, the elusive Connelly was again haring up the middle to present the crowd with an incredible draw. Few could quite remember the like of this remarkable match, or such a turnabout result. It was more a lesson for the prospective champions than the resilient title-holders but Bill Nicholson proved typically phlegmatic with his defence: 'We scored eight goals and still only drew,' he commented in the dressing-room.

Half way to the title finish there was no longer a bookmaker who would accept money on Tottenham. It was a one-horse race. The point and poise of the side was the Blanchflower-White axis, the wry, pale Scot having taken over Harmer's role ('Scottish waif for Cockney wisp' wrote one journalist) to add a more urgent, broader sweep to a side now better able to vary pace and power. Mackay, who seemed to play with a skirl of bagpipes in his game, was the ideal blend of flinty, foraging pirateer opposite his skipper, and the so brave Jones with his jet speed was a scimitar aimed at the heart of any defence. And now Smith and Allen were proving Nicholson's point, that with all the style in the world it was still goals which won matches in the end.

Little Dyson, small enough to be the son of his father, a leading northern jockey, had wrested the other wing place from Medwin with a bit more dash and unorthodoxy, while the defence had now bedded solidly down from keeper Brown and outwards to Baker and Henry, with Norman commanding in the air if occasionally reluctant to tackle on the ground. For the first three seasons after he had moved from Norwich, Maurice Norman had played at full-back, somewhat uneasily for much of the time. He was now in his prefered position in a defence which was, unlike the middle and front lines, built on extremely conventional principles.

In the 1960–61 season's first half they scored 21 more goals and gained 10 more points than they did in the second half. And they won five more games. The point is made for interest, not contention. By kinder weather alone the going should be more favourable, played mostly as it is in the autumn. But in any case, those who had been trying to pick the flaws in Tottenham's runaway leadership had seen ample evidence presented to them that the heavier going would not – and did not – really clog up the Tottenham works. But the fact was that they lost two of their first three League

games in the New Year, 0-2 at Old Trafford against Manchester United, then a 2-3 beating by Leicester City at White Hart Lane. They also finished their greatest ever season with another wobble, beaten 2-4 at Burnley and then by West Bromwich back at the Lane in two of their last three League matches. The West Brom game, played before 51,880 people on 29 April, was a particular disappointment. One more point would have broken Arsenal's First Division record. Instead, Spurs lost 2-1. But they were still masters enough of the First Division to bridge a ten-year gap in the club's history and reclaim the Football League Championship trophy for the Tottenham sideboard as they finished eight points ahead of Sheffield Wednesday and nine in front of Wolves. Appropriately the trophy was won by beating Wednesday.

It was against the Wednesday on 17 April that Spurs avenged their first defeat of the season with the same 2-1 scoreline, this time in their favour. But, as last time, it was no match for the faint-hearted and skill came second to all-out, full-blooded effort which had the smile freezing on the face of 'Smiler' Tommy Dawes, the Norwich referee. He booked both Mackay and Wednesday's Peter Johnson and Spurs fans were to suffer a slight case of shock when Megson, villain of the piece at Hillsborough, smashed home a first half free-kick to give his side the lead. The evening was one of roaring sound as 62,000 bayed for blood and goals; they had come to see Spurs win the Championship, not to appreciate a great football match. The home crowd, silenced momentarily, then set up even greater roars for Spurs to hit back. They did so almost immediately...twice. First Bobby Smith flipped the ball over England's Swan and slammed it home on the half-volley. And they were still acclaiming that goal when Blanchflower's free-kick was headed sideways by the lurking Norman and Allen thumped in a terrific, shoulder high volley. The match got even hotter in the second half; Smith charged Wednesday keeper Ron Springett into a post and the keeper was carried off, only to insist on returning within minutes. Some nail-biting moments for Tottenham's hopes ended with the crowd pouring onto the pitch at the final whistle and sheer pandemonium until skipper Blanchflower led out his players to take the crowd's thanks and appreciation.

'DANNY, DANNY'

The crowd had little doubt where the credit lay, calling specifically for 'Danny, Danny' to come out and take the victory salute. 'Footballer of the Year' for the second time in four years, the judgement of the fans was surely correct, though it is difficult to pin down exactly how Blanchflower made it all work. He was part of the team, but, probably uniquely, not of it; essentially he was the deputy manager. And while many managers would not (and did not) tolerate Blanchflower's insistence on having his own way, Bill Nicholson had the sense and the confidence to harness it rather than fight it. It was probably the best intuition Nicholson ever had. Blanchflower assesses his own contribution in relatively few words: 'I could change the rhythm, change the pace, slow it down if necessary, speed it up when we needed to. I also had the ball much more often

108

than anyone else – so I should have done something with it shouldn't I? And I was a lot older than the rest – 34. I had learned how to play by then, and, at Villa, how not to play.

'Most of all I could read the team as players and as men. I think I knew how to bring out the best. I would never, for instance, direct Maurice Norman openly on the field – I'd ask Peter Baker or Ron Henry to talk to him. But with Dave Mackay you never had to worry about confidence or ego. I remember Terry Medwin getting injured once, being unhappy about staying on. Dave and I suggested Terry go out to the right-wing, where we used to put people who'd been in the wars, for a few minutes till he recovered. Five minutes later he came haring back: "Did you say go on the right-wing? I *was* on the right-wing!" I think I knew the team.'

Blanchflower had long since ceased to be a mere footballing figure and was a publicly feted 'personality'. His television advertisements for a breakfast cereal led to an Irish accented 'Hullo there' becoming a public catch phrase alongside such gems as Bruce Forsyth's 'I'm in charge'. His refusal to appear on *This is Your Life* (the programme's first such embarrassment) was front page news. 'I did it for personal reasons,' he said afterwards, 'If I told you what they were they wouldn't be personal anymore would they?' Blanchflower, like many footballers, has remained unimpressed by television, questioning the apparent assumption that man's pri-

Perhaps the single most worrying moment during the Double season; McPheat's shot flashes into the net for Sunderland to make it 1-1 in the FA Cup quarter-final. Playing at Roker on 25 February 1961, Spurs had taken an early lead through Cliff Jones but Sunderland eventually scored after four corner kicks in a row. The crowd invaded the pitch (BOTTOM) *and this helped the players calm down. Blanchflower, seen about to pick the ball out of the net with Maurice Norman, told the referee: 'Let the fans work it off, we don't mind.' Spurs won the replay 5-0. Nicholson's greatest fear was just this sort of Cup upset: 'Who knows with the Cup? One afternoon on a strange pitch, an awkward ground, one or two things go the opposite way and bingo. You're out.'*

mary goal in life should be to appear on the small screen. His later career with such programmes as *Sportsview* was short-lived and not marked by outstanding displays of harmony with producers and directors who would not allow him the same creative freedom he enjoyed on the Tottenham pitch.

Bill Nicholson, the other half of this on-field/off-field relationship is blunter: 'In a poor side Danny was a luxury. That's why I dropped him. But in a good side his creativity, his unorthodox approach, was priceless – a wonderful asset.' Together they thought about the game and moulded that great side, the one that won the Double.

Nor did the Tottenham triumphs, or Tottenham-connected triumphs, end at that in 1961. With the FA Cup final still to come there was ex-Spur Alf Ramsey guiding his Ipswich Town side into the First Division for the first time in the club's history, plus Nicholson and Ramsey's mentor Arthur Rowe, thankfully back at work again, managing Crystal Palace from the Fourth to Third Division. And, not to be left out of the celebrations, the Spurs reserves were runners-up to Chelsea in the Football Combination and the third team romped away with the Eastern Counties League.

In achieving their League triumph, Tottenham spread their fire-power right across their attack, all five forwards were into double figures even before the halfway stage, proof that the canny Nicholson had the front blend about right. It pleased him that he was carrying on a Tottenham tradition in doing so.

'Supple and imaginative, that's how the game has always been played at Spurs. Or how they have always tried to play it over my years here. It's the man *without* the ball who is the most important. I can remember an old schoolmaster who tried to show me the way. His words stuck and they always apply: "When not in possession get into position." I never forgot that phrase. You should never be just watching. I used to say when any of my players erred in this way, "If I catch you doing that again I'll charge you admission. If you want to watch, then you should pay".'

THE OTHER HALF

There was motivation enough for the Cup, the other leg of the impossible. They had eased the load by piling up the League points until that title was virtually assured well before the season was completed. From the New Year on the Cup trail opened up, with Second Division Charlton pressing Spurs, on an off day, far too close for comfort before going down 3-2 in the third round at White Hart Lane. Crewe Alexandra travelled down again in sheer terror for a fourth round set-to, and, although escaping the 13-2 annihilation of their previous visit, were not exactly flattered at 5-1.

A trip to their Cup bogey ground of Villa Park was the reward in February's fifth round draw. But the fixture list provided first a full dress rehearsal for that match in the shape of a League meeting between the clubs the previous Saturday. Spurs were happy enough with their League returns from Villa Park games (where they had not lost since Blanchflower moved down), distinctly not so when it came to the Cup, where they had, of course, been beaten in the semi-finals of 1948, 1953 and 1956.

The League match suffered from a lot of sparring and weighing-up by both teams trying to learn something for the more glamorous Cup tie ahead, and although there was effort enough there was not much more. Even so, Spurs made history by a 2-1 victory which took them to the fastest 50 points yet achieved. It was the barrel-chested Mackay who took the chief honours a week later in the Cup as Aston Villa went down again, this time 2-0, before an enormous 69,000 crowd. The goals, both from Cliff Jones and one in each half, were first a somewhat fortunate deflection off full-back John Neal, later Middlesbrough and Chelsea manager, the other an unstoppable drive to round off a smooth five-men Tottenham move. Julian Holland said of the astonishingly fast, direct Jones: 'More than any other player, it was he who made Blanchflower's old age comfortable.' No longer burdened by the most expensive footballer tag, Jones was now doing just what he had been bought for.

It was another Jones goal which held Sunderland to a 1-1 draw at Roker Park in the sixth round. Sunderland jolted Spurs out of their elegant stride in a rugged second half

fight-back but later, with a packed 64,797 looking on at the White Hart Lane replay, the Wearsiders were right up against it as five home goals poured past them without reply. And for conclusive proof that the Villa Park pitch held no more Cup terrors for them, Tottenham stilled a gusty, swirling wind sufficiently long enough to tame Jimmy McIlroy and the rest of the renowned Burnley team into a 3-0 submission in the semi-final. McIlroy and Blanchflower were close friends and shared the scheming role for Northern Ireland. The Burnley star was not, however, always entirely overwhelmed by his colleague's charms: 'People ask me why I often don't play as well for Ireland as I do for Burnley. It's simple – Danny always keeps me up all night talking.' Bobby Smith's two goals and a late one from Jones were the passport to a Wembley meeting with Leicester City in the final. The semi would have made a better final, and for Burnley the match was poorly timed, being just three days after their 4-1 European Cup defeat by Hamburg.

Unfortunately the final itself, on 6 May, was spoiled as a spectacle, or the spectacle it should be, by the injury to City's right-back Len Chalmers. He was hurt in a tackle by Les Allen in the 19th minute, a hard tackle but nothing more than a clumsy one, as Chalmers himself was quick to point out later. There are those who believe that in those early minutes, and with Chalmers still in action, Leicester looked the better bet as Cup winners; that Spurs did little justice to themselves as the heralded Team of the Century until the last twenty minutes of the match, and that was when tiredness had taken toll of a City side which battled helplessly against the odds of

having Chalmers, when he returned to the fray, limping bravely but ineffectively along the left wing.

Leicester could only hope to keep some self respect from the result. They did this by holding out until Smith, with a dummy, feint and cracking 67th minute shot which rocketed past young keeper Gordon Banks, and ten minutes later little Dyson, with a deliberately placed header from a precise Smith cross, enabled skipper Blanchflower to lead the way up to the Royal Box to redeem the pledge which he had made to his chairman at the start of the season – the League and the Cup. Forty-eight hours before he had received his second 'Footballer of the Year' award. It was a time for silverware.

Though it had to be whispered at the time, many found the final something of a disappointment. Everyone, except a few unfortunates from the Midlands, had wanted to see Spurs win, and win in style. At White Hart Lane, however, they remembered what had happened to Manchester United just four years before, when they were even hotter favourites for the Double. Certainly Leicester's chances in 1961 looked better than had Villa's in 1957, even if City had taken three appallingly poor games (0-0, 0-0, 2-0) to get past Sheffield United in the semi-finals.

For Spurs it had been a season of Cup finals; every side was desperate to beat them and the opposition raised its game time after time. This is why Blanchflower's ability to change the pace was so important – to slow everything down, absorb pressure, consolidate any gains they had made. In the 1970s, particularly with European teams away from home, such tactics became commonplace; in 1960

Before the great days began: from left to right; Peter Baker, Bill Brown, Dave Dunmore, Danny Blanchflower and a preoccupied Tommy Harmer, apparently concerned about his toes. Full-backs Peter Baker and Ron Henry were actually the only locally-born members of the Double-winning team. At the beginning of the 1960–61 season Blanchflower had told chairman Fred Bearman that he thought the side could do the Double. 'In our last League match of the previous season at Wolverhampton we had been clearly better than the best of the competition, and this was the basis of my confidence,' Blanchflower now says.

they were never really understood. Spurs approached the Cup final in 1961 in a more conservative frame of mind than for any other game they had played all season. It was, for instance, the only match during which Maurice Norman did not go up for corner-kicks. Certainly it is possible that Chalmers' injury was critical, Spurs only taking control in the last half hour when Leicester had been worn down by the combined burdens of knowing that, unlike most underdogs, they would not be popular winners, the understandable apprehension about their opponents, and, much the most relevant, playing with a man short.

Blanchflower felt the anticlimax as much as anyone in the stadium and makes a more general point: 'I did not feel the same emotion before or after as I had with previous rounds. There were too many people there who did not care about the result and, at the end, I didn't have much heart for running around the stadium. I looked upon it as a duty rather than an enjoyment. For the player the reality of a Cup final can never live up to the dream, the promised land, anyway. The dreams are for the fan, not the player, for the lover of the game who will never know what it is like out there. Cup final day is the fans' day.'

Nicholson also mentions disappointment before glories. 'Looking back now the Double

was fabulous,' he says reflectively, 'but there was also disappointment for me when we did not put our Double feat right out of anybody's reach – remember that Arsenal caught up with us ten years later – by doing it for a second year in succession. Which we should have done.' The key to this regret was his old colleague Alf Ramsey and one game in 1962.

IPSWICH AND RAMSEY

Nicholson explains: 'We were due to play Ipswich and in our team chat before the match I was keen that we should change marking tactics and have our wing-halves mark their wingers instead of the full-backs doing the job. This was because they had wily Jimmy Leadbetter pulling the strings back from deep and I believed that if our half-backs could do a smother-job it would enable us to raid forward while, we hoped, Blanchflower and Mackay throttled them before they could set up anything.

'But there was a disagreement about playing it that way and I conceded the point because I did not want them trying to play a tactical plan they were unhappy about. They beat us home and away, 3-1 on our own pitch. If we had beaten them 3-1 at White Hart Lane we would have done the Double again; it is just as simple as that. It was all a question of tactics.

'But the sequel is interesting... as Ipswich won the League title and we again won the Cup, we had to meet for the Charity Shield at the start of the new season, 1962-63. Alf Ramsey won the toss for the game to be played at Portman Road. There was no nonsense this time. I put my foot down and told them very firmly that we would play this one my way. Which we did and we beat them by 5-1.'

The tactics of these two clashes are worth a diversion, for they highlight the astuteness of Nicholson, the reasons why Alf Ramsey was able to win a World Cup and, more pertinently, the relative tactical illiteracy of most English managers at the time. Ipswich, newly promoted, had a mediocre squad at best. It is not too much of an exaggeration to say that Alf Ramsey won the Championship with just two strengths; one was the fact that hardly anyone in the division had met the Ipswich team before, the other was the use of slightly

built Jimmy Leadbetter as a withdrawn left-winger. Instead of pushing Leadbetter to the goal-line, Ramsey had him use the ball in a variety of ways, often slotting it diagonally into the penalty area from up to 50 yards out from goal. The opposing full-back, conventionally believing that the number 11 was nowhere near the danger-area, generally held off. But Leadbetter was a remarkably accurate kicker of the ball and his target was almost invariably the battering ram of a dual spear-

FIRST DIVISION 1960-61												
	P	W	D	L	F	A	W	D	L	F	A	PTS
Tottenham	42	15	3	3	65	28	16	1	4	50	27	66
Sheff Wed	42	15	4	2	45	17	8	8	5	33	30	58
Wolves	42	17	2	2	61	32	8	5	8	42	43	57
Burnley	42	11	4	6	58	40	11	3	7	44	37	51
Everton	42	13	4	4	47	23	9	2	10	40	46	50
Leicester	42	12	4	5	54	31	6	5	10	33	39	45
Man Utd	42	14	5	2	58	20	4	4	13	30	56	45
Blackburn	42	12	3	6	48	34	3	10	8	29	42	43
Aston Villa	42	13	3	5	48	28	4	6	11	30	49	43
WBA	42	10	3	8	43	32	8	2	11	24	39	41
Arsenal	42	12	3	6	44	35	3	8	10	33	50	41
Chelsea	42	10	5	6	61	48	5	2	14	37	52	37
Man City	42	10	5	6	41	30	3	6	12	38	60	37
Nottm F.	42	8	7	6	34	33	6	2	13	28	45	37
Cardiff C.	42	11	5	5	34	26	2	6	13	26	59	37
West Ham	42	12	4	5	53	31	1	6	14	24	57	36
Fulham	42	8	5	8	39	39	6	0	15	33	56	36
Bolton	42	9	5	7	38	29	3	6	12	20	44	35
Birmingham	42	10	4	7	35	31	4	2	15	27	53	34
Blackpool	42	9	3	9	44	34	3	6	12	24	39	33
Newcastle	42	7	7	7	51	49	4	3	14	35	60	32
Preston	42	7	6	8	28	25	3	4	14	15	46	30

head – Ray Crawford and Ted Phillips. Neither was at all subtle, but attacking the centre-half together (this was before the days of twin centre-backs and, remember, the full-backs had stayed wide) they were remarkably effective. Phillips scored 28 goals in his only First Division season of note (the next two years his tally dropped to 9 and then 4), Crawford 33. And no one really found them out until Nicholson revealed the simplicity of the tactic in that Charity Shield match. He brought the Spurs full-backs infield to outnumber Crawford and Phillips, and had the half-backs mark Leadbetter out of the game. Spurs won 5-1.

One of the oddest coincidences of Spurs' two Championship successes was that the trophy was actually won on both occasions against Sheffield Wednesday at White Hart Lane. In 1951 Spurs won 1-0 on 28 April to clinch it, while in 1961 they overcame the Yorkshiremen 2-1 on the evening of Monday 17 April. Spurs were 1-0 down to a Don Megson goal when (OPPOSITE TOP) Bobby Smith flicked the ball over Peter Swan's head and crashed a half-volley home. A few minutes later (LEFT) a Blanchflower free-kick was headed on by Maurice Norman (in right background) and Les Allen (not in picture) hit a shoulder high volley past Ron Springett to make it 2-1. THIS PAGE: Wednesday had been Spurs' nearest challengers all season, eventually finished second in the League and proved perfect opponents for the moment of victory.

OPPOSITE BOTTOM: After winning the Championship minds quickly switched to the Cup, with a predictable loss of League form and Spurs were beaten in two of their last three games. The final home match was against West Bromwich Albion on 29 April and they lost 2-1, thus missing a chance of establishing a First Division points record. At the end of the game, nonetheless, the crowd called for Blanchflower to speak after the Championship trophy had been presented. The players listening are (left to right): Les Allen, Bill Brown, Maurice Norman, Bobby Smith, Peter Baker, Cliff Jones, John White, Terry Dyson and Dave Mackay. Ron Henry is hidden behind Les Allen. Henry, White, Allen and Blanchflower played in every first-class competitive game during the Double season.

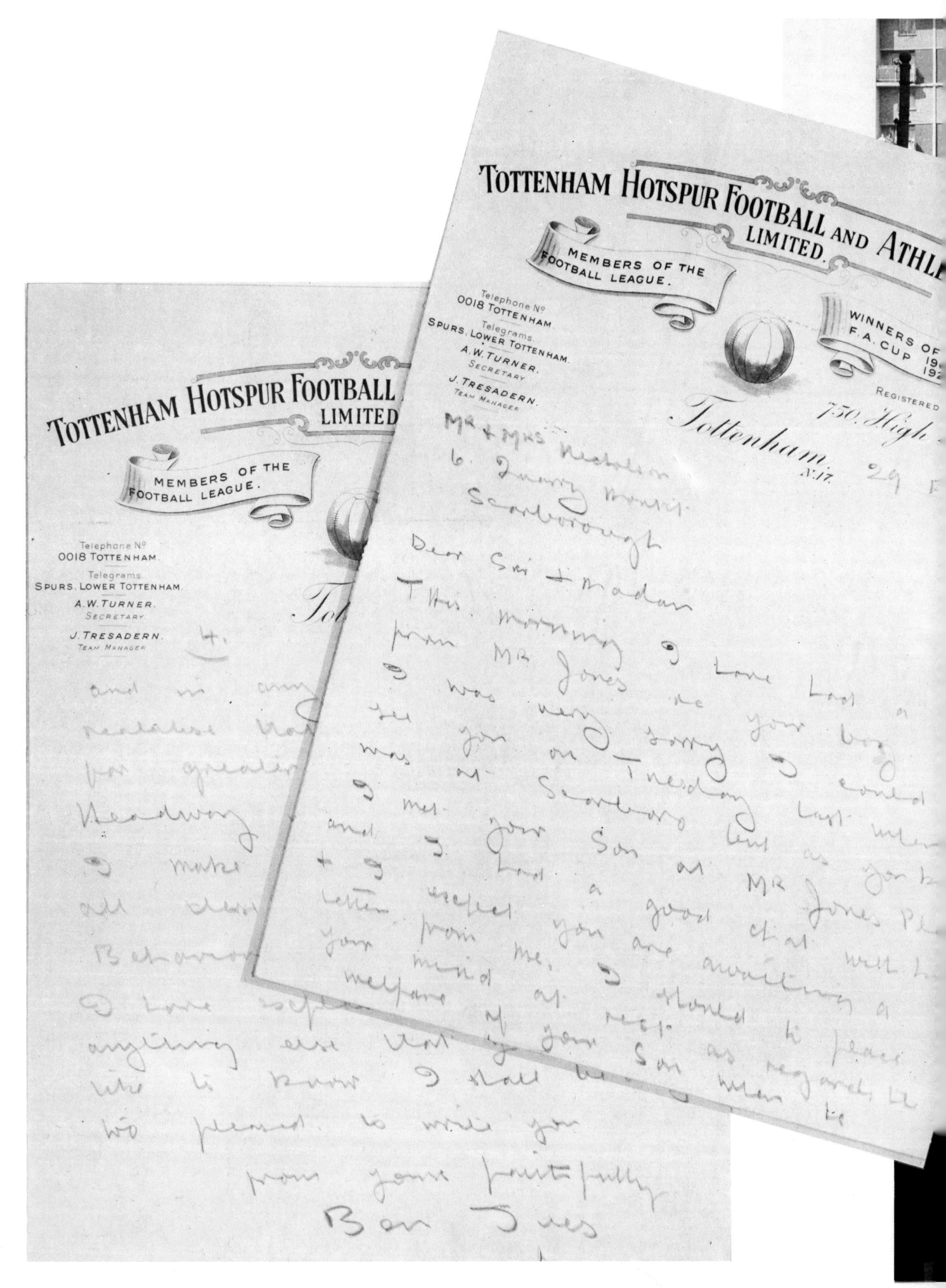

TOTTENHAM HOTSPUR FOOTBALL AND ATHLE
LIMITED.

MEMBERS OF THE
FOOTBALL LEAGUE.

Telephone Nº
OO18 TOTTENHAM.
Telegrams
SPURS, LOWER TOTTENHAM.
A.W. TURNER.
SECRETARY
J. TRESADERN.
TEAM MANAGER

WINNERS OF
F.A. CUP 19
192

REGISTERED
750 High

Tottenham,
N.17   29

Mr & Mrs Nicholson
6. Quarry Mount
Scarborough

Dear Sir & Madam

This morning I have had a
letter from Mr Jones. He
was very sorry I could
tell you on Tuesday last when
I met your son at Mr Jones. Pl
and I had a good chat will t
letter asked you are awaiting a
your mind of reply to pleas
welfare of your son when h
be

from your faithfully

Ben Jones

TOTTENHAM HOTSPUR FOOTBALL
LIMITED.

MEMBERS OF THE
FOOTBALL LEAGUE.

Telephone Nº
OO18 TOTTENHAM.
Telegrams
SPURS, LOWER TOTTENHAM.
A.W. TURNER.
SECRETARY
J. TRESADERN.
TEAM MANAGER

and in any
realalise that
for greater
headway
I make
all these
Behaviour
I have se
anything else Not
like to know I shall
be pleased to write you

OPPOSITE PAGE: *The letter that changed, and made, Tottenham's history. Written by chief scout Ben Ives on 29 February 1936 it invited Bill Nicholson's parents to send their son down to White Hart Lane for a month's trial. While Ives mentions having had a chat with Nicholson, the future manager has no recollection of the meeting. The Mr Jones mentioned was the organiser of Nicholson's local team. The letter came as a complete surprise to all at 6 Quarry Mount, Scarborough. 'My parents had never seen me play; they knew I was keen but had no idea whether I was any good or not. We weren't even exactly sure where Tottenham was,' says Nicholson. The letter goes on to reassure the 16-year-old's parents that: 'You need not fear about him as at present we have about 20 boys his age and we get them good lodgings with personal friends of mine . . . Mr Jones will put him on the night train at York and I shall meet him at Kings X, or should Mr Nicholson like to bring him down himself he would be welcome. The boy seems to be very bright and I am sure he will get on (here) and in any case I trust you realise that he must have a far greater chance of making headway in London than elsewhere.' Nicholson came and, a quarter of a century later, so did the trophies. In the space of three years there were to be four of them.*

LEFT TOP: *Ron Henry and Peter Baker hold the Championship trophy and FA Cup respectively as the Double winners parade up the High Road between Edmonton and Tottenham town halls.*

LEFT BOTTOM: *A year later the FA Cup, in the capable hands of Maurice Norman and Danny Blanchflower, takes the same route after Spurs had become only the fourth club in history to retain the trophy. They missed another Double by just one game – when Ipswich beat them at home.*

BOTTOM CENTRE: *There'll be another bus along next year . . . this time carrying the Cup Winners Cup. Though the cheering crowds couldn't know it, an era was at an end.*

It was a vindication of manager Nicholson's tactical know-how and one could understand the disappointment of a man who had always aimed to be a winner. But it might also have been true to say that Tottenham took their eye off the ball over the last few laps of the League race. Five crucial home points were dropped in the last six matches to be played at White Hart Lane and that was definitely not championship form. Amazingly West Brom yet again beat them in the season's last home match – and again the score was 2-1. It was all too late when, faced with the most difficult ending possible to their programme, they rattled off three away victories at Blackburn, Birmingham and Leicester. That only underlined what might-have-been. Ipswich and Burnley slugged it out in the final matches, both dropping points all over the place, but Ramsey clinched it at the end with a con-vincing 6-2 win over the Lancastrians.

Almost as an afterthought, Spurs did win the Cup again – only the fourth club (after Wanderers, Blackburn Rovers and Newcastle United) ever to do so in consecutive years. The draw was not an easy one for them but they handled it in style. In the third round they drew 3-3 at St Andrew's and won the replay 4-2. The fourth round saw a 5-1 walkover at Plymouth, the fifth 4-2 at The Hawthorns. Spurs' only home draw was in the quarter-finals, when they beat Villa 2-0. Hillsborough, a favourite semi-final ground for the club (they were to win there in 1967 and 1981), was the venue for the penultimate round, and a relatively easy 3-1 defeat of Manchester United. It was a quiet campaign. Fans and Press were diverted by the drama of the European Cup and the intrigue of pursuing incomprehensible Ipswich in the League.

The final was a much better game than the previous year's, and brought together the best two teams of the period. Burnley, without an FA Cup win since 1914, were probably slightly favoured. Spurs had just been knocked out of the European Cup by the odd goal (just as had Burnley when the clubs met in the previous season's semi-final), and the general assessment was that Spurs were past their peak and coming downhill. The pundits were wrong. Jimmy Greaves, a member of the team for six months now, scored an early goal. Robson pulled one back but Smith scored an excellent second and Blanchflower made it safe at 3-1 with a late penalty, only the fourth ever given, and converted, in a Wembley final.

But, as in 1961, there was just a slight sense of anticlimax. Not because of the game, which was a good one this time, but because this wasn't really the Cup players and fans had

wanted to win. The 1962 FA Cup often appears as little more than a footnote to the Double because the real prize, the one that was never won, was the European Cup.

AND SO TO EUROPE

No British club has ever entered the European Cup with more confidence than did Spurs on 13 September 1961 against Gornik Zabrze of Poland. At no time were the supporters of Liverpool, Manchester United or Nottingham Forest ever as sure that this was their year as were the Spurs fans of 1961. This was not only because of the unquestioned excellence of their team, but also because the competition was, at last, wide open. Read Madrid had been beaten, by Barcelona, for the very first time the previous season. Benfica were the new champions – a good side to be sure, but surely not one to live with Spurs?

It was Tottenham's first trip to Europe, and their inexperience showed. Bill Nicholson recounts his advance trip to Poland to have a look at the training facilities and hotels: 'They took me to this terrible place, and told me this is where we would be staying. I told them they would stay at the best hotel in England when they came to us, so I wanted Spurs to stay at the best hotel in Katowice (Gornik's home). They said this *was* the best hotel in Katowice. So we tried nearby Chorzow, but there were no decent hotels at all there, and Warsaw was hours away.' Spurs were one of the first British clubs to experience the total disorientation that trips behind the Iron Curtain can bring. Blanchflower tells more of the story: 'There were prisoners in the streets digging up cobblestones, guarded by men with machine-guns. Going through the park leading to the Slaski Stadium we could see women, on their hands and knees, cutting the grass with what seemed to be large pairs of scissors. The stadium, massive, lit and tall like a distant castle, was the only welcoming thing about the whole place.'

Apparently no-one had told Gornik that this was Spurs' year for the European Cup. Within an hour the Poles were 4-0 up and Tottenham were as good as dead. 'I was bloody upset,' says Nicholson, 'We showed no determination or discipline.' But Jones and Dyson got two late goals back when the Poles let up and Spurs were in with a chance back home.

Perhaps the fondest memory of the great Spurs years of the early sixties is of the magical European nights. Twenty years later men from all over London still speak with damp eyes of those tremendous occasions – the first London had ever experienced and in an era, of course, when European Cup ties were not televised as a matter of course. It was not until these wonderful Wednesday nights that *Glory, Glory, Hallelujah*, the four-sided Tottenham wall of sound, really became established as the most individual and evocative of all English club tunes. As it happens, the club played *McNamara's Band* (and still does) as the 'official' song at the time. 'The sound came from everywhere,' says Blanchflower, 'It was marvellous. When they sang, they all sang together...fathers and sons, old and young. A local vicar used to complain that the whole thing was like a substitute for religion, and I suppose it was in a way. A century before those

OPPOSITE PAGE: *The Double team; standing left to right: Bill Brown, Peter Baker, Ron Henry, Danny Blanchflower, Maurice Norman, Dave Mackay; seated left to right; Cliff Jones, John White, Bobby Smith, Les Allen, Terry Dyson. This is the team that won the Cup in 1961. The following season's final saw Medwin and Greaves replace Dyson and Allen. At the end of the 1960–61 season Blanchflower paraphrased Nicholson's low-key approach saying: 'We've had what our manager might call a rather good year...'*

fathers and sons would have sung in church together – but it wasn't in any way irreligious.' It is rather a sad reflection on the last two decades that the Tottenham crowd at Wembley for the 1981 Charity Shield should be singing 'Can you hear us on the box?' with barely a Glory, Glory to be heard.

To hear tell of it now, one could be excused for thinking that the great European nights went on for years. In actual fact there were really just two seasons and seven games (four in the European Cup and three in the Cup Winners Cup) and the legends that surround them really grew up from one particular game – the return leg against Gornik on 20 September 1961.

This was the night when the Poles found themselves outnumbered 60,000 to 11, when, as they admitted later, the noise from the crowd (who were much closer to the pitch than they were used to) battered them into submission. They never stood a chance, though they did get one goal through the appropriately named Pohl. The ferocity of the support was terrifying, probably frightening the Spurs players as much as their opponents. The defences were soon to be breached, initially by Blanchflower with a penalty, and then the flood gates opened; three for Jones, two for Smith, one apiece for Dyson and White. At the end the crowd slumped back limp just from watching. Sitting or standing it had been an extraordinary experience and anyone who was there will talk about it with the same intensity today.

Nicholson's reactions to the first leg problems were characteristic. Never again would Spurs be caught out that way. Preparations for away legs became intense, every detail was covered, never again would Spurs players find themselves covered in flea bites from bug-ridden beds, or bemused by the social conditions of the countries they had to visit. As Blanchflower repeats: 'You had to go there once, to experience it. It's difficult to win anything first time round.'

The next two legs were much easier. In nearby Rotterdam Feijenoord went down 3-1 (Dyson and young Frank Saul, with two, getting the goals) though Spurs disappointed their fans by playing safe for a 1-1 draw at home. Dyson again got the goal. In the quarter-finals Tottenham lost 1-0 in Prague to Dukla, playing much more cautiously than in Poland, and won 4-1 at home; Smith and Mackay both scored twice.

THE DREAMS DIE

In the semi-finals Spurs drew Cup holders Benfica. The other tie was between Real Madrid and Standard Liege. The prize, then, was as great as could be imagined – almost certainly a final against Real in the Olympic Stadium in Amsterdam.

This is the fourth of those critical five games with which one can write the Spurs story of the early sixties. It is also the only one they lost and, in so doing, probably robs the story of its denouement. When all is said and done Spurs did not, like Liverpool, Manchester United and Forest after them, reach the ultimate goal. They came as close as the woodwork on three occasions, and suffered almost certainly incorrect offside decisions twice, but that often tends to be the margin by which great stories are never told and by

which great prizes are never won.

Nicholson prepared himself well for the tie. He watched Benfica in Nürnberg and took the trouble to see Real beat Juventus in Madrid. 'Real were not the side they had been. I came back thinking that we would beat Real in the final if we could get past Benfica,' he remembers. Bela Guttmann, the Hungarian exile who was coaching that side of Portuguese and Mozambiquans and who had just acquired a young black player called Eusebio, agreed with Nicholson's assessment. He was proved correct – despite a Puskas hat-trick Benfica were to win one of the great finals, 5-3.

Nicholson's tactical planning was also more sophisticated now. For away games he would generally play Tony Marchi as an extra defender. The player left out from the Double side was Les Allen, meaning Spurs had one less attacker. Medwin, who could cover back better than Dyson, generally got the vote to play alongside Smith and Jones up front. Dyson, who had scored in each of the first four European Cup games, was never to play in that competition again. For the semi-final, however, Greaves was eligible, and he took the remaining place in Lisbon in a formation which was effectively a pioneering 4-3-3.

Tottenham always preferred to bring their opponents back to White Hart Lane for the second leg, knowing then what they needed to do. This allowed them to use the first match to get to know their opponents, the initial 45 minutes being played extremely cautiously. The whole scheme fell apart in Lisbon. Within 20 minutes Aguas and Augusto had put Benfica two ahead. Smith got one back, but Augusto headed his second to make it 3-1. The talk was not of the goals that were scored, but of the two that were disallowed – one by Greaves and one by Smith. Greaves, not a bad loser, says now: 'I reckon to this day the Swiss ref, Muellet, refereed us out of the final. I beat the full-back before I scored and was still given offside. Nine minutes from the end I crossed for Smithy to score and Muellet pointed to the centre-circle for 3-2. Then he saw the linesman flagging and disallowed the goal without even talking to him. But I was *ahead* of Smithy when I crossed.' Nicholson was brutal about the defeat: 'We gave away two vital goals because three players in a row made stupid mistakes.'

Spurs had already pulled back a two-goal deficit against Gornik and the crowd expected them to do so again. The ground was packed for the return leg on 5 April 1962, the noise terrifying. The average attendance for these four European Cup matches worked out at 60,430. Twenty years later David Miller of the *Daily Express* called the Benfica game '...the most electrifying ninety minutes of European football I have seen on an English ground,' and few who were there would ever question these sentiments. Bela Guttmann brought his extraordinary tactical and human know-how to succeed in one of his greatest tasks.

Guttmann himself deserves a diversion. He was a member of the Hungarian Olympic team in 1924, and went on to coach in America and the Netherlands before being imprisoned in a Second World War concentration camp. Having survived that, he took Ujpest to the Hungarian championship, coached Kispest

OPPOSITE PAGE: *Bill Brown tips over a Norman Deeley corner during a League match against Wolves at White Hart Lane on Saturday 16 September 1961. Spurs won the game 1-0, the goal coming from Dave Mackay. Brown is well protected by his full-backs Ron Henry (left) and Peter Baker. The Spurs' rearguard was extremely conventional and very unadventurous by the standards of a decade later. Nicholson now says of Baker: 'Danny should be very grateful to him; he had to cover a lot of holes on the right-hand side when Danny was attacking. He was particularly good at coming inside to cut off a break through the middle and to force play out to the wing.' Baker and Henry played together for five full seasons and in that time Baker scored just two League goals and Henry none at all. Bill Brown was one of Nicholson's best, and least publicised, signings. The manager was rightly proud of his ability to sign the right player without press speculation, fuss or competitive bidding: 'Mackay took an hour and a half, White one hour and Bill Brown three-quarters. Greaves dragged on for days but he was worth every penny and every minute.' Four days after this game against Wolves, Spurs faced one of their sternest tests – the European Cup return leg against Gornik which the Londoners began 4-2 down. That was to be the night of Glory, Glory, Hallelujah, when in an emotionally draining hour and a half Spurs destroyed the Poles to win 8-1.*

OVERLEAF: *As the clock shows, it is half-time at White Hart Lane and Bill Nicholson talks tactics to Cliff Jones (right). Elsewhere (left to right) are Peter Baker, keeper John Hollowbread, Tommy Harmer (wrestling with an orange), Tony Marchi, John Ryden (not in kit) and trainer Cecil Poynton. The 'H' on his jug means home team.*

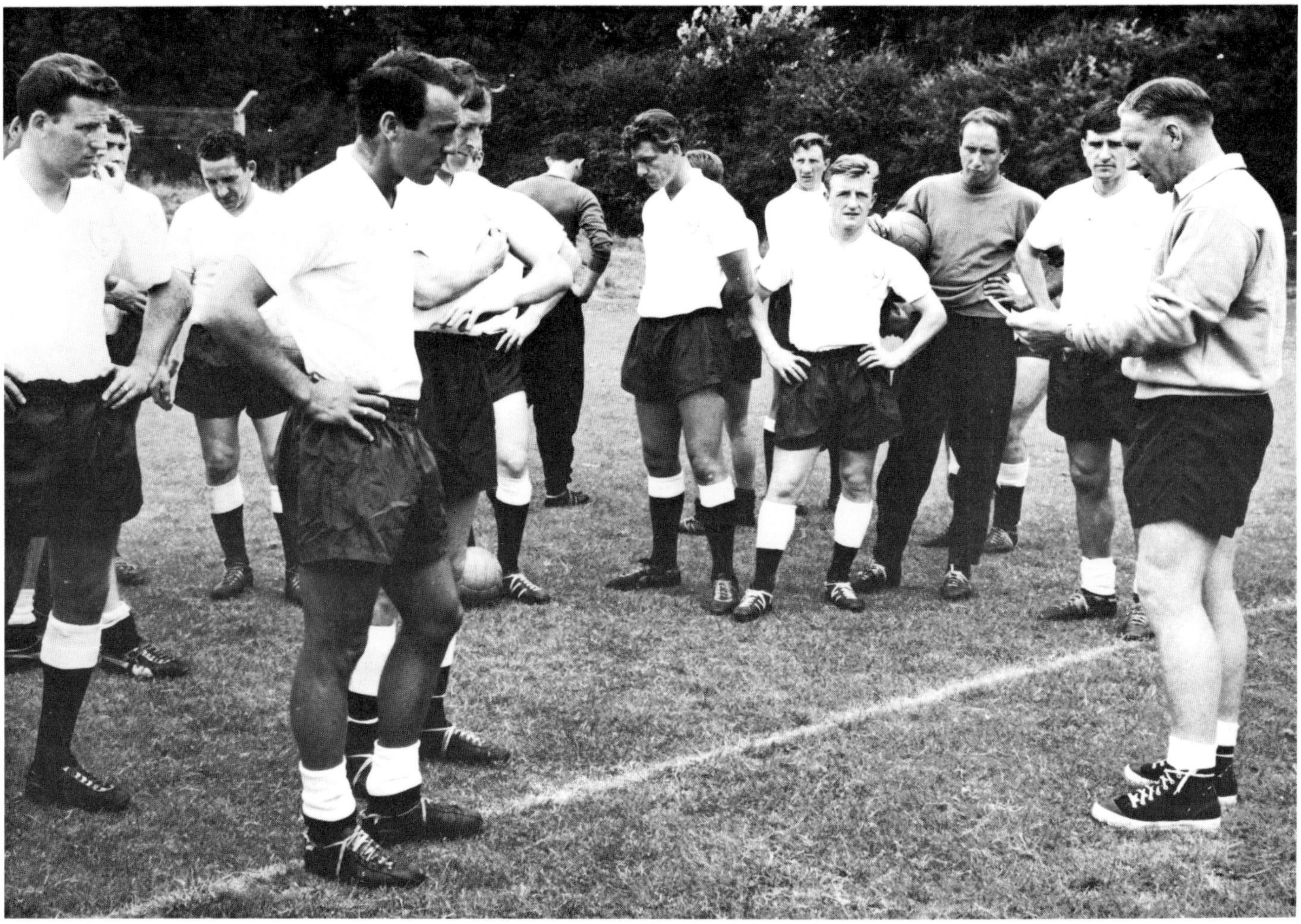

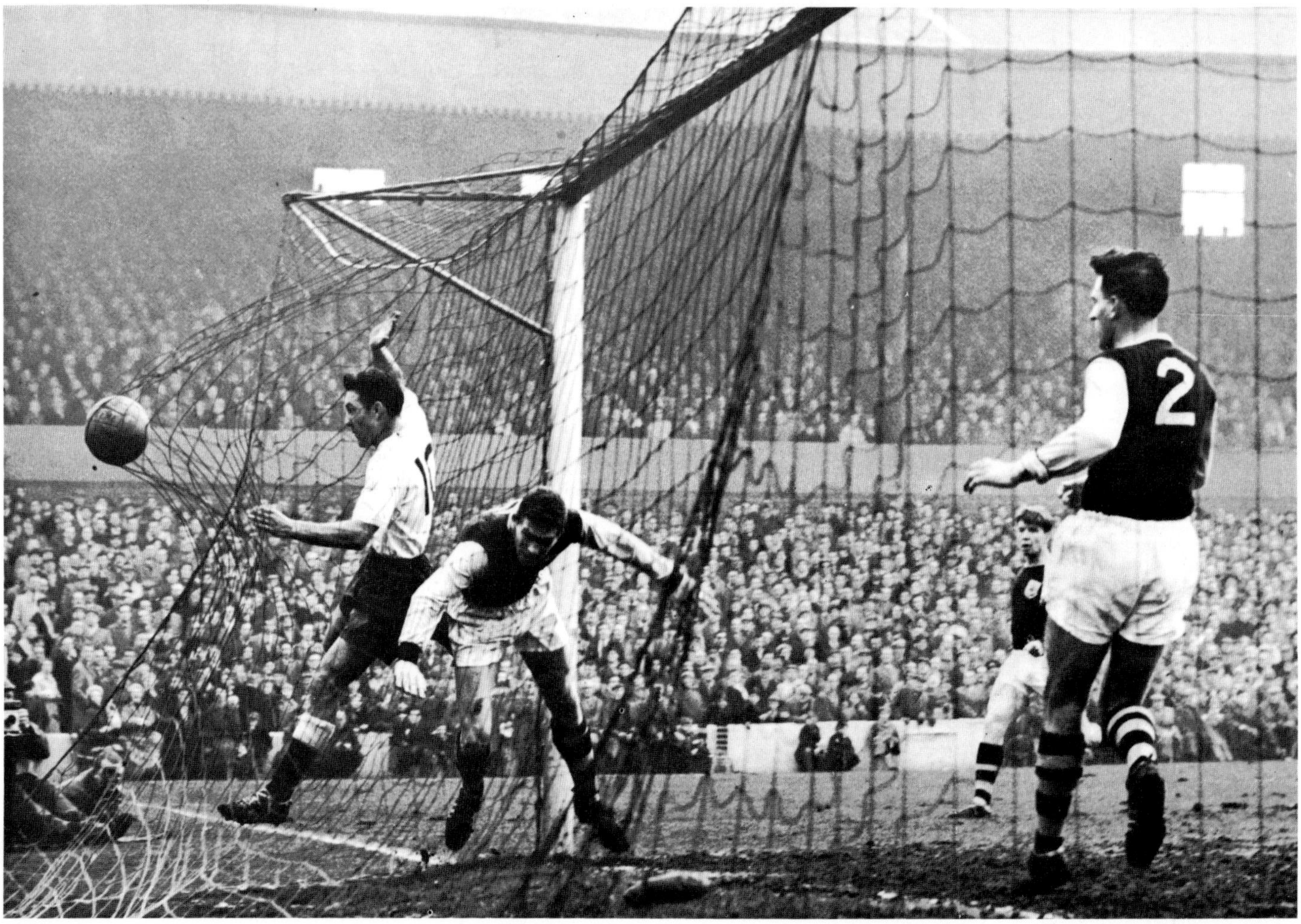

(who, renamed Honved, created something of a stir) and moved on to Italy. Here his AC Milan won the championship and were leading the Italian League when he was sacked for his pains, and he then took over the touring Hungarian side which had escaped the 1956 revolution. Having thus arrived in South America, he coached Sao Paulo to the 1958 Brazilian Championship, and almost certainly created the 4-2-4 system which Vicente Feola adopted for the Brazilian national squad in the World Cup in Sweden that year. Having thus learned to speak Portuguese, he ended up in Lisbon with Benfica.

Guttmann was a worthy opponent for Nicholson and Blanchflower. His gamesmanship was subtle but not extreme. He complained loudly about the physical excesses of Smith and Mackay, and the resulting Press comment seemed to intimidate Danish referee Aage Poulsen (certainly Guttmann thought it worked; he said afterwards: 'Yes, we got more than our share of free-kicks.') He knew the crowd would overawe his players, so he refused to let them warm up. They went straight out to the kick-off so that the atmosphere was not allowed to get to them before the game began.

Within 15 minutes a thoroughly underawed Aguas played a one-two with Simoes and slid the ball home across the rain-sodden six-yard box. Spurs were 4-1 down on aggregate. Then came a replay of one of the disallowed goals in Lisbon. White to Smith to Greaves, who, running between two defenders, scored from close in. The referee gave it, then consulted a linesman who had briefly raised his flag and the goal was disallowed. It was the third marginal decision that had gone against Spurs and it raised justifiable doubts afterwards.

After 38 minutes White finally made a goal for Smith, and then Blanchflower calmly converted another penalty four minutes after the break. Costa Pereira went the wrong way, Spurs were only one goal behind and there were 40 minutes left. History says they did not succeed, that their frantic attacks left them with no reward other than muddy woodwork – three shots that would have gone in another day came back off the posts and bar (though, to be fair, Aguas also hit the bar in the first half). Nicholson and Blanchflower both said afterwards that they thought Spurs were probably a goal better, over the two legs, but they wouldn't have changed their tactics if they had to do it again. 'I lost count of the near misses,' says Nicholson, 'but the one I'll always remember is when Dave (Mackay) hit the crossbar right at the end.' Blanchflower concedes Benfica's abilities: 'You have to remember that Pereira was magnificent against Bobby Smith and that Coluna was marvellous in midfield. I think Guttmann was sharper than we thought. All those years in Europe and South America, all that experience. He told me that Benfica would do it after the game in Lisbon.' Guttmann resigned the Benfica job after the final, eschewing a possible hat-trick, and moving to Penarol in Uruguay. He eventually went to live in Vienna where, so legend has it, he became a pool hustler. The destroyer of Spurs' most cherished dreams was to die there in August 1981.

Spurs themselves did not despair and the following season was to see them become the first British club to win a European trophy, the Cup Winners Cup. This was a new trophy, only three years old, and had yet to acquire its later status but Spurs were, nonetheless, impressive winners.

Nor was their League performance much behind when they finished runners-up to Everton for the Championship. They were six points in arrears of the Merseyside club with Burnley, always their close rivals, a further point behind. But the Lancashire side sampled some revenge for this and that Cup final defeat of the previous year by inflicting Tottenham's first FA Cup defeat for three years when they went to White Hart Lane for their third round meeting and came away clear 3-0 winners. No hat-trick here for Nicholson.

It was a season in which Spurs, with 111 goals, were the liveliest attackers in the Football League, Jimmy Greaves leading the way with a club record 37 goals which beat the jointly-held previous best of 36 by Ted Harper and Bobby Smith. This brighter if not quite as consistent Spurs side scored in each of their first 19 League games and it took new champions Everton to check them in the twentieth, when they earned a 0-0 draw from their visit.

THE CUP WINNERS CUP

In one glorious autumn seven game spree they averaged five goals a go, including nine rammed home against Nottingham Forest, (Forest winger Trevor Hockey said afterwards: 'We scored first and last and they got nine lucky ones in between'), six against Manchester United, five against Leyton Orient away and the sharing of a 4-4 draw with Arsenal. They later hit West Ham for six, Liverpool for seven and Ipswich Town for five and Jimmy Greaves scored four goals against both Forest and Liverpool. The two Liverpool games were particularly entertaining. Having lost 5-2 at Anfield on Good Friday, Spurs won 7-2 at home on Easter Monday. But their failure to stay the course strongly, the 62 goals conceded, and the reallocation of matches following the worst hold-up which League football has ever experienced after the appalling 1962–63 winter, put paid to another title chance. From their last ten matches they took only eight points, winning three, drawing two and losing five of the games. It was the second consecutive season in which a terrible finish probably cost them the title.

The season was, in retrospect, one of hanging on for the final prize. The Cup Winners Cup final against Atletico Madrid in Rotterdam was the fifth and last of the era's critical games, partially because it was literally the last gasp of the Double side and the glory that had gone with their achievements.

The route to Rotterdam had not been a long or exhausting one, consisting of only three preliminary rounds for Spurs. Glasgow Rangers were poor opposition, going down 3-2 at home and 5-2 in London. Two of their defenders did, however, make their mark. A violent sandwich on Blanchflower damaged his knee and the cartilage came out. At his age (37) it took time to repair and he was to miss 22 games in all. John White's growing importance to the team is indicated by how well they played in Blanchflower's absence. The next round saw more Iron Curtain travels

OPPOSITE TOP : *On 30 November 1961 Bill Nicholson made perhaps his best ever signing, bringing Jimmy Greaves back from Milan for £99,999. The fee was set at that figure so that Greaves would not have to carry the tag of being the first player to have cost an English club £100,000. Here the new boy listens with team-mates Blanchflower, Henry, Hopkins, Dyson, Hollowbread and Eddie Clayton to Nicholson's instructions at the Cheshunt training ground. Greaves first senior game for the club was on 16 December 1961, against Blackpool. He got a hat-trick and maintained a record of scoring in every debut game of his career.*

OPPOSITE BOTTOM : *Greaves and ball in a familiar position – the back of the net. The date is Saturday 24 November 1962 and Greaves has just put Spurs 1-0 ahead at Burnley, despite the efforts of defenders Brian Miller, Alex Elder and John Angus (number 2). The day was not to end happily for Spurs, however, Connelly and Pointer scoring in the second half to give Burnley victory. Seven weeks later the Lancastrians were to inflict Spurs' first FA Cup defeat for three years – 3-0 at the Lane.*

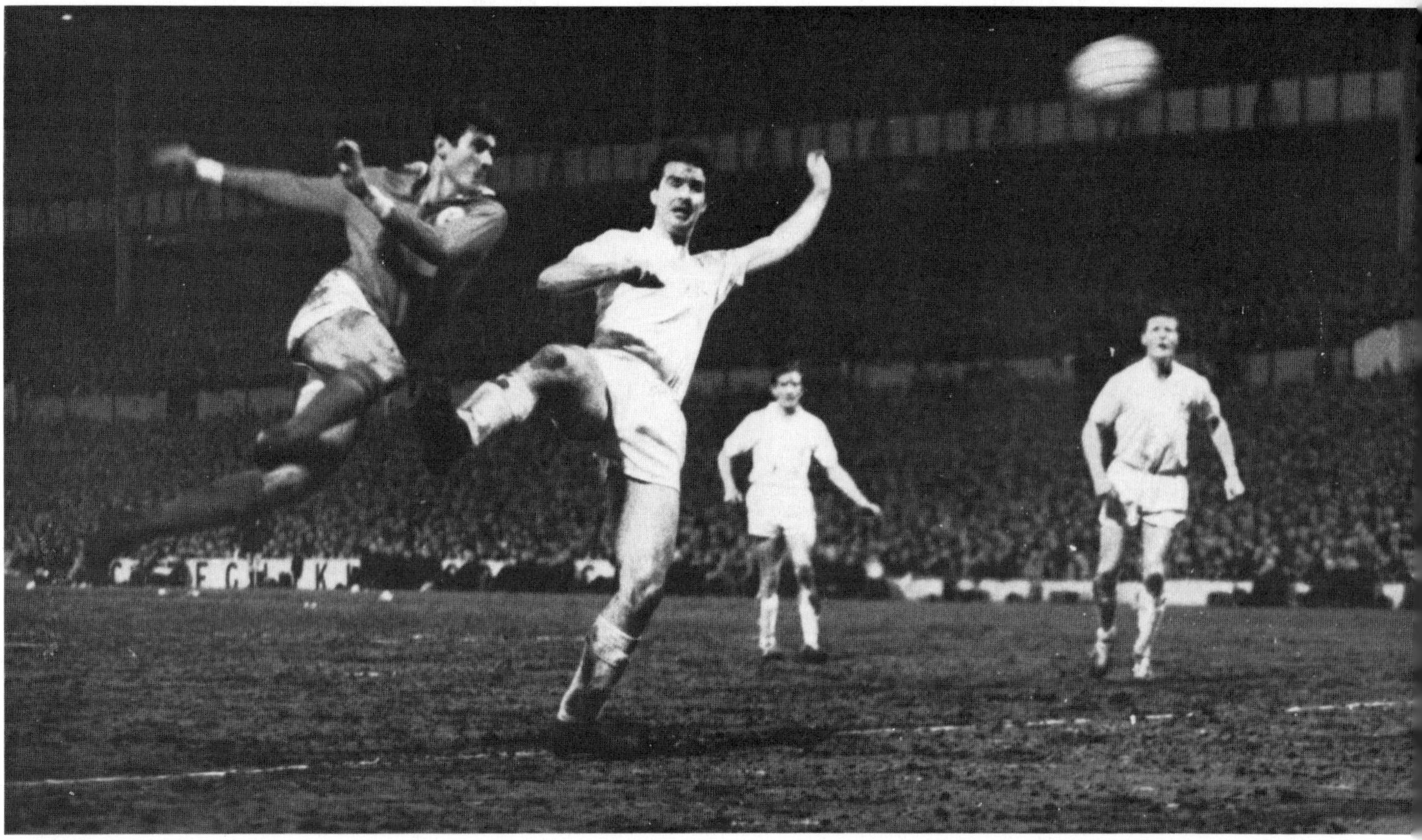

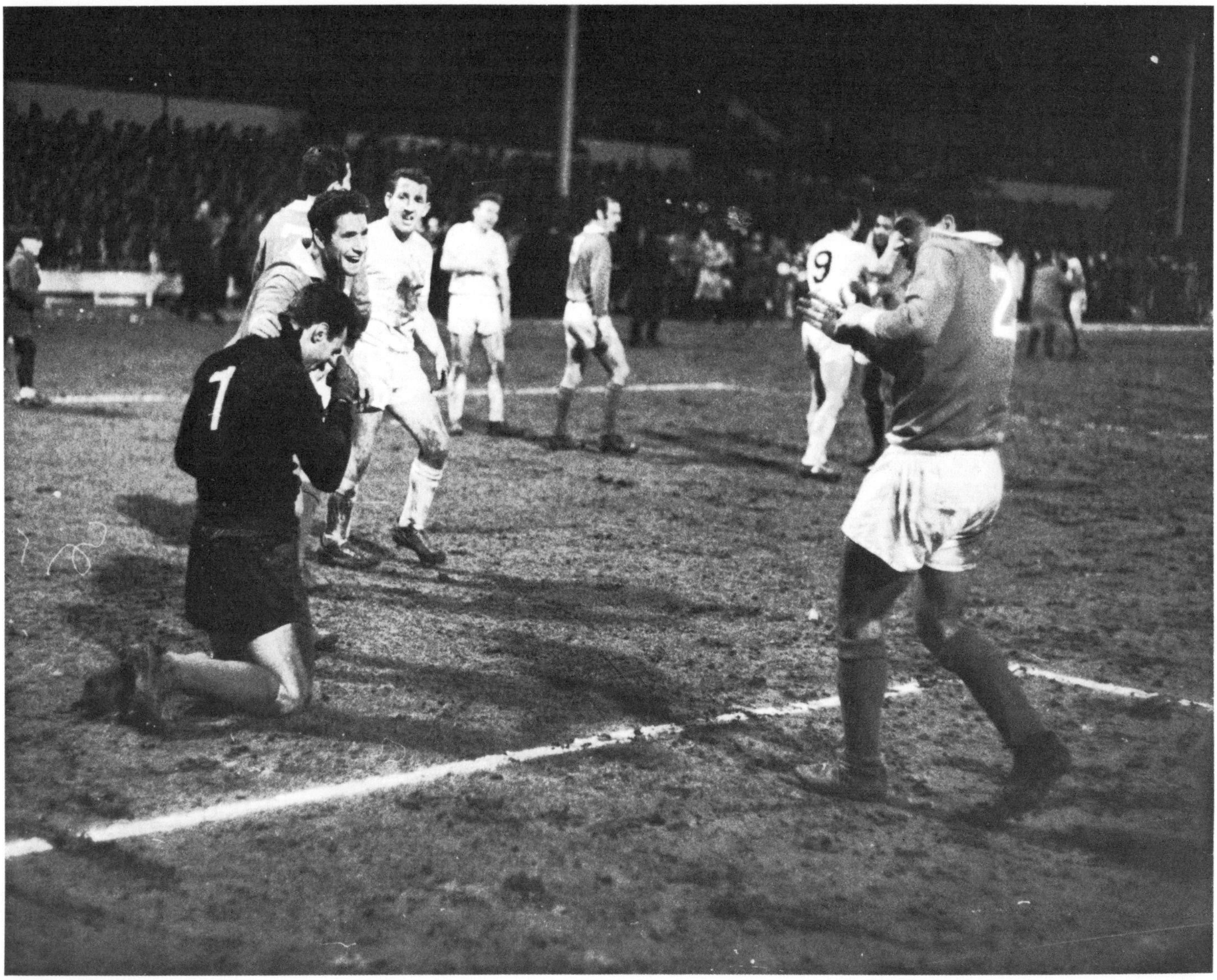

with a draw against Slovan Bratislava. By now Spurs were almost seasoned travellers in Eastern Europe, but Slovan were to pull them apart. Bill Brown, his nose all plastered up after one particularly brave dive at a forward's feet, kept them in the game. Spurs were lucky to keep the score down to 2-0. Blanchflower, from the previous year's experience with Gornik and Dukla, knew that Western Europe disorientated Iron Curtain sides even more than the reverse trip upset Spurs. 'We were never happy over there,' he says, 'but they couldn't believe their eyes when they came to London. We rarely had any trouble at home.' Blanchflower was right, Spurs scoring six without reply in the second leg.

The semi-final against OFK Belgrade was most notable for Jimmy Greaves being sent off – the first man in a Tottenham shirt to be dismissed since 27 October 1928. Greaves played at outside-right, John Smith moved to inside-forward and Maurice Norman turned out with an injured foot. Missing were Cliff Jones and Blanchflower when Tottenham arrived for the first leg in the Red Army Stadium, Belgrade. Greaves was sent off in the 55th minute for retaliation, and one man who could clearly remember the last time it happened, 35 years before, was Spurs trainer Cecil Poynton, for he was the unfortunate it had happened to. Greaves admitted later that he had taken a swing at Krivokuca, the home defender who had been trying to kick lumps out of him. Earlier there had been a free-for-all with the Hungarian referee roughly man-handled when trying to sort things out. The cause of it all was the senseless figure of wing-half Maric lying flat out in the home penalty area after a free-kick had been awarded against him for a horrific tackle on Smith. No-one in London had much doubt as to who had laid him out. Sixty thousand fans still gave ten-men

Spurs a stirring farewell as they left 2-1 winners through White and Dyson and thanks to heroic defence inspired by play-everywhere Mackay. Blanchflower returned for the second leg to make the first goal for Mackay...Belgrade pulled that back; then Jones and a Smith header meant the first one-legged European final for any English club on a 5-2 aggregate.

It was harsh on Nicholson that Dave Mackay, of all people, should miss the final against the holders, Atletico Madrid, in the Feijenoord Stadium in Rotterdam, a stomach injury keeping him on the touchlines. It was certainly not his week...he also came second to Stanley Matthews as 'Footballer of the Year'. Marchi made an admirable deputy for the Scot.

It was the prospect of Mackay's absence which troubled Spurs most as they waited for the final on 15 May 1963. 'With Dave in the team we feel we can beat anyone,' said Cliff Jones before the match. 'He makes things happen. He makes us go. Without him, the odds change.' The odds had changed and Mackay did not play, added to which Spurs lost their last domestic game 0-1 to already relegated Manchester City. Blanchflower was still not fit but, officially now assistant to the manager (*not* assistant manager), he preferred Bill Nicholson to make the critical decision. 'It's a simple choice', he said, 'either me on one leg or John Smith (a skilful reserve bought from West Ham) on two.' Nicholson ordered pain-killing injections for Blanchflower's knee and had him play. He was 37 and this, to all intents and purposes, was his last major match.

The Atletico match has gone down in folklore as the game Blanchflower won without kicking a ball. Nicholson, says David Miller, gave an almost funereal team-talk. 'Nick's confidence seemed to have gone,' said Jimmy Greaves afterwards, 'because we'd lost Dave Mackay and he was our best player. He just went through the Spaniards, player by player, pointing out their strengths. But he just made us worry whether they *were* as good as he had painted them.' Blanchflower took over from Nicholson and told them to listen to what *he* had to say. Greaves recalls the captain's own brand of team-talk: 'He said that if their centre-half was big and ugly then ours, Maurice Norman, was even bigger and uglier. That if they had a fast winger called Jones

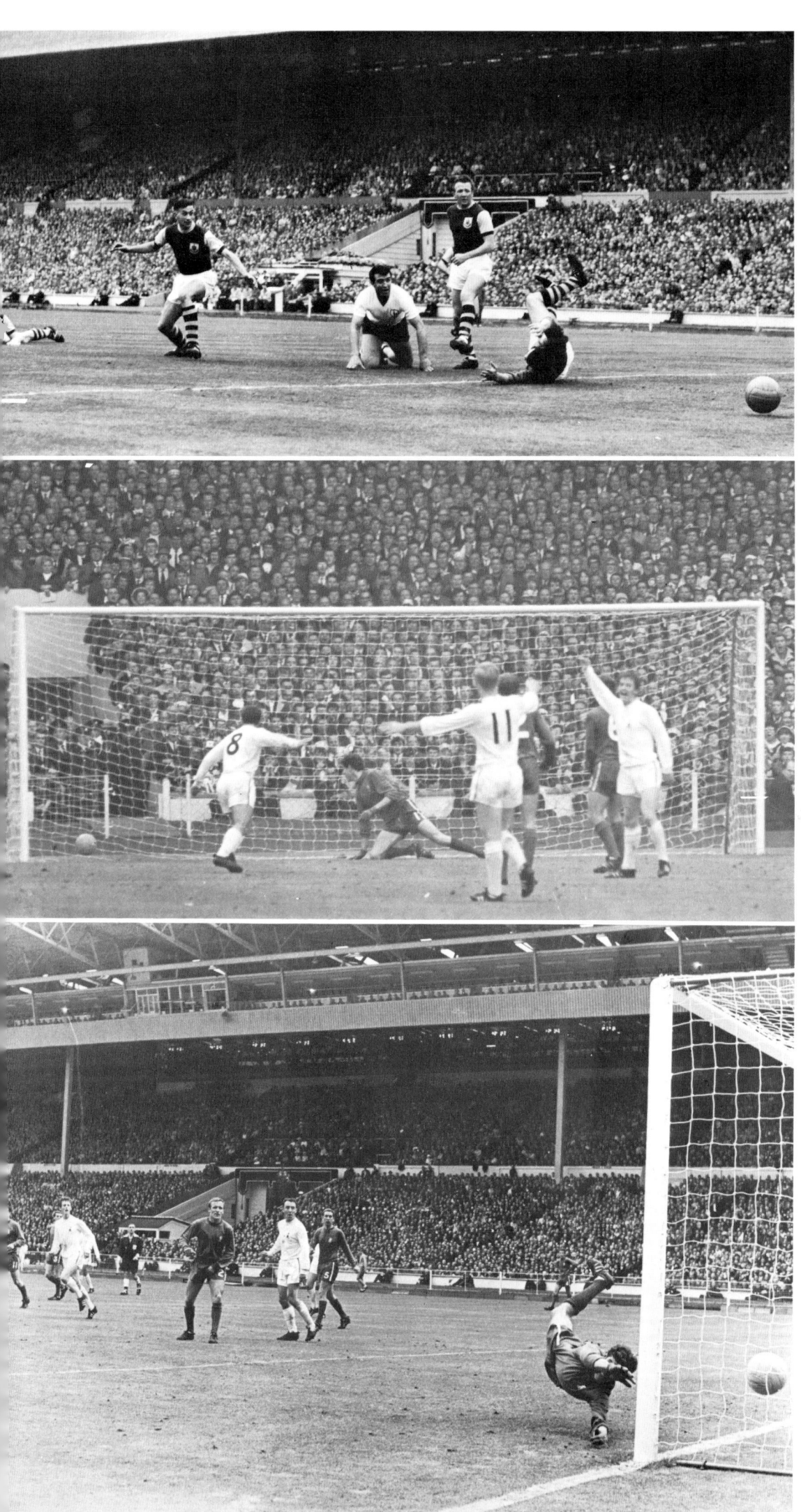

OPPOSITE TOP: *The goal that made the Double safe. In the 77th minute of the 1961 FA Cup final Bobby Smith (furthest left in picture) crossed for Terry Dyson (not in photograph) to head past a despairing Gordon Banks.*

OPPOSITE CENTRE: *Ten minutes earlier Bobby Smith (just rising from ground) had feinted one way, turned the other and put Spurs 1-0 ahead against a Leicester City side reduced to ten men after an injury to Len Chalmers. Danny Blanchflower said afterwards that the final was probably Spurs' worst performance of the whole season.*

CENTRE: *The two goalscorers after the Cup win of 1961; Terry Dyson (left) and Bobby Smith, plus the photographer catching himself in the mirror and, also reflected in the mirror, John White bending over the table.*

OPPOSITE BOTTOM: *A year later and Bobby Smith scores a similar goal against Burnley after a John White run down the left. The Burnley keeper is Adam Blacklaw and Smith's goal made the score 2-1.*

THIS PAGE TOP: *Jimmy Greaves (far left) scores the first goal of the 1962 final after just three minutes. This was the first medal Greaves had won – two more coming in the Cup Winners Cup and the FA Cup final of 1967.*

THIS PAGE CENTRE: *Jimmy Robertson (right) raises his arm in trimph as the ball hits the back of Peter Bonetti's net and opens the scoring in the 1967 final against Chelsea. In the 40th minute Alan Mullery's shot had rebounded off Chelsea defender Allan Harris and left Robertson with a clear opening from the edge of the penalty area.*

THIS PAGE BOTTOM: *After 67 minutes of the 1967 final Frank Saul put the result beyond reasonable doubt with a hooked shot inside Bonetti's near post. Saul, who was standing with his back to goal, is not in the picture, but looking on are John Boyle, Jimmy Robertson, Allan Harris, Jimmy Greaves and Marvin Hinton as Spurs' last Cup final goal of the decade buries itself in the net.*

(which Atletico did – a strange coincidence), then ours was so fast he could catch pigeons.'

That pigeon-catching Cliff Jones played on the right-wing, Terry Dyson on the left, and it was to be Dyson's night. Spurs' first goal came in the 16th minute, a cross from Jones to the impeccable Greaves and into the net. Sixteen minutes later Dyson made it 2-0, but Ron Henry had to give away a penalty at the start of the second half and Collar made it 2-1. Spurs were on the ropes for perhaps twenty minutes, but were saved by a bolt from a highly unlikely source. Dyson, who had been having a good, teasing match against full-back Rivilla beat his man again and slung over a high, teasing cross. It went too close to the keeper, Madinabeytia, but somehow the goalie lost it in flight and it squeezed over his head at the near-post. Dyson claimed this fluke among flukes was the result of his quick thinking when he saw the keeper move out two yards, but it certainly inspired the winger to believe anything was possible. Ten minutes from the end he sent over the cross from which Greaves made it four and then, in the 87th minute, Dyson made the night his by running 30 yards with the ball, dummying right and left and finishing with a 25-yard screamer. He had the immense satisfaction of playing the game of his career at the perfect time, a privilege few footballers ever enjoy. As the 5-1 victors walked back to the dressing-room Bobby Smith said to Terry Dyson: 'You'd better retire now, you'll never play better.'

THE OLD GUARD GOES

Dyson may not have decided to retire, but the next three years was not much more than the gradual dissolution of Nicholson's first great side.

Little Harmer had departed the Tottenham scene just before Spurs hit their jackpot years. At 32 he had to abdicate in favour of the younger White after some 15 years at White Hart Lane, the longest-serving active member of a squad which had seen many changes under the demanding Nicholson. Many clubs were still ready to make room for him in their first teams when Spurs put a £6,000 transfer fee on his head, including his old team-make Alf Ramsey at Ipswich. Harmer chose Watford, where he had worked in a print shop, but the move was not a success for the Third Division was not equipped to follow the advanced promptings of the wee fellow. His still bright talents were not being fully utilised until manager Tommy Docherty stepped in. He saw Harmer as the mastermind to lead his young Chelsea fledglings upwards and into the First Division. It proved to be a master stroke. Besides coaching and spreading his soccer lore around the Stamford Bridge dressing-rooms and training areas, he played in just five of that season's League matches, but was on the winning side every time to make a joke of the £3,000 fee he had cost Chelsea. And the one goal he scored came in the closing game of the season... to beat Sunderland, his club's nearest rivals for promotion, at Roker Park. He converted a centre into a goal with what might euphemistically be called his private parts. With that goal Chelsea went into the First Division, while Sunderland had to wait one more season.

There was satisfaction for Tiny Tom the

following season when he went back to the Lane with Chelsea and had a leading part in both the Chelsea goals which brought a 2-1 away success over his old club. It's an echo of a story Eddie Baily still likes to tell about Harmer, his old colleague of the Arthur Rowe days and much later. Says Eddie: 'I thought I had been put out to grass when I was transferred from Tottenham to Port Vale. We played Nottingham Forest, then around the top of the Second Division, and we beat them 3-1. I must have impressed Forest's manager Billy Walker. I was told he wanted me to join him.

'Freddie Steele, the Port Vale manager had me in his office and asked if I was willing to go. He received more than the £6,000 he paid for me ... and a fair bit besides. We won promotion at Forest, I got a Second Division medal and so in no time I was back at the Spurs, in the First Division. We went to White Hart Lane leading the division in October 1957 and Tommy Harmer was in the Spurs team. I was then 36 and was captain for the day against many old pals I had left behind ... I remember when the score was at 2-2 Tommy coming near to me and calling out, "I don't think much of your team, Eddie". But as we went off at the end I caught him up to tell him, "I think even less of yours, Tom" – we had won 4-3 and stayed top!'

In April 1964 the club lost a much-loved figure, its president, Fred Bearman, at the great age of 91. He had begun as a Spurs director 54 long years before, in 1910, was made chairman in 1943 and president in 1961 after retiring from the board. He had been a real tower of strength during his long association, a caring chairman. Three months later, just as the players were due to report back for pre-season training in July, came the tragic news of John White's death while sheltering from a storm during a round of golf at Crews Hill, Middlesex. It was a sickening blow to all who knew him. He left a wife and young family and a great host of friends and admirers of this pleasant, friendly, freckle-faced young Scotsman. In his near five years since joining from Falkirk he lit many of the fuses which set off the power drive of this great club side.

In a season in which he was to be tested by taking almost every bad knock that could be handed out, Bill Nicholson broke down and wept over the death of the slight 26-year-old young man of so many talents. He had been asked by the police to identify the body and had kept his feelings under his usual iron control until talking to his players after they had reported back.

He had already lost his right-hand man, Danny Blanchflower, who, at 37 and still feeling the recurring effects of that injury against Glasgow Rangers en route to lifting the Cup Winners Cup, had called it a day to switch sideways to reporting and talking football both in print and on television.

But the sad, bad news did not end there. Terry Medwin, on the summer tour of South Africa in 1963, had been injured in the very first match. That more or less ended the tour for him. But, worse for Nicholson's plans, he lost the services of the adaptable Welshman for the whole of 1963–64 season. Came December 1963 and their defence of the Cup Winners Cup. It did not last long, not even beyond the

OPPOSITE TOP: *Bill Brown in pensive mood; signed from Dundee in June 1959, Brown was already a Scottish international and went on to win 28 caps in all, his last against Italy in November 1965.*

OPPOSITE BOTTOM: *The fluke goal which restored Tottenham's composure mid-way through the second half of the European Cup Winners Cup final against Atletico Madrid in Rotterdam on 15 May 1963. Though they were leading 2-1, Spurs were struggling against the Spaniards when Terry Dyson slung over a high cross from the left. It seemed to swerve late and the Atletico keeper, Madinabeytia, lost its flight and could do nothing but flap at the ball as it dropped over his head into the net. Afterwards Dyson claimed he had seen the keeper move out a fraction and decided to shoot; that might even have been true judging by his later goal, a 30-yard run and 25-yard shot which made the score 5-1 and completed a game forever remembered as Terry Dyson's night. 'Terry would do anything for the team and, in particular, for Dave Mackay,' says Nicholson. 'That's why we had such a good left side for three years – they were wonderful together.'*

128

first challenge, despite the two-goal lead gained on the first leg of a domestic dust-up with Manchester United. A week later at Old Trafford the Nicholson furrowed brow took on another line of worry as United wiped out their two-goal deficit and finished 4-1 victors (4-3 on aggregate) to end any further Spurs interest in Europe. But they suffered a far deeper cut after only twenty minutes play when they lost Dave Mackay with a broken leg and inevitably, even though it was ironman Mackay, for the rest of the season. Within a year Nicholson had lost his whole midfield of White, Blanchflower and Mackay, that magical trio which had surely been the key to the Double. A month after Mackay's injury, Chelsea held up a patched up Spurs 1-1 at White Hart Lane in the FA Cup, then put them out 2-0 in the Stamford Bridge replay.

Determined to get back in the senior line-up, Mackay put everything into his efforts to win the thumbs up for a return. He had been out of action for nine months when he turned out against Shrewsbury Town reserves...and that same left leg was broken again. And who else but the indestructable Mackay, with painful sweat pouring down his face, could beg his bearers, 'Don't let Bill Nicholson know, not yet,' thinking of the boss's preoccupation with first team troubles.

Nicholson had a special regard for Mackay, his first signing and the man he called the 'heart' of his teams. The loss of both Blanchflower and Mackay at the same time was like taking the works out of a watch; two players, two men each, in their own individual way, of whom had meant so much to and given so much to Tottenham and Bill Nick. He is interesting when he talks about players like these: 'The character of a player meant as much to me as his skill,' he says. 'After all, he was going to represent my club and me. Most of my fellows were truly genuine. They were good to have around and ready to serve you fully. When the going became tough or rough you could still bank on them. That's when they proved you, and themselves, right or wrong. I pulled out of several deals for top players because I saw that I could not have them around this club. I like to think that I was consistent as a player, and I like consistency in players. You would have a job to go through my lot and say, "He was an inconsistent player."

'Danny Blanchflower was a fine captain. He was respected and could carry out any orders to the team. He was a class player and we always worked together very well. I admired him and still do, as a player and as a man. Dave Mackay was the complete professional, the heart-beat of a team with his fierce will to win in every game of every kind.'

BAILY RETURNS

Towards the mid-sixties Eddie Baily got the call from his old club. 'Bill Nick asked me to join him as coach and assistant manager. I got back just when the great Double side was beginning to break up. I've been so lucky to have been with clubs whose teams had been brought up in the best footballing traditions... Spurs, Nottingham Forest and West Ham. And I happened to be coach when manager Johnny Carey took Leyton Orient to their only season in the First Division back in 1962–63.

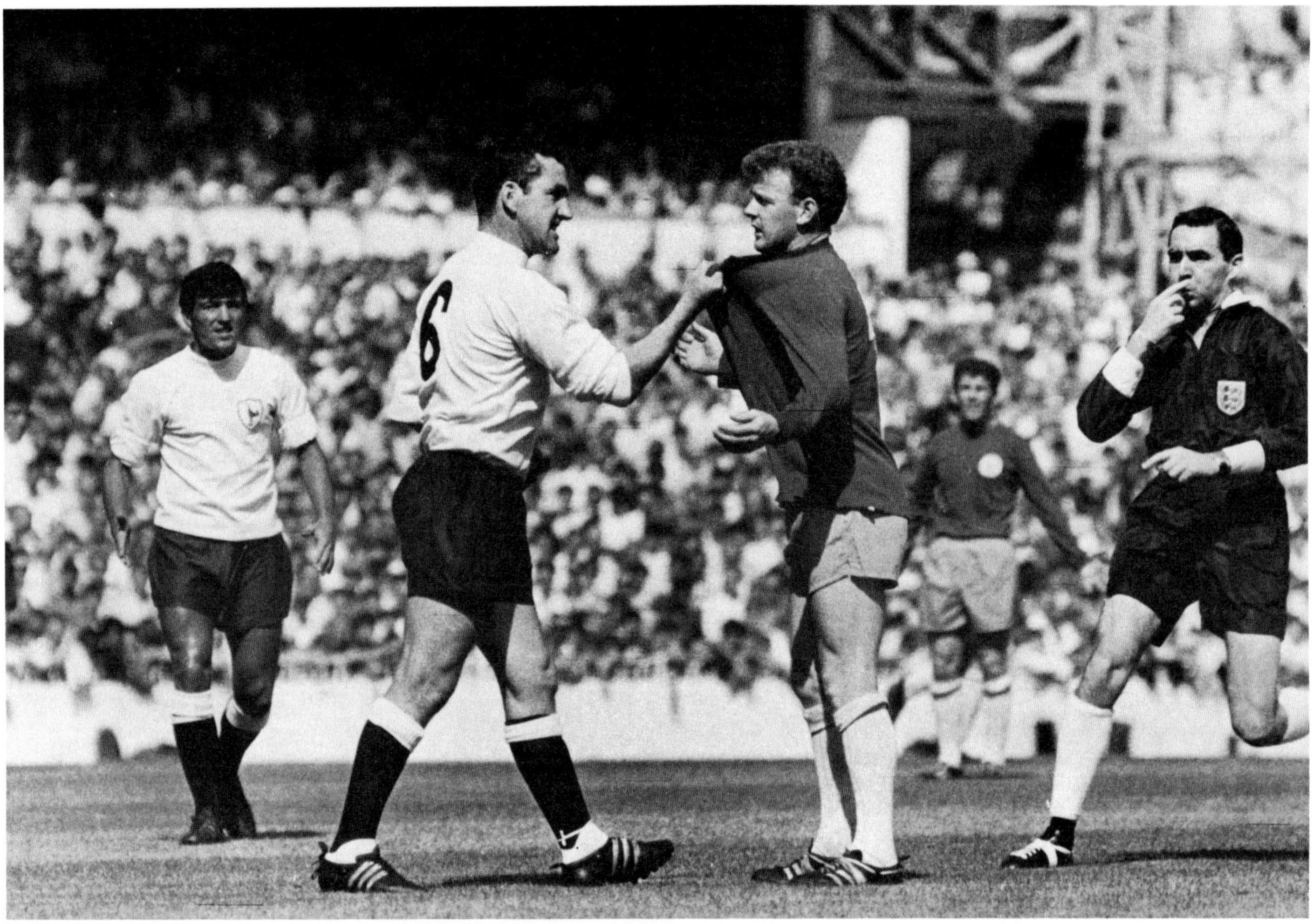

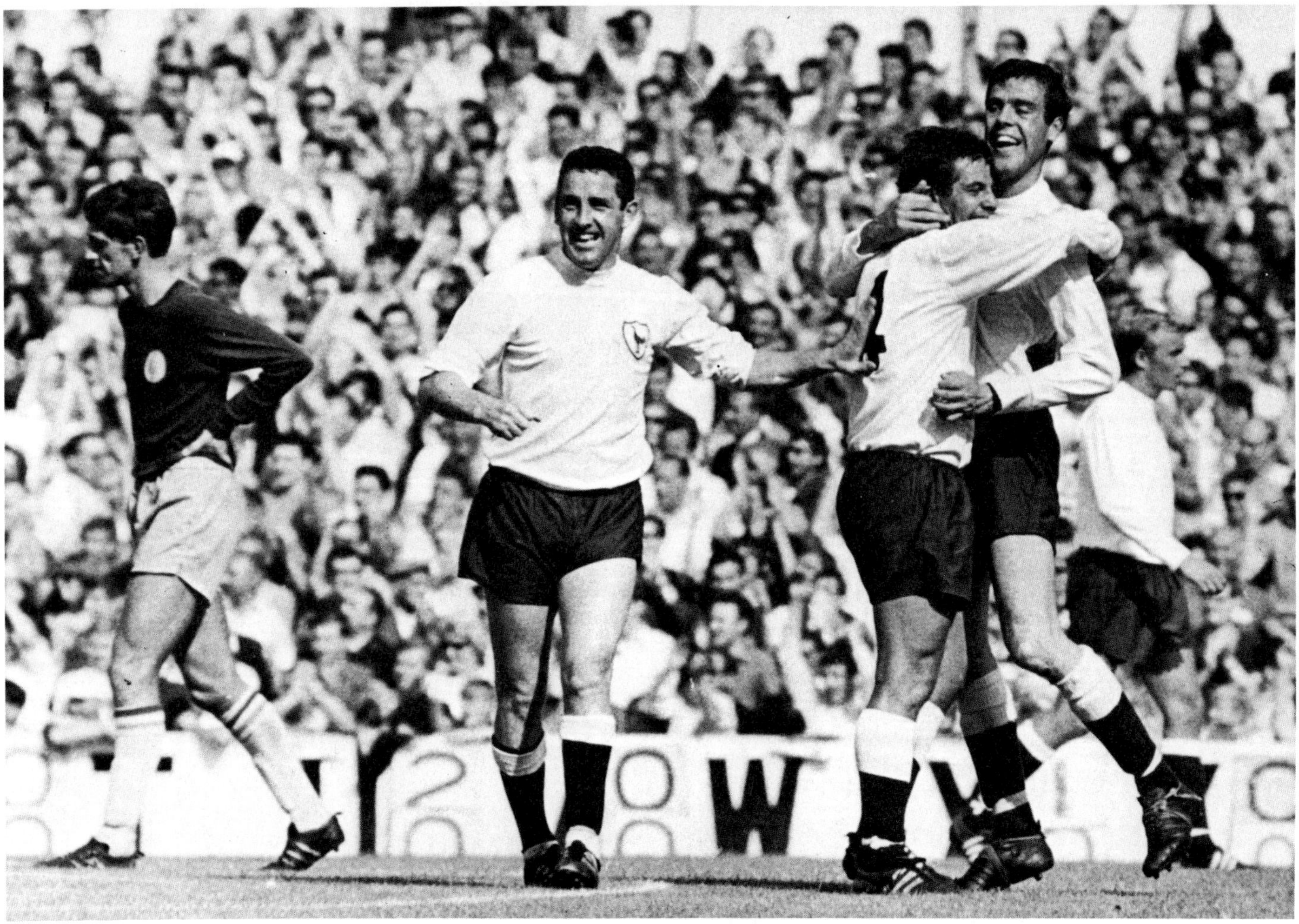
W

We went up with Liverpool and came down with Manchester City!'

He had a long ten-year partnership with Nicholson, his old playing colleague of the push-and-run days, before their break-up in September 1974. Baily was on the outside of the game looking in for two years during which time he worked as a games instructor, at a school in Enfield, teaching both football and cricket. He had been scouting for Chelsea along with the schools job, longing to get back, when Ron Greenwood rang to ask him if he would become West Ham's chief representative as that doyen of soccer scouts, Wally St Pier, was about to retire. When Greenwood took over the job of England manager, Baily was one of his first appointments as an observer, weighing up England's rivals in advance.

Today he tells you: 'The game hasn't changed much, only people have. It's the same ball, same markings, the game's the same. One-touch football is what they are teaching and coaching now, we called it push-and-run so maybe we were a bit ahead of our time. We had forwards, now there are strikers, hit-men, target players; there are numbered formations, it's all done by numbers.' He is being more reflective than critical when he says it. 'Great players are players who haven't got the ball, the hardest thing in the game. But when they've got it, it is simply doing the right thing, picking the right thing to do, not the hard thing. Lesser players shun doing the simple thing.'

The Spurs break-up continued. Peter Baker went off to play in South Africa, Tony Marchi became player-manager of Cambridge City, unlucky Terry Medwin had to call it a day after that injury in South Africa, Terry Dyson joined Fulham, Les Allen went to QPR, where son Clive was to make a name for himself fifteen years later. 1965–66 was really the end of the old days. Bill Brown handed over to Pat Jennings, Ron Henry played just once, his place filled by the nice one, Cyril Knowles, and the old-timer helped coach the reserves and the youngsters. A badly broken leg finished Maurice Norman's career, Cliff Jones found he could no longer catch pigeons and in 1968 contented himself with whatever feathered varieties they have at Fulham. Only Jones and Dave Mackay were left when the decade's final trophy was carried round Wembley, the FA Cup of 1967.

Mackay broke the final link in 1968, a good time to go: 'I could do nothing more for them, nor they for me. If I had stayed I would have got a share of the blame. It meant a new challenge.' He joined the star of the new generation, Brian Clough, at Derby. Far from being finished, he helped Clough bring Derby back to the First Division, and shared a long-deserved 'Footballer of the Year' award with Tony Book in 1969. On 20 September 1969, the Baseball Ground saw its largest ever crowd (41,826) and they saw Derby annihilate Tottenham 5-0. It was a magnificent moment for Mackay, who stayed around the East Midlands during that area's great decade, first to manage Nottingham Forest and then supersede Clough at Derby, where his side won the 1975 Championship, before Mackay drifted away from the limelight.

But all was not gloom and depression in the mid-1960s. Spurs did not cease to exist as a footballing force, and they maintained a respectable League position throughout these years of turbulent change – second in 1962–63, fourth in 1963–64, sixth in 1964–65 and eighth in 1965–66. The addition of Jimmy Greaves was, of course, the first, the most exciting and most significant change to the Double-winning side.

The addition of the goal-power of Jimmy Greaves towards the end of 1961 was simply a case of the alert Nicholson taking his chances as swiftly as the little striker himself took them on the pitch. 'He came in November, but his registration was held up for a time by the Football League,' said Nicholson. 'What a great player he proved for us and he seemed so happy here after the misery of his stay with AC Milan and his fall-outs with trainer-coach Rocco.

'I went for Jimmy because of something I had stored away in my mind, something he had said when I met him going to a dinner at the Café Royal. We got talking and it came up about his proposed transfer from Chelsea to a continental club. He told me that night that he would have loved to have played in our Double team. I stored that away. It wasn't too long after he went to Italy that we began to hear stories of how difficult he was finding trying to settle in Italy. How his game had suffered and that he was homesick. Then I heard he might be available for transfer and that's when I began to get things moving. He had such talent, such wonderful anticipation that he was on the right spot at the right time – the real art of the great striker. His timing was perfect and he was deadly. Once he lined up a goal in his sights the biggest certainty was that he would get it, he was such a deadly finisher.'

Greaves proved all this with his goal-a-game beginning with Tottenham and 20,000 turned out to see him score for the reserves at Plymouth. He hit a hat-trick in his first League match, a 5-2 home win over Blackpool, then went on to score 30 goals in the 31 games, League and Cup, he played in the second half of the 1961–62 season. His third goal against Blackpool was recently recalled by one national newspaper as being one of the greatest ever scored in post-war football, an overhead bicycle kick which made the £99,999 Nicholson had paid appear absurdly cheap. Greaves' goalscoring for Spurs in the next eight seasons was astonishing. His League tallies alone were 21 (in 22 games), 37, 35, 29, 15 (in 29 games), 23, 23 and 27. He led the First Division scorers an unprecedented six times between 1958 and 1969 and is the only man to have headed that list in three consecutive years.

There has not been another goalscorer like him in the post-war game, despite the effort and money the major clubs have put into trying to find a successor. Despite the goals, his relationship with Bill Nicholson was not always perfect. There is the famous story of a game during one of Tottenham's leaner spells. The manager was trying to get Greaves to come back and help the midfield more often, or to run into space more effectively. On one particularly lazy day Greaves' finishing was at its sharpest. He would score a goal, only to disappear for twenty minutes, and then pop up with another. After the game Nicholson was heard to comment: 'All he did this afternoon was score those four goals...' Spurs now had three ex-Chelsea forwards – Allen, Smith and Greaves – and it was Allen who had to make way in the established first choice team.

During the mid-sixties there were other major additions. In 1966 Terry Venables also came from Chelsea, where Tommy Docherty had seemingly dismissed his key playmaker in a fit of disappointment after Chelsea had lost their second consecutive FA Cup semi-final. Venables, the only footballer ever to be capped at every international level for England (Schoolboy, Youth, Amateur, Under-23, Full), was essential to fill the creative hole in midfield, but he found the going difficult. At Chelsea he was in charge of a team of younger players who had been brought up on a faster, longer-ball game. The shorter, subtler Spurs style was not suited to Venables spraying long passes from the centre-circle and, though he won an FA Cup winners' medal against his old club, he never really fitted in as Nicholson had hoped. He and Mullery, signed from Fulham in 1964 for £72,500, suffered most at the hands of the Tottenham crowd and both had some cynical things to say about their experiences. It was their misfortune, of course, to have to try and step into the shoes of Blanchflower, White and, in Mullery's case later, those of the great Mackay. It is no disrespect to them both to suggest that this was simply not possible, that Spurs have never had, nor will probably ever have again, a centre-line quite like that one. No players in the world could have filled that gaping hole and it was unfortunate that the crowd needed the enchantment of distance, via a few years, to appreciate the fact. 'It was bloody awful at the time,' says Mullery now. 'It took me at least two years to win the crowd over and get accepted and I'd have gone anywhere else for a time. I won them over in the end, but it was hard going.' Mullery recalls that he had gone to Tottenham because of Nicholson, and that the manager had predicted well ahead that Spurs would win the Cup again by 1967, which is one reason he had moved from Fulham.

The other major signings were Mike England, £95,000 from Blackburn Rovers to fill Maurice Norman's place, and the man with the three-penny bit shaped head, Alan Gilzean. Gilzean had starred in Dundee's surprise run to the semi-finals of the European Cup in 1963 when they beat FC Köln 8-1, Sporting Lisbon 4-1, and Anderlecht 4-1 away but went out to AC Milan at the penultimate stage. Gilzean had scored hat-tricks against Köln and Sporting, two against Anderlecht and the only goal of the home leg against Milan. His ability to head the ball in any direction was priceless, though Spurs did not reap maximum dividends from it until he was playing slightly behind Chivers in the early 1970s, a time when Gilzean's back header from a long throw into the penalty area might almost have been copyrighted. Like Blanchflower, Gilzean became an old war-horse, continuing until he was 36 in 1974.

There was a negative side to the transfer

market, both financially and domestically. Nicholson never found another really successful winger – going through the likes of Robertson, Saul, Morgan, Coates, Possee, Weller and Pearce. By the late 1960s, after Ramsey's 'penguin side' ('the wingless wonders' as parts of the Press had called them) of 1966 had sown its tactical seed, no major club was regularly playing more than one winger, and the one that remained was often having to double as a marking-back wide midfield man as well. Roger Morgan, one of celebrated identical twins from QPR, was the North London crowd's biggest disappointment. At £110,000 the fans thought they should have got Rodney Marsh (the joke on the terraces was that Rangers had wrapped Morgan in a paper bag and told Spurs they were getting Marsh, only they couldn't open the bag until they got home).

Domestically the problem was that youngsters were put off by Spurs image as the big-money club. Like Liverpool in the 1970s, it seemed that Spurs would always buy to fill the gaps – so what chance did youngsters have of coming through from the ranks? Nicholson denies it, but the fact is that only two of the 1967 Cup winning team (Jennings, Kinnear, Knowles, Mullery, England, Mackay, Robertson, Greaves, Gilzean, Venables and Saul) had come up through the juniors. Those two 'outsiders' were Kinnear and Saul, and the other nine had cost over half a million pounds. In 1982 terms that does not sound a lot but at the time no other club in the country could come

near it. One of Spurs' problems was their sheer success – buying a player a year used up the profits and brought the corporation tax bill down. Under the somewhat absurd Inland Revenue regulations, buying players is tax deductable whereas ground improvements are not, so while profits were good there was actually a *need* to buy expensive players.

1967 – ANOTHER FA CUP

The 1967 Cup win was a surprise, and all the more welcome for that. It is unusual for a club which has had such spectacular success to rebuild a team and come back for a major prize so quickly. Wolves did it in the 1950s, but the Spurs fans of 1967 appreciated the difficulty of the feat and the crowds that greeted the team and the trophy were even bigger than they had been in 1961 and 1962.

The third round draw was away at Millwall – actually a much harder prospect than it sounds. At the time the numbers came out of the hat Millwall had gone 59 League games at The Den without defeat, a record run that had lasted thirty-two months as they rose from the Fourth to the Second Division. As chance would have it, Millwall lost that record to Plymouth Argyle the Saturday before the third round, but Spurs had to weather a hard, goalless draw nonetheless. The replay was almost as tight, Gilzean getting the only goal.

The fourth, fifth and sixth rounds also threw up Second Division opponents. Gilzean got two and Greaves one to remove Portsmouth 3-1 and Bristol City then went down 2-0, both

OPPOSITE PAGE: *Saturday 29 April 1967 and Spurs are back in the FA Cup final. A 2-1 defeat of Nottingham Forest at Tottenham's favourite semi-final ground Hillsborough (where they won in 1921 and 1981) was inspired by a Jimmy Greaves snap shot in the first half and cemented by another from Frank Saul with 15 minutes left. Here Saul challenges full-back Peter Hindley while keeper Grummitt gathers the ball. Looking on are Alan Gilzean and Bobby McKinlay. It was the critical game on the road to Wembley for Spurs, Forest being favourites and finishing one place above them in the League.*
BELOW: *Jimmy Greaves after the game, talking with Terry Venables (left). Greaves was a constant nightmare to Forest, scoring 29 first-class goals against them in his career which included four on no less than three separate occasions.*

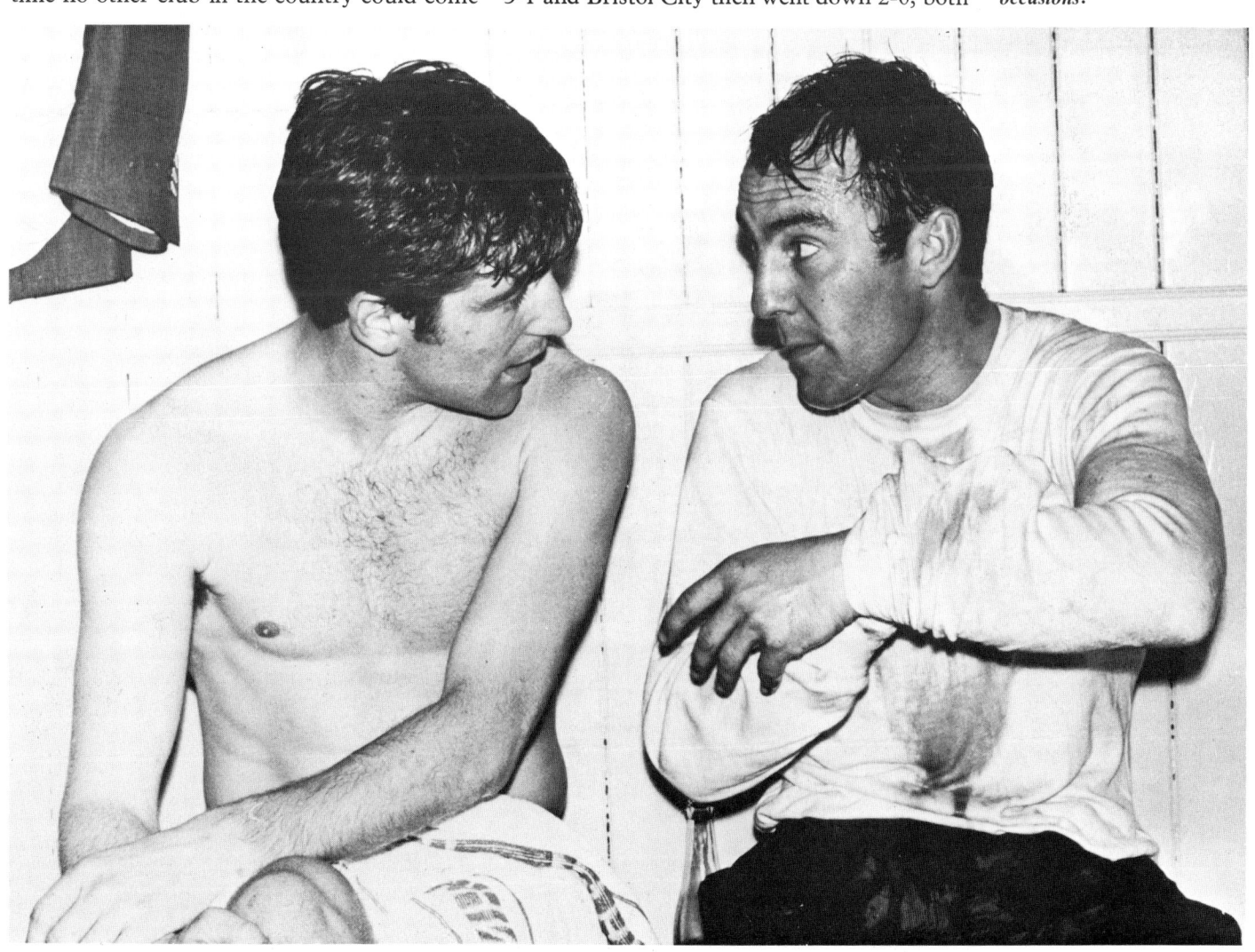

games being at White Hart Lane. Birmingham at St Andrew's in the quarter-finals was much tougher and Spurs were lucky to escape with a goalless draw. Despite Jimmy Robertson's speed on the right Greaves and Gilzean could do little that matched the winger's penetration, and all the good chances fell to Birmingham. The closest was when Jennings dropped a Fenton centre on the line and everyone joined in with their opinion as to whether it was over or not.

To their evident relief Spurs escaped with the draw and then crushed the Midlanders 6-0 on a White Hart Lane paddy field the following week. Venables scored straight from the off, unusually adding his name to the sheet, but soon added a second and Gilzean finally made use of one of Robertson's constant stream of crosses for a third before half-time. Birmingham got no better after the break and virtually gave up trying to control Greaves, who got two, with Frank Saul adding the sixth.

The semi-final at Hillsborough was the season's critical game. Nottingham Forest, second in the League and chasing Manchester United hard, were favourites, but they had lost Joe Baker in their classic quarter-final defeat of Everton and this was to disrupt their whole pattern of play. Despite having three other current or future England internationals up front (Hinton, Wignall and Storey-Moore), they depended on Baker's speed on the turn to win games no less than Spurs needed Greaves.

This game was, indeed, to produce one of Greaves' most memorable goals, a killing psychological blow as much as a single score because of his strange affinity for Forest. During his career Greaves scored far more goals (29) against Forest than any other club – including four on three occasions. Clearly he terrified the Nottingham club and his thirtieth-minute goal demoralised them so much that they lost a game they really should have won. As a goal it was probably not as classic a moment as three others that will always live in the memory – his bicycle kick against Blackpool in his first game for the club, his turn and dribble past four Manchester United defenders at White Hart Lane on 16 October 1965, and his run and shot past three Forest defenders when he never touched the ball but beat them simply by letting it run, dipping his shoulders and dummying left and right. But the semi-final goal was a great goal because of its context, because it got Spurs to a Cup final, because it was one of those goals that only Greaves seemed to be able to score, and because it was proof, if it was needed, that a single player can occasionally win for a team trophies that they would not otherwise have won. In recent years only Jimmy Greaves and George Best fall unquestionably into this category.

Greaves' goal came out of the blue at a time when Forest were clearly on top. A long clearance from Mike England was headed side-ways by Gilzean. As the ball bounced at Greaves' feet, he suddenly twisted and hit it left-footed on the half-volley from about 25-yards. The ball shot along the ground, snicked Grummitt's right-hand post and settled in the far corner of the net. The Forest defence never moved. With a quarter of an hour left Frank Saul robbed Terry Hennessey in the defender's half, set off for goal and whacked a magnificent shot over Grummitt into the net. Forest attacked frantically but could only reply once, from Hennessey himself, and Spurs were through. It was probably the best of all their semi-finals.

They found themselves facing Chelsea in the final; the Pensioners had, at the third consecutive attempt, managed to win a semi-final at last by beating Leeds 1-0. It was the first all-London professional final, which was excellent for the two competing sides but which somehow robbed the game of its national stage – the rest of the country was clearly indifferent to the whole thing. Deryk Brown wrote of the game: 'It was supposed to have been drab, which it wasn't, and supposed to have lacked atmosphere, which it did. This was Tottenham's fault only in that they were too good.'

Spurs did not break their routine at all. They trained as usual and spent just one night away. For the club it was not an overwhelming moment, being their fourth cup final in six years. For Chelsea's youngsters, however, it was rather too much; the Spurs players watched their opponents on television on the morning of the match and were delighted to observe nerve ends showing.

That Tottenham judgement on the Chelsea side was proved accurate; the younger team never settled, nor once looked like winning the game. Only Ron Harris, who kept Greaves out of things, enhanced his reputation. After 40 minutes Jimmy Robertson scored a well deserved goal. Mullery ran at the defence, his shot hit Allan Harris and Robertson buried the rebound from the edge of the area. After 67 minutes Frank Saul, with his back to goal, somehow hooked a shot into the corner of Bonetti's net after a Dave Mackay throw. It was all over, Bobby Tambling's 85th minute header (Jennings effectively punched the ball at his head) barely even being a consolation for Chelsea. It was now Dave Mackay's turn to collect the silverware and Cliff Jones became the first substitute ever to collect a Cup final medal. It was more easily earned than his other mementoes – he never left the bench.

The most significant benefit was, of course, that Spurs were back in the Cup Winners Cup. This time things did not end so happily. Their first rivals were the Yugoslav side Hajduk Split and they returned from the first leg with a 2-0 lead. It all seemed so easy. Then in the return the Spurs fans rejoiced as their team sailed on with a three-goal lead, then got another in the dying minutes. But not before the tough Yugoslavs had bounced back to grab three goals for themselves in a late rally which caused many palpitations.

Alan Mullery was sent off in a riotous second round away clash with the French club Olympique Lyonnais which saw Spurs defeated 1-0. The home side also lost their international centre-forward, André Guy, sent off in the scuffle with Mullery. A series of battles broke out round the terraces and spectators piled onto the pitch. The second leg meant a 4-3 success for Spurs but they went out on the away goals counting double rule. After 1962 and 1963 it was a terrible anticlimax.

The crowd, by now having got used to the fact that they were not going to be watching Blanchflower and White every week, were disappointed rather than depressed. Bill Nicholson remained the biggest critic; having reached the summit it was hard for him to remain camped on the slopes.

A TOTTENHAM LEGEND

A hard man but a fair man is Alan Mullery's summary of Nicholson the manager at this time. There was little artistry but a lot of honesty in his game. But he always wanted to see his teams doing it in style. Ask him, looking at it as a player and a manager, did he enjoy football and he says: 'Enjoy...that is not a word I would think of using. You cannot do that, playing or watching with a direct interest, until after a match. As a player there is the preparation, the feeling of being keyed up, the bending of all your thoughts to the game. You carry these through any game. Same with a manager, there is too much else on when things are happening to say you enjoy it. Only if your side is playing exceptionally well and have gone well in front – very well in front – then maybe you might enjoy it as it happens. But enjoy...' and he leaves the thought in mid-air.

The stories of Tottenham Hotspur and Bill Nicholson are now so intertwined that it is virtually impossible to separate them. For the

record, the future manager was born in Scarborough, one of a family of nine. His father was a groom and horse cab driver and Nicholson was a little special even then, passing scholarship examinations to go to Scarborough High School.

Leaving at 16 he went to work in a laundry and played soccer at weekends for a local team, the Young Liberals. He had no thoughts of becoming a professional footballer at this stage but, out of the blue, Spurs asked him to come for a trial in 1936.

'When the letter came no-one knew what to do. We weren't even sure exactly where Tottenham was. My mother and father had never once seen me play football. They knew I was keen, but they had no idea whether I was any good or not. I honestly had no idea what the world of professional football was about. Our heroes were the local Midland League side – none of my friends had even been to see Hull or York.'

Nicholson thinks that the local Spurs scout, based in York, had heard about him and Ben Ives, the chief scout, then took a trip to see for himself. Nicholson was probably introduced to Ives but has no recollections of the meeting and certainly had no idea of what it might lead to. No other club had ever shown any interest, and from this point on his life in football was to be committed to the cause of Tottenham Hotspur.

He had a month's trial at White Hart Lane, and was taken on as a ground staff boy. 'We were cheap labour really,' he now says, 'I think I painted every single girder under those stands out there, eight to five we worked, every weekday. We trained two afternoons a week, including a lot of running round the pitch. There was no tactical discussion, just what we were able to organise ourselves. But it wasn't all bad, of course. I remember that Willie Hall, who was club captain at the time, was very kind and always took a great interest.'

Nicholson played for the nursery side, Northfleet, and signed as a full professional at 18, on the same day as Ronnie Burgess. The Welshman retains a warm spot in Nicholson's memory: 'If I had to pick out one player in all my time here, a player who had it all, I think I'd pick Ron Burgess. He could do anything. Once Arthur Rowe had sold Ron on his methods then he had no trouble with push-and-run. Convincing Burgess was the most difficult thing Arthur ever had to do, but once it was done, well...yes, if pushed I'd even put him above Blanchflower.'

Burgess and Nicholson had started to play odd games for the first team before 1939, but on the outbreak of war Nicholson joined the Durham Light Infantry. Because he was known to be a professional footballer, he was sent on a PE course and soon became a sergeant-instructor. He continued training new intakes throughout the War, eventually ending up in Italy where he took over a rest camp in Bari from Stan Cullis and then going on to Geoff Dyson's physical education headquarters at Udine.

He probably lost half his playing career to the War but, doesn't regret it because he is convinced that it was those wartime experiences which made what came afterwards possible. 'It was invaluable. What I did for six years in the army taught me how to handle

OVERLEAF: *Like virtually all other successful teams of the post-war era, Spurs great spell lasted just three years, during which they won four trophies. The last was the Cup Winners Cup, photographed here with the squad at the beginning of the 1963–64 season. Standing left to right: Cliff Jones, Ron Henry, Mel Hopkins, Maurice Norman, John Hollowbread, Bill Brown, Bobby Smith, John White, Jimmy Greaves and John Smith. Sitting left to right: Frank Saul, Peter Baker, Dave Mackay, Danny Blanchflower, Tony Marchi, Les Allen, Terry Dyson and Eddie Clayton. The only player from the great days not in this line-up was Terry Medwin, who had been injured on a close-season tour of South Africa and was never to play for the first team again. Within a year far worse was to have happened; John White was killed by lightning on a golf course, Dave Mackay was out having broken his left leg twice, Blanchflower had to retire after being given a terrible run-around by Denis Law at Old Trafford and Brown, Baker, Smith and Allen were no longer first choices.*

people and how to talk to people. It obviously taught me how to get players fit, and I began to think about coaching routines – not in a very organised way, but how it could be done. After the War Freddie Cox asked some of the lads to go on a coaching course, and, with all those years in the army, I didn't find it too difficult. Gradually I got to think more about it.'

In 1946 he went straight into the Tottenham first team at centre-half for two seasons. He moved to right-half and stayed there until Danny Blanchflower took over the position in 1954. Nicholson had suffered a knee-injury and had already said to Arthur Rowe that he felt the time had probably come to find a replacement.

They were good years for Nicholson, though not without their regrets. He was a member of the disastrous World Cup party in 1950 and

won only one cap overall, basically because Billy Wright held the right-half spot throughout Nicholson's career. That debut was as spectacular as his managerial one however; he scored against Portugal after just 19 seconds with his very first kick in international football.

Nicholson became the Spurs first-team coach in 1955. He had already helped Walter Winterbottom on England tours and courses ('He was a wonderful coach, taught me an enormous amount,' says Nicholson) and had trained the Cambridge University side for a time. He went with the England side to Sweden for the 1958 World Cup and, when Jimmy Anderson resigned a couple of month's later, the Tottenham board apparently asked the FA to help in making recommendations for the succession. It is possible that the board were just asking for confirmation of what they already knew. The reply soon came back,

probably from Stanley Rous thinks Nicholson, that the club had already got the very man at White Hart Lane, that they did not need to search any further and that Nicholson had already proved his abilities to the FA, never mind the club.

Bill Nicholson was regularly described as dour and pessimistic during his period as manager, adjectives which are impossible to apply and barely possible to believe talking to him today. The only hint of pessimism comes when discussing the game's present state and prospects for the future: 'I go and watch Second and Third Division games nowadays and I think to myself: "How can even the managers of these teams bear to watch them 46 times a year?" It can be terrible. There's no point anyone pretending that the game has not lost a lot of what made it worth watching.'

Otherwise he is nothing if not positive, particularly about Keith Burkinshaw's current side. His pride also shines through when he talks of the academic successes of his daughters and of his five-year old grandson's enthusiasm for football, but, above all else, when he talks about how the Double side came together.

'People talk about the team's skills, rightly, but they don't seem to recall that the team succeeded because it was very fit and very well organised. That was almost disguised *behind* the skill. People used to come to Cheshunt from all over Europe to watch our training routines – stood there with stop watches and notebooks in their hands, writing it all down.'

When Nicholson became coach the players still often trained at the ground. When it rained they had to train under the stand – where there were girders all over the place. 'Because of those years in the army, I could

One man and his Cup; a contented Bill Nicholson carries the FA Cup away from Tottenham Town Hall on Sunday 21 May 1967, the day after Spurs had beaten Chelsea 2-1 in the first all-London professional Cup final. It was Nicholson's fifth trophy of the decade. 'People talk about the skills of Spurs' sides in that period,' says Nicholson, 'but they don't seem to recall that the side succeeded because it was fit and very well organised. That was almost disguised behind the skill.'

work out indoor routines where the girders didn't get in the way. But I pushed for the indoor training pitch (opened in the early 1960s) and that made a big difference.' Nicholson clearly loved the coaching; devising new routines, analysing how best to coach two-on-one situations, or how to tackle, making defenders play as forwards or vice versa, so that they could appreciate better their own roles. He would look at every facet of the game. Most things could be improved, could be broken down so that they could be coached; he would not accept that players either had or did not have certain skills and could not get better with the right routines.

'I was never a desk manager, like many were at that time. I would tell the directors that they could get me in the office before a quarter to ten. After that I would be out with the team, coaching'.

The side Nicholson took charge of already contained most of the Double side, but there were two or three vital additions to be made later. 'I'd been chasing Dave Mackay for some time but there seemed to be no chance; the club had enough money for a big signing, the directors wanted one and the transfer deadline was coming up. I went down to Wales to see Mel Charles. He wasn't sure and said he'd ring me at the weekend. Then, out of the blue, my sources in Scotland told me that Mackay might just be available. Only I couldn't do anything because of Charles – I couldn't buy

them both and I'd given my word and had to hope he'd say no. So I waited until Saturday night, when Mel Charles thankfully rang to say he wasn't going to sign. I got the sleeper to Edinburgh, signed Mackay from Tommy Walker at Hearts the following morning (which was the deadline) and brought him back. I remember the station-master at Edinburgh nearly went through the roof when he saw us together and realised what had happened. Nobody else got a whisper.

'With John White the problem was stamina. He seemed so frail I wasn't sure he was tough enough. Then someone – Danny, I think – mentioned that he was a cross-country runner. So I rang up White's army unit (he was on national service at the time) and talked to his commandant. "Yes, he's a bloody good footballer," said this officer, "but he'll not be playing football on Saturday. He'll be running for us in a race." We talked about John White and I soon discovered that he was an excellent cross-country runner. That convinced me.'

Les Allen's arrival was also a little different from the way it was reported at the time. 'Actually,' says Nicholson, 'Ted Drake [the Chelsea manager] rang me and said he needed Johnny Brooks. Ted was in trouble fighting relegation at the time, and I didn't really feel Brooks was the right man for his team then. But Ted persisted so I looked at their squad. Les Allen was in the reserves and it struck me as a good swap. Chelsea wanted money as well but I told them what they could do about that. What I liked about Les was that he could ghost into scoring positions, like Martin Peters.' Allen had already been on Spurs' books once, as an amateur, but had preferred to sign professional forms with Chelsea.

'So there was the Double side. There was no single secret to it, just as there's no school for managers where you can go and be told how to win things. The players in that side didn't get the rewards they should have – though that wasn't clear at the time. I'm sorry about that, and that I was always too busy to appreciate the small things about people and about our success, which is a great pity.'

He still lives in the small house close to the ground which has been home to his wife Darkie (so called because she was the darker of twins) and himself for years. Returning to the club he became a positive presence, never seeming to cast shadows over Keith Burkinshaw as Matt Busby did over his successors. Indeed, it was Burkinshaw who insisted that Nicholson rejoin the staff in 1976. 'It's been my life, Tottenham Hotspur, and I love the club,' he readily agrees and he makes the parallel between the Tottenham sides he served as a player and as a manager. Of the 1950 champions he says: 'Other clubs got to know our style . . . it was only for a short time. But the chief factor was that a lot of us went over the hill together. It was impossible to replace them. In a good side you can paper over the cracks with one or even two good players and the loss is not allowed to show too much. You can still play well and get by. But when it involves a lot of players going, then it's a real problem. It happened to me with the 1960 team . . . a lot of them finished at around the same time. That was the saddest thing, but I wouldn't have missed a moment.'

1971

The Glory Game • The numbers game • Four seasons, four finals • League Cups • Chivers and troubled times • Rotterdam again • Nicholson resigns • Terry Neill • Relegation and renewal

On Wednesday 29 May 1974, against a background of rioting by their supporters, Spurs lost the second leg of the UEFA Cup final 2-0 against Feijenoord in Rotterdam. With a 2-2 draw at White Hart Lane eight days earlier paving the way for a Dutch victory, Spurs had, for the first time in their history, lost a major cup final. Suddenly it was the end of Europe and conspicuously the end of an era, the Golden Age of Bill Nicholson. In fifteen glorious years, he had led them to the Double, two more FA Cup wins, two League Cup wins, the Cup Winners' Cup and the UEFA Cup. The heights had been intoxicating, so falling from them was all the harder.

Spurs fans had not only come to expect success, but to demand it. And in 1974, after a decade and a half dominating the breeze, the

bubble finally burst. Almost exactly three months after the UEFA final defeat, on 28 August, Nicholson resigned after the club's worst start to a League season in 62 years. 'Success in soccer,' as he rightly said, 'comes in cycles. It can't go on forever. You must have experienced players to win things, but the problem is that they all grow old together.' By the start of the 1974–75 season, the players who had helped Spurs win three major titles in the early seventies and reach the final of a fourth were, by soccer standards, growing old. Mike England was 31, Martin Peters and Cyril Knowles were 30, Phil Beal and Martin Chivers 29. Only a few weeks earlier Alan Gilzean had played his last game for the club, retiring just before his 36th birthday.

Nicholson realised that to prolong the cycle, or preferably break it, he needed to introduce

Alan Gilzean goes up with Denis Smith (right) and Alan Bloor of Stoke City during a League game in February 1972. Gilzean was signed from Dundee in 1964 and played for Tottenham for ten successful years, retiring at the age of 36. 'Football's not a job or a career – you're meant to enjoy it,' he said in 1972, 'I get paid to enjoy myself!'

The three goals which gave Spurs their two League Cup wins in 1971 and 1973.
TOP: *Martin Chivers scores the first goal of the 1971 final against Aston Villa. In the 78th minute keeper John Dunn could only parry Jimmy Neighbour's shot and Chivers followed up to break a rather poor, deadlocked game.*
CENTRE: *Just three minutes later Chivers scored his second goal of the 1971 final and dispelled any hopes Third Division Villa's supporters might have clung to. Fred Turnbull (number 5) and Dunn could do nothing to conclude a convincing run which had shown Chivers at his best. He had won his first cap just three weeks before, against Malta, and had finally recovered from the disastrous injury which kept him out of the game from September 1968 to August 1969. The length of time it took Chivers to regain his strength and confidence can be gauged from the fact that his first full cap came nearly four years after he won the last of his Under-23 selections. It can be argued that Spurs lost the best years of Chivers' career because of injury.*
BOTTOM: *Substitute Ralph Coates (far right) turns away in delight after scoring the only goal of the 1973 League Cup final against Norwich City. In the 72nd minute a long throw from Chivers was touched on by Peters and Coates pushed the ball past keeper Keelan. It was probably the highlight of Coates' career with Spurs and it settled an extremely poor final throughout which Norwich, in their first Division 1 season, had been on the defensive. For Spurs it meant re-entry to Europe as well as becoming the first club to win the trophy twice. The winning side of 1971 was: Jennings, Kinnear, Knowles, Mullery, Collins, Beal, Gilzean, Perryman, Chivers, Peters and Neighbour. In 1973 England replaced Collins, Pearce replaced Neighbour, and Pratt replaced Mullery, but was injured after only 20 minutes and Coates came on as sub.*

new blood. But times in soccer were changing and for a collection of reasons, some external, some stemming from the character of the man himself, Nicholson was unable to sustain a youth policy as he wanted it, or to buy in the players who could realise his constant vision of new and successful Spurs sides rising out of the ashes of the old. Abolition of the maximum wage had made players wealthy. And the younger ones were impatient for their share of the riches. They were no longer content to sit around waiting for their first team chance. Few were willing to weigh the glorious traditions of White Hart Lane against the lure of hard cash.

'We couldn't keep our young reserves,' says Nicholson, recalling the name of one outstanding Scottish Youth international midfield player who signed as an apprentice in 1969 but left four years later, still hungering for his first team chance. His name? Graeme Souness. There were others like him, too. Derek Possee and Keith Weller, who went on to win England honours, were on Spurs books in the late sixties. 'We didn't want to lose any of them,' says Nicholson, 'but they just wouldn't wait.' To an extent the problem was of Nicholson's own making. The pressures on him for success were enormous. But in his pursuit of excellence, he was caught in a trap: to gain the necessary experience, you need to be playing; to be part of a regular side, you need to play well and the team needs to win; to be winning, you need the experience. In consequence, his younger players were depressed by expensive new signings and held back to the point where the more talented and ambitious simply drifted away.

Nicholson was also frustrated in his attempts to recreate the magic of his Double winners. As a perfectionist who measured all performances by the standards set by Blanchflower's side, he often rejected signings better than the players he had because they were not as good as those he wanted. Those he did sign were not so much replacements for the Double heroes as copies, and as such they suffered in comparison. Chivers on his day was more skilful than Smith but surely lacked his dogged determination and courage; Coates never approached the heights of a Jones; Mullery was never quite in the Blanchflower or Mackay class and would complain of incessant reminders of what Mackay might have done in a given situation. Nicholson summed it all up when he said, 'I can't sit and watch them in comfort, not the way I've done with other teams I've had.'

As they entered the seventies, Spurs also suffered at the hands of changing playing styles, or the 'numbers game' as Nicholson called it. The days of 3-2-2-3 were long gone, even 4-2-4 was well past its peak. This was the era of defensive football, the day of the spoiler, a time epitomised by Arsenal and Peter Storey, Leeds and Norman Hunter. The one-touch game employed by Spurs over nearly two decades was an easy target, open to exploitation and destruction by less ambitious, more ruthless teams. It was also a style which did not lend itself to players whose skills could probably not match those of an earlier generation. It merely added to Nicholson's frustrations to have to change to a safer percentage game, where long passes were driven upfield for target men. As the new decade opened in August 1970, with Spurs suffering their worst start since 1958–59, it was being asked whether they had players with the heart for this type of game.

After a 1-0 fourth round FA Cup replay defeat at Crystal Palace on 28 January 1970, Nicholson made sweeping changes. The Palace defeat was a watershed for Jimmy Greaves, whose great goalscoring skills had rapidly gone into decline. It was his last game for Spurs, dropped along with Gilzean, Knowles and Kinnear. But Nicholson's revamped side fared no better in the next League match against Southampton, losing 1-0. In March Nicholson moved into the transfer market in a deal which brought England World Cup star Martin Peters from West Ham for £200,000. It was ironic that, in breaking the British transfer record for the second time in a decade, Nicholson should part with the player for whom he broke it the first time nine years before. For the deal included Greaves in part-exchange. Greaves' departure cut a further tie with past glories. He'd joined Spurs in November 1961 and, as Spurs' new chairman, Sidney Wale, wrote in the 1970–71 handbook: 'We shall always remember the joy and pleasure Jimmy gave us.' In just over eight years, Greaves scored 267 goals in senior matches, leaving behind him two club records which are still unbroken: his 37 First Division goals in a season (1962–63) and his aggregate League goals, 220 between 1961 and 1970. In his place, Nicholson went for experience rather than promise. Peters, still only 26, with his subtle ball skills and brilliantly timed blindside runs, was a goal-taker and goal-maker who had match-winning experience at the ultimate level. There were, after all, only two players in England who had scored a goal in a World Cup final.

Spurs finished the 1969–70 season eleventh in the First Division, their lowest for eleven years. The stigma of failure was felt most by Wale, who was in his first year as chairman following the death of his father, Frederick. 'This,' he wrote afterwards, 'is obviously not good enough for Tottenham Hotspur.' Spurs responded in the tradition set by their uncanny knack of winning major titles at the start of a new decade. And their victory in the 1971 League Cup final over Aston Villa heralded a revival in their fortunes. They won the new UEFA Cup the following season and the League Cup again in 1973. But none but the most blindly fanatical supporters could pretend that the quality of these latter-day triumphs could match the flair and brilliance shown by Nicholson's earlier sides. A look at Tottenham's for and against columns in the early sixties and seventies is most revealing. In the seasons between 1960 and 1965 they scored 115, 88, 111, 97 and 87 League goals. A decade later the tally was 54, 63, 58, 45 and 52, an average reduction of nearly half. And Spurs were by no means a negative or unsuccessful side by the standards of the early 1970s. In defence the figures were 55, 69, 62, 81 and 71 against 33, 42, 48, 50 and 63, an average fall of over 30%. So while Tottenham's notoriously porous defence (only three other clubs conceded more than fourth-placed Spurs in 1963–64) had certainly tightened up in keeping with the times, the attack had ceased to be the rock on

which success could be guaranteed. It was no criticism of Tottenham, still one of the more popular and entertaining sides, to suggest that football's authorities needed to look no further than the goals scored column to discover why the game was losing its popularity. Not only that, but rather than ask why fans were voting with their feet, it might have been more interesting to find out why so many still bothered to watch at all.

FOUR SEASONS: FOUR FINALS

Nonetheless, trophies came at a time when the emphasis in soccer had shifted even further from entertainment towards success. Winning was clearly the name of the new game; it wasn't just the main thing, for a time it became the only thing. And though it hurt Nicholson to suffer mediocrity while he was searching for perfection, major trophy wins in 1971, 1972 and 1973 were more than any other club could offer its fans. It was a sign of the times when he was forced to admit: 'A bloke is measured by what he wins.' In 1970–71 they were propelled towards Wembley by a mixture of good luck and a change of playing style which saw them perform more as a team than as a team of individuals. If the sum of the individual parts of the Double side had been greater than the whole, the reverse was surely true of Spurs in the early seventies. The last ties with individual flair had been cut with the departure of Greaves. Their style with him up front had been geared to providing chances for the game's greatest goal poacher to polish off. But Greaves' partnership alongside Gilzean had never blossomed, mainly because the Scottish forward wasn't suited to the role of target man and provider. Finding the right position for the gifted Gilzean had also been a problem for Scotland, but at club level it was solved with the switch of Chivers to centre-forward and Gilzean to his preferred position just behind the two front men. With Peters in close support, and Perryman and Mullery adding thrust from midfield, Spurs found a style which at last began to pay dividends in the First Division's new, relentless long-ball, target-man game.

Spurs reached Wembley via four consecutive home ties and a semi-final against a Bristol City side struggling in the Second Division. It was a time when the word 'lucky' switched from its more familar Highbury home to White Hart Lane. Spurs' final opponents, too, weren't the most awesome in the world – Third Division Aston Villa. But a team that had defeated Manchester United to reach Wembley was not to be treated lightly and there was the added ill-omen for Spurs in recent successes by the Third Division over the First in League Cup finals, namely Queen's Park Rangers against West Bromwich and Swindon against Arsenal.

Like their Third Division predecessors, Villa proved no pushovers but, despite hitting the woodwork and forcing a goal-line clearance from Perryman, they couldn't make history repeat itself. With 12 minutes remaining and Villa holding a grip in midfield, Spurs broke the deadlock with two goals from Chivers to win 2-0. It was a drab final but, spectacle or not, victory meant everything to Tottenham: another major trophy, their first League Cup win, success in their lucky year, and to Nichol-son, most of all, it meant Europe once more. For him, matches against continental opposition were the only occasions when Spurs rose above the mundane and appeared to relish the battle. They were occasions when, for Nicholson, expectation and achievement more nearly matched one another. As he was so fond of saying: 'Spurs are not Spurs anymore without Europe.'

With Chivers shaking off the effects of a bad knee injury, sustained three seasons earlier, to produce his best form – 29 goals from 54 games – Spurs enjoyed a resurgence in the League and FA Cup too. Only an inspired performance by Ray Clemence in a quarter-final replay at White Hart Lane prevented them from reaching the FA Cup semi-final at the expense of Liverpool, while in the League a much improved defensive record (33 goals conceded against 55 the previous season) lifted them to third, their best position since 1967. How ironic that their last home game should have been against Arsenal, who were seeking a goalless draw or victory to clinch the Championship and first leg of their own Double exactly ten years on from Spurs' more historic achievement. From the glories of one-touch, the game had deteriorated to a monotonous succession of high balls to a couple of big front-runners and, in John Radford and Ray Kennedy, Arsenal had two worthy masters in heading and shooting. Spurs were reduced to trying to beat Arsenal at their own game and came off second best when George Armstrong eventually found the head of Kennedy to give Arsenal the winning goal they needed to bring the title to Highbury. The contrast in playing styles between 1961 and 1971 was completed five days later when Peter Storey ruthlessly marked Liverpool's Steve Heighway in the Cup final to help Arsenal to a 2-1 extra-time victory which clinched the Double. In ten years, soccer had arguably gone from its most sublime to its most cynical phase.

Wingers had rather gone out of fashion at international level with Ramsey in 1966. Spurs fans used to joke that, as a full-back himself, he had never liked wingers anyway, but they remained a tradition at Tottenham throughout the sixties and into the seventies. From Cliff Jones through Jimmy Robertson to the 1970s crop of Roger Morgan, Jimmy Neighbour and Jimmy Pearce, Spurs had won all their trophies playing with wingers. But as they approached the 1971–72 season it was a position where Nicholson had neither experience nor outstanding talent. Morgan, who had been bought from Queen's Park Rangers for £110,000 in 1969, promised much but delivered little, partially because of injury, while home-grown youngsters Neighbour and Pearce always gave the appearance of being in the first team only as stop-gaps. When Burnley's England winger, Ralph Coates, came up for sale at the end of the 1970–71 season following his club's relegation to the Second Division, Nicholson moved swiftly. In a characteristically cloak-and-dagger deal Coates' move was finalised on a May night at the Staffordshire Post House, just off the M6. One of the reasons for all the secrecy was because both clubs wanted to avoid a public auction for the player, Spurs because they feared his price could go considerably beyond the £190,000 they'd agreed,

and Burnley because they wanted to honour their long-standing promise to give Spurs first option.

Coates' arrival brought Tottenham's England international contingent to five (Peters, Mullery, Knowles and Chivers were the others) and with Gilzean (Scotland), England (Wales), Jennings (Northern Ireland) and Kinnear (Republic of Ireland) completing their international line-up, Spurs had a wealth of experience with which to march again into Europe. The new season saw Chivers continue his prolific goalscoring form – 44 goals in 64 matches – and Spurs create another British club record. On 17 May 1972, they won the new UEFA Cup, the successor to the defunct Inter-Cities Fairs Cup, thus becoming the first British club to win two of the European trophies. Only Liverpool have ever matched this feat. But during a season in which they also finished sixth in the League, reached the quarter-finals of the FA Cup and the semi-finals of the League Cup, the first cracks were beginning to appear in the Nicholson renaissance.

It is a measure of how high standards had been set at White Hart Lane when, in a season as apparently successful as 1971–72, finishing sixth in the League should have been considered only adequate. But as Sidney Wale would never cease reminding everyone, the League was the club's bread and butter. It was vital to do well. When the end came for Nicholson two years later, it wasn't Spurs' failure in Europe, the FA Cup or League Cup which was at the root of the problem, but their inability to win a League match. The paradox of the club's contrasting fortunes at European and domestic level was never more clearly illustrated than by the ten games it took Spurs to reach the UEFA final and, for example, their first ten League games of 1972. In the former they scored 27 goals and conceded just four while in the latter they scored

12 and conceded seven. The anomaly was frequently remarked on but never satisfactorily explained. Nicholson was aware of it but could only say: 'For such an experienced team, a lot of them are not consistent,' while chairman Wale had a reason but no cure: 'It was as if the players had got such a taste for Europe that it was the only competition in which they could raise their game.'

In his controversial book *The Glory Game* journalist Hunter Davies made the same point: 'There seemed something lacking in the team's character all season which made them fade in ordinary League matches...but almost every big occasion had been a joy to watch. During the season Spurs produced consistently high form in every cup match. Was their failure in ordinary matches a group weakness or a weakness in certain individuals in the group?' The question was left unanswered. With the benefit of greater hindsight, it is clear that three factors emerged during that season which were to begin undermining the club's achievements. They were Nicholson's growing disenchantment with the game as a whole, a real disaffection between Nicholson and at least one of his players, and the ageing process which was catching up on his current team. All this could be set aside in European matches, however, as it was in the Battle of Bucharest.

On a cold December afternoon in the Rumanian capital, Spurs once again rose out of their League doldrums to inflict another impressive defeat on European opposition. But it was almost a pyrrhic victory. Against a Rapid Bucharest side determined to kick and punch their way back into the match (they were 3-0 down from the first leg) Spurs had seven players injured and Jimmy Pearce sent off along with Rapid's right-back. Spurs won 2-0 to finish 5-0 aggregate winners, but it was only due to the discipline and self-restraint drummed into the team by Nicholson that their casualties weren't higher. Afterwards

Cyril Knowles chases Liverpool left-winger Steve Heighway during the goalless draw at Anfield on 17 April 1971. A Yorkshireman who had worked in the mines before becoming a professional footballer, Knowles won four England caps. He is, nonetheless, probably best remembered as the inspiration for the record 'Nice One, Cyril' which reached number 14 in the hit parade just before the 1973 League Cup final.

Gilzean and Jennings combine to clear an Ipswich corner on 10 April 1971. The Ipswich defender is Derek Jefferson. Spurs won the game 2-0 (with an own goal and one from Chivers) and finished a creditable third in the League behind Arsenal and Leeds.

Press rightly dubbed 'The Forgotten Final', Spurs survived a tremendous Wolves onslaught in the second leg at White Hart Lane to emerge 3-2 aggregate winners. There was plenty of tension but little good football to excite a purist like Nicholson. Hunter Davies, in *The Glory Game*, remarked that Nicholson was relieved but far from ecstatic. 'As a European final,' said Nicholson, 'it was nothing like our 1963 win. That really was a wonderful occasion. Winning 5-1 against Atletico Madrid was winning in style.' Once again Nicholson's fate had been to suffer mediocrity in success while seeking perfection.

"THE GLORY GAME"

The publishing of *The Glory Game* deserves a diversion in itself. A minor sensation when it appeared, it remains the most controversial inside view of how any Football League club works. At the time journalist Michael Hart commented: 'The exposure is total and absolute. No one is spared. As one player put it to me: "He has dug his holes too deeply. I am surprised the club passed the transcript."' Understandably the heirarchy at Tottenham are not happy with Mr Davies. The players, too, have a few choice phrases for him . . . (but) as one observed: "There's nothing we can do. It's all true".' But Mike Langley in *The People* said on 29 October 1972: 'The book has been scourged over the past few days by reviews of staggering naivety . . . it's been suggested that Chivers, Mullery and even Mrs Nick might make . . . a point of smashing Mr Davies's front teeth down his throat. But no one mentioned that he'd an arrangement with the club. That each player, and fan Morris Keston, read and approved his individual chapter. That the entire book was scrutinised . . . by club chairman Sidney Wale.' Langley went on to say that the management and players were taking part of the profit from the book (implying that it was to their benefit to make it more spicy than usual) and concludes, interestingly, that: '. . . far from doing Spurs down I'd say he's glossed over a few sensitive details.' The club's only deep sensitivity was for Eddie Baily, a Tottenham stalwart for so long, whose contribution and warmth seemed to have been ignored in favour of rather isolated quotations and observations which, while no doubt being strictly accurate, were perhaps prejudicial by being selective.

Nonetheless, reading it a decade later, it is difficult to see what the fuss was all about. Apart from revealing that some of the players and staff had the average man's human prejudices, and that the team did not like garlic on its food, there is little that comes as a surprise. In fact it is almost totally silent on what had already become the most sensitive issue at Tottenham and throughout senior football – the financial demands of the players. And on the positive side it is a book with very real heroes – primarily Bill Nicholson, whose dedication to the club and unstinting effort on its behalf shines through on every page, Pat Jennings and Steve Perryman, who emerges as a thoughtful, generous and devoted player, the kind of hero every father would want for his son. Ten years on, it actually reflects extremely well on the club that the author was allowed the freedom of a whole season with the side to write the book, and that the publish-

Nicholson, normally a restrained man in front of the Press, was moved to say: 'Rapid were the dirtiest side I've come across in 30 years of football. If this is European football, I'd rather have a Combination match.'

Even victory in the UEFA Cup final itself couldn't raise Nicholson's enthusiasm. After Spurs' heady European campaigns, it was a bit of an anticlimax to be facing less than exotic Wolverhampton Wanderers. In a match the

ers were allowed to sell it without any of the devaluing censorship that so often accompanies anything written about football.

Spurs achieved their European successes by Nicholson's shrewd tactical planning, playing 4-3-3 in the home legs while smothering the opposition's 4-2-4 line-ups in the away leg by packing midfield with a 4-4-2 formation. For these games Chivers and Gilzean were the front men, feeding off crosses from Coates and the overlapping full-backs Knowles and Kinnear. Coates had a disappointing debut season. He was tried in midfield and on the wing but, like many players coming to a new club, he was slow to settle in. It is fair to say, with hindsight, that Coates never fulfilled the promise he had shown at Burnley. With Spurs he was always adequate, and often valuable, but just missed out on being a really great club player.

Up front Chivers had his best season to date in terms of goals, but he tended to have too many anonymous matches and was frequently the focal point of Nicholson's criticisms. Constant carping was the manager's way of trying to rouse and motivate the infuriatingly inconsistent striker. On his day, Chivers was a match-winner, as his two excellent goals in the first leg of the UEFA final proved. But too often he faded out of matches altogether, as England were to find to their cost in that astonishing World Cup qualifier against Poland at Wembley. Nicholson's attacks ('He never stopped moaning' Chivers complains in *The Glory Game*) did not reduce the mounting antagonism which was eventually to prove a factor in Nicholson's resignation. For the manager's part, he felt he had just cause in requesting more effort from Chivers. He did not ask for goals every week from the centre-forward, who was hardly a players' player anyway, but he felt entitled to ask for the energy and co-operation which regularly appeared to be lacking.

However, the Spurs manager was faced with a player problem of a different nature as the 1971–72 season drew to a close. In an unprecedented revolt over pay, no less than nine first team players, including Chivers, were in dispute over their contracts. To the consternation of the board there were revelations in the Press about how poorly players were paid in comparison with the rest of the First Division (if not with the country at large) and, worst of all, that players at (admittedly highly successful) Arsenal were paid nearly twice as much. Led by Welsh international centre-half Mike England, the Spurs players optimistically demanded parity with Highbury.

The UEFA final was a personal triumph for club skipper Alan Mullery. Already 30, Mullery's England and Spurs career looked to be coming to a close when he lost his international and club place midway through the season and was shipped back to Fulham on loan. But, in typically tenacious style, Mullery battled his way back. He returned to score a vital first goal in the away leg of the UEFA Cup semi-final against AC Milan (Spurs drew 1-1 to win 3-2 on aggregate) and scored again, fairy tale like, in the 1-1 home draw against Wolves which clinched the Cup. It turned out to be a glorious swan-song for 'Mullers'. In the summer he made a permanent move back to Fulham – the first of the new victims of Nicholson's old enemy, time.

It had been more than a year since Nicholson's last big purchase and with the fans coming to expect the arrival of a big expensive new star at the start of every season, and the club eager to oblige if only to keep the money from the tax man, the one manager in Britain to have spent a million pounds on new players was ready to take another massive plunge into the transfer market. Nicholson had already broken the British transfer record twice with Greaves and Peters and, armed with more than a quarter of a million pounds as the rich pickings of Spurs' European crusades, he had more than enough to do it again. On this occasion, however Nicholson became the victim of his own big spending. In pushing transfer fees well into six figures, he had been one of the principal causes of inflation in the game. Quality players were scarce and clubs were asking astronomic fees. Even Spurs did not have a bottomless well of money, although they were undoubtedly one of the richest clubs in the country. Frustrated at not being able to buy the players he wanted, Nicholson kept faith with his experienced players, despite their growing age and inconsistency, at the expense of his own frustrated reserves.

WEMBLEY AGAIN

The following season repeated the pattern of 1971–72 – good cup performances contrasting with poor league form. The difference this time was that the levels of achievement on all fronts were that much lower. They finished eighth in the League, two places lower than the previous season, were knocked out by Derby in the fourth round of the FA Cup (losing 5-3 in a home replay after leading 3-1 with five minutes to go), lost to Liverpool in the semi-finals of the UEFA Cup on the away goals rule (despite winning 2-1 at White Hart Lane), yet still managed to pull a rabbit out of the hat by lifting the League Cup for the second time in three years when they beat Norwich 1-0. The final was an individual success for Ralph Coates, who came on as substitute for John Pratt to score the winning goal, but was one of the most tedious Wembley finals in history (if not the most tedious) and the club was widely criticised as yet again achieving success at the expense of entertainment. As Sidney Wale remarked, with considerable understatement, in the handbook for the following season: '...the final...was not the classic we should have liked to witness.' Spurs were stifled by Norwich's defensive approach, but they still managed to breathe enough air to keep themselves alive in Europe for just one more season.

Events in football were now being influenced by the worsening economic climate in the country. Big pay packets and spiralling overheads were eating into the profits of those clubs lucky enough to be still making money at all, while others plunged inexorably into the red or were forced to sell their star players to stay solvent. Even a club as rich and successful as Tottenham, with a healthy balance in the bank, was about to feel the pinch. And since a job at Spurs was generally a job for life, there was never any question of Nicholson selling any of his star names. Falling attendances throughout the game, as much a sign of the diminishing entertainment value of soccer as of the general effects of inflation and tight money, added to clubs' financial worries. And, for all their success, Spurs were as badly hit as anyone. In two seasons average home attendances declined from 38,000 in the 1971–72 UEFA Cup winning season to 26,000 in 1973–74, and that after winning the League Cup again and proceeding to the final of the UEFA Cup. Spurs fans demanded success, but not so many were willing to pay for it any more.

The result was that from a profit of £300,000 in their League Cup season of 1972–73, proceeds from the following season tumbled to a mere £35,000. Worse still, forecasts for the following season, 1974–75, when Spurs would be out of Europe for the first time in four years, were for a loss of £250,000. And the club was already committed to spending £200,000 on ground improvements.

August 1973, and for the second season in succession Spurs kicked off without a new signing. Unable to get the players he wanted, Nicholson decided to concentrate instead on his home-grown youngsters. Ray Evans established himself in the right-back position occupied for eight seasons by Joe Kinnear, Cyril Knowles was to make way for Terry Naylor and, in midfield, Nicholson gave an extended run to Chris McGrath, a promising young Belfast boy who had turned professional only 18 months earlier. This belated attempt to rejuvenate his ageing team had mixed results for, despite the weight of experience which again carried them to another European final, Spurs' League form continued its alarming downward trend.

RIOTS IN ROTTERDAM

The disparity was at its greatest in March 1974, when they won even greater admiration in Europe with a memorable fourth round UEFA Cup victory over West Germany's FC Köln (2-1 away and 3-0 at home) while at home their image was being further tarnished by the threat of relegation. They recovered to finish eleventh in the League but Nicholson admitted: 'It was the most disappointing season since my first as manager,' and he talked of a lack of determination and slipping standards. The side scored only 45 League goals, the same as in 1912–13 and their worst total ever. His three-times cup winners were for the most part approaching the autumn of their soccer careers and, while it may be a harsh judgement on the younger players Nicholson was now drafting in, they could not show the skill and application of their predecessors, because, in the final analysis, they were not the *creme de la creme* Spurs were accustomed to. In failing to buy new quality players, and neglecting the best of his youngsters, the Sounesses, Wellers and Possees, Nicholson had fallen between two stools. For the first time in 15 years, there was serious talk of resignation. Sidney Wale hinted that not even the great man's job was safe when he said: 'There will have to be changes one day. It's a question of time and timing.'

For his part, Nicholson considered the board might take the pressure off by making him general manager and appointing a younger man to look after team affairs. One of the criticisms levelled at Nicholson in the Press was that he hadn't already pressed for a younger man to be brought in to bridge the growing generation gap between himself and his younger players, the role that he himself had filled for Jimmy Anderson in the 1950s. Nicholson was 55 and finding it increasingly difficult to maintain a rapport with his team. His assistant, Eddie Baily, was no better placed, being of the same generation as Nicholson and, like him, Spurs man and boy. 'It's more difficult to get loyalty, respect and honesty from players,' said Nicholson at the time. His long-running feud with Chivers was smouldering on, ready to erupt in a final showdown during the summer of 1974; he was still having no success in the transfer market, and, most critical of all at this stage in his career, he lacked a strategy. He could see no long-term solution to the club's problems, as he says in retrospect: 'What could I do? Just carry on. There was no turning point, so you just change gradually to suit your own problems.' Had Spurs beaten Feijenoord in the UEFA Cup final in May 1974, Nicholson says he had intended to resign there and then. 'You're only as good as your last result,' he philosophically reiterated.

But he was denied that coup de grace when, in a grisly sequel to the Battle of Bucharest, Spurs were traumatically beaten in the Riot of Rotterdam, their first defeat in ten major cup finals spanning 73 years. Feijenoord were formidable opposition. They had just won the Dutch championship and in de Jong, Rijsbergen, van Hanegem and Jansen they had four internationals who, two months later, were to help take Holland to the World Cup final against West Germany. By comparison, Spurs went into the first leg at White Hart Lane on 21 May with a mixture of youthful inexperience in players like Evans, Naylor and McGrath, none of whom had ever played in a cup final before, and seasoned campaigners whose international careers (with the exception of Jennings) were drawing to a close; England was out of the Welsh team; Chivers had made his last England appearance in the fateful World Cup qualifier against Poland seven months earlier, and his intermittent career was well past its peak; Coates hadn't played for England since 1971 and Peters' 67th appearance for England, in the Home International against Scotland only three nights earlier, was to be his last. Spurs also preferred young Chris McGrath, who, by contrast, had just won his first three caps for Northern Ireland in the same Home Internationals, to the ageing Gilzean.

Spurs needed a decisive victory to stand any chance of maintaining their record of cup invincibility. But a downpour just before the kick-off made the surface slippery and immediately upset their passing. They were frequently caught by Feijenoord's offside trap, and, though scoring twice, through England and an own goal by van Daele, were finally outmatched by the physical strength and resilience of the Dutch. With four minutes left and Spurs leading 2-1, de Jong stole a late equaliser. The writing was on the wall and everyone at White Hart Lane knew it. The 2-0 defeat at Rotterdam eight days later against a team of Feijenoord's quality was, on Sidney Wale's admission, no disgrace – that belonged to the so-called fans who brought mayhem to the match and to the streets of Europe's biggest port in a night of mindless violence and vandalism. Thousands of pounds worth of damage were caused to shops and cars during a rampage which resulted in 70 arrests and 200 injuries Nicholson personally appealed to fans at the match to stop fighting, but to no avail. The hooliganism merely became one of a list of similar outbreaks of violence perpetrated by British fans abroad in the face of defeat and was strangely out of character for a group of supporters which had never been associated with the Shedites of Chelsea or the Stretford Enders of Manchester United. That Spurs followers might have joined the ranks of those who had done so much to destroy the traditional pleasures of English football was perhaps the most depressing lesson of a thoroughly depressing episode. Now, it had to be assumed, no club was safe from the mindless minority. Because Nicholson went out to talk to the crowd he was unable to give his usual half-time team talk. That did not help the side's composure and everyone was disturbed by what was going on outside. When Nicholson came back Steve Perryman thought he detected tears in the manager's eyes. It must have been one of the final straws for a man who had always acted in the most decent and straightforward way, a terrible climax to an increasingly difficult season.

UEFA's punishment, ordering Spurs to play their next two European home ties at least 250 kilometres from White Hart Lane, was largely academic. There was no more Europe for Spurs in the 1970s, and in 1980 came EUFA's 25th anniversary amnesty. For some reason Spurs were left out of the general lifting of such punishments, and director Geoff Richardson had to appeal on behalf of the club before they were included. 'I think they just forgot about us,' he says.

NICHOLSON'S LAST STAND

Nicholson, his resignation plans temporarily shelved, returned to try and pick up the pieces. He faced problems on nearly all fronts, most of all with Chivers, who had finally made it clear that White Hart Lane was no longer big enough for both of them. It had been Chivers' goals which had kept Spurs afloat over the past few seasons but now his feud with Nicholson erupted into another bitter pay row. Chivers publicly called Spurs' offer 'rubbish' and demanded a transfer. He was joined by one of Nicholson's young proteges, defender Mike Dillon, who had made a handful of senior appearances and was now demanding suitable reward. Nicholson gave the same reply to both: 'No one leaves until I've found replacements.' That was the rub. Replacements were proving almost impossible to find. Nicholson tried to sign Duncan McKenzie from Nottingham Forest, David Hay from Celtic and Chelsea's Bill Garner. But they all said no, McKenzie preferring Leeds, Hay Chelsea and Garner staying where he was.

Nicholson's one transfer success in the summer of 1974 was persuading Alfie Conn, a young left-sided midfield player with hippie-length hair, to sign from Glasgow Rangers for £150,000. Nicholson had £500,000 to spend on

John Toshack tries to evade Alan Mullery in another Anfield clash of the early 1970s. Long regarded as Spurs' bogey ground, Tottenham had not won there since March 1912. Mullery joined the club from Fulham in 1964 and returned there eight years later, but not until after a fairy tale return to the side which saw him score a vital semi-final goal against AC Milan and another against Wolves in the final to help lift the UEFA Cup (see P66). Mullery suffered during his early days at the club by being compared with the great half-back line of the Double year: 'People always told me what Dave Mackay had done. Like telling me the wonders he performed after his injury. You wanted to say it's me, it's my injury, this is how I feel and I'm not putting it on.'

Mullery, as Spurs' captain, lifted the club's second European trophy at White Hart Lane on 17 May 1972. It was also, as it happened, his last ever game for the club.

RIGHT: *Mike England gets above AC Milan defender Karl-Heinz Schnellinger during the UEFA Cup semi-final first leg in London on 5 April 1972. The Italians went into a 1-0 lead but Steve Perryman scored twice, once from 20 yards and again from nearly 35 yards, to give Spurs hope for the second leg. Despite England heading against his own crossbar at San Siro, Tottenham came away from Milan with a 1-1 draw and were through to the final, where they met Wolves.*

RIGHT BELOW: *The clock at Molineux shows 8.40pm as Martin Chivers rises to meet a Mike England free-kick (one of Spurs' rehearsed moves), outjump Frank Munro and put the Londoners 1-0 ahead in the UEFA Cup final first leg. Wolves equalised from a McCalliog free-kick, but Chivers made it 2-1 with perhaps the best goal he ever scored for the club. Picking the ball up near the half-way line, he went past two defenders and shot on the run from all of thirty yards. The return leg was a perfect finale to the season for Spurs, the last game and the biggest crowd – 54,303. Mullery's headed goal made it 1-1 and the trophy was Spurs' – their eighth victory in their eighth cup final.*

new players but, as the new season opened with a series of calamitous defeats, revelations were made in the Press about one of main reasons pinning Spurs to the foot of Division One. Nicholson claimed that several top-class players (not those mentioned here), and especially those from London, were demanding five-figure sums 'under-the-counter' to move. It was Spurs' persistent refusal to pay these sums, as Sidney Wale confirmed, that lay behind Nicholson's failure to bring star names to White Hart Lane in recent years.

Here one reaches one of the game's most delicate areas, one that most fans were unaware of during the 1970s and which was not revealed publicly in all its details until Terry Yorath's attempts to negotiate his own departure from White Hart Lane in 1980. It is a subject which everyone in the game is extremely sensitive about (under-the-counter payments are dubious because they are outside the tax system though, as Nicholson points out, a player can ask for a tax-free sum quite

legitimately – as long as the club is prepared to pay the massive resulting Inland Revenue bill itself) but which has come to dominate the movement of players. Several seemingly incomprehensible moves, and numerous disputes, would be made only too comprehensible if the full financial details were revealed. Spurs have maintained an excellent reputation through this period, being among the foremost of those clubs which have unsuccessfully tried to outlaw illegitimate, unnecessary and excessive payments. In the late 1970s this attitude also began to extend to transfer fees.

When Spurs, clearly in need of a goalscorer, were linked with Andy Gray and, as the traditional Bank of England club, were expected to pay £1.5 million for him, Sidney Wale became exasperated by newspaper pressure on the club to bid. 'We are expected to pay out more than one and a half million pounds for a single player, plus wages. That is more than we took at the gate in the whole of last season. Is it sane economics to spend more than your entire gate money on one man?' It was a policy Spurs pursued with some success and, at the time of writing, they have still to pay more than £800,000 for a single player. The attitude to advertising was also conservative. They were the last of the major clubs to hold out against making their ground a TV-inspired billboard, not allowing hoardings around the pitch until as late as 1972.

Back in 1974 the strain of the Chivers dispute, coupled with the club's deepening League crisis, reached breaking point for Nicholson in a week when Burnley's Martin Dobson became the fourth player to reject a move to White Hart Lane and Spurs, without a point, plunged to their fourth successive League defeat. Dobson, a cultured England player whose pedigree would have brought some much-needed class to the weak midfield, preferred to stay in Lancashire with a £300,000 move to Everton, where he failed to fulfil his massive earlier promise. At White Hart Lane, Spurs, who had lost 1-0 in midweek to newly promoted Carlisle, faced their fourth match of the season at home to Manchester City. It was 28 August, and Nicholson's last stand. He recalled Martin Chivers, who had been dropped for the first three matches, replaced Pratt with McGrath, and, with the exception of Neighbour, fielded the side which had lost in Rotterdam. A crowd of 20,079 watched in dismay as Spurs lost 2-1. It equalled their worst ever League start 62 years before. For Nicholson defeat was the final straw. On the Saturday evening, after 38 years with Tottenham, the last 15 of them as the most successful manager in their history and as one of perhaps the three most successful with any British club ever, he resigned.

'You're only as good as your last result' . . . no-one except a perfectionist such as Nicholson himself would say that his reign had been anything other than outstanding. Yet now there was the danger that, if he stayed any longer, the club and the man would destroy each other. 'The pressures had been building up over several months,' says Sidney Wale. 'Few people knew it at the time but Bill was under a lot of strain. He'd had a bad time over contracts and some players really got him down. The opening results of the season finished him. He felt he just couldn't take any more.'

Although Wale won't say so publicly, there is no doubt that the contract dispute which upset Nicholson most was with Martin Chivers. A passage from *The Glory Game* gives an idea of the two men's relationship. After a poor Spurs performance in a 0-0 draw against Nantes in the 1971–72 UEFA Cup, Nicholson singled out Chivers. They had been debating the side: "You mean we had some poor players?" said Nicholson: 'He hadn't named any names, but there was no doubt which poor player he was referring to. "What do you mean?" said Chivers, suddenly becoming violent and animated.'

Chivers' love-hate relationship with the club through this period was its most intriguing feature. Probably against his own wishes, Chivers became the dominant factor in its success. When he was playing well, and scoring goals, Spurs could win trophies. When he wasn't, they didn't. It is inconceivable that Spurs could have reached those four finals without Chivers up front, and his two goals at Wolverhampton in the UEFA Cup final could probably not have been scored by any other player of the period. Yet this placed too much responsibility on him. If he had a bad game the team tended to have a bad game, because they had lost their goalscoring threat (the need for defences to mark him closely was the primary means Spurs used to create space for *other* players to score goals, particularly at set-pieces). So his bad games were much more noticeable than those of other players, and he would receive much more criticism, both inside and outside the club, because of that. In Chivers' case there can be little doubt that matters were out of balance – the team was simply too dependent on him – and similar recriminations were to be heard after his performance for England against Poland in 1973.

The other strange, almost unreal, factor about Nicholson's (and his team's) perceived problems at this point was that they had reached a cup final in each of the previous four seasons, and won three of them. This, while not unprecedented, is very rare in the modern game. Reactions to Spurs' current side were a statement about Nicholson's past successes, and the levels of expectation which he had engendered in the club and its supporters, more than any detached view of the club's actual situation or the team's abilities. As Nicholson said at one point in this period: 'Here I am contemplating problems and so called failure while someone like Matt Gillies (then manager at Nottingham Forest) would give anything to be in my shoes.' In addition to the four cup finals, Nicholson's side had reached the semi-finals of the League Cup in 1968–69 (beaten 2-1 by Arsenal) and in 1971–72 (beaten 5-4 by Chelsea) as well as the UEFA Cup semi-finals in 1972–73. Seven semi-finals in six seasons was surely enough to keep the most fickle fan interested.

Despite the board's request that he reconsider, Nicholson's decision was final. He would never be thought of as anything but a success, but now he was tired and not a little disillusioned and he was surely right in thinking that the time for a change had come.

Geoff Richardson, now vice-chairman of the club, stresses that the board never asked Nicholson to resign, nor did it ever wish him to leave. Indeed, no one was more delighted than the directors when, after a brief interlude, Nicholson took up his present post.

The option of general manager was never seriously considered by Nicholson, no matter how hard the Press may have pushed it. He had resigned and expected to leave the club. He had no desire for an administrative post and Tottenham, with the example of Matt Busby at Manchester United in the immediate past, would not necessarily have thought it the best solution. If a new man was to come in, faced with the near impossible task of following the legendary Bill Nicholson, then there would have to be changes made.

Nicholson's first choice as successor was his assistant, Eddie Baily. 'The age difference was the same as Shankly and Paisley,' says Nicholson, 'and it worked well enough there.' After Baily he supported Blanchflower and Johnny Giles, either individually or as a team.

It would be foolish to pretend that such a successful era ended, or could have ended, without some regrets and not a little hurt. A new manager, if any outsider took the job, would inevitably be walking on eggs, trying to take account of the sensitivities of staff who had, in some cases, been with the club for decades.

But even the greatest of institutions do have to undergo change from time to time though it is certainly true that the changeover might have been handled more smoothly if one or other of the alternative candidates had been given the job. As it was, the Press, at least, seemed convinced that Danny Blanchflower's time had come.

BLANCHFLOWER REJECTED

The next seven seasons took Spurs through troughs of depression to achievements that didn't seem possible in their darkest hours. There was another change of manager, relegation to the Second Division for the first time since 1935, instant promotion, the arrival of the Argentinian World Cup stars, Ardiles and Villa, and finally, in 1981, the magical first year of the new decade, victory in the FA Cup. Spurs were back in Europe. But success took years of painstaking work and as Spurs crashed from one disaster to another in that traumatic 1974–75 season, Brian James, in his *Daily Mail* column, asked how different things might have been had Nicholson been allowed to name his own successor. He raised the point as Spurs, still struggling near the foot of the First Division under the new managership of Terry Neill, faced a Liverpool side challenging Derby for the League title. Ten months earlier, Spurs and Liverpool had met more nearly as equals, watched and presided over by the two men who had created them, Nicholson and Shankly. A few months later both would be gone. One difference was that Shankly sat in on the board meeting which selected Bob Paisley as his successor, while Nicholson had no say at White Hart Lane. James argued, fairly, that if Spurs had only groomed a successor in the way the well-oiled Liverpool machine had groomed Paisley, the White Hart Lane change-over could have been made without the traumas which followed.

Spurs didn't ask Nicholson's advice because, in the words of Sidney Wale, 'It was the manager's job to manage' and, in keeping with their conservative image, they attempted to make the appointment as straightforward as possible by advertising the post and choosing a successor from the applicants. But they had to contend first with a massive Press campaign in favour of the man said to be the number one choice of the fans, and arguably the one everyone was expecting to take over, Double hero Danny Blanch-flower. Victor Railton confidently predicted in the *London Evening News* that Blanchflower would be appointed, while other names being touted for the job included Gordon Jago of Queen's Park Rangers, Dave Mackay of Derby and Johnny Giles, player-manager of the Irish Republic and soon to retire at Leeds. Of all the likely candidates, Blanch-flower was the most obvious, though he himself would have preferred Johnny Giles alongside him as coach. Immediately identified with the glory years, Blanchflower was a man who shared Nicholson's idealism but was still young enough, at 47, not to share his despair. He had retired from the game in 1964 vowing never to go into management and spending the years instead trying to put an errant soccer world to rights from the platform of sports journalism in the *Sunday Express*.

Nicholson possibly believed he could play king-maker by spending several hours persuading Blanchflower to become a candidate. Plans were hatched, prospective transfers tentatively negotiated. In one deal, Don Givens and Gerry Francis were to come from QPR in exchange for the still uncontracted Chivers. A whole new side was being planned. But at the end of the day, Blanchflower didn't get the job because he didn't apply for it. That, however, was arguably a convenient escape route for the board, who had not been pro-Blanchflower from the outset. 'I know Bill wanted Danny to have the job,' says Wale, 'and I know they discussed it together. I told Bill that if he wanted Danny to be considered, Danny would have to apply like the

Kevin Keegan and Alan Mullery take off during a League game on 4 September 1971. Spurs won 2-0 with goals from Chivers and Peters. Nicholson says of Mullery: 'He was honest and dedicated and, of course, he was there at just the right time in 1972. It couldn't have worked out better for him.'

others. He never did. It's as simple as that.' Wale does not try to hide his own reasons for not being a Blanchflower enthusiast, although he claims: 'I could have been persuaded either way.' Wale says be believed that Blanchflower had been out of the game too long to make a return at the highest level of management without any experience. 'I felt he was out of touch,' says Wale. 'Also, over the years I'd come to look on him, through his columns in the *Sunday Express*, as more of a football critic than a prospective manager. I believe, too, that his subsequent records in charge of Chelsea and Northern Ireland proved me right.'

Privately, the board had other reasons for opposing Blanchflower. They feared that he would challenge their authority as he had done constantly as a player (they remembered how he gave up the club captaincy in that row about how far he could extend his responsibilities), and that he would ruffle the hitherto calm waters of White Hart Lane. Under Nicholson, Spurs had had a low profile manager. ('I'm not a man who's desperate to see his name in the papers' Nicholson once said.) The only news, until the recent troubles, had been good news and directors could sleep soundly at night knowing they wouldn't find the club's name plastered all over the back pages. With his own Press connections, and a long standing dislike of Football Association regulations which in theory prevented any manager or player going into print without his club's approval (when he was a player Blanchflower discussed his newspaper pieces with the club only after insisting that he would not change anything anyway), he could have proved a very independent force. No greater change from the Nicholson cra could probably be imagined.

'I know it sounds hopelessly optimistic,' says Wale, 'but the type of manager we were looking for was someone like Bill, a man who could take over and get on with the job. I don't know if the idea of following in Bill's footsteps put anyone off, but we were very disappointed with the response to our advert.' In light of their requirements, and in what was perceived as a snub for Blanchflower, the board's subsequent appointment was a paradox. Not only that, it upset Nicholson, angered Spurs fans and stunned the soccer business.

In naming Hull City's Terry Neill the board had chosen someone with a good deal more in common with Blanchflower than with Nicholson; moreover, as a former and recent long-serving Arsenal player, Neill was among the very last people the fans wanted. Nicholson's pride was obviously hurt by the board's decision. 'I thought they'd appoint Danny,' he said. 'I don't even know Terry Neill.'

Capped a then record 59 times for Northern Ireland (thus beating the record held by Blanchflower and Billy Bingham), Neill had spent 12 years as centre-half at Arsenal before serving his 'apprenticeship' player-managing Second Division Hull and the Northern Ireland team. Like Blanchflower, Neill came from Belfast, shared the same energetic enthusiasm for the game, though not Blanchflower's brilliance, and had also captained club and country. And, while not as articulate as Blanchflower, he still had plenty to say for

himself; indeed arguably rather too much, as the Spurs board would find to their regret.

Neill's four years at Hull were, by his own admission, an undistinguished start to his new career. The best Hull finished was fifth, and that was in his first season. Since his period in charge they have slowly descended to the Fourth Division. He was 32 when he applied for the Spurs job, offering a happy-go-lucky football philosophy that was in stark contrast to the austere regime of Nicholson. It was Bill Shankly who once said: 'Football's not a matter of life and death – it's more important than that'; Neill said of the Spurs' job: 'If I fail, I've got a wonderful wife and two beautiful daughters to go back to.' And, good for him, he meant it.

His Arsenal connections didn't bother the board for the simple reason that, unlike the fans, they've generally got on well with their Highbury counterparts. So why in the end did Spurs appoint him? Says Sidney Wale, perhaps with a touch of sadness: 'He was clearly the best candidate.' But Neill's selection was a unanimous decision (he was hardly responsible for the quality of the opposition) and he took over as the First Division's youngest manager with a simple but daunting brief: to keep Spurs up. It was 13 September; Spurs were still bottom with just two points from their first six League games and had just been knocked out of the League Cup 4-0 at home by Middlesbrough.

Neill's relaxed approach ('I want you all to go out and enjoy yourselves' he started by telling his struggling team) brought mixed results. They began Neill's term with a 2-1 win over West Ham and a 3-2 away success at Wolves, going on to collect 15 points from their next 13 League matches. Helped by some points-earning goals from his new striker John Duncan, bought from Dundee on 19 October for £125,000, they slowly began to edge away from the bottom. But a New Year relapse once again brought back the spectre of relegation and questions began to be raised in the Press about Neill's apparently unconcerned attitude in the face of crisis.

Neill was under constant fire from the fans, too. 'They made it clear they didn't want me from the outset,' he says. 'My every word and action was scrutinised for its level of devotion towards Tottenham Hotspur. It was a test of loyalty. In other words, what was I doing with THEIR club.' During his early months in charge, Neill correctly identified and tried to rectify one of the malaises which had developed under Nicholson, the problem of over-staffing. 'Competition for first team places is healthy,' says Neill, 'but in Spurs' case, places in the reserves which should have been for up-and-coming players, the Glenn Hoddles, Steve Walfords and Neil McNabs, were being taken by players who had no future at the club. The paths to the top were being blocked.' McNab was a case in point, says Neill. Signed by Nicholson from Morton in February 1974, the teenage Scottish youth international midfielder had been playing games in the South East Counties League for the youth side when he should have been on the fringe of the first team.

For season 1974–75, the staff numbered 32 professionals and 13 apprentices, but by the end of the season those totals would be considerably fewer as Neill cleared the decks for his younger players to emerge and time caught up with the remaining stars from Nicholson's final days.

First to go of the old guard were Martin Peters and Mike England. Following a 3-0 home defeat by Leicester in February, which left Spurs even more firmly embedded in the relegation struggle, Neill sold Peters to Norwich for £40,000 – where he was to enjoy a renaissance under John Bond – while England walked out after a row, to retire from the English game at the age of 32. The normally placid Peters had refused to watch a game against Stoke after rowing about tactics and being substituted. Back in the League, Spurs' dismal run of only three points from their first ten New Year games was halted by three successive wins over Easter. But they continued to live dangerously until the very last game of the season. The drama did wonders for the gates. Only six months earlier, for the home game against newly-promoted Carlisle on 16 October, Spurs had been watched by a mere 12,823 fans, their lowest League gate since the Second World War (though it should be said that it was a midweek game, it had rained all day and Carlisle did not exactly pack the grounds they played). For their penultimate home game against Chelsea, 50,998 watched Spurs win 2-0. A week later 43,762 were at Highbury for a 1-0 defeat by Arsenal which left Spurs needing victory in their last match, at home to Leeds two days later on Monday 28 April, to stay in the First Division. Anything less and they, not Luton, might be relegated. Neill's preparation included calling in a hypnotherapist to convince the team they were going to win. The idea worked, or rather it didn't fail, because in front of a 49,886 crowd Spurs stormed to a 4-2 win with two goals from a back-in-favour Cyril Knowles and one each from Conn and Chivers. It was the sort of Spurs performance of which Nicholson would have been proud. But for Neill victory was a bitter sweet sensation. 'It was as if we'd won the Cup,' he says, 'but I'd worked 24 hours a day, seven days a week to keep Spurs in the First Division and I'd taken a lot of stick from the fans for my trouble. Yet here they all were chanting my name and calling for me to go out on to the pitch and acknowledge their cheers. Did I go? I went straight home. I'd paid my dues.'

BURKINSHAW'S ARRIVAL

Spurs fans don't thank Neill for very much these days but one of his appointments which must warrant their gratitude is Keith Burkinshaw, brought in as coach during the summer of 1975 (Neill's Hull coach, Wilf Dixon, who'd replaced Eddie Baily as assistant manager in the changeover, was moved to youth recruitment). Burkinshaw had been sacked by Newcastle following defeat by Liverpool in the 1974 FA Cup final and, though he didn't know him personally, Neill had heard enough about his qualities to want him at White Hart Lane.

Perhaps it was because the fans couldn't find it in their hearts to say a good word about Neill, that Burkinshaw got much of the praise for helping the club finish a respectable ninth in the First Division the following season and

reach the semi-finals of the League Cup. Certainly Neill didn't do his Tottenham cause any good by disappearing to Highbury so soon after joining, but the facts are that with him Spurs returned from the brink of relegation to within 90 minutes of another cup final, while without him they sank like a stone. The fairest assessment is that, together, Neill and Burkinshaw would have struck up a very successful partnership. In his seven years at Newcastle, the last four of them as first team coach, Burkinshaw's side enjoyed their final years as a First Division force, reaching the FA Cup final in 1974, and, even after his departure, maintaining enough momentum to reach the 1976 League Cup final (ironically, at Spurs' expense in the semi-final). Two seasons later they were relegated. When Burkinshaw arrived at Spurs, Neill had already had five years' managerial experience at Second and First Division level to Burkinshaw's none. The partnership equation of good coach plus experienced manager equals successful team starts to make sense when it's remembered that, after Neill teamed up with Don Howe at Arsenal, the Gunners had their greatest run of success since their own Double year. Burkinshaw would have his day but, like Neill before him, it would take five years.

A combination of economic factors and Neill's desire to streamline his squad saw the turnaround in their fortunes on a playing staff reduced from 32 professionals the previous season to 26 for 1975–76. Their number was strengthened by the arrival in September 1975 of a tall, powerful if inelegant central defender, Willie Young, who cost £80,000 from Aberdeen, and, two months later, striker Gerry Armstrong from Irish club Bangor. As essentially a players' manager, Neill had a cordial but distant relationship with the board. 'During the first 18 months they let me get on with the job without interference,' he now says. But three events during the spring and summer of 1976 brought Neill's brief Tottenham reign to a swift and sour finale.

OVER TO HIGHBURY

First, in autumn 1975, the board heard from the Press (and vetoed) plans to try and bring star Johan Cruyff to Tottenham (they needn't have bothered, since if subsequent attempts to bring Cruyff to a British club are anything to go by, Neill was on a wild goose chase). The incident which followed in the spring of 1976 was a far more serious challenge to Neill's authority, not so much in its nature as in the manner in which it was done. It happened on the morning of Sunday 25 April, as the players prepared to set off on their close-season tour of Australia and the Pacific. Neill had promised a seat on the coach to Heathrow Airport for the only fan travelling with the party, 78-year-old retired bookmaker Mr Fred Rhye, a devoted follower who had missed only three of their matches in 40 years and was popular throughout the club. Rhye's standing at White Hart Lane can be gauged by the fact that he was the only fan to have a place in the official car park. Yet Sidney Wale, for reasons which he goes to some lengths to explain, chose the occasion to embarrass Neill by publicly countermanding his orders. Rhye was told he would have to find alternative transport to the airport (he was paying his own way to follow Spurs) and Neill was left to hurriedly organise a taxi.

London clubs often have difficulty with enthusiastic fans, and the arranging of rival celebration parties after Cup wins has caused both Arsenal and Spurs considerable heartaches in recent years. Rhye was never in this category, though the incident does bring to mind the fact that, when the Supporters Club was founded in 1948, it had to be called the Spurs Supporters Club because permission to use the official club name was withheld.

Wale defends his action, saying: 'It was always a firm club rule that fans were not allowed to travel on the team coach, for insurance reasons among others. If we made an allowance for one fan, we'd get everyone climbing aboard. I knew Fred Rhye well, and, among other things, felt that we were being rash in encouraging him to undertake such an arduous trip when he was ill.' (Rhye subsequently decided to return from Canada.) The incident brought to the surface the personality clash which had been underlying Neill's presence at Spurs almost from the day he arrived. Neill's expansive, aggressive approach was always bound to be at odds with the more cautious Wale and his colleagues and it needed only a contretemps like this to bring it into the open. Neill says: 'I'd been aware for some time of a growing aloofness by the board towards myself and it made it very difficult for me to go into the job with all my heart and soul. The coach affair was the beginning of the end. When a manager can't decide who can and can't travel on the team coach, what next?' The very same point might have been made, of course, by the directors.

With relations soured before the tour had even got under way, and a long and tiring itinerary ahead taking in Canada, New Zealand, Fiji and Australia, the outlook was stormy. Neill won't admit to deliberately provoking the showdown which led to the final breach, but his actions at the end of the tour had that effect. As a reward for winning all nine matches, Neill wanted to give some of his players and backroom staff a bonus out of the proceeds of the tour. He maintains that perfectly straightforward means could have been found to make such payments, but the directors, and Wale in particular, were not prepared to sanction them. Wale insists that Neill was rash in promising the players something he could not guarantee they were going to get – hence the untenable situation in which Neill then found himself. The party arrived back in England on 24 May and Neill handed in his resignation a fortnight later. It was another three weeks, on 30 June, before the board unanimously accepted it after a four hour meeting. They were not hoping Neill would change his mind, rather the delay was because Sidney Wale was not prepared to cut short his holiday to resolve the matter sooner. The parting of the ways was thus mutual. 'I didn't feel it was up to me to ask Terry to change his mind,' says Wale. 'He was still under contract and he'd walked out on us.' Neill says: 'They didn't take me seriously. I was treated like a naughty schoolboy who didn't know how lucky he was.'

As soon as news of Neill's resignation reached Highbury, Arsenal chairman Denis Hill-Wood telephoned Wale to see if the

way was clear to offer Neill a job, and, within a fortnight of quitting Spurs, he was installed as Arsenal manager in succession to Bertie Mee. If it seems strange how, with two clubs as close and as big as Arsenal and Spurs, one should be almost relieved to see the back of their manager while the other strives to take him on, Wale sums up the reasons when he says: 'Terry wasn't the sort of manager we were used to. But as an Arsenal player and club captain, he was highly thought of by Denis Hill-Wood, and rightly so.' Neill was predictably branded a traitor by Spurs fans, but he still insists: 'I know a lot of people thought I was an opportunist and was using Tottenham for my own ends, but I can say in all honesty that I had already made up my mind to resign from Spurs before I knew of the Arsenal vacancy. Spurs still mean something very special to me and I was proud to be asked to manage them.'

Wale was understandably bitter about the Neill affair, writing in the 1977–78 handbook: 'It can be seen that the decline of our club was not halted by the appointment made following the resignation of Bill Nicholson in August 1974.' He might have been more favourably disposed if Neill's brief reign had not merely postponed the inevitable. After 15 years with one manager, the club could not absorb the shock of having three in under two years. The season after Neill's departure they were relegated to the Second Division for the first time since 1935.

Keith Burkinshaw, whose only other claim to fame prior to joining Spurs was that he had been in the same form as Michael Parkinson at Barnsley Grammar School, had stayed well in the background throughout the Neill dispute. He had played mainly for Workington, where he had scored one of the goals in that unsung club's 9-1 defeat of Barrow in the Football League Cup in 1964, still the record for the competition despite the fact that neither club is now in the League. He had gone on to enjoy brief managerial experience at Workington and Scunthorpe and he clearly had aspirations of his own. When Neill took him on as coach, Burkinshaw was shrewd enough to get an assurance that Neill would not stand in his way if a manager's job came up. He could scarcely have believed it would be the Tottenham job itself that he would be applying for inside a year, or given much for his chances of getting it. His only experience in the transfer jungle, for instance, was spending three months trying to raise the £300 Workington needed to pay for a Scottish junior. With Neill's exit leaving the rest of the Spurs backroom staff exposed to a new manager's purge, Burkinshaw acted quickly to leave the directors in no doubt where his loyalties lay. By applying for Neill's job he effectively killed two birds with one stone.

As one of the game's quiet men, Burkinshaw already had a lot going for him so far as Spurs were concerned. A workmanlike wing-half of moderate ability as a player, he had been rejected by Wolves before joining Liverpool. He made a handful of first-team appearances and spent most of his time in the reserves. He had just concluded a seven-year spell as a coach at Newcastle, the last four of them, between 1971 and 1975, in charge of the first team. In his final full season at St James'

Park, Newcastle reached the FA Cup final – their first since 1955. His reward was the sack.

Burkinshaw believed that the good working relationship he had established with the Spurs players helped his claim to the managership. But what clinched the job for him in the summer of 1976 was the impression he made on Sidney Wale during the fateful close season tour. While relations between Wale and Neill were at their lowest ebb, Burkinshaw was quietly getting on with the job in the background. 'Doing the work while Terry appeared on television,' was how Wale put it.

'On the tour I got the chance to get to know Keith,' says Wale. 'I found him hard-working, honest and I knew he was well-liked by the players. It was those qualities which convinced the board when we considered his application.' Burkinshaw's ideas about attacking football were also very much in the Spurs tradition, although it was to take five long years to bring them to fruition.

'I grew up in the era of Read Madrid, di Stefano, Puskas – they were my heroes and they more than anyone else influenced my approach to the game. My philosophy has always been that you've got to entertain, but you can only play like that nowadays if you've got players willing to get back when it matters.'

Burkinshaw's ideal had to be put into cold storage in his first season in command. Spurs were playing with their backs to the wall from the moment they lost 3-1 at Ipswich in the first match of the season. Burkinshaw analyses the problem simply when he says: 'We just weren't good enough.' More specifically they were weak at the back and were beset by problems in attack. John Duncan, who had been top scorer for the previous two seasons, missed the first eleven games with a back injury which limited his first team appearances that season to just nine games, and in which he scored only four times. Defensively, the team started badly and then got worse. In consecutive away games in October and November they conceded 13 goals, including the club's heaviest defeat to date when they went down 8-2 at Derby. The one defender who emerged with his reputation unscathed from the winter blitzkrieg was goalkeeper Pat Jennings. 'He didn't stand a chance,' says Burkinshaw.

Burkinshaw's early forays into the transfer market came before the full extent of the team's shortcomings were apparent. His first buy was £75,000 forward Ian Moores from Stoke in August. Peter Taylor, a winger of capricious skills who had played for England while still in the Third Division, and whom Neill had already tried to sign, came from Crystal Palace for £125,000 in September. When his defence crumbled, Burkinshaw imported John Gorman from Carlisle in November, but still the defeats piled up. On the cup front, the team suffered the ignominy of losing at home to Third Division Wrexham in the third round of the League Cup, and equally embarrassing was their exit at the first hurdle from the FA Cup when they lost 1-0 at Second Division Cardiff.

For the League game against Birmingham on 19 March Burkinshaw played his final card. Steve Perryman, club captain and mid-

field ever present, was switched to the back four where Burkinshaw felt his leadership qualities, quick reading of the game and overall purposefulness could marshall a department which had lost all coordination and confidence. The move helped bring about 12 points from the last 13 League games of the season, but it came too late to save Spurs. The killer result was a 5-0 defeat at Manchester City in the penultimate match. Spurs were relegated for the first time in four decades.

In anyone's knives were out for Burkinshaw, Wale did a remarkably good job of keeping them out of his manager's back. 'I didn't expect the sack,' says Burkinshaw, 'but in view of our performance that season, they would have been justified in getting rid of me. I didn't think I was a failure. I knew where we were going and that what I was doing was right. I could only hope that the board thought the same way.'

Spurs means different things to different people but it is generally a club where players and staff, once settled, stay for a long time. Throughout Burkinshaw's season as manager, he had always received the backing of Wale, even when relegation looked a certainty. 'I remember travelling by car to Manchester City with Keith on the day we were relegated,' says Wale, 'It was one of the saddest days of my life. But as soon as we got home, the first thing I did was to phone Keith's wife Joyce and reassure her that his job was safe.'

At the next board meeting, Wale told his four fellow directors: 'I don't know if any of you have any idea about trying to get rid of

Keith Burkinshaw, but one thing I must remind you of is that it was we five who appointed him.' Not another word was spoken on the subject.

Despite the setbacks of that season, Wale had continued to be impressed by Burkinshaw's dedication and hard work. 'He showed many of the qualities of Bill Nicholson. Like Bill, he was never a publicity-seeker. He was honest, hard-working and, in short, more the sort of manager we'd been used to and we liked.'

THE JENNINGS THUNDERBOLT

Two decisions in his first year in charge, which were to prove of long-lasting significance, reflected Burkinshaw's awareness as a tactician, but his lack of experience as a manager. The single most contentious issue of the decade was, of course, Pat Jennings' sale to Arsenal and it still seems surprising that the club should have allowed the deal to go through. It wasn't so much the sale itself, which on the face of it seemed reasonable at the time, but the buyers which should have caused alarm. Given Burkinshaw's relative inexperience in the transfer market, someone should have at least given him the benefit of one timeworn business dictum: 'Don't sell on your own doorstep.' The repercussions of the Jennings sale rebounded on Burkinshaw with three-fold force. He had already sold Willie Young to Highbury and Jennings's departure was coupled with the sale, also to Arsenal, of defender

Gerry Armstrong and Leicester's Steve Sims fight for the ball on 14 May 1977, Spurs' last day in the First Division. They won the game 2-0 with goals from Jimmy Holmes and John Pratt but it did them little good. They were already condemned to Second Division football for the first time in nearly three decades and eventually finished the season in bottom position. Armstrong had joined Spurs late in 1975 from Irish club Bangor but, with the arrival of Archibald and Crooks, was to move to Watford.

Steve Walford. All three proved bargain buys for Terry Neill, none more so than Jennings, as Spurs fans were never to let Burkinshaw forget. Neill says of the deals: 'They were good for me, but I was conscious that Keith was inexperienced.'

Young was sold right at the climax of the relegation battle because, despite his aerial strength, he possessed few of the ground skills a purist like Burkinshaw required in his players. At 6ft 3in and 14 stone, Young made up in energy and enthusiasm what he lacked in finesse. Fans love a trier, and Young was immediately adopted by Highbury's North Bank in the way he had been by the Park Lane End. But Burkinshaw remained unimpressed. As a former player who perhaps shared Young's relative lack of natural ability, it was all the more important to Burkinshaw to create a team without such shortcomings. With Spurs' defence taking most of the rap for their dismal performances that season, Young was sacrificed when Perryman was switched into the back four. Terry Neill had bought Young in the first place and was still an admirer of the big man's capabilities, so a move to Highbury suited all concerned.

The sale of Jennings was under very different circumstances. He was 31 at the time and the previous season had set a new club appearance record of 449 League matches, passing Ted Ditchburn's total of 418. He'd been voted Football Writers' Footballer of the Year in 1973, the Professional Footballers' Player of the Year in 1975–76 and had been made an MBE in the Queen's Birthday Hon-

ours List the same year. He was also Northern Ireland's most capped player, having passed Terry Neill's record of 59 caps in the 1975–76 season.

Standing 6ft tall with hands as big as frying pans, he was the complete goalkeeper, probably the best in Britain and perhaps the world throughout the 1970s. Bought from Watford by Bill Nicholson in June 1964, for a bargain £30,000, Jennings had spent twelve illustrious years at White Hart Lane, collecting an FA Cup winners' medal in 1967, League Cup winners' medals in 1971 and 1973 and a UEFA Cup winners' medal in 1972. 'Pat,' says Sidney Wale, 'had seen it all and done it all.' Although Jennings never asked for a transfer, it was almost an embarrassment for Spurs to have to ask a goalkeeper of his calibre to play in the Second Division. Understandably, he didn't want to leave the top division.

There were other factors to be considered, too. Cuts would have to be made to help the club pay their way on projected lower gates, and Jennings would be an expensive item on the wage bill. Spurs also believed they had a capable deputy in Barry Daines, and adequate cover in Welsh Under-21 international Mark Kendall. A former Spurs apprentice, Daines was seven years younger than Jennings and had stood in competently for him 19 times during the 1976–77 season when the senior player was injured. More to the point, Daines had told Spurs that he could see no future for himself at the club if Jennings stayed. The club saw it as something of a rerun of the Banks/Shilton debate at Leicester.

Wale agrees that Spurs were wrong in believing Jennings was approaching the end of his career and Burkinshaw is the first to admit that, in the light of experience, he wouldn't do the same thing again. It is interesting that it was Jennings' high quality performances for Arsenal through into the 1980s that finally convinced most league managers that keepers could go on, and arguably get better, into their mid- and even late-thirties. That changing attitude received an ironic twist, of course, when Spurs bought 33-year-old Ray Clemence from Liverpool in August 1981 to replace the more than competent Milija Aleksic. Burkinshaw points out, with some justification, that the consequences of the Jennings' sale would not have rebounded so hard on him if Daines' progress as goalkeeper hadn't been hampered by injury. Says Burkinshaw ruefully: 'Barry never came near to fulfilling his potential, while Pat went from strength to strength. I don't regret my decision, because I thought it was right at the time, but knowing what I now know, I wouldn't do it again.'

Burkinshaw's new tactical plan was drawn up simply to get Spurs out of the Second Division at the first attempt: in a sense, it didn't much matter how. Nonetheless, Burkinshaw's scheme was founded on his faith in attacking football, a brave philosophy in the Second Division, where it is often said that the only successful method is to kick your way out. By contrast Burkinshaw was determined that Spurs would 'play our way out.' To that end he retained the industrious Perryman in the back four, turned Terry Naylor and Jimmy Holmes into a couple of overlapping full-backs ready to attack down

157

the flanks, and took the team on a close-season tour to Scandinavia to see how the experiment worked. Results proved encouraging enough for Burkinshaw to pursue the plan in the club's pre-season triangular tournament at Umea in Sweden against Leicester, who finished eleventh in the First Division the previous season, and Royale Union of Belgium. Spurs won the tournament, defeating Royale 2-0 and Leicester 2-1, and Burkinshaw was ready to put the scheme to the real test in the Second Division. He well remembers the reaction of Leicester after seeing the new-style Spurs in action: 'You'll never get away with playing in the Second Division like that.' But Burkinshaw was convinced he'd got it right, and so were the team. 'Everyone was right behind it,' he says.

He didn't have to wait long to be vindicated. In their first match of the new season, Spurs beat Sheffield United 4-2 with goals from John Duncan, Chris Jones and two penalties from Keith Osgood. And that really was the story of their season. Spurs amassed 83 goals for their highest total since 1965, but their attacking style took its toll in defence where 49 goals were conceded. The result was that, despite being the Second Division's top scorers, Spurs were involved in a nail-biting race for the promotion line with Brighton, Southampton and Bolton. The issue was not resolved until the last Saturday of the season, with Spurs playing at Southampton and needing a draw to be certain of going up at Brighton's expense. With news reaching The Dell that Brighton were beating Blackpool, the wait for chairman Sidney Wale became sheer agony. 'I remember looking at my watch with about a quarter of an hour to go, and again at what I thought was at least five minutes later and the minute hand hadn't moved a millimetre!' His match was still scoreless.

If both scores stood at the final whistle, Spurs would be promoted on goal difference over Brighton. Victories like the 9-0 demolition of Bristol Rovers, the club's biggest win since their record 13-2 victory over Crewe, had given them a comfortable goal advantage over Brighton but the one thing they couldn't afford to do was lose. By a happy coincidence, Southampton also needed only a point to be sure of their promotion place so, with both teams content to defend, the match ended in the goalless draw. It was a result which drew more than a little cynical comment, particularly from along the South Coast at the Goldstone Ground, and an impartial observer who was not aware of all the circumstances would certainly have found it difficult to believe that Spurs and the Saints were desperately battling for a First Division place. If Wale offered a silent prayer of thanks afterwards, he would almost certainly have mentioned Southampton winger Tony Funnell: 'How he missed a couple of chances for them, I just don't know,' he recalls.

So Spurs were back in the First Division at their first attempt. And their return was a triumph not only for Burkinshaw's tactics but for Spurs' attacking style of play. For far from playing to smaller houses in the Second Division, they maintained the upward trend in their gates that Burkinshaw had managed to accelerate even in their relegation season. From a home average of 27,836 in Terry Neill's last season, attendances rose to 30,173 in the season Spurs went down and were swollen by an extra 68,119 fans in the Second Division for an average of 33,417. It was a figure bettered by only six other clubs in the Football League and came at a time when attendances generally were falling fast. 'I suppose people must have liked something we were doing,' said Burkinshaw afterwards.

1981

Keith Burkinshaw • The arrival of the Argentinians • The Sixth FA Cup • Steve Perryman • Glenn Hoddle • A £4,000,000 investment • Fans' favourites • Facing the future

'Wherever Spurs play, whether it's Manchester, Malta or Mauritius, we're famous. Soccer is about big clubs and star names, but most of all it's about people. You can be playing for the biggest club in the world with the biggest stars in the game, but if you don't enjoy it, if you don't get on with the people around you, you're wasting your time. I enjoy Spurs because at this club everyone, from the humblest backroom boy to the highest-paid player, is treated with equal respect. They're all equally important to our success. That's what makes Tottenham Hotspur a great football club.'

Steve Perryman, club captain in the centenary season.

The transfer market is as much part of the mystique of the soccer world as magical goals and memorable cup wins. It figures every bit as much in the fan's imagination as, say, scoring the winning goal at Wembley. It is every schoolboy's dream for his favourite club to sign a star player. For fans in the fifties and sixties, the transfers to Italy and back of Jimmy Greaves, John Charles and Denis Law were just as exciting as almost anything that happened on the pitch. In the seventies the outstanding memory is unquestionably the coup which Keith Burkinshaw pulled off in the summer of 1978. Just as Bill Nicholson had changed the face of soccer 17 years earlier with his Double-winners, so Burkinshaw changed it that July. It was a time when virtually no foreigners played it the Football League, though no one who saw Argentina win the World Cup a month before could have failed to be impressed by the

Osvaldo Ardiles, Ricky Villa, Terry Yorath and Glenn Hoddle, four of the eight internationals on the club's books that season, line up against Crystal Palace on 6 October 1979. Villa scored the only goal in a 1-1 draw.

bewitching skills of their diminutive midfield player, Osvaldo Ardiles.

Every World Cup throws up a star or two who, through the worldwide media of television, radio and newspapers, suddenly become household names. The mesmerising one-twos Ardiles played with Mario Kempes instantly raised the hitherto unknown Argentinian schemer into the superstar bracket. But unlike many World Cups, where the victors merely pack up their kits and silently slip away, heroes today, gone tomorrow, the impact of Ardiles was to reverberate around the clubs, shops, offices, pubs and homes of England like no other soccer event since the 1966 World Cup win. The first inkling that a sensational transfer deal was in the offing came in the few lines Fleet Street newspapers gave to a news agency report from Buenos Aires on Wednesday 28 June that Ardiles was to sign for Manchester United. Indeed the papers that did mention the item turned it into an emphatic denial from Sir Matt Busby that United knew anything about such a deal.

The next report to hit the teleprinters in Fleet Street came on the evening of Tuesday 4 July, nine days after the World Cup final. Again, Spurs were not mentioned. Ardiles' club, Huracan, was reported from Buenos Aires as saying that he had been transferred to Sheffield United for £530,000. The same report quoted Ardiles' World Cup teammate, Ricardo Villa, as saying he had been transferred from Racing Club, Buenos Aires, to Manchester City for £315,000. Several papers ignored this dispatch altogether. Ardiles coming to play in England? At Sheffield United? It must be a joke. Only *The Times* carried the report in full. It was not until three days later, on Friday 7 July, that the real news came out and this time it was on every front page. Ardiles and Villa were joining Spurs in what Jeff Powell in the *Daily Mail* called (with little if any exaggeration – only the transfer of Tommy Lawton to Third Division Notts County is comparable) the most sensational deal in British soccer history. David Lacey summed up a common reaction when he wrote in *The Guardian*: 'When Keith Burkinshaw went shopping and brought back Ardiles, it was as if the janitor had gone out to buy a tin of paint and had returned with a Velasquez. Astonishment that the Argentinians were coming at all is equalled by the incredulity that they were going to play for Spurs, who seemed to have lost faith in major transfers following the muted success of such purchases as Coates, Conn and Taylor.'

How did it all come about? Perhaps it was Bill Nicholson, the man responsible for so many sensational soccer transfers himself, who played the talisman at Tottenham on the morning of Thursday 29 June, a few days after Argentina's 3-1 win over Holland. Nicholson was sitting in his office just across the corridor from where Burkinshaw was having a meeting when the phone rang. It was the Sheffield United manager Harry Haslam on the line, asking to speak to Keith. Burkinshaw, who only minutes earlier had returned from giving his manager's report to the monthly board meeting, takes up the story. 'Bill came in, told me Harry was on the line and I had to go into his office to take the call. Harry told me that both Ardiles and Villa were available for transfer and wanted to play in England. The tie-up was through Antonio Rattin the old Argentinian captain, who was acting as agent but who is obviously still best known here for being sent off at Wembley in 1966. He was a big mate of Harry's and Harry was phoning a few clubs to see if they were interested. Like everyone else I'd watched Argentina in the World Cup. You dream about having players like that in your side but you never think it could come off.'

Burkinshaw lost no time. He went straight back to the board meeting, which was still in progress, got the directors' blessing to fly out

to Buenos Aires to pursue the deal and began to make the necessary preparations. The League ban on overseas players had been lifted a couple of seasons earlier, but Burkinshaw still needed to be certain that the necessary work permit could be obtained and one of his first calls was to the Department of Employment, who told him there should be no problem with a player of that ability. At that stage he was going with the intention of signing just Ardiles. He was due to fly out to Buenos Aires on the Friday evening, a plan which very nearly ran into trouble when he heard that Arsenal's Terry Neill might be intending to do the same.

'I obviously wanted this one all to myself,' says Burkinshaw, who was relieved to find later that the Arsenal manager had decided against the trip. Whether the Arsenal board vetoed the idea has never been revealed, but in conceding this particular victory to his North London rival, Neill has always maintained that, already having Brady and Rix, he didn't need Villa and Ardiles.

Burkinshaw caught the Friday night flight, arrived in Buenos Aires on Saturday morning and checked into the Hotel Libertador. Within a matter of hours he had his first meeting with Ardiles. 'It was one of those occasions when you immediately know something is right,' says Burkinshaw, 'there was an instant rapport. Within twenty minutes of meeting him, he'd agreed to sign.' Ardiles' next words took Burkinshaw by surprise. 'He told me he had a friend, Ricardo Villa, who also wanted to play in England. Could be come too?' At that time Villa was assuming he would be going to Arsenal, and that the two could effectively come to London together.

One of the reasons why Burkinshaw was able to win his board's immediate approval for the trip was because Haslam had told him that Ardiles could be bought for around £350,000 – a bargain price by English standards, even in 1978. With the bankrupt state of Argentinian soccer and the virtually permanent devaluation of the Argentinian peso, clubs were prepared to let their players go for under their international market value just to reduce debts. Perversely, it also meant that they wouldn't then go to any domestic rival. For their part, the players were so poorly paid that, even under the British taxation system, they'd be ten times better off than staying at home. Burkinshaw didn't know much about Villa except that he was the big, bearded player Cesar Menotti had twice sent on as substitute (once for Ardiles) to add some steel to the midfield in two crucial group matches. What he did know was that for around £700,000 he could have two leading members of the squad that had just won the World Cup. To put the figure in perspective, it was £250,000 more than Manchester United had just paid Leeds for Gordon McQueen, whom Burkinshaw had failed to sign earlier in the summer.

Back in England, on the Sunday morning, Sidney Wale was about to have a drink with his wife before lunch when the phone rang. 'It was Keith calling from Buenos Aires,' says Wale, 'He told me he had a bit of a problem. There was another player who wanted to come too. Well, we'd agreed as a board on one but since Keith wanted an answer straight away,

I told him to hang on, and did some quick mental arithmetic. I worked out how much the bank would allow us on overdraft, how much extra we could expect to raise from season ticket sales with all the interest that was bound to be aroused, and I thought, we'll take a chance, so I gave Keith the go-ahead. We were both putting our heads on the chopping block. It was a big gamble to take, but looking back on it now, it was the best decision I ever made.'

Burkinshaw reached agreement with Villa even more swiftly than with Ardiles. 'Within a minute of meeting him, he'd agreed to sign,' says Burkinshaw. The stories about the Argentinian team being keen to get away were obviously no more than the truth. Not only were Spurs able to pay cash on the nail, but in the best traditions of Nicholson's cloak-and-dagger transfers, not a word came out about the true nature of the historic deal until Burkinshaw was ready to announce it.

The arrival of Ardiles and Villa was initially opposed by a PFA fearful of an invasion of foreign stars depriving their British members of a job. One can think of many other unionised trades and professions where such protests would have succeeded, but it is to the credit of football that the voices of welcome far outweighed those of dissent. At the same time, Spurs took no chances. With Keith Burkinshaw having already done his homework on the work permits, chairman Sidney Wale smoothed the path at Home Office level by marshalling some powerful voices to ensure there were no hiccups along the way.

By the time the new League season came around on 19 August, the soccer-going public's attention focussed with excitement and eager anticipation on the debuts of Ardiles and Villa. And the two Argentinians couldn't have asked for a sunnier South American day on which to make their entry into British football. A crowd of 41,223 turned out on a magnificent summer's afternoon at the City Ground, Nottingham, to watch the new champions Forest do battle with the most talked – about team in the League, Tottenham Hotspur. Without TV cameras present, those fans alone had the privilege of witnessing a sensational start to the Argentinians' League careers.

With 26 minutes gone, Spurs were trailing 1-0 to a goal by Martin O'Neill when Peter Shilton was drawn out to a low cross from Ian Moores. But with a deft skill which belies his massive stature, Villa teased the ball away from Shilton's grasp and flicked it past the outstretched leg of Archie Gemmill into the corner of the net.

Villa would have to wait almost three years to score another goal with such public acclaim. But this was more than enough to be going on with. Spurs collected a well-deserved point in their opening match back in the First Division, the Sunday papers proclaimed the result with predictable headlines like 'Viva Villa', and already Spurs were rather prematurely being tipped to win the Championship.

But the honeymoon was soon over. Only four days later, Spurs were brought down to earth with a bump. Playing their first home match before a crowd of 47,892, who laid on a South American-style confetti welcome for their new heroes, Spurs were roundly beaten 4-1 by Aston Villa. A 2-2 home draw against Chelsea followed and then a result which in two words and two figures rudely shattered Burkinshaw's brave new world; Liverpool 7 Tottenham 0. It is the only time in their history that Spurs have been defeated by a margin of seven goals in a Football League match. But their fans did at least see the next League champions that September day – Liverpool. For Keith Burkinshaw, the problem of grafting South American skill on to the muck and nettles of English league soccer was only just beginning.

Looking back on that new era in Spurs' history, Burkinshaw explains the dilemma in which he found himself. 'Over there,' he says, metaphorically pointing to a distant corner of the globe, 'all the attackers attack, and the defenders defend. That means all your midfield players attack as well. Ossie and Ricky didn't know the meaning of the word defend when they first came here. It's a coach's nightmare when you've got five against three – and the three are your's because the midfield's in attack. That's what happened to us at Liverpool and they're the sort of team who punish you for it.'

Ex-Spurs and England winger Peter Taylor asked an obvious question at the time when he said: 'Argentina won the World Cup not picking anyone up, so who's wrong?' Burkinshaw draws this distinction between the way the game is played in South American countries and the English concept of midfield players who combine defence with attack: 'The South Americans have defenders who all have as much skill as Glenn Hoddle. They don't need the support our defenders need because they're so much better equipped. We don't have these players, so we've got to get extra men back.'

Spurs continued to win friends, if not as many matches as they would have liked, throughout the season. The curiosity factor of Ardiles and Villa swelled gates wherever they played, making Spurs the top away attraction in the League. While Villa struggled to secure a regular first team place, Ardiles delighted fans with his darting runs, perceptive passing and use of space. Pictures frequently show him with the ball glued to his right instep, while his eyes are glancing about to see who's in space.

'It's his terrific skill combined with the ability to play with his head up which makes him a world-class footballer,' says Burkinshaw. 'He's 5ft 6in and weighs under ten stone. People said he would be knocked all over the place when the pitches got heavy here in winter. But he's proved them all wrong. He's hardly had an injury since he arrived. There's a very tough character inside that little frame.'

Indeed, it is Ardiles' ability to ride heavy tackles and still maintain his superb balance which has won him almost as much admiration as his marvellous ball skills. But despite his individual success, Spurs finished a moderate 11th in their first season back in Division One. They reached the quarter-finals of the FA Cup before going out 2-0 to Manchester United in an Old Trafford replay, but overall their achievement fell short of the high expectations held for them after such a sensational summer. And Burkinshaw still hadn't solved the problem of how to make the best use of his new acquisitions.

They were tried in defensive midfield, attacking midfield, left midfield, right midfield and central midfield. But Spurs were forgetting one vital point as they searched for the magic

formula. In Argentina's World Cup-winning side, Ardiles was working with two highly mobile, skilful ground players in Leopoldo Luque and Mario Kempes, two players with the acceleration and speed on the turn to make the most of Ardiles' through balls and lightning-quick one-twos on the edge of the box.

Spurs skipper Steve Perryman summed up the problem: 'We'd come up from the Second Division using a winger and overlapping full-backs to provide crosses for tall front men who were good with their heads. But with Ardiles and Villa, we naturally channelled everything through midfield. We were playing shorter, quicker balls, changing our game to a style which our strikers just weren't used to. It was unfair to expect them to play that way.'

Spurs added the combative talents of Welsh international captain Terry Yorath to midfield for the 1979–80 season as they continued to juggle with the permutations. But even Yorath's ball-winning ability – a quality rather lacking in Spurs' armoury until then – failed to make much impression on their overall performance. Unlike the previous season, when their home form let them down, this time it was Spurs' away form which was dis-

appointing, and the club slipped to 14th, scoring a meagre 52 goals while conceding 62.

The season was, however, memorable for one match: Spurs' third round FA Cup victory over Manchester United in yet another titanic struggle between the two clubs. United had beaten Spurs in the previous season's quarter-final replay, knocked them out of the current season's League Cup after two hectic second round legs, and here they were again, poised for their sixth cup meeting in two seasons after United had forced another 1-1 draw and another Old Trafford replay.

Ardiles had often been quoted about his dream of appearing in a Wembley final, but it seemed the chance had once again eluded him. And the prospect of a Spurs victory looked even more improbable when, midway through the Old Trafford match, goalkeeper Milija Aleksic, who had made a brilliant reflex save from Sammy McIlroy earlier in the game, was stretchered off with serious chest and head injuries after a collision with Joe Jordan. But after 'the save of the season', as Aleksic's effort was later voted by the BBC, came 'the goal of my life' by Osvaldo Ardiles.

With Glenn Hoddle in goal for the injured Aleksic, and the game heading for a second replay after 119 minutes without a goal from either side, Villa received the ball on the edge of the United penalty area. What happened next was a piece of South American magic, pure and simple. As Ardiles said: 'Most English players would have gone to the bye-line and crossed. But I knew Ricky's play. I knew he wanted to lay the ball back and I darted back to find space just inside the box. Just as I anticipated, Ricky saw me, rolled the ball back, and I looked up and with all my strength aimed for the top corner.'

The ball curled beyond the despairing Bailey and into the exact spot Ardiles had picked. Seconds later the whistle went and jubilant Spurs had won a match they were expected to lose. Victories followed over Swindon and Birmingham, but again the quarter-finals proved the bogey round. In a tense home game against Liverpool, they lost by the only goal, a typical opportunist effort from the edge of the box by Terry McDermott which won the BBC's 'Goal of the Season' award. Ardiles' dream would have to wait another season... but just another season.

Burkinshaw recognised that if his bold experiment was not to fizzle out in anticlimax, if his cherished vision of a truly great Spurs side was to be accomplished with his current squad, time was running out. Ardiles and Villa each had just one more season of their contracts remaining, while Spurs' other prize possession, the richly gifted Glenn Hoddle, was also approaching the end of his contracted period.

Hoddle, so often an enigma with his breathtaking skills alternating with long periods of anonymity, had just enjoyed his most successful season. He increased his work-rate, conquered his frequently criticised habit of fading from matches well before the final whistle, and scored an impressive 22 goals in all. What was remarkable about Hoddle's feat was that not only did he score them playing from midfield, but that so many came from outside the penalty area. The point was never more clearly illustrated than when he scored on

his England debut on 22 November 1979, with a superb 20-yard volley in the 2-0 win over Bulgaria at Wembley.

It was a dream start to an international career, but somehow Hoddle was unable to establish his England place, a fact that puzzled Burkinshaw as much as Hoddle's many admirers. 'He's so good that by now he should be among the world's best,' says Burkinshaw. 'Just talk to Ossie Ardiles. He says that Glenn is one of the best players he had come across in world football, and that's some accolade.' Burkinshaw believes Hoddle should be given an extended run in the international team to give him the chance to realise his potential: 'Glenn needs to come into the England side on a regular basis for a chance to produce two or three top-class performances and get himself established.'

In May 1980, with the backing of Spurs' new chairman, Arthur Richardson, Burkinshaw made the first of two new purchases that took Spurs' spending that summer to £1.5 million. Sidney Wale, who had surprised everyone at the club with his decision to resign from the board at the end of the 1979–80 season, admits that the advent of the million-pound transfer was one of the reasons that caused him to retire from a soccer world he saw becoming increasingly inflationary. An accountant by profession and a sensibly cautious man with money, Wale liked to try to balance the books and he said: 'It alarmed and saddened me to see so many clubs going deeper and deeper into the red.' Ironically one of Wale's last decisions before his retirement and subsequent appointment as the club's life president was to sanction the building of Spurs' £4¼ million stand, an act he acknowledges, looking at clubs such as Chelsea, Sheffield United and Wolves, that could make or break Spurs.

But he said: 'We had little choice with the building of a new stand, although we could have settled for something a little less ambitious and grandiose. The original stand had wooden floors and was a potential fire hazard. The time had come when we had to do something.'

Whatever Wale's reservations about spending huge sums of money on new players, Arthur Richardson had no such inhibitions. Now 78, he is unusual among chairmen in having been a competent player himself, good enough to have a trial for London Schoolboys at one point – though he never appeared for the side as their fixture against Glasgow Schoolboys was called off because of a railway strike. With their new chairman, if there is any truth in the saying that fortune favours the brave, then Spurs reaped an instant dividend. Steve Archibald, bought in May from Aberdeen for £800,000, and Garth Crooks, a £650,000 August arrival from Stoke, struck up an explosive partnership which yielded 46 goals and helped the club to its first major title for eight years. Having correctly diagnosed Spurs' problems in attack, Burkinshaw had gone for two quicksilver strikers, essentially ground players with the ability to play with their backs to goal, fit into the new midfield pattern, turn their marker, and, above all, score goals. In other words players who could profit from the split-second timing of Ardiles' short-ball game.

Archibald's name had been linked with Spurs for some time but the deal wasn't concluded until Aberdeen's shrewd manager, Alec Ferguson, had made certain of only Pittodrie's second Scottish League championship, and thus a hefty transfer fee for his twenty-goal star. England Under-21 striker Crooks had been a consistent scorer for Stoke over the previous three seasons with nearly fifty goals but, with the Potteries club anxious to pay off some of their debts and Spurs looking for a hunting partner for Archibald, a deal was swiftly concluded which meant that, in the best Spurs tradition, the club was once again starting a new season with a couple of exciting and expensive new stars.

Even skipper Steve Perryman, who has seen so many big names come and go in his 14 years with the club, admits Spurs wouldn't be Spurs without their star signings. 'Our fans have come to expect it, I've come to expect it, I think most of the players have come to expect it,' he says. 'It brings an air of excitement to the club, fans talk about it, it brings them in each season and it means they know we're always trying to get things right.'

Crooks and Archibald got things right from the opening day of the season. Crooks marked his debut with a goal in the 2-0 win over Forest, and propelled by his August hat-trick in the 4-3 win over Crystal Palace, Spurs led the First Division for the first time in nine years. But it was in the FA Cup that they enjoyed their finest hour. Says Perryman: 'We'd felt for a couple of seasons that our best chance of success was in the Cup. We knew

our League form wasn't consistent enough to win the First Division but we thought we had the individual talent in the one-off games to go all the way.'

Playing now with short one-twos around the penalty area to the nimble Archibald and Crooks, Spurs had the agility and mobility to go through defences rather than have to battle it out in the air. Defensively, however, they remained suspect, a price they would have to pay for a team so committed to attack. But while Crooks and Archibald were scoring goals, it was a price they could afford.

Tottenham began their Wembley odyssey without Ardiles, who had been given leave of absence to play for Argentina in the Gold Cup in Uruguay in January 1981. In a defensive match at Loftus Road, Spurs were held to a 0-0 draw by a Queen's Park Rangers side hoping to sneak into the fourth round on the break. Rangers went into the return with the same approach, confident that having stretched Spurs' shaky defence on the first occasion they could breach it on the second. But Tottenham opened up their game at White Hart Lane and, though they were clearly not playing with much confidence, scored a decisive 3-1 victory. The game was a personal triumph for winger Tony Galvin, who scored on his return after eight months recovering from a pelvis operation.

Spurs were next drawn at home to Hull, who, despite their Third Division ranking, held out for 84 minutes before succumbing. The match marked the return of Ardiles, though not without a ripple of controversy.

Steve Archibald dribbles between Billy Bonds and Alvin Martin at West Ham during the League Cup quarter-final at Upton Park on Tuesday 2 December 1980. West Ham won 1-0 with a David Cross goal. Archibald, signed from Aberdeen at the beginning of the season, was the club's top scorer in 1980–81 with 25 first-class goals. Between their FA Cup quarter-final defeat by Liverpool in 1980 and the same stage against Chelsea in March 1982, Spurs played 26 Cup ties in London and this game against West Ham was the only one they lost.

In his absence Spurs had gone six games without defeat, including their first victory over Arsenal in four seasons. Ardiles didn't help his case by returning several days late from South America and promptly found himself dropped for the Arsenal match. The matter was quietly forgotten but Ardiles also sounded a warning about his personal future at the club: 'Spurs want me to stay and I want to play for them for another two years. But we can't agree on a new contract. We're not even close on the financial aspects.'

If Galvin was the success of the third round, it was 20-year-old Garry Brooke who was the star of the fourth. Demoted because of Ardiles' return, there was still room on the substitute's bench because of a knee injury sustained by Villa in the tie with Rangers. Brooke, a home-grown youngster with a deceptively powerful shot from a very short backswing, broke Hull's resistance after coming on in place of Ardiles. Brooke was to figure in a rather more important substitution later in the Cup, but on this occasion he gave due warning of his ability by shooting Spurs ahead in the 84th minute and laying on their second for Archibald four minutes later. Even Ardiles was impressed: 'He made the difference. I love the way he plays. He's a brilliant prospect.'

Spurs were drawn at home a second time with a fifth round tie against Coventry, the team much vaunted for having the youngest average age in the First Division. But a week when they had just been denied their first-ever Wembley appearance by West Ham's League Cup semi-final victory was probably not the best of occasions to pitch a team of shell-shocked teenagers against an increasingly confident Spurs. The result was never in doubt with Ardiles, Archibald and Hughton contributing to the 3-1 victory. Spurs were now in the quarter-finals, the round they'd stumbled at in the previous two seasons.

'We'd had Liverpool and Manchester United those times so we were due a bit of luck,' says Perryman. Spurs duly got it when the draw was made: a home tie with Third Division Exeter. 'We knew then that we could win the Cup,' said the captain. Conquerors of Newcastle and Leicester in the previous rounds, Exeter were no pushovers. Indeed it took a second half injury to midfield player Ian Pearson to throw Exeter's defence into sufficient confusion and allow Spurs to score. Perhaps it was only delaying the inevitable since, while they held Spurs at bay for an hour, Exeter seldom looked likely to score themselves. However Spurs could scarcely have relished the prospect of a trip to Exeter's tiny ground – scene of the Leicester and Newcastle defeats – so it brought some considerable relief when Graham Roberts headed them in front. Paul Miller completed what was then a formality and Spurs marched 2-0 victors into the semi-finals.

THE YEAR OF THE COCKEREL

For those who believe in omens, Tottenham Hotspur's progress towards the winning of the hundredth FA Cup was little less than inevitable. It was, after all, the 'Year of the Cockerel', thoughbeit in the Chinese calendar. Then there were the vaguaries of the draw, so unfavourable in the disastrous campaigns between 1974 and 1978, but now producing only one game out of nine away from London. The superstitious pointed to the catalogue of major trophies gathered to White Hart Lane in the first season of each new decade, and any casual observer could point out that Spurs, of all the major clubs, were the only one never to have lost a game at Wembley (a record still

intact after their eighth appearance, in the Charity Shield, in August 1981). Above all else, perhaps, there was Tottenham's amazing propensity for winning major cup finals. This would be their eleventh, and they had previously lost just one out of ten (against Feijenoord in the 1974 UEFA Cup). Spurs had never lost a single-leg cup final, nor any final match played in England. No other club comes near to matching this amazing record, the closest being Forest with six wins out of seven.

Within the dressing-room, however, an overwhelming sense of realism prevailed, primarily because of Keith Burkinshaw's painful experiences seven years earlier. As coach to Newcastle United he had been on the wrong end of the FA Cup's most one-sided post-war final. Liverpool, inspired by Kevin Keegan, had overrun players who had been drained not just by the occasion but also by an over-lengthy and too open-housed preparation.

Determined that his Tottenham of 1981 should not fall into this trap, Burkinshaw established some ground rules in the week leading up to the semi-final against Wolverhampton Wanderers at Hillsborough. One day, but one day only, was set aside for the requirements of television, radio and newspaper reporters, an exercise to protect the squad which was successfully repeated before the final.

At Cheshunt on that final press day, Ricky Villa, an absentee from the Cup since an injury in the third round, confirmed his fitness to return; Steve Perryman chatted happily of his memories of significant Spurs victories over Wolves in the 1972 UEFA Cup final and 1973 League Cup semi-final, while Milija Aleksic pondered on the prospect of his first FA Cup tie since his shuddering, jaw-breaking collision with Joe Jordan at Old Trafford more than a year before.

Semi-finals often live in the memory more for the result than for the quality of the contest. This one, however, transcended the limits normally imposed by the importance and tension of the match. Tony Galvin established the tone with the first incisive break after just four minutes. From his cross Steve Archibald had only to stretch forward to turn the ball over the line for his 25th goal of the season. But, only minutes later, Wolves were level. Andy Gray, patched up on the morning of the match, guided down the type of header that was to trouble Spurs all afternoon and Ken Hibbitt's low shot arrowed inside Aleksic's left-hand post. Yet by half-time Tottenham were back in the lead with a goal that generated some considerable heat. As Osvaldo Ardiles surged purposefully towards the extremities of the penalty area, George Berry's tackle sent him flying *into* the area. The Spurs appeals were for a penalty, the Wolves defenders believed the challenge to be fair. Referee Clive Thomas judged that a foul had been committed, but just outside the box.

Glenn Hoddle could have been excused some relief at the decision. On the morning of the match he had recalled that the last penalty he had missed had been saved by Paul Bradshaw. But now, from seven yards further out, he totally deceived the goalkeeper. Bradshaw's awareness of the danger from a direct shot over the wall sucked him in right behind

Club captain Steve Perryman and Villa's Tony Morley contest the Spurs' right flank during a First Division game on Saturday 5 September 1981. Villa won 3-1, Ricky Villa scoring the only home goal against his namesakes. Keith Burkinshaw says of Perryman: 'He's just as important as Ardiles or Archibald. The big clubs . . . Leeds, Liverpool . . . they've all enquired about him at some time. They'd take him tomorrow. He knows the game inside-out and can apply that knowledge on the field. The other players know this and listen when he talks.'

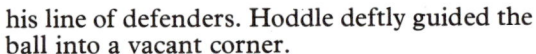

his line of defenders. Hoddle deftly guided the ball into a vacant corner.

In the second half the tempo understandably dropped, only to reach a new crescendo in the final minute of normal time. Television's much-used replay of the central incident clearly showed that in a tackle on Hibbitt, by unlikely Hoddle of all ironies, the ball had been played well before the man if, indeed, the man had ever been touched at all. The tackle was entirely fair. Referee Thomas, without the aid of technological assistance and from a different angle, signalled dramatically for a penalty. Mayhem followed. Archibald and Ardiles argued their claims of injustice to such lengths that they might have been sent off, instead of merely becoming two of the game's eight cautioned players. Burkinshaw intervened to pacify his team before the start of extra-time. Meanwhile Willie Carr had produced an unerring touch from the spot, remarkable circumstances for his first goal of the season. The newspapers the following day were full of admissions – from Hibbitt that it was natural to fall in the area when tackled, from Wolves manager John Barnwell that the game was 'professional' and teams had to do what they had to do, particularly in the closing minutes of a semi-final when they were a goal down. No-one questioned that Clive Thomas had been deceived.

Neither side could muster their flagging resources to settle the tie in the additional thirty minutes, but Tottenham's desperate disappointment was partially mollified by the venue for the replay. At Highbury, it

was virtually a home match. Shortly before the replay's kick-off came significant news on the Wolves team sheet; this time the battle-scarred Gray had not made it, and his influence would inevitably be missed. Soon after the start, Garth Crooks picked up a ball that Wolves should have cleared and Tottenham established a lead that was rarely threatened. On the stroke of half-time the same striker settled the outcome in glorious fashion. Hoddle released a through pass of stunning accuracy and Crooks provided a sprinter's pace and a perfect finish. The final goal belonged to Villa, from a lazy swing of his left foot some thirty yards out that emphasised the latent power of the Argentinian, a power that was too often hidden. So uncertain was his future at the time, it could have provided an epitaph for his days in English football. As it turned out it was just a rehearsal for an even greater spectacular.

WEMBLEY AGAIN

Villa and Ardiles thus became the first two Argentinians to play in an FA Cup final, with Manchester City the opposition after surprising favourites Ipswich Town 1-0 in the other semi-final at Villa Park. Keith Burkinshaw kept faith with his semi-final selection, which meant a Wembley disappointment for important squad members like Don McAllister, Gordon Smith, the injured John Lacy and, particularly, Barry Daines in his testimonial year. So often playing the bridesmaid to victorious goalkeepers, in all those years he had still won nothing of note. The green jersey went to Milija Aleksic, just

past his thirtieth birthday, a self-confessed 'nervy player' who could draw confidence, though, from a Wembley appearance nine years earlier for Stafford Rangers in the FA Trophy final when he kept a clean sheet and Rangers beat Barnet 3-0. Steve Perryman, unselfishly accepting any role if it suited the team, had now been switched to right-back and had just broken the club appearance record previously held by Pat Jennings. Chris Hughton, naturally right-sided, was happier at left-back, though he worried that his only attack of cramp had come at Wembley when playing for the Republic of Ireland fifteen months earlier.

The centre of the defence had come under continual scrutiny in a season in which Tottenham's attractive philosophies had often been at the expense of a vulnerability at the back. The frailty had arguably owed more to their style of play than to individual weaknesses, but persistent pre-match comments on defensive problems exerted extra pressure on the two young centre-backs. At twenty-two Paul Miller had risen from the ranks of the apprentices, and had won back his place just at the right time, before the third round. Alongside him Graham Roberts, a year younger, had proved a versatile acquisition from Weymouth in his first full League season, and was desperate to show Southampton, Bournemouth and Portsmouth how wrong they had been to discard him. Roberts' selection added a romantic note to the hundredth final. Thirteen months earlier he had been working as a fitter in a shipyard with only the memory

of a 1973 appearance at Wembley to cherish
... as a ballboy!

In midfield Osvaldo Ardiles was living out a dream held since he had watched the 1979 final between Arsenal and Manchester United, a sentiment that provoked a highly successful record which swelled the funds of the players' pool of commercial earnings from their achievements. References to Ossie going all trembly and Tott ... ing ... ham can probably bear omission from the story, though the demands of the players' pool did bring forth some unflattering comments; *The Observer* suggested that Ossie's knees had probably gone trembly at the thought of the demands (into four figures) for player interviews. Unlike Ardiles, Ricky Villa had not been selected for the 1978 World Cup final and, surprised that he had bounded back so quickly from three months absence with injury, he described the prospect of the final as the greatest day of his career.

To the right in midfield of the two South Americans Glenn Hoddle could point to two unusual statistics. He had scored in both his Wembley internationals for England, and had contributed a goal in each of his last four games against Manchester City. Hoddle's personal situation within the club led to an even greater desire for victory from Tottenham followers; many believed that a place in Europe the following season would persuade him to decline a number of rich European clubs to whom he would be available at the end of his contract. In the event, all was to be well on that front.

Tony Galvin attracted much less publicity than Hoddle as the final approached, yet his role in the pattern of play had become barely less important. His commitment and energy on the left showed no signs of a major groin operation at the start of the season, although it still gave him considerable pain. The younger brother of a professional, Leeds' and Hull's Chris Galvin, Tony had arrived in the big-time via a Russian degree at Hull University and Goole Town of the Northern Premier League – which was no doubt a unique combination.

For Steve Archibald and Garth Crooks, the Cup campaign provided a splendid climax to a season in which their talents had blended superbly. The investment of almost a million and a half pounds for their services, from Aberdeen and Stoke respectively, had produced its dividends in goals from the quiet, Scotsman and the articulate, ebullient Crooks, who never seemed happier than when leading the singing on the team coach. The substitute's shirt went to Garry Brooke, who had marked his first full league game in December with two goals against Southampton. Now twenty, his development had been aided by a spell on loan in Sweden, and coming off the bench he had already contributed a number of impressive performances.

In the knowledge that Tottenham had never lost a game at Wembley, Keith Burkinshaw took his side away to the seclusion of the Ponsbourne Hotel in Hertfordshire, where the club's own security force protected their privacy. So settled was the base that the manager could happily slip back to his own nearby home on the night before the big game. As usual the television cameras provided the

players with a diversion from the pressures, the highlight being a Friday evening link-up between Villa and Ardiles and their families in Argentina.

Saturday morning was a time to keep to routines. Assistant manager Peter Shreeves drove off to Cheshunt to supervise a light training session preferred by Perryman, Miller and Aleksic. The rest of the squad with Mike Varney, the physiotherapist, at the helm set off for a gentle stroll around the extensive grounds of the hotel. At 1pm they left for the forty-minute drive which transferred them from the hotel's tranquility to the electricity of the greatest occasion in the domestic game. The occasion was more significant than usual, for it was the 100th final and it was fortunate that the draw had brought together two of the game's greatest names and provided a London v Lancashire clash for such a historic match.

Manchester City, meanwhile, were crossing London on their journey north from their headquarters at the Selsdon Park Hotel in Surrey. David Bennett, the young striker who had vowed never to go to the Empire Stadium until he played there, had survived a rigorous examination on a thigh strain, and took his place in the team which had come alive since the November arrival of John Bond in the manager's chair. His side was also that which had won the semi-final: Joe Corrigan, Ray Ranson, Nicky Reid, Tommy Caton and Bobby McDonald, Tommy Hutchison, Steve Mackenzie, Gerry Gow and Paul Power, Dave Bennett and Kevin Reeves, with Tony Henry as substitute.

History will record that the one hundredth FA Cup final lived up to its billing, but not before it threatened to fall horribly flat. The events of Saturday 9 May lasted wearily for two hours with the most memorable experience being that of Tommy Hutchison, who became only the second man ever to score for both sides in a Cup final. City began with the midfield industry that had stifled Ipswich in the semi-final, not to mention the enthusiastic tackling of Gerry Gow. On a pitch dampened by morning rain their cohesive effort created an atmosphere in which the skills of Hoddle and Ardiles were not allowed to flourish. Archibald and Crooks were left isolated, their supply cut off. Without being able to use their possession to dominate, City could still stifle Spurs and deserved the lead they edged into on the half-hour. Hutchison's superb near-post header produced a goal in the same unlikely vein as that of Trevor Brooking's which had won the Cup for West Ham United a year earlier. Most neutrals saw the comparisons being exact, that City would sneak it 1-0 despite Spurs having been everyone's favourites.

Keith Burkinshaw recalls the half-time discussion: 'We felt that they couldn't keep running like that. We had to make sure we played through the middle of the park. We didn't do it enough, though give credit to Manchester City – they didn't give us any space.' As Tottenham initiated some improvements in the second half, they clearly owed nothing to Villa, an anonymous figure to both his own dismay and to that of the millions watching the match live in Argentina. Brooke's arrival in his place offered a perkier alternative, and the replaced Argentinian sought to hide

LEFT: *Graham Roberts seems almost to be protecting the body of a fallen colleague at White Hart Lane late in 1981. Rejected by his three local south coast clubs (Southampton, Bournemouth and Portsmouth), he eventually joined Spurs from Weymouth for £35,000, the record fee paid to any non-League club for a player.*

LEFT BELOW: *Ricky Villa bursts between Alan Devonshire and Billy Bonds at Upton Park, perfectly illustrating the combination of speed and strength which enabled him to score the winner in the 1981 FA Cup final. He joined Spurs from Racing Club of Buenos Aires and, until the transfer of Diego Maradona, was the most costly player in Argentinian football history. Oscar Arce, an Argentinian coaching at Sheffield United, provided the first link in the chain that was to bring Villa and Ardiles to White Hart Lane.*

TOP RIGHT: *The aggressive side of Glenn Hoddle; Ardiles' arrival was a great plus for the England midfield player. 'Glenn has shown greater maturity since they arrived,' said Burkinshaw a few months later, 'He's really begun to turn it on. Ardiles thinks he's a must for England.'*

OPPOSITE RIGHT: *Hoddle brings the ball away from England colleague Bryan Robson, then with West Bromwich Albion.*

OPPOSITE BOTTOM: *Ricky Villa takes on Gordon Cowans.*

THIS PAGE CENTRE: *Garry Brooke gets in a fierce left-foot shot at Middlesbrough. Another local, born in Bethnal Green, he scored the vital goal against Hull in the fourth round of the 1980–81 Cup run.*

THIS PAGE BOTTOM: *Tony Galvin contests possession with Geoff Palmer of Wolves.*

THIS PAGE TOP: *Trainer Johnny Wallis, manager Keith Burkinshaw and physio Mike Varney contemplate in the dug-out before kick-off. Burkinshaw had a relatively undistinguished career as a professional, as he recalls: 'As a 15-year-old I went to Wolves. When you were 17 they decided whether or not they would take you on – they decided against me. So I went to a Midland League club called Denaby United for about 13 weeks when Liverpool took me as a full-time pro. I was also working down the pits at the time. I was at Liverpool for four years (including two on national service) but still in the reserves so I asked for a transfer and went to Workington for eight years. Ken Furphy was manager and we got promotion. After he left I took over as manager for 3 or 4 months, but left after a disagreement with the club and went to Scunthorpe with Freddie Goodwin. After three years I ended up as acting manager but at 33 cartilage trouble made me pack up as a player and I went to Newcastle as a coach for Joe Harvey.'*

his disappointment in the dressing-room rather than watch the remaining minutes of what he was sure would be Tottenham's first FA Cup final defeat. His lonely and very public walk, which ended tearfully in the dressing-room, had reached the mouth of the tunnel when he checked to watch a free-kick ten minutes from time.

With one hand on the Cup, Manchester City lost that grip in a freak moment. Just as, in the semi-final, the threat of Hoddle at free-kicks produced an irrational response from the Wolves defence, this time it was Hutchison who opted to move from his alloted defensive task to run behind the wall and cover the swerve round the outside of the line of defenders. His reading of Hoddle's intentions was exactly right, but with Corrigan covering any danger from the free-kick, the goalkeeper was left stranded as the ball spun off Hutchison's shoulder and into the other corner. Ten minutes from being crowned the hero, Hutchison's unnecessary intervention had made him at least part villain.

The most relieved player in the ground was the one who had just left the pitch. Gradually Ricky Villa swallowed his pride and, by extra-time, had marched back to the bench. On the field the additional period produced little to remember, and John Bond lamented at the end of the affair: 'We could have had penalties, or even played until somebody scored, though it might have ended up two-a-side the way everyone was dropping in extra-time. Everybody was wandering around not knowing what to do. I think that if a game of this importance, with a crowd of this size, ends in a draw, it is an anti-climax.' It was only the second Wembley FA Cup final ever to need a replay.

On the coach back to the post-match banquet at London's Hilton Hotel, Garth Crooks quickly broke the atmosphere by encouraging raucous renditions of *Ossie's Dream*. Graham Roberts, who had lost two front teeth in a collision with Chris Hughton, suffered further pain when an emergency stop by the bus induced a bout of cramp. At the front Keith Burkinshaw was already affirming, despite the poor form of Villa, that his side would be unchanged when the battle continued.

The first ever Wembley replay of an FA Cup final took place on Thursday 14 May, with a controversial edict from the Football Association that penalties would decide things if the match was again drawn after extra-time. With England at home to Brazil on the Tuesday night, and the European Cup Winners Cup final between Dinamo Tbilisi and Carl Zeiss Jena televised from Dusseldorf on the Wednesday, there was enough alternative football to take the limelight from the players for a welcome few days. Recharged, Tottenham Hotspur and Manchester City produced an enthralling contest, arguably one of the great finals.

This time both sides scored inside the opening ten minutes, the first from Villa, whose show of temperament at his substitution five days earlier had looked like a thoroughly unwise snub to his manager. But Burkinshaw's wise reaction to the affair could not have produced a better ending. Villa's goal had its roots in the work of Ardiles, whose attempted shot struck Archibald. The Spurs leading scorer, who was to have no personal good fortune in either match, swung quickly to shoot. The ball ricochetted off the body of Corrigan straight to Villa and, from just outside the six-yard box, he drove it straight into the unprotected net.

Steve Mackenzie's equaliser now lies buried among a welter of memories of this marvellous match. In the context of most other games it would have lived as the abiding memory. Mackenzie, hauled into prominence two years earlier as a seventeen-year-old when Malcolm Allison paid £250,000 before he had played a league game, must have made his mentor smile in satisfaction at a goal of the highest calibre. From just outside the Spurs' penalty area, Hutchison nodded the ball down and Mackenzie's right-footed volley sped past Aleksic. It was to be City's strange fate in this final to score two of the best goals ever seen in an FA Cup final – by Hutchison and Mackenzie – and still finish with the losers' medals.

Though Corrigan continued to be the busier goalkeeper, it was City who made the next inroad early in the second half. Bennett's speed uncovered a soft centre in the defence and Miller and Hughton converged for a combined challenge that demolished the progress of the City striker. Referee Keith Hackett from Sheffield awarded only the fifth penalty in the history of Wembley FA Cup finals. Kevin Reeves joined the names of Mutch, Shimwell, Allen and Blanchflower and kept up the unfailing record by placing his shot to the goalkeeper's left with sufficient power, though Aleksic guessed the right way.

So lethargic in adversity in the first match, Tottenham now produced a response far more in keeping with the quality of their players. Hoddle had already enjoyed a much more productive game when he lit the flame under a grand finale. A controlled lofted pass caught City coming out and found Archibald onside. The Scot was not able to fully digest the offering but the defenders could not recover, and the crumbs were devoured by Crooks for his 22nd goal of the season. Twenty minutes left and at two goals each the ebbs and flows of this captivating match had pushed the miserable memories of Saturday far from the mind.

What followed has now passed into the folklore of the competition; a denouement in the tradition of the Matthews final of 1953 and Everton's comeback in 1966. The very nature of the winning goal would have deserved all its accolades, but the Cup so often reaches beyond the pure world and drama of football to create an extra dimension. Now the same brooding, bearded Latin America figure who had sulked away to the Wembley dressing-room the previous Saturday was to place his name on that roll-call of legendary figures whose deeds will be remembered long after they have gone.

In the 76th minute Ricky Villa collected the ball on the Spurs left outside the penalty area, a long way from, and no direct threat to, Joe Corrigan's goal. Caton and Ranson were the defenders caught momentarily off their guard by the audacity of an Argentinian who was in no mood to settle for a safe square pass. The two young City players were entangled as Villa worked a magical web, with sure-footed changes of direction this way and that and which were coupled with the physical power

OPPOSITE TOP: Villa, Garth Crooks and Ardiles take on West Ham's midfield.
OPPOSITE BOTTOM: Tony Galvin and Glenn Hoddle tackle Manchester City's Ray Ranson in the first of the 1981 Cup finals on 9 May. A tough midfield struggle ended, fairly, at 1-1 after an exhausting 120 minutes.

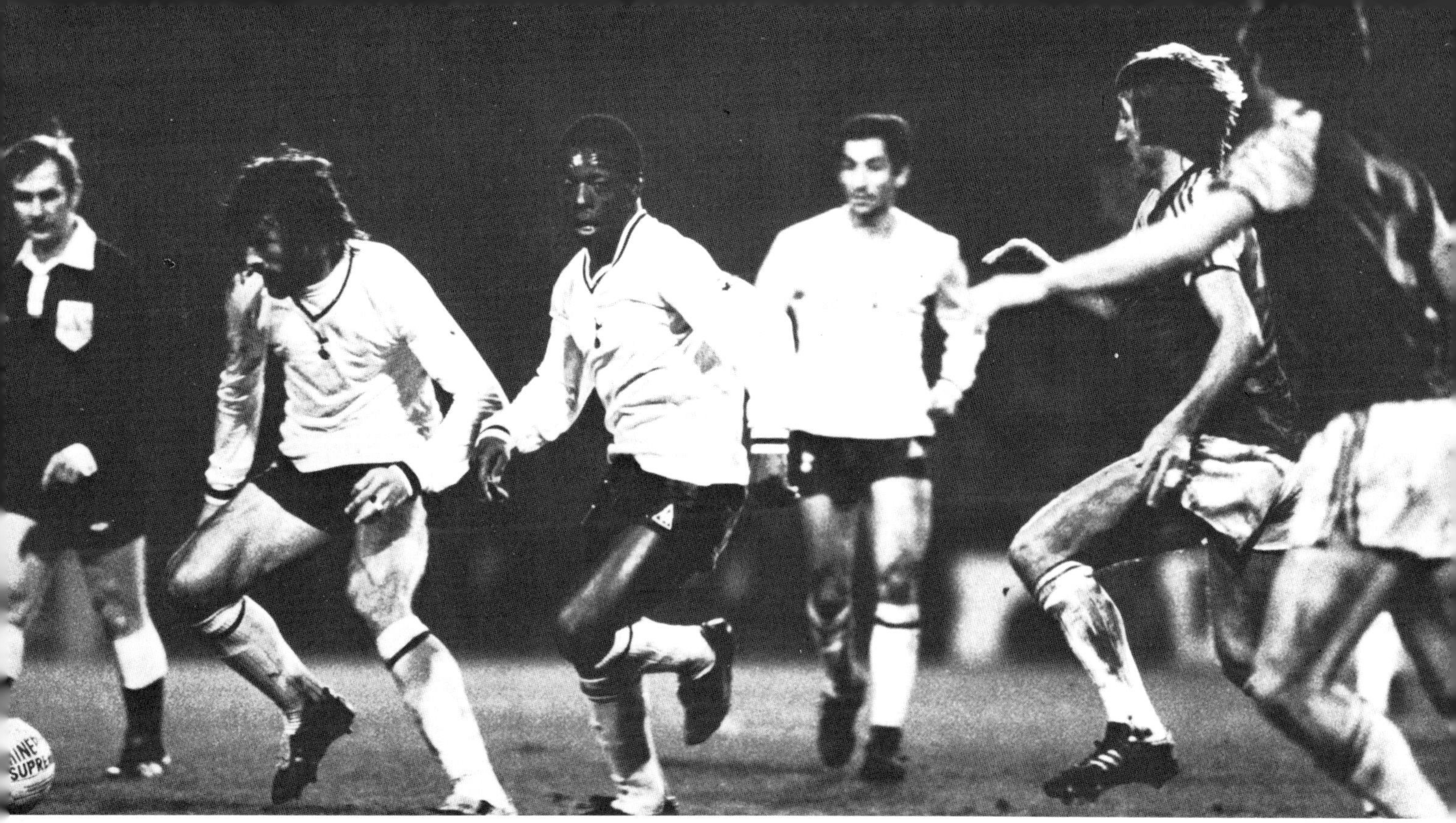

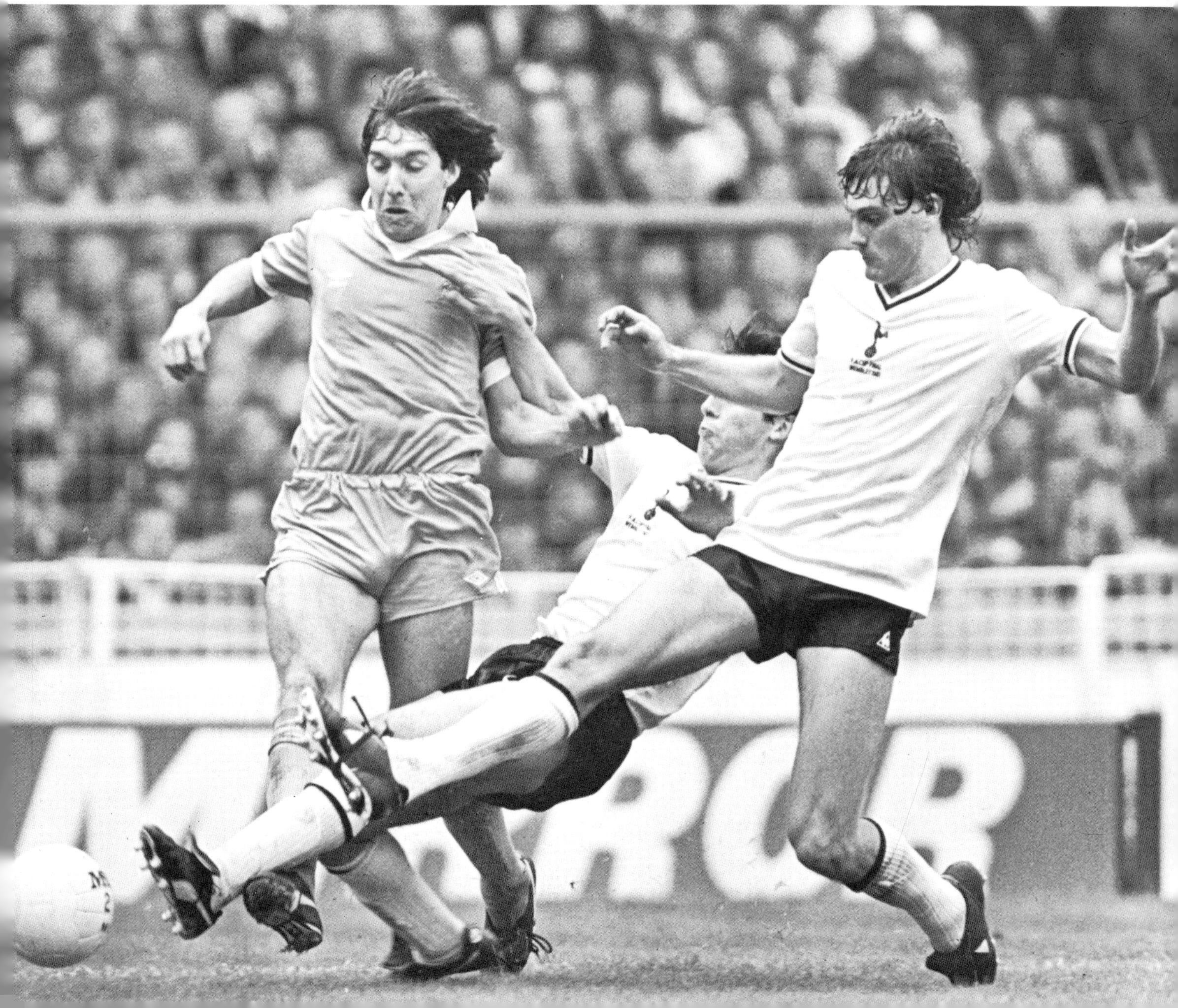

Tottenham's somewhat fortuitous equalising goal in the 81st minute of the first game at Wembley in 1981. Just as Spurs' fans were beginning to believe that they were about to witness Tottenham's first ever FA Cup final defeat, their side was awarded a free-kick on the edge of the penalty area. As Hoddle stood over the ball, City winger Tommy Hutchison took up his appointed position on the left-hand edge (TOP) of the Manchester City wall. But as Hoddle took the kick (CENTRE) Hutchison ran behind the wall, presumably to cover any shot which might curl into the top right corner. In fact, at this stage, there was no danger; keeper Joe Corrigan had that side of the goal well protected and the free-kick was going wide. A few moments later (BOTTOM) the ball struck Hutchison on the angle of shoulder and head and was neatly deflected into the other corner of the net. Joe Corrigan had already made a safety dive and could do nothing. Hutchison thus became only the second man (Bert Turner of Charlton in 1946 was the other) to score for both sides in an FA Cup final, and at a time when he must have begun to think that his excellent first-half diving header had won the trophy for City.

that has always made him such a difficult player to knock off the ball. Corrigan advanced to try to halt the trail of devastation, but Villa retained his balance and took advantage of the goalkeeper committing himself: 3-2. Wembley roared its appreciation of a superb solo goal, and Villa raced away totally unstoppable in his triumph. It was not that it was just an outstanding goal – more, it was a courageous goal. To have the courage to hold onto that ball with 15 minutes of an FA Cup final replay left – that was the ultimate significance of the moment (see artwork on page 67).

'It's great after last Saturday,' enthused Villa, whose command of English was now vastly improved from the silent days of his arrival in 1978 alongside the more talkative Ardiles. 'The ball seemed stuck to my feet. I don't know how many players I beat but the thrill was terrific when the ball went into the net. I just wanted to run anywhere. I say thank you to the manager. He took big chance on me for the semi-final. Before tonight I have not much luck in England, I think.'

Steve Perryman, who had begun to worry as to whether the side would ever win a major trophy under his leadership, collected the FA Cup from Princess Michael of Kent, a reward for his twelve years of unquestioned loyalty to Tottenham Hotspur. Keith Burkinshaw, controlled in the fashion of his native Yorkshire, had seen his team selection vindicated: 'How can you leave out a player of his quality? Ricky showed all his skill tonight. He was pleased that I had so much faith in him. But above all I am thrilled for our fans who have waited a long time for success and now they have their pride back. They did not desert us when we slipped into the Second Division. I hope we have repaid them for their loyalty.'

John Bond retained his dignity, and humour, in defeat: 'This was a magnificent match in terms of what English football is all about. Whatever I feel personally it's been a tremendous night for the game. But you know I said right at the start of the season that it might be Tottenham's year for the Cup. For once I wish I hadn't been right.'

THE CENTENARY SEASON

The centenary season, 1981–82, started in tremendous style. Though attendances were dropping elsewhere in the country, Spurs had become the League's biggest drawing card. Their football was often a delight to watch. Patrick Barclay said in *The Guardian* after one of the season's first games, a Cup final repeat at Maine Road, that: 'If every team played like Tottenham Hotspur, football's only problem would be in pacifying the hordes of supporters unable to get into packed grounds. They bring beauty to the game, and people like that. If all the public wanted was to see one side win and another lose, they would go to the nearest park and save money.'

John Bond was no less complimentary: 'However long you look at football and think of all the great teams, you won't find any who could knock it about better than Tottenham did today. They are not necessarily a great team, they might not win the Championship because they are a bit vulnerable when they haven't got the ball, but they are great for the game.'

Spurs' two major signings before the season began had been the England goalkeeper Ray Clemence, for £300,000, and the Welsh international defender Paul Price from Luton.

With Corrigan already committed, Garth Crooks slides home the rebound from a Steve Archibald shot and Spurs draw level again at 2-2 in the 1981 Cup final replay on Thursday 14 May. This was the first time that an FA Cup final replay had ever been played at Wembley. Indeed, it was only the second replay that had been necessary since the stadium was built nearly 60 years before. The players, left to right, are: Ranson, Perryman, Caton, Hutchison, Corrigan, Miller, Crooks and Archibald.

RIGHT: *A hair-raising moment for Ricky Villa as he is tackled by Nicky Reid during the Argentinian's depressingly poor first Cup final at Wembley. Replaced by Garry Brooke, Villa was observed by millions making a long, lonely and rather humiliating walk back to the dressing-room before Spurs equalised and gave him and his side hope of a replay. Keith Burkinshaw's decision to retain Villa in the same starting line-up for the replay was magnificently vindicated five days later.*
RIGHT BELOW: *Tommy Caton and Garth Crooks contest a high ball during the first game, while Osvaldo Ardiles appears to be considering the rather unorthodox use of the elbow by the Manchester City defender.*

Unfortunately Price was injured early on and Clemence took time to settle into a new defensive pattern, having left such a familiar one behind on Merseyside.

This was never clearer than at Wembley for the 1981 Charity Shield, when his uncharacteristically poor handling helped Aston Villa achieve a 2-2 draw they probably did not deserve. The clubs shared the trophy and Spurs continued their amazing Wembley record – this was the eighth game they had played there and they had yet to be defeated. Clemence also set up a personal record that day – it was his sixth appearance in the season's annual opener. Spurs had now contested the annual Shield (both the Charity and its forerunner the Sheriff of London's) on 8 occasions, winning 5 and drawing 2.

The Charity Shield was also notable for the display of a Spurs reserve, Mark Falco, who scored his side's two goals. Deputising for Garth Crooks, who had undergone a cartilage operation, Falco went on to score nine goals in the season's first twelve games, before suffering a ligament injury himself.

Falco's most notable performance was in Amsterdam, where he scored twice in the highly creditable 3-1 Cup Winners Cup win over once mighty Ajax. The club was concerned that its first European trip since the disaster at Rotterdam should be back to the Netherlands – it would have been preferable to play rather further away where fewer of the troublesome element could afford to travel. There was happily little trouble, though it is a comment on the current interpretation of the term that Jeff Powell could write in the *Daily Mail*: 'Thirteen arrests, mostly for window-breaking and car-scratching, one unconfirmed minor stabbing and the separation of two small groups of squabblers on the terraces were no more than a routine night's work for the Dutch police.'

A £4 MILLION INVESTMENT

The return at White Hart Lane was no less easy – Spurs winning 3-0. Little Dundalk, runners-up in the League of Ireland, proved far tougher opposition in the second round of the Cup Winners Cup, holding Tottenham 1-1 in Ireland and going down to a single goal from Garth Crooks in the return. It was enough, however, to put Spurs through to the quarter-finals in March 1982.

Although Tottenham's signing of Ray Clemence received the summer's headlines, far more significant to the club was the fact that Hoddle, Villa and Ardiles had all renewed their contracts. Vice-chairman Geoff Richardson rightly pointed out that: 'In the current climate, with some players looking to European salaries and with others exercising their new freedom to move where they like at the end of a contract, this was as important as signing three new stars.'

The rewards for staying, however, were not inconsiderable. The Spurs' accounts showed that five of the club's employees, almost certainly including the midfield trio, had earned £50,000 in the previous year, though this did include bonuses for the Cup win.

While the side entertained on the pitch, though stuttering at home (a string of home defeats late in 1981 intrigued rather than concerned most fans), the club's administration was devoting its energies to a far bigger investment than any single player had ever represented.

The building of the new West Stand had rapidly acquired far greater significance than that of simply more comfortable accommodation. As trends in attendances and revenue became more worrying in the late 1970s and early 1980s, Spurs' decision to spend £4¼ million became a clear statement about what lay ahead.

'At some point in the reasonably near future, we could see some form of Super League in Britain. It's essential that Spurs stake their claim for a place in that League,' says Geoff Richardson. 'Having a good team is a major part of it, and we're doing our bit financially on that score in buying the likes of Archibald, Crooks, Price and Clemence. But everything else about the club is like the team as well. If we stand still we'll go into decline.'

The new stand was built partially by choice and partially by necessity. The old stand was 75 years old, largely wooden, and its revenue earning capacity was limited. The new stand is expected to bring in between two and three times the revenue per seat as its predecessor, before allowing for inflation, and the increase in ticket prices is only part of the reason.

'I'll bet that people said Charles Roberts was crazy when the club started to build the old stand in 1905,' says chairman Arthur Richardson, 'but look what a tremendous asset it proved to be. Yes, it's a risk, but so is any major commercial decision.'

The structure is designed to have a far wider range of uses than is usually to be found at a football ground. There are enough entertainment and club facilities for the holding of conferences, dinners and social functions, and the facilities are also perfect for sponsors to use on match days and during the week. The ground's location, right on a main road on the outskirts of London, is also firmly in its favour. Spurs have always been part of their local community, and are now a solidly established mature member of Tottenham society.

The club owns most of the land around the ground, the neighbouring Chanticleer restaurant, two 'Spurs' Shops', the club lottery and a travel agency. This is a strong commercial base for any institution, and one they intend to develop further with the new stand as the centre-piece and symbol of future plans.

Holding 6,500 people, it contains 72 boxes (more than in any other stand) which sell at £10,000 per annum for a three year lease, a Centenary Club for a limited number of members and a whole floor of bars, restaurants and club rooms. 'We were obviously aware of what happened at Chelsea, and of the problems that still worry Wolves and Nottingham Forest, but we looked at every new stand that has been built in the country in recent years and, we hope, combined the best features of all of them,' says Geoff Richardson. 'We can rarely attract crowds of more than 50,000 nowadays, and that will be the new capacity of the ground. Obviously we hope that families will come, that fathers will bring sons and wives. From a financial point of view, the club has to offer the right facilities at a good price to the committed supporter. That will please everyone – I'm sure our own fans don't want to see a bankrupt club either. Nowadays it's

ABOVE: *The Cup final replay of 1981 was to be Ricky Villa's day. In the 7th minute Steve Archibald was stopped on the 6-yard line by Joe Corrigan and the rebound fell easily for Villa (number 5) to slot past a helpless Tommy Caton. A quarter of an hour from time, with the score 2-2, Villa dribbled the ball in from the left touch-line, weaved his way past* (TOP *and* CENTRE) *Ranson, Caton and Reid, and* (BOTTOM) *drew Joe Corrigan out far enough to slip the ball into the net. It was one of Wembley's truly great goals and one certainly fit to win the 100th FA Cup final.*

essential to do everything possible for everyone who does want to watch football. We have even installed facilities in the boxes for action replays on their individual TV screens, and we'll have TV cameras in the stands covering every match.'

'Yes, we've gone into overdraft to build it,' says Arthur Richardson, 'though it isn't substantial, and the bank (Barclays) have been marvellous. They treat us like any other commerical concern – we showed them what we proposed, what it would cost and what the return was likely to be. They could see the financial sense and provided all the backing we needed. We did our homework for 18 months before we began and we've had no financial surprises since.'

'Even the recession has had its blessings,' says Geoff Richardson, 'There have been no cost over-runs and the whole thing was complete just about on time.' If fans are concerned about the money involved reducing what is available for new players, then their fears are almost certainly unfounded. 'We've never told a manager he couldn't have a player because there wasn't the money, nor do we intend to now,' says Arthur Richardson. And Nicholson and Burkinshaw confirm this: 'I never had anything but co-operation from the board when I was manager,' says Nicholson, 'They never interfered with who I bought or sold.' The club is, nonetheless, noted throughout the game for its financial prudence and the attitude towards million pound players which has prevailed for the past four years is not likely to alter – which is not to say that Burkinshaw would ever be denied the money to purchase a player clearly worth that amount. 'But I'm glad I wasn't the chairman responsible for making one or two of the million

pound buys we've seen in the last few years,' says Arthur Richardson today.

THE CLUB OFF THE PITCH

History was to suggest the confidence of the Richardsons was misplaced. The stand probably cost £1 million more than they had counted on and, combined with a downturn in attendances and results, it was ultimately to cause them to lose control of the club. Tottenham Hotspur is not a small organisation by any standards, with a turnover in excess of £3 million per annum and a staff of 80. It is in the manager's office (traditionally on the corner of the High Road) that the decisions which have really shaped the club's history have always been made. So much must have happened there in the century since Spurs first used that same building as their headquarters. Outside the telephone never stops ringing and the office staff never stop working. At Tottenham, for the past three and a half decades, there has always been a big match the next week, and there have always been numerous people who must have tickets for it, must interview the players, must have autographed photographs, or who just want to stand and watch.

The club now has a permanent gateman, match days or not, to keep away the merely curious. Though the staff will eventually move into the new stand, the old gates will stay, a reminder of games gone by. How often, one wonders, have they closed on the disappointed, a full-house already inside – and how often will they do so in the future? 'The biggest crowd we ever had *outside* the ground,' remembers Geoff Richardson, 'was probably for the fifth round replay against Sunderland in the Double year. I'd be prepared to bet well over 100,000 tried to get in that day.' In more

recent times, the crowd that flocked from all over London to see Arsenal take the first leg of *their* Double on 3 May 1971, so ironically at White Hart Lane, was probably as big.

On match days the total swells to over 400 with stewards, gatemen, attendants, programme sellers and doormen. Nor does this include the catering staff, who are employed by an outside contractor, and who serve full meals in the restaurants in the new stand as well as in the 72 boxes if the occupants order them.

The Tottenham management has traditionally been nothing if not low key. Unlike many other clubs, it never had a history of shareholder revolts or power struggles. Starting from the days of Charlie Roberts and Arthur Turner, the shares had tended to be concentrated in relatively few hands and there was a remarkable continuity in the directorships. New faces were not invited to join the board unless they were very well known to at least one board member and, certainly since the First World War, directors were not asked for personal guarantees or promises to invest in the club. At least two directors in the post-war period reached 90 before they retired. As the building of the new stand gradually put pressure on the finances of the club, these traditions came under fire. The challenge to the board in 1982 was actually the first in living memory.

Tottenham had, in fact, entered the history books for legal and commercial reasons as well as footballing ones. One of the classic precedents in company law involved its shareholders. The club had refused to transfer shares from one person to another and the decision was challenged in the courts (this was around the time of the Second World War). The courts found in Spurs' favour and the case was, for many years, used as a precedent by companies who also wished to control the ownership of their shares. In the end, it seemed to be

something of a double-edged sword for the board in 1982. They had, not unreasonably perhaps, presumed that his ruling gave them security from an outside bidder, but they reckoned without the determination of at least two potential shareholders who found a clever way to circumvent the original ruling.

From the boardroom, the future of the club can only be as secure as the future of the game as a whole. By 1985 the pessimism of the early 1980s had again reared its head, partially as a result of some appalling crowd trouble (little of it involving Spurs), partially because of the seeming inability of the game's administrators to decide on a settled approach to the game's attitude to television. The latter point was critical, for television was a mirror on society like no other since Spurs were founded and football could only really find security in a society where television's role was already central. It was no longer possible to pretend that the game could live without the box ... the fans who had gone would not come back just because games were not televised. Indeed, that would probably distance them even more. It is interesting that the new chairman, Irving Scholar, was invited to be one of the League's negotiators with the television companies in 1985 – evidence of Tottenham's importance in the game and the club's newly recognised business acumen.

Most of the tens of thousands who pour through the turnstiles at White Hart Lane every other week have come to watch *their* team. They assess the club solely by what happens in an hour and three-quarters on a Saturday afternoon and it is probable that few are remotely concerned about what paradoxes lie behind that simple truth. It is sometimes very unfair on most of a club's employees – they may run a near-perfect administration, operate ideal ticket arrangements, have an excellent ground and attractive facilities and still be judged failures because one shot hits a post or because a centre-forward is injured. Football clubs are unusual institutions – they are assessed entirely on the tip of the iceberg, the part that shows on the field.

There can be very few fans who have not wondered what it must be like to play for Spurs, or how those eleven on the pitch managed to get there at all, how they negotiated the minefields to become members of that exclusive club of First Division footballers. To say that the battles of White Hart Lane are won on the school playing fields of Southern England is barely an exaggeration. For the eleven players who turn out for Tottenham Hotspur on a Saturday afternoon are largely the end-product of a development programme which has its roots in the network of scouts who scour the soccer pitches of London and the Home Counties looking for the Spurs of tomorrow.

WINNING YOUR SPURS

The route to a place in the first team takes its course through a pool of some 100 outstanding youngsters who train or play regularly with the club (either as associated schoolboys or on an informal basis), two junior sides comprising a mixture of associated schoolboys, invited players and the club's own dozen or so apprentice professionals, and a reserve team. The juniors, split into under-17 and an under-18, play in the South East Counties League while the reserves play in the Football Combination.

Besides the boys who are recommended by scouts, the club can also take their pick from the hundreds of eager young players who write in every year asking for a trial. With the 1981 FA Cup victory, that figure swelled to more than a thousand in the following twelve months, and each is followed up by the club's youth team coach, Ken Oliver, or his chief schools scout, John Moncur.

Boys who write for a trial are generally sent an official application form asking for details of height, weight, age, school, school team, club team and, crucially, their next five club fixtures. 'If they can name those fixtures,' says Oliver, 'we know they must be playing regular club football and it's at a sufficiently well-organised level for us to have a scout look at the boy.' It's Moncur's job to watch boys himself and generally organise the club's scout network, which, although concentrated in London and the South East where he has seven part-timers working for him, also extends throughout the United Kingdom. With one scout in each of the regions, there are around three dozen people around the country who scout for Spurs on a regular basis and, of course, many more who will occasionally write in with names of players they have seen.

The process of becoming a Spur starts at the age of 14 when, with the mutual written agreement of club, boy, parents and headmaster, comes the first contractual arrangement, associated schoolboy forms. This is a two-year, standard agreement during which the player cannot be approached by another League club. During that period he trains and plays in club friendlies, and, on reaching his 15th birthday, becomes eligible to play in the under-17 side in the South East Counties

League. Up to the age of 15, associated schoolboys can do no more than train with the club and play in the odd friendly. These training sessions are held three times a week and are run by Oliver and two assistants, Dave Lister and the Double-side full-back Ron Henry. Altogether there are usually 40 to 50 associated schoolboys on Spurs' books, many coming from as far afield as Kent for the chance to catch the eye of Oliver and his team.

'Different years throw up different standards,' says Oliver, who has joined the club quite recently. 'But on the whole we know what we're looking for. In inviting boys to become associated schoolboys, we look for skill, awareness, and character. If the standard is down in any one year, we won't take the best of a bad bunch.'

Training takes the form of improving ball skills in one of the club's two indoor ball courts at the Paxton Road End of the ground, or perhaps circuit training to build up leg or upper body muscles in the gymnasium.

From the pool of associated schoolboys, plus those from further afield who have been given trials during the school holidays, the club will invite some half-dozen who are approaching their 16th birthday to take the next step in the ladder, that of becoming an apprentice professional. These are the boys chosen by Oliver and Peter Shreeves (the manager has the final decision) to join the club full-time for a further two-year period. In some cases boys who are not offered AP terms are retained as non-contract players, train with the club two or three times a week and play in either the under-17s or under-18s in the South East Counties League. In addition to their associated schoolboys, Spurs have another 40 or so boys of 16 and over who, being above the school-leaving age, are free to make their own arrangements with the club. Inevitably some are late developers and this second-tier scheme acts as a safety net. Chris Hughton was just such a player, an associated schoolboy who wasn't offered an apprenticeship and who had left school and taken a job as a trainee lift engineer before being offered part-time professional terms at the age of 17.

Clubs are allowed up to 15 APs although, for reasons of economics and the high standards they require, Spurs haven't touched that figure for years. In the past, these apprentices would have been known as groundstaff lads but with the streamlining of the game in the late 1960s and early 1970s, the term apprentice professional was coined for young players between their 16th and 18th birthdays.

Contracts, usually signed at school-leaving age and running for two years, finish on the 18th birthday. Players must then either be offered full professional terms or be released. Although there is an old maxim that footballers are born and not made, clubs like Spurs are always looking to mould any sign of natural talent from the earliest possible age – to stop bad habits before they start. Bill Nicholson has an interesting view on this: 'Really a club should put its best coach with its youngest players. That's when you can teach them the right habits and mould the way they'll play for the rest of their careers. If they still have their bad habits at 23 it's very much harder to do anything about it.'

Schoolboy training is only the first step

towards a career in soccer. The AP is on the staff as a full-time employee of the club, although Oliver hastens to point out that while Spurs' apprentices are expected to do some of the chores like cleaning boots and laying out kit, gone are the days when apprentices were used as cheap labour to do everything from painting the stands to cleaning the toilets. But he does see non-soccer jobs as a test of character: 'A boy who's sloppy or thoughtless in what he does off the pitch is likely to be the same on it,' says Oliver.

Monday for Spurs' first-year APs is back-to-school day. 'Since there is no guarantee they will be offered pro terms, it's important to give them some education which will be of practical use whether they become professional footballers or not,' says Oliver. Over the years the club has come to accept that a general course is more use than some of the ambitious schemes which have been tried in the past. 'The club used to have courses in motor mechanics, but with the best will in the world, doing a course like that only once a week is no benefit unless you have the practical experience to go with it. Now we concentrate on things that are likely to prove useful whatever they do with their careers.'

Lessons, for first year boys only, take place at the Kingsway-Princeton College, King's Cross, which runs special courses for apprentices from various London clubs. 'After their first year, it's not compulsory,' says Oliver. 'Most lads join the club to get away from school, not to go back!'

For the rest of Spurs' squad Monday is a free day. The working week begins in earnest on Tuesday morning when the APs report to White Hart Lane at 8.30am. Working on a rota, two or three pack the squad's training kit in skips and load them on a minivan which takes them to the club's Cheshunt training ground about nine miles north of Tottenham. There the kit is unpacked and laid out, together with the players' boots in readiness for the morning training session which starts at 10.30am.

The rest of the squad make their own way to Cheshunt around 10am and, depending on numbers, split into groups. Oliver takes the apprentices, reserve team coach Robbie Stepney, Peter Shreeves and the new main coach and old Spurs player John Pratt take their respective squads. If there are a fair number of injuries, Stepney and Oliver will sometimes join forces, since this may be the opportunity for some of their promising youngsters to join the senior squad. Injuries to Ricardo Villa and Garth Crooks gave young reserves Mark Falco and Mike Hazard just such a chance in the 1981–82 seasons. 'It would be soul-destroying to do nothing but training exercises,' says Oliver. 'Soccer is what they're here for and that's what they want to play so we always include a practice game of some sort.' At one time the APs would take packed lunches while the senior players might go home or have a cold buffet meal at Cheshunt. But with Keith Burkinshaw's conviction that more time should be spent there – 'Why train indoors when the game we play on Saturday is on grass?' he points out – canteen facilities have been added and players can now eat hot meals.

With the onset of winter, however, training may continue at the club's ball-courts during the afternoon. Here the APs repack the kits at Cheshunt and take it back to White Hart

Lane where it goes straight to the laundry or drying room while they clean all the boots and get a fresh set of kit out for the next day's training. Each apprentice is responsible for four or five other players' training boots and, whereas the club employs a professional boot-man to look after the kit used for competitive matches, the 'Cheshunt boots' are the responsibility of the APs.

Towards the end of the week training sessions are geared more and more to the needs of the first team. The apprentices and the reserves may be used to provide specific opposition tactics for first team practice, or to provide particular crosses or passes for the forwards to head or shoot, or give the goal-keepers particular shots to save. The youth team or reserves might also be asked to copy the style of say Manchester United or Liverpool to enable the first team to work out how they will tackle Saturday's match.

While the professionals usually train only in the morning, the apprentices continue in the afternoon either at Cheshunt or in the ball-courts. For a youngster who is fighting with the problem of linking strength to the physical problems of growing, the two-hour morning and afternoon sessions add up to a hard day. But at around 4.45pm they're free to go, back to their digs or home. For those living in digs, the club has a handful of landladies who every year provide a warm and friendly home to go to.

On Fridays the apprentices stay at White Hart Lane while the rest of the squad's activities are governed by whether they're at home or away the following day. After a few sprints round the cinder border of the White Hart Lane ground, the APs start their final round of chores for the week. The dressing rooms – and there are more than the two in use on match days – have to be washed down and scrubbed, including the cleaning of the duck-boards in the showers. For about an hour every apprentice has to put his back into a succession of menial tasks. Friday is also the day the team-sheet goes up, the chance to see if you've made it into the under-17s, or in the case of former APs like Mark Falco, Mike Hazard or Garry Brooke in recent seasons, the big step into the first team.

Match days start with two South East Counties games on a Saturday morning, sometimes both at Cheshunt, and afternoon games for reserves and first team. Oliver will watch one or both junior games, depending on where they are, and if the first team are at home, he may be joined by Peter Shreeves and any number of the club's training staff. It is the manager's final assessment which determines whether an apprentice is offered full professional terms. That time comes three months before the AP's 18th birthday so that the player, if he is not retained, has that period to try to find either another club or a job outside the game.

It's the success stories of Brooke, Falco, and Hazard, to name the most recent, which show the other young pretenders that the size and wealth of the club need not be a barrier to ambition. And as Oliver emphasises, the training received at Spurs is second to none. 'Even if they don't make it here, we believe they have all got the schooling to make good professionals with another club. But the opportunity in the end must come down to the character and ability of the player himself.'

CUPS AND MORE CUPS

As the centenary season settled down, it seemed to North London that Spurs were contesting one non-stop cup tie.

From the beginning of October through to the middle of February, when the League Cup finalists and FA Cup quarter-finalists were decided, Spurs played 25 games of which 12 were cup ties. They were already in process of establishing a record for modern times when, on February 13, they beat Aston Villa in an FA Cup fifth round tie to establish a run of 23 consecutive cup matches without defeat. This covered three competitions – the FA Cup, the League Cup and the Cup Winners Cup. At this stage their last cup setback had been a League Cup tie at Upton Park on 2 December 1980. Far more remarkable, the last occasion on which Tottenham had been drawn away in a cup tie was in the third round at Queen's Park Rangers on 3 January 1981. They had obviously had to play two-legged matches and semi-finals away from White Hart Lane, but had not otherwise had to travel. Fortune indeed seemed to be favouring them. It must have bought tears to the eyes of the push-and-run side who, between 1953 and 1955, played away in 10 consecutive FA Cup rounds, then a twentieth-century record.

The Centenary Year, 1982, could not have got off to a more dramatic start. After nearly one hundred years of almost totally ignoring each other in the FA Cup, Arsenal and Spurs were drawn together at White Hart Lane in the third round on 2 January. It was to be a one-sided game, Garth Crooks winning it

The magnificent new West Stand nears completion at the end of 1981. Built at a cost of £4¼ million, it is the most expensive structure ever to be added to a League ground (though at £3 million in 1973 Chelsea's probably cost more in real terms) and seats over 6,000 people in remarkable comfort. The 72 boxes (again, more than at any other ground) represent the height of football-watching comfort, with their own dining facilities and private action-replay television available from the club's own cameras. The stand was formally opened by Sir Stanley Rous before the game against Wolves on 6 February 1982. The Wanderers were ideal visitors for they had been the opposition for White Hart Lane's very first League game 74 years before. They also contrived to go down 6-1 with Ricky Villa getting his first hat-trick in England.

with the only goal, as well as hitting a post and bar. It will always be remembered, however, for the manner of the goal. An Ardiles pass gave Crooks the chance of a weakly hit left-footed shot. Jennings, returning to his old stamping ground, had the ball well covered, but it somehow slipped under his arm and dribbled over the line. To make the day thoroughly forgettable for Jennings, he later suffered a groin strain in a wild chase and tackle outside the penalty area with Crooks, had to leave the field and was to be out of the game for months. He said afterwards, with no overstatement: 'It's the worst goal I've let in during the whole of my career.'

The one-sided, rather dull (if extremely satisfying for the home supporters) fixture allowed many to reminisce about the only other occasion the two clubs had met before in the Cup – at the same stage 33 years and two Doubles before. The following day one or two reporters seemed to devote more space to the earlier game than the one they had just witnessed. Said Brian Glanville in the *Sunday Times*: 'On that remote afternoon, Tottenham inexplicably dropped their star inside-forward Eddie Baily, replacing him with an obscure reserve called Harry Gilberg, who did nothing. Ronnie Burgess, their attacking wing-half, ran wild, giving the freedom of the park to Arsenal's Jimmy Logie, who then ran them ragged. Roper and Lishman, if I remember correctly, ran in to drive ground shots home in the first half and Ian McPherson was on the far post to head the ball past the celebrated Ted Ditchburn in the second.'

That paragraph was an excellent cameo of the strengths and weaknesses of Spurs' creative department in the 1950s, as well as revealing a tremendous affection for the Tottenham, and the football, of the time.

In 1982 Spurs won just as easily as had Arsenal in 1949, and just as they would do again in the next two rounds, against Leeds (Crooks again scoring the only goal) and against League Champions Villa. The latter game was yet another 1-0 home win, the goal coming from a Falco diving header after an excellent Paul Price run and a Crooks' centre.

For the moment though, attention returned to the League Cup, where the whole country was gearing up for perhaps the most attractive final ever in this previously poor relation of a cup competition. It was to be a clash of the country's best and most popular sides of the moment – Liverpool and Spurs. The Merseysiders had convincingly ejected Ipswich in the League Cup semi-final and, until losing to Chelsea in the FA Cup, had gone undefeated through 1982.

Spurs, for their part, had undergone a difficult path to Wembley. The home and away second round tie was against Manchester United – the fourth time the two sides had been drawn together in Cup competitions in the space of four seasons.

It was inevitably a tight tie. In the first leg Steve Archibald scored the only goal; in the away return, before 56,000 people, Mike Hazard volleyed one in early on and it was all over bar the glum Old Trafford obituaries. The next two rounds were easier – Second Division Wrexham succumbed 2-0 to Hughton and Hoddle goals, while Third Division Fulham conceded just one, again to Mike Hazard,

but it was one too many for them. The fifth round, again at home, against Nottingham Forest was the toughest tie. Forest had the best record of any club in the League Cup, having reached three of the previous four finals. This time it was Spurs against Peter Shilton, the only goal eventually being a mis-hit shot by Ardiles. The game's talking point was, however, a thrice taken penalty by Glenn Hoddle. Shilton saved Hoddle's first effort, diving to his right, but the kick was ordered to be retaken because Forest defenders had been encroaching; Hoddle succeeded with the next, to Shilton's left, but again had to retake it because Mark Falco had entered the area; Hoddle changed direction again, put it just inside Shilton's right-hand post – and this time saw the England keeper save it again. Hoddle's face was saved by Ardiles in the second half and it proved a happy day for the 6,000 fans who occupied the new West Stand for the very first time.

The League Cup semi-final was against West Bromwich, again another tight and hard fought tie and against a side Spurs had not defeated for three seasons. The first leg, in the Midlands, ended goalless after seven names had been taken and Galvin and West Brom's Jol were sent off in the closing minutes. Galvin was singularly unlucky to be dismissed for nothing much more than an arm wave of exasperation after he had been impeded. The second leg, a week later, was far more dignified. After 56 minutes Falco back-headed a ball from Hoddle and Mike Hazard added to his tally of valuable goals. Yet again a single goal won it and, with the same result removing Villa from the FA Cup three days later, Spurs had played their tenth domestic Cup game of the 1981–82 season without defeat. Far more remarkable was the fact that they had yet to concede a goal in either the FA Cup or League Cup. So far, ten games had seen ten goals for and none against; eight had ended 1-0, one 2-0 and the other was goalless. The decision to buy Ray Clemence was looking better by the Saturday.

The remarkable sequence of nine consecutive home ties was finally broken for the FA Cup quarter-finals. Even so Spurs still remained in London. They had played 29 cup matches since they had last been drawn to play outside the capital in a normal domestic single legged tie. That was way back on 26 January 1980 when they had drawn 0-0 at Swindon in the fourth round of the FA Cup. Of those 29 matches all had been played on London grounds except the first semi-final in 1981 against Wolves (at Hillsborough) and the away halves of the two legged League Cup ties against Manchester United and West Bromwich.

The FA Cup quarter-final against Chelsea was perhaps the most exhilarating of all their cup ties in a cup-packed season. Spurs went in for half-time having conceded their first cup goal of the season – a quite magnificent 25-yard free-kick from Mike Fillery. But the Pensioners' hopes were to be shortlived for, within a quarter of an hour of the restart, Spurs were 3-1 ahead and cruising. The goals came in quick succession from Archibald (after Francis failed to hold a Hoddle shot), Hoddle himself after a delightful cross-passing sequence from Archibald to Hazard to Hoddle,

and then a third from Mike Hazard. Alan Mayes made it 3-2 but Spurs had made Chelsea's earlier hopes of a repeat of their win against Liverpool look rather foolish. A few days later Tottenham patiently awaited their chances in the first leg of the Cup Winners Cup quarter-final against Eintracht Frankfurt. Miller and Hazard took their openings late in the second half and Spurs had a two-goal lead to take to Germany for the second leg. Talk had now, a little late but the more insistently for that, turned to the apparent possibility of Spurs winning four prizes. Everyone at the club dismissed this as pure fantasy – it was only a few days before that view was to be confirmed.

THE RECORDS TUMBLE

On Saturday 13 March 1982 Spurs lost their first ever domestic Cup final, at the ninth time of asking; they lost for the first time at Wembley, also their ninth appearance; their run of 25 consecutive cup games without defeat came to an end, though it went into the record books as the longest ever, beating Blackburn's run of 24 set up only four years after Spurs were founded; and, of course, they lost any chance they might have had of winning four trophies in a season.

It was a game with the usual ironies. The two captains, Steve Perryman and Graeme Souness, had played together in Spurs' youth team in 1970 when it had won the FA Youth Challenge Cup (the success was repeated in 1974). Less well known was that Keith Burkinshaw had played just one League game for Liverpool, at the end of 1954, and this was his sole first-team appearance in the upper reaches of the English game. Joining Liverpool in November 1953, he had stayed until December

1957 when, with that one memory, he had gone off to Workington. Bob Paisley, by contrast, had given up playing in 1954 and gone on to the coaching staff at Anfield at the same time.

And it was Liverpool who were to get the cream at the end of the newly-named Milk Cup final, but not before Spurs had appeared to be on their way to a famous and uncharacteristic success until just three minutes from the end of normal time. The details of the game are easily told. Steve Archibald scored after just 11 minutes when he somehow managed to latch on to a lofted pass from Glenn Hoddle, persevere rather than dribble his way past the Liverpool defenders Thompson and Lawrenson, and then beat keeper Grobbelaar, who had already committed himself. For the next 76 minutes Spurs defended, getting behind the ball, bringing forwards back into midfield, closing down the Liverpool powerhouse. It was not a particularly attractive display but it appeared to be effective, bringing back memories of the titanic struggles between Liverpool and Forest in the late 1970s when Forest kept winning with just those tactics.

Had the game ended three minutes early, the following day's reports would have been full of just this kind of praise for Spurs; that Liverpool were never easy to beat, but that there were ways and means of doing so and Spurs had found the right one. Not a great game, but well done Tottenham.

But in that 87th minute concentration lapsed just long enough. Substitute David Johnson, on for McDermott, crossed from the right. Somehow or other the Spurs defence let it through, and there was young Ronnie Whelan, Liverpool's discovery of the season, to place it to Clemence's right.

The staff of the Tottenham Hotspur Football Club proudly lines up at the end of their first season as Champions – 1950–51. The first team is in the centre, Bill Nicholson in the right-half position ahead of Alf Ramsey. At the time the club employed 67 people full-time, of whom half were professional footballers. Nowadays the number is closer to a hundred, with slightly fewer professionals (28 in 1981–82) although Spurs still retain one of the largest playing staffs in the country. On match days the numbers are swollen to around 400 with the addition of gatemen, stewards etc, and this does not include the independent catering staff.

From that moment on the result never seemed in doubt. At the end of 90 minutes the Liverpool players seemed exuberant, raring to go; by contrast the Spurs seemed exhausted. Hoddle had had a poor 90 minutes, apparently suffering from a bruised rib, while Tony Galvin had not proved his superiority over Phil Neal as predicted, perhaps because of an early injury after a tackle by Graeme Souness.

Twenty minutes into extra-time, Ossie Ardiles, clearly the best of the Spurs players on display, gave the ball away to Ian Rush near the penalty area. The ball passed quickly from Rush to Dalglish to Whelan and into the back of the net. Rush added a third in the dying seconds but by then it was all academic. The writing had been on the milk bottle from the moment Whelan scored his first goal. Spurs were brave in the unaccustomed role of vanquished; in a history lasting 99 years and 6 months there had never been the need to hand down lessons on how to be good final losers.

For most clubs, such a traumatic Wembley defeat would have been both the highlight and the end of their season. For Spurs, though naturally disappointed by the result, it was very much business as usual. There were still three prizes to be pursued and such a log-jam of fixtures that many wondered whether they could possibly end the season with even eleven fit professionals; in April and the first three weeks of May alone Tottenham had an absurd 18 fixtures.

It was the familiar failing of British football, simply too much pressure for the better teams, and all the worse for the fact that it was World Cup year as well. Clemence, Hoddle, Archibald and company would be playing first-class English football only two weeks before the start of the World Cup. Argentina, by comparison, had refused to allow their squad to play any club football since mid-February, the only exceptions being the exiles Ardiles and Bertoni.

The Championship remained the most alluring prize, if certainly the toughest. Because of their run of Cup matches, plus exceptional problems during the winter's cold spell, Tottenham had spent most of the season four or five games in arrears of the other challengers. Theoretically they were almost always in a position to eventually head the League, but they would have had to win most of their games in hand to do so – a near impossible feat in recent seasons.

The attempt was to be a brave, if doomed, one. Excellent results such as a 3-2 defeat of Southampton, at a time when the Saints headed the League, a 1-0 Easter win over Ipswich, then second in the division, and a sweet 3-1 success at Highbury two days later, clearly left Spurs in with a chance. But inevitably they were occasionally erratic; a 1-0 defeat at The Hawthorns on 27 March was their first League setback away from home in six months, but a 2-2 home draw with Sunderland just after Easter was rather more crucial. The 1981-82 season was the first which awarded three points for a win, and to take only one point from the then bottom club in the division (particularly after being 2-0 up at half-time) was careless in the extreme. Even so, Spurs might still have won (or, more crucially at the time, might have believed they *could*

have won) the Championship if Liverpool had not run into such devastating form from the turn of the year after having fallen to 12th.

By the time Spurs arrived at Anfield on 15 May, the last Saturday of the season, their chance had gone and, ironically, Liverpool needed to win to secure a record 13th Championship. Spurs had not won at Anfield for 70 years and this was no moment to break the sequence. A glorious Hoddle goal, from nearly 40 yards out and swerving left to right over Grobbelaar's head, provided a delightful memory but Liverpool won 3-1 and confirmed Keith Burkinshaw's prediction made ten games earlier. After a crucial 2-0 defeat for Spurs at Old Trafford he had said: 'Liverpool are such a good team for getting these 1-0 wins, aren't they? I can't honestly say we stand a great chance of catching them now.' And so it was to prove.

It is not really surprising that Spurs could not sustain enough of a challenge to win the League. Bill Nicholson says of his teams in 1961 and 1962 that, as soon as they had won their FA Cup semi-finals, it was almost impossible to keep their minds on League matches. Indeed, in both years Spurs had a very poor spell leading up to Wembley.

Burkinshaw's team appeared slightly less vulnerable to this fluctuating form because of the extremely strong defensive base which had been laid down. The midfield and forward line had developed the confidence not to panic in search of a first goal in even the most vital games – largely because they had developed a reliance on the defence keeping its domain intact during the mid-season run of ten cup games without conceding a goal.

As 1982 progressed, injuries to his front runners meant that Burkinshaw had to be able to permutate Crooks, Archibald, Falco and Chris Jones almost game to game. In midfield things were even more fluid – a choice being made among Ardiles (before his return to Argentina), Villa, Hazard, Brooke, Hoddle, Perryman and Graham Roberts depending on who was fit. Roberts' play was a revelation. He proved that he was not only a strong, forceful centre-back, but also a rather subtle, hard-working midfield tyro when given the chance. Against Southampton he even contrived to score a hat-trick, all three goals coming from open play. This may well be the only occasion in first-class soccer history that a centre-back, playing in midfield, has scored a hat-trick – and against the League leaders.

Tony Galvin's role on the left was also perceived as more critical. With neither Archibald nor Crooks being a natural target man, Galvin's speed down the wing was the essential variety in a mix which would otherwise have depended too heavily on a skilful midfield pushing ground-balls through the middle to utilise the speed of the front-runners. The full-backs also proved themselves valuable overlappers. Chris Hughton had long performed that role, and scored the occasional goal into the bargain, but Steve Perryman's ability to read Glenn Hoddle's intentions became almost telepathic. Perhaps Spurs most delightful move of the season was Hoddle's dropping of a long ball, or quick reverse pass against the direction of play, into the last few yards of the right hand side of the field for Steve Perryman to run on to and centre.

During the 1981-82 season Spurs played 23 cup matches, all of which were in London except for semi-finals and the away halves of two-legged ties. For the second consecutive season they reached the FA Cup final having played only their semi-final outside the capital.
OPPOSITE TOP: *Garth Crooks scores the only goal of the fourth round FA Cup tie against Leeds at White Hart Lane on 23 January 1982. The new stand (background) had been brought into use just five days before.*
OPPOSITE CENTRE: *Same competition, same place, same score but different opposition. After a magnificent run by Paul Price from his own half, Mark Falco heads the only goal of the fifth round against Aston Villa on 13 February. Looking on with differing hopes are Ken McNaught and Graham Roberts. This was Spurs' tenth domestic cup game of the season and they had still to be beaten, having scored ten goals and conceded none.*
OPPOSITE BOTTOM: *Paul Miller disentangles himself from the net after celebrating Steve Archibald's (second left) goal at Stamford Bridge in the FA Cup quarter-final on 6 March 1982. Chelsea keeper Francis had failed to hold a Hoddle free-kick and Spurs were level at 1-1. This game was Spurs 25th consecutive cup match without defeat and broke the long-standing record of 24 undefeated cup matches set up by Blackburn Rovers in 1886, just four years after Spurs were founded.*

191

Steve Archibald battles his way between Liverpool defenders Phil Neal and Phil Thompson to score the first goal of the 1982 League Cup (re-named Milk Cup) final after just 11 minutes. Spurs held on to their lead for another 76 minutes, when Ronnie Whelan's equaliser opened the gates for two more and a 3-1 defeat for Spurs. It was Tottenham's first ever defeat at Wembley (on their ninth appearance), first defeat in a cup final match played in England (the fourteenth time, including replays, that they had taken the field for a cup final) and their first defeat in nine major domestic cup finals.

CUP WINNERS AND CUPS

If the Championship was to slip slowly from Spurs grasp, perhaps the single most likely prize – the European Cup Winners Cup – shot dramatically from that of Ray Clemence in one dreadful moment.

Tottenham had survived the quarter-final second leg away at Eintracht Frankfurt somewhat fortuitously. Two-nil up from the first leg, they conceded two goals very quickly to Eintracht's Borchers and the Korean Bum Kun Cha and seemed on the way out. However a slow, cautious recovery in the final 45 minutes was rewarded when, ten minutes from time, Hoddle delicately placed a 20-yard shot into the corner of the net to put the Londoners into the semi-final.

Initially they seemed fortunate to draw Barcelona in the last four, partially because it meant avoiding favourites Dinamo Tbilisi, but, more relevantly, because Barcelona were to host the final in their own Nou Camp Stadium and it seemed preferable to face them over two games than in a single one on their own patch. As it turned out, that reasoning was defective. Standard Liege won both legs against Dinamo and Barcelona came to London obsessed by the need not to lose.

Playing the final at home would mean a full house for the Spaniards at Nou Camp – extended to hold 120,000 spectators for the World Cup opening match being held there only a couple of weeks later – and almost one million pounds for the club. They therefore arrived in London with a succeed-at-all-costs attitude.

The result was 'The most cynical game I've seen for 10 years,' said Frank McLintock. Barcelona manager Udo Lattek ('the match was sometimes too violent') had sent out a hit-squad very reminiscent of the bunch of Atletico Madrid thugs which disgraced Celtic Park in the 1974 European Cup semi-final. In both cases, the Spaniards did their job. Barcelona went home with a 1-1 result and only one

man – Estella – sent off. He was later suspended for two matches (meaning he missed the final) while both clubs were fined, Barcelona much the more heavily.

Despite all this, Spurs might have survived had it not been for a terrible error by Ray Clemence, his first critical mistake since the Charity Shield eight months before. A speculative 35-yard shot from Barcelona full-back and captain Olmo was aimed straight at the keeper and looked totally harmless. As Clemence stood and gathered the ball it somehow squirmed from his grasp and over the line. It should be said, in mitigation, that it was Clemence's excellent performance in Germany in the previous round that had kept Spurs in the competition at all. Graham Roberts popped up for a late equaliser but it was not to be enough. 'We didn't expect them to play like that,' said Keith Burkinshaw, 'we had heard so much about them being a good side technically, but it never showed through.' A fortnight later in Barcelona Spurs, who had thus far lost only four games away from home all season and hence had cause for some hope, went down 1-0.

The goal was a bad one for Spurs; Quini headed on a free-kick, Ray Clemence apparently yelled 'Away!' but defenders Hughton and Roberts thought he said 'Leave it' in the noise and confusion. As a result no-one went for the ball and Allan Simonsen nipped in to push it home.

It was a sad moment, with inevitable memories of another semi-final in the Iberian peninsula exactly twenty years before, when Benfica denied the seemingly unstoppable claims of Glory, Glory, Hallelujah to a first European prize.

But the Spurs of 1962 were to bounce back from their European Cup semi-final defeat, were to finish third in the League and were to go on to retain the FA Cup they had won the year before. The parallels and omens seemed remarkably close.

After Spurs FA Cup quarter-final defeat of Chelsea the semi-final draw threw up two rather poignant games, while leaving open the possibility of the first all-Second Division final or the attractive and intriguing re-run of the League Cup semi-final between Spurs and West Brom.

Queen's Park Rangers, playing in their first FA Cup semi-final, and West Brom were to meet at Highbury. They had met in only one other crucial game in their history – the first Wembley League Cup final in 1967, when Third Division QPR beat their First Division opponents 3-2. Playing for QPR that day was one Les Allen, of Double fame. Fifteen years later the Londoners' upset the bookies again when one of their forwards stuck out a leg to deflect a defenders' clearance into the West Brom net and win the game 1-0. The forward's name was, of course, Clive Allen and he was the son born to Les Allen and his wife exactly two weeks after Spurs beat Leicester to win the Double. It was Clive's seventh goal in the Cup run, including four against Blackpool in the fourth round.

The other semi-final brought back even stronger memories of that same Double, for Spurs were to play against the very side they had defeated in the 1961 Cup final – Leicester City. The similarities did not end there either. The game was at Villa Park, traditionally Spurs' unlucky semi-final ground after the 1948, 1953 and 1956 defeats, though they had won their semi-final there in the Double year. More significantly, Leicester were to go down by the same score as in the 1961 final – 2-0. Like that game at Wembley twenty-one years before, it could hardly be called a classic. Spurs were trying to reach Wembley for the fifth time in a year; Leicester were hopefully trying to make it fifth time lucky, for they had lost their previous four FA Cup finals. The first half was tight, the most newsworthy item being the Leicester crowd's continual booing of Ardiles.

Argentina had invaded the Falkland Islands 24 hours before the game and there was considerable speculation about what would happen to that country's most popular exports to Britain – Ardiles and Villa. Ardiles was due to return to Buenos Aires the following day anyway but Cesar Menotti, the Argentine manager, had indicated that he might be prepared to let his key midfielder return to England for the Cup final. Menotti was quoted as saying: 'Keith Burkinshaw and all the people at Tottenham are my friends. Always Tottenham have said Yes, Yes and Yes again to Menotti. Now it is impossible for Menotti to say No if they need Ardiles for the Cup final. Ardiles will decide.' The crisis obviously put Ardiles' eventual return in doubt, as did an interview given at Buenos Aires airport on his arrival there.

But if the Villa Park semi-final was to eventually be remembered as Ardiles' last game for Spurs, he certainly made his mark on it. In the 56th minute he moved towards Hoddle as the latter took a corner on the right. In a clearly set-piece move, Hoddle pushed the ball short to Ardiles, who, having lost his marker, was able to turn and put across a low centre for Crooks' to volley home from the six-yard line. Leicester's troubles mounted. In yet another incident reminiscent of 1961 (when they had lost right-back Len Chalmers for most of the final) an innocuous collision between Galvin and Leicester's current right-fullback Tommy Williams left the defender with a hairline fracture of the shin and his side with ten men.

Even more was to come. In the 76th minute, a Galvin cross went begging and was collected about 20 yards from his own goal by Ian Wilson. The Leicester man was under no pressure and had any number of options. He chose a back pass to Mark Wallington, but got too much of his foot under the ball and clipped it perfectly over the goalkeeper's head into the net. It was, if nothing else, one of the most memorable goals scored in a semi-final in

The 1982 FA Cup semi-final at Villa Park on 3 April brought back memories of the Double, for Spurs' opponents were Leicester and City lost by the same score as in the 1961 final, 2-0. Garth Crooks (out of picture ABOVE) *scored the first goal but it was made by Ossie Ardiles (celebrating background right) after a Glenn Hoddle corner. This was to be Ardiles' last game for Spurs before his return to Buenos Aires. Argentina had invaded the Falklands the previous day and Ardiles left to join his country's World Cup squad the following morning.*

ABOVE LEFT: *An unusually sombre conversation between two goalscorers in a semi-final. Garth Crooks consoles Leicester's Ian Wilson after the latter had finished his club's chances of reaching their fifth FA Cup final with a spectacular lobbed own-goal in the 76th minute.*

years and it guaranteed Tottenham's tenth game at Wembley, their thirteenth cup final and a chance to equal the performances of 1961 and 1962 in retaining the FA Cup.

So the final was an unexpected and unpredictable one against Queen's Park Rangers, and it clearly had more than its fair share of interest. It was the fifth time in ten seasons that a Second Division side had reached the final – and no-one at White Hart Lane needed reminding that three of the previous four (Sunderland, Southampton and West Ham) had come away with the Cup. It was also the fourth all-London professional final in fifteen years (Spurs had figured in the first, against Chelsea in 1967), a factor which increased the interest in the capital but rather tended to diminish the event for the country as a whole.

On the personal level, and in addition to the Allen connection, Rangers' manager Terry Venables had, of course, played for Spurs in that 1967 success, while, by coincidence, Rangers were also celebrating their centenary.

Tottenham had no illusions about the task ahead. As recently as the third round in 1981, they had found it no easy task to squeeze past Rangers – drawing 0-0 at Loftus Road and winning the replay 3-1 at home. Rangers run to the final – past Middlesbrough (winning 3-2 away after drawing 1-1 at home), Blackpool, Grimsby, Crystal Palace and West Bromwich – was impressive enough. And it was rather odd, travelling to Wembley, to consider that QPR had almost withdrawn from the 1981-82 FA Cup over their synthetic pitch. The FA would not give them an absolute guarantee that it could be used for Cup matches for more than one season and chairman Jim Gregory had to be disuaded from withdrawing in protest.

Playing a Second Division club at Wembley was certainly going to be no walkover. Spurs knew they would face a tight midfield and a very committed defence. They had also experienced a very lop-sided approach to Wembley. The first three rounds were against relatively strong First Division sides, the next three all against Second Division clubs. Since the formation of the Football League in 1888, only one other club has completely avoided First Division opposition from the last eight onwards.

That club was Newcastle United, who had faced Grimsby, Fulham and Wolves in 1908, and actually lost the final 3-1 to the latter. Strangely, Newcastle enjoyed the same good fortune two years later, in 1910, when they played Leicester Fosse, Swindon and Barnsley. Again they failed to win the final (drawing 1-1 at Crystal Palace) but eventually won the replay 2-0 at Goodison. Spurs share another statistical oddity with Newcastle. They are the only clubs to have retained the FA Cup in the twentieth century. Newcastle did so in 1951 and 1952, Spurs in 1961 and 1962. In the first two years of another decade Spurs were set to maintain the sequence.

But as the club approached the 1982 FA Cup final there was a very real fear that Burkinshaw's side had peaked too early, that it had seen its period of excellence around the middle of what had been an over-long and over-strenuous season. Ardiles had gone back to Buenos Aires, Hoddle seemed prone to nagging injuries and, perhaps, concern about his

England place. In attack neither of the strikers had been as consistent as in the previous year and Archibald had had no better than a mediocre 1982, scoring just six league goals in an injury-upset season.

At the back the best combination had yet to emerge – the mixture of Roberts, Miller and Price suffered a string of injuries and even gave way, as late as the beginning of May, to a further centre-back pairing in the shape of John Lacy and Pat Corbett.

Any instability in the centre of the defence put even more pressure on the side's cornerstone and captain, Steve Perryman. Often referred to as the best uncapped player in the country, it has been convincingly argued that, had Sir Alf Ramsey continued as England manager, then Steve Perryman would have won the international recognition he so richly deserves.

Perryman played his last game for England Schoolboys just days before joining Spurs as an apprentice in 1967. He progressed easily into the Under-23 team, winning 17 caps, and was undoubtedly being groomed for the senior team when a pair of unconnected events probably robbed him of his inheritance.

First Ramsey was sacked from the England job after the failure to reach the 1974 World Cup finals. Then Perryman had to switch positions as Spurs went through their relegation traumas in the mid-1970s. 'I won the Under-23 caps playing in midfield, then I changed to the back four. I realised then that if England wanted two big men at the back, capable of winning everything in the air, I'd never get a look-in,' Perryman concedes.

Brian Glanville of the *Sunday Times*, believes the Ramsey era has a lot to answer for in failing to help a player of Perryman's ability make the international grade. 'We paid a heavy price for World Cup success in the awful sterile years of work rate, neglect of wingers and the primacy of effort over style and skill,' says Glanville. 'At the time Perryman was encouraged to toil and graft rather than to express his natural skill.'

At 30, Perryman is still, in Glanville's words, the eternal cherub. In 15 years at the club, he has passed Pat Jenning's record of 472 League appearances and, short of some disastrous event, looks certain to reach the 600 mark. When he signed as a professional in 1969, he joined names like Gilzean, Greaves and Mullery. 'Spurs were the team to play for then. I was in four finals in my first five years,' he recalls. Perhaps Perryman's greatest qualities are his versatility and durability. Keith Burkinshaw says he is one of the best speed-readers of a ball in the game, but his ability to play a variety of roles to great effect has probably been a reflection of his tremendous staying power as much as anything else.

There were to be more tangible rewards as well. Two weeks before the FA Cup final he was voted Sportswriters Footballer of the Year, the third Spurs' player to win the award after Blanchflower and Jennings. Glenn Hoddle was a close second, reflecting the impression the Spurs side had made on the country through an excellent season. Perryman also joined Hoddle in Ron Greenwood's final forty for the World Cup finals.

In a sense, the real story of the 1982 Cup final had been told before a ball had even been

kicked. Just as Spurs had played their semi-final the day after Argentina invaded the Falklands, so Keith Burkinshaw was faced with a decision whether or not to play Ricky Villa the day after the British task force had landed there. At 11.30am on the morning of the match Burkinshaw was forced to concede that both he and the player felt the situation had become too tense for Villa to play. In itself that was a terrible decision to have to make. What made it so ironic were the memories of a year before, of a Cup final replay in which Villa scored twice and won the match with perhaps the most memorable individual goal scored at Wembley since the War.

Villa himself stayed at home with his family to watch the game on TV – not to avoid the fans or his team-mates, but to try and keep away from insistent media pursuers. At the ground the fans chanted his name with affection and sadness, hoping that they had not seen the last of the two symbols who had so dramatically placed Spurs back on centre-stage four years before.

Sitting on the coach on the way to Wembley Burkinshaw must have been pondering on a fraught end to a strange season. Three months before Spurs might have won four trophies. Now here he was, having agreed a new three-year contract with the club the night before, forced to resign himself to the probable loss of the two talismen who had first brought him to managerial prominence, and also having to cope with three troublesome injuries to the players he did have left. Ray Clemence had a calf injury, Tony Galvin an uncertain knee after a month out of the game, and captain Steve Perryman, who had not missed a match all season, a pulled thigh muscle.

In the event all three took the field, the team having Clemence back in goal; Perryman, Price, Miller and Hughton at the back; Graham Roberts pushed into midfield to join Hazard and Hoddle, and the front runners were the season's first choices – Galvin, Crooks and Archibald.

The clubs may have only played each other once before in the FA Cup (in 1981) but the team members knew each other well enough. Like Graeme Souness, Mike Flanagan had also played with Steve Perryman in the Spurs team which won the 1970 FA Youth Cup. Les Allen, Clive's father, was manager at QPR

when Terry Venables followed him from White Hart Lane to Shepherd's Bush in 1969. Not surprisingly, young Clive had trained for a time at Spurs and had even scored a hat-trick in Tottenham colours when playing for London Schools against Coventry at the Lane.

Before the game David Miller said in the *Daily Express* that: 'Together Ardiles and Burkinshaw have made a statement of principle (about the game) which has possibly been the most important in English football since the era of Moore-Hurst-Peters at West Ham. At an admittedly lean time in the game, Burkinshaw has more than deserved his success and it is what he has done for the game as much as for Tottenham that we should be celebrating today.'

But as Danny Blanchflower said after the 1961 final, the talking was rather better than the playing. Few finals can possibly live up to their previews, but this one was perhaps more guilty than most. It was one-sided but unconvincing. Spurs were playing their 65th first-class game of the season and, particularly in the second-half, looked it. For 115 minutes Ray Clemence (who was equalling Pat Jennings' record of four goalkeeping appearances in FA Cup finals) had just two real shots to stop – and both of those looked marginally off target. QPR were hampered by an early injury to Clive Allen, but Spurs were equally affected by Steve Archibald's poor finishing. Twice he was put through clear, twice he failed to score. Ironically, on the one, similar, occasion he did find the net he was very debatably ruled offside. 0-0 after 90 minutes but Spurs eventually broke the deadlock with just ten minutes of extra-time left. Glenn Hoddle played a one-two with Graham Roberts, hit a low shot from 20 yards and saw it go through Tony Currie's legs, take a slight deflection, and beat Rangers excellent keeper Peter Hucker.

It seemed all over but, with just five minutes left, Spurs were suckered by a QPR set piece. A Stainrod long throw was back-headed by Bob Hazell and nodded in by an unmarked Terry Fenwick. It was the first goal ever scored from open play by a full-back in a Cup final. To nostalgic eyes looking back ten years the whole move could have been a Chivers throw, a Gilzean back-header and a ghosting Peters, but that was hardly an excuse for Spurs being caught out.

Glenn Hoddle's 110th minute shot passes through Tony Currie's legs, takes a slight deflection and beats man-of-the-match Peter Hucker to put Spurs 1-0 up in the first game of the 1982 FA Cup final. It was the second consecutive year that a Hoddle shot had been deflected into the net by an opponent in the Cup final. Spurs, playing in yellow because of the colour clash, held their lead for just five minutes before Terry Fenwick equalised for QPR and, for the second consecutive year though only the third time since the final moved to Wembley in 1923, the match went to a replay.

Seven finals and seven victories as Glenn Hoddle slots home his second goal of the 1982 FA Cup final, a penalty in the sixth minute of the replay. It was his third scoring shot in the four games that had made up Spurs' two consecutive FA Cup successes, but this one did not need a deflection on the way. It was to be the only goal of the game and Tony Currie was again involved, conceding the penalty when he brought down Graham Roberts just inside the area. Fortunately, as it was to decide the game, there was no doubt about the decision, though Queen's Park Rangers had cause to feel that their aggressive, dominating performance perhaps deserved some reward other than the losers' medals. It was, in fact, only the third FA Cup final to be decided by a single penalty goal – the other two being the famous games between Huddersfield and Preston in both 1922 and 1938. In 1982 the FA had already decided that, should scores be level after extra-time, then the final would be the first major match in Britain to be concluded by penalties anyway. How right they were . . .

So for the second year running, and for only the third time since the final moved to Wembley, there was to be a replay. And this time the problems were to be QPR's. Clive Allen's ankle injury ruled him out while Glenn Roeder was suspended after an earlier sending off at Luton and so Tony Currie captained the side. Gary Micklewhite and Warren Neill came into the QPR team while Spurs remained unchanged.

And, at 9.15 pm on Thursday 27 May, only one thing really mattered; that was that Spurs had retained the FA Cup and won the trophy for the seventh time in seven appearances. Only Aston Villa have won it as often. But it is fair to add that not even the most blinkered Tottenham fan could have argued that it was one of his side's greatest performances, certainly not one to compare with a year before, or that QPR did not deserve something more from their replay performance.

There was to be just one goal, scored after a mere six minutes before either side had settled. Graham Roberts set off on a surging run into the right side of the penalty area; three yards inside his legs were swept away by Tony Currie; it was a clear penalty, as Terry Venables agreed at half-time. Glenn Hoddle took the kick without any preamble, placing it in the corner to Hucker's right. This time he didn't need a deflection. As an attacking force, Spurs' final virtually ended there. As on the previous Saturday, they looked like a team that had been playing flat out for months, as indeed they had. Not until the very last minute, when Steve Archibald was put through yet again and this time hit the post, did they look like scoring a second.

But the essence of football is that the best team is the one which scores most goals. The simple fact was that QPR, after attacking for the greater part of the match, did not manage to do so once. Nonetheless they seemed to have succeeded in the 43rd minute when a Gary Micklewhite shot was disallowed because Terry Fenwick was judged to have been offside for an instant. The decision was a let-off – the Spurs players had not protested and it was the sort of goal which would have been allowed on a different day. After 65 minutes QPR went even closer when John Gregory hit the crossbar with a beautifully volleyed chip and for most of the second half it was really a matter of Spurs holding out, not so much for the FA Cup but for some tangible reward at the end of an impossibly exhausting season. Paul Miller and Graham Roberts were the heroes, though, even with Garry Brooke on again as substitute, it was clear that Ardiles was going to be sadly missed.

But if both games left something to be desired there could be no denying that Spurs deserved their prize after a string of five convincing wins on the way to Wembley, achieved without a single replay. The fact that the season and the tiredness had finally caught up with them could not take away the memories and the quality that had achieved all those magnificent results against Ajax, Manchester United, Chelsea and many others.

It was, in fact, the sixteenth time that Spurs had taken the field (including replays) for a cup final match played in England. Astonishingly they had lost just once, the Milk Cup final against Liverpool.

Nonetheless, a strangely quiet Thursday night with the exhausted Cup holders hanging on to a one goal lead is not the archetypal image of the English season's dramatic conclusion. The air of unreality was highlighted by the empty spaces on the terracing. For the only time in the 60 years since the very first Wembley game in 1923, it had been possible to buy tickets at the gate for an FA Cup final. Even then, the stadium was not full. The official attendance was given as 90,000, but it was clearly considerably less. Perhaps this was not so surprising. It was Spurs' sixth appearance at Wembley in two seasons (four FA Cup finals, the Milk Cup final and the Charity Shield), an all-London tie generates little provincial interest and QPR could not expect to carry more than 25,000 supporters at the most.

But, at the end, there could hardly be a more fitting conclusion to the centenary season than the winning of a record seventh FA Cup. It is the FA Cup that has been Spurs' symbol, almost as much as the cockerel. It was their astonishing win in 1901 that gained them not only a place in the history books but a place in the Football League. It was the glory of 1921 which proved the answer to Arsenal's stealing of their First Division place. It was the moment in 1961 which placed the crown on the

best club side the country had ever seen, it was 1962 and 1967 which saw Jimmy Greaves in his rightful place and it was to be 1981 which left the game with the enduring memory of one glorious goal and two Argentinians.

So the 1982 Cup celebrations surely seemed a fitting finale to the centenary story and yet, at that very moment, events were in train to prove that no story ever ends, nor does even a successful centenary prove a time for quiet reflection. As the actual centenary date was reached, in September 1982, negotiations which were to have a far wider effect on the club than any FA Cup win were being quietly concluded.

The symbol and the spur had been the new stand. The intention to build it, declared in mid-1980, had already caused the resignation of one chairman, Sidney Wale. Wale had, however, remained the biggest shareholder. And while the building had gone reasonably to schedule, there was no disguising the fact that the father and son team of chairman and vice-chairman Arthur and Geoff Richardson were, despite their confident earlier assertions, increasingly worried about matching costs with revenues. A basic part of the plan had been to sell the 72 boxes for £30,000 each, covering a three-year lease. That would, in theory, have covered nearly half the cost of the whole enterprise. The problem was that, with the recession deepening and companies becoming very sensitive about visible directors' perks (this was the period when numerous chairmen's Rolls-Royces were quietly sold), the boxes were just not moving. Having set the price at £30,000, it also became very difficult to reduce this figure to create more interest. Those that had committed would, not unreasonably, expect a similar deduction. And, as the bills rolled in, it also

became clear that the original estimate of £4¼ million had been somewhat unrealistic. When the final reckoning came to be made the overall costs were nearly one million higher, and the club was faced with interest and repayments on the loan of around £800,000 per annum. To make matters worse, despite reaching two Cup finals and taking £3 million in receipts (easily their highest ever) the club's profit on the 1981–82 season was only £200,000.

All of this was probably manageable, but it was seen to be combined with a standard of public relations and organisation off the field which bore no relation to that achieved by Keith Burkinshaw and the team on it. At a meeting to discuss the new stand, a prospective purchaser of a private box asked for confirmation that it would be available for European matches, a point which should have been rhetorical. Arthur Richardson seemed unsure, giving an answer that gave an impression of poor planning and even poorer salesmanship, and this was compounded by an unconvincing and uninspiring appearance on a televised brains trust on the future of football. The move into the new stand had thrown the ticket office and administration into ill-disguised chaos. Season ticket holders had first been moved out of the old main stand and then back again, but the new systems were poorly installed and numerous seats were double and even treble booked. Given the fact that this coincided with a run of big attendances and major Cup games, the organization was clearly beset with problems.

Despite all this, the board still felt secure. There had never been a takeover attempt at the club, partially because of its traditions but largely because of the article of association which required that any share transfer had to

Alan Brazil celebrates his recent signing by Spurs with a header which hit the Watford bar on 19 March 1983. The rebound was knocked in by Mark Falco and Spurs won the game 1-0. After a brief career Brazil went (at a profit to Spurs) on to Manchester United where, peculiarly, he was unable to find a place in the first team.

197

Keith Burkinshaw plus friend and colleague Bill Nicholson in August 1983. One of the first acts of the club's new board was to erect, shades of Herbert Chapman, a bronze bust of Nicholson in the entrance hall at White Hart Lane. Both he and Burkinshaw achieved the remarkable feat of reaching four Cup finals in the four seasons prior to their respective resignations.

be authorised by the board. The consequence was that this article of association (effectively a rule of the club) could only be overturned by a vote of the shareholders. But, and here was the catch-22, the board knew all the shareholders, controlled a large percentage of the shares itself and, by its veto, could theoretically prevent any outsider from buying any shares anyway.

The board's confidence was eventually shown to be misplaced in the face of a clever assault by two rich young fans, 31-year-old Paul Bobroff and a 35-year-old multi-millionaire property developer Irving Scholar. Scholar had approached the Richardsons back in 1980, genuinely worried about matters prior to the stand being built, and offering his services as a property consultant free of charge. His motivations were concern for the club as a fan, but his interest was not reciprocated. Bobroff later also offered his company's computer facilities to sort out the problems in the ticket office, but this was not to be taken up either.

By February 1982, while Spurs ploughed on to two Cup finals on the field, matters were equally intense off it. Scholar and Bobroff had devised a plan to get round the problem of the articles of association. They could buy shares, the problem was that the board did not have to recognise the purchase. So, in addition to the shares, they also acquired the proxy voting powers of the previous owner. In other words, they could use the votes whether the board recognised the purchase or not. With half the shares, they could overturn the old rules at the next meeting. At the rapidly escalating share price (which reached £300 per share) it would

cost around £500,000 to buy up enough, always assuming the owners would sell.

The critical moment was when ex-chairman Sidney Wale decided to sell. His son-in-law, Douglas Alexiou, was already on the board and was to become chairman when the coup was carried through. Wale had always disagreed with the building of the stand and, while too gentlemanly to bear a grudge, bore the current board little personal goodwill after his replacement as chairman. By November 1982 Richardson realised that Bobroff and Scholar had enough promises and proxy votes to call an extra-ordinary general meeting and unseat him. He had no choice but to resign and allow Bobroff to join the board. Scholar, the effective owner of the club with Bobroff, remained in Monte Carlo for the time being.

For the next year and a half Spurs made more news off the field than on it. Ossie Ardiles had, of course, gone back to join the Argentinian national squad before the 1982 World Cup, had supposedly commented at Buenos Aires airport that the Malvinas were Argentinian (a perfectly understandable sentiment for anyone of his nationality, especially so public a figure) and that he would never play in England again. As the Falklands War continued through the summer of 1982 it did indeed seem unlikely that he could ever return. Keith Burkinshaw arranged a year's loan to Paris St. Germain, supposedly for £100,000, and it was assumed that that was the last of Ardiles. Burkinshaw's relationship with the Argentinians had always contained a large element of chance, and so it was to prove again. Spurs had invited the Luxembourg national team, who

had just played England at Wembley, to come to the Christmas 1982 party at White Hart Lane. The Luxembourgeois interpreter also acted in the same capacity for Paris St. Germain, and had been involved in the Ardiles transfer. He told Burkinshaw that Ardiles, who had not settled well, was prepared to return and that the French club would probably agree. Burkinshaw flew off again on his second Argentinian-chasing odyssey, concluded the deal, gave St. Germain their money back, and Ardiles was at home in Hoddesden by the New Year, 1983.

The Ardiles story did not continue quite so happily. In only his second game back in England he broke a leg. In a friendly six months later, shades of Dave Mackay, he sustained another fracture. A year later there was an operation for cartilage trouble. He was now 32, a difficult age to make a come back after three such disturbing blows. But Ardiles himself was philosophical, as he told Brough Scott of the *Sunday Times*: 'Alas, people are entitled to think I can't come back. Maybe sometimes I think it myself. But I don't have economic problems and more than anything I love to play football. All my life, from six or seven, I can play very, very good, but they always say I am too small. Now they say I am too old. We'll see.' Indeed, Ardiles had few problems compared with most footballers contemplating the end of their careers. He owned a 1500 acre farm and other property in Argentina, and was close to his final qualifications as a lawyer. It was nonetheless not until the end of the 1983–84 season that he was again seen in the first team, making a particularly important contribution to the second leg of the UEFA

Cup final when he came on as a substitute. But, because of cartilage trouble, little was to be seen of him the following season either until well into 1985, and just months before his £80,000 p.a. contract was due to expire.

Off the field, the club were having an equally controversial, and noticeable, impact. One of the early decisions of the new board was that the club should advertise its 'product' like any other commercial organisation. A relatively sophisticated television and radio campaign, based on the theme of individual fans taking the field against next Saturday's opposition, was mounted on Thames and London Weekend Television, and via the local commercial radio stations, Capital and LBC. As an idea it received a considerable amount of attention and comment; arguably, in a peculiar twist of public relations logic, the discussions about the campaign had more overall impact than the campaign itself. It has to be said that the expenditure on advertising cannot really be counted a success. On of the problems was that it was impossible to guess how many people would have gone to the game if there had not been any advertising anyway (always an acid test of the effectiveness of any form of advert) and, in addition, attendances were being compared with the very successful spell the club had enjoyed through 1980, 1981 and 1982. By the beginning of 1984 crowds were significantly down and the idea had been quietly put to one side.

Questions were beginning to be asked about the team and the direction the club was going in 1984, as the cold wind of the recession seemed to be affecting Spurs more than other major sides. While they tried to match the expenditure and the ambitions of Liverpool, Manchester United and Arsenal, the other members of the current unofficial elite, it did seem that Tottenham's base support fell below that of their rivals. Between mid-January and May 1984, with the club well out of the Championship race, there were only two gates above 25,000 and several below 20,000, well under the effective breakeven. It had become a simple truism that the club needed at least one good Cup run each season to hope to breakeven.

Happily, the overhang of financial worries had been largely solved by a brave and unique step taken by the new board. The decision was made to become the first club to take a full stock-market listing, which meant, simply enough, that absolutely anyone could buy shares in the club through their local bank manager. The new board had already put £1,150,000 into the club early in 1983, and they then raised another £3,800,000 by selling shares to the public. The two injections of cash largely eliminated the bank borrowings, causing many people elsewhere in the game to ask why such a simple and relatively obvious idea had not been tried by other clubs in difficulty. Perhaps the answer was the massive depth of support for the club, particularly in relatively financially sophisticated North London. The shares were put on sale at 100 pence each (3 million in all) and, though they were sold easily enough, the price soon dropped to the 75p–80p level where it has largely remained since.

Despite this fall, the shares and financial state of the club remained something of a favourite with the *Financial Times*. 'Spurs set for promotion' and 'Spurs score in strong second half' became popular if predictable headlines in the normally conservative pink pages, and the results were always treated kindly. 'To the average fan, who completely

Ardiles return was not trouble free. Two fractures and knee problems meant that he rarely appeared for the first team in 1983 or 1984. A rare foray was against Leicester on 11 February 1984, when he was seen robbing Steve Lynex.

dominates the share register, the news that Glenn Hoddle has signed a new contract probably means more than the disclosure that the club has beaten its floatation target by 6 per cent' said the FT about the first year's results. But, more positively, they concluded: 'The annual results show that, with the elimination of the previously crippling burden of debt, playing costs have been strictly controlled in line with operating revenues and to cover the dividend with something to spare. That, if nothing else, is a measure of the new team's (meaning the board's) strike rate this far.' The second year, with a profit of nearly £1 million, was equally encouraging financially and equally well received. 'I've never known a fan or a shareholder complain about the dividend', said Paul Bobroff, 'I don't think that's why they bought the shares.'

Well before the end of the 1983–84 season it had become clear that Keith Burkinshaw would leave at its end. The reasons were complex. He had been in effective control for some time, had been conspiciously successful and was rightly noted as a man who spoke his mind and stuck by his own beliefs. The fall in attendances in 1984 was financially worrying, and the board's frank and publicly stated view was the football team, while the necessary core of the whole business, was only part of the business and other sectors, such as the development of the property on the High Road, were financially significant as well. Expenditures on the team had to be viewed in that light. Burkinshaw also had a season-long running argument with his main striker, the unpredictable Scot Steve Archibald, who continued to play for the team having vowed at one point never to speak to the manager again. At season's end the club conducted a number financially astute deals, especially in obtaining a remarkable £1¾ million by selling Alan Brazil (who had never

Mark Falco shoots past Bayern Munich's Soren Lerby during the UEFA Cup tie on 23 November 1983 but fails to score. Spurs lost this first leg 1-0 but won the tie 2-1 on aggregate with goals from Archibald and Falco. It was adequate revenge for the previous year's defeat in the Cup Winners' Cup.

begun to succeed since his arrival from Ipswich) to Manchester United Reserves and Steve Archibald to Terry Venables in Barcelona where, it must be said, the Scotsman surprised everyone by leading the Spanish scorers as Barcelona and Venables ran away with that country's League Championship. Peter Shreeves, the new manager, spent some of the cash in bringing Clive Allen back to his first, and his father's, club from QPR. Allen had thus perambulated from Loftus Road, to Highbury, to Crystal Palace, back to QPR and on to White Hart Lane in a very brief career which had, for a striker who had cost in aggregate some £3,500,000, supplied relatively limited highlights. While Allen's early linking with the other new purchase, Notts County winger John Chiedozie, seemed encouraging, injuries and loss of form soon led to the striker being replaced up front by the old team of Falco and Crooks.

But this is to run ahead of the highlight of 1984, yet another trophy for the departing Burkinshaw. While domestic events had provided little cheer (Spurs going out to Norwich in a fourth round FA Cup replay and Arsenal in the third round of the Milk Cup), there was always the UEFA Cup. Their run through the competition was not noticeably easy, though it started in style.

In the first round they amassed 14 goals without reply as the Irish part-timers of Drogheda were despatched 6-0 on their own ground and 8-0 at White Hart Lane. A superb performance by Glenn Hoddle, upstaging a much publicised return to the European arena by Johan Cruyff, paved the way to victory in the second round over Dutch side Feijenoord. Spurs couldn't stop Cruyff scoring, however,

and their 4-2 home win was more precarious than it looked until Hughton and Galvin put the result beyond doubt in Rotterdam. Once again there were the same scenes of violence which had marred Spurs' previous visit to the Dutch port in the final of the same competition back in 1974. Tottenham fans left a trail of destruction and 30 injuries. In the event the club was probably fortunate to escape with an £8,000 fine by UEFA.

Spurs scored their most impressive victory in the third round. A goal by Michael Rummenigge, brother of West Germany's World Cup star and European Footballer of the Year Karl-Heinz, gave Bayern a 1-0 home win. Steve Archibald levelled the scores in the home leg and Mark Falco, who was to score another vital goal in the semi-finals, hit their winner.

Security problems dominated the quarter-final tie against Austria Vienna, whose unprotected ground looked a sitting target for trouble-makers. Spurs gave themselves a comfortable 2-0 home lead and the away leg passed without incident except on the pitch where the Austrians fought to a 2-2 draw after Brazil and Ardiles had inflicted further damage.

Spurs were frankly lucky to win their semi-final, against the perennial Yugoslav challengers Hajduk Split. Losing 2-1 on the Adriatic, Falco getting the priceless away goal, Tottenham crept through 1-0 at home when Mike Hazard hit a low, hard drive into the right-hand corner from 20 yards after just 6 minutes. Roberts, Miller and Garry Stevens all performed sterling roles in the middle of the field and at the back to close Split down for the remaining 84 minutes.

Tottenham's opponents in the final, the

club's fourth in Europe, were to be the holders of the trophy, Anderlecht of Brussels. The Belgians, like Spurs, were a little fortunate to be there. Having lost 2–0 at Nottingham Forest in the first leg of their own semi-final, they had won the home half 3–0 after a peculiar long shot from their Italian prodigy Scifo beat Forest's Van Breukelen early on, and the referee had then awarded them a travesty of a non-existent but game winning penalty in the last minute. No doubt Spurs were relieved; it would have been a peculiar coincidence if they had had to play another European final, like that against Wolves in 1972, against a second Midlands club.

The first leg of the UEFA Cup final was in Brussels. It was a hard game with Spurs pleased to come away with a 1–1 draw. They were leading through a 58th minute Paul Miller header – another vital away goal which was to prove Spurs passport right the way through the competition – and held on until six minutes from the end when Anderlecht forced an equaliser. Once more crowd trouble dominated the tie and a Spurs fan was shot dead in a Brussels bar after a disturbance.

The return, and Keith Burkinshaw's last game as manager of the club, was memorable essentially for its conclusion, yet another penalty shoot-out. Almost unknown prior to 1982, these events had become increasingly and irritatingly familiar after the France v West Germany semi-final that year. In 1984, two of the three European competitions (Liverpool defeated Roma in the Champions Cup the same way) went to the same unsatisfactory conclusion. The actual result after 120 minutes was again 1–1, but this concealed the fact that most independent observers thought Ander-

lecht the better team. 'Roberts, who scored the first penalty kick, as much as Parks and the rest of them hung on to beat a better team for Burkinshaw's sake,' said Jeff Powell in the *Daily Mail*. 'It may seem a little churlish to focus attention on the ugly character of Spurs' defensive play in their hour of triumph,' wrote Robert Armstrong in *The Guardian*, 'but there is no doubt that the London side would not have reacted with the same stoical fortitude shown by the Belgians, who declined to retaliate under extreme provocation. The fact that Spurs could muster only a single goal in two hours – and that from Roberts – indicates how fortunate they were to topple Anderlecht.' Indeed, it is odd that a European trophy should be won with just two goals from the two centre-backs, but then Liverpool's full-backs have a similar habit of winning European Cups for their side.

The Belgians had actually gone ahead after an hour when Morten Olsen's beautiful through ball put Alex Czerniatinski away and the Polish miner's son flicked the ball past keeper Tony Parks, who had been standing in for the off form Ray Clemence towards the season's end. The Belgian side, incidentally, was composed of Danes, Dutch, Italians, Icelanders and various other combinations of European blood. Tottenham continued to battle. Roberts, captaining the side in Perryman's absence, was in the thick of everything, his enthusiasm carrying him beyond the bounds of most players' normal physical endurance and often beyond the bounds of most referee's notebooks. He was probably lucky the West German Mr. Roth seemed to view his antics benignly. With just a few minutes left, and the game increasingly looking all over for

Steve Archibald scores the vital first goal in the second leg of the UEFA Cup tie against Bayern Munich on 7 December 1983.

Mark Falco's left-footed shot consigns Bayern to the also-rans and puts Spurs into the next round of the 1983-84 UEFA Cup at White Hart Lane.

the home side, Burkinshaw made his very last decision as Tottenham manager – he sent on his talisman. Off came Miller and Mabbutt, on went Ally Dick and the man whose own career had been so closely linked to Burkinshaw's, Ossie Ardiles. As if by pre-arrangement with the gods, it worked.

Ardiles, with one of his earliest touches, hit the crossbar, the ball came back into a crowded penalty area and Roberts somehow forced it home. There were just six minutes of normal time left. 1–1 and the teams were level on aggregate, 2–2.

The half-hour of extra time produced numbing tiredness but no goals, leaving 21-year-old Tony Parks to face the remarkably daunting task of penalties to decide the destination of the trophy. Roberts took the first and scored. Then the Anderlecht and Danish captain Morten Olsen struck his shot well to Parks left, but the young keeper surprised the whole ground by saving it. 'I could see in the Anderlecht player's eyes where he was going to go', said Parks afterwards, 'so I just dived to the left.' Falco, Stevens and Archibald scored for Spurs, de Groote, Scifo and Vercauteren did the same for Anderlecht. That meant that, if Danny Thomas, signed from Coventry the year before, scored from the fifth kick, the trophy was Spurs'. In the kind of moment which can live with a player for the rest of his career, full-back Thomas ran up, shot unconvincingly, and Munaron saved. It was now 4–3 on penalties and there was only one of the original 10 penalties left. If Anderlecht scored it would be 4–4 and go to sudden death. Parks said later:

'I'd dived left for all four penalties so far, so I thought it was best to change my mind.' Icelander Arnor Gudjohnsen took the kick, Parks threw himself to his right and palmed it away. Up jumped the young reserve and hared off down the pitch. 'You read about this sort of thing in comics,' he said later, 'It's a lovely feeling. I started playing at nine on Hackney Marshes – now all this. I'm only 21 and not so long ago I thought I'd have to move to another club to get a chance.' It was very much Parks' night, and Burkinshaw's.

The manager was going out on a high note, winning a European trophy and having reached four finals in four years. The parallels with Bill Nicholson a decade before were uncanny. He too resigned after reaching four Cup finals in four seasons. He too won three of them, including the UEFA Cup. He too had spent a season in dispute with his principal striker.

Debate about a successor ranged far and wide. Terry Venables, David Pleat and Graham Taylor were favoured. In the end the club maintained its tradition of promoting within. An intelligent new broom has the sense to preserve those ideals which have worked in the past. The man who got the job was Keith Burkinshaw's assistant, Peter Shreeves. Like Burkinshaw, Shreeves had not had a particularly distinguished playing career – appearing or coaching at Reading, Chelmsford, Charlton and Wimbledon. At the tender age of 18 he was just three days away from a Welsh under-23 cap when he broke a leg playing for Reading. The chance never came again. He is Welsh because his parents were evacuated from

Islington to Neath and he was born there during the Battle of Britain. Perhaps the most quoted fact about him is that he has been a taxi-driver, which he was while coaching Chelmsford in the late 1960s. He had to retire from playing at the age of 28 with cartilage trouble and has coached ever since, though John Pratt now acts as trainer of the Spurs first team. Terry Neill brought Shreeves to Spurs in 1975, as youth team coach. One of the advantages he clearly has is that many of his early charges have grown with him into the first team.

That was certainly something of an advantage as the Spurs team went through a fair number of permutations in the first half of the 1984–85 season. Up front Allen, Falco, Crooks, Galvin and Chiedozie fluctuated without any set of three settling down. In midfield neither Hoddle, Stevens, Ardiles, Mabbutt nor Hazard were exactly permanent features. But this did not serve to greatly upset the way the team played. Though they were unexpectedly knocked out of the Milk Cup at home by Sunderland, and almost inevitably lost 1–0 at Anfield in the FA Cup, the League remained open and Spurs well placed in the top three. The fact that the League was, for perhaps the first time since 1981, of interest outside Merseyside was actually due to Liverpool starting the season very badly. Missing Graeme Souness, now with Sampdoria, it took some time for the Liverpool machine to move into gear. The Championship had gone to Liverpool in the three previous seasons, and in 1984–85 it certainly looked likely that the trophy would return to the said city, if not

club. FA Cup holders Everton led the League from early on, with Spurs a steady second in a well-paced chase. The critical day could well have been Saturday March 2nd. While Spurs won 1–0 at Stoke, Garth Crooks capitalising on a dreadful goalkeeping error by his old club, Everton let go a golden opportunity to keep the gap dangerously wide and effectively eliminate the third club, Manchester United, from the chase at the same time. With the score 1–1 at Old Trafford, and less than ten minutes left, Everton were awarded a penalty. Bailey saved from Sheedy and Everton got one point out of United rather than three. Suddenly the race was wide open and, almost as suddenly, Spurs were favourites. Ten of their remaining 15 games were at home.

Two weeks later the omens seemed to have gone into reverse. Having lost 2–1 at home to Manchester United in the interval, Spurs had to travel to a resurgent Liverpool. It was exactly 73 years to the day – 16 March 1912 – that they had last won at Anfield. If Liverpool won, and took the three points, then their claim to a fourth successive championship would begin to look very substantial indeed. If they lost, they would be around ten points adrift, surely too big a gap to make up in a dozen or so games. No one, understandably, thought the latter scenario a possibility. To place Spurs sequence at Anfield in context (it was the longest of its kind in British football), the last time Spurs won there was the year the Titanic sank and, even more remarkably, Barnsley won the FA Cup, having applied for reelection the year before. To the amusement of some, Liver-

Spurs new signing Garry Stevens causes Pat Jennings a little discomfort during the Boxing Day game between Tottenham and Arsenal in 1983. Arsenal won 4-2.

Steve Archibald powers a shot towards the FK Austria Memphis goal during the first leg of the UEFA Cup quarter-final at White Hart Lane on 7 March 1984. Spurs won the game 2-0 and the tie 4-2 on aggregate. Archibald left for Barcleona at the end of the season, netting Spurs £1,160,000 – the most they have ever received for any player.

pool had just beaten the very same Barnsley 4–0 in the FA Cup, though as it happened their memories would be closer to the ice-berg that was Clemence.

Early in the second half, with the score at 0–0, Hoddle nodded a subtle header to the edge of the penalty area, Mike Hazard hit a scorching volley to Grobbelaar's right, the keeper palmed the ball out but there, as he had been at Stoke, was Garth Crooks and Spurs were 1–0 up. Thanks to excellent Clemence goalkeeping (he emphatically denied having been the Liverpool keeper when Spurs last won at Anfield) that's the way the score stayed. Spurs were level top, had thirteen games to play and nine were at home. Everton, ahead on goal difference, had injury problems, and were still in the FA Cup and Cup Winners Cup.

One of Spurs advantages seemed that they had nothing else to concentrate on. The attempt to retain the UEFA Cup had collapsed at the quarter-final stage. Opponents Real Madrid were thought to be little more than a shadow of their former glorious selves; domestically they were far behind the Barcelona of Venables and Archibald. But the current Spurs could not exercise the domination of their old boys. The tie was unsatisfactory in almost every sense, there being just a single goal in the whole 180 minutes. It was an own-goal at that, Steve Perryman deflecting a shot past Ray Clemence in the first leg at White Hart Lane. Spurs were the better team in the Bernabeu Stadium two weeks later and suffered from a disgraceful refereeing decision when an excellent Falco header was disallowed by a referee who was presumably momentarily hallucinating. But even had the goal been allowed, it would only have brought the scores level. With

three minutes left the frustrations boiled over and Steve Perryman ended a tie he will hope to forget by being sent off for a frankly dreadful tackle on Valdano. This time no-one could argue with the referee's decision.

Before the game, it had been the general view among the British press that Spurs would probably win. This highlighted one peculiarity of their season so far – they had played far better away from home than at White Hart Lane. It was a difficult phenomenon to explain, except in terms of their now being a strong defensive unit, capable of absorbing pressure, and a good side on the break. Traditionally these were qualities associated more with near neighbours Arsenal than with the more cultured Spurs. If it was the case, then it does not seem to have been part of any tactical change by Peter Shreeves. Nonetheless, with so many home games left there were real concerns about form at the Lane.

Sadly, these fears were to prove only too justified. In the space of five days what had seemed to be so firmly in Spurs grasp melted away like an early summer mist. In the space of five days on the cusp of March and April two disastrous home defeats left them clutching at straws rather than rungs on the ladder. First came Aston Villa, an admittedly poor side lacking both their regular goalkeeper and central defender Alun Evans. Two breakaway goals, a frustrated Spurs attack and a 2–0 home defeat looked ominous. Five days later came the crunch – the visit of leaders Everton to White Hart Lane. Everton scored twice, from Andy Gray and Trevor Steven, and though both goals were aided by defensive errors they were very well taken and a late Roberts goal could not conceal the fact that Everton were

clearly the better side. In retrospect, it was probably the leg injury to Garry Stevens a month before which had been the turning point. Now virtually an England regular, his ability to play either as central defender or in midfield was invaluable to the team.

Spurs loss of form was a massive disappointment to the club and its fans. Between 1 January and 4 May 1985 they played 8 home games, lost six, drew one and won just once. There were four consecutive home League defeats – against Villa, Everton, Arsenal and Ipswich. But there are seasons and seasons. Even if they had won most of those games it wouldn't actually have won them the trophy. Everton had gone into one of those sequences which make a club unstoppable. Heading for an undefeated run of 30 matches, chasing three trophies and already well past the previous highest ever points total they were frankly uncatchable and clearly the best side in the country. Another year Spurs efforts would have won them the Championship, this year Everton brooked no real contenders.

Chairman Irving Schloar was philosophical about the season's end: 'Ever since I first watched Spurs from the terraces in 1954 I've believed that if the club wins a trophy it is essential that it deserves to win it and is seen to deserve it. This is Everton's year – but it's also our best League performance for around 15 years. Don't forget that.'

Since his arrival at the club at the end of 1982, Scholar's main priority has obviously been putting the financial side in order. He had already had informal discussions in the City about a public floatation prior to the takeover. As soon as there was a change of control he was quick to introduce an efficient computer-controlled ticket system (long Spurs' achilles heel) and arrange a testimonial for Bill Nicholson, who celebrates 50 years with the club in February 1986. The biggest problem was paying for the stand, something Scholar's business career well suited him for: 'It is interesting that every club which has gone in for a major new stand since the early seventies has had major problems as a result. Chelsea and Wolves both nearly went out of business, Forest were fortunate to have the revenue from that amazing spell of their's. Spurs were in a similar position. The reason is quite simple; a new stand is a capital asset and has to be paid for out of capital. A player isn't – you can pay for him out of profits and deduct the transfer fee before paying tax. Basically, if a stand costs, let's say, £5 million, then you need to make profits of around £10 million to pay for it. And who can make that sort of money in football nowadays? The reason we went public was very straightforward; money raised in a share floatation is capital. Hence it could all be used to pay for the capital cost of the building. It made perfect sense.'

Scholar is surprised no other clubs have followed Spurs' route: 'Every kind of business is represented on the Stock Exchange – why not football clubs? It's a conservative game, but the advantages are enormous, not least that you give the fans a chance to have a share, and, as a result, a say in *their* club.'

In May 1985 the club received permission to develop its valuable Cheshunt training ground, a plan which should be worth at least £3 million to Spurs. 'We may develop it ourselves,' says Scholar. 'Why not? It's very sensible for the club to have interests outside football because they provide other sources of income. Of course, football will always be the basis but if we can make money elsewhere then it is bound to benefit the club. The key is to do things gradually, steadily, not to rush major decisions. We are going to continue developing the ground, but a step at a time like Manchester United at Old Trafford. I would like to do something about the corners first, then perhaps move on to a new stand on the East side. But we'll take it slowly – and, until we reach the

ABOVE LEFT: *Keith Burkinshaw says his farewells to the Tottenham crowd before the UEFA Cup final on 23 May 1984. It was a fitting end, Spurs winning the trophy on penalties. Irving Scholar says of Burkinshaw that he constantly needed new challenges: 'It must be very difficult for a manager to come up with new ideas all the time, to keep players interested . . . Keith was always looking for something new, and he's done well.'*
ABOVE: *Burkinshaw's assistant and successor, Peter Shreeves.*

207

ORDINARY SHARE CERTIFICATE

Tottenham Hotspur plc

(Incorporated under the Companies Acts 1948 to 1981. Registered in England No. 1706358.)

Number of Shares

ONE THOUSAND TWO HUNDRED AND THIRTY

Printed by Henry Jaffe Limited, London.

This is to Certify that

PHILIP WILLIAM SOAR ESQ

Joint Holder(s)

is/are the registered holder(s) of fully paid
Ordinary Shares of 25 pence each in
Tottenham Hotspur plc subject to the
Memorandum and Articles of Association
of the Company.

Given under the Seal of the Company.

No transfer of any of the Shares specified herein will be registered unless accompanied by this Certificate. 87103SOAR   PHILIWI/00

Transfer Office: Bourne House, 34 Beckenham Road, Beckenham, Kent BR3 4TU

One thing that can make a Tottenham follower's lot a happy one compared to that of a fan of any other English team ... a part ownership of the club. This modest share certificate is the author's.

point when everyone wants to sit down, then there will always be standing accommodation at White Hart Lane.

'The traditions of the club are vital to me. I've always believed in the way the club plays – the attacking game, the style, the fact that we have always been known as a *positive* club. That will never change while I'm chairman. You have to take the responsibility personally and very seriously. You can never think, or let anyone else think, that the club is not bigger than any individual. The club must always come first and we only want players at White Hart Lane who want to play for Spurs. I remember a discussion with one player recently. It wasn't a serious problem but he wanted a meeting. I said to him straightaway: "Do you want to play for this club?" "Yes, absolutely," he replied, and after that no problem is too difficult to solve. But if he had said no then I wouldn't have wanted him ever to play for Spurs again. That's why we spend as much time, more in fact, investigating a player *off* the field than on it when we make a new signing.'

In 1985 the problems of football were indeed rather more off the field than on it. While Spurs had certainly experienced a reasonably satisfactory season, the game itself was in turmoil. 1984–85 would not be remembered for Everton's Championship or Norman Whiteside's astonishing FA Cup final winner, rather it would go down in the history books as the year of Luton and Chelsea, of Bradford and Birmingham and, of course, the stunning culmination of so many ills at the European Cup final in Brussels. And while Spurs had been relatively blameless in recent seasons, they soon became one of the clubs most affected by the dramatic and entirely understandable public reaction to this final tragedy.

The first thing to go was Spurs' hard-won place in Europe, not just for one season but perhaps for a footballing generation. As with the other major clubs, revenues from television, sponsors and, for that matter, week-by-week gates were suddenly also brought in question. Few major clubs could afford the consequences that loomed before them – Spurs alone would almost certainly be several

With just six minutes of the UEFA Cup final against Anderlecht left on 23 May 1984, Graham Roberts forces the ball over the line and gives Spurs the chance of extra-time.

BELOW: As Tony Parks makes his historic save from Arnor Gudjohnsen's penalty, the Spurs players (from left to right) Ardiles, Stevens, Roberts and Hughton rush to congratulate their young keeper. Spurs beat Anderlecht 4-3 in the penalty shoot-out.

hundred thousand pounds worse off than they had projected by losing European competition in one season alone. It induced a sense of real sadness in more than one way.

Only a year before Spurs had effectively won a European trophy in that very Belgian capital. Their return leg against Anderlecht had, unusually for an English club game, been televised live throughout Europe. While it lacked the quality of European matches two decades before, it certainly compared for excitement. 'It was a wonderful advertisement for the club and for the English game,' says Irving Scholar today. 'It was fast, thrilling and tense. In many respects it was probably the best game seen at White Hart Lane since the legendary Benfica match.' It was sad that it would be many years before we could expect to see its like again.

Tottenham Hotspur is now an institution, well into it's second century. No one survives who can tell us about those days spent playing on the Tottenham Marshes, or even about the way the club eventually arrived at White Hart Lane. None of us will be there to celebrate the Bicentennial in 2082. But there is one thing that we can be sure of; that as long as football continues to be played, then the Spurs will go marching on . . .

EUROPE IN THE 1960s and 1970s

Date							BROWN	BAKER	HENRY	BLANCHFLOWER	NORMAN	MACKAY	JONES	WHITE	R. SMITH	ALLEN	DYSON	MARCHI	SAUL	CLAYTON	MEDWIN	GREAVES	HOPKINS	J. SMITH	JENNINGS	KINNEAR	KNOWLES	MULLERY	ENGLAND	BEAL	ROBERTSON	GILZEAN	VENABLES	HOY	BOND
13 Sep	61	A	L	2-4	ECup	Gornik	1	2	3	4	5	6	7^1	8	9	10	11^1																		
20 Sep	61	H	W	8-1	ECup	Gornik	1	2	3	4^1	5	6	7^3	8^1	9^2	10	11^1																		
1 Nov	61	A	W	3-1	ECup	Feijenoord	1	2	3	4	5		7	8			11^1	6	9^2	10															
15 Nov	61	H	D	1-1	ECup	Feijenoord	1	2	3	4	5	10	7	8			11^1	6	9																
14 Feb	62	A	L	0-1	ECup	Dukla Prague	1	2	3	4	5	10	11	8	9			6			7														
26 Feb	62	H	W	4-1	ECup	Dukla Prague	1	2	3	4	5	10^2	11	8	9^2			6			7														
21 Mar	62	A	L	1-3	ECupsf	Benfica	1	2	3	10	5	6	11	8	9^1			4				7													
5 Apr	62	H	W	2-1	ECupsf	Benfica	1	2	3	4^1	5	6	11	8	9^1						7	10													
31 Oct	62	H	W	5-2	ECWC	Glasgow Rangers	1	2	3	4	5^1	6	11	8^1		9^1					7	10^1													
11 Dec	62	A	W	3-2	ECWC	Glasgow Rangers	1	2	3	4	5	6	11	8	9^2						7	10^1													
5 Mar	63	A	L	0-2	ECWC	Slovan Bratislava	1	2	3		5	6	11	8	9			4	7			10													
14 Mar	63	H	W	6-0	ECWC	Slavan Bratislava	1		3		5	6^1	11^1	8^1	9^1			4	7			10^2	2												
24 Apr	63	A	W	2-1	ECWCsf	OFK Belgrade	1	2	3		5	6		8^1	9		11^1	4				7		10											
1 May	63	H	W	3-1	ECWCsf	OFK Belgrade	1	2	3	4	5	10^1	7^1	8	9^1		11	6																	
15 May	63	*	W	5-1	ECWCFinal	Atletico Madrid	1	2	3	4	5		7	8^1	9		11^2	6				10^2													
3 Dec	63	H	W	2-0	ECWC	Man Utd	1	2	3		5	6^1	7	8	9		11^1	4				10													
10 Dec	63	A	L	1-4	ECWC	Man Utd	1	2	3		5	6	7	8	9		11	4				10^1													
20 Sep	67	A	W	2-0	ECWC	Hadjuk Split													11			8^1			1	2	3	4	5	6	7^1	9	10		
27 Sep	67	H	W	4-3	ECWC	Hadjuk Split							11									8			1	2	3	4	5	6	7^2	9^1	10^1		
29 Nov	67	A	L	0-1	ECWC	Olympique Lyonnais						6	11									8			1	2	3	4			7	9	10	5	
13 Dec	67	H	W	4-3	ECWC	Olympique Lyonnais						6	11^1									8^2			1	2	3				7	9	10^1	5	4
						Total App	**17**	**16**	**17**	**12**	**17**	**17**	**19**	**17**	**14**	**3**	**9**	**12**	**5**	**1**	**5**	**14**	**1**	**1**	**4**	**4**	**4**	**3**	**2**	**2**	**4**	**4**	**4**	**2**	**1**
*** Played at Rotterdam**						**Total Goals**				**2**	**1**	**5**	**7**	**5**	**10**	**1**	**8**		**2**			**10**									**3**	**1**	**2**		

Date							JENNINGS	KINNEAR	KNOWLES	MULLERY	ENGLAND	BEAL	ROBERTSON	GILZEAN	VENABLES	SAUL	HOY	BOND	SOUNESS	COATES	PEARCE	PERRYMAN	CHIVERS	PETERS	EVANS	HOLDER	NEIGHBOUR	MORGAN	PRATT	COLLINS	NAYLOR	DILLION	DAINES	McGRATH	
14 Sep	71	A	W	6-1	UEFA	Keflavik	1	2	3	4^2	5	6		11^3					S	7^1	S	8	9	10											
28 Sep	71	H	W	9-0	UEFA	Keflavik	1		3^1	4	5	6		11^2						7^1		8^1	9^3	10	2	S^1									
20 Oct	71	A	D	0-0	UEFA	Nantes	1	2	3	4	5	6		11								8	9	10			7	S							
2 Nov	71	H	W	1-0	UEFA	Nantes	1		3		5	6		11							S	8	9	10^1	2		7		4						
8 Dec	71	H	W	3-0	UEFA	Rapid Bucharest	1		3		5	6		7						4	S	8	9^2	10^1	2		11								
15 Dec	71	A	W	2-0	UEFA	Rapid Bucharest	1		3			6		11						5	S^1	7	10^1	8	2				9	4	S				
7 Mar	72	A	W	2-0	UEFA	U.T. Arad	1		3		5^1	6		7								8	9	10	2			11^1	4	S					
21 Mar	72	H	D	1-1	UEFA	U.T. Arad	1		3		5			7^1						4		8		10	2			11	9		6				
5 Apr	72	H	W	2-1	UEFAsf	A.C. Milan	1	2	3	11	5			7						4		8^2	9	10			S				6				
19 Apr	72	A	D	1-1	UEFAsf	A.C. Milan	1	2	3	4^1	5	6								11		8	9	10					7						
3 May	72	A	W	2-1	UEFAFinal	Wolves	1	2	3	4	5	6		7						11		8	9^2	10					S						
17 May	72	H	D	1-1	UEFAFinal	Wolves	1	2	3	4^1	5	6		7						11		8	9	10											
13 Sep	72	A	W	6-3	UEFA	Lyn Oslo	1		3		5			7^2							11	8	9^2	10^1	2				4^1		6				
27 Sep	72	H	W	6-0	UEFA	Lyn Oslo	1	2	3		5	6		7						11^2	10^1	8	9^3			S			4		S				
25 Oct	72	H	W	4-0	UEFA	Olympiakos	1		3		5	6		7						11^1	4^2	8	9^1	10	2		S				S				
8 Nov	72	A	L	0-1	UEFA	Olympiakos	1		3		5			7							4	8	9		2				11		10	6			
29 Nov	72	H	W	2-0	UEFA	Red Star Belgrade	1		3		5			7^1							11	8	9^1	10	2				4		6				
13 Dec	72	A	L	0-1	UEFA	Red Star Belgrade	1	6	3		5									7	11	8	9	10	2				4						
7 Mar	73	H	W	1-0	UEFA	Vitoria Setubal	1	2	3		5	6		7						4	11	8	9	10	S^1										
21 Mar	73	A	L	1-2	UEFA	Vitoria Setubal	1	2	3		5	6		7						4	11	8	9^1	10							S				
10 Apr	74	A	L	0-1	UEFAsf	Liverpool	1	2	3		5	6		7						4	S	8	9	10	S				11						
25 Apr	74	H	W	2-1	UEFAsf	Liverpool	1	2	3		5	6		7						4	S	8	9	10^2	S				11						
19 Sep	73	A	W	5-1	UEFA	Grasshoppers	1		3		5	6		S^2						4		8	9^2	10	2^1	S	11		7						
3 Oct	73	H	W	4-1	UEFA	Grasshoppers			3		5^1	6		7						11		8	9	10^2	2				4				1		
24 Oct	73	A	D	1-1	UEFA	Aberdeen		3			5	6		7						11^1		8		10	2		S		4		S		1	9	
7 Nov	73	H	W	4-1	UEFA	Aberdeen	1		3		5	6		7								8	9	10^1	2		11^1		4					S^2	
28 Nov	73	A	D	1-1	UEFA	Dinamo Tbilisi	1		3		5	6								11^1		8	9	10	2				4		7				
12 Dec	73	H	W	5-1	UEFA	Dinamo Tbilisi	1				5	6								11		8	9^2	10^2	2				4		3			7^1	
6 Mar	74	A	W	2-1	UEFA	FC Cologne	1				5	6										8	9	10^1	2				4		3	11		7^1	
20 Mar	74	H	W	3-0	UEFA	FC Cologne	1				5	6								11^1		8	9^1	10^1	2				4		3			7	
10 Apr	74	A	W	2-1	UEFAsf	Lokomotiv Leipzig	1				5	6								11^1		8	9	10^1	2	S	7		4		3				
24 Apr	74	H	W	2-0	UEFAsf	Lokomotiv Leipzig	1	2			5	6								11		8	9^1	10		S			4		3			7^1	
21 May	74	H	D	2-2	UEFAFinal	Feijenoord	.1				5^1	6								11		8	9	10	2				4		3	S		7	
29 May	74	A	L	0-2	UEFAFinal	Feijenoord	1				5	6								11		8	9	10	2	S			4		3			7	
						Full App	**32**	**14**	**26**	**7**	**33**	**28**		**23**						**26**	**8**	**34**	**32**	**32**	**22**		**6**	**2**	**24**	**1**	**13**	**2**	**2**	**7**	
					(3 own goals)	**Total Goals**			**1**	**4**	**3**			**11**						**9**	**4**	**3**	**22**	**13**	**2**	**1**	**1**	**1**	**1**					**5**	
						App as sub								**1s**					**1s**		**6s**				**3s**	**6s**	**3s**	**1s**	**1s**	**1s**	**5s**	**1s**		**1s**	

Spurs versus Arsenal

Spurs versus Arsenal . . . three words to create excitement in the most stoical of North Londoners. With the possible exception of Everton and Liverpool, the latter being an offshoot of the former, no conflict is greater, no English fans are more committed and no neighbours have had such a justifiable basis for their rivalry.

First and foremost, Spurs and Arsenal remain London's leading clubs. Before 1982 Arsenal had won the League eight times, the Cup on five occasions. Spurs had won the League twice and the Cup six times. The whole of the rest of London has managed to accumulate just six trophies among twelve other Football League clubs. But added to that is the physical proximity of the grounds, Arsenal's strange arrival, despite Spurs' protests, in North London in 1913, and the Gunners' quite astonishing vanishing trick

from the Second Division in 1919 – when they fooled the football establishment into handing over Spurs' First Division place. Add to this those two managerial quirks – Spurs half-back Herbert Chapman going on to make Arsenal the dominant club of the inter-war period and Terry Neill's expeditions across North London – and one has the basis for a very real rivalry.

Having said that, it is surprising the clubs have rarely met in a major game. They have never contested a final in either the FA Cup or League Cup and had met in only three first-class cup ties before being drawn together in the third round in 1982. In terms of League games, they have met in only one truly critical match – the last game of the 1971 season when Arsenal needed to win at White Hart Lane to take the Double. But, therein, lies the other remarkable link between the clubs; they are

Aerial ballet at Highbury on Saturday 27 February 1954 as Cliff Holton of Arsenal and Harry Clarke compete at a corner. Looking on are Marchi, Willis, Ditchburn and Ramsey. The other Arsenal forward is Doug Lishman. Spurs won the game 3-0 with two goals from George Robb and one from Sonny Walters. Earlier in the season Arsenal had won just as convincingly at White Hart Lane – 4-1. It was not an outstanding year for either club – Arsenal finished 12th and Spurs 16th.

the only ones in the twentieth century to do the impossible, to win the coveted Double.

But to tell the tale of the North London rivalry from the beginning; the story really revolves around the remarkable Henry Norris. He was a property developer in the Fulham and Wimbledon areas around the turn of the century, had been a member of Fulham Borough Council for many years and was mayor from 1909 to 1919. He became chairman of Fulham Football Club around this time and led his side to the championship of the Southern League in 1906 and 1907. In those same years Spurs finished fifth and sixth. Fulham then went straight into the Second Division of the Football League, where they found the going rather more difficult. Their decisiveness was, however, one of the key triggers for Spurs to make the same move a year later.

Norris was soon convinced that Fulham did not have the potential support to become a really top flight club. By the 1910–11 season they were over £3,000 in debt but, by coincidence, Woolwich Arsenal were suffering similar problems at the same time. Norris had close links with the Woolwich club; Fulham's first two managers, Harry Bradshaw and Philip Kelso, were both ex-Arsenal players (a link which has continued to the present day – nine of Fulham's fourteen managers since they joined the League have previously been with Arsenal). In 1910 Norris proposed that the two struggling clubs should merge, though it was unclear whether the combined organisation would have played in Fulham or Woolwich, or possibly both. The League and FA refused to let the merger go through, largely because of objections from other League clubs in the capital. But Norris had by now embarked on what amounted to a personal crusade – the building of a great London club which could compete with the best from the North and the Midlands. At the time only Spurs had made inroads into their dominance (and then no more than fleetingly) and no Southern club had ever won the League. Norris sensed that Woolwich Arsenal were the more pliable of his two options and soon transferred his patronage, and cash, south of the river. He effectively took control of Arsenal in 1910, when they temporarily went into liquidation. There was no quick improvement, for the 1912–13 season was the worst in the club's history, seeing them finish bottom of Division One with a record low 18 points.

ARSENAL MOVE TO HIGHBURY

Arsenal had been founded in 1886 at the Ordnance factory in Woolwich. Originally called Dial Square, the club played its first game on 8 January 1887 on Plumstead Common and progressed at an amazing pace. We have read earlier of their first game against Spurs, on the Marshes on 19 November 1887. In 1893, well before Spurs had seriously considered professionalism, Arsenal had applied for and been accepted by the Football League. Times were hard as the only Football League club south of Birmingham, but Woolwich Arsenal (for a time they were called Royal Arsenal) prospered and entered the First Division in 1904. From then until the move from Plumstead in 1913, the club drifted along,

never indicating that it might one day scale the dizzy heights for which Norris yearned.

Norris knew that Plumstead, hemmed in by the Thames to the north and miles from central London, was never going to support a Championship or Cup winning side. He made his decision to move after he had decided that the existing possibilities for Fulham and Arsenal were exhausted. All that remained was to find a suitable place to play. The London School of Divinity, in Avenell Road, N5, proved ideal and Norris bought the site from the Ecclesiastical Commissioners. It had enough land but, more important as it eventually turned out, it was right next door to a tube station. Gillespie Road station, on the Great Northern, Piccadilly and Brompton Railway (later simply the Piccadilly Line of the London Underground) had been opened in December 1906. It was to give Arsenal what few other London clubs had, direct access via a comprehensive transport network to the whole of London's working-class population. Chelsea might be nearer the West End, but Arsenal was the more convenient. Highbury is still only a 15-minute tube ride from Piccadilly Circus, a convenience with which White Hart Lane has never been able to compete and which was to prove critical to Norris's plans. What it did was to give Arsenal the *potential* to become a great club.

Spurs and Clapton Orient objected vociferously to the move – but to no avail. The League had no regulation preventing a club moving if they wished, though one was added soon afterwards. It was then unprecedented and in fact only South Shields Adelaide, who moved to Gateshead in 1930, have ever left their home in a similar way. It is unlikely that Norris was much concerned with Spurs' protests; he had what he wanted and, in the event, North London, with its comprehensive rail network, has provided more than adequate support for two major clubs since.

Arsenal's move was enormously hurried. By the time of their first game of the 1913–14 season, on Saturday 6 September, the stands were far from completed, there were no dressing-room facilities (the players just washed in bowls of cold water brought in from outside) and the only first-aid provision was a milk cart provided by the local dairy and on which one unfortunate player was removed from the ground. Norris had poured a fortune, estimated then at £125,000, into the club but any hopes for a rapid return on his outlay were dashed by the First World War. At the end of the 1914–15 season Arsenal had finished fifth in the Second Division – Derby had 53 points, Preston 50, Barnsley 47, Wolves 45 with Arsenal, Birmingham and Hull having 43 each. What happened next is largely a matter for conjecture. Norris was not without friends in the League and he was particularly close to Liverpool's John McKenna, then the President. Tottenham, as we have seen, had finished bottom of the First Division in 1914–15, with Chelsea nineteenth. The League decided to extend the First Division to 22 clubs in 1919–20 and, in the normal course of events, Chelsea and Spurs would have expected to remain in Division 1 with Derby and Preston promoted to join them. This had happened on every other occasion on which the First Division had been extended.

ARSENAL THE ROBBERS

Such an outcome seemed even more likely in the light of some dubious goings on at the end of the 1914–15 season. With the League certain to be suspended for the duration of the War, some results in April 1915 were under suspicion. In particular, the match between Manchester United and Liverpool on 2 April 1915 was, after a long libel case, firmly determined to have been fixed by some of the players. United won that game 2–0, but the significance for Spurs was that the Manchester side thus ended with 30 points, Chelsea with 29 and Spurs with 28. The League decided to leave United (the club itself was blameless) with their two points, but, even if they had been deducted, Spurs would still have finished bottom as they had a much worse goal average than United. Nonetheless, the incident did throw considerable doubt on the final placings and suggested that there could not possibly be any alternative but to re-elect the bottom clubs after the War.

It was not to be. Somehow or other Norris's desperation for success (and concern about his investment) communicated itself to the management committee and, instead of automatically promoting Derby and Preston (which did happen) and leaving it at that, they invited applications to fill Chelsea and Tottenham's spots. Furthermore, the President announced to the meeting that there were special reasons why Chelsea should not be asked to go to the vote and the management committee suggested they be elected unopposed – which they were. Chelsea would have finished *above* United had the two debatable points against Liverpool been deducted and it was this which was behind McKenna's statement. But it was not as if Spurs had performed abysmally in that pre-War season. They had, after all, only one point fewer than Chelsea and there was not the slightest suggestion that Spurs had been involved in any malpractice.

This was all very well, but the President's next announcement was a bombshell. He urged the meeting to vote for Arsenal on the grounds that they had been members of the League for longer than Tottenham and that their loyalty should be rewarded. The suggestion made little sense; Wolves, who had been founder members of the League in 1888 and who had finished above Arsenal in 1915, were also applying, as were Birmingham who, as Small Heath, had entered the Second Division a year before Arsenal, in 1892.

The meeting clearly picked up the mood – that the management committee had some good reason for replacing Spurs with Arsenal, though these good reasons remained unspoken, were not revealed afterwards and no convincing explanation has ever been offered since. The voting went Arsenal 18, Spurs 8, Barnsley 5, Wolves 4, Nottingham Forest 3, Birmingham 2, Hull 1. Arsenal were thus elected to the First Division and have remained there since, the only club in the Football League not to have earned its current position.

This astonishing incident – which is as intriguing now as it was then – is really the source of the North London rivalry, particularly coming so soon on the League management committee's refusal to heed Spurs' protests about Arsenal's arrival at Highbury. But the actual proximity of the two clubs has

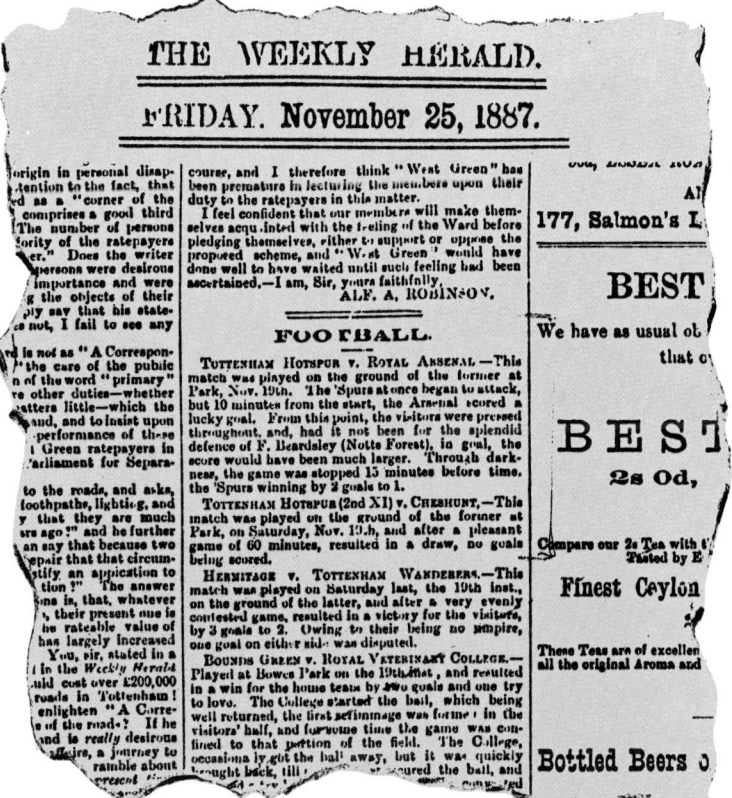

never really been a source of friction. Spurs were promoted back a year later, in 1920, and it can be convincingly argued that the rivalry has been of great benefit to both clubs.

The Norris story is worth concluding. He continued to rule Arsenal with an iron hand until, in 1925, he persuaded that ex-Spurs reserve Herbert Chapman to leave his Huddersfield side for the highly unpromising pastures of Highbury. Chapman rapidly became the iron man himself, throwing out some of Norris's more restrictive controls (such as not spending more than £1,000 on a player) and, of course, eventually making Arsenal the best known club side in the world.

In 1927 the FA censured Norris and another Arsenal director for various financial irregularities and Norris sued them for libel. The FA contended that Norris's series of special payments to players (particularly to Charlie Buchan) were against FA regulations, that there were other financial irregularities involved (the club paid for his chauffeur for instance), and that they had the right to discipline him. Norris lost the case and was effectively exiled from the game. He died on 30 July 1934, the same year as Chapman, and before his club completed its own celebrated hat-trick of Championships. It was almost a Greek tragedy of an ending for a great footballing man.

CHAPMAN THE SPUR

Despite Arsenal's elevation to the First Division in 1919, Spurs were unquestionably North London's leading club for the next six years. Between Tottenham's return to Division 1 in 1920 and the 1925–26 season Arsenal led Spurs in the League just once (that was in 1922–23 when they were 11th and 12th re-

spectively), White Hart Lane was attracting far more fans than Highbury, and The Arsenal were in increasing danger of relegation – they finished 19th, only one point clear, in 1924 and 20th in 1925.

What changed matters in 1925 was the arrival of Herbert Chapman. Within twelve months Arsenal were League runners-up, equalling Spurs performance in 1921–22, and Spurs were 13 points behind in 15th place. Chapman is particularly significant in the Spurs-Arsenal story because it has often been said that one of the major reasons behind his desire to make Arsenal a great club was his relative failure as a player at White Hart Lane.

He had appeared for numerous clubs, usually as an amateur, before he reached Spurs – Stalybridge Rovers, Rochdale, Grimsby, Swindon, Sheppey United (Spurs' first ever Southern League opponents), Northampton (he scored two goals *against* Spurs on 19 October 1901), Sheffield United, Notts County and Northampton a second time. The Cobblers were a run-of-the-mill Southern League club at the time but Chapman's performances at wing-half and centre-forward attracted Spurs' attention and, when 'Bristol' Jones died of typhoid, they filled the gap for £70 with the purchase of one Herbert Chapman.

He scored in his first game for the club, a 1-1 draw against Brighton on 18 March 1905, but that was apparently the peak of his career and, according to Stephen Studd, author of *Football Emperor*, the fans were angry when Spurs retained him at the end of the season. In two years he was to play 42 times in the Southern League and score 15 goals. By then, the *Herald* was commenting that '. . . Chapman began by getting goals but for some time past he has been no better than the others. . .'

In March 1907 Northampton asked him to persuade a Spurs colleague, Walter Bull, to become their secretary-manager. Bull eventually decided to continue playing for another season and suggested Chapman apply instead. In the end he was Northampton's third choice (they had also been turned down by Manchester City half-back Sam Ashworth) but he got the job and moved immediately after playing his last game for Spurs, against Queen's Park Rangers at White Hart Lane on Saturday 27 April 1907. On that date Northampton were six points adrift at the bottom of the Southern League. Within two years they were champions.

His spell at White Hart Lane as a player was the longest he ever had with one club, and while Spurs were to meander up and down for the next two decades, Chapman was to go from strength to strength. After Northampton he moved to Leeds City, where he won the Wartime League Championship, then on to Huddersfield, who won the FA Cup in 1922 and the League in 1923–24 and 1924–25.

The challenge of Arsenal was obvious to the most successful manager in football. London had never welcomed the League Championship, the only London professional club to win the FA Cup was Spurs, and yet Highbury was only 15 minutes by tube from the centre of the biggest and richest city in the world. If there was no potential at Highbury, then where did it exist?

By a delightful stroke of luck, Chapman's first game in charge of Arsenal was at High-bury on 29 August 1925 against. . . Spurs! It was also the very first day on which games were played under the new offside law, which had changed 'three defenders nearer the goal' to 'two defenders. . .'.

Spurs won 1-0, with Jimmy Dimmock scoring the goal and Jimmy Seed playing in midfield to provide the link between attack and defence and helping fill the gap caused by having to move the centre-half back. Chapman was to solve the problems caused by the new law far more quickly than Peter McWilliam at Tottenham, and Arsenal were runners-up in the First Division in 1925–26. Spurs continued to prove something of a bogey team to them at Highbury, however, and it was not until 20 October 1934 that Arsenal beat their neighbours at home – a rather convincing 5-1.

THE OFF-FIELD RIVALRY

Those results do anything but reflect the relative playing success of the two clubs between Chapman's arrival at Highbury and the Second World War. While Spurs spent all but five of those seasons in the Second Division, Arsenal won five League Championships and reached four Cup finals, winning two. Both of Chapman's League clubs – Huddersfield and Arsenal – were to complete a hat-trick of championships, the only sides ever to do so.

Considering that they have been London's premier clubs for so long, perhaps the most intriguing feature of the Spurs – Arsenal rivalry is that they have hardly ever met in a truly critical game. They have never contested a Cup final, and only once been drawn together in a semi-final – for a 1968 League Cup final place. On only two occasions in nearly 100 years since Arsenal were formed have they met in the FA Cup, statistically a remarkably small number of meetings given their status in the game, and just once more in the League Cup, in 1980.

The Spurs v Arsenal rivalry, therefore, is probably unique among major derby conflicts in being based on off-field events rather than any significant on-field clashes. It is also probably best illustrated by a triangle, with the two sets of fans in opposite corners, boxing-style, at the bottom, the players and managers forming the two converging sides, and the directors meeting in peace and harmony at the apex. For as Spurs life-president and past chairman Sidney Wale will tell you, the two clubs have always retained very friendly relations at board and managerial level, at least since the 1930s.

The clubs have done business over the years and never fallen out, even though Spurs have come off decidedly second best in some deals. The sale of Pat Jennings is one such example; but though that perhaps is the skeleton in Keith Burkinshaw's cupboard, Bill Nicholson was blamed by Spurs' fans for another unprofitable deal with Arsenal, swapping the popular Jimmy Robertson for David Jenkins. Nicholson didn't have any more success with Laurie Brown when he bought the former Northampton defender from Highbury for £40,000 and tried unsuccessfully to turn him into a striker.

Skipper Steve Perryman's earliest recollection of a Spurs-Arsenal cup match was the 1968 two-leg League Cup semi-final when he

OPPOSITE BOTTOM: *The Spurs' team group photograph taken before the start of the 1905–06 Southern League season. This was Herbert Chapman's first full season with the club (he is circled), and he ended it as top scorer with 11 goals in 28 games. No other player reached double figures, but it was his only year of note at White Hart Lane. In two and a half seasons he made only 42 Southern League appearances, scoring 15 goals, playing either at wing-half or as a forward. Manager John Cameron is standing second from left on the third row, chairman Charles Roberts is third from right on the same row. Holding the ball is captain Sandy Tait.*
OPPOSITE TOP: *Chapman left Tottenham in April 1907 and went on to manage Northampton, Leeds City and Huddersfield. He won Championship trophies with all of them before returning to London as manager of The Arsenal in 1925. The very first game they played under Chapman's management was at Highbury on 29 August 1925. . . against Spurs! The picture of that game shows Spurs' centre-forward William Lane failing to reach the ball before Arsenal keeper Robson. It was also the first day of the new offside law and Spurs won the match 1-0 with a Jimmy Dimmock goal. Jimmy Seed, seen between Robson and Lane, fell back to act as a deeper lying midfield link, but it took Herbert Chapman two months to fully appreciate the tactical changes needed. As soon as he did so Arsenal became the major football force in London, finishing the season as League runners-up. Spurs finished 15th and were not to seriously challenge Arsenal's dominance in the capital for another quarter of a century.*

was still an apprentice. The clubs had met only once previously in a cup match, back on 8 January 1949 at Highbury, where Arsenal won 3-0 in the FA Cup third round. If this League Cup encounter is any indication, perhaps it's just as well they haven't met more often. After Spurs had lost the Highbury leg 1-0 – the goal coming from John Radford 30 seconds from time – the return boiled over as the tension turned to desperation. Radford and Cyril Knowles were involved in a punch-up, Mike England and Arsenal's Ian Ure fought a running battle, and Arsenal goalkeeper Bob Wilson left the ground on crutches. There was trouble on the terraces, too, with one fan stabbed amid a wave of fights. Greaves put Spurs back in the game with an equaliser but Radford made the difference with another late winner. If there was any consolation for Spurs' fans, it might have been Arsenal's humiliation in the final by Third Division Swindon.

The clubs' more recent League Cup meeting, on 4 November 1980, was a far quieter affair, and this time Spurs won – their first victory over Arsenal in eight meetings spanning four years. Again it was in the League Cup, and 42,000 fans broke into the *Glory, Glory, Hallelujah* chorus as Ardiles scored the only goal of the fourth round tie. Keith Burkinshaw spoke for everyone at Spurs when he said: 'It's always nice to win, But to beat that lot is the icing on the cake.'

Perryman, who had the chance to join Arsenal but turned them down – 'I didn't find them as warm a club as Spurs' he recalls – has one particularly vivid recollection of a Spurs-Arsenal League match, probably the most crucial the two clubs have ever played. It was the 1971 Double 'decider' at White Hart Lane when Arsenal won 1-0 to clinch the League title. 'I remember arriving at White Hart Lane station for the game at about six o'clock,' says Perryman. 'It's only 500 yards to the ground, but it took me until ten past

seven to get inside. The road was jammed solid with fans.'

With a degree of professionalism that transcends inter-club rivalry, Perryman admits he has a sneaking admiration for Arsenal's performance that year, despite the usually disparaging Press comparisons with Spurs' own feat a decade before: 'They were well organised and had a style perfectly adapted to their players. It was no mean achievement.'

Board relations are so friendly that Sidney Wale didn't bat an eyelid when, in the late 1970s, he received a phone call from Arsenal chairman Denis Hill-Wood inviting him to discuss a plan to share a new stadium. It wasn't a new idea, for another ground-sharing scheme had been put forward in 1968 by a consortium planning a £30 million leisure development less than a mile from Spurs' ground. That idea never got off the drawing board, if ever it got onto it, but the proposal Hill-Wood put to Wale was taken sufficiently seriously by both clubs for a meeting to be arranged. This plan revolved around the conversion of Alexandra Palace into a prestige soccer stadium to rival Wembley and bid for international matches. But it never got beyond a first meeting with GLC chiefs. Local residents protested so vociferously about the prospect of having their Saturday afternoon peace shattered every week of the football season that the plan was quickly dropped. Alas, or perhaps thank heaven, depending on where you live, the Ally Pally was burned down in 1980 and such a scheme is unlikely to be revived in the present economic climate.

So while Spurs lead Arsenal in victories over the years, they have scored virtually the same number of goals against each other and have rather similar rolls of honour. The basic difference seems to reflect their styles – Arsenal's moments have really come in the League, Spurs, the more popular club, have surely found their's in the FA Cup.

Terry Yorath and Brian Talbot symbolize the mood of clashes between the clubs in recent years, which have tended to develop into hard, midfield struggles. For nearly a decade neither of the clubs scored more than 2 goals in a game – though admittedly when they broke the sequence the results were spectacular. At Christmas 1978 Spurs lost 5-0 at home and then won by the same score in April 1983. Arsenal got their revenge next season, winning 3-2 and 4-2 in the League. That must have brought back memories of the Blanchflower era when the clubs drew 4-4 on three separate occasions between 1958 and 1963.

Spurs versus Arsenal — the complete record

Date	Competition	Venue	Score (T-A)
19 Nov 1887	F	Marshes	2-1*
22 Sep 1888	F	Plumstead Comm	1-0+
9 Mar 1889	F	Northumb. Park	0-1
21 Sep 1889	F	Plumstead	1-10
1 Oct 1892	F	Northumb. Park	3-0
16 Mar 1896	F	Plumstead	3-1
26 Mar 1896	F	Northumb. Park	1-3
30 Apr 1896	F	Northumb. Park	3-2
9 Nov 1896	ULge	Plumstead	1-2
25 Feb 1897	ULge	Northumb. Park	++
25 Dec 1897	ULge	Northumb. Park	3-2
8 Apr 1898	ULge	Plumstead	1-0
28 Apr 1898	F	Plumstead	0-3
11 Mar 1899	ULge	Plumstead	1-2
29 Apr 1899	ULge	Northumb. Park	3-2
17 Apr 1900	SDC	WHL	4-2
24 Apr 1900	SDC	Plumstead	1-2§
16 Sep 1901	LLge	WHL	2-0
4 Nov 1901	LLge	WHL	5-0
23 Apr 1902	SDCC	Plumstead	0-0
29 Apr 1902	SDCCr	WHL	2-1
17 Nov 1902	LLge	Plumstead	1-2
1 Dec 1902	LLge	WHL	1-0
10 Oct 1904	SCC	Plumstead	3-1
23 Apr 1906	SCC	Plumstead	0-0
28 Apr 1906	SCCr	Plumstead	0-5
1 Feb 1908	F	WHL	0-1
1 Nov 1909	LPCF	WHL	3-0
4 Dec 1909	Lge	Plumstead	0-1
16 Apr 1910	Lge	WHL	1-1
3 Dec 1910	Lge	WHL	3-1
8 Apr 1911	Lge	Plumstead	0-2
25 Dec 1911	Lge	WHL	5-0
26 Dec 1911	Lge	Plumstead	1-0
29 Apr 1912	F	Shepherd's Bush	0-3[1]
14 Dec 1912	Lge	Plumstead	3-0
19 Apr 1913	Lge	WHL	1-1
10 Nov 1913	LCCsf	Stamford Bridge	2-1
22 Aug 1914	F	WHL	1 5[2]
4 Sep 1915	WAR	Highbury	0-2
13 Nov 1915	WAR	WHL	3-3
4 Mar 1916	WAR	Highbury	3-0
8 Apr 1916	WAR	WHL	3-2
9 Sep 1916	WAR	Highbury	1-1
2 Dec 1916	WAR	Highbury	4-1
6 Apr 1917	WAR	Homerton	0-0
9 Apr 1917	WAR	Highbury	2-3
22 Sep 1917	WAR	Highbury	1-2
17 Nov 1917	WAR	Homerton	1-0
12 Jan 1918	WAR	Highbury	4-1
9 Mar 1918	WAR	Highbury	1-4
12 Oct 1918	WAR	Highbury	0-3
7 Dec 1918	WAR	Highbury	1-0
1 Feb 1919	WAR	Highbury	3-2
29 Sep 1919	F	Highbury	1-0
29 Mar 1919	WAR	Highbury	0-1
25 Oct 1920	LPCF	WHL	2-0
1 Nov 1920	LCC	WHL	3-1
15 Jan 1921	Lge	WHL	2-1
22 Jan 1921	Lge	Highbury	2-3
14 Nov 1921	LCCsf	Stamford Bridge	0-0
21 Nov 1921	LCCsfr	Homerton	1-2
15 Apr 1922	Lge	WHL	2-0
22 Apr 1922	Lge	Highbury	0-1
23 Sep 1922	Lge	WHL	1-2
30 Sep 1922	Lge	Highbury	2-0
23 Oct 1922	LCC	Highbury	2-3
17 Nov 1923	Lge	Highbury	1-1
24 Nov 1923	Lge	WHL	3-0
25 Oct 1924	Lge	Highbury	0-1
28 Feb 1925	Lge	WHL	2-0
29 Aug 1925	Lge	Highbury	1-0
2 Jan 1926	Lge	WHL	1-1
18 Dec 1926	Lge	Highbury	4-2
7 May 1927	Lge	WHL	0-4
2 Jan 1928	Lge	Highbury	1-1
7 Apr 1928	Lge	WHL	2-0
4 May 1931	LCCf	Stamford Bridge	1-2
16 Sep 1933	Lge	WHL	1-1
31 Jan 1934	Lge	Highbury	3-1
20 Oct 1934	Lge	Highbury	1-5
6 Mar 1935	Lge	WHL	0-6
19 Aug 1939	F	WHL	0-1[3]
18 Nov 1939	WAR	Highbury	1-2
25 Jan 1940	WAR	WHL	0-1
30 Mar 1940	WAR	WHL	1-1
24 Apr 1940	WAR	Highbury	4-2
16 Nov 1940	WAR	Highbury	1-1
5 Apr 1941	WAR	Highbury	1-2
12 Apr 1941	WAR	WHL	1-1
3 May 1941	WAR	WHL	3-3
21 May 1941	WAR	Highbury	3-0
30 Sep 1941	WAR	Highbury	0-3
27 Dec 1941	WAR	WHL	1-2
7 Nov 1942	WAR	WHL	1-0
13 Feb 1943	WAR	Highbury	0-1
8 May 1943	F	WHL	1-2
18 Dec 1943	WAR	WHL	2-1
22 Apr 1944	WAR	Highbury	3-3
2 Sep 1944	WAR	WHL	4-0
9 Dec 1944	WAR	Highbury	3-2
19 May 1945	F	WHL	4-0
9 Feb 1946	WAR	Highbury	1-1
16 Feb 1946	WAR	WHL	2-0
25 Jan 1947	F	WHL	2-0
8 Jan 1949	FC	Highbury	0-3
26 Aug 1950	Lge	Highbury	2-2
23 Dec 1950	Lge	WHL	1-0
14 May 1951	F	Selhurst Park	0-0[4]
29 Sep 1951	Lge	Highbury	1-1
9 Feb 1952	Lge	WHL	1-2
20 Sep 1952	Lge	WHL	1-3
7 Feb 1953	Lge	Highbury	0-4
4 May 1953	F	Highbury	2-0
10 Oct 1953	Lge	WHL	1-4
27 Feb 1954	Lge	Highbury	3-0
4 Sep 1954	Lge	Highbury	0-2
15 Jan 1955	Lge	WHL	0-1
2 Mar 1955	F	Highbury	1-4
10 Sep 1955	Lge	Highbury	3-1
14 Jan 1956	Lge	Highbury	1-0
20 Oct 1956	Lge	Highbury	1-3
13 Mar 1957	Lge	Highbury	1-3
12 Oct 1957	Lge	WHL	3-1
22 Feb 1958	Lge	Highbury	4-4
13 Sep 1958	Lge	Highbury	1-3
31 Jan 1959	Lge	WHL	1-4
5 Sep 1959	Lge	Highbury	1-1
16 Jan 1960	Lge	WHL	3-0
10 Sep 1960	Lge	Highbury	3-2
21 Jan 1961	Lge	WHL	4-2
26 Aug 1961	Lge	Highbury	4-3
23 Dec 1961	Lge	Highbury	1-2
6 Oct 1962	Lge	WHL	4-4
26 Jan 1963	F	WHL	2-0
23 Feb 1963	Lge	Highbury	3-2
15 Oct 1963	Lge	Highbury	4-4
22 Feb 1964	Lge	WHL	3-1
10 Oct 1964	Lge	Highbury	3-1
23 Jan 1965	Lge	Highbury	1-3
11 Sep 1965	Lge	WHL	2-2
8 Mar 1966	Lge	Highbury	1-1
3 Sep 1966	Lge	WHL	3-1
7 Jan 1967	Lge	Highbury	2-0
16 Sep 1967	Lge	Highbury	0-4
20 Jan 1968	Lge	WHL	1-0
10 Aug 1968	Lge	WHL	1-2
20 Nov 1968	FLCsf	Highbury	0-1
4 Dec 1968	FLCsf	WHL	1-1
24 Mar 1969	Lge	Highbury	0-1
16 Sep 1969	Lge	Highbury	3-2
2 May 1970	Lge	WHL	1-0
5 Sep 1970	Lge	Highbury	0-2
3 May 1971	Lge	WHL	0-1
24 Nov 1971	Lge	WHL	1-1
11 May 1972	Lge	Highbury	2-0
9 Dec 1972	Lge	WHL	1-2
14 Apr 1973	Lge	Highbury	1-1
13 Oct 1973	Lge	WHL	2-0
16 Feb 1974	Lge	Highbury	1-0
19 Oct 1974	Lge	WHL	2-0
26 Apr 1975	Lge	Highbury	0-1
27 Sep 1975	Lge	WHL	0-0
22 Oct 1975	T	WHL	2-2
3 Apr 1976	Lge	Highbury	2-0
9 Oct 1976	Lge	Highbury	2-1
23 Nov 1976	T	WHL	3-2
27 Dec 1976	Lge	WHL	2-2
11 Apr 1977	Lge	Highbury	0-1
22 Nov 1977	T	Highbury	3-1
12 May 1978	T	WHL	3-5
23 Dec 1978	Lge	WHL	0-5
10 Apr 1979	Lge	Highbury	0-1
26 Dec 1979	Lge	Highbury	0-1
7 Apr 1980	Lge	WHL	1-2
30 Aug 1980	Lge	Highbury	0-2
4 Nov 1980	FLC	WHL	1-0
17 Jan 1981	Lge	WHL	2-0
2 Jan 1982	FC	WHL	1-0
27 Dec 1982	Lge	Highbury	0-2
4 Apr 1983	Lge	WHL	5-0
9 Nov 1983	FLC	WHL	1-2
26 Dec 1983	Lge	WHL	2-4
21 Apr 1984	Lge	Highbury	2-3
1 Jan 1985	Lge	Highbury	2-1
17 Apr 1985	Lge	WHL	0-2

NOTES TO TABLES:

Arsenal were known as Royal Arsenal from 1886 to 1892, Woolwich Arsenal from 1892 to 1913, The Arsenal until 1927 and plain Arsenal since that date.

* This game was abandoned after 75 minutes

+ Plumstead Common was not the same ground as Plumstead

++ No record exists of the final score of this game

§ This Southern District Combination match was abandoned after 55 minutes due to crowd trouble and was never replayed.

[1] Titanic Fund match

[2] War Relief Fund match

[3] Football League Jubilee match

[4] Festival of Britain match

Taking all matches played by the two clubs between 19 November 1887 and 17 April 1985, and including the two games which were abandoned, the complete results are:

Played: 185 Spurs wins: 78
Arsenal wins: 73
Drawn: 33 (plus one unknown)
Spurs goals scored: 289
Arsenal goals scored: 286

KEY TO TOURNAMENTS:

Lge	Football League (First Division — the clubs have never met in the Second Division)
FC	FA Cup
FLC	Football League Cup
WAR	Wartime competitions
ULge	United League
F	Friendly
SDC	Southern District Combination
SCC	Southern Charity Cup
LLge	London League
LPCF	London Professional Charity Fund
LCC	London Challenge Cup
T	Testimonial game
sf/f	Semi-final/final
r	Replay

TOTTENHAM HOTSPUR —
the complete first class record

The Hotspurs did not have a recognised fixture list until their third season; the first official 'list' was published in the *Weekly Herald* on 24 October 1884. Between their formation in 1882 and season 1892–93, all games can be classified as friendlies except for a small number of appearances in local cup competitions, when the specific competition is mentioned. Between 1884 and 1892 only games which were included on the fixture list at the beginning of the season and were reported by the *Herald* have been included. For the other seasons prior to 1896–97, when the club joined the Southern League, only games covered by the *Herald* as first team matches have been included. The club obviously arranged other games on free Saturdays, but there are no means of distinguishing, at this distance, whether those games were first, second or third team fixtures. In seasons where the *Herald* gives the team's final record as including more games than were actually reported, then this fact has been noted. Again, it is probable that the paper included some second team matches in its summary. The *Herald*, incidentally, is referred to in various sources as the *Weekly Herald*, *Tottenham Herald* and *Tottenham Weekly Herald* but these are all the same newspaper. In 1882–83 only one game, against Latymer, was reported by the *Herald* and it is therefore more than likely that the team's other fixtures were against local scratch sides. The Latymer fixture was only covered because the Edmonton club was quite prominent at the time — otherwise the Hotspurs' first season would have been ignored completely.

In a number of cases in the first decade, games were definitely played but no record of the result remains. This is usually because the *Herald* did not cover the game, but occasionally it was because the result was disputed and the paper did not wish to offend either team by stating one result. At other times, games had to be called off because of bad light and, on at least two occasions, because the ball burst and there was no replacement.

Between 1896 and 1908, Spurs played in at least two first class leagues and sometimes in three. In theory all of these games were first class, for the reserve teams contested other leagues such as the South East Counties and the London Combination (reserve leagues and games are not covered here). It does not seem possible, however, that all of the Thames and Medway League, United League, Southern District Combination or even Western League games can have been contested by the first team. They were, nonetheless, published as first team fixtures and have been included here. The same problem applies to friendlies, which are always difficult to classify. In general, friendlies where it is known that most of the first team turned out have been included, but the reader must assess for himself or herself how seriously these games would have been taken by the club.

Several discrepancies in the various league tables, particularly prior to 1900, have been identified but not always altered. These generally occur when the for and against columns do not add up (or do not correspond to those results which are known), or where some results are missing or are contradictory in different sources. While every effort has been made to ensure that the Spurs figures are correct, at this distance it is impossible to find the missing information, or to resolve contradictory scores and results for other clubs. Given the choice between leaving these tables out or reproducing them as published at the time, with their errors,

we have chosen to do the latter. The same problems apply to early Southern League appearances and to goalscorers (who were occasionally not recorded as late as 1939). Even in the 1970s, there are goalscoring discrepancies between newspaper reports, club programmes and annual aggregates. These often arise through interpretation of what constitutes an own goal. We have tried to be as accurate as is now possible in all these cases but there are occasions where, for instance, early appearances do not add up to the required totals and there is no way of correcting the figures. In recent seasons substitutes have added a further complication, and our rule has been to include a substitute as having made an appearance if he actually came on the field. The appearances and goals columns apply only to Southern League and Football League matches throughout.

Key to Competitions

AC	Amateur Cup
CS	Charity Shield
CUP	Minor wartime cup competitions
EC	European Cup
ECWC	European Cup Winners Cup
EEC	East End Cup
f	Final (of a Cup competition)
F	Friendly
FC	FA Cup
FLC	Football League Cup
LCC	London Challenge Cup (sometimes referred to as London Charity Cup)
LCup	London Wartime Cup
LGC	Wartime League Cup
Lge	Football League (or, in wartime years, whichever League was operating [Football League South, London Combination, Regional League South, London League] as shown by the League table that season).
LLge	London League
LnC	London Cup (known also as the London Association Cup and the London Senior Cup)
LPCF	London Professional Charity Fund
LSupp	London Supplementary Wartime Competition
LuCC	Luton Charity Cup
MC	Middlesex Cup
r	Replay (of a Cup tie)
SAll	Southern Alliance
SCC	Southern Charity Cup
SDC	Southern District Combination
SDCC	Southern District Charity Cup
sf	Semi-final (of a Cup competition)
SLge	Southern League
SLS	Sheriff of London's Charity Shield (occasionally referred to as Dewar Shield)
TEX	Texaco Cup
TLge	Thames and Medway League
UEFA	UEFA Cup
ULge	United League
VC	Victory Cup
WDC	Wolverton and District Charity Cup
WLge	Western League
WRF	War Relief Fund

Blank spaces in early years represent local friendlies — the only sort of game at that time apart from occasional cup matches.

The columns in each league table are, in order, played, won, drawn, lost, for, against and points.

SEASON 1882/83

6 Jan		A	Latymer	L 1-8

SEASON 1883/84

6 Oct	H	Brownlow Rvs	W 9-0		27 Dec	H	Latymer	W 2-0
13 Oct	H	Evelyn	W 5-1*		29 Dec	H	Star	W 3-0
20 Oct	A	Grange Pk	L 1-3		12 Jan	A	Woodgrange	L 0-1
27 Oct	H	Leyton Rvs	W 1-0		19 Jan	A	Grafton	W 1-0
10 Nov	A	Brownlow Rvs	W 1-0		9 Feb	H	Albion	W 3-0
24 Nov	H	Sekforde Rvs	W 2-0		16 Feb	H	Hanover Utd	L 1-2
8 Dec	A	Leyton Rvs	L 1-3		23 Feb	H	Grange Pk	W 1-0‡
15 Dec	H	Claremont	W 2-0†		15 Mar	A	Latymer	W 2-0
26 Dec	H	Oak	W 6-0		22 Mar	H	Remington	W 2-0

* Hotspurs score recorded as 'five goals and one disputed goal'
† Game lasted only 60 minutes
‡ Grange Park played with only 10 men

SEASON 1884/85

27 Sep	*	J. Jull XI	5-4		3 Jan	A	Hadley	‡
4 Oct	H	Remington	W 4-0*		10 Jan	A	Abbey	D 1-1
11 Oct	H	Abbey	W 1-0		17 Jan	A	Grange Pk	L 0-1
18 Oct	H	Woodgrange	L 4-5		24 Jan	H	Victoria	W 5-0
25 Oct	H	Grange Pk	W 4-0		31 Jan	H	St Martins	‡
1 Nov	A	Sekforde Rvs	W 4-0		7 Feb	H	Fillebrook	W 3-0
8 Nov	H	Marlbro Rvs	W 1-0		14 Feb	H	Latymer	D 0-0
15 Nov	A	Latymer	W 2-1		21 Feb	H	St Peters	‡
22 Nov	H	St Peters	W 3-2		28 Feb	A	Bedford Rvs	D 1-1
29 Nov	H	Hadley	‡		7 Mar	A	Marlbro Rvs	‡
6 Dec	H	Tottenham	W 4-0†		14 Mar	A	Victoria Wand	‡
13 Dec	A	Woodgrange	D 0-0		21 Mar	A	Remington	‡
20 Dec	H	Sekforde	W 5 0		28 Mar	A	St Martins	‡
26 Dec	H	Grove	‡		4 Apr	H	Mars	‡
27 Dec	H	Enfield	W 3-0		11 Apr	A	Grove	‡

* Jack Jull's XI versus Billy Harston's XI
† Tottenham were a different side from Hotspurs
‡ Scores either unknown or disputed by the two clubs

SEASON 1885/86

3 Oct		A	Silesia Coll	W 4-3		16 Jan	A	Woodgrnge Pk	L 0-2
10 Oct		A	Grange Pk	L 0-3		6 Feb	H	Edmonton Ind	W 4-1
17 Oct	LnC	H	St Albans	W 5-2		20 Feb	H	Sth Hackney	W 8-0
24 Oct		H	Westmstr Rvs	W *		27 Feb	H	Silesia Coll	D 1-1
7 Nov	LnC	A	Casuals	L 0-8		6 Mar	H	Ilford	W 6-1
14 Nov		A	Fairfield	L 0-1		13 Mar	H	Rutland	W 5-0
28 Nov		H	Dalston Rvs	W 3-0		27 Mar	H	Enfield Lock	W 6-1
26 Dec		A	Bowes Pk	W 2-0		3 Apr	H	Park	W 8-0
2 Jan		H	St Martins	W 3-0		17 Apr	H	Hermitage	W 3-0

* Score not available
According to the Tottenham Weekly Herald a total of 37 games were played at all levels this season, of which 24 were won and only 11 lost. Total goals for were 111 with 51 against. Nonetheless, the Herald only records the results of the 18 matches above.

SEASON 1886/87

2 Oct		H	Sth Hackney	W 13-1		15 Jan	EEC	H	Park	W 2-0
9 Oct		H	Woodford Bdg	W 2-0		22 Jan		H	Foxes	W 2-1
16 Oct	LnC	H	Upton Pk	L 0-6		5 Feb		A	Park	W 4-1
29 Oct		H	Old St Pauls	D 1-1		13 Feb		A	Fillebrook	W 3-0
13 Nov		A	Silesia Coll	L 2-3		19 Feb	EECsf	H	St Lukes	W 2-1
27 Nov		A	Fillebrook	L 1-4		5 Mar		H	Edmonton Ass	W 2-1
4 Dec		A	Iona	W 5-0		16 Apr	EECf	A	Caledonians	L 0-1
18 Dec	EEC	H	Phoenix	W 6-0		23 Apr		H	Enfield Lock	W 6-0*
27 Dec		H	Dreadnought	W 6-0						

* Herald gives score as 'six goals and one disputed goal to nil'. The Herald gives the club's record for the season as played 20, won 14, lost 5, for 59, against 22. Results of two games against City Ramblers and another possibly against Silesia College were not recorded by the Herald.

SEASON 1887/88

1 Oct		H	Buckhurst Hill	W 6-1		3 Dec	A	Luton Town	W 2-1
8 Oct	LnC	A	Hendon	L 0-6		10 Dec	A	Priory	W 3-0
29 Oct		H	St Augustines	W 5-1		7 Jan	H	St Brides	W 3-2
19 Nov		H	Royal Arsenal	W 2-1*		17 Mar	A	St Brides	W 3-0

* Abandoned after 75 minutes because of bad light

SEASON 1888/89

22 Sep		A	Royal Arsenal	W 1-0		22 Dec	A	Bowes Pk	W 4-0
13 Oct	LnC	H	Old Etonians	L 2-8		1 Mar	A	Windsor Phnx	L 1-2
20 Oct		H	Clapton	L 2-5		9 Mar	H	Royal Arsenal	L 0-1
24 Nov		H	Plaistow (Knt)	W 4-0		16 Mar	H	Edmonton	D 1-1
1 Dec		H	Old St Marks	W 5-1		13 Apr	H	Orion Gym	W 6-1

SEASON 1889/90

21 Sep		A	Royal Arsenal	L 1-10		1 Feb		H	Robin Hood	W 1-0
28 Sep		H	Westminster	W 13-0		8 Feb		H	Vulcan	W 2-1
5 Oct		H	Vulcan	W 5-1		15 Feb	MC	H	Clapton	L †
12 Oct	LnC	H	Iona	W 10-0		1 Mar		A	Swindon	L 1-2*
19 Oct	LnC	A	Edmonton	L 2-3		8 Mar		H	Unity	W 3-1
23 Nov		H	Hampstead	W 1-0		15 Mar		H	Edmonton	L 1-4
30 Nov		A	Sutherland	W 1-0		4 Apr		H	Dreadnought	L 0-1
4 Jan		H	Foxes	D 1-1		5 Apr		A	Uxbridge	D 2-2
11 Jan		A	Romford	D 0-0		7 Apr		A	Maidenhead	W 3-2
18 Jan	MC	A	Old St Stphns	W 4-2						

† Score not available
* According to the Herald Swindon won by 'one goal and one disputed goal to one'. The Herald says that the club played 45 games in all this season, winning 22 and drawing 10, but they record only the results of the 19 above.

SEASON 1890/91

Date	Comp	H/A	Opponent	Result
27 Sep		H	Hampstead	W 6-3
18 Oct		A	Luton Town	L 1-4
25 Oct		H	Northumbrlnd Fusiliers	W 1-0
1 Nov	LnC	A	QPR	D 1-1
8 Nov	LnCr	H	QPR	W 2-1
15 Nov		H	City Ramblers	W 1-0
22 Nov	LnC	H	Barking	W 3-0
6 Dec		A	Unity	D 1-1
24 Jan	LnC	A	Barnes	W 1-0
31 Jan	LnC	A	Millwall Ath	L 1-5
7 Feb	MC	H	Orion	*
28 Feb		H	Old St Stphns	W 3-0

* Score not available

SEASON 1891/92

Date	Comp	H/A	Opponent	Result
26 Sep		H	Hampstead	W 6-2
3 Oct		H	Grange Pk	W 4-2
10 Oct	LnC	H	Caledonian Ath	W 4-3
24 Oct		H	Clapton	L 1-2
31 Oct	LnC	A	Hampstead	W 3-2
7 Nov	LuCC	H	Coldstream	D 3-3
14 Nov	LuCCr	H	Coldstream	W 7-2
21 Nov	LnC	A	City Ramblers	L 1-4
28 Nov		H	Old St Stphns	D 0-0
5 Dec	MC	A	Minerva	L 0-2
12 Dec		H	Forest Swifts	D 1-1
19 Dec	LuCC	A	1st Scots Gds	L 0-4
26 Dec		A	Kings Lynn	*
2 Jan		H	Uxbridge	W 3-0
9 Jan		H	QPR	L 1-2
23 Jan		H	Westminster	D 2-2
30 Jan		H	Old St Lukes	W 3-1
6 Jan		A	St Albans	L 1-2
13 Feb		A	Clapton	D 1-1
27 Feb		H	Grenadier Gds	W 9-0
12 Mar		H	Casuals	W 3-1

* Score not available

SEASON 1892/93

Date	Comp	H/A	Opponent	Result
17 Sep		H	Paddington	W 10-0
24 Sep	SAll	A	Polytechnic	W 2-1
1 Oct		H	Royal Arsenal	W 3-0
8 Oct		H	Coldstrm Gds	W 6-0
15 Oct	SAll	A	Old St Stphns	W 3-0
22 Oct		H	Coldstrm Gds	W 3-2
29 Oct		H	2nd Scts Gds	L 2-4
5 Nov	SAll	A	Windsor	W 2-1
12 Nov		H	Clapton	L 1-2
19 Nov	SAll	H	Erith	W 3-2
26 Nov		H	Calednian Ath	W 5-0
3 Dec	LnC	A	Polytechnic	D 2-2
17 Dec	LnCr	H	Polytechnic	W 3-0
14 Jan	SAll	A	Erith	L 1-2
21 Jan	SAll	A	Slough	D 3-3
28 Jan	LnC	H	Casuals	L 0-1
4 Feb	SAll	H	Slough	W 5-2
11 Feb	SAll	H	Polytechnic	D 2-2
18 Feb		H	London Welsh	D 2-2
25 Feb	SAll	H	Upton Pk	W 1-0
4 Mar	SAll	H	Windsor	W 5-2
11 Mar		H	QPR	W 1-0
25 Mar	SAll	H	Old St Stphns	L 1-2
1 Apr		H	City Ramblers	W 1-0
8 Apr	SAll	A	Upton Pk	L 1-4
15 Apr	WDC	*	Smethwick	L 0-2

* Played at Wolverton

The Herald gives Spurs full first team record for the season as played 31, won 17, drawn 6, for 79 and against 46. They fail to record the results of five of these matches, however.

Southern Alliance 1892–93

1 Old St Stphns	12	10	1	1	44:15	21
2 Erith	11	8	1	2	29:14	17
3 TOTTENHAM	12	7	2	3	29:21	16
4 Polytechnic	8	4	0	4	18:12	8
5 Slough	11	2	2	7	21:33	6
6 Windsor/Eton	10	2	1	7	14:37	5
7 Upton Pk	10	1	0	9	7:36	2

Only two other fixtures were known to have been played—Slough v Upton Park on 29 April and Windsor v Polytechnic on 23 April. The results of these games are not recorded and, as far as known, the league was left incomplete. The Southern Alliance was disbanded at the end of this season.

SEASON 1893/94

Date	Comp	H/A	Opponent	Result
16 Sep		A	Enfield	L 1-5
23 Sep		H	Romford	D 2-2
30 Sep		H	Casuals	L 0-1
7 Oct		H	City Ramblers	W 2-0
14 Oct		H	London Welsh	W 1-0
21 Oct	LnC	H	Old St Marks	D 0-0
28 Oct	LnCr	H	Old St Marks	L 1-6
4 Nov		H	1st Scts Gds	L 1-2
11 Nov	AC	H	Vampires	W 3-1
18 Nov		H	London Welsh	W 2-1
9 Dec	LCC	H	Crusaders	L 2-5
16 Dec		H	Erith	L 0-1
19 Dec		H	Friars	W 2-1
23 Dec		H	Wolverton	D 2-2
26 Dec		A	Southampton	L 0-1
30 Dec		A	Uxbridge	L 0-1
13 Jan	MC	H	3rd Gren Gds	D 1-1
20 Jan	MCr	H	3rd Gren Gds	L 0-2
27 Jan	WDC	H	Chesham	D 2-2
3 Feb		H	City Ramblers	D 0-0
10 Feb		H	Polytechnic	W 5-0
17 Feb		H	Highland Iftry	D 2-2
24 Feb	WDC	A	Chesham	W 3-1
2 Mar		H	Uxbridge	D 1-1
10 Mar	WDC	*	Smethwick	L 0-1
23 Mar		H	Scots Gds	W 3-1
24 Mar		H	Slough	W 3-0
26 Mar		A	N/Brompton	D 3-3
31 Mar		H	Polytechnic	D 0-0
7 Apr		H	Old St Stphns	D 1-1
14 Apr		H	Ilford	L 0-1
21 Apr		H	Crouch End	D 2-2

* Played at Wolverton

SEASON 1894/95

Date	Comp	H/A	Opponent	Result
15 Sep		A	Uxbridge	L 0-2
22 Sep		H	Casuals	W 3-1
29 Sep		A	Lon Caledonian	L 1-3
6 Oct		H	3rd Gren Gds	D 1-1
13 Oct	FC	H	West Herts	W 3-2
20 Oct	AC	H	O/Harrovians	W 7-0
27 Oct		A	Crouch End	D 2-2
3 Nov	FC	H	Wolverton	W 5-3
10 Nov	AC	H	City Ramblers	W 6-1
17 Nov		H	Hglnd Lt Ifnt	D 1-1
24 Nov	FC	A	Clapton	W 4-0
1 Dec	AC	A	Romford	W 8-0
8 Dec	LCC	H	Crusaders	W 4-2
15 Dec	FC	H	Luton Town	D 2-2
19 Dec	FCr	A	Luton Town	L 0-4
22 Dec	AC	H	Lon Welsh	D 1-1
25 Dec		H	Sheff & Dist	W 7-1
26 Dec		H	Wst Liverpool	W 3-0
29 Dec		H	Vampires	W 4-1
5 Jan	ACr	H	Lon Welsh	D 3-3
19 Jan	ACr	*	Lon Welsh	W 4-2
26 Jan	LnC	H	Lon Welsh	W 5-0
23 Feb	AC	H	Beeston	W 2-0
2 Mar	LnC	A	Old Westmstr	D 3-3
9 Mar	LnCr	H	Old Westmstr	L 4-5
16 Mar	AC	H	O/Carthusians	L 0-5
19 Mar	LCC	H	O/Carthusians	L 0-3
23 Mar		H	Lon Caledonian	W 5-1
30 Mar		H	City Ramblers	W 2-0
6 Apr		H	Casuals	L 1-2
12 Apr		H	Lpool Casuals	W 6-0
13 Apr		H	2nd Scts Gds	D 1-1
15 Apr		A	Southampton	D 0-0
16 Apr		A	Bristl Sth End	W 7-0
25 Apr		H	Lon Caledonian	W 2-0

* Second replay at Spotted Dog Ground

SEASON 1895/96

Date	Comp	H/A	Opponent	Result
7 Sep		A	Royal Engs	L 0-3
14 Sep		H	Royal Scots	W 3-2
21 Sep		H	Casuals	W 3-2
28 Sep		H	Ryl Ordnance	W 2-0
5 Oct		A	Claptn Orient	L 4-5
12 Oct	FC	H	Luton Town	W 2-0
19 Oct		H	Ilford	W 2-0
26 Oct		H	Ryl Artillery	L 1-2
2 Nov	FC	A	Vampires	L 2-4*
6 Nov		H	Luton Town	L 0-2
9 Nov		H	Old Westmstrs	W 2-1
16 Nov	FC	H	Vampires	W 2-1
23 Nov	FC	A	Ilford	W 5-1
30 Nov		A	Lon Welsh	W 3-2
7 Dec		H	Caledonian	L 0-3
14 Dec	FC	H	Old St Stphns	W 2-1
21 Dec		H	Casuals	W 3-1
25 Dec		A	Millwall Ath	L 3-5
26 Dec		H	Accrington	W 3-0
28 Dec		H	Freemantle	D 2-2
4 Jan		H	Reading	W 2-1
11 Jan		H	Millwall	D 1-1
18 Jan		H	Ilford	W 2-1
25 Jan		H	Notts County	L 1-5
1 Feb	FC	A	Stoke	L 0-5
8 Feb		H	Royal Scots	W 2-1
10 Feb		A	Luton Town	L 0-9
15 Feb		A	Ryl Ordnance	L 1-2
22 Feb		H	Clapton	W 4-0
1 Mar		H	Burslm Prt Vle	W 3-1
4 Mar		A	Gravesend	D 1-1
7 Mar		H	1st Scts Gds	W 8-0
9 Mar		A	Ryl Ordnance	L 1-3
14 Mar		H	Uxbridge	W 4-0
16 Mar		A	Woolwich Asnl	W 3-1
19 Mar		H	Ryl Ordnance	D 2-2
21 Mar		H	Mancstr Reg	W 8-0
26 Mar		H	Woolwich Asnl	L 1-3
28 Mar		A	Lon Caledonian	W 5-0
3 Apr		A	Reading	W 3-2
4 Apr		H	Ostwsle Rvs	W 4-0
6 Apr		H	Middlesbrough	W 5-0
7 Apr		H	Swindon	L 2-3
11 Apr		H	Aston Villa	L 1-3
18 Apr		A	Southampton	L 1-4
22 Apr		A	Gravesend	D 1-1
25 Apr		H	Wellingboro	W 3-0
30 Apr		H	Woolwich Asnl	W 3-2

* Replayed because Vampires pitch was 'improperly marked'

SEASON 1896/97

Date	Comp	H/A	Opponent	Result
3 Sep	F	H	Rossendale	W 7-0
5 Sep	SLge	A	Sheppey Utd	D 3-3
10 Sep	F	H	London Caled	D 3-3
12 Sep	SLge	A	Wolverton	W 1-0
17 Sep	F	H	Casuals	W 4-0
19 Sep	ULge	A	Millwall	L 5-6
24 Sep	F	H	Luton Town	D 0-0†
26 Sep	F	A	Casuals	W 4-1
3 Oct	SLge	A	Gravesend	W 3-1
10 Oct	SLge	H	Chatham	L 2-3
17 Oct	SLge	H	Gravesend	W 4-0
24 Oct	SLge	A	Ryl Ordnance	W 2-1‡
31 Oct	SLge	A	Chatham	W 2-1
2 Nov	ULge	A	Rushden	L 0-2
7 Nov	SLge	H	Sheppey Utd	W 3-2
9 Nov	ULge	A	Woolwich Asnl	L 1-2
14 Nov	SLge	H	Swindon	W 3-1
16 Nov	F	A	Luton Town	L 0-3
28 Nov	SLge	H	Millwall	L 1-3
5 Dec	SLge	A	Reading	L 1-2
12 Dec	FC	H	Old St Stphns	W 4-0
19 Dec	F	A	Clapton	W 2-1
25 Dec	SLge	A	Millwall	L 0-4
26 Dec	F	H	Vampires	*
26 Dec	F	A	Vampires	*
6 Jan	FC	H	Maidenhead	W 6-0
9 Jan	SLge	A	Swindon	L 0-1
16 Jan	FC	A	Luton	L 0-3
30 Jan	ULge	A	Wellingbro'	††
10 Feb	F	A	Gravesend	††
13 Feb	SLge	H	Northfleet	W 5-0
20 Feb	Slge	A	N/Brompton	L 1-2
25 Feb	ULge	H	Woolwich Asnl	††
27 Feb	ULge	H	Loughbrough	††
4 Mar	ULge	H	Rushden	††
6 Mar	SLge	A	Northfleet	L 0-2
13 Mar	ULge	H	Luton	††
15 Mar	ULge	A	Kettering	††
20 Mar	SLge	H	Reading	D 4-4
25 Mar	F	H	Gravesend	††
27 Mar	SLge	H	N/Brompton	W 6-0
29 Mar	SLge	A	Southampton	D 1-1
1 Apr	SLge	A	Wolverton	W 2-0
3 Apr	SLge	H	Millwall	††
8 Apr	SLge	H	Southampton	D 2-2
10 Apr	ULge	A	Luton	††
16 Apr	F	H	Nottm Forest	††
17 Apr	ULge	A	Kettering	††
19 Apr	ULge	H	Wellingbro'	††
20 Apr	F	H	Lincoln	††
22 Apr	F	A	London Caled	††
24 Apr	ULge	A	Loughborough	††

* One game played in morning, one in afternoon; scores not available
† abandoned
‡ void after Royal Ordnance resigned from Southern League
†† scores not available; final table of United League games known, but not exact scores

Player	SL App	Goals	Player	SL App	Goals
Allen	9		Lanham	1	
Almond	16	1	McElhaney	19	8
Ambler	19		Main	1	
Briggs	7	1	Markham	3	
Burrows	16		Milliken	19	7
Clements	20	10	Montgomery	20	
Collins	2		Newbigging	9	2
Crump	18	2	Payne	18	5
Devlin	20	1	Robertson	1	3
Fleming	2	2	Wilson	5	1
Hatfield	1				

United League 1896–97

1	Millwall Ath	14	11	1	2	43:22	23
2	Luton	14	10	1	3	52:16	21
3	Woolwich A	14	6	3	5	28:34	15
4	Loughborough	14	6	1	7	29:31	13
5	Rushden	14	6	1	7	25:42	13
6	Kettering	14	4	4	6	23:24	12
7	Wellingborough	14	3	3	8	17:39	9
8	TOTTENHAM	14	1	4	9	25:34	6

Southern League 1896–97

1	Soton St Marys	20	15	5	0	63:18	35
2	Millwall Ath	20	13	5	2	63:24	31
3	Chatham	20	13	1	6	54:29	27
4	TOTTENHAM	20	9	4	7	44:32	22
5	Gravesend Utd	20	9	4	7	35:34	22
6	Swindon	20	8	3	9	33:37	19
7	Reading	20	8	3	9	31:49	19
8	N/Brompton	20	7	2	11	32:42	16
9	Northfleet	20	5	4	11	24:46	14
10	Sheppey Utd	20	5	1	14	34:47	11
11	Wolverton	20	2	0	18	17:74	4

SEASON 1897/98

Date	Comp	H/A	Opponent	Result
2 Sep	F	H	Glossop	W 3-2
4 Sep	SLge	A	Sheppey Utd	D 1-1
9 Sep	F	H	Ryl S. Fuslrs	W 12-0
11 Sep	F	H	Chorley	W 3-1
16 Sep	ULge	H	Kettering	D 1-1
18 Sep	SLge	H	Southampton	W 2-0
23 Sep	F	A	2nd Scts Gds	W 4-1
25 Sep	SLge	H	Millwall	W 7-0
29 Sep	ULge	A	Loughbro'	W 2-1
2 Oct	SLge	A	N/Brompton	L 0-1
7 Oct	F	H	3rd Gren Gds	W 4-0
9 Oct	SLge	A	Gravesend	W 2-0
11 Oct	ULge	A	Luton	L 0-5
16 Oct	ULge	A	Millwall	D 0-0
20 Oct	F	H	Reading	W 2-1
23 Oct	SLge	A	Southampton	L 1-4
30 Oct	FC	A	2nd Cold Gds	W 7-0
2 Nov	F	A	Eastbourne	W 2-0
6 Nov	SLge	A	Reading	D 3-3
9 Nov	F	H	N/Brompton	W 3-0
13 Nov	SLge	H	Bristol City	D 2-2
20 Nov	FC	H	Luton	L 3-4
27 Nov	SLge	A	Bristol City	L 1-3
1 Dec	F	A	Gravesend	L 0-3
4 Dec	ULge	H	Wellingbro'	W 5-0
11 Dec	F	H	Kettering	D 1-1
18 Dec	SLge	H	Wolverton	W 2-1
25 Dec	ULge	H	Woolwich Asnl	W 3-2
27 Dec	F	H	Ilkeston	W 4-2
28 Dec	F	H	Stockton	W 3-0
1 Jan	ULge	A	Rushden	L 2-5
8 Jan	ULge	H	Rushden	W 3-1
10 Jan	ULge	A	Kettering	L 2-4
15 Jan	ULge	H	Northfleet	W 4-0
19 Jan	ULge	A	Southampton	D 2-2
22 Jan	SLge	H	Wolverton	W 7-1
27 Jan	F	H	Gravesend	L 1-2
29 Jan	SLge	A	Chatham	L 2-4
3 Feb	ULge	H	Luton	D 2-2
5 Feb	SLge	A	Swindon	L 0-3
9 Feb	F	A	Sussex	W 2-1
12 Feb	F	H	Sheff Utd	D 1-1
15 Feb	F	H	St Bernards	W 4-0
19 Feb	SLge	A	Northfleet	W 3-1
26 Feb	SLge	H*	Reading	D 1-1
28 Feb	F	A	Chesham	W 4-2
5 Mar	SLge	A	Gravesend	W 2-1
9 Mar	F	A	Tunbridge W	W 5-0
12 Mar	ULge	H	Millwall	W 3-2
17 Mar	ULge	H	Loughbro'	W 5-0
19 Mar	SLge	H	Sheppey Utd	W 4-0
24 Mar	ULge	H	Southampton	W 7-0
26 Mar	F	A	Sunderland	L 0-2
2 Apr	SLge	H	N/Brompton	W 3-1
8 Apr	ULge	A	Woolwich Asnl	W 1-0
9 Apr	SLge	H	Chatham	W 2-1
11 Apr	SLge	H	Swindon	W 2-0
12 Apr	F	H	Lincoln	W 2-1
16 Apr	SLge	A	Millwall	L 1-3
20 Apr	F	H	Reading	D 3-3
23 Apr	ULge	A	Wellingbro'	D 2-2
25 Apr	F	H	Aston Villa	L 2-3
28 Apr	F	A	Woolwich Asnl	L 0-3
30 Apr	F	H	Bolton	D 2-2

* Game versus Reading played at Millwall as White Hart Lane suspended after attacks on Luton players

Player	SL App	Goals	Player	SL App	Goals
Ambler	1		Jones J.L.	20	1
Black D.	20	8	Joyce W.	19	16
Briggs S.	1		Knowles J.	19	
Burrows L.	9		Madden J.	2	
Cullen J.	21		Meade T.	10	5
Crump	11		Montgomery J.	16	
Davidson J.	17	8	Stormont R.	22	3
Downie	7		Tannahill R.	11	3
Hall A.	21		Own Goal		1
Hartley A.	15	7			

United League 1897–98

1	Luton	16	13	2	1	49:11	28
2	TOTTENHAM	16	8	5	3	40:27	21
3	Arsenal	16	8	5	3	35:24	21
4	Kettering	16	9	1	6	28:25	19
5	Rushden	16	7	1	8	24:26	15
6	Southampton	16	6	3	7	23:28	13*
7	Millwall	16	4	4	8	27:27	12
8	Wellingborough	16	3	3	10	17:41	9
9	Loughborough	16	1	2	13	8:42	4

* two points deducted

Southern League 1897–98

1	Southampton	22	18	1	3	53:18	37
2	Bristol C	22	13	7	2	67:33	33
3	TOTTENHAM	22	12	4	6	52:31	28
4	Chatham	22	12	4	6	50:34	28
5	Reading	22	8	7	7	39:31	23
6	N/Brompton	22	9	4	9	37:37	22
7	Sheppey Utd	22	10	1	11	40:49	21
8	Gravesend	22	7	6	9	28:39	20
9	Millwall Ath	22	8	2	12	48:45	18
10	Swindon	22	7	2	13	36:48	16
11	Northfleet	22	4	3	15	29:60	11
12	Wolverton	22	3	1	18	28:82	7

Thames & Medway League 1898–99

1	N/Brompton	16	13	1	2	47:15	27
2	Gravesend	16	12	1	3	53:21	25
3	Chatham	16	10	3	3	41:11	23
4	TOTTENHAM	16	11	0	5	34:28	22
5	Thames Irnwks	16	7	2	7	23:24	16
6	Sheppey Utd	16	7	1	8	31:31	15
7	RETB	16	2	2	12	24:49	6
8	Grays Utd	16	2	2	12	11:42	6
9	Dartford	16	2	0	14	21:64	4

SEASON 1898/99

Date	Comp	H/A	Opponent	Result	Score
1 Sep	F	H	Gainsbro'	W	6-2
3 Sep	TLge	H	Thames Iron	W	3-0
5 Sep	ULge	H	Luton	W	1-0
10 Sep	SLge	H	Bedminster	D	1-1
12 Sep	F	H	Surrey Wandrs	W	5-0
17 Sep	SLge	H	Sheppey Utd	W	3-2
19 Sep	ULge	A	Luton	W	4-3
24 Sep	SLge	H	Warmley	W	7-1*
26 Sep	TLge	A	Sheppey Utd	W	3-2
1 Oct	F	H	Burton Wand	W	5-2
3 Oct	TLge	H	Gravesend	W	3-1
5 Oct	ULge	A	Brighton Utd	W	2-1
8 Oct	SLge	H	Chatham	W	2-0
10 Oct	ULge	H	Southampton	W	4-0
15 Oct	ULge	A	Bristol	W	1-0
17 Oct	TLge	H	N/Brompton	W	2-1
22 Oct	SLge	A	Millwall	L	2-4
26 Oct	TLge	A	Dartford	W	3-2
29 Oct	FC	H	Wolverton	W	4-0
2 Nov	TLge	A	RETB	W	6-2
5 Nov	SLge	H	Reading	W	3-0
9 Nov	ULge	A	Reading	L	0-1
12 Nov	ULge	H	Bristol City	W	2-1
19 Nov	FC	A	Clapton	D	1-1
23 Nov	FCr	H	Clapton	W	2-1
26 Nov	SLge	A	Ryl Artillery	W	3-2
3 Dec	SLge	A	Bristol City	L	1-2
5 Dec	ULge	H	Kettering	W	3-0
10 Dec	FC	H	Luton	D	1-1
14 Dec	FCr	A	Luton	D	1-1
17 Dec	SLge	A	Sheppey Utd	L	2-3
19 Dec	FCr	A	Luton	W	2-0
21 Dec	F	A	Surrey Wandrs	D	1-1
24 Dec	SLge	A	Warmley	W	5-1*
26 Dec	SLge	A	Southampton	D	1-1
27 Dec	F	H	Ilkeston	W	1-0
31 Dec	SLge	A	Swindon	L	3-4
2 Jan	TLge	A	Chatham	W	5-0
7 Jan	SLge	H	Ryl Artillery	W	1-0
9 Jan	TLge	H	Chatham	L	0-4
14 Jan	SLge	A	Gravesend	L	2-4
16 Jan	TLge	H	Sheppey Utd	W	3-0
21 Jan	SLge	A	Brighton Utd	W	1-0
23 Jan	ULge	H	Reading	D	1-1
28 Jan	FC	A	Newton Heath	D	1-1
1 Feb	FCr	A	Newton Heath	W	5-3
4 Feb	SLge	A	Reading	L	0-2
6 Feb	TLge	H	Grays Utd	W	2-1
11 Feb	FC	H	Sunderland	W	2-1
15 Feb	ULge	A	Southampton	L	1-2
18 Feb	SLge	H	Bristol City	W	3-2
20 Feb	SLge	A	Rushden	L	1-2
25 Feb	FC	A	Stoke	L	1-4
27 Feb	ULge	A	Kettering	W	1-0
4 Mar	ULge	H	Millwall	L	1-2
8 Mar	TLge	A	Gravesend	W	3-0
11 Mar	ULge	A	Woolwich Asnl	L	1-2
13 Mar	SLge	A	N/Brompton	D	1-1
16 Mar	TLge	A	Thames Iron	L	1-2
18 Mar	SLge	H	N/Brompton	W	3-0
20 Mar	TLge	H	RETB	L	1-2
22 Mar	TLge	A	Grays	L	0-1
25 Mar	SLge	H	Brighton Utd	L	1-3
27 Mar	ULge	A	Rushden	D	0-0
31 Mar	SLge	H	Southampton	L	0-1
1 Apr	SLge	H	Gravesend	W	3-0
3 Apr	SLge	H	Swindon	D	1-1
4 Apr	SLge	H	Brighton Utd	W	3-0
8 Apr	SLge	A	Chatham	L	0-1
10 Apr	TLge	A	N/Brompton	L	4-5
13 Apr	TLge	H	Dartford	W	9-0
15 Apr	SLge	A	Bedminster	L	0-1
17 Apr	ULge	A	Wellingbro'	L	1-3
22 Apr	SLge	H	Millwall	W	3-1
24 Apr	ULge	H	Wellingbro'	W	5-2
26 Apr	ULge	A	Millwall	L	1-3
29 Apr	ULge	H	Woolwich Asnl	W	3-2

* Warmley resigned from Southern League on 21 January 1899 so their results void

Player	SL App	Goals	Player	SL App	Goals
Ambler	2		Leach	4	2
Atherton	2		McKay C.	17	4
Bradshaw	22	3	McNaught J.	19	
Cain R.	22		Meade T.	5	
Cameron J.	23	11	Melia J.	13	
Cullen J.	19		Rule A.G.	3	2
Downie E.	4		Smith T.	24	5
Erentz H.	22		Stormont R.	21	
Hall A.	2		Payne E.	1	
Hartley A.	3	1	Waller W.H.	3	
Jones J.L.	14		Own Goals		2
Joyce W.	19	10			

United League 1898–99

		P	W	D	L	F:A	Pts
1	Millwall Ath	20	14	3	3	42:19	31
2	Southampton	20	12	1	7	53:32	25
3	Woolwich Asnl	20	10	4	6	30:30	24
4	TOTTENHAM	20	11	2	7	36:25	24
5	Bristol C	20	11	0	9	43:31	22
6	Reading	20	8	5	7	36:25	21
7	Brighton Utd	20	10	1	9	41:42	21
8	Wellingborough	20	7	1	12	32:40	15
9	Kettering	20	8	1	11	25:38	15*
10	Rushden	20	6	1	13	26:45	13
11	Luton Town	20	2	3	15	24:71	7

* two points deducted

Southern League 1898–99

		P	W	D	L	F:A	Pts
1	Southampton	24	15	5	4	54:24	35
2	Bristol C	24	15	3	6	55:33	33
3	Millwall Ath	24	12	6	6	59:35	30
4	Chatham	24	10	8	6	32:23	28
5	Reading	24	9	8	7	31:24	26
6	N/Brompton	24	10	5	9	38:30	25
7	TOTTENHAM	24	10	4	10	40:36	24
8	Bedminster	24	10	4	10	35:39	24
9	Swindon	24	9	5	10	43:49	23
10	Brighton Utd	24	9	2	13	37:48	20
11	Gravesend Utd	24	7	5	12	42:52	19
12	Sheppey Utd	24	5	3	16	23:53	13
13	Ryl Artillery	24	4	4	16	17:60	12

SEASON 1899/1900

Date	Comp	H/A	Opponent	Result	Score
2 Sep	SLge	A	Millwall	W	3-1
4 Sep	F	H	Notts Co	W	4-1
9 Sep	SLge	H	QPR	W	1-0
13 Sep	F	A	Richmond	W	3-1
16 Sep	SLge	A	Chatham	W	3-2
18 Sep	SDC	H	Portsmouth	W	2-0
23 Sep	SLge	H	Reading	W	2-1
26 Sep	F	A	Clapton	W	4-1
30 Sep	F	A	Southampton	L	1-2
2 Oct	SLge	H	Gravesend	W	4-0
7 Oct	SLge	H	Brighton Utd	W	6-1†
11 Oct	SDC	A	Reading	L	1-2
14 Oct	SLge	A	Bedminster	L	1-2
16 Oct	SDC	H	Millwall	L	1-2
21 Oct	SLge	H	Bristol Rvs	W	1-0*
23 Oct	SDC	A	QPR	W	3-1
28 Oct	F	H	Southampton	W	4-3
30 Oct	SDC	H	Reading	W	3-0
4 Nov	SLge	H	Thames Iron	W	7-0
6 Nov	SDC	H	Chatham	W	8-0
11 Nov	F	H	Ilkeston	W	7-0
15 Nov	SDC	A	Bristol City	D	3-3
18 Nov	F	H	Bolton	W	4-0
20 Nov	SDC	H	QPR	W	3-1
25 Nov	F	H	Corinthians	W	5-1
27 Nov	F	H	Kaffirs	W	6-4
2 Dec	SLge	A	Swindon	W	2-0
4 Dec	SDC	A	Chatham	W	1-0
9 Dec	SLge	A	Bristol City	D	2-2
11 Dec	F	H	Players/South	W	3-2
16 Dec	SLge	A	Cowes	W	6-1†
18 Dec	F	H	HRBourkesXI	W	12-2
25 Dec	SLge	A	Portsmouth	W	3-0
26 Dec	SLge	A	Southampton	L	1-3
30 Dec	SLge	H	Millwall	W	2-1
1 Jan	F	A	Middlesbro'	D	2-2
2 Jan	F	A	Sunderland	W	3-1
6 Jan	SLge	A	QPR	D	0-0
8 Jan	SDC	H	Southampton	W	3-2
13 Jan	SLge	H	Chatham	W	2-1
17 Jan	SDC	A	Portsmouth	D	2-2
20 Jan	SLge	A	Reading	W	1-0
27 Jan	FC	A	Preston	L	0-1
3 Feb	SLge	A	Sheppey Utd	W	4-1
5 Feb	F	H	Oxford Univ	W	7-2
10 Feb	SLge	A	Brighton Utd	W	3-0†
17 Feb	SLge	H	Bedminster	W	5-2
24 Feb	SLge	A	Bristol Rvs	D	2-2
3 Mar	SLge	A	Portsmouth	L	0-1
5 Mar	F	H	Stoke	W	6-0
10 Mar	SLge	A	Thames Iron	D	0-0
12 Mar	SDC	A	Bristol City	W	2-0
17 Mar	F	A	Corinthians	W	3-1
19 Mar	SLge	H	Bristol Rvs	W	5-1
24 Mar	SLge	A	N/Brompton	W	1-0
31 Mar	SLge	H	Gravesend	W	6-2
2 Apr	F	A	Thames Iron	W	3-0
7 Apr	SLge	H	Swindon	W	3-0
13 Apr	SLge	H	Southampton	W	2-0
14 Apr	SLge	A	Bristol City	L	0-3
16 Apr	SLge	H	Sheppey Utd	W	3-0
17 Apr	SDC	H	Woolwich Asnl	W	4-2
21 Apr	F	A	Aston Villa	L	3-4
24 Apr	SDC	A	Woolwich Asnl	L	1-2‡
26 Apr	SDC	A	Millwall	D	0-0
28 Apr	SLge	A	N/Brompton	W	2-1
30 Apr	SDC	A	Southampton	W	4-1

* Abandoned after 55 minutes

† Games void: Brighton United resigned from Southern League on 10 March, Cowes resigned from Southern League on 18 December

‡ Game not completed because of crowd trouble

Players	SL App	Goals	Players	SL App	Goals
Cameron J.	25	11	Melia J.	12	
Clawley G.	7		Morris T.	20	4
Copeland D.	24	12	Munro	1	
Chapman	1	1	Pratt T.	26	19
Erentz H.	16		Riley	2	
Haddow D.	20		Rule A.G.	4	
Hughes E.	1		Smith T.	24	6
Hyde L.	6	2	Stormont R.	22	1
Jones J.L.	18		Tait A.	28	
Kirwan J.	26	10	Waller W.H.	1	
McNaught J.	24		Own Goal		1

Southern League 1899–1900

		P	W	D	L	F:A	Pts
1	TOTTENHAM	28	20	4	4	67:26	44
2	Portsmouth	28	20	1	7	59:29	41
3	Southampton	28	17	1	10	70:33	35
4	Reading	28	15	2	11	41:28	32
5	Swindon Town	28	15	2	11	50:42	32
6	Bedminster	28	13	2	13	44:45	28
7	Millwall	28	12	3	13	36:37	27
8	QPR	28	12	2	14	49:57	26
9	Bristol City	28	9	7	12	43:46	25
10	Bristol Rvs	28	11	3	14	46:55	25
11	N/Brompton	28	9	6	13	39:49	24
12	Gravesend Utd	28	10	4	14	38:58	24
13	Chatham	28	10	3	15	38:58	23
14	Thames Irnwks	28	8	5	15	30:45	21
15	Sheppey Utd	28	3	7	18	24:66	13

Southern District Combination 1899–1900

		P	W	D	L	F:A	Pts
1	Millwall	16	12	2	2	30:10	26
2	TOTTENHAM*	15	10	3	2	40:16	23
3	Portsmouth	16	9	2	5	30:16	20
4	Woolwich Asnl*	15	7	1	7	25:21	15
5	Bristol C	16	5	3	8	25:32	13
6	Southampton	16	5	2	9	23:30	12
7	Reading	16	4	4	8	16:28	12
8	Chatham	16	5	2	9	12:35	12
9	QPR	16	4	1	11	19:28	9

* Match between Woolwich Arsenal and Spurs at Plumstead abandoned after 55 minutes because of crowd trouble (score stood at 2-1). Never replayed.

SEASON 1900/01

Date	Comp	H/A	Opponent	Result	Score
1 Sep	SLge	H	Millwall	L	0-3
3 Sep	F	A	Bristol Rvs	L	0-1
8 Sep	F	A	Southampton	W	3-1
10 Sep	F	H	Reading	D	3-3
15 Sep	F	H	Chatham	W	5-0†
17 Sep	F	A	Millwall	W	2-1
22 Sep	SLge	A	Bristol City	D	1-1
24 Sep	F	H	Richmond Ass	W	8-0
27 Sep	F	A	Notts Co	L	1-4
29 Sep	SLge	H	Swindon	W	2-0
3 Oct	F	A	Reading	D	1-1
6 Oct	SLge	A	Watford	L	1-2
8 Oct	F	H	Notts Co	D	1-1
13 Oct	F	H	Corinthians	D	2-2
15 Oct	F	H	Millwall	W	2-1
20 Oct	SLge	A	QPR	L	1-2
22 Oct	F	A	Luton	L	1-3
27 Oct	SLge	H	West Ham	D	0-0
31 Oct	F	H	QPR	W	7-0
3 Nov	F	A	Portsmouth	W	3-1
5 Nov	F	H	Camb Univ	W	3-1
10 Nov	SLge	A	N/Brompton	W	2-1
12 Nov	F	A	Luton	L	0-1
17 Nov	WLge	H	Portsmouth	W	8-1
24 Nov	SLge	A	Reading	L	1-3
26 Nov	WLge	H	Bristol City	W	4-1
1 Dec	SLge	H	Kettering	W	1-0
5 Dec	WLge	A	Swindon	W	1-0
8 Dec	WLge	H	Millwall	D	1-1
10 Dec	WLge	H	Bristol Rvs	W	6-0
15 Dec	SLge	A	Millwall	W	2-1
17 Dec	F	H	Preston	D	1-1
22 Dec	WLge	H	Southampton	W	2-0
25 Dec	SLge	H	Portsmouth	W	4-1
26 Dec	SLge	A	Southampton	L	1-3
29 Dec	F	H	Newark	W	3-0
5 Jan	F	H	Clapton	W	3-0
8 Jan	F	H	German XI	W	9-6
12 Jan	SLge	A	Swindon	D	1-1
14 Jan	F	H	CWBrowns XI	W	4-2
19 Jan	SLge	H	Watford	W	7-0
26 Jan	SLge	H	Bristol Rvs	W	4-0
4 Feb	F	H	Oxford Univ	W	5-2
9 Feb	FC	H	Preston	D	1-1
13 Feb	FCr	A	Preston	W	4-2
16 Feb	SLge	A	West Ham	W	4-1
18 Feb	WLge	H	Reading	W	3-2
23 Feb	FC	H	Bury	W	2-1
27 Feb	WLge	H	Swindon	W	5-0
2 Mar	SLge	H	N/Brompton	W	2-1
6 Mar	WLge	A	Reading	D	1-1
9 Mar	SLge	A	Bristol Rvs	L	0-1
11 Mar	WLge	A	Southampton	D	1-1
16 Mar	SLge	H	Reading	W	1-0
18 Mar	WLge	A	QPR	D	1-1
23 Mar	FC	A	Reading	D	1-1
27 Mar	WLge	A	Bristol City	L	1-4*
28 Mar	FCr	H	Reading	W	4-1
30 Mar	SLge	H	QPR	W	4-1
3 Apr	SLge	A	Gravesend	L	1-2
5 Apr	SLge	H	Southampton	W	1-0
6 Apr	SLge	H	Bristol City	W	1-0
8 Apr	FCsf	‡	WBA	W	4-0
13 Apr	WLge	A	Millwall	W	1-0
15 Apr	WLge	H	QPR	D	2-2
17 Apr	WLge	A	Portsmouth	L	0-1
20 Apr	FCf	‡	Sheff Utd	D	2-2
22 Apr	WLge	A	Bristol Rvs	L	0-4
24 Apr	SLge	A	Portsmouth	L	0-4
25 Apr	SLge	H	Luton	W	3-2
27 Apr	FCfr	‡	Sheff Utd	W	3-1
27 Apr	SLge	H	Gravesend	W	5-0*
29 Apr	SLge	A	Luton	W	4-2
30 Apr	SLge	A	Kettering	D	1-1

* Reserves played these fixtures as first team playing Cup tie
† Match void as Chatham resigned from Southern League on 20 December 1900
‡ Semi-final played at Villa Park, Cup final at Crystal Palace and Cup final replay at Bolton

Players	SL App	Goals	Players	SL App	Goals
Anson	2		Jones J.L.	17	3
Brown A.	20	10	Kirwan J.	20	5
Burton	3	1	McNaught J.	18	
Buckingham	5		Melia J.	10	1
Cameron J.	21	6	Moffat	5	3
Clawley G.	25		Moles J.	3	
Erentz H.	21		Morris T.	19	3
Forthum	2	1	Pangbourn T.	2	
Haddow D.	3		Smith T.	17	2
Hawley	3	2	Stevenson	3	
Hudson	1		Stormont R.	22	5
Hughes E.	19	2	Tait A.	22	
Hyde L.	8	4	Woodward V.J.	2	2
Jones A.E.	6	1	Own Goal		1

Southern League 1900–01

1	Southampton	28	18	5	5	58:26	41
2	Bristol C	28	17	6	6	54:27	39
3	Portsmouth	28	17	4	7	56:32	38
4	Millwall	28	17	2	9	55:32	36
5	TOTTENHAM	28	16	4	8	55:33	36
6	West Ham	28	14	5	9	40:28	33
7	Bristol Rvs	28	14	4	10	46:35	32
8	QPR	28	11	4	13	43:48	26
9	Luton Town	28	11	2	15	43:49	24
10	Reading	28	8	8	12	24:25	24
11	Kettering	28	7	9	12	33:46	23
12	N/Brompton	28	7	5	16	34:51	19
13	Gravesend Utd	28	6	7	15	32:85	19
14	Watford	28	6	4	18	24:52	16
15	Swindon	28	3	8	17	19:47	14

Western League 1900–01

1	Portsmouth	16	11	2	3	36:23	24
2	Millwall	16	9	5	2	33:14	23
3	TOTTENHAM	16	8	5	3	37:19	21
4	QPR	16	7	4	5	39:24	18
5	Bristol C	16	6	4	6	27:24	16
6	Reading	16	5	5	6	23:31	15
7	Southampton	16	5	2	9	19:29	12
8	Bristol Rvs	16	4	1	11	18:42	9
9	Swindon	16	2	2	12	9:35	6

SEASON 1901/02

Date	Comp	H/A	Opponent	Result	Score
2 Sep	F	H	Hearts	D	0-0
7 Sep	SLge	H	Millwall	W	2-0
9 Sep	WLge	H	Reading	W	4-0
14 Sep	SLge	H	QPR	W	2-0
16 Sep	LLge	A	Woolwich Asnl	W	2-0
21 Sep	SLge	A	Reading	D	1-1
23 Sep	F	A	Sheff Utd	L	1-3
28 Sep	WLge	H	Southampton	W	5-0
30 Sep	SLge	H	QPR	W	3-1
5 Oct	SLge	A	Bristol Rvs	W	2-1
7 Oct	WLge	H	Millwall	W	3-1
12 Oct	SLge	H	N/Brompton	W	3-1
14 Oct	WLge	H	West Ham	W	2-1
16 Oct	F	H	Rest Sth Lge	W	2-0
19 Oct	SLge	A	Northampton	L	1-3
21 Oct	WLge	H	Bristol Rvs	W	4-1
26 Oct	SLge	H	Watford	W	8-1
2 Nov	SLge	A	West Ham	W	1-0
4 Nov	LLge	A	Woolwich Asnl	W	5-0
9 Nov	SLge	A	Wellingborough	W	1-0
11 Nov	WLge	H	Swindon	W	6-0
13 Nov	F	A	West Norwood	W	3-1
16 Nov	WLge	A	Portsmouth	L	1-3
18 Nov	WLge	A	Bristol Rvs	W	4-0
23 Nov	SLge	A	Swindon	W	3-1
2 Dec	F	A	Army Assoc	W	2-1
7 Dec	SLge	A	Kettering	W	2-0
9 Dec	WLge	H	QPR	W	3-2
14 Dec	F	A	Corinthians	L	0-3
16 Dec	LLge	A	West Ham	L	1-3
21 Dec	SLge	A	Millwall	D	1-1
25 Dec	SLge	H	Portsmouth	L	1-2
26 Dec	SLge	A	Southampton	L	0-1
28 Dec	SLge	A	QPR	W	3-0
1 Jan	F	A	Everton	L	1-3
2 Jan	F	A	Hearts	L	1-3
4 Jan	SLge	H	Reading	W	4-2
6 Jan	LLge	A	Millwall	D	1-1
11 Jan	WLge	A	Southampton	L	1-5
15 Jan	WLge	A	Reading	W	1-0
18 Jan	SLge	H	Bristol Rvs	W	1-0
25 Jan	FC	H	Southampton	D	1-1
29 Jan	FCr	A	Southampton	D	2-2
1 Feb	SLge	H	Northampton	W	1-0
3 Feb	FCr	*	Southampton	L	1-2
8 Feb	SLge	A	Watford	W	3-0
10 Feb	LLge	H	QPR	L	1-5
15 Feb	SLge	H	West Ham	L	1-2
17 Feb	WLge	A	Millwall	W	3-1
22 Feb	SLge	H	Wellingborough	W	3-0
1 Mar	SLS	H	Corinthians	W	5-2
8 Mar	SLge	H	Swindon	W	7-1
10 Mar	WLge	A	West Ham	D	1-1
15 Mar	SLge	A	Brentford	L	1-2
17 Mar	WLge	H	Portsmouth	D	0-0
22 Mar	SLge	H	Kettering	W	4-0
24 Mar	LLge	H	Millwall	D	1-1
28 Mar	SLge	H	Southampton	D	2-2
29 Mar	SLge	A	Luton	D	0-0
31 Mar	SLge	A	Portsmouth	L	0-1
1 Apr	F	H	Sheff Utd	W	3-2
5 Apr	SLge	A	N/Brompton	D	0-0
9 Apr	WLge	A	Swindon	W	1-0
12 Apr	SLge	H	Luton	D	0-0
14 Apr	LLge	A	QPR	W	2-1
21 Apr	LLge	H	West Ham	D	2-2
23 Apr	SDCC	A	Woolwich Asnl	D	0-0
26 Apr	SLge	H	Brentford	W	3-0
28 Apr	F	H	Preston	L	1-2
29 Apr	SDCCr	A	Woolwich Asnl	W	2-1
30 Apr	F	A	Portsmouth	W	2-0

* FA Cup 2nd replay (at Reading FC)

Player	SL App	Goals	Player	SL App	Goals
Barlow J.	3	1	Hyde L.	2	
Brown A.	26	18	Jones J.L.	26	1
Burton J.H.	2		Kirwan J.	28	10
Cameron J.	24	13	McNaught J.	17	
Clawley G.	20		Moles J.	1	
Copeland D.	29	9	Morris T.	26	3
Erentz H.	30		Soulsby T.	1	
Fitchie T.T.	1		Smith T.	23	4
Gilhooly P.	9	1	Stevenson	1	
Griffiths F.J.	9		Tait A.	26	
Haig-Brown A.R.	2		Woodward V.J.	2	
Hughes E.	22	1			

Southern League 1901–02

1	Portsmouth	30	20	7	3	67:24	47
2	TOTTENHAM	30	18	6	6	61:22	42
3	Southampton	30	18	6	6	71:28	42
4	West Ham	30	17	6	7	45:28	40
5	Reading	30	16	7	7	57:24	39
6	Luton Town	30	11	10	9	31:36	32
7	Millwall	30	13	6	11	48:31	32
8	Kettering	30	12	5	13	44:39	29
9	Bristol Rvs	30	12	5	13	43:39	29
10	N/Brompton	30	10	7	13	39:38	27
11	Northampton	30	11	5	14	53:64	27
12	QPR	30	8	7	15	34:56	23
13	Watford	30	9	4	17	36:60	22
14	Wellingborough	30	9	4	17	34:72	22
15	Brentford	30	7	6	17	34:61	20
16	Swindon	30	2	3	25	17:92	7

Western League 1901–02

1	Portsmouth	16	13	1	2	53:16	27
2	TOTTENHAM	16	11	3	2	42:17	25
3	Reading	16	7	3	6	29:22	17
4	Millwall	16	8	1	7	25:29	17
5	Bristol Rvs	16	8	0	8	25:31	16
6	Southampton	16	7	1	8	30:28	15
7	West Ham	16	6	2	8	30:20	14
8	QPR	16	5	1	10	17:43	11
9	Swindon	16	0	2	14	8:53	2

London League 1901–02

1	West Ham	8	5	1	2	18: 9	11
2	TOTTENHAM	8	3	3	2	15:13	9
3	Millwall	8	2	4	2	9:13	8
4	QPR	8	2	2	4	11:14	6
5	Woolwich A	8	2	2	4	9:13	6

SEASON 1902/03

Date	Comp	H/A	Opponent	Res	Score
6 Sep	SLge	H	QPR	D	0-0
8 Sep	SCC	A	West Ham	W	2-1
13 Sep	WLge	A	Southampton	D	1-1
15 Sep	WLge	H	Millwall	W	4-3
20 Sep	SLge	H	Wellingborough	W	6-1
22 Sep	WLge	A	QPR	W	2-0
27 Sep	SLge	A	Bristol Rvs	L	2-3
29 Sep	SLge	H	Reading	W	2-1
4 Oct	SLge	H	Northampton	W	2-0
6 Oct	LLge	A	Brentford	W	5-1
11 Oct	SLge	A	Watford	W	2-1
13 Oct	WLge	H	Bristol Rvs	L	0-1
18 Oct	SLge	H	Brentford	W	3-1
20 Oct	LLge	A	West Ham	D	0-0
25 Oct	SLge	A	Millwall	L	0-2
29 Oct	WLge	A	Reading	L	0-3
1 Nov	SLge	H	West Ham	D	1-1
3 Nov	SLge	H	QPR	W	3-0
8 Nov	WLge	H	Portsmouth	D	0-0
10 Nov	F	H	Camb Univ	W	2-1
15 Nov	F	A	Corinthians	W	3-1
17 Nov	LLge	A	Woolwich A	L	1-2
22 Nov	SLge	H	Swindon	W	2-0
24 Nov	SCC	H	Reading	D	1-1
29 Nov	WLge	A	Portsmouth	D	2-2
1 Dec	LLge	H	Woolwich A	W	1-0
6 Dec	SLge	H	Luton	D	1-1
8 Dec	F	H	London FA	D	2-2
10 Dec	F	A	West Norwood	W	9-0
13 Dec	F	H	Corinthians	D	2-2
15 Dec	LLge	H	West Ham	W	4-0
20 Dec	SLge	A	QPR	W	4-0
25 Dec	SLge	H	Portsmouth	D	2-2
26 Dec	SLge	A	Southampton	W	1-0
27 Dec	WLge	H	Southampton	D	0-0
3 Jan	SLge	A	Wellingborough	W	2-0
5 Jan	SLge	H	N/Brompton	W	3-1
10 Jan	SLge	H	Bristol Rvs	W	3-0
12 Jan	LLge	H	Brentford	W	1-0
14 Jan	SCC	A	Reading	L	2-3
17 Jan	SLge	A	Northampton	L	1-3
22 Jan	F	A	Camb Univ	W	1-0
24 Jan	SLge	H	Watford	D	1-1
28 Jan	WLge	A	Millwall	D	1-1
31 Jan	SLge	A	Brentford	D	1-1
7 Feb	FC	H	WBA	D	0-0
11 Feb	FCr	A	WBA	W	2-0
14 Feb	SLge	A	West Ham	L	0-1
16 Feb	WLge	H	West Ham	W	1-0
21 Feb	FC	H	Bristol City	W	1-0
23 Feb	WLge	A	Bristol Rvs	L	0-2
2 Mar	LLge	A	Millwall	W	3-0
7 Mar	FC	A	Aston Villa	L	2-3
19 Mar	SLge	A	Brentford	D	0-0
14 Mar	SLge	H	Kettering	W	4-0
16 Mar	LLge	A	QPR	L	0-1
19 Mar	WLge	A	West Ham	D	0-0
21 Mar	SLge	A	Luton	L	0-3
23 Mar	LLge	H	Millwall	W	1-0
26 Mar	WLge	H	Brentford	W	4-0
28 Mar	SLge	H	Reading	W	2-0
30 Mar	LLge	H	QPR	W	3-0
4 Apr	SLge	A	Reading	D	0-0
6 Apr	F	H	QPR	W	1-0
10 Apr	SLge	H	Southampton	W	2-1
11 Apr	SLge	A	N/Brompton	L	0-3
13 Apr	SLge	A	Portsmouth	L	0-2
14 Apr	SLge	H	Millwall	W	2-0
22 Apr	SLge	A	Swindon	L	0-2
25 Apr	SLge	A	Kettering	L	0-1
30 Apr	F	H	Nottm Forest	W	2-1

Player — 1902/03

Player	SL App	Goals	Player	SL App	Goals
Barlow J.	4	1	Houston R.	9	4
Brown C.	12		Hughes E.	20	3
Burton J.H.	11	1	Jones J.	8	3
Cameron J.	14	2	Jones J.L.	17	
Chalmers J.	4		Kirwan J.	26	7
Clawley G.	30		Morris T.	27	1
Copeland D.	28	8	Tait A.	25	1
Dryburgh T.	17	2	Warner A.	20	8
Erentz H.	25		Watson J.	13	
Fredericks	1		Woodward V.J.	12	2
Gilhooly P.	6	3	Own Goal		1
Haig-Brown A.R.	1				

Southern League 1902–03

		P	W	D	L	F:A	Pts
1	Southampton	30	20	8	2	83:20	48
2	Reading	30	19	7	4	72:30	45
3	Portsmouth	30	17	7	6	69:32	41
4	**TOTTENHAM**	**30**	**14**	**7**	**9**	**47:31**	**35**
5	Bristol Rvs	30	13	8	9	46:34	34
6	N/Brompton	30	11	11	8	37:35	33
7	Millwall	30	14	3	13	52:37	31
8	Northampton	30	12	6	12	39:48	30
9	QPR	30	11	6	13	34:42	28
10	West Ham	30	9	10	11	35:49	28
11	Luton Town	30	10	7	13	43:44	27
12	Swindon	30	10	7	13	38:46	27
13	Kettering	30	8	11	11	33:40	27
14	Wellingborough	20	11	3	16	36:56	25
15	Watford	30	6	4	20	35:87	16
16	Brentford	30	2	1	27	16:84	5

Western League 1902–03

		P	W	D	L	F:A	Pts
1	Portsmouth	16	10	4	2	34:14	24
2	Bristol Rvs	16	9	2	5	36:22	20
3	Southampton	16	7	6	3	32:20	20
4	**TOTTENHAM**	**16**	**6**	**7**	**3**	**20:14**	**19**
5	Millwall	16	6	3	7	23:29	15
6	Reading	16	7	0	9	20:21	14
7	QPR	16	6	2	8	18:31	14
8	Brentford	16	3	4	9	16:34	10
9	West Ham	16	2	4	10	15:29	8

London League Premier Division 1902-03

		P	W	D	L	F:A	Pts
1	**TOTTENHAM**	**10**	**7**	**1**	**2**	**19: 4**	**15**
2	West Ham	10	5	3	2	15:13	13
3	Woolwich A	10	6	0	4	14:10	12
4	Millwall	10	3	4	3	18:14	10
5	QPR	10	2	3	5	9:15	7
6	Brentford	10	1	1	8	9:28	3

This was the last season in which the first team contested the London League. From 1903-04 onwards it was a reserve team league.

SEASON 1903/04

Date	Comp	H/A	Opponent	Res	Score
5 Sep	SLge	A	Fulham	D	0-0
7 Sep	WLge	H	Reading	W	3-1
12 Sep	SLge	H	Millwall	L	0-1
14 Sep	SLge	A	Brentford	D	0-0
19 Sep	SLge	A	QPR	L	0-2
23 Sep	F	A	N/Brompton	L	0-3
26 Sep	SLge	H	Plymouth	L	0-2
28 Sep	SCC	A	Millwall	L	1-3
3 Oct	SLge	A	Reading	D	2-2
5 Oct	WLge	H	QPR	W	3-0
10 Oct	SLge	H	Wellingbor'	W	1-0
14 Oct	WLge	H	Reading	W	2-0
17 Oct	SLge	A	Bristol Rvs	L	0-1
19 Oct	F	A	N/Brompton	W	4-2
24 Oct	SLge	A	Brighton	D	2-2
31 Oct	WLge	A	Portsmouth	W	3-0
2 Nov	WLge	H	Brentford	D	1-1
7 Nov	SLge	H	Northampton	W	2-1
9 Nov	WLge	A	QPR	L	0-2
21 Nov	SLge	H	West Ham	W	2-1
28 Nov	F	H	Brighton	W	7-0
30 Nov	WLge	H	Bristol Rvs	W	2-1
5 Dec	SLge	A	Luton	L	2-3
7 Dec	F	A	Burnley	W	4-0
12 Dec	F	A	Corinthians	W	5-1
14 Dec	WLge	H	West Ham	W	4-1
19 Dec	SLge	H	Kettering	D	3-3
25 Dec	SLge	H	Portsmouth	D	1-1
26 Dec	SLge	A	Southampton	L	0-1
28 Dec	WLge	H	Southampton	W	1-0
2 Jan	SLge	H	Fulham	W	1-0
9 Jan	SLge	A	Millwall	W	1-0
16 Jan	SLge	H	QPR	D	2-2
23 Jan	SLge	A	Plymouth	W	3-1
30 Jan	SLge	H	Reading	W	7-4
6 Feb	FC	A	Everton	W	2-1
13 Feb	SLge	H	Bristol Rvs	W	5-1
20 Feb	FC	H	Aston Villa		0-1*
22 Feb	SLge	A	Swindon	W	1-0
25 Feb	FCr	A	Aston Villa	W	1-0
27 Feb	WLge	H	Portsmouth	D	1-1
29 Feb	WLge	H	Plymouth	W	5-1
5 Mar	FC	H	The Wednsdy	D	1-1
10 Mar	FCr	A	The Wednsdy	L	0-2
12 Mar	SLge	H	Brentford	D	1-1
19 Mar	SLge	A	West Ham	W	2-0
26 Mar	SLge	A	Swindon	D	0-0
28 Mar	WLge	A	Brentford	W	2-1
1 Apr	SLge	H	Southampton	W	2-1
2 Apr	SLge	H	Luton	D	1-1
4 Apr	SLge	A	Portsmouth	L	0-1
5 Apr	SLge	H	N/Brompton	W	1-0
9 Apr	SLge	A	N/Brompton	W	1-0
13 Apr	SLge	A	Brighton	W	2-1
16 Apr	SLge	H	Kettering	W	5-1
18 Apr	WLge	A	West Ham	W	1-0
20 Apr	WLge	A	Plymouth	D	0-0
23 Apr	WLge	A	Southampton	L	0-1
25 Apr	SLge	A	Northampton	W	1-0
27 Apr	WLge	A	Bristol Rvs	W	4-2
30 Apr	SLge	A	Wellingbor'	D	3-3

* Abandoned after crowd invasion. FA ordered replay to be played at Villa Park and fined Spurs £350

Player — 1903/04

Player	SL App	Goals	Player	SL App	Goals
Berry	3		McConachie A.	6	
Brearley H.	16	3	McNaught J.	13	
Brown C.	2		Mapley	5	
Burton J.H.	5		Mearns F.	5	
Burton O.	15		Milton	1	
Cameron J.	3		Morris T.	22	2
Chalmers J.	6	1	Quinn	1	
Copeland D.	32	5	Tait A.	25	
Erentz H.	16		Walton J.	12	4
Gilhooly P.	1		Warner A.	17	3
Hughes E.	24		Watson J.	17	
Jones J.	25	15	Williams C.	29	
Jones J.L.	20	1	Woodward V.J.	17	10
Kirwan J.	28	4	Turner A.D.	5	5
Leach-Lewis A.	1		Own Goal		1

Southern League 1903–04

		P	W	D	L	F:A	Pts
1	Southampton	34	22	6	6	75:30	50
2	**TOTTENHAM**	**34**	**16**	**11**	**7**	**54:37**	**43**
3	Bristol Rvs	34	17	8	9	66:42	42
4	Portsmouth	34	17	8	9	41:38	42
5	QPR	34	15	11	8	53:37	41
6	Reading	34	14	13	7	48:35	41
7	Millwall Ath	34	16	8	10	64:42	40
8	Luton Town	34	14	12	8	38:33	40
9	Plymouth	34	13	10	11	44:34	36
10	Swindon	34	10	11	13	30:42	31
11	Fulham	34	9	12	13	34:35	30
12	West Ham	34	10	7	17	39:44	27
13	Brentford	34	9	9	16	34:48	27
14	Wellingborough	34	11	5	18	44:63	27
15	Northampton	34	10	7	17	36:60	27
16	N/Brompton	34	6	13	15	26:43	25
17	Brighton	34	6	12	16	45:69	24
18	Kettering	34	6	7	21	39:78	19

Western League 1903–04

		P	W	D	L	F:A	Pts
1	**TOTTENHAM**	**16**	**11**	**3**	**2**	**32:12**	**25**
2	Southampton	16	9	3	4	30:18	21
3	Plymouth	16	8	4	4	22:18	20
4	Portsmouth	16	7	2	7	24:23	16
5	Brentford	16	6	4	6	19:22	16
6	QPR	16	5	5	6	15:21	15
7	Reading	16	4	4	8	16:26	12
8	Bristol Rvs	16	4	3	9	29:29	11
9	West Ham	16	2	4	10	13:31	8

SEASON 1904/05

Date	Comp	H/A	Opponent	Result	Score
3 Sep	SLge	H	Fulham	L	0-1
7 Sep	WLge	A	Reading	W	1-0
10 Sep	SLge	A	Watford	W	1-0
12 Sep	F	H	Brighton	W	3-1
17 Sep	SLge	H	Plymouth	W	2-0
19 Sep	WLge	H	QPR	W	4-1
24 Sep	SLge	A	West Ham	D	0-0
26 Sep	SLge	H	Bristol Rvs	W	1-0
1 Oct	SLge	H	Reading	L	1-3
3 Oct	WLge	A	Millwall	L	2-3
8 Oct	SLge	A	Bristol Rvs	L	1-3
10 Oct	SCC	A	Woolwich Asnl	W	3-1
15 Oct	SLge	H	Northampton	L	0-1
19 Oct	WLge	A	Plymouth	L	0-5
22 Oct	WLge	A	Portsmouth	L	0-1
24 Oct	WLge	H	West Ham	L	0-1
29 Oct	SLge	H	Brentford	D	1-1
31 Oct	F	H	London FA	W	4-1
2 Nov	F	A	Littlehampton	W	7-0
5 Nov	SLge	A	QPR	W	2-1
7 Nov	WLge	H	Reading	D	2-2
12 Nov	SLge	H	Millwall	W	1-0
12 Nov	WLge	A	Fulham	D	0-0*
19 Nov	SLge	A	Brighton	D	1-1
21 Nov	WLge	H	Plymouth	W	2-0
26 Nov	SLge	A	Luton	L	0-1
28 Nov	F	H	Camb Univ	D	2-2
3 Dec	SLge	H	Swindon	W	6-3
5 Dec	F	H	G. Robey's XI	W	2-1
10 Dec	SLge	A	N/Brompton	D	1-1
17 Dec	SLge	H	Wellingborough	W	8-1
26 Dec	SLge	A	Southampton	D	1-1
27 Dec	SLge	H	Portsmouth	D	1-1
31 Dec	SLge	A	Fulham	L	0-1
2 Jan	WLge	H	Fulham	L	0-5
7 Jan	SLge	A	Watford	W	2-0
19 Jan	F	H	Corinthians	L	0-2
21 Jan	SLge	H	West Ham	W	1-0
24 Jan	F	A	Camb Univ	D	4-4
28 Jan	SLge	A	Reading	L	2-3
4 Feb	FC	A	Middlesbrough	D	1-1
9 Feb	FCr	H	Middlesbrough	W	1-0
11 Feb	SLge	A	Northampton	W	3-0
18 Feb	FC	H	Newcastle	D	1-1
22 Feb	FCr	A	Newcastle	L	0-4
25 Feb	SLge	A	Brentford	D	0-0
27 Feb	WLge	H	Millwall	W	4-1
4 Mar	SLge	H	QPR	W	5-1
6 Mar	WLge	A	Bristol Rvs	L	1-2
11 Mar	SLge	A	Millwall	W	2-0
18 Mar	SLge	H	Brighton	D	1-1
20 Mar	WLge	A	QPR	D	1-1
25 Mar	SLge	H	Luton	W	1-0
27 Mar	WLge	A	West Ham	D	1-1
29 Mar	WLge	H	Southampton	D	1-1
1 Apr	SLge	A	Swindon	L	1-2
3 Apr	WLge	A	Brentford	L	0-2
5 Apr	SLge	A	Plymouth	L	1-2
8 Apr	SLge	H	N/Brompton	W	2-0
11 Apr	WLge	H	Brentford	D	0-0
15 Apr	SLge	A	Wellingborough	W	1-0
17 Apr	WLge	H	Portsmouth	L	0-1
21 Apr	SLge	H	Southampton	L	1-2
22 Apr	WLge	A	Southampton	L	0-1
24 Apr	SLge	A	Portsmouth	L	2-3
25 Apr	F	H	Sheff Utd	D	0-0
27 Apr	SCC	A	Reading	D	0-0
29 Apr	SLge	H	Bristol Rvs	W	1-0
4 May	F	A	Hohen Warte	W	6-0†
7 May	F	A	Everton	L	0-2†
10 May	F	A	Vienna Ath	W	4-1†
12 May	F	A	Torna	W	7-1‡
14 May	F	A	Testgyakor	W	12-1‡
16 May	F	A	Everton	L	0-1‡
21 May	F	A	Slavia	W	8-1‡

* Reserve team appeared at Fulham   † In Vienna   ‡ In Budapest

Player	SL App	Goals	Player	SL App	Goals
Berry	8		McNaught J.	8	
Brearley H.	19	3	Morris T.	29	3
Bull W.	26	2	Murray	8	
Burton J.	9		O'Hagen	14	5
Chapman H.	3	1	Stansfield H.	23	5
Copeland D.	18	2	Swann	2	
Eggett	27		Tait A.	24	1
Freeborough	1		Walton J.	19	6
George	3	1	Warner A.	10	6
Glen	19	11	Watson J.	25	
Hughes E.	15	2	Williams C.	7	
Kirwan J.	26	3	Woodward V.	20	7
McCurdy	12		Own Goal		1

Southern League 1904–05

1	Bristol Rvs	34	20	8	6	74:36	48
2	Reading	34	18	7	9	57:38	43
3	Southampton	34	18	7	9	54:39	43
4	Plymouth	34	18	5	11	57:39	41
5	**TOTTENHAM**	34	15	8	11	53:34	38
6	Fulham	34	14	10	10	46:34	38
7	QPR	34	14	8	12	51:46	36
8	Portsmouth	34	16	4	14	61:56	36
9	N/Brompton	34	11	11	12	40:40	33
10	Watford	34	15	3	16	43:45	33
11	West Ham	34	12	8	14	48:42	32
12	Brighton	34	13	6	15	44:45	32
13	Northampton	34	12	8	14	43:54	32
14	Brentford	34	10	9	15	33:38	29
15	Millwall Ath	34	11	7	16	38:47	29
16	Swindon	34	12	5	17	41:59	29
17	Luton	34	12	3	19	45:54	27
18	Wellingborough	34	5	3	26	25:107	13

Western League 1904–05

1	Plymouth	20	13	4	3	52:18	30
2	Brentford	20	11	6	3	30:23	28
3	Southampton	20	11	2	7	45:22	24
4	Portsmouth	20	10	3	7	29:30	23
5	West Ham	20	8	4	8	37:43	20
6	Fulham	20	7	3	10	29:32	17
7	Millwall Ath	20	7	3	10	32:39	17
8	**TOTTENHAM**	20	5	6	9	20:28	16
9	Reading	20	6	3	11	28:37	15
10	QPR	20	6	3	11	27:45	15
11	Bristol Rvs	20	7	1	12	32:44	15

SEASON 1905/06

Date	Comp	H/A	Opponent	Result	Score
2 Sep	SLge	A	Reading	D	1-1
4 Sep	SLge	H	Reading	W	5-1
9 Sep	SLge	H	Watford	W	1-0
11 Sep	WLge	A	QPR	D	1-1
16 Sep	SLge	A	Brighton	L	0-2
23 Sep	SLge	H	West Ham	W	2-0
25 Sep	WLge	H	Bristol Rvs	L	0-1
30 Sep	SLge	H	Fulham	D	0-0
2 Sep	WLge	H	Plymouth	L	0-2
7 Oct	SLge	H	QPR	W	2-1
11 Oct	WLge	A	Reading	D	0-0
14 Oct	SLge	A	Bristol Rvs	W	2-0
16 Oct	WLge	H	Fulham	W	1-0
21 Oct	SLge	H	N/Brompton	W	6-0
23 Oct	WLge	H	Millwall	W	5-0
28 Oct	WLge	A	Portsmouth	D	0-0
4 Nov	SLge	H	Swindon	W	2-1
6 Nov	WLge	A	West Ham	L	1-4
8 Nov	SCC	H	QPR	W	2-0
11 Nov	SLge	A	Millwall	L	1-2
13 Nov	WLge	H	Brentford	L	2-3
18 Nov	SLge	H	Luton	W	1-0
20 Nov	WLge	A	Fulham	W	3-0
25 Nov	SLge	A	Northampton	W	2-0
27 Nov	F	H	Camb Univ	W	2-1
2 Dec	SLge	A	Brentford	W	3-0
16 Dec	SLge	A	Plymouth	L	1-2
23 Dec	WLge	A	Southampton	W	5-0
25 Dec	SLge	H	Portsmouth	W	3-1
26 Dec	SLge	A	Southampton	L	0-1
30 Dec	SLge	H	Reading	W	1-0
6 Jan	SLge	A	Watford	D	0-0
13 Jan	FC	H	Burnley	W	2-0
20 Jan	SLge	H	Brighton	W	3-1
24 Jan	F	A	Camb Univ	L	1-4
27 Jan	WLge	A	West Ham	L	1-2?
29 Jan	WLge	H	QPR	L	1-2?
3 Feb	FC	H	Reading	W	3-2
10 Feb	SLge	A	QPR	D	0-0
12 Feb	SLge	H	Fulham	L	0-1
17 Feb	SLge	H	Bristol Rvs	D	2-2
19 Feb	WLge	A	Millwall	D	1-1
24 Feb	FC	H	Birmingham	D	1-1
26 Feb	WLge	H	Brentford	W	1-0
28 Feb	FCr	A	Birmingham	L	0-2
3 Mar	WLge	H	Portsmouth	D	1-1
5 Mar	SLge	A	N/Brompton	L	0-1
10 Mar	SLge	A	Swindon	L	0-2
17 Mar	SLge	H	Millwall	W	3-1
19 Mar	WLge	A	Bristol Rvs	D	0-0
21 Mar	WLge	A	Plymouth	D	0-0
24 Mar	SLge	A	Luton	L	0-2
26 Mar	WLge	H	West Ham	W	1-0
31 Mar	SLge	A	Northampton	D	0-0
7 Apr	SLge	H	Brentford	W	4-1
13 Apr	SLge	H	Southampton	D	1-1
14 Apr	SLge	A	Norwich	L	1-4
16 Apr	SLge	A	Portsmouth	L	0-1
17 Apr	SLge	H	Norwich	W	3-0
21 Apr	SLge	H	Plymouth	L	0-1
23 Apr	SCC	H	Woolwich Asnl	D	0-0
25 Apr	WLge	H	Southampton	L	0-1
28 Apr	SCCr	A	Woolwich Asnl	L	0-5

Player	SL App	Goals	Player	SL App	Goals
Berry	4	1	Kyle	25	8
Brearley H.	16	1	Leach-Lewis A.	2	2
Bull W.	30	2	Morris T.	32	2
Burton O.	6		Murray	13	
Carrick C.	15	4	O'Hagan	7	
Chaplin	2		Page G.	1	
Chapman H.	28	11	Shackleton	3	1
Darnell J.	10		Stansfield H.	7	1
Derry	1		Tait A.	27	1
Eggett	34		Walton J.	21	5
Freeborough	1		Watson J.	33	
George	1		Whyman A.	7	
Glen A.	14	2	Woodward V.J.	12	5
Hughes E.	22				

Southern League 1905–06

1	Fulham	34	19	12	3	44:15	50
2	Southampton	34	19	7	8	58:39	45
3	Portsmouth	34	17	9	8	61:35	43
4	Luton	34	17	7	10	64:40	41
5	**TOTTENHAM**	34	16	7	11	46:29	39
6	Plymouth	34	16	7	11	52:33	39
7	Norwich	34	13	10	11	46:38	36
8	Bristol Rvs	34	15	5	14	56:56	35
9	Brentford	34	14	7	13	43:52	35
10	Reading	34	12	9	13	53:46	33
11	West Ham	34	14	5	15	42:39	33
12	Millwall	34	11	11	12	38:41	33
13	QPR	34	12	7	15	58:44	31
14	Watford	34	8	10	16	38:57	26
15	Swindon	34	9	7	18	31:52	25
16	Brighton	34	9	7	18	30:55	25
17	N/Brompton	34	7	8	19	20:62	22
18	Northampton	34	8	5	21	32:79	21

Western League 1905–06

1	QPR	20	11	4	5	33:27	26
2	Southampton	20	10	5	5	41:35	25
3	Plymouth	20	8	8	4	34:23	24
4	**TOTTENHAM**	20	7	7	6	28:17	21
5	Bristol Rvs	20	8	3	9	34:34	19
6	Millwall Ath	20	7	5	8	28:29	19
7	Portsmouth	20	6	7	7	26:29	19
8	West Ham	20	7	5	8	32:35	19
9	Reading	20	6	6	8	28:35	18
10	Fulham	20	5	10	5	23:32	15
11	Brentford	20	6	3	11	25:36	15

SEASON 1906/07

Date	Comp	H/A	Opponent	Result	Score
1 Sep	SLge	H	West Ham	L	1-2
3 Sep	WLge	H	Plymouth	D	0-0
5 Sep	SLge	A	Watford	D	1-1
8 Sep	SLge	A	Bristol Rvs	L	2-3
10 Sep	WLge	H	Southampton	L	2-3
13 Sep	F	H	London Cal	W	6-4
15 Sep	SLge	A	Swindon	D	0-0
17 Sep	F	H	Ilford	D	4-4
22 Sep	SLge	H	Norwich	D	2-2
24 Sep	SLge	H	Fulham	W	5-1
29 Sept	SLge	A	Luton	L	0-2
3 Oct	WLge	A	Southampton	L	0-2
6 Oct	SLge	H	C. Palace	W	3-0
8 Oct	WLge	A	West Ham	L	0-5
13 Oct	SLge	A	Brentford	D	2-2
20 Oct	WLge	H	Millwall	W	1-0
22 Oct	SCC	H	West Ham	W	2-0
27 Oct	SLge	A	Leyton	D	1-1
29 Oct	SLge	A	Fulham	L	1-2
3 Nov	SLge	H	Portsmouth	D	1-1
7 Nov	WLge	A	Portsmouth	L	0-1
10 Nov	SLge	A	N/Brompton	W	1-0
12 Nov	F	H	Camb Univ	W	4-2
14 Nov	F	A	Corinthians	L	1-6
19 Nov	F	H	Oxford Univ	W	2-1
24 Nov	SLge	A	Brighton	L	0-2
26 Nov	WLge	H	Portsmouth	W	4-2
1 Dec	SLge	H	Reading	W	2-0
8 Dec	F	H	Corinthians	W	5-0
12 Dec	WLge	A	Plymouth	D	2-2*
12 Dec	SLge	H	Plymouth	W	4-2*
15 Dec	SLge	H	Northampton	W	6-0
22 Dec	SLge	A	QPR	L	1-3
25 Dec	SLge	H	Millwall	W	3-1
26 Dec	SLge	A	Southampton	L	1-2
29 Dec	SLge	A	West Ham	L	2-4
5 Jan	SLge	A	Bristol Rvs	W	4-0
12 Jan	FC	H	Hull City	D	0-0
17 Jan	FCr	A	Hull City	D	0-0
19 Jan	SLge	H	Swindon	W	3-0
21 Jan	FCr	H	Hull City	W	1-0
26 Jan	SLge	A	Norwich	L	0-5
2 Feb	FC	H	Blackburn	D	1-1
7 Feb	FCr	A	Blackburn	D	1-1
9 Feb	SLge	A	C. Palace	W	1-0
11 Feb	FCr	§	Blackburn	W	1-0
16 Feb	SLge	H	Brentford	W	2-1
23 Feb	FC	A	Notts Co	L	0-4
2 Mar	SLge	H	Leyton	D	0-0
9 Mar	SLge	A	Portsmouth	L	1-3
16 Mar	SLge	H	N/Brompton	W	2-0
23 Mar	SLge	A	Plymouth	D	0-0
25 Mar	SLge	H	Luton	L	1-2
29 Mar	SLge	H	Southampton	W	2-0
30 Mar	SLge	H	Brighton	W	3-0
1 Apr	SLge	A	Millwall	L	0-2
2 Apr	F	H	Spurs 1901 XI	L	1-4†
3 Apr	SCC	H	QPR	W	4-0
6 Apr	SLge	A	Reading	L	0-2
8 Apr	WLge	H	West Ham	W	4-2
13 Apr	SLge	H	Watford	D	0-0
15 Apr	F	H	W.Browns XI	W	2-1
20 Apr	SLge	A	Northampton	L	0-2
22 Apr	WLge	A	Millwall	D	0-0
27 Apr	SLge	H	QPR	W	2-0
29 Apr	SCC	H	Southampton	W	2-0
26 May	F	A	Ostend Club	W	8-1‡
27 May	F	A	Fulham	W	2-1‡

* Spurs played Plymouth twice on the same day in both Southern and Western Leagues. The reserves played the Western League match

† Charity match: current Spurs side v 1901 side. Benefit for S. Mountford

‡ Played in Ostend, Belgium   § Played at Villa Park

Player	SL App	Goals
Badenoch	1	
Berry	1	
Bull W.	27	2
Burton O.	4	
Brearley H.	18	
Chaplin J.	34	
Chapman H.	11	3
Darnell	2	
Dow	9	3
Eames	7	2
Eggett	5	
Hewitt	31	11
Hughes E.	25	
Jones W.H.	9	
McDiarmid	7	
Morris T.	33	2
Pickett A.	15	4
Reid	26	16
Reilly C.H.	1	
Reilly G.	19	
Stansfield H.	10	2
Steel D.	6	
Tait A.	24	
Walker	9	
Walton J.	34	9
Watson J.	12	
Whitebourne J.	14	
Whyman A.	3	1
Wilkinson	2	
Woodward V.J.	19	8

Southern League 1906–07

		P	W	D	L	F:A	Pts
1	Fulham	38	20	13	5	58:32	53
2	Portsmouth	38	22	7	9	63:36	51
3	Brighton	38	18	9	11	53:43	45
4	Luton	38	18	9	11	52:52	45
5	West Ham	38	15	14	9	60:41	44
6	TOTTENHAM	38	17	9	12	63:45	43
7	Millwall	38	18	6	14	71:50	42
8	Norwich	38	15	12	11	57:48	42
9	Watford	38	13	16	9	46:43	42
10	Brentford	38	17	8	13	57:56	42
11	Southampton	38	13	9	16	49:56	35
12	Reading	38	14	6	18	57:47	34
13	Leyton	38	11	12	15	36:60	34
14	Bristol Rvs	38	12	9	17	55:54	33
15	Plymouth	38	10	13	15	43:50	33
16	Swindon	38	11	11	16	43:54	33
17	N/Brompton	38	12	9	17	47:59	33
18	QPR	38	11	10	17	47:55	32
19	C. Palace	38	8	9	21	46:66	25
20	Northampton	38	5	9	24	29:87	19

Western League 'B' 1906–07

		P	W	D	L	F:A	Pts
1	West Ham	10	7	1	2	25:14	15
2	Plymouth	10	5	3	2	16:10	13
3	Portsmouth	10	4	2	4	16:19	10
4	TOTTENHAM	10	3	3	4	13:15	9
5	Southampton	10	4	0	6	14:16	8
6	Millwall	10	1	3	6	5:15	5

SEASON 1907/08

Date	Comp	H/A	Opponent	Result	Score
2 Sep	SLge	A	QPR	D	3-3
7 Sep	SLge	A	West Ham	D	1-1
9 Sep	SLge	H	Bristol Rvs	W	10-0
14 Sep	SLge	H	QPR	W	3-2
18 Sep	WLge	A	Bristol Rvs	L	1-2
21 Sep	SLge	H	N/Brompton	W	2-1
23 Sep	WLge	A	Millwall	L	0-2
28 Sep	SLge	A	Swindon	L	0-1
30 Sep	SCC	H	Millwall	L	0-1
2 Oct	WLge	A	Reading	W	2-1
5 Oct	SLge	H	C. Palace	L	1-2
7 Oct	WLge	H	West Ham	W	2-1
12 Oct	SLge	A	Luton	L	1-3
14 Oct	WLge	H	Reading	L	0-2
19 Oct	SLge	A	Brighton	D	1-1
21 Oct	F	H	Ilford	W	10-0
23 Oct	SLge	A	C. Palace	L	1-2
26 Oct	SLge	A	Portsmouth	W	2-1
28 Oct	F	H	Clapton	W	2-0
2 Nov	WLge	H	Bradford PA	D	0-0
4 Nov	WLge	A	West Ham	W	3-1
9 Nov	SLge	A	Millwall	W	2-1
16 Nov	SLge	H	Brentford	W	1-0
18 Nov	SCC	A	Millwall	L	1-2
23 Nov	WLge	A	Bristol Rvs	D	0-0
25 Nov	WLge	H	Millwall	L	0-3
30 Nov	SLge	H	Leyton	W	1-0
2 Dec	WLge	H	C. Palace	W	1-0
7 Dec	SLge	A	Reading	L	1-3
9 Dec	WLge	A	Luton	W	5-1
14 Dec	SLge	H	Watford	W	5-0
16 Dec	SLge	H	Luton	W	2-0
21 Dec	SLge	H	Norwich	W	3-0
25 Dec	SLge	H	Northampton	W	2-0
26 Dec	SLge	A	Southampton	D	1-1
28 Dec	SLge	A	Northampton	L	1-2
4 Jan	SLge	H	West Ham	W	3-2
11 Jan	FC	A	Everton	L	0-1
18 Jan	SLge	A	N/Brompton	W	2-1
20 Jan	SLge	H	Plymouth	W	0-1
25 Jan	SLge	H	Swindon	W	1-0
1 Feb	F	H	Woolwich Asnl	L	0-1
8 Feb	SLge	H	Luton	L	1-2
12 Feb	SLge	A	C. Palace	W	2-0
15 Feb	SLge	A	Brighton	L	0-2
22 Feb	F	A	Chelsea	D	1-1
29 Feb	SLge	A	Bradford PA	W	2-1
7 Mar	SLge	H	Millwall	L	1-2
14 Mar	SLge	A	Brentford	L	0-3
21 Mar	SLge	H	Bristol Rvs	L	1-2
28 Mar	SLge	A	Leyton	W	5-2
4 Apr	SLge	H	Reading	W	2-0
6 Apr	SLge	H	Portsmouth	L	2-3
11 Apr	SLge	A	Watford	D	2-2
17 Apr	SLge	H	Southampton	W	3-0
18 Apr	SLge	A	Norwich	L	1-2
20 Apr	SLge	A	Plymouth	L	0-1
30 Apr	F	A	Clapton	L	0-2

Player	SL App	Goals
Brewster	1	
Bull W.	21	3
Burton O.	31	
Chaplin J.	30	
Coquet E.	6	
Cousins	2	
Darnell J.	22	
Dixon A.	5	
Gray	15	
Hughes E.	1	
McNair W.	15	6
Manning G.	33	
Middlemiss H.	25	8
Minter W.J.	9	4
Morris T.	32	
Pass J.E.	18	5

Player	SL App	Goals
Payne G.	6	3
Pickett A.E.	13	2
Reid	11	2
Seeburg M.P.	15	4
Stansfield H.	8	1
Steel D.	25	1
Tait A.	1	
Walker R.H.	11	2
Walton J.	21	1
Watson J.	3	
Whitbourne J.G.	5	
Whyman A.	8	
Woodruff C.L.	5	3
Woodward V.J.	20	10
Own Goals		4

Southern League 1907–08

		P	W	D	L	F:A	Pts
1	QPR	38	21	9	8	82:57	51
2	Plymouth	38	19	11	8	50:31	49
3	Millwall Ath	38	19	8	11	49:32	46
4	C. Palace	38	17	10	11	54:51	44
5	Swindon	38	16	10	12	55:40	42
6	Bristol Rvs	38	16	10	12	59:56	42
7	TOTTENHAM	38	17	7	14	59:48	41
8	Northampton	38	15	11	12	50:41	41
9	Portsmouth	38	17	6	15	64:52	40
10	West Ham	38	15	10	13	47:48	40
11	Southampton	38	16	6	16	51:60	38
12	Reading	38	15	6	17	55:50	36
13	Bradford PA	38	12	12	14	53:54	36
14	Watford	38	12	10	16	47:59	34
15	Brentford	38	14	5	19	49:52	33
16	Norwich	38	12	9	17	46:49	33
17	Brighton	38	12	8	18	46:59	32
18	Luton	38	12	6	20	33:56	30
19	Leyton	38	8	11	19	51:74	27
20	N/Brompton	38	9	7	22	44:75	25

Western League 'B' 1907–08

		P	W	D	L	F:A	Pts
1	Millwall	12	9	2	1	31:15	20
2	TOTTENHAM	12	7	0	5	26:13	14
3	Bristol Rvs	12	6	2	4	22:29	14
4	Luton	12	4	4	4	16:21	12
5	Reading	12	4	3	5	20:25	11
6	C. Palace	12	3	4	5	16:17	10
7	West Ham	12	1	1	10	16:27	3

SEASON 1908/09

Date	Comp	H/A	Opponent	Result	Score
1 Sep	Lge	H	Wolves	W	3-0
5 Sep	Lge	A	Leeds	L	0-1
12 Sep	Lge	H	Barnsley	W	4-0
19 Sep	Lge	H	Bolton	W	2-1
26 Sep	Lge	A	Hull	L	0-1
3 Oct	Lge	H	Derby	D	0-0
5 Oct	LCC	H	QPR	W	1-0
10 Oct	Lge	A	Blackpool	D	1-1
17 Oct	Lge	H	Chesterfield	W	4-0
24 Oct	Lge	A	Glossop	D	1-1
31 Oct	Lge	H	Stockport	D	0-0
2 Nov	LCC	H	Clapton	D	1-1
7 Nov	Lge	A	WBA	L	0-3
14 Nov	Lge	H	Birmingham	W	4-0
21 Nov	Lge	A	Gainsbro'	W	2-0
28 Nov	Lge	H	Grimsby	W	2-0
30 Nov	LCC	A	West Ham	W	2-0
5 Dec	Lge	A	Fulham	W	3-2
12 Dec	Lge	H	Burnley	W	4-2
19 Dec	Lge	A	Bradford PA	W	2-0
25 Dec	Lge	A	Oldham	L	0-1
26 Dec	Lge	H	Oldham	W	3-0
28 Dec	Lge	A	Wolves	L	0-1
2 Jan	Lge	H	Leeds	W	3-0
9 Jan	Lge	A	Barnsley	D	1-1
16 Jan	FC	A	Man City	W	4-3
23 Jan	Lge	A	Bolton	W	1-0
30 Jan	Lge	H	Hull	D	0-0
6 Feb	FC	H	Fulham	W	1-0
13 Feb	Lge	H	Blackpool	W	4-1
20 Feb	FC	H	Burnley	D	0-0
24 Feb	FCr	A	Burnley	L	1-3
27 Feb	Lge	H	Glossop	D	3-3
6 Mar	Lge	A	Stockport	W	3-1
8 Mar	Lge	A	Chesterfield	W	3-1
13 Mar	Lge	H	WBA	L	1-3
20 Mar	Lge	A	Birmingham	D	3-3
22 Mar	LCC	A	Millwall	L	0-2
27 Mar	Lge	H	Gainsbro'	D	1-1
3 Apr	Lge	A	Grimsby	W	2-1
9 Apr	Lge	H	Clapton	L	0-1
10 Apr	Lge	H	Fulham	W	1-0
12 Apr	Lge	A	Clapton	D	0-0
17 Apr	Lge	A	Burnley	W	2-1
24 Apr	Lge	H	Bradford PA	W	3-0
28 Apr	Lge	A	Derby	D	1-1
29 Apr	F	A	Clapton	W	3-2

Player	Lg App	Goals	Player	Lg App	Goals
Boreham F.	8		Middlemiss H.	38	14
Brough J.	1		Minter W.J.	34	14
Bull W.	12		Morris T.	24	1
Burton O.	33		Morton J.	2	
Coquet E.	37		Seeburg M.P.	1	
Curtis J.	2	1	Steel R.	37	12
Darnell J.	37		Steel D.	38	1
Hewitson R.	30		Watson J.	24	2
Leslie T.	2		Wilkes F.	6	
MacFarlane D.	16	2	Woodruff C.L.	8	1
Massey F.J.	1		Woodward V.J.	27	19

Final table for Second Division

1	Bolton	38	24	4	10	59:28	52
2	**TOTTENHAM**	38	20	11	7	67:32	51
3	West Bromwich	38	19	13	6	56:27	51
4	Hull	38	19	6	13	63:39	44
5	Derby	38	16	11	11	55:41	43
6	Oldham	38	17	6	15	55:43	40
7	Wolverhampton	38	14	11	13	56:48	39
8	Glossop	38	15	8	15	57:53	38
9	Gainsbro'	38	15	8	15	49:70	38
10	Fulham	38	13	11	14	58:48	37
11	Birmingham	38	14	9	15	58:61	37
12	Leeds C.	38	14	7	17	43:53	35
13	Grimsby	38	14	7	17	41:54	35
14	Burnley	38	13	7	18	51:58	33
15	Clapton O.	38	12	9	17	37:49	33
16	Bradford P.A.	38	13	6	19	51:59	32
17	Barnsley	38	11	10	17	48:57	32
18	Stockport	38	14	3	21	39:71	31
19	Chesterfield T.	38	11	8	19	37:67	30
20	Blackpool	38	9	11	18	46:68	29

SEASON 1909/10

Date	Comp	H/A	Opponent	Result	Score
1 Sep	Lge	A	Sunderland	L	1-3
4 Sep	Lge	A	Everton	L	2-4
11 Sep	Lge	H	Man Utd	D	2-2
18 Sep	Lge	A	Brad City	L	1-5
20 Sep	LCC	A	Nunhead	W	9-0
25 Sep	Lge	H	Sheff Wed	W	3-0
29 Sep	F	A	Reading	W	3-2
2 Oct	Lge	A	Bristol C	D	0-0
9 Oct	Lge	H	Bury	W	1-0
11 Oct	LCC	H	Croydon	W	7-1
16 Oct	Lge	H	Middlesbro	L	1-3
30 Oct	Lge	H	Notts Co	L	1-3
1 Nov	LPCF	H	Arsenal	W	3-0
6 Nov	Lge	A	Newcastle	L	0-1
8 Nov	LCCsf	* QPR	D	0-0
13 Nov	Lge	H	Liverpool	W	1-0
15 Nov	LCCsfr	† QPR	W	4-1
20 Nov	Lge	A	Aston Villa	L	2-3
22 Nov	Lge	A	Preston	L	1-4
27 Nov	Lge	H	Sheff Utd	W	2-1
4 Dec	Lge	A	Arsenal	L	0-1
6 Dec	LCCf	* Fulham	L	1-4
11 Dec	Lge	H	Bolton	D	1-1
18 Dec	Lge	A	Chelsea	L	1-2
25 Dec	Lge	H	Nottm For	D	2-2
27 Dec	Lge	A	Nottm For	D	2-2
1 Jan	Lge	A	Blackburn	L	0-2
8 Jan	Lge	H	Everton	W	3-0
15 Jan	FC	A	Plymouth	D	1-1
19 Jan	FCr	H	Plymouth	W	7-1
22 Jan	Lge	A	Man Utd	L	0-5
29 Jan	Lge	A	Bradford C	D	0-0
5 Feb	FC	A	Chelsea	W	1-0
12 Feb	Lge	H	Bristol C	W	3-2
19 Feb	FC	A	Swindon	L	2-3
26 Feb	Lge	A	Middlesbro	L	3-4
5 Mar	Lge	H	Preston	W	2-1
12 Mar	Lge	A	Notts Co	L	0-3
14 Mar	Lge	A	Sheff Utd	D	1-1
19 Mar	Lge	H	Newcastle	L	0-4
25 Mar	Lge	H	Sunderland	W	5-1
26 Mar	Lge	A	Liverpool	L	0-2
29 Mar	Lge	H	Blackburn	W	4-0
2 Apr	Lge	H	Aston Villa	D	1-1
9 Apr	Lge	A	Sheff Utd	D	1-1
16 Apr	Lge	H	Arsenal	D	1-1
20 Apr	Lge	A	Bury	L	1-3
23 Apr	Lge	A	Bolton	W	2-0
30 Apr	Lge	H	Chelsea	W	2-1

* played at Chelsea
† played at Fulham

Player	Lg App	Goals	Player	Lg App	Goals
Bentley F.W.	19		Leslie T.	7	
Boreham F.	12		Lunn T.H.	2	
Brown D.C.	1		Lyle A.	1	
Brown I.	8		MacFarlane D.	5	
Burton O.	4		Middlemiss H.	36	9
Coquet E.	27		Minter W.J.	38	15
Curtis J.	37	3	Morris T.	26	1
Darnell J.	25		Newman E.	1	
Drabble F.	1		Steel A.	1	
Elkin R.H.	8		Steel D.	36	2
Harris W.	7		Steel R.	38	9
Humphreys P.	20	13	Tull W.D.	7	1
Joyce J.W.	23		Wilkes F.	23	
Kennedy J.J.	2		Woodruff C.L.	2	
Kerry A.H.G.	1				

Final table for First Division

1	Aston Villa	38	23	7	8	84:42	53
2	Liverpool	38	21	6	11	78:57	48
3	Blackburn	38	18	9	11	73:55	45
4	Newcastle	38	19	7	12	70:56	45
5	Manchester U.	38	19	7	12	69:61	45
6	Sheffield U.	38	16	10	12	62:41	42
7	Bradford C.	38	17	8	13	64:47	42
8	Sunderland	38	18	5	15	66:51	41
9	Notts Co.	38	15	10	13	67:59	40
10	Everton	38	16	8	14	51:56	40
11	The Wednesday	38	15	9	14	60:63	39
12	Preston	38	15	5	18	52:58	35
13	Bury	38	12	9	17	62:66	33
14	Nottingham F.	38	11	11	16	54:72	33
15	**TOTTENHAM**	38	11	10	17	53:69	32
16	Bristol C.	38	12	8	18	45:60	32
17	Middlesbrough	38	11	9	18	56:73	31
18	Woolwich Asnl	38	11	9	18	37:67	31
19	Chelsea	38	11	7	20	47:70	29
20	Bolton	38	9	6	23	44:71	24

SEASON 1910/11

Date	Comp	H/A	Opponent	Res	Score
1 Sep	Lge	A	Everton	L	0-2
3 Sep	Lge	H	Sheff Wed	W	3-1
10 Sep	Lge	A	Bristol C	W	2-0
17 Sep	Lge	H	Newcastle	L	1-2
19 Sep	LCC	H	Clapton	W	1-0
24 Sep	Lge	A	Oldham	L	0-2
1 Oct	Lge	A	Middlesbrough	L	0-2
3 Oct	LPCF	A	Chelsea	W	3-0
8 Oct	Lge	H	Preston	D	1-1
10 Oct	LCC	H	Chelsea	W	3-0
15 Oct	Lge	A	Notts Co	L	0-1
22 Oct	Lge	H	Man Utd	D	2-2
29 Oct	Lge	A	Liverpool	L	1-2
5 Nov	Lge	H	Bury	W	5-0
7 Nov	LCCsf	A	Millwall	D	2-2*
12 Nov	Lge	A	Sheff Utd	L	0-3
19 Nov	Lge	H	Aston Villa	L	1-2
21 Nov	LCCsfr	A	Millwall	W	2-0*
26 Nov	Lge	A	Sunderland	L	0-4
3 Dec	Lge	H	Arsenal	W	3-1
5 Dec	LCCf	†	Fulham	W	2-1
10 Dec	Lge	A	Brad City	L	0-3
17 Dec	Lge	H	Blackburn	D	2-2
24 Dec	Lge	A	Nottm Forest	W	2-1
26 Dec	Lge	H	Nottm Forest	L	1-4
27 Dec	Lge	H	Man City	D	1-1
31 Dec	Lge	A	Sheff Wed	L	1-2
3 Jan	Lge	A	Man City	L	1-2
7 Jan	Lge	H	Bristol City	W	3-2
14 Jan	FC	H	Millwall	W	2-1
21 Jan	Lge	A	Newcastle	D	1-1
4 Feb	FC	A	Blackburn	D	0-0
9 Feb	FCr	H	Blackburn	L	0-2
11 Feb	Lge	A	Preston	L	0-2
13 Feb	Lge	H	Middlesbrough	W	6-2
18 Feb	Lge	H	Notts Co	W	3-0
25 Feb	Lge	A	Aston Villa	L	0-4
4 Mar	Lge	H	Liverpool	W	1-0
11 Mar	Lge	A	Bury	L	1-2
15 Mar	Lge	A	Man Utd	L	2-3
18 Mar	Lge	H	Sheff Wed	W	2-1
27 Mar	Lge	H	Oldham	W	2-0
1 Apr	Lge	H	Sunderland	D	1-1
8 Apr	Lge	A	Arsenal	L	0-2
15 Apr	Lge	H	Brad City	W	2-0
17 Apr	Lge	H	Everton	L	0-1
22 Apr	Lge	A	Blackburn	L	0-3
7 May	F	‡	Nth German XI	W	4-1
13 May	F	‡	Preussen	W	7-0
14 May	F	‡	Hertha	W	4-1
20 May	F	‡	Wacker	W	8-1
21 May	F	‡	Eintracht F.	W	4-1
25 May	F	‡	Kickers Vict	W	6-0

* Played at Leyton
† Final played at Stamford Bridge
‡ German tour

Player	Lg App	Goals
Bentley F.W.	16	
Birnie E.L.	4	1
Brown I.	4	
Bulling E.	2	
Collins T.	25	
Coquet E.	13	
Crompton E.	5	
Curtis J.	30	1
Darnell J.	38	2
Elkin R.H.	17	
Foreman T.	2	1
Gosnell A.A.	5	
Humphreys P.	24	10
Joyce J.W.	4	
Kennedy J.J.	7	1
Leslie T.	1	
Lunn T.H.	34	
McTavish J.K.	7	
McTavish R.	11	2
Middlemiss H.	30	4
Minter W.J.	38	19
Morris T.	11	
Newman E.	2	1
Rance C.S.	11	
Steel D.	26	
Steel R.	29	9
Tull W.D.	3	1
Wilkes F.	19	

Final table for First Division

1	Manchester U.	38	22	8	8	72:40	52
2	Aston Villa	38	22	7	9	69:41	51
3	Sunderland	38	15	15	8	67:48	45
4	Everton	38	19	7	12	50:36	45
5	Bradford C.	38	20	5	13	51:42	45
6	The Wednesday	38	17	8	13	47:48	42
7	Oldham	38	16	9	13	44:41	41
8	Newcastle	38	15	10	13	61:43	40
9	Sheffield U.	38	15	8	15	49:43	38
10	Woolwich Asnl	38	13	12	13	41:49	38
11	Notts Co.	38	14	10	14	37:45	38
12	Blackburn	38	13	11	14	62:54	37
13	Liverpool	38	15	7	16	53:53	37
14	Preston	38	12	11	15	40:49	35
15	**TOTTENHAM**	**38**	**13**	**6**	**19**	**52:63**	**32**
16	Middlesbrough	38	11	10	17	49:63	32
17	Manchester C.	38	9	13	16	43:58	31
18	Bury	38	9	11	18	43:71	29
19	Bristol C.	38	11	5	22	43:66	27
20	Nottingham F.	38	9	7	22	55:75	25

SEASON 1911/12

Date	Comp	H/A	Opponent	Res	Score
2 Sep	Lge	A	Everton	D	2-2
4 Sep	Lge	H	Sheff Wed	W	3-1
9 Sep	Lge	H	WBA	W	1-0
16 Sep	Lge	A	Sunderland	D	1-1
18 Sep	LCC	A	Brentford	L	1-4
23 Sep	Lge	H	Blackburn	L	0-2
30 Sep	Lge	A	Sheff Wed	L	0-4
7 Oct	Lge	H	Bury	W	2-1
14 Oct	Lge	A	Middlesbro	L	0-2
21 Oct	Lge	H	Notts Co	D	2-2
23 Oct	LPCF	H	Fulham	W	3-0
28 Oct	Lge	H	Preston	W	6-2
4 Nov	Lge	A	Man Utd	W	2-1
11 Nov	Lge	H	Liverpool	W	2-0
18 Nov	Lge	A	Aston Villa	D	2-2
25 Nov	Lge	A	Newcastle	L	1-2
2 Dec	Lge	A	Sheff Utd	W	2-1
9 Dec	Lge	H	Oldham	W	4-0
16 Dec	Lge	A	Bolton	L	0-1
23 Dec	Lge	H	Bradford C	L	2-3
25 Dec	Lge	H	Woolwich A.	W	5-0
26 Dec	Lge	A	Woolwich A.	L	1-3
30 Dec	Lge	H	Everton	L	0-1
13 Jan	FC	A	WBA	L	0-3
20 Jan	Lge	H	Sunderland	D	0-0
27 Jan	Lge	A	Blackburn	D	0-0
3 Feb	F	H	C. Orient	W	3-2
10 Feb	Lge	A	Bury	L	1-2
17 Feb	Lge	H	Middlesbro	W	2-1
24 Feb	Lge	A	Newcastle	D	2-2
2 Mar	Lge	A	Preston	W	1-0
13 Mar	Lge	A	WBA	L	0-2
16 Mar	Lge	A	Liverpool	W	2-1
23 Mar	Lge	H	Aston Villa	W	2-1
30 Mar	Lge	A	Newcastle	L	0-2
5 Apr	Lge	A	Man City	L	0-2
6 Apr	Lge	H	Sheff Utd	D	1-1
8 Apr	Lge	H	Man City	L	0-2
9 Apr	Lge	H	Man United	D	1-1
13 Apr	Lge	A	Oldham	L	1-2
18 Apr	F	A	Northampton	L	0-2
20 Apr	Lge	H	Bolton	W	1-0
27 Apr	Lge	A	Bradford C	L	0-3
29 Apr	F	*	Woolwich A.	L	0-3
12 May	F	†	Hull City	L	0-2
16 May	F	‡	Bewegungs	W	3-1
20 May	F	‡	Sport Vienna	W	5-3
24 May	F	‡	Woolwich A.	L	0-4
27 May	F	‡	Varosi Torna	W	4-1
28 May	F	‡	Olympic XI	D	2-2
30 May	F	‡	Olympic XI	W	4-3
2 Jun	F	‡	Olympic XI	L	0-3

* Titanic fund charity match at Shepherd's Bush (QPR ground)
† Bedekker Cup match in Brussels
‡ Tour of Leipzig (first game) and Vienna (remaining six games)

Player	Lg App	Goals
Bentley F.W.	1	
Bliss H.	5	1
Bowering G.	7	
Brittan R.C.	26	
Collins T.	33	
Crompton E.	3	
Curtis J.	9	
Darnell J.	34	1
Elliot J.	5	2
Foreman T.	6	
Grimsdell A.	2	
Humphreys P.	1	
Joyce J.W.	4	
Kennedy J.J.	4	
Lightfoot E.J.	21	
Lunn T.H.	34	
McTavish J.K.	30	3
Mason T.L.	7	1
Middlemiss H.	32	11
Minter W.J.	35	18
Morris T.	2	
Newman E.	19	6
Rance C.S.	17	
Steel D.	29	
Steel R.	30	7
Tattersall W.	2	
Webster F.	6	
Wilkes F.	9	
Young A.	5	3

Final table for First Division

1	Blackburn	38	20	9	9	60:43	49
2	Everton	38	20	6	12	46:42	46
3	Newcastle	38	18	8	12	64:50	44
4	Bolton	38	20	3	15	54:43	43
5	The Wednesday	38	16	9	13	69:49	41
6	Aston Villa	38	17	7	14	76:63	41
7	Middlesbrough	38	16	8	14	56:45	40
8	Sunderland	38	14	11	13	58:51	39
9	West Bromwich	38	15	9	14	43:47	39
10	Woolwich Asnl	38	15	8	15	55:59	38
11	Bradford C.	38	15	8	15	46:50	38
12	**TOTTENHAM**	**38**	**14**	**9**	**15**	**53:53**	**37**
13	Manchester U.	38	13	11	14	45:60	37
14	Sheffield U.	38	13	10	15	63:56	36
15	Manchester C.	38	13	9	16	56:58	35
16	Notts Co.	38	14	7	17	46:63	35
17	Liverpool	38	12	10	16	49:55	34
18	Oldham	38	12	10	16	46:54	34
19	Preston	38	13	7	18	40:57	33
20	Bury	38	6	9	23	32:59	21

SEASON 1912/13

Date	Comp		Opponent		Score
2 Sep	Lge	H	Everton	L	0-2
7 Sep	Lge	H	Sheff Wed	L	2-4
14 Sep	Lge	A	Blackburn	L	1-6
21 Sep	Lge	H	Derby	L	1-2
23 Sep	LCC	H	Bromley	W	3-0
28 Sep	Lge	A	Sunderland	D	2-2
5 Oct	Lge	A	Middlesbro	D	1-1
14 Oct	LPCF	A	Fulham	L	0-1
19 Oct	Lge	A	Man Utd	L	0-2
26 Oct	Lge	H	Aston Villa	D	3-3
28 Oct	LCC	H	C. Palace	D	3-3
2 Nov	Lge	A	Liverpool	L	1-4
4 Nov	Lge	H	Notts Co.	L	0-3
9 Nov	Lge	H	Bolton	L	0-1
11 Nov	LCC	A	C. Palace	L	1-4
16 Nov	Lge	A	Sheff Utd	L	0-4
23 Nov	Lge	H	Newcastle	W	1-0
30 Nov	Lge	A	Oldham	L	1-4
7 Dec	Lge	H	Chelsea	W	1-0
14 Dec	Lge	A	Woolwich A.	W	3-0
21 Dec	Lge	H	Bradford C.	W	2-1
25 Dec	Lge	A	Man City	D	2-2
26 Dec	Lge	H	Man City	W	4-0
28 Dec	Lge	A	Sheff Wed	L	1-2
1 Jan	Lge	A	Everton	W	2-1
4 Jan	Lge	H	Blackburn	L	0-1
11 Jan	FC	H	Blackpool	D	1-1
16 Jan	FCr	* Blackpool		W	6-1
18 Jan	Lge	A	Dorby	L	0-5
25 Jan	Lge	H	Sunderland	L	1-2
1 Feb	FC	A	Reading	L	0-1
8 Feb	Lge	H	Middlesbro	W	5-3
15 Feb	Lge	H	Notts Co.	W	1-0
22 Feb	Lge	H	Sheff Utd	W	1-0
1 Mar	Lge	A	Aston Villa	L	0-1
8 Mar	Lge	H	Liverpool	W	1-0
15 Mar	Lge	A	Bolton	L	0-2
21 Mar	Lge	H	WBA	W	3-1
24 Mar	Lge	A	WBA	L	1-4
29 Mar	Lge	A	Newcastle	L	0-3
31 Mar	Lge	H	Man Utd	D	1-1
5 Apr	Lge	H	Oldham	W	1-0
9 Apr	F	A	Watford	D	0-0
12 Apr	Lge	A	Chelsea	L	0-1
19 Apr	Lge	H	Woolwich A.	D	1-1
26 Apr	Lge	A	Bradford C.	L	1-3
1 Mar	F	‡ Red Star		W	4-1
4 May	F	‡ French XI		W	9-0

‡ Played in Paris
* Blackpool sold home advantage; game played at White Hart Lane

Player	Lg App	Goals	Player	Lg App	Goals
Bliss H.	18	7	Middlemiss H.	38	8
Brittan R.C.	14		Minter W.J.	37	11
Cantrell J.	25	12	Newman E.	3	
Collins T.	28	1	Rance C.S.	32	
Curtis J.	4		Steel R.	19	1
Darnell J.	4		Tate J.A.	2	
Elliott J.	6	1	Tattersall W.	30	3
Grimsdell A.	25		Upton S.	2	
Jones G.	7		Walden F.	1	
Joyce J.W.	20		Webster F.	34	
Lightfoot E.J.	15		Weir F.	34	1
Lunn T.H.	16		Young C.	4	

Final table for First Division

1	Sunderland	38	25	4	9	86:43	54
2	Aston Villa	38	19	12	7	86:52	50
3	The Wednesday	38	21	7	10	75:55	49
4	Manchester U.	38	19	8	11	69:43	46
5	Blackburn	38	16	13	9	79:43	45
6	Manchester C.	38	18	8	12	53:37	44
7	Derby	38	17	8	13	69:66	42
8	Bolton	38	16	10	12	62:63	42
9	Oldham	38	14	14	10	50:55	42
10	West Bromwich	38	13	12	13	57:50	38
11	Everton	38	15	7	16	48:54	37
12	Liverpool	38	16	5	17	61:71	37
13	Bradford C.	38	12	11	15	50:60	35
14	Newcastle	38	13	8	17	47:47	34
15	Sheffield U.	38	14	6	18	56:70	34
16	Middlesbrough	38	11	10	17	55:69	32
17	**TOTTENHAM**	**38**	**12**	**6**	**20**	**45:72**	**30**
18	Chelsea	38	11	6	21	51:73	28
19	Notts Co.	38	7	9	22	28:56	23
20	Woolwich Asnl	38	3	12	23	26:74	18

SEASON 1913/14

Date	Comp		Opponent		Score
1 Sep	Lge	A	Sheff Utd	W	4-1
6 Sep	Lge	A	Chelsea	W	3-1
8 Sep	Lge	H	Sheff Utd	W	2-1
13 Sep	Lge	H	Derby	D	1-1
20 Sep	Lge	A	Oldham	L	0-3
22 Sep	LCC	H	Metrogas	W	11-2
27 Sep	Lge	H	Man City	W	3-1
4 Oct	Lge	A	Man Utd	L	1-3
11 Oct	Lge	H	Bradford C.	D	0-0
14 Oct	LCC	A	Fulham	W	2-0
18 Oct	Lge	A	Burnley	L	1-3
25 Oct	Lge	H	Blackburn	D	3-3
27 Oct	LPCF	H	C. Palace	L	1-2
1 Nov	Lge	A	Preston	W	2-1
8 Nov	Lge	H	Sunderland	L	1-4
10 Nov	LCCsf	* Arsenal		W	2-1
15 Nov	Lge	A	Newcastle	L	0-2
22 Nov	Lge	H	Everton	W	4-1
29 Nov	Lge	A	Liverpool	L	1-2
6 Dec	Lge	H	WBA	W	3-0
8 Dec	LCCf	† C. Palace		L	1-2
13 Dec	Lge	A	Aston Villa	D	3-3
20 Dec	Lge	H	Sheff Wed	D	1-1
26 Dec	Lge	H	Middlesbro	L	0-1
27 Dec	Lge	H	Chelsea	L	1-2
1 Jan	Lge	A	Bolton	L	0-3
3 Jan	Lge	A	Derby	L	0-4
10 Jan	FC	A	Leicester	D	5-5
15 Jan	FCr	H	Leicester	W	2-0
17 Jan	Lge	H	Oldham	W	3-1
24 Jan	Lge	A	Man City	l	1-2
31 Jan	FC	A	Man City	L	1-2
7 Feb	Lge	H	Man Utd	W	2-1
14 Feb	Lge	A	Bradford C	L	1-2
21 Feb	Lge	H	Burnley	W	2-0
28 Feb	Lge	A	Blackburn	D	1-1
5 Mar	F	H	Mus. Hall Arts	W	3-0
7 Mar	Lge	H	Preston	W	3-0
14 Mar	Lge	A	Sunderland	L	0-2
21 Mar	Lge	H	Newcastle	D	0-0
28 Mar	Lge	A	Everton	D	1-1
4 Apr	Lge	H	Liverpool	D	0-0
10 Apr	Lge	H	Bolton	W	3-0
11 Apr	Lge	A	WBA	D	1-1
13 Apr	Lge	A	Middlesbro	L	0-6
18 Apr	Lge	H	Aston Villa	L	0-2
25 Apr	Lge	A	Sheff Wed	L	0-2
3 May	F	‡ Hanover		W	6-3
6 May	F	‡ Nuremburg		D	1-1
9 May	F	‡ Bayern FC		W	6-0
10 May	F	‡ Furth		D	2-2
13 May	F	‡ Milan		W	5-0
17 May	F	‡ Zurich		W	6-0
21 May	F	‡ St Gallen		W	3-0
23 May	F	‡ Pforzheim		W	5-0
24 May	F	‡ Stuttgart		W	1-0

* Played at Stamford Bridge
† Played at Highbury
‡ Tour of Germany and Switzerland

Player	Lg App	Goals	Player	Lg App	Goals
Banks J.A.	12		King A.	19	
Bauchop J.R.	10	6	Lightfoot E.J.	2	1
Bliss H.	29	6	Middlemiss H.	34	4
Bowler G.	3		Minter W.J.	16	5
Cantrell J.	33	15	Newman E.	5	
Cartwright W.	13		Oliver W.	2	
Clay T.	15		Sparrow H.	3	4
Collins T.	15		Steel R.	37	
Crowl S.R.	1		Tate J.A.	2	
Darnell J.	1		Tattersall W.	7	
Elliot J.E.	1		Walden F.	30	5
Fleming J.B.M.	8	1	Webster F.	33	
Grimsdell A.	37	1	Weir F.	33	
Joyce J.W.	17	1	Own Goal		1

Final table for First Division

1	Blackburn	38	20	11	7	78:42	51
2	Aston Villa	38	19	6	13	65:50	44
3	Middlesbrough	38	19	5	14	77:60	43
4	Oldham	38	17	9	12	55:45	43
5	West Bromwich	38	15	13	10	46:42	43
6	Bolton	38	16	10	12	65:52	42
7	Sunderland	38	17	6	15	63:52	40
8	Chelsea	38	16	7	15	46:55	39
9	Bradford C.	38	12	14	12	40:40	38
10	Sheffield U.	38	16	5	17	63:60	37
11	Newcastle	38	13	11	14	39:48	37
12	Burnley	38	12	12	14	61:53	36
13	Manchester C.	38	14	8	16	51:53	36
14	Manchester U.	38	15	6	17	52:62	36
15	Everton	38	12	11	15	46:55	35
16	Liverpool	38	14	7	17	46:62	35
17	**TOTTENHAM**	**38**	**12**	**10**	**16**	**50:62**	**34**
18	The Wednesday	38	13	8	17	53:70	34
19	Preston	38	12	6	20	52:69	30
20	Derby	38	8	11	19	55:71	27

SEASON 1914/15

22 Aug	WRF	H	Arsenal	L	1-5		26 Dec	Lge	H	Sheff Wed	W	6-1
2 Sep	Lge	H	Everton	L	1-3		1 Jan	Lge	A	Everton	D	1-1
5 Sep	Lge	H	Chelsea	D	1-1		2 Jan	Lge	A	Chelsea	D	1-1
12 Sep	Lge	A	Bradford C,	D	2-2		9 Jan	FC	H	Sunderland	W	2-1
19 Sep	Lge	H	Burnley	L	1-3		16 Jan	Lge	A	Bradford C.	D	0-0
21 Sep	LCC	A	Nunhead	W	2-1		23 Jan	Lge	A	Burnley	L	1-3
26 Sep	Lge	A	Man City	L	1-2		30 Jan	FC	A	Norwich	L	2-3
28 Sep	Lge	H	WBA	W	2-0		6 Feb	F	H	Fulham	D	2-2
3 Oct	Lge	A	Newcastle	L	0-4		13 Feb	Lge	A	Middlesbro	L	5-7
10 Oct	Lge	H	Middlesbro	D	3-3		20 Feb	Lge	H	Notts Co	W	2-0
15 Oct	F	A	Chelsea	D	1-1		27 Feb	Lge	A	Aston Villa	L	1-3
17 Oct	Lge	A	Sheff Utd	D	1-1		6 Mar	Lge	H	Liverpool	D	1-1
19 Oct	LCC	A	C. Palace	L	1-3		13 Mar	Lge	A	Bradford PA	L	1-5
24 Oct	Lge	H	Aston Villa	L	0-2		15 Mar	Lge	H	Man City	D	2-2
28 Oct	LPCF	A	C. Palace	D	2-2		20 Mar	Lge	H	Oldham	W	1-0
31 Oct	Lge	A	Liverpool	L	2-7		27 Mar	Lge	A	Man Utd	D	1-1
7 Nov	Lge	H	Bradford PA	W	3-0		2 Apr	Lge	H	Newcastle	D	0-0
14 Nov	Lge	A	Oldham	L	1-4		3 Apr	Lge	H	Bolton	W	4-2
21 Nov	Lge	H	Man Utd	W	2-0		6 Apr	Lge	A	WBA	L	2-3
28 Nov	Lge	A	Bolton	L	2-4		10 Apr	Lge	A	Blackburn	L	1-4
5 Dec	Lge	H	Blackburn	L	0-4		17 Apr	F	H	Cameron High.	L	1-2
12 Dec	Lge	A	Notts Co.	W	2-1		19 Apr	Lge	H	Sheff Utd	D	1-1
19 Dec	Lge	H	Sunderland	L	0-6		24 Apr	Lge	A	Sunderland	L	0-5
25 Dec	Lge	A	Sheff Wed	L	2-3							

Player	Lg App	Goals	Player	Lg App	Goals
Banks J.A.	5		Lowe H.	2	
Bliss H.	33	21	Middlemiss H.	33	3
Cantrell J.	26	14	Minter W.J.	26	5
Clay T.	38	4	Pearson J.	17	
Collins T.	12		Rance C.S.	3	
Darnell J.	11		Sparrow H.	15	3
Eadon J.	5		Steel R.	36	2
Fleming J.B.M.	11	2	Tattersall W.	5	
Grimsdell A.	8		Walden F.	38	1
Jacques W.	28		Webster F.	9	
Joyce J.W.	5		Weir F.	29	1
Lightfoot E.J.	23	1			

Final table for First Division

1	Everton	38	19	8	11	76:47	46
2	Oldham	38	17	11	10	70:56	45
3	Blackburn	38	18	7	13	83:61	43
4	Burnley	38	18	7	13	61:47	43
5	Manchester C.	38	15	13	10	49:39	43
6	Sheffield U.	38	15	13	10	49:41	43
7	The Wednesday	38	15	13	10	61:54	43
8	Sunderland	38	18	5	15	81:72	41
9	Bradford P.A.	38	17	7	14	69:65	41
10	West Bromwich	38	15	10	13	51:43	40
11	Bradford C.	38	13	14	11	55:51	40
12	Middlesbrough	38	13	12	13	62:74	38
13	Liverpool	38	14	9	15	65:75	37
14	Aston Villa	38	13	11	14	62:72	37
15	Newcastle	38	11	10	17	46:48	32
16	Notts Co.	28	9	13	16	41:57	31
17	Bolton	38	11	8	19	68:84	30
18	Manchester U.	38	9	12	17	46:62	30
19	Chelsea	38	8	13	17	51:65	29
20	**TOTTENHAM**	**38**	**8**	**12**	**18**	**57:90**	**28**

SEASON 1915/16

4 Sep	Lge	A	Arsenal	L	0-2		15 Jan	Lge	A	Watford	W	1-0
11 Sep	Lge	H	Brentford	D	1-1		22 Jan	Lge	H	Millwall	D	2-2
18 Sep	Lge	A	West Ham	D	1-1		29 Jan	F	H	C. Orient	L	0-1
25 Sep	Lge	H	Chelsea	L	1-3		5 Feb	LSupp	A	West Ham	L	0-2
2 Oct	Lge	H	C. Palace	L	2-4		12 Feb	LSupp	A	Croydon Comm	W	1-0
9 Oct	Lge	A	QPR	W	4-0		19 Feb	LSupp	A	Fulham	L	1-3
16 Oct	Lge	H	Fulham	W	3-1		26 Feb	LSupp	H	Luton	W	7-4
23 Oct	Lge	A	C. Orient	D	0-0		4 Mar	LSupp	A	Arsenal	W	3-0
30 Oct	Lge	H	Watford	W	3-0		11 Mar	LSupp	H	QPR	D	0-0
6 Nov	Lge	A	Millwall	L	2-3		18 Mar	LSupp	A	Croydon	D	3-3
13 Nov	Lge	H	Arsenal	D	3-3		25 Mar	LSupp	H	Fulham	W	4-0
20 Nov	Lge	A	Brentford	D	1-1		1 Apr	LSupp	A	Luton	W	2-1
27 Nov	Lge	H	West Ham	W	3-0		8 Apr	LSupp	H	Arsenal	W	3-2
4 Dec	Lge	A	Chelsea	L	1-8		15 Apr	LSupp	A	QPR	W	3-1
11 Dec	Lge	A	C. Palace	L	2-4		21 Apr	LSupp	H	C. Palace	W	3-1
18 Dec	Lge	H	QPR	W	2-1		24 Apr	LSupp	A	C. Palace	L	0-4
25 Dec	Lge	H	Croydon Comm	W	3-0		26 Apr	F	A	Norwich	D	1-1
27 Dec	Lge	A	Croydon Comm	D	0-0		29 Apr	LSupp	H	West Ham	D	1-1
1 Jan	Lge	A	Fulham	W	2-0		6 May	F	A	C. Orient	L	2-3
8 Jan	Lge	H	C. Orient	D	1-1							

Player	War Lg App	Goals	Player	War Lg App	Goals
Banks J.	17	7	Knighton T.	4	2
Barton P.	29	1	Lloyd H.	12	6
Bassett E.	28	9	Minter A.	3	1
Bliss H.	33	23	Morris J.	35	3
Chaplin A.	4		Page J.	1	
Clay T.	32	4	Page R.	3	
Darnell J.	15		Ralston A.	17	
Doyle J.	1		Rance C.	36	4
Elliott J.	33		Steel R.	29	6
Fricker F.	1		Thomas D.	9	1
Glen P.	1	1	Travers G.	3	
Hopkins T.	3	1	Watkins W.	1	
Jacques W.	18		Weir F.	1	
Joyce J.	17		Wilson A.	10	

London Combination 1915–16

1	Chelsea	22	17	3	2	71:18	37
2	Millwall	22	12	6	4	46:24	30
3	Arsenal	22	10	5	7	43:46	25
4	West Ham	22	10	4	8	47:35	24
5	Fulham	22	10	4	8	45:37	24
6	**TOTTENHAM**	**22**	**8**	**8**	**6**	**38:35**	**24**
7	Brentford	22	6	8	8	36:40	20
8	QPR	22	8	3	11	27:41	19
9	C. Palace	22	8	3	11	35:55	19
10	Watford	22	8	1	13	37:46	17
11	Clapton O.	22	4	6	12	22:44	14
12	Croydon Comm	22	3	5	14	24:50	11

Supplementary Tournament Group 1915–16

1	Chelsea	14	10	1	3	50:15	21
2	**TOTTENHAM**	**14**	**8**	**3**	**3**	**31:22**	**19**
3	Millwall	14	8	2	4	30:22	18
4	Watford	14	5	3	6	22:20	13
5	Brentford	14	5	2	7	29:33	12
6	Clapton O.	14	3	4	7	17:27	10
7	Reading	14	3	2	9	23:64	8

SEASON 1916/17

Date	Comp		Opponent	Result	Score
2 Sep	Lge	H	Chelsea	L	0-2
9 Sep	Lge	A	Arsenal	D	1-1
16 Sep	Lge	*	Luton	L	2-3
23 Sep	Lge	A	Reading	W	4-2
30 Sep	Lge	A	Millwall	L	1-4
7 Oct	Lge	A	Watford	W	2-0
14 Oct	Lge	A	C. Orient	W	4-2
21 Oct	Lge	A	Fulham	L	1-2
28 Oct	Lge	†	QPR	L	4-5
4 Nov	Lge	A	West Ham	L	1-5
11 Nov	Lge	A	Southampton	L	0-1
18 Nov	Lge	*	C. Palace	W	3-1
25 Nov	Lge	A	Chelsea	W	4-2
2 Dec	Lge	*	Arsenal	W	4-1
9 Dec	Lge	A	Luton	W	3-1
16 Dec	Lge	*	Portsmouth	W	1-0‡
23 Dec	Lge	A	Millwall	D	3-3
25 Dec	Lge	A	Brentford	W	5-1
26 Dec	Lge	†	Brentford	W	5-2
30 Dec	Lge	*	Watford	W	3-0
6 Jan	Lge	A	C. Orient	W	2-1
13 Jan	Lge	†	Fulham	W	1-0
20 Jan	Lge	A	QPR	D	1-1
27 Jan	Lge	*	West Ham	D	0-0
3 Feb	Lge	*	Southampton	W	3-1
10 Feb	Lge	A	C. Palace	W	1-0
17 Feb	Lge	A	Portsmouth	W	4-2
24 Feb	Lge	*	C. Palace	W	4-1
3 Mar	Lge	*	Luton	W	3-2
10 Mar	Lge	A	Southampton	W	4-2
17 Mar	Lge	*	C. Orient	W	5-2
24 Mar	Lge	A	West Ham	L	0-3
31 Mar	Lge	*	Portsmouth	W	10-0
6 Apr	Lge	†	Arsenal	D	0-0
7 Apr	Lge	A	C. Palace	W	3-0
9 Apr	Lge	A	Arsenal	L	2-3
10 Apr	Lge	*	Portsmouth	W	2-1
14 Apr	Lge	A	Luton	L	4-5
21 Apr	Lge	†	Southampton	W	4-0
28 Apr	Lge	A	C. Orient	W	8-0
5 May	F	A	West Ham	D	3-3

* White Hart Lane commissioned by War Office. Home games played at Highbury
† Home games played at Homerton, ground of Clapton Orient
‡ Abandoned

Player	War Lg App	Goals	Player	War Lg App	Goals
Banks J.	31	30	Jacques W.	38	
Barton P.	37	5	Lloyd H.	23	1
Bassett J.	36	26	McVey J.	2	
Bearman F.	1		Middlemiss H.	2	1
Bliss H.	26	19	Morris J.	4	1
Caldwell T.	1		Potter H.	13	4
Clay T.	30	3	Powell H.	1	
Clayton A.	1		Ralston A.	37	
Croft F.	2		Rance C.	23	1
Croft W.	2		Slade H.	1	
Crossley J.	1		Smith J.	1	
Crowl S.	12	1	Thwaites W.	9	3
Darnell J.	14	2	Travers G.	3	1
Elliott J.	36	3	Walden F.	30	6
Grimes W.	3	1	Watkin W.	1	
Hannaford C.	1	1	Weir F.	3	
Hawkins W.	9	2	Williamson E.	1	
Hoad S.	4		Own Goal		1
Hunt K.	1				

London Combination 1916–17

	Team	P	W	D	L	F:A	Pts
1	West Ham	40	30	5	5	110:45	65
2	Millwall	40	26	6	8	85:48	58
3	Chelsea	40	24	5	11	93:48	53
4	TOTTENHAM	40	24	5	11	112:62	53
5	Arsenal	40	19	10	11	62:47	48
6	Fulham	40	21	3	16	102:63	45
7	Luton	39	20	3	16	101:82	43
8	C. Palace	38	14	7	17	68:72	35
9	Southampton	39	13	8	18	57:80	34
10	QPR	39	10	9	20	48:86	29
11	Watford	39	8	9	22	69:115	25
12	Brentford	40	9	7	24	56:99	25
*13	Portsmouth	40	9	4	27	58:117	22
14	Clapton O.	40	6	7	27	49:104	19

* Took over record of Reading who had played and lost 7 games with 8 goals for and 34 against.
Note C. Palace v Luton, QPR v Watford, Southampton v C. Palace were never played. Each team played the others twice and then played *any* 7 of their rivals according to fixture availability.

SEASON 1917/18

Date	Comp		Opponent	Result	Score
1 Sep	Lge	A	C. Palace	W	4-2
8 Sep	Lge	*	Chelsea	L	0-4
15 Sep	Lge	A	Brentford	L	2-5
22 Sep	Lge	*	Arsenal	L	1-2
29 Sep	Lge	A	West Ham	L	0-1
6 Oct	Lge	A	Fulham	W	1-0
13 Oct	Lge	A	QPR	W	3-2
20 Oct	Lge	†	C. Orient	W	2-1
27 Oct	Lge	*	C. Palace	W	1-0
3 Nov	Lge	A	Chelsea	D	0-0
10 Nov	Lge	*	Brentford	W	6-1
17 Nov	Lge	†	Arsenal	W	1-0
24 Nov	Lge	*	West Ham	W	2-0
1 Dec	Lge	A	Fulham	L	3-4
8 Dec	Lge	†	QPR	L	0-1
15 Dec	Lge	A	C. Orient	W	4-2
22 Dec	Lge	A	C. Palace	W	3-2
25 Dec	Lge	A	Millwall	W	5-0
26 Dec	Lge	†	Millwall	L	0-1
29 Dec	Lge	*	Chelsea	W	2-0
5 Jan	Lge	A	Brentford	W	3-2
12 Jan	Lge	A	Arsenal	W	4-1
19 Jan	Lge	A	West Ham	D	2-2
26 Jan	Lge	*	Fulham	L	0-1
2 Feb	Lge	A	QPR	W	7-2
9 Feb	Lge	†	Millwall	W	4-2
16 Feb	Lge	*	C. Palace	W	8-0
23 Feb	Lge	A	Chelsea	L	0-3
2 Mar	Lge	A	Brentford	W	3-0
9 Mar	Lge	A	Arsenal	L	1-4
16 Mar	Lge	*	West Ham	L	0-5
23 Mar	Lge	A	Fulham	W	3-0
29 Mar	Lge	A	C. Orient	W	3-2
30 Mar	Lge	†	QPR	L	1-2
1 Apr	Lge	†	C. Orient	W	5-2
6 Apr	Lge	A	Millwall	W	1-0
13 Apr	F	A	Chelsea	D	1-1
20 Apr	F	*	Chelsea	L	0-1
27 Apr	F	A	Fulham	L	0-3
4 May	F	‡	Fulham	L	2-3

* Home games played at Highbury
† Home games played at Homerton
‡ Played at Upton Park

Player	War Lg App	Goals	Player	War Lg App	Goals
Ayres	2		Jacques W.	29	
Baldwin	1		Laurence A.	5	1
Banks J.	33	21	Lightfoot E.	2	
Barnard	1	2	Lindsay A.	8	
Barton P.	4		Lindsay D.	5	2
Bassett E.	7	1	Lloyd H.	1	
Beaton	2		Middlemiss H.	6	2
Bird	1		Minter W.	3	4
Bliss H.	2		Nuttall J.	18	9
Brown R.	2		Peake	15	7
Clay T.	20		Potter H.	5	
Coomber G.	14	2	Ralston A.	36	
Crosswell T.	11		Rance C.	36	3
Crowl S.	1		Robinson	1	
Darnell J.	20		Saunders	1	1
Elliott J.	36	1	Spencer	1	1
Fleming J.	1		Thomas D.	7	1
Goldthorpe	7	5	Thwaites W.	2	
Halle W.	1		Tomkin	12	
Hawkins W.	36	10	Walden F.	33	7
Hill	2		Wren	1	
Hoffman	1		Own Goal		1
Jack	6	4			

London Combination 1917–18

	Team	P	W	D	L	F:A	Pts
1	Chelsea	36	21	8	7	82:39	50
2	West Ham	36	20	9	7	103:51	49
3	Fulham	36	20	7	9	75:60	47
4	TOTTENHAM	36	22	2	12	85:55	46
5	Arsenal	36	16	5	15	76:56	37
6	Brentford	36	16	3	17	81:95	35
7	C.Palace	36	13	4	19	54:83	30
8	QPR	36	14	2	20	48:73	30
9	Millwall	36	12	4	20	52:72	28
10	C. Orient	36	2	4	30	34:104	8

Date	Comp		Opponent	Res	Score
31 Aug	F	A	RAMC XI	D	1-1
7 Sep	Lge	A	Fulham	D	2-2
14 Sep	Lge	†	Brentford	D	1-1
21 Sep	Lge	A	West Ham	W	1-0
28 Sep	Lge	†	C. Orient	W	2-0
5 Oct	Lge	*	Chelsea	W	2-1
12 Oct	Lge	A	Arsenal	L	0-3
19 Oct	Lge	*	C. Palace	W	2-0
26 Oct	Lge	A	Millwall	W	2-0
2 Nov	Lge	†	Fulham	W	1-0
9 Nov	Lge	A	Brentford	L	1-7
16 Nov	Lge	†	West Ham	L	1-4
23 Nov	Lge	A	C. Orient	W	3-0
30 Nov	Lge	A	Chelsea	L	1-3
7 Dec	Lge	*	Arsenal	W	1-0
14 Dec	Lge	A	C. Palace	L	3-6
21 Dec	Lge	†	Millwall	L	0-3
25 Dec	Lge	A	QPR	D	1-1
26 Dec	Lge	†	QPR	D	0-0
28 Dec	Lge	A	Fulham	L	1-3
4 Jan	Lge	*	Brentford	D	1-1
11 Jan	Lge	A	West Ham	L	0-2
18 Jan	Lge	†	C. Orient	L	2-4
25 Jan	Lge	*	Chelsea	D	1-1
1 Feb	Lge	A	Arsenal	W	3-2
8 Feb	Lge	*	C. Palace	W	4-2
15 Feb	Lge	A	QPR	L	1-7
22 Feb	Lge	†	Fulham	L	0-2
1 Mar	Lge	A	Brentford	L	1-4
8 Mar	Lge	†	West Ham	L	0-1
15 Mar	Lge	A	C. Orient	W	2-1
22 Mar	Lge	A	Chelsea	W	2-1
29 Mar	Lge	*	Arsenal	L	0-1
5 Apr	Lge	A	C. Palace	D	2-2
12 Apr	Lge	*	QPR	L	2-3
18 Apr	Lge	*	Millwall	D	2-2
19 Apr	VC	‡	Fulham	L	0-2
21 Apr	Lge	A	Millwall	W	4-2
26 Apr	F	A	C. Orient	L	1-6

* Home games at Highbury
† Home games at Homerton
‡ Played at Stamford Bridge

Player	War Lg App	Goals	Player	War Lg App	Goals
Banks J.	27	5	Hoffman	1	
Barnard	7	2	Jack	13	3
Barton	14		Jacques W.	16	
Beaton S.	6		Jennings	1	
Bennett	4	1	Lindsay A.	16	
Blake H.	1		Lindsay C.	3	
Bliss H.	2	2	Lindsay D.	14	4
Bowlier	1		Lloyd	1	
Brown R.	1		McCalmont	1	1
Buley	1		McIver	3	
Cain	1	1	Middlemiss H.	4	3
Cantrell J.	2		Minter W.	9	9
Chester	2		Parsons	1	
Clay T.	24		Patterson	1	
Couchman	1		Peake	4	1
Darnell J.	21		Potter	2	
Dockray	11		Ralston A.	10	
Duncan	1		Rance C.	34	3
Eaden	1		Simmons	3	2
Elliott J.	18	1	Smith E.	4	
Fraser	1		Smith J.	5	1
Freeman	2		Thomas	8	4
Gee	2		Tomkins	21	
Goldthorpe	10	4	Walden F.	4	1
Grimsdell A.	9		Walters C.	1	
Hadyn-Price	9	3	Williams C.	3	1
Harbridge	2		Worral	11	
Hawkins	21				

London Combination 1918–19

1	Brentford	36	20	9	7	94:46	49
2	Arsenal	36	20	5	11	85:56	45
3	West Ham	36	17	7	12	65:51	41
4	Fulham	36	17	6	13	70:55	40
5	QPR	36	16	7	13	69:60	39
6	Chelsea	36	13	11	12	70:53	37
7	C. Palace	36	14	6	16	66:73	34
8	**TOTTENHAM**	36	13	8	15	52:72	34
9	Millwall	36	10	9	17	50:67	29
10	C. Orient	36	3	6	27	35:123	12

Date	Comp		Opponent	Res	Score
30 Aug	Lge	A	Coventry	W	5-0
1 Sep	Lge	H	Leicester	W	4-0
6 Sep	Lge	H	Coventry	W	4-1
11 Sep	Lge	A	Leicester	W	4-2
13 Sep	Lge	H	Sth Shields	W	2-0
20 Sep	Lge	A	Sth Shields	W	3-0
22 Sep	LnC	H	Millwall	W	6-0
27 Sep	Lge	H	Lincoln	W	6-1
29 Sep	F	A	Arsenal	W	1-0
4 Oct	Lge	A	Lincoln	D	1-1
6 Oct	LnC	A	C. Palace	L	2-3
11 Oct	Lge	H	C. Orient	W	2-1
18 Oct	Lge	A	C. Orient	W	4-0
27 Oct	Lge	A	Port Vale	W	1-0
1 Nov	Lge	H	Port Vale	W	1-0
8 Nov	Lge	A	Bury	L	1-2
15 Nov	Lge	H	Bury	W	2-1
22 Nov	Lge	A	Nottm Forest	D	1-1
29 Nov	Lge	H	Nottm Forest	W	5-2
6 Dec	Lge	A	Fulham	W	4-1
13 Dec	Lge	H	Fulham	W	4-0
15 Dec	F	H	Corinthians	W	4-1
20 Dec	Lge	A	Barnsley	L	0-3
25 Dec	Lge	H	Hull City	W	4-0
26 Dec	Lge	A	Hull City	W	3-1
27 Dec	Lge	H	Barnsley	W	4-0
3 Jan	Lge	A	Stockport	W	2-1
10 Jan	FC	A	Bristol Rvs	W	4-1
17 Jan	Lge	H	Stockport	W	2-0
24 Jan	Lge	A	Huddersfield	D	1-1
31 Jan	FC	H	West Stanley	W	4-0
7 Feb	Lge	A	Blackpool	W	1-0
14 Feb	Lge	H	Blackpool	D	2-2
16 Feb	Lge	H	Huddersfield	W	2-0
21 Feb	FC	H	West Ham	W	3-0
25 Feb	Lge	A	Bristol City	W	2-1
28 Feb	Lge	H	Bristol City	W	2-0
6 Mar	FC	H	Aston Villa	L	0-1
13 Mar	Lge	H	West Ham	L	1-2
20 Mar	Lge	H	Rotherham	W	2-0
22 Mar	Lge	H	West Ham	W	2-0
27 Mar	Lge	A	Rotherham	D	1-1
2 Apr	Lge	H	Wolves	W	4-2
3 Apr	Lge	H	Stoke	W	2-0
5 Apr	Lge	A	Wolves	W	3-1
10 Apr	Lge	A	Stoke	W	3-1
17 Apr	Lge	H	Grimsby	W	3-1
19 Apr	F	A	Mid Rhondda	D	0-0*
24 Apr	Lge	A	Grimsby	L	0-2
26 Apr	Lge	H	Birmingham	D	0-0
1 May	Lge	A	Birmingham	W	1-0
8 May	LCC	A	Norwich	W	4-0
15 May	CS	H	WBA	L	0-2

* Abandoned after 25 minutes

Player	Lg App	Goals	Player	Lg App	Goals
Archibald J.	13		Lorimer H.H.	4	
Banks J.A.	19	2	Lowe H.	1	
Bliss H.	42	31	McDonald R.J.	1	
Brown R.S.	20		Middlemiss H.	3	
Cantrell J.	30	19	Minter W.J.	19	7
Castle S.R.	2		Pearson J.	21	
Chipperfield J.	15	6	Rance C.S.	26	
Clay T.	27	2	Sage W.	1	
Dimmock J.H.	27	5	Seed J.M.	5	1
Elliott J.E.	1		Skinner J.F.	3	
Goodman A.A.	16	1	Smith B.	40	2
Grimsdell A.	37	14	Walden F.	32	4
Jacques W.	41		Walters C.	1	
Leese F.H.	1		Wilson C.	11	7
Lindsay A.F.	3		Own Goal		1

Final table for Second Division

1	**TOTTENHAM**	42	32	6	4	102:32	70
2	Huddersfield	42	28	8	6	97:38	64
3	Birmingham	42	24	8	10	85:34	56
4	Blackpool	42	21	10	11	65:47	52
5	Bury	42	20	8	14	60:44	48
6	Fulham	42	19	9	14	61:50	47
7	West Ham	42	19	9	14	47:40	47
8	Bristol C.	42	13	17	12	46:43	43
9	South Shields	42	15	12	15	58:48	42
10	Stoke	42	18	6	18	60:54	42
11	Hull	42	18	6	18	78:72	42
12	Barnsley	42	15	10	17	61:55	40
13	Port Vale	42	16	8	18	59:62	40
14	Leicester	42	15	10	17	41:61	40
15	Clapton Orient	42	16	6	20	51:59	38
16	Stockport	42	14	9	19	52:61	37
17	Rotherham Co.	42	13	8	21	51:83	34
18	Nottingham F.	42	11	9	22	43:73	31
19	Wolverhampton	42	10	10	22	55:80	30
20	Coventry	42	9	11	22	35:73	29
21	Lincoln	42	9	9	24	44:101	27
22	Grimsby	42	10	5	27	34:75	25

SEASON 1920/21

Date	Comp	H/A	Opponent	Res	Score
28 Aug	Lge	H	Blackburn	L	1-2
30 Aug	Lge	A	Derby	D	2-2
4 Sep	Lge	A	Blackburn	D	1-1
6 Sep	Lge	H	Derby	W	2-0
11 Sep	Lge	A	Aston Villa	L	2-4
18 Sep	Lge	H	Aston Villa	L	1-2
25 Sep	Lge	A	Man Utd	W	1-0
2 Oct	Lge	H	Man Utd	W	4-1
9 Oct	Lge	H	Chelsea	W	5-0
11 Oct	LCC	A	Barking	W	4-1
16 Oct	Lge	A	Chelsea	W	4-0
23 Oct	Lge	H	Burnley	L	1-2
25 Oct	LPCF	H	Arsenal	W	2-0
30 Oct	Lge	A	Burnley	L	0-2
1 Nov	LCC	H	Arsenal	W	3-1
6 Nov	Lge	H	Oldham	W	5-1
13 Nov	Lge	A	Oldham	W	5-2
18 Nov	F	A	Oxford Univ	L	0-1
20 Nov	Lge	H	Preston	L	1-2
27 Nov	Lge	A	Preston	L	1-4
4 Dec	Lge	H	Sheff Utd	W	4-1
11 Dec	Lge	A	Sheff Utd	D	1-1
18 Dec	Lge	H	Bolton	W	5-2
25 Dec	Lge	A	Newcastle	D	1-1
27 Dec	Lge	H	Newcastle	W	2-0
1 Jan	Lge	A	Bolton	L	0-1
8 Jan	FC	H	Bristol Rvs	W	6-2
15 Jan	Lge	H	Arsenal	W	2-1
22 Jan	Lge	A	Arsenal	L	2-3
29 Jan	FC	H	Bradford C	W	4-0
3 Feb	Lge	H	Bradford PA	W	2-0
5 Feb	Lge	A	Bradford PA	D	1-1
12 Feb	Lge	H	Man City	W	2-0
19 Feb	FC	A	Southend	W	4-1
23 Feb	Lge	A	West Brom	L	1-3
26 Feb	Lge	H	West Brom	W	1-0
5 Mar	FC	H	Aston Villa	W	1-0
9 Mar	Lge	A	Man City	L	0-2
12 Mar	Lge	H	Everton	W	2-0
19 Mar	FCsf	*	Preston	W	2-1
25 Mar	Lge	A	Liverpool	D	1-1
26 Mar	Lge	A	Sunderland	W	1-0
28 Mar	Lge	H	Liverpool	W	1-0
2 Apr	Lge	H	Sunderland	D	0-0
9 Apr	Lge	A	Bradford C	L	0-1
11 Apr	LCC	†	C. Orient	L	1-2
16 Apr	Lge	H	Bradford C	W	2-0
23 Apr	FCf	‡	Wolves	W	1-0
25 Apr	Lge	A	Huddersfield	L	0-2
27 Apr	Lge	A	Everton	D	0-0
30 Apr	Lge	H	Huddersfield	W	1-0
2 May	Lge	A	Middlesbrough	L	0-1
7 May	Lge	H	Middlesbrough	D	2-2
14 May	F	A	Fulham	W	4-0
16 May	CS	H	Burnley	W	2-0

* at Hillsborough
† at Highbury
‡ at Stamford Bridge

Player	Lg App	Goals	Player	Lg App	Goals
Archibald J.	6	1	Lindsay A.F.	5	
Banks J.A.	20	3	Lowe H.	5	
Bliss H.	36	17	McDonald R.J.	36	
Brown R.S.	2		Pearson J.	5	
Cantrell J.	23	7	Rance C.S.	14	
Castle S.R.	3		Seed J.M.	37	12
Clay T.	35	1	Skinner J.F.	2	
Dimmock J.H.	41	9	Smith B.	36	3
Forester M.	7		Thompson A.	3	
Grimsdell A.	38	3	Walden F.	22	5
Hunter A.C.	11		Walters C.	25	
Jacques W.	30		Wilson C.	20	9

Final table for First Division

1	Burnley	42	23	13	6	79:36	59
2	Manchester C.	42	24	6	12	70:50	54
3	Bolton	42	19	14	9	77:53	52
4	Liverpool	42	18	15	9	63:35	51
5	Newcastle	42	20	10	12	66:45	50
6	**TOTTENHAM**	**42**	**19**	**9**	**14**	**70:48**	**47**
7	Everton	42	17	13	12	66:55	47
8	Middlesbrough	42	17	12	13	53:53	46
9	The Arsenal	42	15	14	13	59:63	44
10	Aston Villa	42	18	7	17	63:70	43
11	Blackburn	42	13	15	14	57:59	41
12	Sunderland	42	14	13	15	57:60	41
13	Manchester U.	42	15	10	17	64:68	40
14	West Bromwich	42	13	14	15	54:58	40
15	Bradford C.	42	12	15	15	61:63	39
16	Preston	42	15	9	18	61:65	39
17	Huddersfield	42	15	9	18	42:49	39
18	Chelsea	42	13	13	16	48:58	39
19	Oldham	42	9	15	18	49:86	33
20	Sheffield U.	42	6	18	18	42:68	30
21	Derby	42	5	16	21	32:58	26
22	Bradford PA	42	8	8	26	43:76	24

SEASON 1921/22

Date	Comp	H/A	Opponent	Res	Score
27 Aug	Lge	A	Cardiff	W	1-0
29 Aug	Lge	H	Bolton	L	1-2
3 Sep	Lge	A	Cardiff	W	4-1
5 Sep	Lge	A	Bolton	L	0-1
10 Sep	Lge	A	Middlesbro	L	2-4
12 Sep	LPCF	A	West Ham	L	0-1
17 Sep	Lge	A	Middlesbro	D	0-0
19 Sep	F	A	Partick This.	L	1-3
22 Sep	F	A	Inverness Cale.	L	3-6
24 Sep	Lge	A	Aston Villa	W	3-1
1 Oct	Lge	A	Aston Villa	L	1-2
6 Oct	F	H	Corinthians	W	2-1
8 Oct	Lge	H	Man Utd	D	2-2
15 Oct	Lge	A	Man Utd	L	1-2
17 Oct	LCC	H	London Cal	W	5-0
22 Oct	Lge	A	Liverpool	L	0-1
29 Oct	Lge	A	Liverpool	D	1-1
31 Oct	LCC	H	Brentford	D	1-1
5 Nov	Lge	A	Newcastle	W	4-0
7 Nov	LCCr	A	Brentford	W	3-2
12 Nov	Lge	A	Newcastle	W	2-0
14 Nov	LCCsf	*	Arsenal	D	0-0
19 Nov	Lge	H	Burnley	D	1-1
21 Nov	LCCsfr	†	Arsenal	L	1-2
26 Nov	Lge	A	Burnley	L	0-1
1 Dec	F	A	Oxford Univ	W	1-0
3 Dec	Lge	H	Sheff Utd	W	2-1
10 Dec	Lge	A	Sheff Utd	L	0-1
17 Dec	Lge	H	Chelsea	D	0-0
24 Dec	Lge	A	Chelsea	W	2-1
26 Dec	Lge	H	Bradford C.	W	1-0
27 Dec	Lge	A	Bradford C.	W	4-0
31 Dec	Lge	H	Preston	W	5-0
7 Jan	FC	A	Brentford	W	2-0
14 Jan	Lge	A	Preston	W	2-1
21 Jan	Lge	A	WBA	L	0-3
28 Jan	FC	H	Watford	W	1-0
30 Jan	Lge	H	WBA	W	2-0
4 Feb	Lge	A	Man City	D	3-3
11 Feb	Lge	H	Man City	W	3-1
13 Feb	F	H	Oxford Univ	W	4-3
18 Feb	FC	H	Man City	W	2-1
25 Feb	Lge	H	Everton	W	2-0
4 Mar	FC	A	Cardiff	D	1-1
9 Mar	FCr	H	Cardiff	W	2-1
11 Mar	Lge	H	Sunderland	W	1-0
15 Mar	Lge	A	Everton	D	0-0
18 Mar	Lge	H	Huddersfield	W	1-0
25 Mar	FCsf	‡	Preston	L	1-2
27 Mar	Lge	A	Huddersfield	D	1-1
1 Apr	Lge	A	Birmingham	W	3-0
5 Apr	Lge	A	Sunderland	L	0-2
8 Apr	Lge	H	Birmingham	W	2-1
14 Apr	Lge	H	Oldham	W	3-1
15 Apr	Lge	H	Arsenal	W	2-0
17 Apr	Lge	H	Oldham	L	0-1
22 Apr	Lge	A	Arsenal	L	0-1
29 Apr	Lge	H	Blackburn	W	2-1
6 May	Lge	A	Blackburn	D	1-1

* at Stamford Bridge   † at Homerton   ‡ at Hillsborough

Player	Lg App	Goals	Player	Lg App	Goals
Archibald J.	5		Lorimer H.H.	1	
Banks J.A.	11	1	Lowe H.	12	
Blake H.E.	8		McDonald R.J.	40	
Bliss H.	23	7	Pearson J.	3	
Cantrell J.	13	3	Seed J.M.	36	10
Clay T.	37	8	Skinner J.F.	16	2
Dimmock J.H.	42	7	Smith B.	25	
Forster M.	4		Thompson A.	18	6
Grimsdell A.	35	3	Walden F.	28	2
Handley C.H.J.	1		Walters C.	33	
Hunter A.C.	12		Wilson C.	21	11
Jacques W.	22		Own Goals		2
Lindsay A.F.	16	3			

Final table for First Division

1	Liverpool	42	22	13	7	63:36	57
2	**TOTTENHAM**	**42**	**21**	**9**	**12**	**65:39**	**51**
3	Burnley	42	22	5	15	72:54	49
4	Cardiff	42	19	10	13	61:53	48
5	Aston Villa	42	22	3	17	74:55	47
6	Bolton	42	20	7	15	68:59	47
7	Newcastle	42	18	10	14	59:45	46
8	Middlesbrough	42	16	14	12	79:69	46
9	Chelsea	42	17	12	13	40:43	46
10	Manchester C.	42	18	9	15	65:70	45
11	Sheffield U.	42	15	10	17	59:54	40
12	Sunderland	42	16	8	18	60:62	40
13	West Bromwich	42	15	10	17	51:63	40
14	Huddersfield	42	15	9	18	53:54	39
15	Blackburn	42	13	12	17	54:57	38
16	Preston	42	13	12	17	42:65	38
17	The Arsenal	42	15	7	20	47:56	37
18	Birmingham	42	15	7	20	48:60	37
19	Oldham	42	13	11	18	38:50	37
20	Everton	42	12	12	18	57:55	36
21	Bradford C.	42	11	10	21	48:72	32
22	Manchester U.	42	8	12	22	41:73	28

SEASON 1922/23

Date	Comp		Opponent	Result	Score
26 Aug	Lge	H	Cardiff	D	1-1
2 Sep	Lge	A	Cardiff	W	3-2
4 Sep	Lge	H	Everton	W	2-0
9 Sep	Lge	H	Burnley	L	1-3
11 Sep	F	A	Corinthians	W	2-1
16 Sep	Lge	A	Burnley	W	1-0
23 Sep	Lge	H	Arsenal	L	1-2
30 Sep	Lge	A	Arsenal	W	2-0
2 Oct	LPCF	H	West Ham	W	2-1
7 Oct	Lge	A	Aston Villa	L	0-2
14 Oct	Lge	H	Aston Villa	L	1-2
16 Oct	F	A	Llanelli	L	1-2
21 Oct	Lge	H	WBA	W	3-1
23 Oct	LCC	A	Arsenal	L	2-3
28 Oct	Lge	A	WBA	L	1-5
4 Nov	Lge	H	Liverpool	L	2-4
11 Nov	Lge	A	Liverpool	D	0-0
16 Nov	F	H	Camb Univ	W	5-1
18 Nov	Lge	H	Newcastle	L	0-1
25 Nov	Lge	A	Newcastle	D	1-1
30 Nov	F	A	Oxford Univ	W	3-0
2 Dec	Lge	H	Nottm Forest	W	2-1
9 Dec	Lge	A	Nottm Forest	W	1-0
16 Dec	Lge	A	Chelsea	D	0-0
23 Dec	Lge	H	Chelsea	W	3-1
25 Dec	Lge	H	Sheff Utd	W	2-1
26 Dec	Lge	A	Sheff Utd	L	0-2
30 Dec	Lge	A	Middlesbrough	L	0-2
1 Jan	Lge	A	Everton	L	1-3
6 Jan	Lge	H	Middlesbrough	W	2-0
13 Jan	FC	A	Worksop Town	D	0-0*
15 Jan	FCr	H	Worksop Town	W	9-0
20 Jan	Lge	A	Oldham	W	3-0
27 Jan	Lge	H	Oldham	W	3-0
3 Feb	FC	H	Man Utd	W	4-0
10 Feb	Lge	A	Blackburn	L	0-1
14 Feb	Lge	H	Blackburn	W	2-0
17 Feb	Lge	H	Bolton	L	0-1
19 Feb	F	H	Oxford Univ	L	1-2
24 Feb	FC	H	Cardiff	W	3-2
3 Mar	Lge	H	Man City	W	3-1
10 Mar	FC	H	Derby	L	0-1
14 Mar	Lge	A	Man City	L	0-3
17 Mar	Lge	A	Stoke	D	0-0
24 Mar	Lge	H	Stoke	W	3-1
30 Mar	Lge	H	Preston	W	3-1
31 Mar	Lge	A	Sunderland	L	0-2
2 Apr	Lge	A	Preston	L	0-2
7 Apr	Lge	H	Sunderland	L	0-1
11 Apr	Lge	A	Bolton	W	2-0
14 Apr	Lge	H	Birmingham	L	1-2
21 Apr	Lge	H	Birmingham	W	2-0
28 Apr	Lge	A	Huddersfield	L	0-1
5 May	Lge	H	Huddersfield	D	0-0
7 May	F	H	West Ham	W	5-2

* Worksop agreed to play first match at White Hart Lane

Player	Lg App	Goals	Player	Lg App	Goals
Banks J.A.	2		Lindsay A.F.	34	11
Barnett F.W.	2		Lowe H.	14	
Blake H.E.	36		McDonald R.J.	17	
Bliss H.	8	3	Maddison G.	5	
Brooks S.	7	1	Pearson J.	1	
Brown R.S.	12		Ross J.	6	
Cantrell J.	10	4	Seed J.M.	36	9
Clay T.	34	3	Sharp B.	2	
Dimmock J.H.	42	6	Skinner J.F.	15	1
Forster M.	12		Smith B.	32	2
Grimsdell A.	40	21	Thompson A.	2	
Handley C.H.J.	30	5	Walden F.	30	3
Hartley F.	1		Walters C.	29	
Jacques W.	1		Wilson C.	2	

Final table for First Division

1	Liverpool	42	26	8	8	70:31	60
2	Sunderland	42	22	10	10	72:54	54
3	Huddersfield	42	21	11	10	60:32	53
4	Newcastle	42	18	12	12	45:37	48
5	Everton	42	20	7	15	63:59	47
6	Aston Villa	42	18	10	14	64:51	46
7	West Bromwich	42	17	11	14	58:49	45
8	Manchester C.	42	17	11	14	50:49	45
9	Cardiff	42	18	7	17	73:59	43
10	Sheffield U.	42	16	10	16	68:64	42
11	The Arsenal	42	16	10	16	61:62	42
12	**TOTTENHAM**	**42**	**17**	**7**	**18**	**50:50**	**41**
13	Bolton	42	14	12	16	50:58	40
14	Blackburn	42	14	12	16	47:62	40
15	Burnley	42	16	6	20	58:59	38
16	Preston	42	13	11	18	60:64	37
17	Birmingham	42	13	11	18	41:57	37
18	Middlesbrough	42	13	10	19	57:63	36
19	Chelsea	42	9	18	15	45:53	36
20	Nottingham F.	42	13	8	21	41:70	34
21	Stoke	42	10	10	22	47:67	30
22	Oldham	42	10	10	22	35:65	30

SEASON 1923/24

Date	Comp		Opponent	Result	Score
25 Aug	Lge	H	Preston	W	2-0
27 Aug	Lge	A	Chelsea	W	1-0
1 Sep	Lge	A	Preston	D	2-2
3 Sep	Lge	H	Chelsea	L	0-1
8 Sep	Lge	A	Middlesbrough	W	2-1
15 Sep	Lge	A	Middlesbrough	W	1-0
22 Sep	Lge	H	Bolton	D	0-0
29 Sep	Lge	A	Bolton	L	1-3
6 Oct	Lge	A	Notts Co	D	0-0
8 Oct	LPCF	H	Clapton O.	L	1-3
13 Oct	Lge	H	Notts Co	L	1-3
20 Oct	Lge	A	Sunderland	L	0-1
22 Oct	LCC	A	C. Palace	D	1-1
25 Oct	F	A	Norwich	W	3-2
27 Oct	Lge	H	Sunderland	D	1-1
29 Oct	LCC	H	C. Palace	W	2-1
3 Nov	Lge	A	Nottm Forest	D	0-0
5 Nov	LCC	A	Clapton O.	L	0-2
10 Nov	Lge	H	Nottm Forest	W	3-0
15 Nov	F	A	Camb Univ	W	6-5
17 Nov	Lge	A	Arsenal	D	1-1
24 Nov	Lge	H	Arsenal	W	3-0
1 Dec	Lge	H	WBA	D	0-0
4 Dec	F	A	Oxford Univ	W	5-0
8 Dec	Lge	A	WBA	L	1-4
15 Dec	Lge	H	Blackburn	W	2-1
22 Dec	Lge	A	Blackburn	W	1-0
25 Dec	Lge	H	Huddersfield	W	1-0
26 Dec	Lge	A	Huddersfield	L	1-2
29 Dec	Lge	H	Birmingham	D	1-1
1 Jan	Lge	A	Man City	L	0-1
5 Jan	Lge	A	Birmingham	L	2-3
12 Jan	FC	A	C. Palace	L	0-2
19 Jan	FC	H	Newcastle	W	2-0
26 Jan	Lge	A	Newcastle	D	2-2
2 Feb	F	A	Chelsea	D	0-0
9 Feb	F	A	West Ham	D	0-0
16 Feb	Lge	H	Cardiff	D	1-1
18 Feb	F	H	Oxford Univ	W	8-1
1 Mar	Lge	H	Sheff Utd	L	1-2
8 Mar	Lge	A	Sheff Utd	L	2-6
15 Mar	Lge	A	Aston Villa	D	0-0
22 Mar	Lge	H	Aston Villa	L	2-3
29 Mar	Lge	A	Liverpool	L	0-1
5 Apr	Lge	H	Liverpool	D	1-1
7 Apr	Lge	A	Cardiff	L	1-2
12 Apr	Lge	H	Everton	L	2-5
16 Apr	F	H	Inter Varsities	W	7-1
19 Apr	Lge	A	Everton	L	2-4
21 Apr	Lge	H	Man City	W	4-1
22 Apr	Lge	H	West Ham	L	0-1
26 Apr	Lge	A	Burnley	D	2-2
3 May	Lge	H	Burnley	W	1-0

Player	Lg App	Goals	Player	Lg App	Goals
Barnett F.W.	2		Maddison G.	35	
Blake H.E.	7		Osborne F.R.	12	1
Brooks S.	3		Poynton C.	10	1
Brown R.S.	3		Ross J.	1	
Clay T.	40	1	Sage W.	7	
Dimmock J.H.	25	2	Seed J.M.	21	2
Elkes J.E.	37	11	Skinner J.F.	2	
Forster M.	35		Smith B.	41	1
Grimsdell A.	27	1	Thompson A.	7	1
Handley C.H.J.	22	5	Walden F.	34	1
Hargreaves H.	7	3	Walters C.	15	
Lindsay A.F.	39	19	White S.E.	5	
Lowe H.	22		Own Goal		1
McDonald R.J.	3				

Final table for First Division

1	Huddersfield	42	23	11	8	60:33	57
2	Cardiff	42	22	13	7	61:34	57
3	Sunderland	42	22	9	11	71:54	53
4	Bolton	42	18	14	10	68:34	50
5	Sheffield U.	42	19	12	11	69:49	50
6	Aston Villa	42	18	13	11	52:37	49
7	Everton	42	18	13	11	62:53	49
8	Blackburn	42	17	11	14	54:50	45
9	Newcastle	42	17	10	15	60:54	44
10	Notts Co.	42	14	14	14	44:49	42
11	Manchester C.	42	15	12	15	54:71	42
12	Liverpool	42	15	11	16	49:48	41
13	West Ham	42	13	15	14	40:43	41
14	Birmingham	42	13	13	16	41:49	39
15	**TOTTENHAM**	**42**	**12**	**14**	**16**	**50:56**	**38**
16	West Bromwich	42	12	14	16	51:62	38
17	Burnley	42	12	12	18	55:60	36
18	Preston	42	12	10	20	52:67	34
19	The Arsenal	42	12	9	21	40:63	33
20	Nottingham F.	42	10	12	20	42:64	32
21	Chelsea	42	9	14	19	31:53	32
22	Middlesbrough	42	7	8	27	37:60	22

SEASON 1924/25

Date	Comp	Venue	Opponent	Result	Score
30 Aug	Lge	H	Bolton	W	3-0
3 Sep	Lge	A	Birmingham	W	2-0
6 Sep	Lge	A	Notts Co.	D	0-0
8 Sep	Lge	A	WBA	L	0-2
13 Sep	Lge	H	Everton	D	0-0
20 Sep	Lge	A	Sunderland	L	1-4
22 Sep	Lge	H	WBA	L	0-1
27 Sep	Lge	H	Cardiff	D	1-1
4 Oct	Lge	A	Preston	W	3-0
11 Oct	Lge	H	Burnley	D	1-1
18 Oct	Lge	A	Leeds Utd	L	0-1
25 Oct	Lge	A	Arsenal	L	0-1
27 Oct	LCC	H	Fulham	W	5-1
1 Nov	Lge	H	Aston Villa	L	1-3
3 Nov	LPCF	A	C. Orient	L	1-2†
6 Nov	F	A	Oxford Univ	W	2-1
8 Nov	Lge	A	Huddersfield	W	2-1
10 Nov	Lge	H	Man City	D	1-1
15 Nov	Lge	H	Blackburn	W	5-0
17 Nov	LCC	H	Kingstonians	W	5-0
22 Nov	Lge	A	West Ham	D	1-1
24 Nov	LCC	*	C. Orient	L	1-2
29 Nov	Lge	H	Sheff Utd	W	4-1
6 Dec	Lge	A	Newcastle	D	1-1
13 Dec	Lge	H	Liverpool	D	1-1
20 Dec	Lge	A	Nottm Forest	L	0-1
25 Dec	Lge	H	Bury	D	1-1
27 Dec	Lge	A	Bolton	L	0-3
1 Jan	Lge	A	Bury	L	2-5
3 Jan	Lge	H	Notts Co.	D	1-1
10 Jan	FC	H	Northampton	W	3-0
17 Jan	Lge	A	Everton	L	0-1
24 Jan	Lge	H	Sunderland	W	1-0
31 Jan	FC	H	Bolton	D	1-1
3 Feb	FCr	A	Bolton	W	1-0
7 Feb	Lge	H	Preston	W	2-0
14 Feb	Lge	A	Burnley	W	4-1
21 Feb	FC	H	Blackburn	D	2-2
26 Feb	FCr	A	Blackburn	L	1-3
28 Feb	Lge	H	Arsenal	W	2-0
7 Mar	Lge	A	Aston Villa	W	1-0
9 Mar	Lge	H	Leeds Utd	W	2-1
14 Mar	Lge	H	Huddersfield	L	1-2
18 Mar	Lge	A	Cardiff	W	2-0
21 Mar	Lge	A	Blackburn	D	1-1
28 Mar	Lge	H	West Ham	D	1-1
4 Apr	Lge	A	Sheff Utd	L	0-2
10 Apr	Lge	H	Birmingham	L	0-1
11 Apr	Lge	H	Newcastle	W	3-0
18 Apr	Lge	A	Liverpool	L	0-1
25 Apr	Lge	H	Nottm Forest	W	1-0
2 May	Lge	A	Man City	L	0-1
9 May	F	A	Basel Old Boys	W	3-0
10 May	F	A	Zurich	W	2-0
17 May	F	A	Winterthur	W	4-0
18 May	F	A	Lausanne	W	6-1
20 May	F	A	La Chaux de Fonds	W	8-1
21 May	F	A	Bern	W	5-0
24 May	F	A	Basel	W	1-0

† abandoned after 70 minutes

* at Highbury

Player	Lg App	Goals	Player	Lg App	Goals
Clay T.	21	2	Osborne F.R.	23	
Dimmock J.H.	29	5	Poynton C.	24	
Elkes J.E.	33	10	Sage W.	1	
Forster M.	21		Seed J.M.	41	17
Grimsdell A.	14		Sharp B.	1	
Handley C.H.J.	14	3	Skinner J.F.	34	
Hargreaves H.	20	3	Skitt H.	27	
Hinton F.	42		Smith B.	37	1
Lane W.H.C.	17	6	Thompson A.	20	3
Lindsay A.F.	18	2	Walters C.	22	
Lowe H.	6		White S.E.	5	
McDonald R.J.	12				

Final table for First Division

1	Huddersfield	42	21	16	5	69:28	58
2	West Bromwich	42	23	10	9	58:34	56
3	Bolton	42	22	11	9	76:34	55
4	Liverpool	42	20	10	12	63:55	50
5	Bury	42	17	15	10	54:51	49
6	Newcastle	42	16	16	10	61:42	48
7	Sunderland	42	19	10	13	64:51	48
8	Birmingham	42	17	12	13	49:53	46
9	Notts Co.	42	16	13	13	42:31	45
10	Manchester C.	42	17	9	16	76:68	43
11	Cardiff	42	16	11	15	56:51	43
12	TOTTENHAM	42	15	12	15	52:43	42
13	West Ham	42	15	12	15	62:60	42
14	Sheffield U.	42	13	13	16	55:63	39
15	Aston Villa	42	13	13	16	58:71	39
16	Blackburn	42	11	13	18	53:66	35
17	Everton	42	12	11	19	40:60	35
18	Leeds	42	11	12	19	46:59	34
19	Burnley	42	11	12	19	46:75	34
20	The Arsenal	42	14	5	23	46:58	33
21	Preston	42	10	6	26	37:74	26
22	Nottingham F.	42	6	12	24	29:65	24

SEASON 1925/26

Date	Comp	Venue	Opponent	Result	Score
29 Aug	Lge	A	Arsenal	W	1-0
31 Aug	Lge	A	Sheff Utd	W	3-2
3 Sep	F	H	Real Madrid	W	4-0
5 Sep	Lge	H	Man City	W	1-0
7 Sep	Lge	H	Sheff Utd	W	3-2
12 Sep	Lge	A	Everton	D	1-1
14 Sep	Lge	H	Cardiff	L	1-2
15 Sep	LCC	H	Brentford	L	1-2
19 Sep	Lge	H	Huddersfield	D	5-5
21 Sep	Lge	A	Cardiff	W	1-0
26 Sep	Lge	A	Sunderland	L	0-3
3 Oct	Lge	H	Blackburn	W	4-2
10 Oct	Lge	A	Bury	L	0-3
17 Oct	Lge	A	Man Utd	D	0-0
22 Oct	F	A	Norwich	L	2-3*
24 Oct	Lge	H	Liverpool	W	3-1
31 Oct	Lge	A	Leicester	L	3-5
7 Nov	Lge	H	West Ham	W	4-2
12 Nov	F	A	Camb Univ	L	1-2
14 Nov	Lge	A	Newcastle	L	1-3
16 Nov	LPCF	H	QPR	W	1-0
21 Nov	Lge	A	Bolton	L	2-3
26 Nov	F	A	Oxford Univ	W	4-1
28 Nov	Lge	A	Notts Co	L	2-4
5 Dec	Lge	H	Aston Villa	D	2-2
12 Dec	Lge	A	Burnley	W	2-1
19 Dec	Lge	H	Leeds	W	3-2
25 Dec	Lge	A	Birmingham	L	1-3
26 Dec	Lge	H	Birmingham	W	2-1
2 Jan	Lge	H	Arsenal	D	1-1
9 Jan	FC	H	West Ham	W	5-0
16 Jan	Lge	A	Man City	D	0-0
23 Jan	Lge	H	Everton	L	1-1
30 Jan	FC	H	Man Utd	D	2-2
3 Feb	FCr	A	Man Utd	L	0-2
6 Feb	Lge	H	Sunderland	L	0-2
13 Feb	Lge	A	Blackburn	L	2-4
20 Feb	Lge	H	Bury	W	4-2
27 Feb	Lge	H	Man Utd	L	0-1
3 Mar	Lge	A	Huddersfield	L	1-2
6 Mar	Lge	H	Liverpool	D	0-0
13 Mar	Lge	H	Leicester	L	1-3
20 Mar	Lge	A	West Ham	L	1-3
25 Mar	Lge	H	Newcastle	W	1-0
27 Mar	F	A	Hull	L	0-5
2 Apr	Lge	H	WBA	W	3-2
3 Apr	Lge	A	Bolton	D	1-1
5 Apr	Lge	A	WBA	L	0-1
10 Apr	Lge	H	Notts Co	W	4-0
17 Apr	Lge	A	Aston Villa	L	0-3
24 Apr	Lge	H	Burnley	L	0-2
1 May	Lge	A	Leeds	L	1-4
3 May	F	A	West Ham	D	1-1

* Played at Bury St Edmunds

Player	Lg App	Goals	Player	Lg App	Goals
Bann W.	8		Lowe H.	2	
Britton J.	9		Osborne F.R.	39	25
Clay T.	34	2	Roe T.W.	4	1
Dimmock J.H.	40	14	Sage W.	3	
Elkes J.E.	31	11	Seed J.M.	30	6
Forster M.	42		Skinner J.F.	17	
Grimsdell A.	13		Skitt H.	35	
Handley C.H.J.	2		Smith B.	38	
Hargreaves H.	8	1	Smith J.	7	
Hinton I.F.	15		Thompson A.	35	4
Kaine W.E.	11		Walters C.	1	
Lane W.H.C.	5		White S.E.	10	
Lindsay A.F.	23	2			

Final table for First Division

1	Huddersfield	42	23	11	8	92:60	57
2	The Arsenal	42	22	8	12	87:63	52
3	Sunderland	42	21	6	15	96:80	48
4	Bury	42	20	7	15	85:77	47
5	Sheffield U.	42	19	8	15	102:82	46
6	Aston Villa	42	16	12	14	86:76	44
7	Liverpool	42	14	16	12	70:63	44
8	Bolton	42	17	10	15	75:76	44
9	Manchester U.	42	19	6	17	66:73	44
10	Newcastle	42	16	10	16	84:75	42
11	Everton	42	12	18	12	72:70	42
12	Blackburn	42	15	11	16	91:80	41
13	West Bromwich	42	16	8	18	79:78	40
14	Birmingham	42	16	8	18	66:81	40
15	TOTTENHAM	42	15	9	18	66:79	39
16	Cardiff	42	16	7	19	61:76	39
17	Leicester	42	14	10	18	70:80	38
18	West Ham	42	15	7	20	63:76	37
19	Leeds	42	14	8	20	64:76	36
20	Burnley	42	13	10	19	85:108	36
21	Manchester C.	42	12	11	19	89:100	35
22	Notts Co.	42	13	7	22	54:74	33

SEASON 1926/27

Date	Comp		Opponent		Result
28 Aug	Lge	H	Everton	W	2-1
30 Aug	Lge	H	Sheff Wed	W	7-3
4 Sep	Lge	A	Blackburn	L	0-1
6 Sep	Lge	H	Leicester	D	2-2
11 Sep	Lge	H	Huddersfield	D	3-3
13 Sep	Lge	H	Leicester	D	2-2
18 Sep	Lge	A	Sunderland	L	2-3
20 Sep	F	H	Bohemians	W	1-0
25 Sep	Lge	H	WBA	W	3-0
27 Sep	LCC	A	Millwall	L	2-5
2 Oct	Lge	A	Bury	D	0-0
9 Oct	Lge	H	Birmingham	W	6-1
16 Oct	Lge	H	Sheff Utd	W	3-1
23 Oct	Lge	A	Derby	L	1-4
30 Oct	Lge	H	Bolton	W	1-0
4 Nov	F	H	Camb Univ	W	3-2
6 Nov	Lge	A	Aston Villa	W	3-2
8 Nov	LPCF	H	C. Orient	W	3-1
11 Nov	F	A	Oxford Univ	W	7-0
13 Nov	Lge	H	Cardiff	W	4-1
20 Nov	Lge	A	Burnley	L	0-5
27 Nov	Lge	H	Newcastle	L	1-3
29 Nov	F	A	Corinthians	W	2-0
4 Dec	Lge	A	Leeds	D	1-1
11 Dec	Lge	H	Liverpool	L	1-2
18 Dec	Lge	A	Arsenal	W	4-2
25 Dec	Lge	H	Man Utd	D	1-1
27 Dec	Lge	A	Man Utd	L	1-2
28 Dec	Lge	A	Sheff Wed	L	1-3
8 Jan	FC	A	West Ham	L	2-3
15 Jan	Lge	A	Everton	W	2-1
22 Jan	Lge	H	Blackburn	D	1-1
29 Jan	Lge	A	Huddersfield	L	0-2
5 Feb	Lge	H	Sunderland	L	0-2
12 Feb	Lge	A	WBA	L	0-5
19 Feb	Lge	H	Bury	W	1-0
26 Feb	Lge	A	Birmingham	L	0-1
5 Mar	Lge	A	Sheff Utd	D	3-3
12 Mar	Lge	H	Derby	W	3-2
19 Mar	Lge	A	Bolton	D	2-2
26 Mar	Lge	H	Aston Villa	L	0-1
2 Apr	Lge	A	Cardiff	W	2-1
9 Apr	Lge	H	Burnley	W	4-1
15 Apr	Lge	A	West Ham	L	1-3
16 Apr	Lge	A	Newcastle	L	2-3
18 Apr	Lge	H	West Ham	W	4-1
23 Apr	Lge	H	Leeds	W	4-1
30 Apr	Lge	A	Liverpool	L	0-1
7 May	Lge	H	Arsenal	L	0-4

Player	Lg App	Goals
Barnett F.W.	1	
Bellamy W.R.	1	
Blair J.G.	24	10
Britton J.	18	
Clay T.	16	
Dimmock J.H.	41	19
Elkes J.E.	40	2
Forster M.	35	
Grimsdell A.	2	
Handley C.H.J.	24	10
Lane W.H.C.	4	1
Lindsay A.F.	37	
Lowe H.	1	
Nicholls J.H.	1	
O'Callaghan E.	13	5
Osborne F.R.	34	9
Poynton C.	31	
Richardson J.	2	
Roe T.W.	3	3
Sanders A.W.	12	7
Seed J.M.	23	7
Skitt H.	22	
Smith B.	24	
Smith J.	23	
Thompson A.	30	3

Final table for First Division

1	Newcastle	42	25	6	11	96:58	56
2	Huddersfield	42	17	17	8	76:60	51
3	Sunderland	42	21	7	14	98:70	49
4	Bolton	42	19	10	13	84:62	48
5	Burnley	42	19	9	14	91:80	47
6	West Ham	42	19	8	15	86:70	46
7	Leicester	42	17	12	13	85:70	46
8	Sheffield U.	42	17	10	15	74:86	44
9	Liverpool	42	18	7	17	69:61	43
10	Aston Villa	42	18	7	17	81:83	43
11	The Arsenal	42	17	9	16	77:86	43
12	Derby	42	17	7	18	86:73	41
13	**TOTTENHAM**	**42**	**16**	**9**	**17**	**76:78**	**41**
14	Cardiff	42	16	9	17	55:65	41
15	Manchester U.	42	13	14	15	52:64	40
16	The Wednesday	42	15	9	18	75:92	39
17	Birmingham	42	17	4	21	64:73	38
18	Blackburn	42	15	8	19	77:96	38
19	Bury	42	12	12	18	68:77	36
20	Everton	42	12	10	20	64:90	34
21	Leeds	42	11	8	23	69:88	30
22	West Bromwich	42	11	8	23	65:86	30

SEASON 1927/28

Date	Comp		Opponent		Result
27 Aug	Lge	H	Birmingham	W	1-0
31 Aug	Lge	A	Middlesbrough	L	1-3
3 Sep	Lge	A	Newcastle	L	1-4
10 Sep	Lge	H	Huddersfield	D	2-2
12 Sep	Lge	H	Middlesbrough	W	4-2
17 Sep	Lge	A	Portsmouth	L	0-3
22 Sep	Lge	H	Leicester	W	2-1
24 Sep	Lge	A	Man Utd	L	0-3
1 Oct	Lge	H	Everton	L	1-3
8 Oct	Lge	A	Cardiff	L	1-2
13 Oct	F	A	Norwich	D	1-1
15 Oct	Lge	H	Blackburn	D	1-1
17 Oct	LCC	A	Fulham	L	2-5
22 Oct	Lge	H	Sunderland	W	3-1
26 Oct	F	A	Reading	W	5-2
29 Oct	Lge	A	Derby	D	1-1
3 Nov	F	A	Camb Univ	L	1-2
5 Nov	Lge	H	West Ham	W	5-3
7 Nov	LPCF	H	Clapton O.	W	4-3
10 Nov	F	A	Oxford Univ	W	5-2
12 Nov	Lge	A	Aston Villa	W	2-1
19 Nov	Lge	H	Sheff Utd	D	2-2
3 Dec	Lge	H	Burnley	W	5-0
5 Dec	F	H	West Ham	D	1-1
10 Dec	Lge	A	Bury	W	2-1
17 Dec	Lge	H	Liverpool	W	3-1
24 Dec	Lge	A	Leicester	L	1-6
26 Dec	Lge	A	Bolton	L	1-4
31 Dec	Lge	A	Birmingham	L	2-3
2 Jan	Lge	A	Arsenal	D	1-1
7 Jan	Lge	H	Newcastle	W	5-2
14 Jan	FC	A	Bristol C.	W	2-1
21 Jan	Lge	A	Huddersfield	L	2-4
28 Jan	FC	H	Oldham	W	3-0
4 Feb	Lge	H	Man Utd	W	4-1
6 Feb	Lge	H	Bolton	L	1-2
11 Feb	Lge	H	Everton	W	5-2
18 Feb	FC	A	Leicester	W	3-0
25 Feb	Lge	A	Blackburn	L	1-2
3 Mar	FC	A	Huddersfield	L	1-6
5 Mar	Lge	H	Cardiff	W	1-0
10 Mar	Lge	H	Derby	L	1-2
17 Mar	Lge	A	West Ham	D	1-1
19 Mar	Lge	H	Portsmouth	L	0-3
26 Mar	Lge	H	Aston Villa	W	2-1
28 Mar	Lge	A	Sunderland	D	0-0
31 Mar	Lge	A	Sheff Utd	L	1-3
6 Apr	Lge	A	Sheff Wed	L	1-3
7 Apr	Lge	H	Arsenal	W	2-0
10 Apr	Lge	A	Sheff Wed	L	2-4
14 Apr	Lge	A	Burnley	D	2-2
21 Apr	Lge	H	Bury	L	1-4
23 Apr	F	A	Norwich	L	0-3
25 Apr	F	A	Ebbw Vale	W	7-3
28 Apr	Lge	A	Liverpool	L	0-2
6 May	F	A	Olympic XI	W	5-2
9 May	F	A	Den Haag	W	6-2
13 May	F	A	All Holland XI	W	3-0
16 May	F	A	Rotterdam	W	3-0

Player	Lg App	Goals
Armstrong J.W.	11	4
Austin P.	1	
Barnett F.W.	5	
Bellamy W.R.	4	
Blair J.G.	5	4
Britton J.	13	
Clay T.	16	
Dimmock J.H.	38	12
Elkes J.E.	22	5
Evans A.A.	3	
Forster M.	32	
Grimsdell A.	35	2
Handley C.H.J.	27	4
Hartley F.	2	
Helliwell S.	2	
Lowdell A.	34	
Lindsay A.F.	18	3
Nicholls J.H.	3	
O'Callaghan E.	42	19
Osborne F.R.	31	18
Poynton C.	14	
Richardson J.	24	
Sanders A.W.	1	
Skitt H.	38	
Smith B.	8	
Spiers C.H.	26	
Thompson A.	4	
Townley J.C.	3	2
Own Goal		1

Final table for First Division

1	Everton	42	20	13	9	102:66	53
2	Huddersfield	42	22	7	13	91:68	51
3	Leicester	42	18	12	12	96:72	48
4	Derby	42	17	10	15	96:83	44
5	Bury	42	20	4	18	80:80	44
6	Cardiff	42	17	10	15	70:80	44
7	Bolton	42	16	11	15	81:66	43
8	Aston Villa	42	17	9	16	78:73	43
9	Newcastle	42	15	13	14	79:81	43
10	Arsenal	42	13	15	14	82:86	41
11	Birmingham	42	13	15	14	70:75	41
12	Blackburn	42	16	9	17	66:78	41
13	Sheffield U.	42	15	10	17	79:86	40
14	The Wednesday	42	13	13	16	81:78	39
15	Sunderland	42	15	9	18	74:76	39
16	Liverpool	42	13	13	16	84:87	39
17	West Ham	42	14	11	17	81:88	39
18	Manchester U.	42	16	7	19	72:80	39
19	Burnley	42	16	7	19	82:98	39
20	Portsmouth	42	16	7	19	66:90	39
21	**TOTTENHAM**	**42**	**15**	**8**	**19**	**74:86**	**38**
22	Middlesbrough	42	11	15	16	81:88	37

SEASON 1928/29

Date	Comp	H/A	Opponent	Result	Score		Date	Comp	H/A	Opponent	Result	Score
25 Aug	Lge	H	Oldham	W	4-1		29 Dec	Lge	A	Oldham	L	1-3
27 Aug	Lge	H	Middlesbrough	L	2-5		1 Jan	Lge	A	Middlesbrough	L	0-3
1 Sept	Lge	A	Southampton	D	1-1		5 Jan	Lge	H	Southampton	W	3-2
8 Sep	Lge	H	Wolves	W	3-2		12 Jan	FC	A	Reading	L	0-2
15 Sep	Lge	A	Notts Co	L	0-2		19 Jan	Lge	A	Wolves	L	2-4
22 Sep	Lge	H	Millwall	W	2-1		26 Jan	Lge	H	Notts Co	W	3-0
29 Sep	Lge	A	Port Vale	L	1-2		2 Feb	Lge	A	Millwall	L	1-5
4 Oct	F	A	Norwich	W	4-2		9 Feb	Lge	H	Port Vale	W	4-2
6 Oct	Lge	H	Hull	W	4-1		23 Feb	Lge	H	Bradford	W	3-2
13 Oct	Lge	A	Bradford	L	1-4		2 Mar	Lge	A	Grimsby	L	0-2
15 Oct	LCC	H	London Cal	W	2-1		9 Mar	Lge	H	Stoke	W	1-0
20 Oct	Lge	H	Grimsby	W	2-1		16 Mar	Lge	A	C. Orient	W	3-2
27 Oct	Lge	A	Stoke	L	0-2		23 Mar	Lge	H	Swansea	D	1-1
29 Oct	LCC	A	QPR	D	1-1		29 Mar	Lge	A	Preston	D	2-2
3 Nov	Lge	H	Clapton O.	W	2-1		30 Mar	Lge	A	Nottm Forest	D	2-2
5 Nov	LCC	H	QPR	W	3-1		1 Apr	Lge	H	Preston	W	2-0
10 Nov	Lge	A	Swansea	L	0-4		6 Apr	Lge	H	Bristol City	D	1-1
15 Nov	F	H	Camb Univ	W	12-3		13 Apr	Lge	A	Barnsley	L	1-4
17 Nov	Lge	H	Nottm Forest	W	2-1		15 Apr	Lge	A	Hull City	D	1-1
21 Nov	F	A	Oxford Univ	W	4-2		20 Apr	Lge	H	Chelsea	W	4-1
24 Nov	Lge	A	Bristol City	L	1-2		27 Apr	Lge	A	Blackpool	D	2-2
26 Nov	LCCsf	*	Charlton	W	5-3		4 May	Lge	H	WBA	W	2-0
1 Dec	Lge	H	Barnsley	W	2-0		6 May	LCCf	†	Millwall	W	5-1
3 Dec	LPCF	A	Clapton O.	W	4-2		11 May	F	A	Sliema	W	7-1
8 Dec	Lge	A	Chelsea	D	1-1		12 May	F	A	Valletta	W	2-1
15 Dec	Lge	H	Blackpool	L	1-2		16 May	F	A	British Army	W	5-0
22 Dec	Lge	A	West Brom	L	2-3		18 May	F	A	British Navy	W	1-0
25 Dec	Lge	H	Reading	D	2-2		19 May	F	A	Floriana	W	2-1
26 Dec	Lge	A	Reading	L	3-4		21 May	F	A	Pick/Malta XI	W	5-1

* at Upton Park   † at Highbury

Player	Lg App	Goals	Player	Lg App	Goals
Armstrong J.W.	12	3	Herod E.R.B.	13	
Bann W.E.	4		Knight J.G.	1	
Barnett F.W.	6	1	Lindsay A.F.	6	
Bellamy W.R.	9		Lowdell A.	39	
Cable T.H.	2		Nicholls J.	11	
Clay T.	5		O'Callaghan E.	36	10
Crompton A.	8	1	Osborne F.R.	33	16
Dimmock J.H.	30	11	Poynton C.	23	1
Elkes J.E.	27	10	Richardson J.	12	
Evans A.A.	2		Roberts W.T.	4	2
Forster M.	33		Scott J.	12	4
Galloway R.	3	2	Skitt H.	29	
Grimsdell A.	11		Smith B.	10	
Handley C.H.J.	1		Smy J.	4	
Harper E.C.	11	11	Spiers C.H.	31	
Hartley F.	3	1	Thompson A.	13	1
Helliwell S.	6		Wilding H.T.	12	1

Final table for Second Division

1	Middlesbrough	42	22	11	9	92:57	55
2	Grimsby	42	24	5	13	82:61	53
3	Bradford PA	42	22	4	16	88:70	48
4	Southampton	42	17	14	11	74:60	48
5	Notts Co.	42	19	9	14	78:65	47
6	Stoke	42	17	12	13	74:51	46
7	West Bromwich	42	19	8	15	80:79	46
8	Blackpool	42	19	7	16	92:76	45
9	Chelsea	42	17	10	15	64:65	44
10	**TOTTENHAM**	**42**	**17**	**9**	**16**	**75:81**	**43**
11	Nottingham F.	42	15	12	15	71:70	42
12	Hull	42	13	14	15	58:63	40
13	Preston	42	15	9	18	78:79	39
14	Millwall	42	16	7	19	71:86	39
15	Reading	42	15	9	18	63:86	39
16	Barnsley	42	16	6	20	69:66	38
17	Wolverhampton	42	15	7	20	77:81	37
18	Oldham	42	16	5	21	54:75	37
19	Swansea	42	13	10	19	62:75	36
20	Bristol C.	42	13	10	19	58:72	36
21	Port Vale	42	15	4	23	71:86	34
22	Clapton O.	42	12	8	22	45:72	32

SEASON 1929/30

Date	Comp	H/A	Opponent	Result	Score		Date	Comp	H/A	Opponent	Result	Score
31 Aug	Lge	A	Bradford PA	L	1-2		26 Dec	Lge	A	Southampton	L	0-1
2 Sep	Lge	A	Millwall	W	5-2		28 Dec	Lge	H	Bradford PA	D	1-1
7 Sep	Lge	H	Barnsley	W	2-1		4 Jan	Lge	A	Barnsley	L	0-2
14 Sep	Lge	A	Blackpool	L	2-3		11 Jan	FC	H	Man City	D	2-2
21 Sep	Lge	H	Bury	D	2-2		14 Jan	FCr	A	Man City	L	1-4
23 Sep	Lge	H	Millwall	D	1-1		18 Jan	Lge	H	Blackpool	W	6-1
28 Sep	Lge	A	Chelsea	L	0-3		25 Jan	Lge	A	Bury	L	1-2
5 Oct	Lge	H	Nottm Forest	D	1-1		1 Feb	Lge	H	Chelsea	D	3-3
9 Oct	Lge	H	Stoke	W	3-1		8 Feb	Lge	A	Nottm Forest	D	0-0
10 Oct	F	A	Norwich	L	0-1		15 Feb	Lge	H	Oldham	W	2-1
12 Oct	Lge	A	Oldham	L	0-2		22 Feb	Lge	H	Wolves	W	4-2
13 Oct	LCC	A	C. Orient	L	1-2		1 Mar	Lge	A	Bradford C	W	2-0
19 Oct	Lge	A	Wolves	L	0-3		8 Mar	Lge	H	Swansea	W	3-0
26 Oct	Lge	H	Bradford C	D	1-1		15 Mar	Lge	A	Cardiff	L	0-1
2 Nov	Lge	A	Swansea	W	1-0		22 Mar	Lge	H	Preston	W	1-0
4 Nov	LPCF	H	Crystal P.	W	5-0		29 Mar	Lge	A	Bristol C	L	0-1
9 Nov	Lge	H	Cardiff	L	1-2		5 Apr	Lge	H	Notts Co	W	2-0
16 Nov	Lge	A	Preston	L	0-4		12 Apr	Lge	A	Reading	L	0-3
23 Nov	Lge	A	Bristol C.	W	2-1		18 Apr	Lge	H	WBA	L	0-2
30 Nov	Lge	A	Notts Co.	W	1-0		19 Apr	Lge	H	Charlton	W	3-0
7 Dec	Lge	H	Reading	D	0-0		21 Apr	Lge	A	WBA	L	3-4
14 Dec	Lge	A	Charlton	L	0-1		26 Apr	Lge	A	Hull City	L	0-2
21 Dec	Lge	H	Hull City	D	2-2		3 May	Lge	A	Stoke City	L	0-1
25 Dec	Lge	H	Southampton	W	3-2							

Player	Lg App	Goals	Player	Lg App	Goals
Armstrong J.W.	5		Lowdell A.	13	
Bellamy W.R.	12	2	Meads T.	33	2
Cable T.H.	34		O'Callaghan E.	10	4
Cook G.W.	32	9	Osborne F.R.	32	9
Crompton A.	7	1	Poynton C.	16	1
Davies W.	14	2	Reddish J.	3	
Dimmock J.H.	32	6	Rowley R.W.M.	9	4
Evans T.	3		Scott J.	5	
Harper E.C.	19	14	Skitt H.	37	
Hartley F.	1		Smy J.	7	2
Forster M.	15		Spiers C.H.	42	
Herod E.R.B.	41		Thompson A.	21	2
Illingworth J.	9		Own Goal		1
Lindsay A.F.	10				

Final table for Second Division

1	Blackpool	42	27	4	11	98:67	58
2	Chelsea	42	22	11	9	74:46	55
3	Oldham	42	21	11	10	90:51	53
4	Bradford PA	42	19	12	11	91:70	50
5	Bury	42	22	5	15	78:67	49
6	West Bromwich	42	21	5	16	105:73	47
7	Southampton	42	17	11	14	77:76	45
8	Cardiff	42	18	8	16	61:59	44
9	Wolverhampton	42	16	9	17	77:79	41
10	Nottingham F.	42	13	15	14	55:69	41
11	Stoke	42	16	8	18	74:72	40
12	**TOTTENHAM**	**42**	**15**	**9**	**18**	**59:61**	**39**
13	Charlton	42	14	11	17	59:63	39
14	Millwall	42	12	15	15	57:73	39
15	Swansea	42	14	9	19	57:61	37
16	Preston	42	13	11	18	65:80	37
17	Barnsley	42	14	8	20	56:71	36
18	Bradford C.	42	12	12	18	60:77	36
19	Reading	42	12	11	19	54:67	35
20	Bristol C.	42	13	9	20	61:83	35
21	Hull	42	14	7	21	51:78	35
22	Notts Co.	42	9	15	18	54:70	33

239

SEASON 1930/31

Date	Comp		Opponent	Res	Score
30 Aug	Lge	H	Reading	W	7-1
1 Sep	Lge	H	Burnley	W	8-1
6 Sep	Lge	A	Wolves	L	1-3
8 Sep	Lge	A	Preston	L	1-2
13 Sep	Lge	H	Bradford PA	W	3-2
15 Sep	Lge	H	Preston	D	0-0
20 Sep	Lge	A	Stoke	L	1-2
27 Sep	Lge	H	Millwall	W	4-1
4 Oct	Lge	A	Oldham	W	2-1
11 Oct	Lge	H	Nottm Forest	W	2-1
13 Oct	LCC	H	Charlton	W	6-0
18 Oct	Lge	H	Bury	W	3-1
25 Oct	Lge	A	Everton	L	2-4
27 Oct	LCC	A	Chelsea	W	2-1
30 Oct	F	A	Oxford Univ	W	3-0
1 Nov	Lge	H	Charlton	W	5-0
3 Nov	LPCF	A	C. Palace	D	2-2
8 Nov	Lge	A	Bradford C	L	0-2
13 Nov	F	H	Camb Univ	W	8-0
15 Nov	Lge	H	Swansea	D	1-1
17 Nov	LCCsf	* Ilford	W	8-1
22 Nov	Lge	A	WBA	W	2-0
29 Nov	Lge	H	Port Vale	W	5-0
6 Dec	Lge	A	Plymouth	L	0-2
8 Dec	F	A	West Ham	W	2-1
13 Dec	Lge	H	Bristol C	W	4-1
20 Dec	Lge	A	Barnsley	W	1-0
25 Dec	Lge	H	Southampton	L	1-3
26 Dec	Lge	A	Southampton	W	3-0
27 Dec	Lge	H	Reading	W	2-1
3 Jan	Lge	H	Wolves	W	1-0
10 Jan	FC	H	Preston	W	3-1
17 Jan	Lge	A	Bradford PA	L	1-4
24 Jan	FC	A	WBA	L	0-1
26 Jan	Lge	H	Stoke City	W	3-0
31 Jan	Lge	A	Millwall	W	3-2
7 Feb	Lge	H	Oldham	W	4-0
14 Feb	Lge	A	Nottm Forest	D	2-2
21 Feb	Lge	A	Bury	L	0-2
28 Feb	F	H	Huddersfield	L	2-4
7 Mar	Lge	A	Charlton	L	0-1
14 Mar	Lge	H	Bradford C	W	3-1
16 Mar	Lge	H	Everton	W	1-0
21 Mar	Lge	A	Swansea	W	2-1
28 Mar	Lge	H	WBA	D	2-2
3 Apr	Lge	H	Cardiff	D	2-2
4 Apr	Lge	A	Port Vale	L	0-3
6 Apr	Lge	A	Cardiff	D	0-0
11 Apr	Lge	H	Plymouth	D	1-1
18 Apr	Lge	A	Bristol C	L	1-2
25 Apr	Lge	H	Barnsley	W	4-2
2 May	Lge	A	Burnley	L	0-1
4 May	LCCf	† Arsenal	L	1-2

* at Upton Park   † at Stamford Bridge

Player	Lg App	Goals	Player	Lg App	Goals
Ashford W.J.	14		Meads T.	41	
Bellamy W.R.	17	4	Messer A.T.	39	2
Cable T.H.	4		O'Callaghan E.	37	10
Cook G.W.	31	12	Osborne F.R.	6	
Davies W.	42	4	Poynton C.	5	
Dimmock J.H.	13	4	Rowley R.W.M.	8	3
Harper E.C.	30	36	Scott J.	1	
Herod E.R.B.	3		Skitt H.	24	
Hodgkinson H.	39		Smailes J.	11	3
Howe L.	3		Smy J.	6	4
Hunt G.S.	9	4	Spiers C.H.	42	
Lyons A.	37	2			

Final table for Second Division

1	Everton	42	28	5	9	121:66	61
2	West Bromwich	42	22	10	10	83:49	54
3	**TOTTENHAM**	**42**	**22**	**7**	**13**	**88:55**	**51**
4	Wolverhampton	42	21	5	16	84:67	47
5	Port Vale	42	21	5	16	67:61	47
6	Bradford PA	42	18	10	14	97:66	46
7	Preston	42	17	11	14	83:64	45
8	Burnley	42	17	11	14	81:77	45
9	Southampton	42	19	6	17	74:62	44
10	Bradford C.	42	17	10	15	61:63	44
11	Stoke	42	17	10	15	64:71	44
12	Oldham	42	16	10	16	61:72	42
13	Bury	42	19	3	20	75:82	41
14	Millwall	42	16	7	19	71:80	39
15	Charlton	42	15	9	18	59:86	39
16	Bristol C.	42	15	8	19	54:82	38
17	Nottingham F.	42	14	9	19	80:85	37
18	Plymouth	42	14	8	20	76:84	36
19	Barnsley	42	13	9	20	59:79	35
20	Swansea	42	12	10	20	51:74	34
21	Reading	42	12	6	24	72:96	30
22	Cardiff	42	8	9	25	47:87	25

SEASON 1931/32

Date	Comp		Opponent	Res	Score
29 Aug	Lge	A	Wolves	L	0-4
31 Aug	Lge	H	Preston	W	4-0
5 Sep	Lge	H	Bradford PA	D	3-3
7 Sep	Lge	A	Southampton	L	1-2
12 Sep	Lge	A	Man Utd	D	1-1
14 Sep	Lge	H	Southampton	W	5-2
19 Sep	Lge	H	Barnsley	W	4-2
26 Sep	Lge	H	Nottm Forest	L	1-3
3 Oct	Lge	A	Chesterfield	L	2-4
10 Oct	Lge	H	Burnley	D	1-1
11 Oct	LCC	H	Brentford	W	4-1
17 Oct	Lge	A	Notts Co	L	1-3
24 Oct	Lge	H	Plymouth	L	0-1
28 Oct	LCC	A	Kingstonian	W	3-1
31 Oct	Lge	A	Bristol C	D	1-1
5 Nov	F	A	Camb Univ	W	9-3
7 Nov	Lge	H	Swansea	W	6-2
14 Nov	Lge	A	Bury	D	1-1
16 Nov	LCCsf	‡ C. Palace	L	0-2
19 Nov	F	H	Oxford Univ	D	5-5
21 Nov	Lge	H	Port Vale	W	9-3
28 Nov	Lge	A	Millwall	W	2-1
5 Dec	Lge	H	Bradford C	L	1-5
12 Dec	Lge	A	Leeds	L	0-1
19 Dec	Lge	H	Oldham	W	3-2
25 Dec	Lge	H	Charlton	L	0-1
26 Dec	Lge	A	Charlton	W	5-2
2 Jan	Lge	H	Wolves	D	3-3
9 Jan	FC	H	Sheff Wed	D	2-2
13 Jan	FCr	A	Sheff Wed	L	1-3
16 Jan	Lge	A	Bradford PA	L	1-2
23 Jan	Lge	H	Man Utd	W	4-1
30 Jan	Lge	A	Barnsley	L	2-3
6 Feb	Lge	H	Nottm Forest	W	3-1
13 Feb	Lge	A	Chesterfield	D	3-3
20 Feb	Lge	A	Burnley	L	0-2
27 Feb	Lge	H	Notts Co	W	2-0
5 Mar	Lge	A	Plymouth	L	1-4
12 Mar	Lge	H	Bristol C	W	2-1
19 Mar	Lge	A	Swansea	D	1-1
25 Mar	Lge	H	Stoke	D	3-3
26 Mar	Lge	H	Bury	D	0-0
28 Mar	Lge	A	Stoke	D	2-2
2 Apr	Lge	A	Port Vale	W	3-1
9 Apr	Lge	H	Millwall	W	1-0
16 Apr	Lge	A	Bradford C	L	0-2
23 Apr	Lge	H	Leeds	W	3-1
30 Apr	Lge	A	Oldham	W	2-1
7 May	Lge	A	Preston	L	0-2
12 May	F	A	Guernsey XI	W	2-1
16 May	F	A	Jersey XI	W	9-0

‡ Played at Upton Park. After this date, Tottenham no longer put out their first team in London Challenge Cup matches

Player	Lg App	Goals	Player	Lg App	Goals
Alsford W.J.	10		Marshall W.H.	1	
Bellamy W.R.	12	3	Meads T.	27	3
Brain J.	32	8	Messer A.T.	11	
Cable T.H.	2		Moran J.	12	
Colquhoun D.M.	36	1	Nicholls J.H.	2	
Davies W.	38	12	O'Callaghan E.	34	16
Evans T.	12	3	Poynton C.	25	
Evans W.	28	5	Reddish J.	3	
Felton W.	10		Rowe A.S.	29	
Greenfield G.	12	5	Rowley R.W.M.	7	3
Harper E.C.	3	1	Smailes J.	5	
Hodgkinson H.	17		Spiers C.H.	17	
Hunt G.S.	37	25	Taylor A.	23	
Lyons A.	17	1	Own Goal		1

Final table for Second Division

1	Wolverhampton	42	24	8	10	115:49	56
2	Leeds	42	22	10	10	78:54	54
3	Stoke	42	19	14	9	69:48	52
4	Plymouth	42	20	9	13	100:66	49
5	Bury	42	21	7	14	70:58	49
6	Bradford PA	42	21	7	14	72:63	49
7	Bradford C.	42	16	13	13	80:61	45
8	**TOTTENHAM**	**42**	**16**	**11**	**15**	**87:78**	**43**
9	Millwall	42	17	9	16	61:61	43
10	Charlton	42	17	9	16	61:66	43
11	Nottingham F.	42	16	10	16	77:72	42
12	Manchester U.	42	17	8	17	71:72	42
13	Preston	42	16	10	16	75:77	42
14	Southampton	42	17	7	18	66:77	41
15	Swansea	42	16	7	19	73:75	39
16	Notts Co.	42	13	12	17	75:75	38
17	Chesterfield	42	13	11	18	64:86	37
18	Oldham	42	13	10	19	62:84	36
19	Burnley	42	13	9	20	59:87	35
20	Port Vale	42	13	7	22	58:89	33
21	Barnsley	42	12	9	21	55:91	33
22	Bristol C.	42	6	11	25	39:78	23

Date	Comp	H/A	Opponent	Result	Score
27 Aug	Lge	H	Charlton	W	4-1
29 Aug	Lge	A	Nottm Forest	L	1-3
3 Sep	Lge	A	Stoke	L	0-2
5 Sep	Lge	H	Nottm Forest	W	0-0
10 Sep	Lge	H	Man Utd	W	6-1
17 Sep	Lge	A	Bury	L	0-1
24 Sep	Lge	A	Grimsby	L	2-3
1 Oct	Lge	H	Oldham	D	1-1
8 Oct	Lge	A	Preston	W	6-2
15 Oct	Lge	H	Burnley	W	4-1
22 Oct	Lge	H	Southampton	W	5-0
27 Oct	F	A	Oxford Univ	W	6-0
29 Oct	Lge	A	Millwall	W	4-1
3 Nov	F	A	Camb Univ	D	3-3
5 Nov	Lge	H	Port Vale	W	4-0
12 Nov	Lge	A	Lincoln	D	2-2
19 Nov	Lge	H	Chesterfield	W	4-1
26 Nov	Lge	A	Bradford C.	W	1-0
3 Dec	Lge	H	Swansea	W	7-0
10 Dec	Lge	A	Fulham	D	2-2
17 Dec	Lge	H	West Ham	D	2-2
24 Dec	Lge	A	Notts Co.	L	0-3
26 Dec	Lge	A	Bradford PA	D	3-3
27 Dec	Lge	H	Bradford PA	W	2-0
31 Dec	Lge	A	Charlton	W	3-0
7 Jan	Lge	H	Stoke City	W	3-2
14 Jan	FC	A	Oldham	W	6-0
21 Jan	Lge	A	Man Utd	L	1-2
28 Jan	FC	A	Luton	L	0-2
1 Feb	Lge	H	Bury	W	2-1
4 Feb	Lge	H	Grimsby	W	4-3
11 Feb	Lge	A	Oldham	W	5-1
18 Feb	Lge	H	Preston	D	1-1
4 Mar	Lge	A	Southampton	D	1-1
11 Mar	Lge	H	Millwall	W	2-1
18 Mar	Lge	A	Port Vale	D	1-1
25 Mar	Lge	H	Lincoln	W	3-2
1 Apr	Lge	A	Chesterfield	D	1-1
8 Apr	Lge	H	Bradford C	D	1-1
14 Apr	Lge	A	Plymouth	D	0-0
15 Apr	Lge	A	Swansea	W	2-0
17 Apr	Lge	A	Plymouth	D	2-2
22 Apr	Lge	H	Fulham	D	0-0
24 Apr	Lge	A	Burnley	D	1-1
29 Apr	Lge	A	West Ham	L	0-1
6 May	Lge	H	Notts Co	W	3-1
11 May	F	A	Chanl Isle XI	W	6-0
13 May	F	A	Guernsey XI	W	8-0
18 May	F	A	Jersey XI	W	5-1

Player	Lg App	Goals	Player	Lg App	Goals
Allen A.	1	1	Hunt G.S.	41	32
Alsford W.J.	2		Levene D.	5	
Bellamy W.R.	3		McCormick J.	9	
Brain J.	12	2	Meads T.	35	
Colquhoun D.	29	1	Morrison J.A.	1	1
Davies W.	15	1	Nicholls J.H.	37	
Evans T.	16	1	O'Callaghan E.	32	15
Evans W.	42	28	Poynton C.	4	
Felton W.	41		Rowe A.S.	41	
Greenfield G.	13	6	Taylor A.	5	
Hall G.W.	21	1	Whatley W.J.	39	
Lowe L.	18	7			

Final table for Second Division

1	Stoke	42	25	6	11	78:39	56
2	**TOTTENHAM**	**42**	**20**	**15**	**7**	**96:51**	**55**
3	Fulham	42	20	10	12	78:65	50
4	Bury	42	20	9	13	84:59	49
5	Nottingham F.	42	17	15	10	67:59	49
6	Manchester U.	42	15	13	14	71:68	43
7	Millwall	42	16	11	15	59:57	43
8	Bradford PA	42	17	8	17	77:71	42
9	Preston	42	16	10	16	74:70	42
10	Swansea	42	19	4	19	50:54	42
11	Bradford C.	42	14	13	15	65:61	41
12	Southampton	42	18	5	19	66:66	41
13	Grimsby	42	14	13	15	79:84	41
14	Plymouth	42	16	9	17	63:67	41
15	Notts Co.	42	15	10	17	67:78	40
16	Oldham	42	15	8	19	67:80	38
17	Port Vale	42	14	10	18	66:79	38
18	Lincoln	42	12	13	17	72:87	37
19	Burnley	42	11	14	17	67:79	36
20	West Ham	42	13	9	20	75:93	35
21	Chesterfield	42	12	10	20	61:84	34
22	Charlton	42	12	7	23	60:91	31

Date	Comp	H/A	Opponent	Result	Score
26 Aug	Lge	A	Sheff Utd	D	0-0
28 Aug	Lge	H	Wolves	W	4-0
2 Sep	Lge	H	Aston Villa	W	3-2
4 Sep	Lge	A	Wolves	l	0-1
9 Sep	Lge	A	Leicester	W	3-1
16 Sep	Lge	H	Arsenal	D	1-1
23 Sep	Lge	A	Liverpool	L	0-3
30 Sep	Lge	A	Chelsea	W	4-0
7 Oct	Lge	H	Sunderland	W	3-1
14 Oct	Lge	A	Portsmouth	W	1-0
21 Oct	Lge	A	Everton	D	1-1
28 Oct	Lge	H	Middlesbrough	W	2-0
2 Nov	F	H	Oxford Univ	W	3-1
4 Nov	Lge	A	WBA	W	2-1
11 Nov	Lge	H	Newcastle	W	4-0
18 Nov	Lge	H	Leeds	D	0-0
23 Nov	F	A	Camb Univ	W	6-0
25 Nov	Lge	H	Derby	L	1-2
2 Dec	Lge	A	Man City	L	0-2
9 Dec	Lge	H	Birmingham	W	3-2
16 Dec	Lge	A	Sheff Wed	L	1-2
23 Dec	Lge	A	Blackburn	W	4-1
25 Dec	Lge	H	Huddersfield	L	1-3
26 Dec	Lge	A	Huddersfield	L	0-2
30 Dec	Lge	H	Sheff Utd	W	4-1
1 Jan	Lge	A	Blackburn	L	0-1
6 Jan	Lge	A	Aston Villa	W	5-1
13 Jan	FC	H	Everton	W	3-0
20 Jan	Lge	H	Leicester	L	0-1
27 Jan	FC	H	West Ham	W	4-1
31 Jan	Lge	A	Arsenal	W	3-1
3 Feb	Lge	A	Liverpool	L	1-3
10 Feb	Lge	H	Chelsea	W	2-1
17 Feb	FC	H	Aston Villa	L	0-1
21 Feb	Lge	A	Sunderland	L	0-6
24 Feb	Lge	H	Portsmouth	D	0-0
3 Mar	Lge	H	Everton	W	3-0
5 Mar	F	H	The Army	W	4-1
10 Mar	Lge	A	Middlesbrough	D	1-1
17 Mar	Lge	H	WBA	W	2-1
24 Mar	Lge	A	Newcastle	W	3-1
30 Mar	Lge	H	Stoke	D	0-0
31 Mar	Lge	H	Leeds	W	5-1
2 Apr	Lge	A	Stoke	L	0-2
7 Apr	Lge	A	Derby	L	3-4
14 Apr	Lge	H	Man City	W	5-1
21 Apr	Lge	A	Birmingham	L	0-2
28 Apr	Lge	H	Sheff Wed	W	4-3
30 Apr	F	A	Luton	D	2-2
2 May	SLS	H	Corinthians	W	7-4

Player	Lg App	Goals	Player	Lg App	Goals
Alsford W.J.	13		Hedley F.	1	
Bellamy W.R.	5		Howe L.	10	6
Bolan L.A.	1		Hunt G.S.	40	32
Channell F.C.	22		Felton W.	22	1
Colquhoun D.M.	13		McCormick J.	40	9
Day A.	3		Meads T.	30	1
Evans T.	26		Nicholls J.H.	42	
Evans W.	36	16	O'Callaghan E.	32	11
Hall B.A.C.	2		Rowe A.S.	42	
Hall G.W.	42	3	Whatley W.J.	40	

Final table for First Division

1	Arsenal	42	25	9	8	75:47	59
2	Huddersfield	42	23	10	9	90:61	56
3	**TOTTENHAM**	**42**	**21**	**7**	**14**	**79:56**	**49**
4	Derby	42	17	11	14	68:54	45
5	Manchester C.	42	17	11	14	65:72	45
6	Sunderland	42	16	12	14	81:56	44
7	West Bromwich	42	17	10	15	78:70	44
8	Blackburn	42	18	7	17	74:81	43
9	Leeds	42	17	8	17	75:66	42
10	Portsmouth	42	15	12	15	52:55	42
11	Sheffield W.	42	16	9	17	62:67	41
12	Stoke	42	15	11	16	58:71	41
13	Aston Villa	42	14	12	16	78:75	40
14	Everton	42	12	16	14	62:63	40
15	Wolverhampton	42	14	12	16	74:86	40
16	Middlesbrough	42	16	7	19	68:80	39
17	Leicester	42	14	11	17	59:74	39
18	Liverpool	42	14	10	18	79:87	38
19	Chelsea	42	14	8	20	67:69	36
20	Birmingham	42	12	12	18	54:56	36
21	Newcastle	42	10	14	18	68:77	34
22	Sheffield U.	42	12	7	23	58:101	31

SEASON 1934/35

Date	Comp	H/A	Opponent	Res	Score
25 Aug	Lge	H	Everton	D	1-1
27 Aug	Lge	H	Preston	L	1-2
1 Sep	Lge	A	Huddersfield	D	0-0
3 Sep	Lge	A	Preston	L	0-1
8 Sep	Lge	H	Wolves	W	3-1
15 Sep	Lge	A	Chelsea	W	3-1
22 Sep	Lge	H	Aston Villa	L	0-2
29 Sep	Lge	A	Derby	L	1-2
6 Oct	Lge	H	Leicester	D	2-2
13 Oct	Lge	A	Sunderland	W	2-1
20 Oct	Lge	A	Arsenal	L	1-5
27 Oct	Lge	H	Portsmouth	W	4-1
1 Nov	F	A	Oxford Univ	W	4-3
5 Nov	Lge	A	Man City	L	1-3
7 Nov	SLS	H	Corinthians	W	7-2
10 Nov	Lge	H	Middlesbrough	W	3-1
14 Nov	Lge	H	Camb Univ	W	4-0
17 Nov	Lge	A	WBA	L	0-4
24 Nov	Lge	H	Sheff Wed	W	3-2
1 Dec	Lge	A	Birmingham	L	1-2
8 Dec	Lge	H	Stoke	W	3-2
15 Dec	Lge	H	Liverpool	L	1-4
22 Dec	Lge	H	Leeds	D	1-1
25 Dec	Lge	A	Grimsby	L	0-3
26 Dec	Lge	H	Grimsby	W	2-1
29 Dec	Lge	A	Everton	L	2-5
1 Jan	Lge	A	Blackburn	L	0-2
5 Jan	Lge	H	Huddersfield	D	0-0
12 Jan	FC	H	Man City	W	1-0
19 Jan	Lge	A	Wolves	L	2-6
26 Jan	FC	H	Newcastle	W	2-0
30 Jan	Lge	H	Chelsea	L	1-3
2 Feb	Lge	A	Aston Villa	L	0-1
9 Feb	Lge	H	Derby	D	2-2
16 Feb	FC	H	Bolton	D	1-1
20 Feb	FCr	A	Bolton	D	1-1
23 Feb	Lge	H	Sunderland	D	1-1
25 Feb	FCr	*	Bolton	L	0-2
6 Mar	Lge	H	Arsenal	L	0-6
9 Mar	Lge	A	Portsmouth	D	1-1
16 Mar	Lge	A	Man City	D	0-0
23 Mar	Lge	A	Middlesbrough	L	1-3
28 Mar	Lge	A	Leicester	L	0-6
30 Mar	Lge	H	WBA	L	0-1
6 Apr	Lge	A	Sheff Wed	L	0-4
13 Apr	Lge	H	Birmingham	D	1-1
19 Apr	Lge	H	Blackburn	W	1-0
20 Apr	Lge	A	Stoke	L	1-4
24 Apr	F	A	Burton Town	D	2-2
27 Apr	Lge	H	Liverpool	W	5-1
4 May	Lge	A	Leeds	L	3-4
16 May	F	A	Chanl Isle XI	W	5-0
18 May	F	A	Guernsey XI	W	5-0

* Played at Villa Park

Player	Lg App	Goals	Player	Lg App	Goals
Alsford W.J.	21		Howe L.F.	32	2
Bell S.	8	2	Hunt D.A.	12	4
Bellamy W.R.	7	1	Hunt G.S.	30	10
Bolan L.A.	9	3	Illingworth J.	1	
Brain J.	1		Jones C.	8	
Burgon A.	4		King	1	
Channell F.C.	41	1	Levene D.	3	
Colquhoun D.M.	3		Meads T.	18	
Day A.	9		McCormick J.	28	6
Duncan A.	6		Morrison J.A.	2	1
Evans T.	28		Nicholls J.H.	21	
Evans W.	32	12	O'Callaghan E.	16	4
Fullwood J.	2		Phypers E.	2	
Goldsmith G.	1		Rowe A.S.	18	
Greenfield G.	6		Sargent F.A.	1	
Hall A.G.	12	3	Taylor A.	18	
Hall G.W.	18	3	Whatley W.J.	37	
Hedley F.	3	1	Own Goal		1
Hooper P.G.	3				

Final table for First Division

1	Arsenal	42	23	12	7	115:46	58
2	Sunderland	42	19	16	7	90:51	54
3	Sheffield W.	42	18	13	11	70:64	49
4	Manchester C.	42	20	8	14	82:67	48
5	Grimsby	42	17	11	14	78:60	45
6	Derby	42	18	9	15	81:66	45
7	Liverpool	42	19	7	16	85:88	45
8	Everton	42	16	12	14	89:88	44
9	West Bromwich	42	17	10	15	83:83	44
10	Stoke	42	18	6	18	71:70	42
11	Preston	42	15	12	15	62:67	42
12	Chelsea	42	16	9	17	73:82	41
13	Aston Villa	42	14	13	15	74:88	41
14	Portsmouth	42	15	10	17	71:72	40
15	Blackburn	42	14	11	17	66:78	39
16	Huddersfield	42	14	10	18	76:71	38
17	Wolverhampton	42	15	8	19	88:94	38
18	Leeds	42	13	12	17	75:92	38
19	Birmingham	42	13	10	19	63:81	36
20	Middlesbrough	42	10	14	18	70:90	34
21	Leicester	42	12	9	21	61:86	33
22	**TOTTENHAM**	**42**	**10**	**10**	**22**	**54:93**	**30**

SEASON 1935/36

Date	Comp	H/A	Opponent	Res	Score
31 Aug	Lge	A	Bradford C.	W	1-0
2 Sep	Lge	H	Hull	W	3-1
7 Sep	Lge	H	Newcastle	L	1-2
9 Sep	Lge	A	Hull	L	0-1
14 Sep	Lge	A	Sheff Utd	D	1-1
16 Sep	Lge	H	Barnsley	W	3-0
21 Sep	Lge	A	Man Utd	D	0-0
28 Sep	Lge	H	Port Vale	W	5-2
5 Oct	Lge	A	Fulham	W	2-1
12 Oct	Lge	H	Burnley	W	5-1
19 Oct	Lge	H	Bradford	W	4-0
26 Oct	Lge	A	Leicester	L	1-4
2 Nov	Lge	A	Swansea	W	7-2
9 Nov	Lge	A	West Ham	D	2-2
16 Nov	Lge	H	Bury	W	4-3
21 Nov	F	H	Oxford Univ	W	4-2
23 Nov	Lge	A	Southampton	L	0-2
28 Nov	F	A	Camb Univ	L	0-1
30 Nov	Lge	A	Blackpool	W	3-1
7 Dec	Lge	A	Nottm Forest	L	1-4
14 Dec	Lge	H	Norwich	W	2-1
21 Dec	Lge	A	Doncaster	L	1-4
25 Dec	Lge	A	Plymouth	L	1-2
26 Dec	Lge	A	Plymouth	L	1-2
28 Dec	Lge	H	Bradford C	W	4-0
4 Jan	Lge	A	Newcastle	W	4-1
11 Jan	FC	H	Southend	D	4-4
15 Jan	FCr	A	Southend	W	2-1
18 Jan	Lge	H	Sheff Utd	D	1-1
25 Jan	FC	H	Huddersfield	W	1-0
1 Feb	Lge	A	Port Vale	W	5-1
5 Feb	Lge	H	Man Utd	D	0-0
8 Feb	Lge	H	Fulham	D	2-2
15 Feb	FC	A	Bradford PA	D	0-0
17 Feb	FCr	H	Bradford PA	W	2-1
22 Feb	Lge	A	Bradford PA	W	5-2
29 Feb	FC	A	Sheff Utd	L	1-3
4 Mar	Lge	H	Nottm Forest	D	1-1
7 Mar	Lge	A	Bury	D	1-1
14 Mar	Lge	H	West Ham	L	1-3
21 Mar	Lge	A	Swansea	D	1-1
28 Mar	Lge	H	Southampton	W	8-0
4 Apr	Lge	A	Blackpool	W	4-2
10 Apr	Lge	H	Charlton	D	1-1
11 Apr	Lge	H	Leicester	D	1-1
13 Apr	Lge	A	Charlton	L	1-2
18 Apr	Lge	A	Newcastle	L	0-1
20 Apr	Lge	A	Burnley	D	0-0
25 Apr	Lge	H	Doncaster	W	3-1
2 May	Lge	A	Barnsley	D	0-0

Player	Lg App	Goals	Player	Lg App	Goals
Alsford W.J.	14		Howe L.	33	6
Bell S.	5	3	Hunt D.A.	4	2
Buckingham V.F.	16		Hunt G.S.	15	11
Channell F.C.	32		Jones C.	10	
Day A.	1		McCormick J.	21	3
Duncan A.	24	6	Meek J.	10	5
Edrich W.J.	9	1	Morrison J.A.	32	25
Evans T.	8		Nicholls J.H.	7	
Evans W.	33	15	Phypers E.	26	
Fullwood J.	12	1	Rowe A.S.	28	
Grice F.	7		Sargent F.A.	16	5
Hall A.E.	1		Taylor A.	14	
Hall A.G.	4		Ward R.A.	8	
Hall G.W.	32	6	Whatley W.J.	19	
Hooper P.G.	21		Own Goals		2

Final table for Second Division

1	Manchester U.	42	22	12	8	85:43	56
2	Charlton	42	22	11	9	85:58	55
3	Sheffield U.	42	20	12	10	79:50	52
4	West Ham	42	22	8	12	90:68	52
5	**TOTTENHAM**	**42**	**18**	**13**	**11**	**91:55**	**49**
6	Leicester	42	19	10	13	79:57	48
7	Plymouth	42	20	8	14	71:57	48
8	Newcastle	42	20	6	16	88:79	46
9	Fulham	42	15	14	13	76:52	44
10	Blackpool	42	18	7	17	93:72	43
11	Norwich	42	17	9	16	72:65	43
12	Bradford C.	42	15	13	14	55:65	43
13	Swansea	42	15	9	18	67:76	39
14	Bury	42	13	12	17	66:84	38
15	Burnley	42	12	13	17	50:59	37
16	Bradford PA	42	14	9	19	62:84	37
17	Southampton	42	14	9	19	47:65	37
18	Doncaster	42	14	9	19	51:71	37
19	Nottingham F.	42	12	11	19	69:76	35
20	Barnsley	42	12	9	21	54:80	33
21	Port Vale	42	12	8	22	56:106	32
22	Hull	42	5	10	27	47:111	20

SEASON 1936/37

Date	Comp	H/A	Opponent	Result	Score
29 Aug	Lge	A	West Ham	L	1-2
31 Aug	Lge	A	Blackpool	D	0-0
5 Sep	Lge	H	Norwich	L	2-3
12 Sep	Lge	A	Newcastle	W	1-0
14 Sep	Lge	H	Leicester	W	4-2
19 Sep	Lge	H	Bradford	W	5-1
21 Sep	Lge	H	Blackpool	L	1-2
26 Sep	Lge	A	Barnsley	L	0-1
3 Oct	Lge	H	Sheff Utd	D	2-2
10 Oct	Lge	A	Burnley	L	1-3
17 Oct	Lge	H	Southampton	W	4-0
24 Oct	Lge	A	Swansea	L	1-2
31 Oct	Lge	H	Bradford C	W	5-1
7 Nov	Lge	A	Aston Villa	D	1-1
14 Nov	Lge	H	Chesterfield	W	5-1
16 Nov	F	H	Corinthians	W	5-1
19 Nov	F	A	Oxford Univ	W	2-0
26 Nov	F	A	Camb Univ	W	6-2
28 Nov	Lge	H	Plymouth	L	1-3
5 Dec	Lge	A	Coventry	L	0-1
12 Dec	Lge	H	Doncaster	W	2-0
19 Dec	Lge	A	Fulham	D	3-3
25 Dec	Lge	A	Blackburn	W	4-0
26 Dec	Lge	H	West Ham	L	2-3
28 Dec	Lge	H	Blackburn	W	5-1
2 Jan	Lge	A	Norwich	W	3-2
9 Jan	Lge	H	Newcastle	L	0-1
16 Jan	FC	A	Portsmouth	W	5-0
23 Jan	Lge	A	Bradford	L	2-3
30 Jan	FC	H	Plymouth	W	1-0
3 Feb	Lge	H	Barnsley	W	3-0
6 Feb	Lge	A	Sheff Utd	L	2-3
13 Feb	Lge	H	Burnley	W	3-0
20 Feb	FC	A	Everton	D	1-1
22 Feb	FCr	H	Everton	W	4-3
24 Feb	Lge	A	Southampton	L	0-1
27 Feb	Lge	H	Swansea	W	3-1
6 Mar	FC	H	Preston	L	1-3
10 Mar	Lge	A	Bradford C	D	2-2
13 Mar	Lge	H	Aston Villa	D	2-2
20 Mar	Lge	A	Chesterfield	W	3-1
26 Mar	Lge	A	Bury	L	3-5
27 Mar	Lge	H	Nottm Forest	W	2-1
29 Mar	Lge	H	Bury	W	2-0
3 Apr	Lge	A	Plymouth	D	2-2
10 Apr	Lge	H	Coventry	W	3-1
17 Apr	Lge	A	Doncaster	D	1-1
21 Apr	Lge	A	Nottm Forest	L	0-3
24 Apr	Lge	H	Fulham	D	1-1
1 May	Lge	A	Leicester	L	1-4

Player	Lg App	Goals	Player	Lg App	Goals
Alexander S.	9	1	Cooper P.G.	3	
Alsford W.J.	7		Howe L.	28	
Bell S.	2	1	Hunt D.A.	1	
Blyth J.	11		Hunt G.S.	13	10
Brown J.	4		Ludford G.A.	1	
Buckingham V.F.	25		McCormick J.	35	8
Duncan A.	29	9	Meek J.	28	9
Edrich W.J.	11	3	Miller L.	23	12
Evans T.	1		Morrison J.A.	32	29
Evans W.	7	2	Page A.E.	15	
Fullwood J.	5		Phypers E.	2	
Grice F.	22		Ringrose A.	10	
Hall A.E.	1		Rowe A.S.	15	
Hall G.W.	19	1	Ward R.A.	32	3
Hall J.	39		Whatley W.J.	32	

Final table for Second Division

1	Leicester	42	24	8	10	89:57	56
2	Blackpool	42	24	7	11	88:53	55
3	Bury	42	22	8	12	74:55	52
4	Newcastle	42	22	5	15	80:56	49
5	Plymouth	42	18	13	11	71:53	49
6	West Ham	42	19	11	12	73:55	49
7	Sheffield U.	42	18	10	14	66:54	46
8	Coventry	42	17	11	14	66:54	45
9	Aston Villa	42	16	12	14	82:70	44
10	TOTTENHAM	42	17	9	16	88:66	43
11	Fulham	42	15	13	14	71:61	43
12	Blackburn	42	16	10	16	70:62	42
13	Burnley	42	16	10	16	57:61	42
14	Barnsley	42	16	9	17	50:64	41
15	Chesterfield	42	16	8	18	84:89	40
16	Swansea	42	15	7	20	50:65	37
17	Norwich	42	14	8	20	63:71	36
18	Nottingham F.	42	12	10	20	68:90	34
19	Southampton	42	11	12	19	53:77	34
20	Bradford PA	42	12	9	21	52:88	33
21	Bradford C.	42	9	12	21	54:94	30
22	Doncaster	42	7	10	25	30:84	24

SEASON 1937/38

Date	Comp	H/A	Opponent	Result	Score
28 Aug	Lge	H	Coventry	D	0-0
30 Aug	Lge	H	Burnley	W	4-0
4 Sep	Lge	A	Nottm Forest	L	1-3
6 Sep	Lge	A	Burnley	L	1-2
11 Sep	Lge	H	Newcastle	D	2-2
16 Sep	Lge	A	Sheff Wed	W	3-0
18 Sep	Lge	A	Luton	W	4-2
25 Sep	Lge	H	Barnsley	W	3-0
2 Oct	Lge	A	Stockport	L	2-3
9 Oct	Lge	H	Man Utd	L	0-1
16 Oct	Lge	A	Fulham	L	1-3
23 Oct	Lge	A	Plymouth	W	3-2
30 Oct	Lge	A	Chesterfield	D	2-2
6 Nov	Lge	H	Swansea	W	2-0
13 Nov	Lge	A	Norwich	L	1-2
18 Nov	F	H	Oxford Univ	W	3-2
20 Nov	Lge	H	West Ham	W	2-0
25 Nov	F	A	Camb Univ	L	2-3
27 Nov	Lge	A	Bradford PA	L	1-3
4 Dec	Lge	H	Aston Villa	W	2-1
11 Dec	Lge	A	Southampton	L	1-2
18 Dec	Lge	H	Blackburn	W	3-1
25 Dec	Lge	A	Bury	W	2-1
26 Dec	Lge	H	Bury	L	1-3
1 Jan	Lge	A	Coventry	L	1-2
8 Jan	FC	H	Blackburn	W	3-2
15 Jan	Lge	H	Nottm Forest	W	3-0
22 Jan	FC	A	N/Brighton	D	0-0
26 Jan	FCr	H	N/Brighton	W	5-2
29 Jan	Lge	H	Luton	W	3-0
2 Feb	Lge	A	Newcastle	L	0-1
5 Feb	Lge	A	Barnsley	D	1-1
12 Feb	FC	H	Chesterfield	D	2-2
16 Feb	FCr	H	Chesterfield	W	2-1
19 Feb	Lge	A	Man Utd	W	1-0
23 Feb	Lge	H	Stockport	W	2-0
26 Feb	Lge	H	Fulham	D	1-1
7 Mar	FC	H	Sunderland	L	0-1*
9 Mar	Lge	A	Plymouth	D	2-2
12 Mar	Lge	H	Chesterfield	W	2-0
19 Mar	Lge	A	Swansea	L	2-3
26 Mar	Lge	H	Norwich	W	4-0
2 Apr	Lge	A	West Ham	W	3-1
9 Apr	Lge	H	Bradford PA	W	2-1
15 Apr	Lge	H	Sheff Utd	L	1-2
16 Apr	Lge	A	Aston Villa	L	0-2
18 Apr	Lge	A	Sheff Utd	L	0-1
23 Apr	Lge	H	Southampton	W	5-0
30 Apr	Lge	A	Blackburn	L	1-2
7 May	Lge	H	Sheff Wed	L	1-2

* Tottenham's record attendance (75,038)

Player	Lg App	Goals	Player	Lg App	Goals
Buckingham V.F.	29		Ludford G.A.	1	
Duncan A.	13	2	Lyman C.C.	24	4
Fullwood J.	15		McCormick J.	3	
Gibbons A.H.	27	13	Meek J.	7	1
Grice F.	17	1	Miller L.	16	5
Hall A.E.	6		Morrison J.A.	39	23
Hall G.W.	30	4	Page A.E.	23	
Hall J.	12		Rowe A.S.	9	
Hitchins A.W.	10		Sargent F.A.	42	14
Hooper P.G.	30		Spelman I.	8	
Howe L.	33	4	Ward R.A.	42	4
Jeffrey G.	1	1	Whatley W.J.	25	

Final table for Second Division

1	Aston Villa	42	25	7	10	73:35	57
2	Manchester U.	42	22	9	11	82:50	53
3	Sheffield U.	42	22	9	11	73:56	53
4	Coventry	42	20	12	10	66:45	52
5	TOTTENHAM	42	19	6	17	76:54	44
6	Burnley	42	17	10	15	54:54	44
7	Bradford PA	42	17	9	16	69:56	43
8	Fulham	42	16	11	15	61:57	43
9	West Ham	42	14	14	14	53:52	42
10	Bury	42	18	5	19	63:60	41
11	Chesterfield	42	16	9	17	63:63	41
12	Luton	42	15	10	17	89:86	40
13	Plymouth	42	14	12	16	57:65	40
14	Norwich	42	14	11	17	56:75	39
15	Southampton	42	15	9	18	55:77	39
16	Blackburn	42	14	10	18	71:80	38
17	Sheffield W.	42	14	10	18	48:56	38
18	Swansea	42	13	12	17	45:73	38
19	Newcastle	42	14	8	20	51:58	36
20	Nottingham F.	42	14	8	20	47:60	36
21	Barnsley	42	11	14	17	50:64	36
22	Stockport	42	11	9	22	43:70	31

SEASON 1938/39

Date	Comp	H/A	Opponent	Res	Score		Date	Comp	H/A	Opponent	Res	Score
27 Aug	Lge	A	Southampton	W	2-1		7 Jan	FC	H	Watford	W	7-1
29 Aug	Lge	H	Sheff Wed	D	3-3		14 Jan	Lge	H	Nottm Forest	W	4-1
3 Sep	Lge	H	Coventry	W	2-1		21 Jan	FC	A	West Ham	D	3-3
10 Sep	Lge	A	Nottm Forest	L	1-2		28 Jan	Lge	H	WBA	D	2-2
12 Sep	Lge	H	Sheff Utd	D	2-2		30 Jan	FCr	H	West Ham	D	1-1
17 Sep	Lge	H	Newcastle	W	1-0		2 Feb	FCr	*	West Ham	L	1-2
24 Sep	Lge	A	WBA	L	3-4		4 Feb	Lge	A	Norwich	W	2-1
1 Oct	Lge	H	Norwich	W	4-1		11 Feb	Lge	H	Luton	L	0-1
8 Oct	Lge	A	Luton	D	0-0		18 Feb	Lge	A	Fulham	L	0-1
15 Oct	Lge	H	Fulham	W	1-0		25 Feb	Lge	H	Blackburn	W	4-3
22 Oct	Lge	A	Blackburn	L	1-3		1 Mar	Lge	A	Newcastle	W	1-0
29 Oct	Lge	H	West Ham	W	2-1		4 Mar	Lge	A	West Ham	W	2-0
5 Nov	Lge	A	Man City	L	0-2		11 Mar	Lge	H	Man City	L	2-3
12 Nov	Lge	H	Bradford PA	D	2-2		18 Mar	Lge	A	Bradford PA	D	0-0
19 Nov	Lge	A	Swansea	D	1-1		25 Mar	Lge	H	Swansea	W	3-0
26 Nov	Lge	H	Chesterfield	D	2-2		1 Apr	Lge	A	Chesterfield	L	1-3
3 Dec	Lge	A	Tranmere	W	2-0		7 Apr	Lge	H	Plymouth	W	1-0
10 Dec	Lge	H	Millwall	W	4-0		8 Apr	Lge	A	Tranmere	W	3-1
17 Dec	Lge	A	Bury	L	1-3		10 Apr	Lge	A	Plymouth	W	1-0
24 Dec	Lge	H	Southampton	D	1-1		15 Apr	Lge	A	Millwall	L	0-2
26 Dec	Lge	A	Burnley	L	0-1		22 Apr	Lge	H	Bury	W	4-3
27 Dec	Lge	H	Burnley	W	1-0		29 Apr	Lge	A	Sheff Wed	L	0-1
31 Dec	Lge	A	Coventry	L	0-4		6 May	Lge	A	Sheff Utd	L	1-6

* Played at Highbury

Player	Lg App	Goals	Player	Lg App	Goals
Buckingham V.F.	41	1	Lyman C.C.	22	6
Burgess W.A.R.	17	1	McCormick J.	1	
Cox F.J.A.	9	2	Miller L.	17	5
Duncan A.	21	5	Morrison J.A.	27	9
Grice F.	1		Nicholson W.E.	8	
Hall A.E.	24	10	Page A.E.	17	
Hall G.W.	40	9	Sargent F.A.	34	4
Hall J.	2		Spelman I.	20	2
Hitchins A.W.	25	1	Sproston B.	9	
Cooper P.G.	40		Tomkin A.H.	2	
Howe L.	8	1	Ward R.A.	33	3
Ludford G.A.	10	6	Whatley W.J.	34	2

Second Division 1938–39

1	Blackburn	42	25	5	12	94:60	55
2	Sheffield U.	42	20	14	8	69:41	54
3	Sheffield W.	42	21	11	10	88:59	53
4	Coventry	42	21	8	13	62:45	50
5	Manchester C.	42	21	7	14	96:72	49
6	Chesterfield	42	20	9	13	69:52	49
7	Luton	42	22	5	15	82:66	49
8	TOTTENHAM	42	19	9	14	67:62	47
9	Newcastle	42	18	10	14	61:48	46
10	West Bromwich	42	18	9	15	89:72	45
11	West Ham	42	17	10	15	70:52	44
12	Fulham	42	17	10	15	61:55	44
13	Millwall	42	14	14	14	64:53	42
14	Burnley	42	15	9	18	50:56	39
15	Plymouth	42	15	8	19	49:55	38
16	Bury	42	12	13	17	65:74	37
17	Bradford PA	42	12	11	19	61:82	35
18	Southampton	42	13	9	20	56:82	35
19	Swansea	42	11	12	19	50:83	34
20	Nottingham F.	42	10	11	21	49:82	31
21	Norwich	42	13	5	24	50:91	31
22	Tranmere	42	6	5	31	39:99	17

SEASON 1939/40

Date	Comp	H/A	Opponent	Res	Score		Date	Comp	H/A	Opponent	Res	Score
19 Aug	J†	H	Arsenal	L	0-1		25 Jan	Lge	H	Arsenal	L	0-1
26 Aug	Lge*	H	Birmingham	D	1-1		10 Feb	Lge	A	West Ham	L	0-2
31 Aug	Lge*	A	Newport	D	1-1		17 Feb	Lge	H	Charlton	W	2-0
2 Sep	Lge*	A	WBA	W	4-3		24 Feb	Lge	A	Chelsea	W	2-0
23 Sep	F	A	Chelmsford	L	2-4		28 Feb	Lge	A	C. Palace	D	1-1
30 Sep	F	A	Chelsea	L	2-4		2 Mar	Lge	H	Southampton	W	4-1
7 Oct	F	H	West Ham	L	0-2		9 Mar	Lge	H	Brentford	D	1-1
21 Oct	Lge	A	Southend	W	2-1		16 Mar	Lge	H	Portsmouth	W	2-1
28 Oct	Lge	H	Millwall	W	3-0		22 Mar	Lge	H	Millwall	L	1-2
4 Nov	Lge	A	West Ham	L	1-2		23 Mar	Lge	A	Fulham	W	3-2
11 Nov	Lge	H	Watford	W	8-2		25 Mar	Lge	A	Millwall	D	1-1
18 Nov	Lge	A	Arsenal	L	1-2		30 Mar	Lge	A	Arsenal	D	1-1
25 Nov	Lge	H	Charlton	W	4-2		6 Apr	Lge	H	West Ham	L	2-6
2 Dec	Lge	A	C. Orient	L	1-2		10 Apr	Lge	H	Fulham	W	3-1
9 Dec	Lge	H	C. Palace	L	1-3		13 Apr	Lge	A	Charlton	W	4-2
16 Dec	Lge	A	Norwich	L	2-5		20 Apr	CUP	A	C. Palace	L	1-4
23 Dec	Lge	A	Southend	L	3-4‡		24 Apr	Lge	A	Arsenal	L	4-2
25 Dec	Lge	A	Millwall	L	1-5		27 Apr	CUP	H	C. Palace	W	2-1
26 Dec	Lge	H	West Ham	L	0-1		4 May	Lge	A	Brentford	W	3-2
30 Dec	Lge	A	Watford	L	1-6		11 May	Lge	H	Portsmouth	W	4-1
13 Jan	Lge	A	Charlton	W	5-1		18 May	Lge	A	Southampton	D	3-3
17 Jan	Lge	A	Southend	L	2-4		25 May	Lge	H	Chelsea	W	3-2
20 Jan	Lge	H	C. Orient	L	2-3		27 May	Lge	H	Norwich	D	2-2

J† Football League Jubilee match

* Three Football League fixtures which were played before the season was abandoned. Other League matches this season were in the two Regional Leagues South.   ‡ Match abandoned but score stood

Player	Lg App	Goals	Player	Lg App	Goals
Buckingham V.F.	3		Lyman C.C.	1	
Burgess W.A.R.	3	1	Morrison J.A.	1	3
Dix R.W.	3	1	Nicholson W.E.	3	
Hall G.W.	3		Page A.E.	1	
Hitchins A.W.	2		Sargent F.A.	3	1
Hooper P.G.	3		Tomkin A.H.	2	
Ludford G.A.	2		Ward R.A.	3	

Player	War Lg App	Goals	Player	War Lg App	Goals
Bennett L.	11	6	Ludford G.	11	7
Buckingham V.	14		Lyman C.	6	1
Burchell	1		McCormick J.	6	
Burgess R.	14	2	McEwan	3	
Cox F.	10	1	Medley L.	23	10
Ditchburn E.	2		Morrison J.	29	21
Dix R.	14	6	Ottewell*	1	
Dorling	12		Page A.	7	
Dowers	2		Piper	1	
Duncan A.	16	4	Sargent F.	15	5
Evans	1		Spelman I.	11	
Hall A.E.	4	2	Stephens	1	
Hall G.W.	26	4	Tomkin A.	1	
Hitchens	32		Ward R.	21	2
Hooper P.	33		Whatley G.	33	2
Howe L.	31	5	Wilbert G.	1	
Hunt D.	2	2			

* Guest

Second Division 1939–40 ▶

1	Luton	3	2	1	0	7:1	5
2	Birmingham	3	2	1	0	5:1	5
3	Coventry	3	1	2	0	8:6	4
4	Plymouth	3	2	0	1	4:3	4
5	West Ham	3	2	0	1	5:4	4
6	Leicester	3	2	0	1	6:5	4
7	TOTTENHAM	3	1	2	0	6:5	4
8	Nottingham F.	3	2	0	1	5:5	4
9	Millwall	3	1	1	1	5:4	3
10	Newport	3	1	1	1	5:4	3
11	Manchester C.	3	1	1	1	6:5	3
12	WBA	3	1	1	1	8:8	3
13	Bury	3	1	1	1	4:5	3
14	Newcastle	3	1	0	2	8:6	2
15	Chesterfield	2	1	0	1	2:2	2
16	Barnsley	3	1	0	2	7:8	2
17	Southampton	3	1	0	2	5:6	2
18	Sheffield W.	3	1	0	2	3:5	2
19	Swansea	3	1	0	2	5:11	2
20	Fulham	3	0	1	2	3:6	1
21	Burnley	2	0	1	1	1:3	1
22	Bradford	3	0	1	2	2:7	1

These were the Football League standings at the point the competition was abandoned.

Regional League South 'A' 1939–40

1	Arsenal	18	13	4	1	62:22	30
2	West Ham	18	12	1	5	57:33	25
3	Millwall	18	8	5	5	46:38	21
4	Watford	18	9	3	6	44:38	21
5	Norwich	18	7	6	5	41:36	20
6	Charlton	18	8	1	9	61:58	17
7	C. Palace	18	5	3	10	39:56	13
8	C. Orient	18	5	3	10	28:60	13
9	TOTTENHAM	18	5	2	11	37:43	12
10	Southend	18	4	0	14	30:61	8

Regional League South 'C' 1939–40

1	TOTTENHAM	18	11	4	3	43:30	26
2	West Ham	18	10	4	4	53:28	24
3	Arsenal	18	9	5	4	41:26	23
4	Brentford	18	8	4	6	42:34	20
5	Millwall	18	7	5	6	36:30	19
6	Charlton	18	7	4	7	39:36	18
7	Fulham	18	8	1	9	38:42	17
8	Southampton	18	5	3	10	28:55	13
9	Chelsea	18	4	3	11	33:53	11
10	Portsmouth	18	3	3	12	26:45	9

SEASON 1940/41

Date	Comp	H/A	Opponent	Result		Date	Comp	H/A	Opponent	Result
31 Aug	Lge	H	West Ham	L 2-3		1 Feb	LCup	H	West Ham	L 1-2
7 Sep	Lge	A	West Ham	W 4-1*		8 Feb	LCup	A	West Ham	L 2-3
14 Sep	Lge	H	Chelsea	W 3-2*		15 Feb	LGC	H	Bournemouth	W 4-1
21 Sep	Lge	A	Chelsea	L 1-4		22 Feb	LGC	A	Bournemouth	W 6-1
28 Sep	Lge	H	Charlton	L 1-3		1 Mar	LGC	H	Northampton	W 4-0
5 Oct	Lge	A	QPR	D 1-1		8 Mar	LGC	A	Northampton	W 3-1
12 Oct	Lge	H	QPR	L 2-3*		15 Mar	Lge	H	Millwall	L 0-1
19 Oct	Lge	A	Charlton	L 0-4		22 Mar	LGC	H	Cardiff	D 3-3
26 Oct	Lge	H	Portsmouth	L 1-2		29 Mar	LGC	A	Cardiff	W 3-2
2 Nov	Lge	A	Luton	D 1-1		5 Apr	LGC	A	Arsenal	L 1-2
16 Nov	Lge	A	Arsenal	D 1-1		12 Apr	LGC	H	Arsenal	D 1-1
23 Nov	Lge	H	Luton	W 2-1*		14 Apr	LCup	H	Reading	D 2-2
30 Nov	Lge	A	Southend	L 2-3†		19 Apr	LCup	A	Reading	D 2-2
7 Dec	Lge	H	QPR	L 2-3		26 Apr	Lge	A	Aldershot	W 3-2
21 Dec	Lge	H	C. Orient	W 9-0		3 May	LCup	H	Arsenal	D 3-3
25 Dec	Lge	H	Millwall	D 3-3		10 May	Lge	H	C. Palace	D 1-1
28 Dec	Lge	H	C. Orient	W 7-0		17 May	Lge	A	Leicester	W 2-1
4 Jan	LCup	H	C. Orient	W 3-0		21 May	LCup	A	Arsenal	W 3-0
11 Jan	LCup	A	C. Orient	W 9-1		24 May	Lge	H	Leicester	W 3-0
18 Jan	LCup	A	Millwall	W 3-1		31 May	LCupsf	H	Brentford	L 0-2
25 Jan	LCup	H	Millwall	W 4-0		7 Jun	Lge	H	Fulham	W 2-1

* Matches abandoned
† Played at Chelmsford

Player	War Lg App	Goals		Regional League South 1940–41							
Arnold*	1			1 C. Palace	27	16	4	7	86:44	1.954
Bennett L.	5			2 West Ham	25	14	6	5	70:39	1.794
Broadis I.	4	2		3 Coventry	10	5	3	2	28:16	1.750
Brown J.	1			4 Arsenal	19	10	5	4	66:38	1.736
Buckingham V.	14			5 Cardiff	24	12	5	7	75:50	1.500
Burdett	1			6 Reading	26	14	5	7	73:51	1.431
Burgess R.	9	8		7 Norwich	19	9	2	8	73:55	1.327
Duncan A.	17	5		8 Watford	35	15	6	14	96:73	1.315
Flack*	5			9 Portsmouth	31	16	2	13	92:71	1.296
Gibbons A.	8	9		**10 TOTTENHAM**	**23**	**9**	**5**	**9**	**53:41**	**1.292**
Goodman*	1			11 Millwall	31	16	5	10	73:57	1.280
Hall G.W.	15	3		12 Walsall	32	14	7	11	100:80	1.250
Henley*	1			13 WBA	28	13	5	10	83:69	1.202
Hitchens	22			14 Leicester	33	17	5	11	87:73	1.191
Hooper P.	14			15 Northampton	30	14	3	13	84:71	1.183
Howe L.	4	2		16 Bristol C.	20	10	2	8	55:48	1.145
Ludford G.	23	11		17 Mansfield	29	12	6	11	77:68	1.132
McCarthy	1			18 Charlton	19	7	4	8	37:34	1.088
McCormick J.	2			19 Aldershot	24	14	2	8	73:68	1.073
Medley L.	6	2		20 Brentford	23	9	3	11	51:51	1.000
Newman A.	1			21 Chelsea	23	10	4	9	57:58	0.981
O'Callaghan F.	8	1		22 Birmingham	16	7	1	8	38:43	0.883
Paton*	4			23 Fulham	30	10	7	13	62:73	0.849
Piper	3			24 Luton	35	11	7	17	82:100	0.820
Sainsbury	1			25 Stoke	36	9	9	18	76:96	0.791
Sargent F.	6	1		26 QPR	23	8	3	12	47:60	0.783
Saunders*	3			22 Brighton	25	8	7	10	51:75	0.680
Skinner	3	1		28 Nottingham F.	25	7	3	15	50:77	0.649
Sperrin J.	4	2		29 Bournemouth	27	9	3	15	59:92	0.641
Sperrin W.	8	3		30 Notts Co.	21	8	3	10	42:66	0.636
Wallace J.	1			31 Southend	29	12	4	13	64:101	0.633
Wallis J.	2			32 Southampton	31	4	4	23	53:111	0.477
Ward R.	22	2		33 Swansea	10	2	1	7	12:33	0.363
Whartley W.	20			34 C. Orient	15	1	3	11	19:66	0.287
White R.	13									
Own Goal		1		Final placings were decided solely on goal average.

* Guest

SEASON 1941/42

Date	Comp	H/A	Opponent	Result		Date	Comp	H/A	Opponent	Result
30 Aug	Lge	H	Watford	W 5-0		3 Jan	Lge	A	QPR	L 0-1
6 Sep	Lge	A	Aldershot	L 2-3		10 Jan	Lge	H	Reading	W 2-1
13 Sep	Lge	H	Millwall	W 3-0		17 Jan	Lge	A	Brighton	L 2-5
20 Sep	Lge	A	Arsenal	L 0-3		31 Jan	Lge	A	C. Palace	D 2-2
27 Sep	Lge	H	QPR	W 3-1		14 Feb	Lge	A	C. Orient	W 3-2
4 Oct	Lge	A	Reading	D 1-1		21 Feb	Lge	H	Portsmouth	D 1-1
11 Oct	Lge	H	Brighton	L 1-2		28 Feb	Lge	H	Chelsea	W 2-0
18 Oct	Lge	A	Brentford	W 4-1		7 Mar	Lge	H	Charlton	W 2-0
25 Oct	Lge	A	C. Palace	D 1-1		14 Mar	Lge	A	West Ham	W 3-2
1 Nov	Lge	A	Fulham	D 2-2		21 Mar	CUP	A	Reading	W 2-1
8 Nov	Lge	H	C. Orient	W 2-0		28 Mar	CUP	H	Watford	W 5-2
15 Nov	Lge	A	Portsmouth	W 2-1		4 Apr	CUP	H	Reading	W 2-1
22 Nov	Lge	A	Chelsea	D 1-1		6 Apr	CUP	A	Watford	D 0-0
29 Nov	Lge	A	Charlton	L 1-2		11 Apr	CUP	H	Charlton	L 0-3
6 Dec	Lge	H	West Ham	D 1-1		18 Apr	CUP	A	Charlton	L 0-4
13 Dec	Lge	A	Watford	W 2-1		25 Apr	Lge	H	Brentford	W 2-1
20 Dec	Lge	H	Aldershot	D 1-1		2 May	Lge	H	Fulham	W 7-1
25 Dec	Lge	A	Millwall	W 2-1		25 Mar	F	A	C. Palace	W 5-3
27 Dec	Lge	H	Arsenal	L 1-2						

Player	War Lg App	Goals		Player	War Lg App	Goals
Bennett F.	4			Ludford G.	24	15
Bennett L.	1	1		Mannion W.*	4	
Broadis I.	29	11		McCormick J.	1	
Buckingham V.	1			Noble*	6	3
Burgess R.	5	2		Pearson*	2	
Cox F.	2			Revell*	1	1
Ditchburn E.	10			Sainsbury	3	
Duncan A.	24	3		Sibley	3	1
Edwards R.	1			Sperrin J.	3	
Finch*	1			Sperrin W.	8	
Fitzgerald*	1			Stevens	1	2
Gibbons A.	23	18		Tickridge	30	
Gilberg H.	2			Trailer	1	
Hall G.W.	29	1		Ward R.	30	
Hitchens	26			Whatley W.	5	
Hooper P.	16			White R.	24	2
Howe L.	4	1		Williams*	3	
Joliffe	1			Woodward	1	

* Guest

London League 1941–42

1	Arsenal	30	23	2	5	108:43	48
2	Portsmouth	30	20	2	8	105:59	42
3	West Ham	30	17	5	8	81:44	39
4	Aldershot	30	17	5	8	85:56	39
5	**TOTTENHAM**	**30**	**15**	**8**	**7**	**61:41**	**38**
6	C. Palace	30	14	6	10	70:53	34
7	Reading	30	13	8	9	76:58	34
8	Charlton	30	14	5	11	72:64	33
9	Brentford	30	14	2	14	80:76	30
10	QPR	30	11	3	16	52:59	25
11	Fulham	30	10	4	16	79:99	24
12	Brighton	30	9	4	17	71:108	22
13	Chelsea	30	8	4	18	56:88	20
14	Millwall	30	7	5	18	53:82	19
15	C. Orient	30	5	7	18	42:94	17
16	Watford	30	6	4	20	47:114	16

SEASON 1942/43

Date	Comp		Opponent	Res	Score		Date	Comp		Opponent	Res	Score
29 Aug	Lge	H	C. Palace	L	1-3		9 Jan	Lge	A	Aldershot	W	3-1
5 Sep	Lge	A	QPR	W	1-0		16 Jan	Lge	A	Millwall	W	3-0
12 Sep	Lge	H	Charlton	W	6-1		23 Jan	Lge	H	Reading	D	2-2
19 Sep	Lge	A	West Ham	L	1-3		30 Jan	Lge	H	Portsmouth	W	5-2
26 Sep	Lge	H	Southampton	D	1-1		6 Feb	Lge	A	Chelsea	W	1-0
3 Oct	Lge	H	Aldershot	W	4-0		13 Feb	Lge	A	Arsenal	L	0-1
10 Oct	Lge	H	Millwall	W	2-1		20 Feb	Lge	H	Luton	W	4-1
17 Oct	Lge	A	Reading	W	6-2		27 Feb	Lge	A	Watford	W	3-0
24 Oct	Lge	A	Portsmouth	L	0-1		6 Mar	CUP	H	Chelsea	W	2-0
31 Oct	Lge	H	Chelsea	D	1-1		13 Mar	CUP	A	Reading	D	1-1
7 Nov	Lge	H	Arsenal	W	1-0		20 Mar	CUP	H	Millwall	W	5-0
14 Nov	Lge	A	Luton	D	3-3		27 Mar	CUP	A	Chelsea	W	2-0
21 Nov	Lge	H	Watford	W	6-0		3 Apr	CUP	H	Reading	L	1-2
28 Nov	Lge	A	C. Palace	D	0-0		10 Apr	CUP	A	Millwall	W	1-0
5 Dec	Lge	H	QPR	W	6-0		17 Apr	F	A	QPR	D	1-1
12 Dec	Lge	A	Charlton	W	3-0		24 Apr	F	H	Charlton	W	2-1
19 Dec	Lge	H	West Ham	W	2-0		26 Apr	F	H	Fulham	W	3-0
25 Dec	Lge	H	Brentford	D	1-1		1 May	F	H	C. Orient	W	4-3
26 Dec	Lge	A	Brentford	L	1-2		8 May	F	H	Arsenal	L	1-2
2 Jan	Lge	A	Southampton	L	1-2							

Player	War Lg App	Goals	Player	War Lg App	Goals
Barron	1		Hares*	1	
Beasley*	21	10	Hooper P.	16	
Bennett L.	1		Howe L.	16	
Briggs*	2		Jackson*	2	
Broadis I.	9	2	Ludford G.	23	15
Browne	3		Marshall*	1	
Burgess R.	4		Martin*	19	6
Chapman*	1		McCormick J.*	2	
Chisholm	28		Muir	1	
Cox F.	3	2	Nicholson W.	1	
Ditchburn E.	9		O'Callaghan E.	6	2
Dix R.	1		Pattison*	12	3
Duncan A.	1		Sainsbury	1	
Eastham*	1		Sargent	1	1
Edwards R.	3	1	Sperrin W.	3	2
Finlay	3		Staley*	1	
Gibbons A.	23	17	Ward R.	26	1
Gurr	1		Whatley W.	11	
Hall G.W.	25	6	White R.	25	

* Guest

Football League South 1942–43

1	Arsenal	28	21	1	6	102:40	43
2	TOTTENHAM	28	16	6	6	68:28	38
3	QPR	28	18	2	8	64:49	38
4	Portsmouth	28	16	3	9	66:52	35
5	Southampton	28	14	5	9	86:58	33
6	West Ham	28	14	5	9	80:66	33
7	Chelsea	28	14	4	10	52:45	32
8	Aldershot	28	14	2	12	87:77	30
9	Brentford	28	12	5	11	64:63	29
10	Charlton	28	13	3	12	68:75	29
11	C. Orient	28	11	5	12	54:72	27
12	Brighton	28	10	5	13	64:72	25
13	Reading	28	9	6	13	67:74	24
14	Fulham	28	10	2	16	69:78	22
15	C. Palace	28	7	5	16	49:75	19
16	Millwall	28	6	5	17	66:88	17
17	Watford	28	7	2	19	51:88	16
18	Luton	28	4	6	18	48:100	14

SEASON 1943/44

Date	Comp		Opponent	Res	Score		Date	Comp		Opponent	Res	Score
28 Aug	Lge	H	C. Palace	D	1-1		1 Jan	Lge	H	West Ham	W	1-0
4 Sep	Lge	A	QPR	L	0-1		8 Jan	Lge	H	Brentford	W	1-0
11 Sep	Lge	H	Charlton	W	4-2		15 Jan	Lge	A	Southampton	W	3-2
18 Sep	Lge	A	West Ham	D	3-3		22 Jan	Lge	A	Aldershot	W	1-0
25 Sep	Lge	H	Southampton	D	2-2		29 Jan	Lge	A	Brighton	W	2-0
2 Oct	Lge	H	Aldershot	W	5-2		5 Feb	Lge	H	Reading	D	2-2
9 Oct	Lge	H	Brighton	W	2-0		12 Feb	Lge	H	Luton	W	8-1
16 Oct	Lge	A	Reading	W	3-2		19 Feb	CUP	*	Millwall	W	1-0
23 Oct	Lge	A	Luton	L	2-4		26 Feb	CUP	H	Portsmouth	W	1-0
30 Oct	Lge	H	Chelsea	W	5-1		4 Mar	CUP	A	Aldershot	L	1-2
6 Nov	Lge	A	Brentford	W	2-0		11 Mar	CUP	H	Millwall	W	1-0
13 Nov	Lge	A	C. Orient	W	4-0		18 Mar	CUP	A	Portsmouth	W	2-1
20 Nov	Lge	H	Watford	W	4-2		25 Mar	CUP	H	Aldershot	W	2-0
27 Nov	Lge	A	C. Palace	L	0-3		1 Apr	CUPsf	†	Charlton	L	0-3
4 Dec	Lge	H	QPR	D	2-2		8 Apr	Lge	A	Chelsea	D	1-1
11 Dec	Lge	A	Charlton	W	2-0		10 Apr	F	A	Millwall	D	0-0
18 Dec	Lge	H	Arsenal	W	2-1		22 Apr	Lge	H	Arsenal	D	3-3
25 Dec	Lge	H	Fulham	W	2-0		29 Apr	Lge	H	C. Orient	W	1-0
27 Dec	Lge	A	Fulham	W	2-0		6 May	Lge	A	Watford	D	1-1

* Played at Selhurst Park
† Played at Stamford Bridge

Player	War Lg App	Goals	Player	War Lg App	Goals
Adams	4		Howe L.	5	1
Beasley	28	11	Jones*	16	7
Bennett L.	1	1	Ludford G.	13	1
Briggs*	1		Manley*	1	
Browne	2		Martin*	14	3
Bryant	3	1	Mogford*	4	
Buckingham V.	6		Mosley	3	1
Burgess R.	19	7	O'Callaghan E.	2	
Chisholm	24		O'Donnell*	11	7
Clayton*	2	1	Page	2	
Cox F.	9	1	Rowley*	18	19
Davie*	1		Sainsbury	1	
Ditchburn E.	21		Smith T.*	2	1
Dix R.	2		Walters	9	4
Downer*	1		Ward R.	30	1
Edwards R.	2		Whatley W.	21	
Flack*	2		Whent	2	1
Gibbins	1		White R.	22	1
Gilberg H.	1		Willis	6	
Hall G.W.	6		Wilson*	1	
Harris*	1		Young*	2	
Hooper P.	8		Own Goals		2

* Guest

Football League South 1943–44

1	TOTTENHAM	30	19	8	3	71:36	46
2	West Ham	30	17	7	6	76:39	41
3	QPR	30	14	12	4	69:54	40
4	Arsenal	30	14	10	6	72:42	38
5	C. Palace	30	16	5	9	75:53	37
6	Portsmouth	30	16	5	9	68:59	37
7	Brentford	30	14	7	9	71:51	35
8	Chelsea	30	16	2	12	79:55	34
9	Fulham	30	11	9	10	80:73	31
10	Millwall	30	13	4	13	70:66	30
11	Aldershot	30	12	6	12	64:73	30
12	Reading	30	12	3	15	73:62	27
13	Southampton	30	10	7	13	67:88	27
14	Charlton	30	9	7	14	57:73	25
15	Watford	30	6	8	16	58:80	20
16	Brighton	30	9	2	19	55:82	20
17	C. Orient	30	4	3	23	32:87	11
18	Luton	30	3	5	22	42:104	11

SEASON 1944/45

Date	Comp	V	Opponent	Res	Score		Date	Comp	V	Opponent	Res	Score
19 Aug	F	A	Coventry	L	1-3		30 Dec	Lge	A	Portsmouth	D	0-0
26 Aug	Lge	H	West Ham	D	2-2		6 Jan	Lge	H	Southampton	W	4-0
2 Sep	Lge	H	Arsenal	W	4-0		13 Jan	Lge	A	Charlton	W	2-1
9 Sep	Lge	A	Reading	D	0-0		20 Jan	Lge	H	C. Palace	W	3-1
16 Sep	Lge	H	Portsmouth	D	1-1		27 Jan	Lge	A	Chelsea	W	2-1
23 Sep	Lge	A	Southampton	W	3-1		3 Feb	CUP	H	QPR	D	1-1
30 Sep	Lge	H	Charlton	W	2-1		10 Feb	CUP	A	West Ham	L	0-1
7 Oct	Lge	A	C. Palace	W	3-1		17 Feb	CUP	H	Aldershot	W	6-1
14 Oct	Lge	H	Chelsea	L	1-5		24 Feb	CUP	A	QPR	L	0-1
21 Oct	Lge	A	Luton	W	9-1		3 Mar	CUP	H	West Ham	W	4-0
28 Oct	Lge	H	Brentford	D	2-2		10 Mar	CUP	A	Aldershot	W	2-0
4 Nov	Lge	H	Aldershot	W	7-0		24 Mar	Lge	A	Brentford	W	2-0
11 Nov	Lge	A	Millwall	W	4-3		1 Apr	Lge	A	Aldershot	W	2-1
18 Nov	Lge	A	C. Orient	W	2-0		7 Apr	F	A	C. Palace	L	1-3
25 Nov	Lge	H	Fulham	W	2-1		14 Apr	Lge	H	Millwall	W	4-0
2 Dec	Lge	A	West Ham	W	1-0		21 Apr	Lge	H	C. Orient	W	4-0
9 Dec	Lge	A	Arsenal	W	3-2		28 Apr	Lge	A	Fulham	W	4-2
16 Dec	Lge	H	Reading	W	3-2		5 May	Lge	H	Luton	W	1-0
23 Dec	Lge	A	QPR	D	0-0		19 May	F	H	Arsenal	W	4-0
25 Dec	Lge	H	QPR	W	4-2		26 May	F	H	Fulham	D	2-2

Player	War Lg App	Goals		Player	War Lg App	Goals
Adams	4			Jackson*	2	
Anderson*	1			Ludford G.	12	5
Beasley*	24	9		Martin*	1	
Boulton*	1			Medley L.	7	1
Broadis	6	2		Mogford	3	
Brown*	3			Muir*	1	
Burgess R.	23	10		Oakes*	1	
Burke*	10			O'Donnell*	2	1
Burnett*	1	2		Page	3	
Chisholm	6			Pryde*	1	
Dix	1			Rowley*	2	2
Duke*	2			Smith K.*	1	
Dunn*	1			Stevens	11	5
Flavell*	11			Swift	1	
Foreman*	5	8		Wallis	4	
Gibbons A.	11	10		Walters	30	8
Gilberg H.	8	6		Ward R.	30	5
Goodman	1			Whatley W.	1	
Hall A.E.	5	2		White R.	24	
Hall F.*	14			Whittingham*	1	1
Henley*	1	1		Willis	27	
Howe L.	5	1		Own Goals		2
Hughes*	21					

* Guest

Football League South 1944–45

1	TOTTENHAM	30	23	6	1	81:30	52
2	West Ham	30	22	3	5	96:47	47
3	Brentford	30	17	4	9	87:57	38
4	Chelsea	30	16	5	9	100:55	37
5	Southampton	30	17	3	10	96:69	37
6	C. Palace	30	15	5	10	74:70	35
7	Reading	30	14	6	10	78:68	34
8	Arsenal	30	14	3	13	77:67	31
9	QPR	30	10	10	10	70:61	30
10	Watford	30	11	6	13	66:84	28
11	Fulham	30	11	4	15	79:83	26
12	Portsmouth	30	11	4	15	56:61	26
13	Charlton	30	12	2	16	72:81	26
14	Brighton	30	10	2	18	66:95	22
15	Luton	30	6	7	17	56:104	19
16	Aldershot	30	7	4	19	44:85	18
17	Millwall	30	5	7	18	50:84	17
18	Clapton O.	30	5	7	18	39:86	17

SEASON 1945/46

Date	Comp	V	Opponent	Res	Score		Date	Comp	V	Opponent	Res	Score
25 Aug	Lge	H	Wolves	L	1-4		10 Jan	FC	A	Brentford	L	0-2*
1 Sep	Lge	A	Wolves	L	2-4		12 Jan	Lge	A	Luton	L	1-3
8 Sep	Lge	A	West Ham	D	1-1		19 Jan	Lge	H	Luton	L	2-3
12 Sep	Lge	H	Leicester	W	6-2		26 Jan	Lge	H	Coventry	W	2-0
15 Sep	Lge	H	West Ham	L	2-3		2 Feb	Lge	A	Aston Villa	L	1-5
22 Sep	Lge	A	West Brom	L	0-5		9 Feb	Lge	A	Arsenal	D	1-1
29 Sep	Lge	H	West Brom	W	4-2		16 Feb	Lge	H	Arsenal	W	3-0
6 Oct	Lge	A	Birmingham C.	L	0-8		23 Feb	Lge	H	Charlton	W	2-1
13 Oct	Lge	H	Birmingham C.	L	0-1		2 Mar	F	H	Chelsea	W	4-2
20 Oct	Lge	A	Swansea	L	2-4		9 Mar	Lge	A	Fulham	D	1-1
27 Oct	Lge	A	Swansea	W	3-1		16 Mar	Lge	H	Fulham	L	1-3
3 Nov	Lge	H	Brentford	W	1-0		23 Mar	Lge	H	Plymouth	W	2-0
10 Nov	Lge	A	Brentford	W	3-1		30 Mar	Lge	A	Plymouth	W	1-0
17 Nov	Lge	A	Chelsea	W	2-1		6 Apr	Lge	A	Portsmouth	W	1-0
24 Nov	Lge	H	Chelsea	W	3-2		13 Apr	Lge	H	Portsmouth	W	2-0
1 Dec	Lge	H	Millwall	W	5-1		17 Apr	Lge	A	Charlton	L	0-1
8 Dec	Lge	A	Millwall	L	2-3		19 Apr	Lge	H	Nottm Forest	W	3-2
15 Dec	Lge	A	Southampton	L	2-3		20 Apr	Lge	A	Newport	W	4-1
22 Dec	Lge	H	Southampton	W	4-3		22 Apr	Lge	A	Nottm Forest	W	2-0
25 Dec	Lge	H	Derby	L	2-5		27 Apr	Lge	H	Newport	W	1-0
26 Dec	Lge	A	Derby	L	0-2		4 May	Lge	A	Coventry	W	1-0
29 Dec	Lge	A	Leicester	L	0-4		7 May	F	H	FA XI	W	4-1†
5 Jan	FC	H	Brentford	D	2-2							

* Second leg, not a replay   † Willie Hall testimonial

Player	War Lg App	Goals		Player	War Lg App	Goals
Acquroff J.*	2	2		Howe L.	1	
Adams	1			Howshall*	1	
Baily E.	1			Hughes W.	27	
Beasley	2			Jinks J.*	1	2
Bennett L.	11			Joslin*	4	
Blair J.	2	1		Ludford G.	30	3
Broadis I.	9	5		Lyman G.	21	7
Buckingham V.	19			McCormick J.	3	1
Burgess R.	37	7		Medley L.	17	3
Chisholm	1			Morrison J.	1	
Cox F.	1			Nicholson W.	11	
Ditchburn E.	2			Page	16	
Dix R.	26	4		Rundle C.	4	
Duquemin L.	1			Sargent	2	
Ferrier*	1			Skinner G.	11	2
Fletcher	1			Smith*	4	
Ford*	3			Stevens L.	13	1
Foreman G.	10	13		Walters W.	2	
Garwood L.	1			Ward R.	26	4
Gibbons A.	21	14		Whitchurch C.	17	4
Gilberg H.	1			White A.	1	
Hall A.E.	24	5		White R.	24	
Hall F.	6			Willis A.	32	
Hall J.	9			Young*	1	

* Guest

Football League South 1945–46

1	Birmingham	42	28	5	9	96:45	61
2	Aston Villa	42	25	11	6	106:58	61
3	Charlton	42	25	10	7	92:45	60
4	Derby	42	24	7	11	101:62	55
5	WBA	42	22	8	12	104:69	52
6	Wolves	42	20	11	11	75:48	51
7	West Ham	42	20	11	11	94:76	51
8	Fulham	42	20	10	12	93:73	50
9	TOTTENHAM	42	22	3	17	78:81	47
10	Chelsea	42	19	6	17	92:80	44
11	Arsenal	42	16	11	15	76:73	43
12	Millwall	42	17	8	17	79:105	42
13	Coventry	42	15	10	17	70:69	40
14	Brentford	42	14	10	18	82:72	38
15	Nottingham F.	42	12	13	17	72:73	37
16	Southampton	42	14	9	19	97:105	37
17	Swansea	42	15	7	20	90:112	37
18	Luton	42	13	7	22	60:92	33
19	Portsmouth	42	11	6	25	66:87	28
20	Leicester	42	8	7	24	57:101	23
21	Newport	42	9	2	31	52:125	20
22	Plymouth	42	3	8	31	39:120	14

SEASON 1946/47

Date	Comp	H/A	Opponent	Result			Date	Comp	H/A	Opponent	Result	
31 Aug	Lge	H	Birmingham	L	1-2		11 Jan	FC	H	Stoke	D	2-2
7 Sep	Lge	A	WBA	L	2-3		15 Jan	FCr	A	Stoke	L	0-1
9 Sep	Lge	H	Southampton	W	2-1		18 Jan	Lge	A	Newcastle	L	0-1
14 Sep	Lge	H	Newcastle	D	1-1		25 Jan	F	H	Arsenal	W	2-0
19 Sep	Lge	A	Newport	W	4-2		27 Jan	Lge	A	Swansea	W	3-1
21 Sep	Lge	A	Swansea	W	2-0		1 Feb	Lge	A	Man City	L	0-1
28 Sep	Lge	H	Man City	D	0-0		18 Feb	Lge	A	Burnley	D	0-0
5 Oct	Lge	H	Burnley	D	1-1		1 Mar	Lge	A	Sheff Wed	L	1-5
7 Oct	Lge	H	Newport	W	3-1		8 Mar	Lge	H	Fulham	D	1-1
12 Oct	Lge	A	Barnsley	W	3-1		22 Mar	Lge	H	Luton	W	2-1
19 Oct	Lge	A	West Ham	D	2-2		29 Mar	Lge	A	Plymouth	W	4-3
26 Oct	Lge	H	Sheff Wed	W	2-0		4 Apr	Lge	H	Nottm Forest	W	2-0
31 Oct	F	A	Oxford Univ	W	2-0		5 Apr	Lge	H	Leicester	W	2-1
2 Nov	Lge	A	Fulham	D	1-1		7 Apr	Lge	A	Nottm Forest	D	1-1
9 Nov	Lge	H	Bury	W	2-1		12 Apr	Lge	A	Chesterfield	D	0-0
16 Nov	Lge	A	Luton	L	2-3		19 Apr	Lge	H	Millwall	W	2-1
20 Nov	F	A	Camb Univ	L	3-4		26 Apr	Lge	A	Bradford PA	L	1-2
23 Nov	Lge	H	Plymouth	W	2-1		3 May	Lge	A	Bury	W	2-1
30 Nov	Lge	A	Leicester	D	1-1		10 May	Lge	A	Southampton	L	0-1
7 Dec	Lge	H	Chesterfield	L	3-4		12 May	F	A	Norwich	W	2-0
14 Dec	Lge	A	Millwall	W	3-0		17 May	Lge	H	West Ham	D	0-0
21 Dec	Lge	H	Bradford PA	D	3-3		7 Jun	Lge	H	Barnsley	D	1-1
25 Dec	Lge	A	Coventry	L	1-3		13 Jun	F	A	Marseille	L	1-2
26 Dec	Lge	H	Coventry	D	0-0		15 Jun	F	A	Toulouse	L	1-2
28 Dec	Lge	A	Birmingham	L	0-1		19 Jun	F	A	Montpelier	W	1-0
4 Jan	Lge	H	WBA	W	2-0		21 Jun	F	A	St Etienne	W	2-0

Player	Lg App	Goals		Player	Lg App	Goals
Baily E.F.	1			Medley L.D.	10	4
Bennett L.D.	38	14		Nicholson W.E.	39	
Buckingham V.F.	27			Rundle C.R.	18	10
Burgess W.A.R.	40	5		Skinner G.	1	
Cox F.J.A.	25	5		Stevens L.W.J.	30	1
Ditchburn E.G.	41			Ludford G.A.	41	2
Dix R.W.	31	5		Tickeridge S.	14	
Foreman G.A.	36	15		Trailor C.H.	1	
Gilberg H.	1			Walters W.E.	1	1
Hall A.E.	8			Whitchurch C.H.	8	2
Hughes W.A.	1			Willis A.	37	
Jones W.E.A.	1			Woodward H.J.	11	
Joseph L.	1			Own Goal		1

Final table for Second Division

1	Manchester C.	42	26	10	6	78:35	62
2	Burnley	42	22	14	6	65:29	58
3	Birmingham	42	25	5	12	74:33	55
4	Chesterfield	42	18	14	10	58:44	50
5	Newcastle	42	19	10	13	95:62	48
6	**TOTTENHAM**	**42**	**17**	**14**	**11**	**65:53**	**48**
7	West Bromwich	42	20	8	14	88:75	48
8	Coventry	42	16	13	13	66:59	45
9	Leicester	42	18	7	17	69:64	43
10	Barnsley	42	17	8	17	84:86	42
11	Nottingham F.	42	15	10	17	69:74	40
12	West Ham	42	16	8	18	70:76	40
13	Luton	42	16	7	19	71:73	39
14	Southampton	42	15	9	18	69:76	39
15	Fulham	42	15	9	18	63:74	39
16	Bradford PA	42	14	11	17	65:77	39
17	Bury	42	12	12	18	80:78	36
18	Millwall	42	14	8	20	56:79	36
19	Plymouth	42	14	5	23	79:96	33
20	Sheffield W.	42	12	8	22	67:88	32
21	Swansea	42	11	7	24	55:83	29
22	Newport	42	10	3	29	61:133	23

SEASON 1947/48

Date	Comp	H/A	Opponent	Result			Date	Comp	H/A	Opponent	Result	
23 Aug	Lge	A	WBA	L	0-1		3 Jan	Lge	A	Sheff Wed	L	0-1
27 Aug	Lge	A	Bury	L	0-2		10 Jan	FC	A	Bolton	W	2-0
30 Aug	Lge	H	Sheff Wed	W	5-1		17 Jan	Lge	H	Cardiff	W	2-1
1 Sep	Lge	H	Bury	D	2-2		24 Jan	FC	H	WBA	W	3-1
6 Sep	Lge	A	Cardiff	W	3-0		31 Jan	Lge	A	Bradford	W	2-1
8 Sep	Lge	A	West Ham	D	1-1		7 Feb	FC	H	Leicester	W	5-2
13 Sep	Lge	H	Bradford PA	W	3-1		14 Feb	Lge	A	Doncaster	D	1-1
15 Sep	Lge	H	West Ham	D	2-2		21 Feb	Lge	H	Southampton	D	0-0
20 Sep	Lge	A	Nottm Forest	L	0-1		28 Feb	FC	A	Southampton	W	1-0
27 Sep	Lge	H	Doncaster	W	2-0		6 Mar	Lge	A	Plymouth	D	1-1
4 Oct	Lge	A	Southampton	D	1-1		13 Mar	FCsf	*	Blackpool	L	1-3
11 Oct	Lge	A	Barnsley	L	1-2		15 Mar	Lge	A	Barnsley	L	0-3
18 Oct	Lge	H	Plymouth	W	2-0		20 Mar	Lge	A	Brentford	L	0-2
25 Oct	Lge	A	Luton	D	0-0		26 Mar	Lge	A	Millwall	D	0-0
30 Oct	F	A	Oxford Univ	W	4-1		27 Mar	Lge	H	Leicester	D	0-0
1 Nov	Lge	A	Brentford	W	4-0		29 Mar	Lge	H	Millwall	W	3-2
8 Nov	Lge	A	Leicester	W	3-0		3 Apr	Lge	A	Leeds	W	3-1
15 Nov	Lge	H	Leeds	W	3-1		5 Apr	Lge	H	Luton	L	0-1
22 Nov	Lge	A	Fulham	W	2-0		10 Apr	Lge	H	Fulham	L	0-2
29 Nov	Lge	H	Coventry	W	2-1		12 Apr	Lge	H	Nottm Forest	L	0-3
6 Dec	Lge	A	Newcastle	L	0-1		17 Apr	Lge	A	Coventry	D	1-1
13 Dec	Lge	A	Birmingham	L	1-2		24 Apr	Lge	H	Newcastle	D	1-1
20 Dec	Lge	H	WBA	D	1-1		1 May	Lge	A	Birmingham	D	0-0
25 Dec	Lge	H	Chesterfield	W	3-0		12 May	F	A	Jersey	W	3-0
27 Dec	Lge	A	Chesterfield	L	1-3		15 May	F	A	Guernsey	W	7-0

* Semi-final played at Villa Park

Player	Lg App	Goals		Player	Lg App	Goals
Baily E.F.	22	5		Jordan J.W.	23	10
Bennett L.D.	36	8		Ludford G.A.	8	
Buckingham V.F.	42			Medley L.D.	2	
Burgess W.A.R.	31	2		Nicholson W.E.	38	
Chisholm J.R.	2			Rundle C.R.	6	1
Cox F.J.A.	34	4		Stevens L.W.J.	22	4
Ditchburn E.G.	41			Tickridge S.	39	
Dix R.W.	5			Trailor C.H.	9	
Duquemin L.S.	36	16		Walters W.E.	1	
Flint K.	5	1		Willis A.	3	
Gilberg H.	1			Withers C.F.	1	
Hughes W.A.	1			Woodward H.J.	35	1
Jones W.E.A.	19	3		Own Goal		1

Final table for Second Division

1	Birmingham	42	22	15	5	55:24	59
2	Newcastle	42	24	8	10	72:41	56
3	Southampton	42	21	10	11	71:53	52
4	Sheffield W.	42	20	11	11	66:53	51
5	Cardiff	42	18	11	13	61:58	47
6	West Ham	42	16	14	12	55:53	46
7	West Bromwich	42	18	9	15	63:58	45
8	**TOTTENHAM**	**42**	**15**	**14**	**13**	**56:43**	**44**
9	Leicester	42	16	11	15	60:57	43
10	Coventry	42	14	13	15	59:52	41
11	Fulham	42	15	10	17	47:46	40
12	Barnsley	42	15	10	17	62:64	40
13	Luton	42	14	12	16	56:59	40
14	Bradford PA	42	16	8	18	68:72	40
15	Brentford	42	13	14	15	44:61	40
16	Chesterfield	42	16	7	19	54:55	39
17	Plymouth	42	9	20	13	40:58	38
18	Leeds	42	14	8	20	62:72	36
19	Nottingham F.	42	12	11	19	54:60	35
20	Bury	42	9	16	17	58:68	34
21	Doncaster	42	9	11	22	40:66	29
22	Millwall	42	9	11	22	44:74	29

Date	Comp	H/A	Opponent	Result	Score		Date	Comp	H/A	Opponent	Result	Score
21 Aug	Lge	H	Sheff Wed	W	3-2		27 Dec	Lge	H	Leicester	D	1-1
23 Aug	Lge	A	Coventry	L	0-2		1 Jan	Lge	H	Lincoln	L	1-2
28 Aug	Lge	A	Lincoln	D	0-0		8 Jan	FC	A	Arsenal	L	0-3
30 Aug	Lge	H	Coventry	W	4-0		15 Jan	Lge	A	Chesterfield	L	0-1
4 Sep	Lge	H	Chesterfield	W	4-0		22 Jan	Lge	H	WBA	W	2-0
8 Sep	Lge	A	Leeds	D	0-0		29 Jan	F	A	Middlesbrough	W	4-1
11 Sep	Lge	A	WBA	D	2-2		5 Feb	Lge	A	Bury	D	1-1
13 Sep	Lge	H	Leeds	D	2-2		12 Feb	Lge	H	Nottm Forest	W	2-1
18 Sep	Lge	H	Bury	W	3-1		19 Feb	Lge	H	West Ham	D	1-1
20 Sep	F	A	Chelmsford	W	5-1		26 Feb	Lge	A	Blackburn	D	1-1
25 Sep	Lge	A	West Ham	L	0-1		5 Mar	Lge	H	Cardiff	L	0-1
2 Oct	Lge	H	Blackburn	W	4-0		12 Mar	Lge	A	QPR	D	0-0
9 Oct	Lge	A	Cardiff	W	1-0		19 Mar	Lge	H	Luton	W	2-1
16 Oct	Lge	H	QPR	W	1-0		26 Mar	Lge	A	Bradford PA	D	1-1
23 Oct	Lge	A	Luton	D	1-1		2 Apr	Lge	H	Southampton	L	0-1
28 Oct	F	A	Oxford Univ	W	7-0		9 Apr	Lge	A	Barnsley	L	1-4
30 Oct	Lge	H	Bradford PA	W	5-1		15 Apr	Lge	H	Brentford	W	2-0
6 Nov	Lge	A	Southampton	L	1-3		16 Apr	Lge	H	Grimsby	W	5-2
13 Nov	Lge	H	Barnsley	W	4-1		18 Apr	Lge	A	Brentford	D	1-1
20 Nov	Lge	A	Grimsby	D	1-1		23 Apr	Lge	A	Nottm Forest	D	2-2
25 Nov	F	A	Camb Univ	W	4-1		25 Apr	F	H	Hibernian	L	2-5
4 Dec	Lge	A	Fulham	D	1-1		30 Apr	Lge	H	Fulham	D	1-1
11 Dec	Lge	H	Plymouth	W	3-0		7 May	Lge	A	Plymouth	W	5-0
18 Dec	Lge	A	Sheff Wed	L	1-3		9 May	F	A	Crnwall Co XI	W	2-0
25 Dec	Lge	A	Leicester	W	2-1							

Player	Lg App	Goals		Player	Lg App	Goals
Baily E.F.	41	11		Medley L.D.	6	3
Bennett L.D.	42	19		Nicholson W.E.	41	2
Buckingham V.F.	25			Rundle C.R.	4	1
Burgess W.A.R.	40	3		Stevens L.W.J.	2	
Clarke H.A.	10			Tickridge S.	41	
Cox F.J.A.	31	4		Toulouse C.H.	2	
Ditchburn E.G.	42			Walters W.E.	12	1
Duquemin L.S.	37	15		Willis A.	10	
Garwood L.F.	2			Withers C.F.	12	
Jones W.E.A.	35	12		Woodward H.J.	17	
Ludford G.A.	10			Own Goal		1

Final table for Second Division

1	Fulham	42	24	9	9	77:37 57
2	West Bromwich	42	24	8	10	69:39 56
3	Southampton	42	23	9	10	69:36 55
4	Cardiff	42	19	13	10	62:47 51
5	**TOTTENHAM**	42	17	16	9	72:44 50
6	Chesterfield	42	15	17	10	51:45 47
7	West Ham	42	18	10	14	56:58 46
8	Sheffield W.	42	15	13	14	63:56 43
9	Barnsley	42	14	12	16	62:61 40
10	Luton	42	14	12	16	55:57 40
11	Grimsby	42	15	10	17	72:76 40
12	Bury	42	17	6	19	67:76 40
13	QPR	42	14	11	17	44:62 39
14	Blackburn	42	15	8	19	53:63 38
15	Leeds	42	12	13	17	55:63 37
16	Coventry	42	15	7	20	55:64 37
17	Bradford PA	42	13	11	18	65:78 37
18	Brentford	42	11	14	17	42:53 36
19	Leicester	42	10	16	16	62:79 36
20	Plymouth	42	12	12	18	49:64 36
21	Nottingham F.	42	14	7	21	50:54 35
22	Lincoln	42	8	12	22	53:91 28

Date	Comp	H/A	Opponent	Result	Score		Date	Comp	H/A	Opponent	Result	Score
20 Aug	Lge	A	Brentford	W	4-1		21 Jan	Lge	A	Bury	W	2-1
22 Aug	Lge	H	Plymouth	W	4-1		28 Jan	FC	H	Sunderland	W	5-1
27 Aug	Lge	H	Blackburn	L	2-3		4 Feb	Lge	H	Leicester	L	0-2
31 Aug	Lge	A	Plymouth	W	2-0		11 Feb	FC	A	Everton	L	0-1
3 Sep	Lge	A	Cardiff	W	1-0		18 Feb	Lge	A	Bradford	W	3-1
5 Sep	Lge	H	Sheff Wed	W	1-0		25 Feb	Lge	H	Southampton	W	4-0
10 Sep	Lge	H	Leeds	W	2-0		4 Mar	Lge	A	Coventry	W	1-0
17 Sep	Lge	H	Bury	W	3-1		11 Mar	Lge	A	Luton	W	2-0
24 Sep	Lge	A	Leicester	W	2-1		18 Mar	Lge	A	Barnsley	L	0-2
1 Oct	Lge	H	Bradford	W	5-0		25 Mar	Lge	H	West Ham	W	4-1
8 Oct	Lge	A	Southampton	D	1-1		1 Apr	Lge	A	QPR	W	2-0
15 Oct	Lge	H	Coventry	W	3-1		7 Apr	Lge	H	Hull	D	0-0
22 Oct	Lge	A	Luton	D	1-1		8 Apr	Lge	H	Preston	W	3-2
27 Oct	F	A	Camb Univ	L	2-3		10 Apr	Lge	A	Hull	L	0-1
29 Oct	Lge	H	Barnsley	W	2-0		15 Apr	Lge	A	Sheff Utd	L	1-2
5 Nov	Lge	A	West Ham	W	1-0		22 Apr	Lge	H	Grimsby	L	1-2
10 Nov	F	A	Oxford Univ	W	3-1		24 Apr	F	A	Chelmsford	W	4-1
12 Nov	Lge	H	Sheff Utd	W	7-0		29 Apr	Lge	A	Swansea	L	0-1
19 Nov	Lge	A	Grimsby	W	3-2		1 May	F	H	Hibernian	L	0-1
26 Nov	Lge	H	QPR	W	3-0		6 May	Lge	A	Sheff Wed	D	0-0
3 Dec	Lge	A	Preston	W	3-1		8 May	F	A	Norwich	D	2-2
10 Dec	Lge	A	Swansea	W	3-1		14 May	F	A	Hanover	W	3-0
17 Dec	Lge	H	Brentford	D	1-1		18 May	F	A	Tennis-Borussia	W	2-0
24 Dec	Lge	A	Blackburn	W	2-1		21 May	F	A	Wacker Innsbruck	W	5-2
26 Dec	Lge	H	Chesterfield	W	1-0		24 May	F	A	Borussia-Dortmund	W	4-0
27 Dec	Lge	A	Chesterfield	D	1-1		27 May	F	A	Ryl Beerschot	L	1-2
31 Dec	Lge	H	Cardiff	W	2-0							
7 Jan	FC	A	Stoke	W	1-0							
14 Jan	Lge	A	Leeds	L	0-3							

Player	Lg App	Goals		Player	Lg App	Goals
Baily E.F.	40	8		Medley L.D.	42	18
Bennett L.D.	35	14		Nicholson W.E.	39	2
Burgess W.A.R.	39			Ramsey A.E.	41	4
Clarke H.A.	42			Rees W.	11	3
Cook R.	3			Scarth J.	4	2
Ditchburn E.G.	42			Tickridge S.	1	
Duquemin L.S.	40	16		Walters W.E.	35	14
Ludford G.A.	4			Willis A.	2	
Marchi A.V.	2			Withers C.F.	40	

Final table for Second Division

1	**TOTTENHAM**	42	27	7	8	81:35 61
2	Sheffield W.	42	18	16	8	67:48 52
3	Sheffield U.	42	19	14	9	68:49 52
4	Southampton	42	19	14	9	64:48 52
5	Leeds	42	17	13	12	54:45 47
6	Preston	42	18	9	15	60:49 45
7	Hull	42	17	11	14	64:72 45
8	Swansea	42	17	9	16	53:49 43
9	Brentford	42	15	13	14	44:49 43
10	Cardiff	42	16	10	16	41:44 42
11	Grimsby	42	16	8	18	74:73 40
12	Coventry	42	13	13	16	55:55 39
13	Barnsley	42	13	13	16	64:67 39
14	Chesterfield	42	15	9	18	43:47 39
15	Leicester	42	12	15	15	55:65 39
16	Blackburn	42	14	10	18	55:60 38
17	Luton	42	10	18	14	41:51 38
18	Bury	42	14	9	19	60:65 37
19	West Ham	42	12	12	18	53:61 36
20	QPR	42	11	12	19	40:57 34
21	Plymouth	42	8	16	18	44:65 32
22	Bradford PA	42	10	11	21	51:77 31

SEASON 1950/51

Date	Comp		Opponent	Result	
19 Aug	Lge	H	Blackpool	L	1-4
23 Aug	Lge	A	Bolton	W	4-1
26 Aug	Lge	A	Arsenal	D	2-2
28 Aug	Lge	H	Bolton	W	4-2
2 Sep	Lge	A	Charlton	D	1-1
6 Sep	Lge	A	Liverpool	L	1-2
9 Sep	Lge	H	Man Utd	W	1-0
16 Sep	Lge	A	Wolves	L	1-2
18 Sep	F	H	Lovells Ath.	W	8-0
23 Sep	Lge	H	Sunderland	D	1-1
30 Sep	Lge	A	Aston Villa	W	3-2
7 Oct	Lge	H	Burnley	W	1-0
14 Oct	Lge	A	Chelsea	W	2-0
21 Oct	Lge	H	Stoke	W	6-1
28 Oct	Lge	A	WBA	W	2-1
4 Nov	Lge	H	Portsmouth	W	5-1
9 Nov	F	A	Camb Univ	W	2-1*
9 Nov	F	A	Oxford Univ	D	1-1*
11 Nov	Lge	A	Everton	W	2-1
18 Nov	Lge	H	Newcastle	W	7-0
25 Nov	Lge	A	Huddersfield	L	2-3
2 Dec	Lge	H	Middlesbro	D	3-3
9 Dec	Lge	A	Sheff Wed	D	1-1
16 Dec	Lge	A	Blackpool	W	1-0
23 Dec	Lge	H	Arsenal	W	1-0
25 Dec	Lge	A	Derby	D	1-1
26 Dec	Lge	H	Derby	W	2-1
30 Dec	Lge	H	Charlton	W	1-0
6 Jan	FC	A	Huddersfield	L	0-2
13 Jan	Lge	A	Man Utd	L	1-2
20 Jan	Lge	H	Wolves	W	2-1
27 Jan	F	A	Cardiff	W	3-2
3 Feb	Lge	A	Sunderland	D	0-0
6 Feb	F	A	Standard Liege	W	4-1
17 Feb	Lge	H	Aston Villa	W	3-2
24 Feb	Lge	A	Burnley	L	0-2
3 Mar	Lge	H	Chelsea	W	2-1
10 Mar	Lge	A	Stoke	D	0-0
17 Mar	Lge	H	WBA	W	5-0
23 Mar	Lge	A	Fulham	W	1-0
24 Mar	Lge	A	Portsmouth	D	1-1
26 Mar	Lge	H	Fulham	W	2-1
31 Mar	Lge	H	Everton	W	3-0
7 Apr	Lge	H	Newcastle	W	1-0
14 Apr	Lge	H	Huddersfield	L	0-2
21 Apr	Lge	A	Middlesbro	D	1-1
23 Apr	F	A	Hibernian	D	0-0
28 Apr	Lge	H	Sheff Wed	D	1-0
30 Apr	F	A	Chelmsford	W	7-3
5 May	Lge	A	Liverpool	W	3-1
7 Mar	F	H	FC Austria	L	0-1
10 May	F	H	Scunthorpe	D	0-0
12 May	F	H	Bor. Dortmund	W	2-1
14 May	F	†	Arsenal	D	0-0
16 May	F	A	Racing Club Paris	W	4-2
29 May	F	A	Danish XI	W	4-2
30 May	F	A	Danish XI	D	2-2
31 May	F	A	Danish XI	W	2-0

* Half first team played at Oxford, half at Cambridge. At the time Oxford were being coached by Vic Buckingham and Cambridge by Bill Nicholson. † Festival of Britain match played at Selhurst P.

Player	Lg App	Goals	Player	Lg App	Goals
Baily E.F.	40	12	Nicholson W.E.	41	1
Brittan C.	8		Ramsey A.E.	40	4
Bennett L.D.	25	7	Scarth J.	1	
Burgess W.A.R.	35	2	Tickridge S.	1	
Clarke H.A.	42		Uphill D.E.	2	1
Ditchburn E.G	42		Walters W.E.	40	15
Duquemin L.S.	33	14	Willis A.	39	
McClellan S.B.	7	3	Withers C.F.	4	
Medley L.D.	35	11	Wright A.M.	2	1
Murphy P.	25	9	Own Goals		2

Final table for First Division

1	TOTTENHAM	42	25	10	7	82:44	60
2	Manchester U.	42	24	8	10	74:40	56
3	Blackpool	42	20	10	12	79:53	50
4	Newcastle	42	18	13	11	62:53	49
5	Arsenal	42	19	9	14	73:56	47
6	Middlesbrough	42	18	11	13	76:65	47
7	Portsmouth	42	16	15	11	71:68	47
8	Bolton	42	19	7	16	64:61	45
9	Liverpool	42	16	11	15	53:59	43
10	Burnley	42	14	14	14	48:43	42
11	Derby	42	16	8	18	81:75	40
12	Sunderland	42	12	16	14	63:73	40
13	Stoke	42	13	14	15	50:59	40
14	Wolverhampton	42	15	8	19	74:61	38
15	Aston Villa	42	12	13	17	66:68	37
16	West Bromwich	42	13	11	18	53:61	37
17	Charlton	42	14	9	19	63:80	37
18	Fulham	42	13	11	18	52:68	37
19	Huddersfield	42	15	6	21	64:92	36
20	Chelsea	42	12	8	22	53:65	32
21	Sheffield W.	42	12	8	22	64:83	32
22	Everton	42	12	8	22	48:86	32

SEASON 1951/52

Date	Comp		Opponent	Result	
18 Aug	Lge	A	Middlesbro'	L	1-2
20 Aug	Lge	H	Fulham	W	1-0
25 Aug	Lge	H	WBA	W	3-1
29 Aug	Lge	A	Fulham	W	2-1
1 Sep	Lge	A	Newcastle	L	2-7
3 Sep	Lge	A	Burnley	D	1-1
8 Sep	Lge	H	Bolton	W	2-1
10 Sep	Lge	H	Burnley	D	1-1
15 Sep	Lge	A	Stoke C.	W	6-1
22 Sep	Lge	H	Man Utd	W	2-0
29 Sep	Lge	A	Arsenal	D	1-1
6 Oct	Lge	H	Man City	L	1-2
10 Oct	F	H	Copenhagen XI	W	2-1
13 Oct	Lge	A	Derby	L	2-4
20 Oct	Lge	A	Aston Villa	W	2-0
27 Oct	Lge	A	Sunderland	W	1-0
3 Nov	Lge	H	Wolves	W	4-2
10 Nov	Lge	A	Huddersfield	D	1-1
17 Nov	Lge	H	Chelsea	W	3-2
24 Nov	Lge	A	Portsmouth	L	0-2
1 Dec	Lge	H	Liverpool	L	2-3
8 Dec	Lge	A	Blackpool	L	0-1
15 Dec	Lge	H	Middlesbro'	W	3-1
22 Dec	Lge	A	WBA	L	1-3
25 Dec	Lge	A	Charlton	W	3-0
26 Dec	Lge	H	Charlton	L	2-3
29 Dec	Lge	H	Newcastle	W	2-1
5 Jan	Lge	A	Bolton	D	1-1
12 Jan	FC	A	Scunthorpe	W	3-0
19 Jan	Lge	H	Stoke	W	2-0
26 Jan	Lge	A	Man Utd	L	0-2
2 Feb	FC	H	Newcastle	L	0-3
9 Feb	Lge	H	Arsenal	L	1-2
16 Feb	Lge	A	Man City	D	1-1
23 Feb	Lge	H	Preston	W	1-0
1 Mar	Lge	H	Derby	W	5-0
8 Mar	Lge	A	Aston Villa	W	3-0
15 Mar	Lge	H	Sunderland	W	2-0
22 Mar	Lge	A	Wolves	D	1-1
26 Mar	F	A	FC Austria	D	2-2
2 Apr	Lge	H	Huddersfield	W	1-0
12 Apr	Lge	H	Portsmouth	W	3-1
14 Apr	Lge	A	Preston	D	1-1
19 Apr	Lge	A	Liverpool	D	1-1
23 Apr	F	H	Hibernian	L	1-2
26 Apr	Lge	H	Blackpool	W	2-0
30 Apr	Lge	A	Chelsea	W	2-0
3 May	F	A	Racing, Paris	W	2-1
5 May	F	A	Ipswich	D	2-2
22 May	F		Toronto	W	7-0*
26 May	F		Saskatchewan	W	18-1*
31 May	F		British Col.	W	9-2*
2 Jun	F		Victoria	W	7-0*
4 Jun	F		British Col.	W	8-2*
7 Jun	F		Alberta	W	11-0*
9 Jun	F		Manitoba	W	5-0*
14 Jun	F		Man Utd	W	5-0*
15 Jun	F		Man Utd	W	7-1*
18 Jun	F		Quebec	W	8-0*

* End of season tour of Canada

Player	Lg App	Goals	Player	Lg App	Goals
Adams C.J.	5	1	Murphy P.	13	5
Baily E.F.	30	4	Nicholson W.E.	37	1
Bennett L.D.	35	19	Ramsey A.E.	38	5
Brittan C.	6		Robb G.W.	1	1
Burgess W.A.R.	40		Robshaw H.K.	1	
Clarke H.A.	33		Scarth J.W.	2	1
Ditchburn E.G.	42		Uphill D.E.	2	
Duquemin L.S.	25	12	Walters W.E.	37	11
Farley B.R.	1		Wetton R.	7	
Harmer T.C.	13	3	Willis A.	17	
King D.A.	2		Withers C.F.	29	
McClellan S.B.	12	3	Own Goals		2
Medley L.D.	34	8			

Final table for First Division

1	Manchester U.	42	23	11	8	95:52	57
2	TOTTENHAM	42	22	9	11	76:51	53
3	Arsenal	42	21	11	10	80:61	53
4	Portsmouth	42	20	8	14	68:58	48
5	Bolton	42	19	10	13	65:61	48
6	Aston Villa	42	19	9	14	79:70	47
7	Preston	42	17	12	13	74:54	46
8	Newcastle	42	18	9	15	98:73	45
9	Blackpool	42	18	9	15	64:64	45
10	Charlton	42	17	10	15	68:63	44
11	Liverpool	42	12	19	11	57:61	43
12	Sunderland	42	15	12	15	70:61	42
13	West Bromwich	42	14	13	15	74:77	41
14	Burnley	42	15	10	17	56:63	40
15	Manchester C.	42	13	13	16	58:61	39
16	Wolverhampton	42	12	14	16	73:73	38
17	Derby	42	15	7	20	63:80	37
18	Middlesbrough	42	15	6	21	64:88	36
19	Chelsea	42	14	8	20	52:72	36
20	Stoke	42	12	7	23	49:88	31
21	Huddersfield	42	10	8	24	49:82	28
22	Fulham	42	8	11	23	58:77	27

SEASON 1952/53

Date	Comp	H/A	Opponent	Result	Score		Date	Comp	H/A	Opponent	Result	Score
23 Aug	Lge	H	WBA	L	3-4		24 Jan	Lge	H	Sheff Wed	W	2-1
27 Aug	Lge	A	Man City	W	1-0		31 Jan	FC	A	Preston	D	2-2
30 Aug	Lge	A	Newcastle	D	1-1		4 Feb	FCr	H	Preston	W	1-0
1 Sep	Lge	H	Man City	D	3-3		7 Feb	Lge	A	Arsenal	L	0-4
6 Sep	Lge	H	Cardiff	W	2-1		14 Feb	FC	A	Halifax	W	3-0
10 Sep	Lge	A	Liverpool	L	1-2		17 Feb	Lge	H	Burnley	L	2-3
13 Sep	Lge	A	Sheff Wed	L	0-2		21 Feb	Lge	H	Preston	D	4-4
15 Sep	Lge	H	Liverpool	W	3-1		28 Feb	FC	A	Birmingham	D	1-1
20 Sep	Lge	H	Arsenal	L	1-3		4 Mar	FCr	H	Birmingham	D	2-2
27 Sep	Lge	H	Burnley	W	2-1		7 Mar	Lge	A	Blackpool	L	0-2
4 Oct	Lge	A	Preston	L	0-1		9 Mar	FCr	*	Birmingham	W	1-0
11 Oct	Lge	A	Derby	D	0-0		12 Mar	Lge	H	Derby	W	5-2
18 Oct	Lge	H	Blackpool	W	4-0		14 Mar	Lge	H	Chelsea	L	2-3
25 Oct	Lge	A	Chelsea	L	1-2		21 Mar	FCsf	†	Blackpool	L	1-2
27 Oct	F	A	Gloucester	L	1-2		25 Mar	Lge	A	Man Utd	L	2-3
1 Nov	Lge	H	Man Utd	L	1-2		28 Mar	Lge	H	Portsmouth	D	3-3
5 Nov	F	A	Oxford Univ	W	3-0		3 Apr	Lge	H	Stoke	W	1-0
6 Nov	F	A	Camb Univ	D	2-2		4 Apr	Lge	A	Bolton	W	3-2
8 Nov	Lge	A	Portsmouth	L	1-2		6 Apr	Lge	A	Stoke	L	0-2
15 Nov	Lge	H	Bolton	D	1-1		11 Apr	Lge	H	Aston Villa	D	1-1
22 Nov	Lge	A	Aston Villa	W	3-0		15 Apr	F	A	West Ham	L	1-2
29 Nov	Lge	H	Sunderland	D	2-2		18 Apr	Lge	A	Sunderland	D	1-1
6 Dec	Lge	A	Wolves	D	0-0		20 Apr	F	A	Reading	W	4-0
13 Dec	Lge	H	Charlton	W	2-0		25 Apr	Lge	H	Wolves	W	3-2
20 Dec	Lge	A	WBA	L	1-2		30 Apr	Lge	A	Charlton	L	2-3
25 Dec	Lge	H	Middlesbro'	W	7-1		4 May	F	A	Arsenal	W	2-0
27 Dec	Lge	A	Middlesbro'	W	4-0		11 May ‡		A	Hibernian	D	1-1
3 Jan	Lge	H	Newcastle	W	3-2		12 May ‡		A	Hibernian	L	1-2
10 Jan	FC	A	Tranmere	D	1-1		15 May	F	A	Hearts	L	0-2
12 Jan	FCr	H	Tranmere	W	9-1		30 May	F	A	Racing, Paris	D	1-1
17 Jan	Lge	A	Cardiff	D	0-0							

* Second replay at Molineux   † Semi-final at Villa Park   ‡ Coronation Cup

Player	Lg App	Goals	Player	Lg App	Goals
Adams C.J.	1		Hopkins M.	2	
Baily E.F.	30	6	King P.A.	10	
Baker P.R.B.	1		McClellan S.B.	17	8
Bennett L.D.	30	14	Marchi A.V.	5	
Brittan C.	9		Medley L.D.	21	1
Brooks J.	1		Nicholson W.E.	31	
Burgess W.A.R.	30	2	Ramsey A.E.	37	6
Clarke H.A.	31		Robb G.W.	6	2
Ditchburn E.G.	42		Stokes A.F.	2	1
Duquemin L.S.	38	18	Uphill D.E.	2	1
Dicker L.R.	10	2	Walters W.E.	26	8
Gibbins E.	1		Wetton R.	12	
Groves V.G.	3	2	Willis A.	27	1
Grubb A.J.	2		Withers C.F.	15	
Harmer T.C.	17	4	Own Goal		1
Hollis R.W.	3	1			

Final table for First Division

1	Arsenal	42	21 12 9	97:64	54
2	Preston	42	21 12 9	85:60	54
3	Wolverhampton	42	19 13 10	86:63	51
4	West Bromwich	42	21 8 13	66:60	50
5	Charlton	42	19 11 12	77:63	49
6	Burnley	42	18 12 12	67:52	48
7	Blackpool	42	19 9 14	71:70	47
8	Manchester U.	42	18 10 14	69:72	46
9	Sunderland	42	15 13 14	68:82	43
10	TOTTENHAM	42	15 11 16	78:69	41
11	Aston Villa	42	14 13 15	63:61	41
12	Cardiff	42	14 12 16	54:46	40
13	Middlesbrough	42	14 11 17	70:77	39
14	Bolton	42	15 9 18	61:69	39
15	Portsmouth	42	14 10 18	74:83	38
16	Newcastle	42	14 9 19	59:70	37
17	Liverpool	42	14 8 20	61:82	36
18	Sheffield W.	42	12 11 19	62:72	35
19	Chelsea	42	12 11 19	56:66	35
20	Manchester C.	42	14 7 21	72:87	35
21	Stoke	42	12 10 20	53:66	34
22	Derby	42	11 10 21	59:74	32

SEASON 1953/54

Date	Comp	H/A	Opponent	Result	Score		Date	Comp	H/A	Opponent	Result	Score
19 Aug	Lge	H	Aston Villa	W	1-0		2 Jan	Lge	A	Middlesbrough	L	0-3
22 Aug	Lge	A	Sheff Wed	L	1-2		9 Jan	FC	A	Leeds	D	3-3
26 Aug	Lge	H	Charlton	W	3-1		13 Jan	FCr	H	Leeds	W	1-0
29 Aug	Lge	H	Middlesbrough	W	4-1		16 Jan	Lge	H	WBA	L	0-1
3 Sep	Lge	A	Charlton	W	1-0		23 Jan	Lge	A	Liverpool	D	2-2
5 Sep	Lge	A	WBA	L	0-3		30 Jan	FC	A	Man City	W	1-0
7 Sep	Lge	H	Burnley	L	2-4		6 Feb	Lge	H	Newcastle	W	3-0
12 Sep	Lge	H	Liverpool	W	2-1		13 Feb	Lge	A	Man Utd	L	0-2
16 Sep	Lge	A	Burnley	L	2-3		20 Feb	FC	A	Hull	D	1-1
19 Sep	Lge	A	Newcastle	W	3-1		24 Feb	FCr	H	Hull	W	2-0
21 Sep	F	A	Hibernian	W	1-0		27 Feb	Lge	A	Arsenal	W	3-0
26 Sep	Lge	H	Man Utd	D	1-1		3 Mar	Lge	H	Bolton	W	3-2
29 Sep	F	H	Racing Club	W	5-3		6 Mar	Lge	H	Cardiff	L	0-1
3 Oct	Lge	A	Bolton	L	0-2		13 Mar	FC	A	WBA	L	0-3
10 Oct	Lge	H	Arsenal	L	1-4		17 Mar	Lge	A	Man City	L	1-4
17 Oct	Lge	A	Cardiff	L	0-1		20 Mar	Lge	H	Sunderland	L	0-3
19 Oct	F	A	Millwall	W	2-0		27 Mar	Lge	A	Chelsea	L	0-1
24 Oct	Lge	H	Man City	W	3-0		3 Apr	Lge	H	Blackpool	D	2-2
28 Oct	F	H	FC Austria	W	3-2		5 Apr	F	H	Hibernian	W	3-2
31 Oct	Lge	A	Sunderland	L	3-4		10 Apr	Lge	A	Huddersfield	W	5-2
7 Nov	Lge	H	Chelsea	W	2-1		16 Apr	Lge	A	Preston	L	1-2
14 Nov	Lge	A	Blackpool	L	0-1		17 Apr	Lge	H	Sheff Utd	W	2-1
21 Nov	Lge	H	Huddersfield	W	1-0		19 Apr	Lge	H	Preston	L	2-6
28 Nov	Lge	A	Sheff Utd	L	2-5		24 Apr	Lge	A	Wolves	L	0-2
5 Dec	Lge	H	Wolves	L	2-3		28 Apr	F	A	Austria Select	L	0-2
12 Dec	Lge	A	Aston Villa	W	2-1		1 May	F	A	Stuttgart	L	1-3
19 Dec	Lge	H	Sheff Wed	W	3-1		5 May	F	A	Eintracht	L	0-1
25 Dec	Lge	H	Portsmouth	D	1-1		7 May	F	A	Hamburg SV	D	2-2
26 Dec	Lge	A	Portsmouth	D	1-1							

Player	Lg App	Goals	Player	Lg App	Goals
Baily E.F.	33	5	King D.A.	2	
Baker P.R.B.	4	1	Marchi A.V.	8	1
Bennett L.D.	26	4	McClellan S.B.	5	
Brittan C.	3	1	Nicholson W.E.	30	
Brooks J.	18	2	Owen A.W.	1	
Burgess W.A.R.	24		Ramsey A.E.	37	2
Clarke H.A.	41		Reynolds R.S.M.	3	
Ditchburn E.G.	39		Robb G.W.	37	16
Dunmore D.G.I.	10	2	Stokes A.F.	2	1
Duquemin L.S.	27	9	Walters W.E.	37	14
Groves V.G.	1	1	Wetton R.	21	
Harmer T.C.	6	2	Willis A.	9	
Hopkins M.	2		Withers C.F.	31	
Hutchinson G.H.	5	1	Own Goals		3

Final table for First Division

1	Wolverhampton	42	25 7 10	96:56	57
2	West Bromwich	42	22 9 11	86:63	53
3	Huddersfield	42	20 11 11	78:61	51
4	Manchester U.	42	18 12 12	73:58	48
5	Bolton	42	18 12 12	75:60	48
6	Blackpool	42	19 10 13	80:69	48
7	Burnley	42	21 4 17	78:67	46
8	Chelsea	42	16 12 14	74:68	44
9	Charlton	42	19 6 17	75:77	44
10	Cardiff	42	18 8 16	51:71	44
11	Preston	42	19 5 18	87:58	43
12	Arsenal	42	15 13 14	75:73	43
13	Aston Villa	42	16 9 17	70:68	41
14	Portsmouth	42	14 11 17	81:89	39
15	Newcastle	42	14 10 18	72:77	38
16	TOTTENHAM	42	16 5 21	65:76	37
17	Manchester C.	42	14 9 19	62:77	37
18	Sunderland	42	14 8 20	80:89	36
19	Sheffield W.	42	15 6 21	70:91	36
20	Sheffield U.	42	11 11 20	69:90	33
21	Middlesbrough	42	10 10 22	60:91	30
22	Liverpool	42	9 10 23	68:97	28

SEASON 1954/55

Date	Comp	H/A	Opponent	Result	Score
14 Aug	F	A	Lille Olym	D	1-1
21 Aug	Lge	A	Aston Villa	W	4-2
25 Aug	Lge	H	Wolves	W	3-2
28 Aug	Lge	H	Sunderland	L	0-1
30 Aug	Lge	A	Wolves	L	2-4
4 Sep	Lge	A	Arsenal	L	0-2
8 Sep	Lge	H	Man Utd	L	0-2
11 Sep	Lge	A	Sheff Wed	D	2-2
15 Sep	Lge	A	Man Utd	L	1-2
18 Sep	Lge	H	Portsmouth	D	1-1
25 Sep	Lge	A	Blackpool	L	1-5
2 Oct	Lge	H	Charlton	L	1-4
9 Oct	Lge	H	WBA	W	3-1
11 Oct	F	A	QPR	L	1-2
16 Oct	Lge	A	Newcastle	D	4-4
18 Oct	F	H	Sptklub Vienna	L	1-2
23 Oct	Lge	H	Preston	W	3-1
30 Oct	Lge	A	Sheff Utd	L	1-4
2 Nov	F	H	Essen Rot Weiss	W	4-2
6 Nov	Lge	H	Cardiff	L	0-2
13 Nov	Lge	A	Chelsea	L	1-2
15 Nov	F	H	Finchley	D	2-2
20 Nov	Lge	H	Leicester	W	5-1
27 Nov	Lge	A	Burnley	W	2-1
29 Nov	F	A	Accrington St.	D	0-0
4 Dec	Lge	H	Everton	L	1-3
11 Dec	Lge	A	Man City	D	0-0
18 Dec	Lge	H	Aston Villa	D	1-1
25 Dec	Lge	A	Bolton	W	2-1
27 Dec	Lge	H	Bolton	W	2-0
1 Jan	Lge	A	Sunderland	D	1-1
8 Jan	FC	A	Gateshead	W	2-0
15 Jan	Lge	H	Arsenal	L	0-1
22 Jan	Lge	H	Sheff Wed	W	7-2
29 Jan	FC	H	Port Vale	W	4-2
5 Feb	Lge	A	Portsmouth	W	3-0
12 Feb	Lge	H	Blackpool	W	3-2
19 Feb	FC	A	York	L	1-3
2 Mar	F	H	Arsenal	L	1-4
5 Mar	Lge	H	Man City	D	2-2
9 Mar	F	H	Racing, Paris	W	6-0
12 Mar	Lge	A	Preston	L	0-1
14 Mar	F	A	Hibernian	D	1-1
19 Mar	Lge	H	Sheff Utd	W	5-0
26 Mar	Lge	A	Cardiff	W	2-1
30 Mar	F	H	FC Servette	W	5-1
2 Apr	Lge	H	Chelsea	L	2-4
9 Apr	Lge	A	Everton	L	0-1
11 Apr	Lge	H	Huddersfield	D	1-1
12 Apr	Lge	A	Huddersfield	L	0-1
16 Apr	Lge	H	Burnley	L	0-3
23 Apr	Lge	A	Leicester	L	0-2
27 Apr	Lge	A	WBA	W	2-1
30 Apr	Lge	H	Newcastle	W	2-1
5 May	Lge	A	Charlton	W	2-1
11 May	F	A	FC Austria	L	2-6
15 May	F	A	Kinizi, Hungary	L	1-4
18 May	F	A	Vegas, Hun.	L	2-4
19 May	F	A	Pecs Doza	W	1-0
25 May	F	A	Racing; Paris	D	0-0

Player	Lg App	Goals	Player	Lg App	Goals
Baily E.F.	41	12	Henry R.P.	1	
Baker P.R.B.	8		Hopkins M.	32	
Bennett L.D.	6	2	King D.A.	5	
Blanchflower R.D.	22		McClellan S.B.	11	8
Brittan C.	10		Marchi A.V.	32	
Brooks J.	31	7	Nicholson W.E.	10	
Clarke H.A.	36		Ramsey A.E.	33	3
Ditchburn E.G.	16		Reynolds R.S.M.	26	
Dowsett G.J.	1	1	Robb G.W.	36	8
Dunmore D.G.I.	22	7	Walters W.E.	7	2
Duquemin L.S.	19	8	Wetton R.	5	
Dyson T.K.	1		Withers C.F.	11	
Gavin J.T.	29	13	Woods A.E.	6	
Harmer T.C.	5		Own Goal		1

Final table for First Division

1	Chelsea	42	20 12 10	81:57	52
2	Wolverhampton	42	19 10 13	89:70	48
3	Portsmouth	42	18 12 12	74:62	48
4	Sunderland	42	15 18 9	64:54	48
5	Manchester U.	42	20 7 15	84:74	47
6	Aston Villa	42	20 7 15	72:73	47
7	Manchester C.	42	18 10 14	76:69	46
8	Newcastle	42	17 9 16	89:77	43
9	Arsenal	42	17 9 16	69:63	43
10	Burnley	42	17 9 16	51:48	43
11	Everton	42	16 10 16	62:68	42
12	Huddersfield	42	14 13 15	63:68	41
13	Sheffield U.	42	17 7 18	70:86	41
14	Preston	42	16 8 18	83:64	40
15	Charlton	42	15 10 17	76:75	40
16	**TOTTENHAM**	**42**	**16 8 18**	**72:73**	**40**
17	West Bromwich	42	16 8 18	76:96	40
18	Bolton	42	13 13 16	62:69	39
19	Blackpool	42	14 10 18	60:64	38
20	Cardiff	42	13 11 18	62:76	37
21	Leicester	42	12 11 19	74:86	35
22	Sheffield W.	42	8 10 24	63:100	26

SEASON 1955/56

Date	Comp	H/A	Opponent	Result	Score
20 Aug	Lge	H	Burnley	L	0-1
24 Aug	Lge	A	Man Utd	D	2-2
27 Aug	Lge	A	Luton	L	1-2
31 Aug	Lge	H	Man Utd	L	1-2
3 Sep	Lge	H	Charlton	L	2-3
5 Sep	Lge	A	Sheff Utd	L	0-2
10 Sep	Lge	A	Arsenal	W	3-1
17 Sep	Lge	H	Everton	L	1-2
24 Sep	Lge	H	Newcastle	W	3-1
1 Oct	Lge	A	Birmingham	L	0-3
8 Oct	Lge	A	Bolton	L	0-3
12 Oct	F	H	FC Vasas	L	1-2
15 Oct	Lge	A	Chelsea	L	0;2
22 Oct	Lge	H	Sunderland	L	2-3
24 Oct	F	A	Plymouth	D	0-0
29 Oct	Lge	A	Portsmouth	L	1-4
5 Nov	Lge	H	Cardiff	D	1-1
12 Nov	Lge	A	Man City	W	2-1
14 Nov	F	A	Partick Thistle	L	0-1
19 Nov	Lge	H	Wolves	W	2-1
26 Nov	Lge	A	Aston Villa	W	2-0
3 Dec	Lge	H	Blackpool	D	1-1
6 Dec	F	H	Swansea	W	4-1
10 Dec	Lge	A	Huddersfield	L	0-1
17 Dec	Lge	A	Burnley	L	0-2
24 Dec	Lge	H	Luton	W	2-1
26 Dec	Lge	H	WBA	W	4-1
27 Dec	Lge	A	WBA	L	0-1
31 Dec	Lge	A	Charlton	W	2-1
7 Jan	FC	H	Boston Utd	W	4-0
14 Jan	Lge	A	Arsenal	W	1-0
21 Jan	Lge	H	Everton	W	2-1
28 Jan	FC	H	Middlesbrough	W	3-1
4 Feb	Lge	A	Newcastle	W	2-1
11 Feb	Lge	H	Birmingham	L	0-1
18 Feb	Lge	A	Doncaster	W	2-0
25 Feb	Lge	H	Chelsea	W	4-0
3 Mar	FC	H	West Ham	D	3-3
8 Mar	FCr	A	West Ham	W	2-1
10 Mar	Lge	H	Portsmouth	D	1-1
17 Mar	FCsf	† Man City	L	0-1	
21 Mar	Lge	A	Bolton	L	2-3
24 Mar	Lge	H	Man City	W	2-1
30 Mar	Lge	H	Preston	L	0-4
31 Mar	Lge	A	Sunderland	L	2-3
2 Apr	Lge	A	Preston	D	3-3
7 Apr	Lge	H	Aston Villa	W	4-3
14 Apr	Lge	A	Blackpool	W	2-0
18 Apr	Lge	H	Wolves	L	1-5
21 Apr	Lge	H	Huddersfield	L	1-2
23 Apr	Lge	A	Cardiff	D	0-0
28 Apr	Lge	H	Sheff Utd	W	3-1

† Semi-final played at Villa Park

Player	Lg App	Goals	Player	Lg App	Goals
Baily E.F.	18	1	Henry R.P.	1	
Baker P.R.B.	5		Hopkins M.	41	
Blanchflower R.D.	40		McClellan S.B.	16	7
Brittan C.	1		Marchi A.V.	42	1
Brooks J.	39	10	Norman M.	27	1
Clarke H.A.	39	4	Reynolds R.S.M.	28	
Ditchburn E.G.	14		Robb G.W.	41	7
Dulin M.C.	6		Ryden J.J.	3	1
Dunmore D.G.I.	10	1	Smith R.A.	21	10
Duquemin L.S.	17	5	Stokes A.F.	11	5
Dyson T.K.	3		Whalley E.	2	
Gavin J.T.	3	2	Walters W.E.	14	1
Harmer T.C.	10	5	Withers C.F.	10	

Final table for First Division

1	Manchester U.	42	25 10 7	83:51	60
2	Blackpool	42	20 9 13	86:62	49
3	Wolverhampton	42	20 9 13	89:65	49
4	Manchester C.	42	18 10 14	82:69	46
5	Arsenal	42	18 10 14	60:61	46
6	Birmingham	42	18 9 15	75:57	45
7	Burnley	42	18 8 16	64:54	44
8	Bolton	42	18 7 17	71:58	43
9	Sunderland	42	17 9 16	80:95	43
10	Luton	42	17 8 17	66:64	42
11	Newcastle	42	17 7 18	85:70	41
12	Portsmouth	42	16 9 17	78:85	41
13	West Bromwich	42	18 5 19	58:70	41
14	Charlton	42	17 6 19	75:81	40
15	Everton	42	15 10 17	55:69	40
16	Chelsea	42	14 11 17	64:77	39
17	Cardiff	42	15 9 18	55:69	39
18	**TOTTENHAM**	**42**	**15 7 20**	**61:71**	**37**
19	Preston	42	14 8 20	73:72	36
20	Aston Villa	42	11 13 18	52:69	35
21	Huddersfield	42	14 7 21	54:83	35
22	Sheffield U.	42	12 9 21	63:77	33

SEASON 1956/57

Date	Comp	H/A	Opponent	Result	Score
18 Aug	Lge	A	Preston	W	4-1
22 Aug	Lge	A	Man City	D	2-2
25 Aug	Lge	H	Leeds	W	5-1
29 Aug	Lge	H	Man City	W	3-2
1 Sep	Lge	A	Bolton	L	0-1
3 Sep	Lge	A	Blackpool	L	1-4
8 Sep	Lge	A	Wolves	W	4-1
11 Sep	F	H	Racing, Paris	W	2-0
15 Sep	Lge	A	Aston Villa	W	4-2
17 Sep	F	A	Hibernian	W	5-1
22 Sep	Lge	H	Luton	W	5-0
26 Sep	F	H	Partick Thistle	W	4-1
29 Sep	Lge	A	Sunderland	W	2-0
6 Oct	Lge	A	Chelsea	W	4-2
13 Oct	Lge	H	Cardiff	W	5-0
15 Oct	F	A	Hearts	L	2-3
20 Oct	Lge	A	Arsenal	L	1-3
27 Oct	Lge	H	Burnley	W	2-0
31 Oct	F	H	Hibernian	D	3-3
3 Nov	Lge	A	Portsmouth	W	3-2
10 Nov	Lge	H	Newcastle	W	3-1
12 Nov	F	H	Hearts	W	4-2
17 Nov	Lge	A	Sheff Wed	L	1-4
24 Nov	Lge	H	Man Utd	D	2-2
26 Nov	F	A	Partick Thistle	L	0-2
1 Dec	Lge	A	Birmingham	D	0-0
3 Dec	F	H	Red Banner	W	7-1
8 Dec	Lge	H	WBA	D	2-2
15 Dec	Lge	H	Preston	D	1-1
25 Dec	Lge	H	Everton	W	6-0
26 Dec	Lge	A	Everton	D	1-1
29 Dec	Lge	H	Bolton	W	4-0
5 Jan	FC	H	Leicester	W	2-0
12 Jan	Lge	A	Wolves	L	0-3
19 Jan	Lge	H	Aston Villa	W	3-0
26 Jan	FC	H	Chelsea	W	4-0
2 Feb	Lge	A	Luton	W	3-1
9 Feb	Lge	H	Sunderland	W	5-2
16 Feb	FC	A	Bournemouth	L	1-3
20 Feb	Lge	H	Chelsea	L	3-4
2 Mar	Lge	A	Leeds Utd	D	1-1
9 Mar	Lge	A	WBA	D	1-1
13 Mar	Lge	H	Arsenal	L	1-3
16 Mar	Lge	H	Portsmouth	W	2-0
19 Mar	F	A	Comb. Antwerp	W	2-1
23 Mar	Lge	A	Newcastle	D	2-2
30 Mar	Lge	H	Sheff Wed	D	1-1
6 Apr	Lge	A	Man Utd	D	0-0
13 Apr	Lge	H	Birmingham	W	5-1
19 Apr	Lge	A	Charlton	D	1-1
20 Apr	Lge	A	Cardiff	W	3-0
22 Apr	Lge	H	Charlton	W	6-2
27 Apr	Lge	H	Blackpool	W	2-1
29 Apr	Lge	A	Burnley	L	0-1
19 May	F		Celtic	W	4-3*
22 May	F		Essex Co. XI	W	8-1*
25 May	F		Ontario All Stars	W	7-0*
29 May	F		Alberta	W	6-1*
1 Jun	F		Celtic	W	6-3*
3 Jun	F		British Col.	L	0-2*
4 Jun	F		Manitoba All Stars	W	12-0*
8 Jun	F		Celtic	W	3-1*
9 Jun	F		Celtic	L	0-1*

* Canadian tour

Player	Lg App	Goals	Player	Lg App	Goals
Baker P.R.B.	38		Hopkins M.	35	
Blanchflower R.D.	39	1	Marchi A.V.	42	
Brittan C.	1		Medwin T.C.	37	14
Brooks J.	23	11	Norman M.	16	
Clarke H.A.	21		Reynolds R.S.M.	13	
Ditchburn E.G.	29		Robb G.W.	37	14
Dulin M.C.	1		Ryden J.J.	15	
Dunmore D.G.I.	5	3	Stokes A.F.	21	18
Duquemin L.S.	2	1	Smith R.A.	33	18
Dyson T.K.	8	3	Whalley E.	2	
Harmer T.C.	42	17	Wilkie R.M.	1	
Henry R.P.	1		Own Goals		4

Final table for First Division

1	Manchester U.	42	28	8	6	103:54	64
2	TOTTENHAM	42	22	12	8	104:56	56
3	Preston	42	23	10	9	84:56	56
4	Blackpool	42	22	9	11	93:65	53
5	Arsenal	42	21	8	13	85:69	50
6	Wolverhampton	42	20	8	14	94:70	48
7	Burnley	42	18	10	14	56:50	46
8	Leeds	42	15	14	13	72:63	44
9	Bolton	42	16	12	14	65:65	44
10	Aston Villa	42	14	15	13	65:55	43
11	West Bromwich	42	14	14	14	59:61	42
=12	Birmingham	42	15	9	18	69:69	39
=12	Chelsea	42	13	13	16	73:73	39
14	Sheffield W.	42	16	6	20	82:88	38
15	Everton	42	14	10	18	61:79	38
16	Luton	42	14	9	19	58:76	37
17	Newcastle	42	14	8	20	67:87	36
18	Manchester C.	42	13	9	20	78:88	35
19	Portsmouth	42	10	13	19	62:92	33
20	Sunderland	42	12	8	22	67:88	32
21	Cardiff	42	10	9	23	53:88	29
22	Charlton	42	9	4	29	62:120	22

SEASON 1957/58

Date	Comp	H/A	Opponent	Result	Score
3 Aug	F	A	IFB Stuttgart	D	2-2
24 Aug	Lge	H	Chelsea	D	1-1
28 Aug	Lge	A	Portsmouth	L	1-5
31 Aug	Lge	A	Newcastle	l	1-3
4 Sep	Lge	A	Portsmouth	L	3-5
7 Sep	Lge	H	Burnley	W	3-1
11 Sep	Lge	A	Birmingham	D	0-0
14 Sep	Lge	H	Preston	L	1-3
18 Sep	Lge	H	Birmingham	W	7-1
21 Sep	Lge	H	Sheff Wed	W	4-2
28 Sep	Lge	A	Man City	L	1-5
2 Oct	Lge	A	Wolves	L	0-4
5 Oct	Lge	H	Nottm Forest	L	3-4
12 Oct	Lge	H	Arsenal	W	3-1
14 Oct	F	A	Hibernian	L	2-5
19 Oct	Lge	A	Bolton	L	2-3
23 Oct	F	A	Swiss Nat. XI	W	5-4
26 Oct	Lge	H	Leeds	W	2-0
2 Nov	Lge	A	Sunderland	D	1-1
6 Nov	F	A	Bristol C.	L	3-4
9 Nov	Lge	H	Everton	W	6-2
11 Nov	F	H	IFB Stuttgart	W	3-2
16 Nov	Lge	A	Aston Villa	D	1-1
23 Nov	Lge	H	Luton	W	3-1
30 Nov	Lge	A	Man Utd	W	4-3
7 Dec	Lge	H	Leicester	L	1-4
14 Dec	Lge	A	Blackpool	W	2-0
21 Dec	Lge	A	Chelsea	W	4-2
26 Dec	Lge	H	Wolves	W	1-0
28 Dec	Lge	H	Newcastle	D	3-3
4 Jan	FC	A	Leicester	W	4-0
11 Jan	Lge	A	Burnley	L	0-1
18 Jan	Lge	H	Preston	D	3-3
25 Jan	FC	H	Sheff Utd	L	0-3
1 Feb	Lge	A	Sheff Wed	L	0-2
8 Feb	Lge	H	Man City	W	5-1
15 Feb	Lge	A	Nottm Forest	W	2-1
22 Feb	Lge	A	Arsenal	D	4-4
1 Mar	F	H	Partick Thistle	W	4-1
8 Mar	Lge	A	Leeds U.	W	2-1
12 Mar	Lge	H	Bolton	W	4-1
15 Mar	Lge	H	Sunderland	L	0-1
22 Mar	Lge	A	Luton	D	0-0
27 Mar	F	A	Rotterdam XI	W	4-1
29 Mar	Lge	H	Aston Villa	W	6-2
4 Apr	Lge	H	WBA	D	0-0
5 Apr	Lge	A	Everton	W	4-3
7 Apr	Lge	A	WBA	W	2-0
12 Apr	Lge	H	Man Utd	W	1-0
14 Apr	F	H	Hibernian	W	4-0
19 Apr	Lge	A	Leicester	W	3-1
24 Apr	F	H	Canto de Rio	W	4-1
26 Apr	Lge	H	Blackpool	W	2-1

Player	Lg App	Goals	Player	Lg App	Goals
Baker P.R.B.	18		Hopkins M.	26	
Bing T.E.	1		Iley J.	19	
Blanchflower R.D.	40		Ireland J.J.C.	1	
Brittan C.	3		Jones C.W.	10	1
Brooks J.	25	10	Medwin T.C.	39	14
Clayton E.	5	3	Norman M.	33	1
Ditchburn E.G.	26		Reynolds R.S.M.	16	
Dulin M.C.	3	2	Robb G.W.	15	3
Dunmore D.G.I.	5	2	Ryden J.J.	35	
Dyson T.K.	12	2	Smith R.A.	38	36
Harmer T.C.	40	9	Stokes A.F.	15	8
Henry R.P.	15		Walley E.	1	
Hills J.R.	21		Own Goals		2

Final table for First Division

1	Wolverhampton	42	28	8	6	103:47	64
2	Preston	42	26	7	9	100:51	59
3	TOTTENHAM	42	21	9	12	93:77	51
4	West Bromwich	42	18	14	10	92:70	50
5	Manchester C.	42	22	5	15	104:100	49
6	Burnley	42	21	5	16	80:74	47
7	Blackpool	42	19	6	17	80:67	44
8	Luton	42	19	6	17	69:63	44
9	Manchester U.	42	16	11	15	85:75	43
10	Nottingham F.	42	16	10	16	69:63	42
11	Chelsea	42	15	12	15	83:79	42
12	Arsenal	42	16	7	19	73:85	39
13	Birmingham	42	14	11	17	76:89	39
14	Aston Villa	42	16	7	19	73:86	39
15	Bolton	42	14	10	18	65:87	38
16	Everton	42	13	11	18	65:75	37
17	Leeds	42	14	9	19	51:63	37
18	Leicester	42	14	5	23	91:112	33
19	Newcastle	42	12	8	22	73:81	32
20	Portsmouth	42	12	8	22	73:88	32
21	Sunderland	42	10	12	20	54:97	32
22	Sheffield W.	42	12	7	23	69:92	31

SEASON 1958/59

Date	Comp		Opponent		Score		Date	Comp		Opponent		Score
23 Aug	Lge	H	Blackpool	L	2-3		3 Jan	Lge	H	Blackburn	W	3-1
27 Aug	Lge	A	Chelsea	L	2-4		10 Jan	FC	H	West Ham	W	2-0
30 Aug	Lge	A	Blackburn	L	0-5		17 Jan	Lge	A	Newcastle	W	2-1
3 Sep	Lge	H	Chelsea	W	4-0		24 Jan	FC	H	Newport	W	4-1
6 Sep	Lge	H	Newcastle	L	1-3		31 Jan	Lge	H	Arsenal	L	1-4
10 Sep	Lge	A	Nottm Forest	D	1-1		7 Feb	Lge	H	Man Utd	L	1-3
13 Sep	Lge	A	Arsenal	L	1-3		14 Feb	FC	H	Norwich	D	1-1
17 Sep	Lge	H	Nottm Forest	W	1-0		18 Feb	FCr	A	Norwich	L	0-1
20 Sep	Lge	A	Man Utd	D	2-2		21 Feb	Lge	H	Portsmouth	D	4-4
27 Sep	Lge	H	Wolves	W	2-1		28 Feb	Lge	A	Everton	L	1-2
4 Oct	Lge	A	Portsmouth	D	1-1		2 Mar	Lge	A	Wolves	D	1-1
11 Oct	Lge	H	Everton	W	10-4		7 Mar	Lge	H	Leicester	W	6-0
14 Oct	F	H	Bella Vista	W	3-1		14 Mar	Lge	A	Leeds	L	1-3
18 Oct	Lge	A	Leicester	W	4-3		21 Mar	Lge	H	Man City	W	3-1
25 Oct	Lge	H	Leeds Utd	L	2-3		27 Mar	Lge	A	Aston Villa	W	3-2
1 Nov	Lge	A	Man City	L	1-5		28 Mar	Lge	A	Bolton	L	1-4
8 Nov	Lge	H	Bolton	D	1-1		30 Mar	Lge	H	Aston Villa	D	1-1
10 Nov	F	H	Hibernian	W	5-2		4 Apr	Lge	A	Luton	W	3-0
15 Nov	Lge	A	Luton	W	2-1		8 Apr	Lge	H	Burnley	D	2-2
22 Nov	Lge	H	Birmingham	L	0-4		11 Apr	Lge	A	Birmingham	L	1-5
29 Nov	Lge	A	WBA	L	3-4		18 Apr	Lge	H	WBA	W	5-0
6 Dec	Lge	H	Preston	L	1-2		25 Apr	Lge	A	Preston	D	2-2
8 Dec	F	H	Bucharest Sel.	W	4-2		27 May	F	A	Moscow Torpedo	W	1-0
13 Dec	Lge	A	Burnley	L	1-3		1 Jun	F	A	Dynamo Kiev	W	2-1
20 Dec	Lge	A	Blackpool	D	0-0		4 Jun	F	A	Com Russian XI	L	1-3
25 Dec	Lge	A	West Ham	L	1-2							
26 Dec	Lge	H	West Ham	L	1-4							

Player	Lg App	Goals	Player	Lg App	Goals
Baker P.R.B.	36		Hopkins M.	34	
Blanchflower R.D.	36	1	Iley J.	34	1
Brooks J.	25	3	Ireland J.J.C.	2	
Clayton E.	11	4	Jones C.W.	22	5
Ditchburn E.G.	2		Mackay D.C.	4	1
Dodge W.C.	5		Medwin T.C.	35	14
Dunmore D.G.I.	13	6	Norman M.	35	3
Dyson T.K.	7		Ryden J.J.	10	1
Harmer T.C.	35	4	Robb G.W.	9	2
Henry R.P.	8		Sharpe F.C.	2	1
Hills J.R.	7		Smith R.A.	36	32
Hollowbread J.F.	40		Stokes A.F.	14	7

Final table for First Division

1	Wolverhampton	42	28	5	9	110:49	61
2	Manchester U.	42	24	7	11	103:66	55
3	Arsenal	42	21	8	13	88:68	50
4	Bolton	42	20	10	12	79:66	50
5	West Bromwich	42	18	13	11	88:68	49
6	West Ham	42	21	6	15	85:70	48
7	Burnley	42	19	10	13	81:70	48
8	Blackpool	42	18	11	13	66:49	47
9	Birmingham	42	20	6	16	84:68	46
10	Blackburn	42	17	10	15	76:70	44
11	Newcastle	42	17	7	18	80:80	41
12	Preston	42	17	7	18	70:77	41
13	Nottingham F.	42	17	6	19	71:74	40
14	Chelsea	42	18	4	20	77:98	40
15	Leeds	42	15	9	18	57:74	39
16	Everton	42	17	4	21	71:87	38
17	Luton	42	12	13	17	68:71	37
18	**TOTTENHAM**	**42**	**13**	**10**	**19**	**85:95**	**36**
19	Leicester	42	11	10	21	67:98	32
20	Manchester C.	42	11	9	22	64:95	31
21	Aston Villa	42	11	8	23	58:87	30
22	Portsmouth	42	6	9	27	64:112	21

SEASON 1959/60

Date	Comp		Opponent		Score		Date	Comp		Opponent		Score
22 Aug	Lge	A	Newcastle	W	5-1		28 Dec	Lge	H	Leeds	L	1-4
26 Aug	Lge	H	WBA	D	2-2		2 Jan	Lge	A	Birmingham	W	1-0
29 Aug	Lge	H	Birmingham	D	0-0		9 Jan	FC	A	Newport	W	4-0
2 Sep	Lge	A	WBA	W	2-1		16 Jan	Lge	A	Arsenal	W	3-0
5 Sep	Lge	A	Arsenal	D	1-1		23 Jan	Lge	H	Man Utd	W	2-1
9 Sep	Lge	H	West Ham	D	2-2		30 Jan	FC	A	Crewe	D	2-2
12 Sep	Lge	A	Man Utd	W	5-1		3 Feb	FCr	H	Crewe	W	13-2
14 Sep	Lge	A	West Ham	W	2-1		6 Feb	Lge	A	Preston	D	1-1
19 Sep	Lge	H	Preston	W	5-1		13 Feb	Lge	H	Leicester	L	1-2
26 Sep	Lge	A	Leicester	D	1-1		20 Feb	FC	H	Blackburn	L	1-3
3 Oct	Lge	H	Burnley	D	1-1		27 Feb	Lge	A	Blackburn	W	4-1
10 Oct	Lge	H	Wolves	W	5-1		1 Mar	Lge	A	Burnley	L	0-2
17 Oct	Lge	A	Sheff Wed	L	1-2		5 Mar	Lge	H	Sheff Wed	W	4-1
21 Oct	F	A	Reading	W	5-2		12 Mar	Lge	A	Nottm Forest	W	3-1
24 Oct	Lge	H	Nottm Forest	W	2-1		19 Mar	Lge	H	Fulham	D	1-1
31 Oct	Lge	A	Man City	W	2-1		26 Mar	Lge	A	Bolton	L	1-2
7 Nov	Lge	H	Bolton	L	0-2		2 Apr	Lge	H	Luton	D	1-1
14 Nov	Lge	A	Luton	L	0-1		9 Apr	Lge	A	Everton	L	1-2
16 Nov	F	H	Moscow Torpedo	W	3-2		15 Apr	Lge	A	Chelsea	W	3-1
21 Nov	Lge	H	Everton	W	3-0		16 Apr	Lge	H	Man City	L	0-1
28 Nov	Lge	A	Blackpool	D	2-2		18 Apr	Lge	H	Chelsea	L	0-1
5 Dec	Lge	H	Blackburn	W	2-1		23 Apr	Lge	A	Wolves	W	3-1
12 Dec	Lge	A	Fulham	D	1-1		30 Apr	Lge	H	Blackpool	W	4-1
19 Dec	Lge	H	Newcastle	W	4-0		2 May	F	A	C. Palace	D	2-2
26 Dec	Lge	A	Leeds	W	4-2		25 May	F	A	Juventus	L	0-2

Player	Lg App	Goals	Player	Lg App	Goals
Allen L.W.	15	7	Hopkins M.	14	
Baker R.P.B.	41		Harmer T.C.	37	3
Blanchflower R.D.	40	2	Jones C.W.	38	20
Brooks J.	4	2	Mackay D.C.	38	11
Brown W.D.F.	40		Marchi A.V.	14	1
Clayton E.	1		Medwin T.C.	26	4
Dodge W.C.	1		Norman M.	39	
Dunmore D.G.I.	10	2	Smith J.	1	
Dyson T.K.	6		Smith R.A.	40	25
Henry R.P.	25		White J.A.	28	5
Hills J.R.	1		Worley L.F.	1	
Hollowbread J.F.	2		Own Goals		4

Final table for First Division

1	Burnley	42	24	7	11	85:61	55
2	Wolverhampton	42	24	6	12	106:67	54
3	**TOTTENHAM**	**42**	**21**	**11**	**10**	**86:50**	**53**
4	West Bromwich	42	19	11	12	83:57	49
5	Sheffield W.	42	19	11	12	80:59	49
6	Bolton	42	20	8	14	59:51	48
7	Manchester U.	42	19	7	16	102:80	45
8	Newcastle	42	18	8	16	82:78	44
9	Preston	42	16	12	14	79:76	44
10	Fulham	42	17	10	15	73:80	44
11	Blackpool	42	15	10	17	59:71	40
12	Leicester	42	13	13	16	66:75	39
13	Arsenal	42	15	9	18	68:80	39
14	West Ham	42	16	6	20	75:91	38
15	Everton	42	13	11	18	73:78	37
16	Manchester C.	42	17	3	22	78:84	37
17	Blackburn	42	16	5	21	60:70	37
18	Chelsea	42	14	9	19	76:91	37
19	Birmingham	42	13	9	20	63:80	36
20	Nottingham F.	42	13	9	20	50:74	35
21	Leeds	42	12	10	20	65:92	34
22	Luton	42	9	12	21	50:73	30

THE DOUBLE SEASON—1960/61

Date			Score	Comp	Opponent	Att	BROWN	BAKER	HENRY	BL'FLOWER	NORMAN	MACKAY	JONES	WHITE	R. SMITH	ALLEN	DYSON	MEDWIN	SAUL	MARCHI	DODGE	ATKINSON	COLLINS	HOLLOWB'D	BARTON	J. SMITH
Aug 20	H	W	2-0	Lge	Everton	47,440	1	2	3	4	5	6	7	8	9¹	10¹	11									
Aug 22	A	W	3-1	Lge	Blackpool	27,656	1	2	3	4	5	6		8	9	10	11²	7¹								
Aug 27	A	W	4-1	Lge	Blackburn	26,700	1	2	3	4	5	6		8	9²	10¹	11¹	7								
Aug 31	H	W	3-1	Lge	Blackpool	45,684	1	2	3	4	5	6		8	9³	10	11	7								
Sep 3	H	W	4-1	Lge	Man Utd	55,445	1	2	3	4	5	6		8	9²	10²	11	7								
Sep 7	A	W	2-1	Lge	Bolton	41,151	1	2	3	4	5	6		8¹		10¹	11	7	9							
Sep 10	A	W	3-2	Lge	Arsenal	60,088	1	2	3	4	5	6		8		10¹	11¹	7	9¹							
Sep 14	H	W	3-1	Lge	Bolton	43,559	1	2	3	4¹	5	6	7	8	9²	10	11									
Sep 17	A	W	2-1	Lge	Leicester	30,129	1	2	3	4	5	6	7	8	9²	10	11									
Sep 24	H	W	6-2	Lge	Aston Villa	61,356	1	2	3	4	5	6¹	7	8²	9¹	10¹	11¹									
Oct 1	A	W	4-0	Lge	Wolves	55,000	1	2	3	4¹	5		7¹	8	9	10¹	11¹			6						
Oct 10	H	D	1-1	Lge	Man City	58,916	1	2	3	4	5	6	7	8	9¹	10	11									
Oct 15	A	W	4-0	Lge	Nottm Forest	37,198	1	2	3	4	5	6¹	7²	8¹	9	10	11									
Oct 24	H	L	3-5	F	Army XI	5,947	1	2	3		5					10¹	11		9	6	4	7¹	8			
Oct 29	A	W	4-3	Lge	Newcastle	51,369	1	2	3	4	5¹	6	7¹	8¹	9¹	10	11									
Nov 2	H	W	3-2	Lge	Cardiff	47,605	1	2	3	4¹	5	6		8	9	10	11¹	7¹								
Nov 5	H	W	5-1	Lge	Fulham	56,270	1	2	3	4	5	6	7²	8¹	9	10²	11									
Nov 12	A	L	1-2	Lge	Sheffield Wed	56,363	1	2	3	4	5¹	6	7	8	9	10	11									
Nov 14	H	W	5-2	F	Dinamo Tbilisi	38,649	1	2	3	4	5	6²		8	9	10	11¹	7²								
Nov 19	H	W	6-0	Lge	Birmingham	46,010	1	2	3	4	5	6	7²	8¹	9¹	10	11²									
Nov 26	A	W	3-1	Lge	WBA	37,800	1	2	3	4	5	6	7	8	9²	10¹	11									
Dec 3	H	D	4-4	Lge	Burnley	58,737	1	2	3	4	5¹	6¹	7²	8	9	10	11									
Dec 10	A	W	1-0	Lge	Preston	21,657	1	2	3	4	5	6	7	8¹		10	11		9							
Dec 17	A	W	3-1	Lge	Everton	61,052	1	2	3	4	5	6¹	7	8¹	9	10¹	11									
Dec 24	H	W	2-0	Lge	West Ham	54,930	1	2	3	4	5	6	7	8¹	9	10¹	11¹									
Dec 26	A	W	3-0	Lge	West Ham	34,481		2	3	4	5	6		8¹	9	10¹	11	7							1	
Dec 31	H	W	5-2	Lge	Blackburn	48,742	1	2	3	4¹	5			8	9²	10²	11	7		6						
Jan 7	H	W	3-2	FC	Charlton	54,969	1	2	3	4	5	6		8	9	10²	11¹	7								
Jan 16	A	L	0-2	Lge	Man Utd	65,295	1		3	4	5	6		8	9	10	11								2	7
Jan 21	H	W	4-2	Lge	Arsenal	65,251	1	2	3	4¹	5	6	7	8	9¹	10²	11									
Jan 28	H	W	5-1	FC	Crewe	53,721	1	2	3	4	5	6¹	7¹	8	9¹	10¹	11¹									
Feb 4	H	L	2-3	Lge	Leicester	53,627	1	2	3	4¹	5	6	7	8	9	10¹	11									
Feb 11	A	W	2-1	Lge	Aston Villa	50,810	1	2	3	4	5	6	7	8	9¹	10	11¹									
Feb 18	A	W	2-0	FC	Aston Villa	69,000	1	2	3	4	5	6	7²	8	9	10	11									
Feb 22	H	D	1-1	Lge	Wolves	62,261	1	2	3	4	5	6	7	8	9¹	10	11									
Feb 25	A	W	1-0	Lge	Man City	40,278	1	2	3	4		6		8	9	10	11	7¹		5						
Mar 4	A	D	1-1	FC	Sunderland	63,000	1	2	3	4	5	6	7¹	8	9	10	11									
Mar 8	H	W	5-0	FCr	Sunderland	64,797	1	2	3	4	5	6¹	7	8	9¹	10¹	11²									
Mar 11	A	L	2-3	Lge	Cardiff	58,000	1	2	3	4	5	6	7	8	9	10¹	11¹									
Mar 18		W	3-0	FCsf	Burnley (Villa Park)	69,968	1	2	3	4	5	6	7¹	8	9²	10	11									
Mar 22	H	L	1-2	Lge	Newcastle	46,470	1	2	3	4	5	6	7	8	9	10¹	11									
Mar 25	A	D	0-0	Lge	Fulham	38,536	1	2	3	4	5		7	8		10	11		9	6						
Mar 31	H	W	4-2	Lge	Chelsea	65,032	1	2	3	4	5		7²	8		10	11		9¹	6						
Apr 1	H	W	5-0	Lge	Preston	46,325	1	2	3	4	5	6	7³	8¹		10		11	9¹							
Apr 3	A	W	3-2	Lge	Chelsea	57,103	1	2	3	4	5¹	6	7	8	9¹	10		11¹		'						
Apr 8	A	W	3-2	Lge	Birmingham	40,960	1	2	3	4	5	6	7	8¹	9¹	10¹	11									
Apr 17	H	W	2-1	Lge	Sheffield Wed	62,000	1	2	3	4	5	6	7	8	9¹	10¹	11									
Apr 22	A	L	2-4	Lge	Burnley	28,397	1	2¹	3	4	5	6		8	9¹	10	11	7								
Apr 26	H	W	1-0	Lge	Nottm Forest	35,743	1	2	3	4	5			8	9	10	11	7¹		6						
Apr 29	H	L	1-2	Lge	WBA	51,880	1	2	3	4	5	6	7	8	9¹	10	11									
May 6		W	2-0	FCf	Leicester (Wembley)	100,000	1	2	3	4	5	6	7	8	9¹	10	11¹									
May 15	A	W	2-1	F	Feijenoord	40,000	1	2	3	4	5	6		8	9	10¹	11	7¹								
May 17	A	W	3-0	F	Amsterdam XI	30,000	1	2	3	4	5	6		8¹	9	10¹	11¹	7								
					Total League App		41	41	42	42	41	37	29	42	36	42	40	14	6	6				1	1	1
(one own goal)					**Total League Goals**			1		6	4	4	15	13	28	22	12	5	3							

Date	Comp	H/A	Opponent	Result	Score
12 Aug	CS	H	England Sel. XI	W	3-2
19 Aug	Lge	A	Blackpool	W	2-1
23 Aug	Lge	H	West Ham	D	2-2
26 Aug	Lge	H	Arsenal	W	4-3
28 Aug	Lge	A	West Ham	L	1-2
2 Sep	Lge	H	Cardiff	W	3-2
4 Sep	Lge	A	Sheff Utd	D	1-1
9 Sep	Lge	A	Man Utd	L	0-1
13 Sep	EC	A	Gornik	L	2-4
16 Sep	Lge	H	Wolves	W	1-0
20 Sep	EC	H	Gornik	W	8-1
23 Sep	Lge	A	Nottm Forest	L	0-2
30 Sep	Lge	H	Aston Villa	W	1-0
9 Oct	Lge	A	Bolton	W	2-1
14 Oct	Lge	H	Man City	W	2-0
21 Oct	Lge	A	Ipswich	L	2-3
28 Oct	Lge	H	Burnley	W	4-2
1 Nov	EC	A	Feijenoord	W	3-1
4 Nov	Lge	A	Everton	L	0-3
11 Nov	Lge	H	Fulham	W	4-2
15 Nov	EC	H	Feijenoord	D	1-1
18 Nov	Lge	A	Sheff Wed	D	0-0
25 Nov	Lge	H	Leicester	L	1-2
2 Dec	Lge	A	WBA	W	4-2
9 Dec	Lge	H	Birmingham	W	3-1
16 Dec	Lge	H	Blackpool	W	5-2
23 Dec	Lge	A	Arsenal	L	1-2
26 Dec	Lge	H	Chelsea	W	2-0
30 Dec	Lge	A	Chelsea	W	5-2
6 Jan	FC	A	Birmingham	D	3-3
10 Jan	FCr	H	Birmingham	W	4-2
13 Jan	Lge	A	Cardiff	D	1-1
20 Jan	Lge	H	Man Utd	D	2-2
27 Jan	FC	A	Plymouth	W	5-1
3 Feb	Lge	A	Wolves	L	1-3
10 Feb	Lge	H	Nottm Forest	W	4-2
14 Feb	EC	A	Dukla Prague	L	0-1
17 Feb	FC	H	WBA	W	4-2
21 Feb	Lge	A	Aston Villa	D	0-0
24 Feb	Lge	H	Bolton	D	2-2
26 Feb	EC	H	Dukla Prague	W	4-2
3 Mar	Lge	A	Man City	L	2-6
10 Mar	FC	H	Aston Villa	W	2-0
14 Mar	Lge	H	Ipswich	L	1-3
17 Mar	Lge	A	Burnley	D	2-2
21 Mar	ECsf	A	Benfica	L	1-3
24 Mar	Lge	H	Everton	W	3-1
31 Mar	FCsf	*	Man Utd	W	3-1
5 Apr	ECsf	H	Benfica	W	2-1
7 Apr	Lge	H	Sheff Wed	W	4-0
9 Apr	Lge	H	Sheff Utd	D	3-3
17 Apr	Lge	A	Fulham	D	1-1
20 Apr	Lge	H	Blackburn	W	4-1
21 Apr	Lge	H	WBA	L	1-2
23 Apr	Lge	A	Blackburn	W	1-0
28 Apr	Lge	A	Birmingham	W	3-2
30 Apr	Lge	A	Leicester	W	3-2
5 May	FCf	†	Burnley	W	3-1
26 May	F	A	Tel Aviv Select	W	2-1
30 May	F	A	Haifa Select	W	5-0

* Semi-final at Hillsborough   † Final at Wembley

Player	Lg App	Goals	Player	Lg App	Goals
Allen L.W.	23	9	Hopkins M.	5	
Baker P.R.B.	36		Jones C.W.	38	16
Barton K.R.	2		Mackay D.C.	26	8
Blanchflower R.D.	39	2	Marchi A.V.	21	
Clayton E.	7	3	Medwin T.C.	20	5
Brown W.D.F.	35		Norman M.	40	
Collins J.	2		Saul F.L.	8	3
Dyson T.K.	23	6	Smith J.	5	
Greaves J.P.	22	21	Smith R.A.	26	6
Henry R.P.	41		White J.A.	36	8
Hollowbread J.F.	7		Own Goal		1

Final table for First Division

1	Ipswich	42	24	8	10	93:67	56
2	Burnley	42	21	11	10	101:67	53
3	**TOTTENHAM**	42	21	10	11	88:69	52
4	Everton	42	20	11	11	88:54	51
5	Sheffield U.	42	19	9	14	61:69	47
6	Sheffield W.	42	20	6	16	72:58	46
7	Aston Villa	42	18	8	16	65:56	44
8	West Ham	42	17	10	15	76:82	44
9	West Bromwich	42	15	13	14	83:67	43
10	Arsenal	42	16	11	15	71:72	43
11	Bolton	42	16	10	16	62:66	42
12	Manchester C.	42	17	7	18	78:81	41
13	Blackpool	42	15	11	16	70:75	41
14	Leicester	42	17	6	19	72:71	40
15	Manchester U.	42	15	9	18	72:75	39
16	Blackburn	42	14	11	17	50:58	39
17	Birmingham	42	14	10	18	65:81	38
18	Wolverhampton	42	13	10	19	73:86	36
19	Nottingham F.	42	13	10	19	63:79	36
20	Fulham	42	13	7	22	66:74	33
21	Cardiff	42	9	14	19	50:81	32
22	Chelsea	42	9	10	23	63:94	28

Date	Comp	H/A	Opponent	Result	Score
11 Aug	CS	A	Ipswich	W	5-1
18 Aug	Lge	H	Birmingham	W	3-0
20 Aug	Lge	A	Aston Villa	L	1-2
25 Aug	Lge	A	West Ham	W	6-1
29 Aug	Lge	A	Aston Villa	W	4-2
1 Sep	Lge	H	Man City	W	4-2
8 Sep	Lge	A	Blackpool	W	2-1
12 Sep	Lge	H	Wolves	L	1-2
15 Sep	Lge	H	Blackburn	W	4-1
19 Sep	Lge	A	Wolves	D	2-2
22 Sep	Lge	A	Sheff Utd	L	1-3
29 Sep	Lge	H	Nottm Forest	W	9-2
6 Oct	Lge	H	Arsenal	D	4-4
13 Oct	Lge	A	WBA	W	2-1
20 Oct	Lge	H	Man Utd	W	6-2
27 Oct	Lge	A	Leyton Orient	W	5-1
31 Oct	ECWC	H	Rangers	W	5-2
3 Nov	Lge	H	Leicester	W	4-0
10 Nov	Lge	A	Fulham	W	2-0
14 Nov	F	A	Zamalek	W	7-3
17 Nov	Lge	H	Sheff Wed	D	1-1
24 Nov	Lge	A	Burnley	L	1-2
1 Dec	Lge	H	Everton	D	0-0
8 Dec	Lge	H	Bolton	L	0-1
11 Dec	ECWC	A	Rangers	W	3-2
15 Dec	Lge	A	Birmingham	W	2-0
22 Dec	Lge	H	West Ham	D	4-4
26 Dec	Lge	H	Ipswich	W	5-0
16 Jan	FC	H	Burnley	L	0-3
19 Jan	Lge	H	Blackpool	W	2-0
26 Jan	F	H	Arsenal	W	2-0
2 Feb	F	A	Portsmouth	W	3-2
23 Feb	Lge	A	Arsenal	W	3-2
2 Mar	Lge	H	WBA	W	2-1
5 Mar	ECWC	A	Slovan Bratislava	L	0-2
9 Mar	Lge	A	Man Utd	W	2-0
14 Mar	ECWC	H	Slovan Bratislava	W	6-0
16 Mar	Lge	A	Ipswich	W	4-2
23 Mar	Lge	A	Leicester	D	2-2
27 Mar	Lge	H	Leyton Orient	W	2-0
30 Mar	Lge	H	Burnley	D	1-1
8 Apr	Lge	A	Sheff Wed	L	1-3
12 Apr	Lge	A	Liverpool	L	2-5
13 Apr	Lge	H	Fulham	D	1-1
15 Apr	Lge	H	Liverpool	W	7-2
20 Apr	Lge	A	Everton	L	0-1
24 Apr	ECWCsf	A	OFK Belgrade	W	2-1
27 Apr	Lge	H	Bolton	W	4-1
1 May	ECWCsf	H	OFK Belgrade	W	3-1
4 May	Lge	H	Sheff Utd	W	4-2
11 May	Lge	A	Man City	L	0-1
15 May	ECWCf	†	Atletico Madrid	W	5-1
18 May	Lge	A	Nottm Forest	D	1-1
20 May	Lge	A	Blackburn Rvs	L	0-3

† European Cup Winners Cup final played in Rotterdam

Player	Lg App	Goals	Player	Lg App	Goals
Allen L.W.	25	5	Mackay D.C.	37	6
Baker P.R.B.	33		Marchi A.V.	22	3
Blanchflower R.D.	24	3	Medwin T.C.	26	9
Brown W.D.F.	40		Norman M.	38	1
Clayton E.	3		Piper R.D.	1	
Dyson T.K.	13	2	Saul F.P.	10	4
Greaves J.P.	41	37	Smith J.	7	1
Henry R.P.	42		Smith R.A.	15	8
Hollowbread J.F.	2		White J.A.	37	8
Hopkins M.	9		Own Goals		4
Jones C.W.	37	20			

Final table for First Division

1	Everton	42	25	11	6	84:42	61
2	**TOTTENHAM**	42	23	9	10	111:62	55
3	Burnley	42	22	10	10	78:57	54
4	Leicester	42	20	12	10	79:53	52
5	Wolverhampton	42	20	10	12	93:65	50
6	Sheffield W.	42	19	10	13	77:63	48
7	Arsenal	42	18	10	14	86:77	46
8	Liverpool	42	17	10	15	71:59	44
9	Nottingham F.	42	17	10	15	67:69	44
10	Sheffield U.	42	16	12	14	58:60	44
11	Blackburn	42	15	12	15	79:71	42
12	West Ham	42	14	12	16	73:69	40
13	Blackpool	42	13	14	15	58:64	40
14	West Bromwich	42	16	7	19	71:79	39
15	Aston Villa	42	15	8	19	62:68	38
16	Fulham	42	14	10	18	50:71	38
17	Ipswich	42	12	11	19	59:78	35
18	Bolton	42	15	5	22	55:75	35
19	Manchester U.	42	12	10	20	67:81	34
20	Birmingham	42	10	13	19	63:90	33
21	Manchester C.	42	10	11	21	58:102	31
22	Leyton Orient	42	6	9	27	37:81	21

SEASON 1963/64

Date	Comp	H/A	Opponent	Result	Score
24 Aug	Lge	A	Stoke City	L	1-2
28 Aug	Lge	A	Wolves	W	4-1
31 Aug	Lge	H	Nottm Forest	W	4-1
4 Sep	Lge	H	Wolves	W	4-3
7 Sep	Lge	A	Blackburn	L	2-7
14 Sep	Lge	H	Blackpool	W	6-1
16 Sep	Lge	A	Aston Villa	W	4-2
21 Sep	Lge	A	Chelsea	W	3-0
28 Sep	Lge	H	West Ham	W	3-0
2 Oct	Lge	H	Birmingham	W	6-1
5 Oct	Lge	A	Sheff Utd	D	3-3
15 Oct	Lge	A	Arsenal	D	4-4
19 Oct	Lge	H	Leicester	D	1-1
26 Oct	Lge	A	Everton	L	0-1
2 Nov	Lge	H	Fulham	W	1-0
9 Nov	Lge	A	Man Utd	L	1-4
16 Nov	Lge	H	Burnley	W	3-2
23 Nov	Lge	A	Ipswich	W	3-2
30 Nov	Lge	H	Sheff Wed	D	1-1
3 Dec	ECWC	H	Man Utd	W	2-0
7 Dec	Lge	A	Bolton	W	3-1
10 Dec	ECWC	A	Man Utd	L	1-4
14 Dec	Lge	H	Stoke	W	2-1
21 Dec	Lge	A	Nottm Forest	W	2-1
26 Dec	Lge	A	WBA	D	4-4
28 Dec	Lge	H	WBA	L	0-2
5 Jan	FC	H	Chelsea	D	1-1
8 Jan	FCr	A	Chelsea	L	0-2
11 Jan	Lge	H	Blackburn	W	4-1
18 Jan	Lge	A	Blackpool	W	2-0
25 Jan	Lge	H	Aston Villa	W	3-1
1 Feb	Lge	H	Chelsea	L	1-2
8 Feb	Lge	A	West Ham	L	0-4
15 Feb	Lge	H	Sheff Utd	D	0-0
22 Feb	Lge	H	Arsenal	W	3-1
29 Feb	Lge	A	Birmingham	W	2-1
7 Mar	Lge	H	Everton	L	2-4
21 Mar	Lge	H	Man Utd	L	2-3
27 Mar	Lge	A	Liverpool	L	1-3
28 Mar	Lge	A	Fulham	D	1-1
30 Mar	Lge	A	Liverpool	L	1-3
4 Apr	Lge	H	Ipswich	W	6-3
13 Apr	Lge	A	Sheff Wed	L	0-2
18 Apr	Lge	H	Bolton	W	1-0
21 Apr	Lge	A	Burnley	L	2-7
25 Apr	Lge	A	Leicester	W	1-0
28 Apr	F	A	Coventry	W	6-5

Player	Lg App	Goals
Allen L.W.	8	1
Beal P.	16	
Baker P.R.B.	35	1
Barton K.R.	1	
Blanchflower R.D.	15	
Brown L.	9	1
Brown W.D.F.	27	
Clayton E.	1	
Dyson T.K.	39	11
Greaves J.P.	41	35
Henry R.P.	29	
Hollowbread J.F.	15	
Hopkins M.	19	
Jones C.W.	39	14
Mackay D.C.	17	3
Marchi A.V.	21	1
Mullery A.P.	9	1
Norman M.	42	3
Possee D.J.	1	1
Robertson J.	3	1
Saul F.L.	2	
Smith J.	7	
Smith R.A.	26	13
White J.A.	40	6
Own Goals		5

Final table for First Division

1	Liverpool	42	26	5	11	92:45	57
2	Manchester U.	42	23	7	12	90:62	53
3	Everton	42	21	10	11	84:64	52
4	**TOTTENHAM**	42	22	7	13	97:81	51
5	Chelsea	42	20	10	12	72:56	50
6	Sheffield W.	42	19	11	12	84:67	49
7	Blackburn	42	18	10	14	89:65	46
8	Arsenal	42	17	11	14	90:82	45
9	Burnley	42	17	10	15	71:64	44
10	West Bromwich	42	16	11	15	70:61	43
11	Leicester	42	16	11	15	61:58	43
12	Sheffield U.	42	16	11	15	61:64	43
13	Nottingham F.	42	16	9	17	64:68	41
14	West Ham	42	14	12	16	69:74	40
15	Fulham	42	13	13	16	58:65	39
16	Wolverhampton	42	12	15	15	70:80	39
17	Stoke	42	14	10	18	77:78	38
18	Blackpool	42	13	9	20	52:73	35
19	Aston Villa	42	11	12	19	62:71	34
20	Birmingham	42	11	7	24	54:92	29
21	Bolton	42	10	8	24	48:80	28
22	Ipswich	42	9	7	26	56:121	25

SEASON 1964/65

Date	Comp	H/A	Opponent	Result	Score
5 Aug	F	A	Glasgow Sel	L	2-4
8 Aug	F	A	Feijenoord	L	3-4
22 Aug	Lge	H	Sheff Utd	W	2-0
25 Aug	Lge	A	Burnley	D	2-2
29 Aug	Lge	A	Everton	L	1-4
2 Sep	Lge	H	Burnley	W	4-1
5 Sep	Lge	A	Birmingham	W	4-1
9 Sep	Lge	A	Stoke	L	0-2
12 Sep	Lge	H	West Ham	L	2-3
17 Sep	Lge	H	Stoke	W	2-1
19 Sep	Lge	H	WBA	W	1-0
23 Sep	F	A	Copenhagen XI	L	1-2
26 Sep	F	A	Man Utd	L	1-4
28 Sep	Lge	A	Blackpool	D	1-1
5 Oct	Lge	H	Fulham	W	3-0
10 Oct	Lge	A	Arsenal	W	3-1
17 Oct	Lge	A	Leeds	L	1-3
24 Oct	Lge	H	Chelsea	D	1-1
31 Oct	Lge	A	Leicester	L	2-4
7 Nov	Lge	H	Sunderland	W	3-0
11 Nov	*	H	Scotland XI	L	2-6
14 Nov	Lge	A	Wolves	L	1-3
21 Nov	Lge	H	Aston Villa	W	4-0
28 Nov	Lge	A	Liverpool	D	1-1
5 Dec	Lge	H	Sheff Wed	W	3-2
8 Dec	F	A	Leytonstone	W	5-0
12 Dec	Lge	A	Sheff Utd	D	3-3
19 Dec	Lge	A	Everton	D	2-2
26 Dec	Lge	A	Nottm Forest	W	2-1
28 Dec	Lge	H	Nottm Forest	W	4-0
2 Jan	Lge	A	Birmingham	L	0-1
9 Jan	FC	A	Torquay Utd	D	3-3
16 Jan	Lge	H	West Ham	W	3-2
18 Jan	FCr	H	Torquay Utd	W	5-1
23 Jan	Lge	A	WBA	L	0-2
30 Jan	FC	H	Ipswich	W	5-0
6 Feb	FC	H	Man Utd	W	1-0
13 Feb	Lge	H	Fulham	L	1-4
20 Feb	FC	A	Chelsea	L	0-1
23 Feb	Lge	A	Arsenal	L	1-3
27 Feb	Lge	H	Leeds Utd	D	0-0
10 Mar	Lge	A	Chelsea	L	1-3
13 Mar	Lge	H	Blackpool	W	4-1
20 Mar	Lge	A	Sunderland	L	1-2
27 Mar	Lge	A	Wolves	W	7-4
3 Apr	Lge	H	Aston Villa	L	0-1
9 Apr	Lge	H	Liverpool	W	3-0
16 Apr	Lge	H	Blackburn	W	5-2
17 Apr	Lge	A	Sheff Wed	L	0-1
19 Apr	Lge	A	Blackburn	L	1-3
24 Apr	Lge	H	Leicester	W	6-2
27 Apr	F	A	Anderlecht	L	2-4
29 Apr	F	A	Coventry	W	3-0
18 May	F	A	DWS Amsterdam	L	0-1
22 May	F	A	Telstar	W	3-2
21 Jun	F	A	Hakoah	W	3-1†
24 Jun	F	A	Maccabi Sel	W	3-2†

* John White testimonial match † Tour of Israel

Player	Lg App	Goals
Allen L.W.	6	2
Baker P.	3	
Beal P.	8	
Brown L.	16	1
Brown W.D.F.	19	
Clayton E.	15	1
Dyson T.K.	32	5
Gilzean A.J.	20	11
Greaves J.P.	41	29
Henry R.P.	41	1
Jennings P.A.	23	
Jones C.W.	39	13
Knowles C.B.	38	
Low A.R.	6	1
Marchi A.V.	17	
Mullery A.P.	42	2
Norman M.	30	1
Possee D.J.	1	
Robertson J.G.	36	7
Saul F.L.	23	11
Weller K.	6	
Own Goals		2

Final table for First Division

1	Manchester U.	42	26	9	7	89:39	61
2	Leeds	42	26	9	7	83:52	61
3	Chelsea	42	24	8	10	89:54	56
4	Everton	42	17	15	10	69:60	49
5	Nottingham F.	42	17	13	12	71:67	47
6	**TOTTENHAM**	42	19	7	16	87:71	45
7	Liverpool	42	17	10	15	67:73	44
8	Sheffield W.	42	16	11	15	57:55	43
9	West Ham	42	19	4	19	82:71	42
10	Blackburn	42	16	10	16	83:79	42
11	Stoke	42	16	10	16	67:66	42
12	Burnley	42	16	10	16	70:70	42
13	Arsenal	42	17	7	18	69:75	41
14	West Bromwich	42	13	13	16	70:65	39
15	Sunderland	42	14	9	19	64:74	37
16	Aston Villa	42	16	5	21	57:82	37
17	Blackpool	42	12	11	19	67:78	35
18	Leicester	42	11	13	18	69:85	35
19	Sheffield U.	42	12	11	19	50:64	35
20	Fulham	42	11	12	19	60:78	34
21	Wolverhampton	42	13	4	25	59:89	30
22	Birmingham	42	8	11	23	64:96	27

SEASON 1965/66

Date	Comp		Opponent	Result	Score		Date	Comp		Opponent	Result	Score
14 Aug	F	A	Valencia	W	2-1		5 Feb	Lge	A	Blackpool	D	0-0
15 Aug	F	A	Standard Liege	W	1-0		12 Feb	FC	H	Burnley	W	4-3
25 Aug	Lge	H	Leicester	W	4-2		19 Feb	Lge	H	Fulham	W	4-3
27 Aug	Lge	H	Blackpool	W	4-0		5 Mar	FC	A	Preston	L	1-2
1 Sep	Lge	A	Leicester	D	2-2		8 Mar	Lge	A	Arsenal	D	1-1
4 Sep	Lge	A	Fulham	W	2-0		12 Mar	Lge	A	Liverpool	L	0-1
8 Sep	Lge	H	Leeds	W	3-2		19 Mar	Lge	H	Aston Villa	D	5-5
11 Sep	Lge	H	Arsenal	D	2-2		26 Mar	Lge	A	Sunderland	L	0-2
15 Sep	Lge	A	Leeds	L	0-2		2 Apr	Lge	H	Nottm Forest	L	2-3
18 Sep	Lge	H	Liverpool	W	2-1		8 Apr	Lge	A	West Ham	L	1-4
22 Sep	F	A	Walton & Hersham	W	8-1		9 Apr	Lge	A	Sheff Wed	D	1-1
25 Sep	Lge	A	Aston Villa	L	2-3		16 Apr	Lge	H	Northampton	D	1-1
6 Oct	Lge	H	Sunderland	W	3-0		23 Apr	Lge	A	Stoke City	W	1-0
9 Oct	Lge	A	Everton	L	1-3		25 Apr	Lge	A	West Ham	L	0-2
16 Oct	Lge	H	Man Utd	W	5-1		30 Apr	Lge	H	Burnley	L	0-1
23 Oct	Lge	A	Newcastle	D	0-0		3 May	F	A	Legia Warsaw	L	0-2
30 Oct	Lge	H	WBA	W	2-1		7 May	Lge	A	WBA	L	1-2
6 Nov	Lge	A	Nottm Forest	L	0-1		9 May	Lge	A	Blackburn	W	1-0
13 Nov	Lge	H	Sheff Wed	L	2-3		15 May	F	A	Sarpsborg	W	3-0*
18 Nov	F	H	Hungarian Sel	W	4-0		19 May	F	A	Bermuda Sel	W	3-2*
20 Nov	Lge	A	Northampton	W	2-0		21 May	F	A	Celtic	L	0-1*
27 Nov	Lge	H	Stoke	D	2-2		25 May	F	A	Hartford USA XI	W	3-0*
4 Dec	Lge	A	Burnley	D	1-1		29 May	F	A	Bologna	L	0-1*
11 Dec	Lge	H	Chelsea	W	4-2		1 Jun	F	A	Celtic	L	1-2*
18 Dec	Lge	A	Man Utd	L	1-5		4 Jun	F	A	Celtic	D	1-1*
27 Dec	Lge	H	Sheff Utd	W	1-0		5 Jun	F	A	Vancouver Sel	W	3-0*
28 Dec	Lge	A	Sheff Utd	W	3-1		12 Jun	F	A	Mexico Sel	W	1-0*
1 Jan	Lge	H	Everton	D	2-2		15 Jun	F	A	Mexico Americano	W	2-0*
8 Jan	Lge	A	Chelsea	L	1-2		17 Jun	F	A	Bayern Munich	W	3-0*
15 Jan	Lge	H	Newcastle	D	2-2		19 Jun	F	A	Bayern Munich	D	1-1*
22 Jan	FC	H	Middlesbrough	W	4-0							
29 Jan	Lge	H	Blackburn	W	4-0							

* North American tour matches

Player	Lg App		Goals	Player	Lg App		Goals
Beal P.	21			Kinnear J.P.	8		
Brown L.	37		1	Knowles C.B.	41		3
Brown W.D.F.	20			Low A.R.	1	(1)	
Clayton E.	38		9	Mackay D.C.	41		6
Collins J.L.	2			Mullery A.P.	40		1
Gilzean A.J.	40		12	Norman M.	16		1
Greaves J.P.	29		15	Pitt S.W.	1		
Henry R.P.	1			Possee D.J.	17		3
Hoy R.E.	5			Robertson J.G.	33		6
Jennings P.A.	22			Saul F.L.	26		8
Johnson N.	10	(1)	1	Venables T.	1		
Jones C.W.	9		8	Weller K.	5		1

Note: first season using substitutes, with appearances as sub in brackets. League appearances include full appearances **plus** occasions when player came on as sub. Sub not leaving bench is not recorded.

Final table for First Division

1	Liverpool	42	26	9	7	79:34	61
2	Leeds	42	23	9	10	79:38	55
3	Burnley	42	24	7	11	79:47	55
4	Manchester U.	42	18	15	9	84:59	51
5	Chelsea	42	22	7	13	65:53	51
6	West Bromwich	42	19	12	11	91:69	50
7	Leicester	42	21	7	14	80:65	49
8	**TOTTENHAM**	**42**	**16**	**12**	**14**	**75:66**	**44**
9	Sheffield U.	42	16	11	15	56:59	43
10	Stoke	42	15	12	15	65:64	42
11	Everton	42	15	11	16	56:62	41
12	West Ham	42	15	9	18	70:83	39
13	Blackpool	42	14	9	19	55:65	37
14	Arsenal	42	12	13	17	62:75	37
15	Newcastle	42	14	9	19	50:63	37
16	Aston Villa	42	15	6	21	69:80	36
17	Sheffield W.	42	14	8	20	56:66	36
18	Nottingham F.	42	14	8	20	56:72	36
19	Sunderland	42	14	8	20	51:72	36
20	Fulham	42	14	7	21	67:85	35
21	Northampton	42	10	13	19	55:92	33
22	Blackburn	42	8	4	30	57:88	20

SEASON 1966/67

Date	Comp		Opponent	Result	Score		Date	Comp		Opponent	Result	Score
14 Aug	F	A	Malaga	W	2-1		7 Jan	Lge	A	Arsenal	W	2-0
15 Aug	F	A	Benfica	W	2-1		14 Jan	Lge	A	Man Utd	L	0-1
20 Aug	Lge	H	Leeds	W	3-1		21 Jan	Lge	H	Burnley	W	2-0
24 Aug	Lge	A	Stoke	L	0-2		28 Jan	FC	A	Millwall	D	0-0
27 Aug	Lge	A	Newcastle	W	2-0		1 Feb	FCr	H	Millwall	W	1-0
31 Aug	Lge	H	Stoke	W	2-0		4 Feb	Lge	A	Nottm Forest	D	1-1
3 Sep	Lge	H	Arsenal	W	3-1		11 Feb	Lge	H	Fulham	W	4-2
6 Sep	Lge	A	Sheff Utd	L	1-2		18 Feb	FC	H	Portsmouth	W	3-1
10 Sep	Lge	H	Man Utd	W	2-1		25 Feb	Lge	H	Man City	D	1-1
14 Sep	FLC	A	West Ham	L	0-1		4 Mar	Lge	A	Aston Villa	D	3-3
17 Sep	Lge	A	Burnley	D	2-2		11 Mar	FC	A	Bristol City	W	2-0
24 Sep	Lge	H	Nottm Forest	W	2-1		18 Mar	Lge	H	Chelsea	D	1-1
1 Oct	Lge	A	Fulham	W	4-3		22 Mar	Lge	A	Everton	W	1-0
8 Oct	Lge	H	Man City	W	2-1		25 Mar	Lge	A	Leicester	W	1-0
10 Oct	F	A	Dundee	W	3-2		27 Mar	Lge	H	Everton	W	2-0
15 Oct	Lge	H	Blackpool	L	1-3		1 Apr	Lge	H	Liverpool	W	2-1
26 Oct	Lge	A	Chelsea	L	0-3		8 Apr	FC	A	Birmingham	D	0-0
29 Oct	Lge	A	Aston Villa	L	0-1		12 Apr	FCr	H	Birmingham	W	6-0
5 Nov	Lge	A	Blackpool	D	2-2		15 Apr	Lge	H	Sheff Wed	W	2-1
12 Nov	Lge	H	West Ham	L	3-4		22 Apr	Lge	A	Southampton	W	1-0
19 Nov	Lge	A	Sheff Wed	L	0-1		29 Apr	FCsf	*	Nottm Forest	W	2-1
23 Nov	F	A	Polish Sel XI	W	2-1		3 May	Lge	H	Sunderland	W	1-0
26 Nov	Lge	H	Southampton	W	3-0		6 May	Lge	A	Liverpool	D	0-0
3 Dec	Lge	H	Sunderland	W	1-0		9 May	Lge	A	West Ham	W	2-0
10 Dec	Lge	A	Leicester	W	2-0		13 May	Lge	H	Sheff Utd	W	2-0
17 Dec	Lge	A	Leeds	L	2-3		20 May	FCf	†	Chelsea	W	2-1
26 Dec	Lge	A	WBA	L	0-3		30 May	F	A	FC Zurich	W	2-0
27 Dec	Lge	H	WBA	D	0-0		1 Jun	F	A	Yng Boys Bern	W	3-2
31 Dec	Lge	H	Newcastle	W	4-0		7 Jun	F	A	Servette	W	4-1

* Semi-final played at Hillsborough   † Final played at Wembley

Player	Lg App		Goals	Player	Lg App		Goals
Beal P.	26			Knowles C.B.	42		1
Bond D.	1	(1)		Low A.R.	1	(1)	
Brown W.D.F.	1			Mackay D.C.	39		3
Clayton E.	9	(3)		Mullery A.P.	39		5
England M.	42		1	Robertson J.G.	40		6
Gilzean A.J.	40		18	Saul F.L.	22	(2)	4
Greaves J.P.	38		23	Venables T.	41		3
Jennings P.A.	41			Weller K.	10	(2)	
Jones C.W.	20		6	Own Goal			1
Kinnear J.P.	20	(1)					

Final table for First Division

1	Manchester U.	42	24	12	6	84:45	60
2	Nottingham F.	42	23	10	9	64:41	56
3	**TOTTENHAM**	**42**	**24**	**8**	**10**	**71:48**	**56**
4	Leeds	42	22	11	9	62:42	55
5	Liverpool	42	19	13	10	64:47	51
6	Everton	42	19	10	13	65:46	48
7	Arsenal	42	16	14	12	58:47	46
8	Leicester	42	18	8	16	78:71	44
9	Chelsea	42	15	14	13	67:62	44
10	Sheffield U.	42	16	10	16	52:59	42
11	Sheffield W.	42	14	13	15	56:47	41
12	Stoke	42	17	7	18	63:58	41
13	West Bromwich	42	16	7	19	77:73	39
14	Burnley	42	15	9	18	66:76	39
15	Manchester C.	42	12	15	15	43:52	39
16	West Ham	42	14	8	20	80:84	36
17	Sunderland	42	14	8	20	58:72	36
18	Fulham	42	11	12	19	71:83	34
19	Southampton	42	14	6	22	74:92	34
20	Newcastle	42	12	9	21	39:81	33
21	Aston Villa	42	11	7	24	54:85	29
22	Blackpool	42	6	9	27	41:76	21

SEASON 1967/68

Date	Comp	H/A	Opponent	Result			Date	Comp	H/A	Opponent	Result	
5 Aug	F	A	Celtic	D	3-3		23 Dec	Lge	A	West Ham	L	1-2
12 Aug	CS	A	Man Utd	D	3-3		26 Dec	Lge	H	Fulham	D	2-2
19 Aug	Lge	A	Leicester	W	3-2		30 Dec	Lge	A	Fulham	W	2-1
23 Aug	Lge	H	Everton	D	1-1		17 Jan	Lge	A	Sheff Wed	W	2-1
26 Aug	Lge	H	West Ham	W	5-1		20 Jan	Lge	H	Arsenal	W	1-0
29 Aug	Lge	A	Everton	W	1-0		28 Jan	FC	A	Man Utd	D	2-2
2 Sep	Lge	A	Burnley	L	1-5		31 Jan	FCr	H	Man Utd	W	1-0
6 Sep	Lge	H	Wolves	W	2-1		3 Feb	Lge	H	Man Utd	L	1-2
9 Sep	Lge	H	Sheff Wed	W	2-1		10 Feb	Lge	A	Sunderland	W	1-0
16 Sep	Lge	A	Arsenal	L	0-4		17 Feb	FC	H	Preston	W	3-1
20 Sep	ECWC	A	Hadjuk Split	W	2-0		26 Feb	Lge	A	Sheff Utd	L	2-3
23 Sep	Lge	A	Man Utd	L	1-3		1 Mar	Lge	H	WBA	D	0-0
27 Sep	ECWC	H	Hadjuk Split	W	4-3		9 Mar	FC	A	Liverpool	D	1-1
30 Sep	Lge	H	Sunderland	W	3-0		12 Mar	FCr	A	Liverpool	L	1-2
7 Oct	Lge	H	Sheff Utd	D	1-1		16 Mar	Lge	A	Nottm Forest	D	0-0
14 Oct	Lge	A	Coventry	W	3-2		23 Mar	Lge	H	Stoke	W	3-0
25 Oct	Lge	H	Nottm Forest	D	1-1		30 Mar	Lge	H	Burnley	W	5-0
28 Oct	Lge	A	Stoke	L	1-2		6 Apr	Lge	H	Southampton	W	6-1
4 Nov	Lge	H	Liverpool	D	1-1		12 Apr	Lge	H	Leeds	W	2-1
11 Nov	Lge	A	Southampton	W	2-1		13 Apr	Lge	A	Chelsea	L	0-2
18 Nov	Lge	H	Chelsea	W	2-0		17 Apr	Lge	A	Leeds	L	0-1
25 Nov	Lge	A	WBA	L	0-2		20 Apr	Lge	H	Coventry	W	4-2
29 Nov	ECWC	A	Olymp. Lyon	L	0-1		27 Apr	Lge	A	Newcastle	W	3-1
2 Dec	Lge	H	Newcastle	D	1-1		29 Apr	Lge	A	Liverpool	D	1-1
9 Dec	Lge	A	Man City	L	1-4		4 May	Lge	H	Man City	L	1-3
13 Dec	ECWC	H	Olymp. Lyon	W	4-3		11 May	Lge	A	Wolves	L	1-2
16 Dec	Lge	H	Leicester	L	0-1		15 May	F	A	Panathinaikos	D	2-2

SEASON 1968/69

Date	Comp	H/A	Opponent	Result			Date	Comp	H/A	Opponent	Result	
31 Jul	F	H	Rangers	W	3-1		14 Dec	Lge	H	Man City	D	1-1
3 Aug	F	A	FK Austria	D	2-2		21 Dec	Lge	A	Liverpool	L	0-1
10 Aug	Lge	H	Arsenal	L	1-2		4 Jan	FC	A	Walsall	W	1-0
17 Aug	Lge	A	Everton	W	2-0		11 Jan	Lge	A	Stoke	D	1-1
21 Aug	Lge	H	WBA	D	1-1		18 Jan	Lge	H	Leeds	D	0-0
24 Aug	Lge	H	Sheff Wed	L	1-2		25 Jan	FC	H	Wolves	W	2-1
28 Aug	Lge	A	Man Utd	L	1-3		29 Jan	Lge	H	QPR	W	3-2
31 Aug	Lge	A	Chelsea	D	2-2		1 Feb	Lge	A	Sunderland	D	0-0
4 Sep	FLC	A	Aston Villa	W	4-1		12 Feb	FC	H	Aston Villa	W	3-2
7 Sep	Lge	H	Burnley	W	7-0		15 Feb	Lge	A	QPR	D	1-1
14 Sep	Lge	A	West Ham	D	2-2		22 Feb	Lge	H	Wolves	D	1-1
17 Sep	Lge	H	Coventry	W	2-1		1 Mar	FC	A	Man City	L	0-1
21 Sep	Lge	H	Nottm Forest	W	2-1		8 Mar	Lge	A	Everton	D	1-1
25 Sep	FLC	H	Exeter	W	6-3		18 Mar	Lge	H	Ipswich	D	2-2
28 Sep	Lge	A	Newcastle	D	2-2		22 Mar	Lge	H	Chelsea	W	1-0
5 Oct	Lge	H	Leicester	W	3-2		24 Mar	Lge	A	Arsenal	L	0-1
9 Oct	Lge	H	Man Utd	D	2-2		29 Mar	Lge	A	Burnley	D	2-2
12 Oct	Lge	A	Man City	L	0-4		2 Apr	Lge	H	Newcastle	L	0-1
16 Oct	FLC	H	Peterborough	W	1-0		4 Apr	Lge	H	Coventry	W	2-0
19 Oct	Lge	H	Liverpool	W	2-1		7 Apr	Lge	A	WBA	L	3-4
26 Oct	Lge	A	Ipswich	W	1-0		12 Apr	Lge	A	Nottm Forest	W	2-0
30 Oct	FLC	H	Southampton	W	1-0		19 Apr	Lge	H	West Ham	W	1-0
2 Nov	Lge	H	Stoke	D	1-1		22 Apr	Lge	H	Southampton	W	2-1
9 Nov	Lge	A	Leeds	D	0-0		29 Apr	Lge	A	Leicester	L	0-1
16 Nov	Lge	H	Sunderland	W	5-1		12 May	Lge	A	Sheff Wed	D	0-0
20 Nov	FLCsf	A	Arsenal	L	0-1		15 May	F	A	West Ham	W	4-3*
23 Nov	Lge	A	Southampton	L	1-2		17 May	F	A	Aston Villa	D	2-2*
4 Dec	FLCsf	H	Arsenal	D	1-1		28 May	F	A	Fiorentina	L	0-3*
7 Dec	Lge	A	Wolves	L	0-2		1 Jun	F	A	Rangers	W	4-3*

* Games played on tour of North America; West Ham in Baltimore, Villa in Atlanta, Fiorentina and Rangers in Toronto

Season 1967/68 players

Player	Lg App		Goals	Player	Lg App		Goals
Beal P.	35	(1)		Kinnear J.P.	30	(1)	1
Bond D.	6	(1)		Knowles C.B.	42		
Chivers M.	18		7	Mackay D.C.	29		1
Clayton E.	2	(1)		Mullery A.P.	41		2
England M.	31		3	Robertson J.G.	34	(1)	5
Gilzean A.J.	34	(2)	8	Saul F.L.	19	(2)	4
Greaves J.P.	39		23	Venables T.	36	(1)	2
Hoy R.E.	5			Want A.G.	2		
Jennings P.A.	42			Own Goals			2
Jones C.W.	30	(3)	12				

Season 1968/69 players

Player	Lg App		Goals	Player	Lg App		Goals
Beal P.	39		1	Johnson N.	16	(3)	3
Bond D.	2			Jones C.W.	7	(1)	5
Chivers M.	10		3	Kinnear J.P.	24		
Collins J.L.	1			Knowles C.B.	37	(1)	2
Collins P.	24	(3)		Morgan R.	13		3
England M.	36		3	Mullery A.P.	41		1
Evans R.	6	(1)		Pearce J.	27	(3)	3
Gilzean A.J.	37		7	Pratt J.	9	(1)	
Greaves J.P.	42		27	Robertson J.G.	11	(3)	1
Jenkins D.	11	(1)	2	Venables T.	37		
Jennings P.A.	42			Want A.G.	8	(1)	

Final table for First Division (1967/68)

	Team	P	W	D	L	F:A	Pts
1	Manchester C.	42	26	6	10	86:43	58
2	Manchester U.	42	24	8	10	89:55	56
3	Liverpool	42	22	11	9	71:40	55
4	Leeds	42	22	9	11	71:41	53
5	Everton	42	23	6	13	67:40	52
6	Chelsea	42	18	12	12	62:68	48
7	**TOTTENHAM**	**42**	**19**	**9**	**14**	**70:59**	**47**
8	West Bromwich	42	17	12	13	75:62	46
9	Arsenal	42	17	10	15	60:56	44
10	Newcastle	42	13	15	14	54:67	41
11	Nottingham F.	42	14	11	17	52:64	39
12	West Ham	42	14	10	18	73:69	38
13	Leicester	42	13	12	17	64:69	38
14	Burnley	42	14	10	18	64:71	38
15	Sunderland	42	13	11	18	51:61	37
16	Southampton	42	13	11	18	66:83	37
17	Wolverhampton	42	14	8	20	66:75	36
18	Stoke	42	14	7	21	50:73	35
19	Sheffield W.	42	11	12	19	51:63	34
20	Coventry	42	9	15	18	51:71	33
21	Sheffield U.	42	11	10	21	49:70	32
22	Fulham	42	10	7	25	56:98	27

Final table for First Division (1968/69)

	Team	P	W	D	L	F:A	Pts
1	Leeds	42	27	13	2	66:26	67
2	Liverpool	42	25	11	6	63:24	61
3	Everton	42	21	15	6	77:36	57
4	Arsenal	42	22	12	8	56:27	56
5	Chelsea	42	20	10	12	73:53	50
6	**TOTTENHAM**	**42**	**14**	**17**	**11**	**61:51**	**45**
7	Southampton	42	16	13	13	57:48	45
8	West Ham	42	13	18	11	66:50	44
9	Newcastle	42	15	14	13	61:55	44
10	West Bromwich	42	16	11	15	64:67	43
11	Manchester U.	42	15	12	15	57:53	42
12	Ipswich	42	15	11	16	59:60	41
13	Manchester C.	42	15	10	17	64:55	40
14	Burnley	42	15	9	18	55:82	39
15	Sheffield W.	42	10	16	16	41:54	36
16	Wolverhampton	42	10	15	17	41:58	35
17	Sunderland	42	11	12	19	43:67	34
18	Nottingham F.	42	10	13	19	45:57	33
19	Stoke	42	9	15	18	40:63	33
20	Coventry	42	10	11	21	46:64	31
21	Leicester	42	9	12	21	39:68	30
22	QPR	42	4	10	28	39:95	18

SEASON 1969/70

Date	Comp	H/A	Opponent	Result	Score
2 Aug	F	A	Hearts	D	1-1
4 Aug	F	A	Rangers	W	1-0
9 Aug	Lge	A	Leeds	L	1-3
13 Aug	Lge	H	Burnley	W	4-0
16 Aug	Lge	H	Liverpool	L	0-2
19 Aug	Lge	A	Burnley	W	2-0
23 Aug	Lge	A	Crystal P.	W	2-0
27 Aug	Lge	H	Chelsea	D	1-1
30 Aug	Lge	H	Ipswich	W	3-2
3 Sep	FLC	A	Wolves	L	0-1
6 Sep	Lge	A	West Ham	W	1-0
13 Sep	Lge	H	Man City	L	0-3
16 Sep	Lge	A	Arsenal	W	3-2
20 Sep	Lge	A	Derby	L	0-5
27 Sep	Lge	H	Sunderland	L	0-1
4 Oct	Lge	A	Southampton	D	2-2
7 Oct	Lge	A	Liverpool	D	0-0
11 Oct	Lge	H	Wolves	L	0-1
18 Oct	Lge	H	Newcastle	W	2-1
25 Oct	Lge	A	Stoke	D	1-1
1 Nov	Lge	H	Sheff Wed	W	1-0
8 Nov	Lge	A	Nottm Forest	D	2-2
15 Nov	Lge	H	WBA	W	2-0
22 Nov	Lge	A	Man Utd	L	1-3
6 Dec	Lge	A	Coventry	L	2-3
13 Dec	Lge	A	Man City	D	1-1
17 Dec	Lge	H	Everton	D	0-0
20 Dec	Lge	H	West Ham	L	0-2
26 Dec	Lge	H	Crystal P.	W	2-0
27 Dec	Lge	A	Ipswich	L	0-2
3 Jan	FC	A	Bradford C	D	2-2
7 Jan	FCr	H	Bradford C	W	5-0
10 Jan	Lge	H	Derby	W	2-1
17 Jan	Lge	A	Sunderland	L	1-2
24 Jan	FC	H	Crystal P.	D	0-0
28 Jan	FCr	A	Crystal P.	L	0-1
31 Jan	Lge	A	Southampton	L	0-1
7 Feb	Lge	A	Wolves	D	2-2
14 Feb	Lge	H	Leeds	D	1-1
21 Feb	Lge	H	Stoke	W	1-0
28 Feb	Lge	A	Newcastle	W	2-1
11 Mar	Lge	H	Everton	L	0-1
14 Mar	Lge	A	Everton	L	2-3
21 Mar	Lge	H	Coventry	L	1-2
27 Mar	Lge	H	Nottm Forest	W	4-1
28 Mar	Lge	A	WBA	D	1-1
30 Mar	Lge	A	Sheff Wed	W	1-0
4 Apr	Lge	A	Chelsea	L	0-1
13 Apr	Lge	H	Man Utd	W	2-1
2 May	Lge	H	Arsenal	W	1-0
13 May	F	A	Valletta	W	3-0
16 May	F	A	Sliema Wand	W	2-1
17 May	F	A	Malta Sel	L	0-1

Player	Lg App		Goals	Player	Lg App		Goals
Beal P.	31	(2)		Kinnear J.P.	9		
Bond D.	12		1	Knowles C.B.	33		
Chivers M.	31	(4)	11	Morgan R.	37		4
Collins P.	18	(2)	2	Mullery A.P.	41		4
England M.	36		1	Naylor T.	3		
Evans R.	16	(1)		Pearce J.	31	(6)	7
Gilzean A.J.	36	(2)	10	Perryman S.	23		1
Greaves J.P.	28		8	Peters M.	7		2
Hancock K.	1			Pratt J.	12		1
Jenkins D.	3	(2)		Want A.G.	29	(3)	
Jennings P.A.	41			Woolcott R.	1		
Johnson N.	5		1	Own Goal			1

Final table for First Division

1	Everton	42	29	8	5	72:34	66
2	Leeds	42	21	15	6	84:49	57
3	Chelsea	42	21	13	8	70:50	55
4	Derby	42	22	9	11	64:37	53
5	Liverpool	42	20	11	11	65:42	51
6	Coventry	42	19	11	12	58:48	49
7	Newcastle	42	17	13	12	57:35	47
8	Manchester U.	42	14	17	11	66:61	45
9	Stoke	42	15	15	12	56:52	45
10	Manchester C.	42	16	11	15	55:48	43
11	TOTTENHAM	42	17	9	16	54:55	43
12	Arsenal	42	12	18	12	51:49	42
13	Wolverhampton	42	12	16	14	55:57	40
14	Burnley	42	12	15	15	56:61	39
15	Nottingham F.	42	10	18	14	50:71	38
16	West Bromwich	42	14	9	19	58:66	37
17	West Ham	42	12	12	18	51:60	36
18	Ipswich	42	10	11	21	40:63	31
19	Southampton	42	6	17	19	46:67	29
20	Crystal Palace	42	6	15	21	34:68	27
21	Sunderland	42	6	14	22	30:68	26
22	Sheffield W.	42	8	9	25	40:71	25

SEASON 1970/71

Date	Comp	H/A	Opponent	Result	Score
3 Aug	F	H	Rangers	W	2-0
7 Aug	F	A	IFC Koln	L	0-1
8 Aug	F	A	Atletico Mad.	L	0-1
15 Aug	Lge	H	West Ham	D	2-2
19 Aug	Lge	H	Leeds	L	0-2
22 Aug	Lge	A	Wolves	W	3-0
25 Aug	Lge	A	Southampton	D	0-0
29 Aug	Lge	H	Coventry	W	1-0
1 Sep	Lge	A	Huddersfield	D	1-1
5 Sep	Lge	A	Arsenal	L	0-2
9 Sep	FLC	H	Swansea	W	3-0
12 Sep	Lge	H	Blackpool	W	3-0
16 Sep	TEX	H	Dunfermline	W	4-0
19 Sep	Lge	A	Crystal P.	W	3-0
26 Sep	Lge	H	Man City	W	2-0
29 Sep	TEX	A	Dunfermline	W	3-0
3 Oct	Lge	A	Derby	D	1-1
7 Oct	FLC	A	Sheff Utd	W	2-1
10 Oct	Lge	H	Liverpool	W	1-0
17 Oct	Lge	A	West Ham	D	2-2
21 Oct	TEX	A	Motherwell	W	3-2
24 Oct	Lge	H	Stoke	W	3-0
28 Oct	FLC	H	WBA	W	5-0
31 Oct	Lge	A	Nottm Forest	W	1-0
3 Nov	TEX	A	Motherwell	L	1-3
7 Nov	Lge	H	Burnley	W	4-0
14 Nov	Lge	A	Chelsea	W	2-0
18 Nov	FLC	H	Coventry	W	4-1
21 Nov	Lge	H	Newcastle	L	1-2
28 Nov	Lge	A	Everton	D	0-0
5 Dec	Lge	H	Man Utd	D	2-2
12 Dec	Lge	A	WBA	L	1-3
16 Dec	FLCsf	A	Bristol City	D	1-1
19 Dec	Lge	H	Wolves	D	0-0
23 Dec	FLCsf	H	Bristol City	W	2-0
2 Jan	FC	H	Sheff Wed	W	4-1
9 Jan	Lge	A	Leeds	W	2-1
16 Jan	Lge	H	Southampton	L	1-3
23 Jan	FC	A	Carlisle	W	3-2
30 Jan	Lge	H	Everton	W	2-1
6 Feb	Lge	A	Man Utd	L	1-2
13 Feb	FC	H	Nottm Forest	W	2-1
17 Feb	Lge	H	WBA	D	2-2
20 Feb	Lge	A	Newcastle	L	0-1
27 Feb	FLCf	*	Aston Villa	W	2-0
6 Mar	FC	A	Liverpool	D	0-0
10 Mar	Lge	H	Nottm Forest	L	0-1
13 Mar	Lge	H	Chelsea	W	2-1
16 Mar	FCr	A	Liverpool	L	0-1
20 Mar	Lge	A	Burnley	D	0-0
23 Mar	Lge	A	Ipswich	W	2-1
3 Apr	Lge	A	Coventry	D	0-0
7 Apr	Lge	H	Derby	W	2-1
10 Apr	Lge	H	Ipswich	W	2-0
12 Apr	Lge	A	Blackpool	D	0-0
17 Apr	Lge	A	Liverpool	D	0-0
24 Apr	Lge	H	C. Palace	W	2-0
28 Apr	Lge	H	Huddersfield	D	1-1
1 May	Lge	A	Man City	W	1-0
3 May	Lge	H	Arsenal	L	0-1
5 May	Lge	A	Stoke	W	1-0
29 May	F	A	All Japan XI	W	6-0
3 Jun	F	A	All Japan XI	W	7-2
9 Jun	F	A	All Japan XI	W	3-0

* Played at Wembley

Player	Lg App		Goals	Player	Lg App		Goals
Beal P.	32			Knowles C.B.	38		
Bond D.	2	(1)		Morgan R.	8		1
Chivers M.	42		21	Mullery A.P.	41		6
Collins P.	26			Naylor T.	4	(1)	
England M.	22		1	Neighbour J.	17	(5)	
Evans R.	7			Pearce J.	32	(10)	2
Gilzean A.J.	38		9	Perryman S.	42		3
Hancock K.	2			Peters M.	42		9
Jennings P.A.	40			Pratt J.	7	(2)	
Johnson N.	3	(3)		Want A.G.	4		
Kinnear J.P.	35			Own Goals			2

Final table for First Division

1	Arsenal	42	29	7	6	71:29	65
2	Leeds	42	27	10	5	72:30	64
3	TOTTENHAM	42	19	14	9	54:33	52
4	Wolverhampton	42	22	8	12	64:54	52
5	Liverpool	42	17	17	8	42:24	51
6	Chelsea	42	18	15	9	52:42	51
7	Southampton	42	17	12	13	56:44	46
8	Manchester U.	42	16	11	15	65:66	43
9	Derby	42	16	10	16	56:54	42
10	Coventry	42	16	10	16	37:38	42
11	Manchester C.	42	12	17	13	47:42	41
12	Newcastle	42	14	13	15	44:46	41
13	Stoke	42	12	13	17	44:48	37
14	Everton	42	12	13	17	54:60	37
15	Huddersfield	42	11	14	17	40:49	36
16	Nottingham F.	42	14	8	20	42:61	36
17	West Bromwich	42	10	15	17	58:75	35
18	Crystal Palace	42	12	11	19	38:57	35
19	Ipswich	42	12	10	20	42:48	34
20	West Ham	42	10	14	18	47:60	34
21	Burnley	42	7	13	22	29:63	27
22	Blackpool	42	4	15	23	34:66	23

SEASON 1971/72

Date	Comp	H/A	Opponent	Result	Score
7 Aug	F	A	Hearts	L	1-2
9 Aug	F	A	Rangers	L	0-1
14 Aug	Lge	A	Wolves	D	2-2
18 Aug	Lge	H	Newcastle	D	0-0
21 Aug	Lge	H	Huddersfield	W	4-1
25 Aug	Lge	A†	Leeds	D	1-1
28 Aug	Lge	A	Man City	L	0-4
1 Sep	*	A	Torino	W	1-0
4 Sep	Lge	H	Liverpool	W	2-0
8 Sep	FLC	A	WBA	W	1-0
11 Sep	Lge	A	Sheff Utd	D	2-2
14 Sep	UEFA	A	Keflavik	W	6-1
18 Sep	Lge	H	C. Palace	W	3-0
22 Sep	*	H	Torino	W	2-0
25 Sep	Lge	A	Coventry	L	0-1
28 Sep	UEFA	H	Keflavik	W	9-0
2 Oct	Lge	H	Ipswich	W	2-1
6 Oct	FLC	A	Torquay	W	4-1
9 Oct	Lge	A	Derby	D	2-2
16 Oct	Lge	H	Wolves	W	4-1
20 Oct	UEFA	A	Nantes	D	0-0
23 Oct	Lge	H	Nottm Forest	W	6-1
27 Oct	FLC	H	Preston	D	1-1
30 Oct	Lge	A	Stoke	L	0-2
2 Nov	UEFA	H	Nantes	W	1-0
6 Nov	Lge	H	Everton	W	3-0
8 Nov	FLCr	A	Preston	W	2-1
13 Nov	Lge	A	Man Utd	L	1-3
17 Nov	FLC	H	Blackpool	W	2-0
20 Nov	Lge	H	WBA	W	3-2
24 Nov	Lge	H	Arsenal	D	1-1
27 Nov	Lge	A	Chelsea	L	0-1
4 Dec	Lge	H	Southampton	W	1-0
8 Dec	UEFA	H	Rapid Bucarest	W	3-0
11 Dec	Lge	A	Leicester	W	1-0
15 Dec	UEFA	A	Rapid Bucarest	W	2-0
18 Dec	Lge	A	Liverpool	D	0-0
22 Dec	FLCsf	A	Chelsea	L	2-3
27 Dec	Lge	H	West Ham	L	0-1
1 Jan	Lge	A	Crystal P.	D	1-1
5 Jan	FLCsf	H	Chelsea	D	2-2
8 Jan	Lge	H	Man City	D	1-1
15 Jan	FC	H	Carlisle	D	1-1
18 Jan	FCr	A	Carlisle	W	3-1
22 Jan	Lge	A	Newcastle	L	1-3
29 Jan	Lge	H	Leeds U.	W	1-0
5 Feb	FC	H	Rotherham	W	2-0
12 Feb	Lge	A	Nottm Forest	W	1-0
19 Feb	Lge	H	Stoke	W	2-0
26 Feb	FC	A	Everton	W	2-0
1 Mar	Lge	A	Everton	D	1-1
4 Mar	Lge	H	Man Utd	W	2-0
7 Mar	UEFA	A	UT Arad	W	2-0
11 Mar	Lge	H	Derby	L	0-1
18 Mar	FC	A	Leeds	L	1-2
21 Mar	UEFA	H	UT Arad	D	1-1
25 Mar	Lge	H	Sheff Utd	W	2-0
28 Mar	Lge	A	Huddersfield	D	1-1
31 Mar	Lge	H	Coventry	W	1-0
1 Apr	Lge	A	West Ham	L	0-2
3 Apr	Lge	A	Ipswich	L	1-2
5 Apr	UEFAsf	H	AC Milan	W	2-1
8 Apr	Lge	A	WBA	D	1-1
15 Apr	Lge	H	Chelsea	W	3-0
19 Apr	UEFAsf	A	AC Milan	D	1-1
22 Apr	Lge	A	Southampton	D	0-0
29 Apr	Lge	H	Leicester	W	4-3
3 May	UEFAf	A	Wolves	W	2-1
11 May	Lge	A	Arsenal	W	2-0
17 May	UEFAf	H	Wolves	D	1-1
7 Jun	F	A	Maccabi	W	3-2

* Anglo-Italian League Cup Winners Cup (two legs) † Played at Boothferry Park

Player	Lg App	Goals	Player	Lg App	Goals
Beal P.	32		Knowles C.B.	34	2
Chivers M.	39	25	Morgan R.	10 (2)	
Coates R.	32	2	Mullery A.	18	3
Collins P.	7 (1)		Naylor T.	12	
Daines B.	1		Neighbour J.	14 (2)	1
England M.	38	2	Pearce J.	15 (6)	5
Evans R.	22		Perryman S.	40 (1)	
Gilzean A.	38	11	Peters M.	35	10
Holder P.	6 (2)		Pratt J.	23 (8)	1
Jennings P.A.	41		Want A.G.	7	
Kinnear J.P.	21 (1)		Own Goal		1

Final table for First Division

1	Derby	42	24 10 8	69:33	58
2	Leeds	42	24 9 9	73:31	57
3	Liverpool	42	24 9 9	64:30	57
4	Manchester C.	42	23 11 8	77:45	57
5	Arsenal	42	22 8 12	58:40	52
6	TOTTENHAM	42	19 13 10	63:42	51
7	Chelsea	42	18 12 12	58:49	48
8	Manchester U.	42	19 10 13	69:61	48
9	Wolverhampton	42	18 11 13	65:57	47
10	Sheffield U.	42	17 12 13	61:60	46
11	Newcastle	42	15 11 16	49:52	41
12	Leicester	42	13 13 16	41:46	39
13	Ipswich	42	11 16 15	39:53	38
14	West Ham	42	12 12 18	47:51	36
15	Everton	42	9 18 15	37:48	36
16	West Bromwich	42	12 11 19	42:54	35
17	Stoke	42	10 15 17	39:56	35
18	Coventry	42	9 15 18	44:67	33
19	Southampton	42	12 7 23	52:80	31
20	Crystal Palace	42	8 13 21	39:65	29
21	Nottingham F.	42	8 9 25	47:81	25
22	Huddersfield	42	6 13 23	27:59	25

SEASON 1972/73

Date	Comp	H/A	Opponent	Result	Score
29 Jul	F	A	Bournemouth	W	4-2
2 Aug	F	A	Aston Villa	D	0-0
7 Aug	F	A	Celtic	L	0-1
12 Aug	Lge	H	Coventry	W	2-1
16 Aug	Lge	A	WBA	W	1-0
19 Aug	Lge	A	Wolves	L	2-3
23 Aug	Lge	H	Birmingham	W	2-0
26 Aug	Lge	H	Leeds Utd	D	0-0
30 Aug	Lge	A	Newcastle	D	1-1
2 Sep	Lge	A	Ipswich	D	1-1
6 Sep	FLC	H	Huddersfield	W	2-1
9 Sep	Lge	H	C. Palace	W	2-1
13 Sep	UEFA	A	Lyn Oslo	W	6-3
16 Sep	Lge	A	Man City	L	1-2
23 Sep	Lge	H	West Ham	W	1-0
27 Sep	UEFA	H	Lyn Oslo	W	6-0
30 Sep	Lge	A	Derby	L	1-2
3 Oct	FLC	A	Middlesbrough	D	1-1
7 Oct	Lge	H	Stoke	W	4-3
11 Oct	FLCr	H	Middlesbrough	D	0-0
14 Oct	Lge	A	Norwich	L	1-2
17 Oct	*	H	Feijenoord	W	2-1
21 Oct	Lge	A	Chelsea	L	0-1
25 Oct	UEFA	A	Olympiakos	W	4-0
28 Oct	Lge	A	Man Utd	W	4-1
30 Oct	FLCr	H	Middlesbrough	W	2-1
1 Nov	FLC	H	Millwall	W	2-0
4 Nov	Lge	A	Birmingham	D	0-0
8 Nov	UEFA	A	Olympiakos	L	0-1
11 Nov	Lge	H	WBA	D	1-1
18 Nov	Lge	A	Leicester	W	1-0
25 Nov	Lge	H	Liverpool	L	1-2
29 Nov	UEFA	H	Red Star	W	2-0
2 Dec	Lge	A	Southampton	D	1-1
4 Dec	FLC	A	Liverpool	D	1-1
6 Dec	FLCr	H	Liverpool	W	3-1
9 Dec	Lge	H	Arsenal	L	1-2
13 Dec	UEFA	A	Red Star	l	0-1
16 Dec	Lge	A	Everton	L	1-3
20 Dec	FLCsf	A	Wolves	W	2-1
23 Dec	Lge	H	Sheff Utd	W	2-0
26 Dec	Lge	A	West Ham	D	2-2
30 Dec	FLCsf	H	Wolves	D	2-2
6 Jan	Lge	A	Leeds	L	1-2
13 Jan	FC	H	Margate	W	6-0
20 Jan	Lge	A	Ipswich	L	0-1
27 Jan	Lge	A	C. Palace	D	0-0
3 Feb	FC	A	Derby	D	1-1
7 Feb	FCr	H	Derby	L	3-5
10 Feb	Lge	H	Man City	L	2-3
17 Feb	Lge	A	Coventry	W	1-0
24 Feb	Lge	H	Everton	W	3-0
3 Mar	FLCf	†	Norwich	W	1-0
7 Mar	UEFA	H	Vitoria Setubal	W	1-0
10 Mar	Lge	H	Norwich	W	3-0
14 Mar	Lge	A	Stoke	D	1-1
21 Mar	UEFA	A	Vitoria Setubal	L	1-2
24 Mar	Lge	H	Man Utd	D	1-1
31 Mar	Lge	A	Liverpool	D	1-1
3 Apr	Lge	A	Chelsea	W	1-0
7 Apr	Lge	H	Southampton	L	1-2
10 Apr	UEFAsf	A	Liverpool	L	0-1
14 Apr	Lge	A	Arsenal	D	1-1
18 Apr	Lge	H	Derby	W	1-0
21 Apr	Lge	H	Leicester	D	1-1
25 Apr	UEFAsf	H	Liverpool	W	2-1
28 Apr	Lge	H	Newcastle	W	3-2
30 Apr	Lge	H	Wolves	D	2-2
2 May	Lge	A	Sheff Utd	L	2-3

* Jimmy Greaves testimonial † Played at Wembley

Player	Lg App	Goals	Player	Lg App	Goals
Beal P.	24		Jennings P.	40	
Chivers M.	38	17	Kinnear J.	24	1
Clarke R.	1 (1)		Knowles C.	35	
Coates R.	32 (3)	2	Naylor T.	16 (2)	
Collins P.	7	2	Neighbour J.	7 (1)	1
Daines B.	2		Pearce J.	35 (8)	4
Dillon M.	8		Perryman S.	41	2
England M.	31	1	Peters M.	41	15
Evans R.	24 (1)		Pratt J.	38 (1)	5
Gilzean A.	35	5	Own Goals		3

Final table for First Division

1	Liverpool	42	25 10 7	72:42	60
2	Arsenal	42	23 11 8	57:43	57
3	Leeds	42	21 11 10	71:45	53
4	Ipswich	42	17 14 11	55:45	48
5	Wolverhampton	42	18 11 13	66:54	47
6	West Ham	42	17 12 13	67:53	46
7	Derby	42	19 8 15	56:54	46
8	TOTTENHAM	42	16 13 13	58:48	45
9	Newcastle	42	16 13 13	60:51	45
10	Birmingham	42	15 12 15	53:54	42
11	Manchester C.	42	15 11 16	57:60	41
12	Chelsea	42	13 14 15	49:51	40
13	Southampton	42	11 18 13	47:52	40
14	Sheffield U.	42	15 10 17	51:59	40
15	Stoke	42	14 10 18	61:56	38
16	Leicester	42	10 17 15	40:46	37
17	Everton	42	13 11 18	41:49	37
18	Manchester U.	42	12 13 17	44:60	37
19	Coventry	42	13 9 20	40:55	35
20	Norwich	42	11 10 21	36:63	32
21	C. Palace	42	9 12 21	41:58	30
22	West Bromwich	42	9 10 23	38:62	28

SEASON 1973/74

Date	Comp	H/A	Opponent	Result
8 Aug	F	A	Ajax	L 1-4
11 Aug	F	A	Cardiff	W 3-1
18 Aug	F	A	Sunderland	W 1-0
25 Aug	Lge	A	Coventry	L 0-1
28 Aug	Lge	A	Birmingham	W 2-1
1 Sep	Lge	H	Leeds	L 0-3
5 Sep	Lge	H	Burnley	L 2-3
8 Sep	Lge	A	West Ham	W 1-0
11 Sep	Lge	A	Burnley	D 2-2
15 Sep	Lge	H	Sheff Utd	L 1-2
19 Sep	UEFA	A	Grasshoppers	W 5-1
22 Sep	Lge	A	Liverpool	L 2-3
29 Sep	Lge	A	Derby	W 1-0
3 Oct	UEFA	H	Grasshoppers	W 4-1
6 Oct	Lge	A	Ipswich	D 0-0
8 Oct	FLC	A	QPR	L 0-1
13 Oct	Lge	H	Arsenal	W 2-0
20 Oct	Lge	A	Norwich	D 1-1
24 Oct	UEFA	A	Aberdeen	D 1-1
27 Oct	Lge	H	Newcastle	L 0-2
3 Nov	Lge	A	Everton	D 1-1
7 Nov	UEFA	H	Aberdeen	W 4-1
10 Nov	Lge	H	Man Utd	W 2-1
17 Nov	Lge	A	Southampton	D 1-1
24 Nov	Lge	H	Wolves	L 1-3
28 Nov	UEFA	A	Dinamo Tbilisi	D 1-1
1 Dec	Lge	A	Leicester	L 0-3
3 Dec	*	H	Bayern Munich	D 2-2
8 Dec	Lge	H	Stoke	W 2-1
12 Dec	UEFA	H	Dinamo Tbilisi	W 5-1
15 Dec	Lge	H	Man City	L 0-2
22 Dec	Lge	A	Derby	L 0-2
26 Dec	Lge	H	QPR	D 0-0
29 Dec	Lge	H	West Ham	W 2-0
1 Jan	Lge	A	Leeds	D 1-1
5 Jan	FC	A	Leicester	L 0-1
12 Jan	Lge	A	Sheff Utd	D 2-2
19 Jan	Lge	H	Coventry	W 2-1
2 Feb	Lge	A	Man City	D 0-0
6 Feb	Lge	H	Birmingham	W 4-2
16 Feb	Lge	A	Arsenal	W 1-0
23 Feb	Lge	H	Ipswich	D 1-1
2 Mar	Lge	A	QPR	L 1-3
6 Mar	UEFA	A	IFC Koln	W 2-1
16 Mar	Lge	H	Norwich	D 0-0
20 Mar	UEFA	H	IFC Koln	W 3-0
23 Mar	Lge	A	Man Utd	W 1-0
30 Mar	Lge	H	Everton	L 0-2
3 Apr	Lge	H	Chelsea	L 1-2
6 Apr	Lge	A	Wolves	D 1-1
10 Apr	UEFAsf	A	Locomotiv Leipzig	W 2-1
13 Apr	Lge	H	Southampton	W 3-1
15 Apr	Lge	A	Chelsea	D 0-0
20 Apr	Lge	A	Stoke	L 0-1
24 Apr	UEFAsf	H	Lokomotiv Leipzig	W 2-0
27 Apr	Lge	A	Leicester	W 1-0
8 May	Lge	A	Liverpool	D 1-1
11 May	Lge	A	Newcastle	W 2-0
21 May	UEFAf	H	Feijenoord	D 2-2
29 May	UEFAf	A	Feijenoord	L 0-2

*Testimonial for Phil Beal

Player	Lg App		Goals	Player	Lg App		Goals
Beal P.	41			Knowles C.	20		2
Chivers M.	40	(1)	17	Lee T.	1		
Coates R.	36		3	McGrath C.	25	(3)	5
Daines B.	5			McNab N.	1	(1)	
Dillon M.	16	(3)	1	Naylor T.	28	(1)	
England M.	33			Neighbour J.	14	(3)	
Evans R.	40		2	Osgood K.	1	(1)	
Gilzean A.	25	(4)	3	Perryman S.	39		1
Holder P.	7	(2)	1	Peters M.	35		6
Jennings P.	36			Pratt J.	35		4
Kinnear J.	7	(4)					

Final table for First Division

1	Leeds	42	24 14 4	66:31	62
2	Liverpool	42	22 13 7	52:31	57
3	Derby	42	17 14 11	52:42	48
4	Ipswich	42	18 11 13	67:58	47
5	Stoke	42	15 16 11	54:42	46
6	Burnley	42	16 14 12	56:53	46
7	Everton	42	16 12 14	50:48	44
8	QPR	42	13 17 12	56:52	43
9	Leicester	42	13 16 13	51:41	42
10	Arsenal	42	14 14 14	49:51	42
11	**TOTTENHAM**	**42**	**14 14 14**	**45:50**	**42**
12	Wolverhampton	42	13 15 14	49:49	41
13	Sheffield U.	42	14 12 16	44:49	40
14	Manchester C.	42	14 12 16	39:46	40
15	Newcastle	42	13 12 17	49:48	38
16	Coventry	42	14 10 18	43:54	38
17	Chelsea	42	12 13 17	56:60	37
18	West Ham	42	11 15 16	55:60	37
19	Birmingham	42	12 13 17	52:64	37
20	Southampton	42	11 14 17	47:68	36
21	Manchester U.	42	10 12 20	38:48	32
22	Norwich	42	7 15 20	37:62	29

SEASON 1974/75

Date	Comp	H/A	Opponent	Result
3 Aug	F	A	Hearts	D 1-1
7 Aug	F	A	Portsmouth	W 2-0
10 Aug	F	A	Fulham	W 1-0
17 Aug	Lge	H	Ipswich	L 0-1
21 Aug	Lge	A	Man City	L 0-1
24 Aug	Lge	A	Carlisle	L 0-1
28 Aug	Lge	H	Man City	L 1-2
31 Aug	Lge	H	Derby	W 2-0
7 Sep	Lge	A	Liverpool	L 2-5
11 Sep	FLC	H	Middlesbrough	L 0-4
14 Sep	Lge	H	West Ham	W 2-1
21 Sep	Lge	A	Wolves	W 3-2
28 Sep	Lge	A	Middlesbrough	L 1-2
5 Oct	Lge	H	Burnley	L 2-3
12 Oct	Lge	H	Chelsea	L 0-1
16 Oct	Lge	H	Carlisle	D 1-1
19 Oct	Lge	H	Arsenal	W 2-0
26 Oct	Lge	A	Luton	D 1-1
2 Nov	Lge	A	Stoke	D 2-2
9 Nov	Lge	H	Everton	D 1-1
16 Nov	Lge	A	Leicester	W 2-1
23 Nov	Lge	H	Birmingham	D 0-0
27 Nov	*	H	Red Star	W 2-0
30 Nov	Lge	A	Sheff Utd	W 1-0
4 Dec	Lge	A	Leeds	L 1-2
7 Dec	Lge	H	Newcastle	W 3-0
14 Dec	Lge	A	Ipswich	L 0-4
21 Dec	Lge	H	QPR	L 1-2
26 Dec	Lge	A	West Ham	D 1-1
28 Dec	Lge	H	Coventry	D 1-1
4 Jan	FC	A	Nottm Forest	D 1-1
8 Jan	FCr	H	Nottm Forest	L 0-1
11 Jan	Lge	A	Newcastle	W 5-2
18 Jan	Lge	H	Sheff Utd	L 1-3
24 Jan	F	A	Watford	W 3-2
27 Jan	F	A	Enfield	W 2-1
1 Feb	Lge	A	Everton	L 0-1
8 Feb	Lge	H	Stoke	L 0-1
15 Feb	Lge	A	Coventry	D 1-1
18 Feb	Lge	A	Birmingham	L 0-1
22 Feb	Lge	H	Leicester	L 0-3
26 Feb	F	A	Red Star	W 1-0
1 Mar	Lge	A	Derby	L 1-3
15 Mar	Lge	A	Middlesbrough	L 0-3
22 Mar	Lge	H	Liverpool	L 0-2
28 Mar	Lge	H	Wolves	W 3-0
29 Mar	Lge	A	QPR	W 1-0
5 Apr	Lge	H	Luton	W 2-1
12 Apr	Lge	A	Burnley	L 2-3
19 Apr	Lge	H	Chelsea	W 2-0
26 Apr	Lge	A	Arsenal	L 0-1
28 Apr	Lge	H	Leeds	W 4-2

*Testimonial for Alan Gilzean

Player	Lg App		Goals	Player	Lg App		Goals
Beal P.	28			Knowles C.	31		4
Chivers M.	28	(1)	10	McAllister D.	8	(1)	
Coates R.	30	(4)	1	McGrath C.	9	(4)	
Conn A.	17	(1)	6	McNab N.	2		
Daines B.	1			Naylor T.	38	(1)	
Duncan J.	28		12	Neighbour T.	25	(4)	3
England M.	31		2	Osgood K.	10		
Evans R.	21	(1)		Perryman S.	42		6
Jennings P.	41			Peters M.	29		4
Jones C.	16		1	Pratt J.	29	(2)	1
Kinnear J.	17			Own Goals			2

Final table for First Division

1	Derby	42	21 11 10	67:49	53
2	Liverpool	42	20 11 11	60:39	51
3	Ipswich	42	23 5 14	66:44	51
4	Everton	42	16 18 8	56:42	50
5	Stoke	42	17 15 10	64:48	49
6	Sheffield U.	42	18 13 11	58:51	49
7	Middlesbrough	42	18 12 12	54:40	48
8	Manchester C.	42	18 10 14	54:54	46
9	Leeds	42	16 13 13	57:49	45
10	Burnley	42	17 11 14	68:67	45
11	QPR	42	16 10 16	54:54	42
12	Wolverhampton	42	14 11 17	57:54	39
13	West Ham	42	13 13 16	58:59	39
14	Coventry	42	12 15 15	51:62	39
15	Newcastle	42	15 9 18	59:72	39
16	Arsenal	42	13 11 18	47:49	37
17	Birmingham	42	14 9 19	53:61	37
18	Leicester	42	12 12 18	46:60	36
19	**TOTTENHAM**	**42**	**13 8 21**	**52:63**	**34**
20	Luton	42	11 11 20	47:65	33
21	Chelsea	42	9 15 18	42:72	33
22	Carlisle	42	12 5 25	43:59	29

SEASON 1975/76

Date		Venue	Opponent	Result	Score
23 Jul	F	A	Rot Weiss	D	1-1
25 Jul	F	A	Karlsruhe	L	1-2
29 Jul	F	A	Hanover	D	1-1
3 Aug	F	A	NAC Breda	W	1-0
8 Aug	F	A	Bristol Rvs	W	4-1
16 Aug	Lge	H	Middlesbrough	W	1-0
20 Aug	Lge	H	Ipswich	D	1-1
23 Aug	Lge	A	Liverpool	L	2-3
25 Aug	Lge	A	West Ham	L	0-1
30 Aug	Lge	H	Norwich	L	1-2
6 Sep	Lge	A	Man Utd	L	2-3
9 Sep	FLC	A	Watford	W	1-0
13 Sep	Lge	H	Derby	L	2-3
20 Sep	Lge	A	Leeds	D	1-1
27 Sep	Lge	H	Arsenal	D	0-0
29 Sep	F	A	Le Stade Rennais	D	1-1
4 Oct	Lge	A	Newcastle	D	0-0
8 Oct	FLC	A	Crewe	W	2-0
11 Oct	Lge	A	Aston Villa	D	1-1
18 Oct	Lge	H	Man City	D	2-2
22 Oct	*	H	Arsenal	D	2-2
25 Oct	Lge	A	Leicester	W	3-2
27 Oct	F	A	Millwall	L	1-3
1 Nov	Lge	H	Wolves	W	2-1
8 Nov	Lge	A	QPR	D	0-0
12 Nov	FLC	H	West Ham	D	0-0
15 Nov	Lge	H	Stoke	D	1-1
22 Nov	Lge	A	Man City	L	1-2
24 Nov	FLCr	A	West Ham	W	2-0
29 Nov	Lge	H	Burnley	W	2-1
3 Dec	FLC	H	Doncaster	W	7-2
6 Dec	Lge	A	Sheff Utd	W	2-1
10 Dec	Lge	H	Everton	D	2-2
13 Dec	Lge	H	Liverpool	L	0-4
20 Dec	Lge	A	Middlesbrough	L	0-1
26 Dec	Lge	H	Birmingham	L	1-3
27 Dec	Lge	A	Coventry	D	2-2
3 Jan	FC	H	Stoke	D	1-1
10 Jan	Lge	A	Derby	W	3-2
14 Jan	FLCsf	H	Newcastle	W	1-0
17 Jan	Lge	H	Man Utd	D	1-1
21 Jan	FLCsf	A	Newcastle	L	1-3
24 Jan	FCr	A	Stoke	L	1-2
31 Jan	Lge	A	Ipswich	W	2-1
7 Feb	Lge	H	West Ham	D	1-1
14 Feb	Lge	H	QPR	L	0-3
21 Feb	Lge	A	Stoke	W	2-1
24 Feb	Lge	A	Everton	L	0-1
28 Feb	Lge	H	Leicester	D	1-1
6 Mar	Lge	A	Norwich	L	1-3
13 Mar	Lge	H	Aston Villa	W	5-2
16 Mar	Lge	A	Wolves	W	1-0
20 Mar	Lge	A	Burnley	W	2-1
23 Mar	†	A	Brighton	W	6-1
27 Mar	Lge	H	Sheff Utd	W	5-0
3 Apr	Lge	A	Arsenal	W	2-0
10 Apr	Lge	H	Leeds	D	0-0
17 Apr	Lge	A	Birmingham	L	1-3
19 Apr	Lge	H	Coventry	W	4-1
21 Apr	F	A	Nrth Herts XI	L	1-2
24 Apr	Lge	A	Newcastle	L	0-3
27 Apr	F	A	Toronto Metros	W	1-0
1 May	F	A	Fiji Select	W	4-0
3 May	F	A	Auckland XI	W	5-3
5 May	F	A	Wellington XI	W	3-2
9 May	F	A	Victoria	W	3-1
12 May	F	A	N. Sth Wales	W	5-1
16 May	F	A	Australian XI	W	3-2
18 May	F	A	South Aust.	W	5-2
23 May	F	A	Western Aust.	W	4-0

* Testimonial for Cyril Knowles † Testimonial for Joe Kinnear

Player	Lg App		Goals	Player	Lg App		Goals
Brotherston N.	1			McGrath C.	4	(1)	
Chivers M.	35	(4)	7	McNab N.	15	(4)	
Coates R.	24	(3)	2	Naylor T.	36		
Conn A.	8	(1)		Neighbour J.	35		3
Daines B.	2			Osgood K.	42		3
Duncan J.	37	(2)	20	Perryman S.	40		6
Hoddle G.	7	(1)	1	Pratt T.	41		10
Jennings P.	40			Robinson M.	2	(1)	1
Jones C.	34	(9)	5	Smith I.	2		
Kinnear J.	1			Stead M.	4		
Knowles C.	10			Walford S.	2	(1)	
McAllister D.	35		2	Young W.	35		3

Final table for First Division

1	Liverpool	42	23 14 5	66:31	60
2	QPR	42	24 11 7	67:33	59
3	Manchester U.	42	23 10 10	68:42	56
4	Derby	42	21 11 10	75:58	53
5	Leeds	42	21 9 12	65:46	51
6	Ipswich	42	16 14 12	54:48	46
7	Leicester	42	13 19 10	48:51	45
8	Manchester C.	42	16 12 15	64:46	43
9	TOTTENHAM	42	14 15 13	63:63	43
10	Norwich	42	16 10 16	58:58	42
11	Everton	42	15 12 15	60:66	42
12	Stoke	42	15 11 16	48:50	41
13	Middlesbrough	42	15 10 17	46:45	40
14	Coventry	42	13 14 15	47:57	40
15	Newcastle	42	15 9 18	71:62	39
16	Aston Villa	42	11 17 14	51:59	39
17	Arsenal	42	13 10 19	47:53	36
18	West Ham	42	13 10 19	48:71	36
19	Birmingham	42	13 7 22	57:75	33
20	Wolverhampton	42	10 10 22	51:68	30
21	Burnley	42	9 10 23	43:66	28
22	Sheffield U.	42	6 10 26	33:82	22

SEASON 1976/77

Date		Venue	Opponent	Result	Score
24 Jul	F	A	Osnabruck	W	3-1
28 Jul	F	A	Eintracht	L	1-4
31 Jul	F	A	IFC Koln	L	1-3
10 Aug	F	A	Swindon	L	1-3
16 Aug	F	H	Ryl Antwerp	D	1-1
21 Aug	Lge	A	Ipswich	L	1-3
25 Aug	Lge	H	Newcastle	L	0-2
28 Aug	Lge	H	Middlesbrough	D	0-0
31 Aug	FLC	A	Middlesbrough	W	2-1
4 Sep	Lge	A	Man Utd	W	3-2
11 Sep	Lge	H	Leeds Utd	W	1-0
18 Sep	Lge	A	Liverpool	L	0-2
22 Sep	FLC	H	Wrexham	L	2-3
25 Sep	Lge	H	Norwich	D	1-1
2 Oct	Lge	A	WBA	L	2-4
9 Oct	F †	A	Arsenal	W	2-1
16 Oct	Lge	A	Derby	L	2-8
20 Oct	Lge	H	Birmingham	W	1-0
23 Oct	Lge	H	Coventry	L	0-1
30 Oct	Lge	H	Everton	D	3-3
6 Nov	Lge	A	West Ham	L	3-5
13 Nov	Lge	H	Bristol City	L	0-1
20 Nov	Lge	A	Sunderland	L	1-2
23 Nov	F*	A	Arsenal	W	3-2
27 Nov	Lge	H	Stoke	W	2-0
11 Dec	Lge	H	Man City	D	2-2
18 Dec	Lge	A	Leicester	L	1-2
27 Dec	Lge	H	Arsenal	D	2-2
1 Jan	Lge	H	West Ham	W	2-1
8 Jan	FC	A	Cardiff	L	0-1
11 Jan	Lge	A	QPR	L	1-2
22 Jan	Lge	H	Ipswich	W	1-0
5 Feb	Lge	A	Middlesbrough	L	0-2
12 Feb	Lge	H	Man Utd	L	1-3
19 Feb	Lge	A	Leeds	L	1-2
26 Feb	Lge	A	Newcastle	L	0-2
5 Mar	Lge	A	Norwich	W	3-1
9 Mar	Lge	H	Liverpool	W	1-0
12 Mar	Lge	H	WBA	L	0-2
19 Mar	Lge	A	Birmingham	W	2-1
23 Mar	Lge	H	Derby	D	0-0
26 Mar	Lge	A	Everton	L	0-4
2 Apr	Lge	A	Coventry	D	1-1
9 Apr	Lge	H	QPR	W	3-0
11 Apr	Lge	A	Arsenal	L	0-1
12 Apr	Lge	A	Bristol City	L	0-1
16 Apr	Lge	H	Sunderland	D	1-1
20 Apr	Lge	A	Aston Villa	L	1-2
23 Apr	Lge	A	Stoke	D	0-0
30 Apr	Lge	H	Aston Villa	W	3-1
7 May	Lge	A	Man City	L	0-5
14 May	Lge	H	Leicester	W	2-0

* Pat Jennings Testimonial   † Peter Simpson Testimonial

Player	Lg App		Goals	Player	Lg App		Goals
Armstrong G.	21	(1)	3	McAllister D.	12	(2)	1
Coates R.	31	(3)	3	McNab N.	10	(4)	
Conn A.	13	(1)		Moores I.	17	(1)	2
Daines B.	19			Naylor T.	40		
Duncan J.	9		4	Neighbour J.	7		
Gorman J.	15			Osgood K.	42		7
Hoddle G.	39		4	Perryman S.	42		1
Holmes J.	10		1	Pratt J.	34	(4)	4
Jennings P.	23			Stead M.	8		
Jones C.	31		9	Taylor P.	32	(1)	8
Keeley G.	6	(1)		Young W.	19		1

Final table for First Division

1	Liverpool	42	23 11 8	62:33	57
2	Manchester C.	42	21 14 7	60:34	56
3	Ipswich	42	22 8 12	66:39	56
4	Aston Villa	42	22 7 13	76:50	51
5	Newcastle	42	18 13 11	64:49	49
6	Manchester U.	42	18 11 13	71:62	47
7	West Bromwich	42	16 13 13	62:56	45
8	Arsenal	42	16 11 15	64:59	43
9	Everton	42	14 14 14	62:64	42
10	Leeds	42	15 12 15	48:51	42
11	Leicester	42	12 18 12	47:60	42
12	Middlesbrough	42	14 13 15	40:45	41
13	Birmingham	42	13 12 17	63:61	38
14	QPR	42	13 12 17	47:52	38
15	Derby	42	9 19 14	50:55	37
16	Norwich	42	14 9 19	47:64	37
17	West Ham	42	11 14 17	46:65	36
18	Bristol C.	42	11 13 18	38:48	35
19	Coventry	42	10 15 17	48:59	35
20	Sunderland	42	11 12 19	46:54	34
21	Stoke	42	10 14 18	28:51	34
22	TOTTENHAM	42	12 9 21	48:72	33

SEASON 1977/78

Date	Comp	H/A	Opponent	Result	Score
7 Aug		A	Royale Union	W	2-0*
10 Aug		A	Leicester	W	2-1*
12 Aug		A	Norsjo	W	3-2*
20 Aug	Lge	H	Sheff Utd	W	4-2
24 Aug	Lge	A	Blackburn	D	0-0
27 Aug	Lge	H	Notts Co.	W	2-1
31 Aug	FLC	H	Wimbledon	W	4-0
3 Sep		A	Cardiff	D	0-0
10 Sep	Lge	H	Fulham	W	1-0
17 Sep	Lge	A	Blackpool	W	2-0
24 Sep	Lge	H	Luton	W	2-0
1 Oct	Lge	A	Orient	D	1-1
4 Oct	Lge	A	Hull	W	2-0
8 Oct	Lge	H	Oldham	W	5-1
15 Oct	Lge	A	Charlton	L	1-4
22 Oct	FLC	H	Coventry	L	2-3
26 Oct	Lge	H	Bristol Rvs	W	9-0
29 Oct	Lge	A	Stoke	W	3-1
5 Nov	Lge	H	Burnley	W	3-0
12 Nov	Lge	A	Crystal P.	W	2-1
19 Nov	Lge	H	Brighton	D	0-0
22 Nov	F	A	Arsenal	W	3-1
26 Nov	Lge	A	Bolton	L	0-1
3 Dec	Lge	H	Southampton	D	0-0
10 Dec	Lge	A	Sunderland	W	2-1
17 Dec	Lge	H	Crystal P.	D	2-2
26 Dec	Lge	A	Millwall	W	3-1
27 Dec	Lge	H	Mansfield	D	1-1
31 Dec	Lge	H	Blackburn	W	4-0
2 Jan	Lge	A	Sheff Utd	D	2-2
7 Jan	FC	H	Bolton	D	2-2
10 Jan	FCr	A	Bolton	L	1-2
14 Jan	Lge	A	Notts Co.	D	3-3
21 Jan	Lge	H	Cardiff	W	2-1
4 Feb	Lge	A	Fulham	D	1-1
11 Feb	Lge	H	Blackpool	D	2-2
22 Feb	Lge	A	Luton	W	4-1
25 Feb	Lge	H	Orient	D	1-1
4 Mar	Lge	A	Oldham	D	1-1
11 Mar	Lge	H	Charlton	W	2-1
18 Mar	Lge	A	Bristol Rvs	W	3-2
22 Mar	Lge	H	Stoke	W	3-1
25 Mar	Lge	A	Mansfield	D	3-3
27 Mar	Lge	H	Millwall	D	3-3
1 Apr	Lge	A	Burnley	L	1-2
8 Apr	Lge	H	Bolton	W	1-0
15 Apr	Lge	A	Brighton	L	1-3
22 Apr	Lge	A	Sunderland	L	2-3
26 Apr	Lge	H	Hull	W	1-0
29 Apr	Lge	A	Southampton	D	0-0
3 May	F	A	Truro City	W	8-2
5 May	F	A	Orient	W	3-1
8 May	F	A	Aleppo Select	W	1-0
10 May	F	A	Syrian Select	W	4-0
12 May	†	H	Arsenal	L	3-5

* Scandinavian tour
† Testimonial for John Pratt

Player	Lg App		Goals
Armstrong G.	19	(9)	2
Coates R.	3	(2)	
Daines B.	42		
Duncan J.	27		16
Hoddle G.	41		12
Holmes J.	38		
Jones C.	20		8
Lee C.	25	(2)	11
McAllister D.	25		4
McNab N.	42		3
Moores I.	10	(3)	4
Naylor T.	37		
Osgood K.	18		3
Perryman S.	42		1
Pratt J.	42		7
Robinson M.	4		1
Stead M.	3	(1)	
Taylor P.	41		11

Final table for Second Division

		P	W	D	L	F:A	Pts
1	Bolton	42	24	10	8	63:33	58
2	Southampton	42	22	13	7	70:39	57
3	**TOTTENHAM**	42	20	16	6	83:49	56
4	Brighton	42	22	12	8	63:38	56
5	Blackburn	42	16	13	13	56:60	45
6	Sunderland	42	14	16	12	67:59	44
7	Stoke	42	16	10	16	53:49	42
8	Oldham	42	13	16	13	54:58	42
9	Crystal P.	42	13	15	14	50:47	41
10	Fulham	42	14	13	15	49:49	41
11	Burnley	42	15	10	17	56:64	40
12	Sheffield U.	42	16	8	18	62:73	40
13	Luton	42	14	10	18	54:52	38
14	Orient	42	10	18	14	43:49	38
15	Notts Co.	42	11	16	15	54:62	38
16	Millwall	42	12	14	16	49:57	38
17	Charlton	42	13	12	17	55:68	38
18	Bristol R.	42	13	12	17	61:77	38
19	Cardiff	42	13	12	17	51:71	38
20	Blackpool	42	12	13	17	59:60	37
21	Mansfield	42	10	11	21	49:69	31
22	Hull	42	8	12	22	34:52	28

SEASON 1978/79

Date	Comp	H/A	Opponent	Result	Score
5 Aug	F	A	Aberdeen	L	1-3
8 Aug	F	A	Ryl Antwerp	W	3-1
10 Aug	F	A	Venlo	L	0-1
12 Aug	F	A	Bohemians	W	4-0
19 Aug	Lge	A	Nottm Forest	D	1-1
23 Aug	Lge	H	Aston Villa	L	1-4
26 Aug	Lge	H	Chelsea	D	2-2
29 Aug	FLC	A	Swansea	D	2-2
2 Sep	Lge	A	Liverpool	L	0-7
6 Sep	FLCr	H	Swansea	L	1-3
9 Sep	Lge	H	Bristol C.	W	1-0
16 Sep	Lge	A	Leeds	W	2-1
19 Sep	F	A	Aldershot	D	1-1
23 Sep	Lge	A	Man City	L	0-2
26 Sep	F	A	IFK Gothnburg	L	0-1
30 Sep	Lge	H	Coventry	D	1-1
7 Oct	Lge	A	WBA	W	1-0
9 Oct	F	A	Saudi Arab XI	W	4-2
14 Oct	Lge	H	Birmingham	W	1-0
16 Oct	F	A	Wolves	L	1-2
21 Oct	Lge	A	Derby	D	2-2
28 Oct	Lge	H	Bolton	W	2-0
4 Nov	Lge	A	Norwich	D	2-2
11 Nov	Lge	H	Nottm Forest	L	1-3
18 Nov	Lge	A	Chelsea	W	3-1
22 Nov	Lge	H	Liverpool	D	0-0
25 Nov	Lge	H	Wolves	W	1-0
4 Dec	F	A	West Ham	L	2-4
9 Dec	Lge	H	Ipswich	W	1-0
16 Dec	Lge	A	Man Utd	L	0-2
18 Dec	F	A	El Nasr	W	1-0
23 Dec	Lge	H	Arsenal	L✓	0-5
26 Dec	Lge	A	QPR	D	2-2
30 Dec	Lge	A	Everton	D	1-1
10 Jan	FC	H	Altrincham	D	1-1
13 Jan	Lge	A	Bristol C.	D	0-0
16 Jan	FCr	A	Altrincham	W	3-0*
20 Jan	Lge	H	Leeds	L	1-2
3 Feb	Lge	H	Man City	L	0-3
10 Feb	Lge	A	Coventry	W	3-1
12 Feb	FC	H	Wrexham	D	3-3
21 Feb	FCr	A	Wrexham	W	3-2
24 Feb	Lge	A	Birmingham	L	0-1
28 Feb	FC	A	Oldham	W	1-0
3 Mar	Lge	H	Derby	W	2-0
10 Mar	FC	H	Man Utd	D	1-1
14 Mar	FCr	A	Man Utd	L	0-2
17 Mar	Lge	H	Norwich	D	0-0
24 Mar	Lge	A	Aston Villa	W	3-2
28 Mar	Lge	H	Southampton	D	0-0
31 Mar	Lge	A	Middlesbrough	L	0-1
3 Apr	Lge	A	Wolves	L	2-3
7 Apr	Lge	H	Middlesbrough	L	1-2
10 Apr	Lge	A	Arsenal	L	0-1
14 Apr	Lge	H	QPR	D	1-1
16 Apr	Lge	A	Southampton	D	3-3
21 Apr	Lge	H	Man Utd	D	1-1
24 Apr	F	A	QPR	W	3-1
28 Apr	Lge	A	Ipswich	L	1-2
30 Apr	†	H	West Ham	D	2-2
5 May	Lge	H	Everton	D	1-1
8 May	Lge	A	Bolton	W	3-1
14 May	Lge	H	WBA	W	1-0
16 May	F	A	Kuwait Army	W	2-1
23 May	F	A	Singapore Sel	W	4-0
27 May	F	A	Indonesia	W	6-0‡
29 May	F	A	Japan XI	W	2-0‡
31 May	F	A	Fiorentina	D	1-1‡
2 Jun	F	A	San Lorenzo	W	5-3‡
5 Jun	F	A	Dundee Utd	W	2-0‡
6 Jun	F	A	Bermuda Sel	W	3-1‡

* Played at Maine Road   † Testimonial for Steve Perryman
‡ Games played during 'Japan Cup' tournament

Player	Lg App		Goals
Aleksic M.	5		
Ardiles O.	38		3
Armstrong G.	10	(3)	1
Beavon S.	1		
Daines B.	14		
Duncan J.	2		1
Falco M.	1		1
Galvin T.	1		
Gorman J.	15		
Hoddie G.	35	(1)	7
Holmes J.	33		1
Jones C.	19	(1)	5
Kendall M.	23		
Lacy J.	35		
Lee C.	27	(1)	8
McAllister D.	38		1
McNab N.	2		
Miller P.	7		
Moores I.	2		
Naylor T.	22		
Perryman S.	42		1
Pratt J.	38	(1)	4
Smith G.	2	(1)	
Taylor P.	33	(1)	10
Villa R.	32	(6)	2
Own Goals			3

Final table for First Division

		P	W	D	L	F:A	Pts
1	Liverpool	42	30	8	4	85:16	68
2	Nottingham F.	42	21	18	3	61:26	60
3	West Bromwich	42	24	11	7	72:35	59
4	Everton	42	17	17	8	52:40	51
5	Leeds	42	18	14	10	70:52	50
6	Ipswich	42	20	9	13	63:49	49
7	Arsenal	42	17	14	11	61:48	48
8	Aston Villa	42	15	16	11	59:49	46
9	Manchester U.	42	15	15	12	60:63	45
10	Coventry	42	14	16	12	58:68	44
11	**TOTTENHAM**	42	13	15	14	48:61	41
12	Middlesbrough	42	15	10	17	57:50	40
13	Bristol C.	42	15	10	17	47:51	40
14	Southampton	42	12	16	14	47:53	40
15	Manchester C.	42	13	13	16	58:56	39
16	Norwich	42	7	23	12	51:57	37
17	Bolton	42	12	11	19	54:75	35
18	Wolverhampton	42	13	8	21	44:68	34
19	Derby	42	10	11	21	44:71	31
20	QPR	42	6	13	23	45:73	25
21	Birmingham	42	6	10	26	37:64	22
22	Chelsea	42	5	10	27	44:92	20

SEASON 1979/80

Date	Comp		Opponent	Res	Score		Date	Comp		Opponent	Res	Score
2 Aug	F	A	Gillingham	D	1-1		5 Jan	FC	H	Man Utd	D	1-1
4 Aug	F	A	Oxford	L	1-2		9 Jan	FCr	A	Man Utd	W	1-0
7 Aug	F	A	Dundee Utd	L	2-3		12 Jan	Lge	A	Man City	D	1-1
8 Aug	F	A	Aberdeen	L	0-2		19 Jan	Lge	A	Brighton	W	2-0
11 Aug	F	A	Orient	D	1-1		26 Jan	FC	A	Swindon	D	0-0
18 Aug	Lge	H	Middlesbrough	L	1-3		30 Jan	FCr	H	Swindon	W	2-1
22 Aug	Lge	A	Norwich	L	0-4		2 Feb	Lge	H	Southampton	D	0-0
25 Aug	Lge	A	Stoke	L	1-3		9 Feb	Lge	A	WBA	L	1-2
29 Aug	FLC	H	Man Utd	W	2-1		16 Feb	FC	H	Birmingham	W	3-1
1 Sep	Lge	H	Man City	W	2-1		23 Feb	Lge	A	Derby	L	1-2
5 Sep	FLC	A	Man Utd	L	1-3		27 Feb	Lge	H	Coventry	W	4-3
8 Sep	Lge	H	Brighton	W	2-1		1 Mar	Lge	H	Leeds	W	2-1
15 Sep	Lge	A	Southampton	L	2-5		8 Mar	FC	H	Liverpool	L	0-1
22 Sep	Lge	H	WBA	D	1-1		11 Mar	Lge	A	Nottm Forest	L	0-4
29 Sep	Lge	A	Coventry	D	1-1		15 Mar	Lge	H	Crystal P.	D	0-0
6 Oct	Lge	A	Crystal P.	D	1-1		22 Mar	Lge	A	Bolton	L	1-2
10 Oct	Lge	H	Norwich	W	3-2		29 Mar	Lge	H	Liverpool	W	2-0
13 Oct	Lge	H	Derby	W	1-0		2 Apr	Lge	H	Ipswich	L	0-2
20 Oct	Lge	A	Leeds	W	2-1		5 Apr	Lge	A	Wolves	W	2-1
27 Oct	Lge	H	Nottm Forest	W	1-0		7 Apr	Lge	H	Arsenal	L	1-2
3 Nov	Lge	A	Middlesbrough	D	0-0		12 Apr	Lge	A	Man Utd	L	1-4
6 Nov	F	A	Widad Moroc	W	4-2		15 Apr	F	A	Crystal P.	W	3-2
10 Nov	Lge	H	Bolton	W	2-0		23 Apr	Lge	H	Wolves	D	2-2
17 Nov	Lge	A	Liverpool	L	1-2		26 Apr	Lge	A	Aston Villa	L	0-1
24 Nov	Lge	A	Everton	D	1-1		29 Apr	*	H	Crystal P.	L	0-2
1 Dec	Lge	H	Man Utd	L	1-2		3 May	Lge	H	Bristol C.	D	0-0
9 Dec	Lge	A	Bristol C.	W	3-1		5 May	F	A	Bournemouth	W	2-1
15 Dec	Lge	H	Aston Villa	L	1-2		7 May	F	A	Hertford Town	W	4-0
21 Dec	Lge	A	Ipswich	L	1-3		11 May	F	A	Vienna Select	L	0-3
26 Dec	Lge	A	Arsenal	L	0-1		13 May	F	A	Sturm Graz	L	0-2
29 Dec	Lge	H	Stoke	W	1-0							

* Testimonial for Terry Naylor

Player	Lg App		Goals	Player	Lg App		Goals
Aleksic M.	8			Lacy J.	4		
Armstrong G.	30	(2)	4	Lee C.	10	(2)	
Ardiles O.	40		3	McAllister D.	36	(1)	1
Beavon S.	3	(1)		Miller P.	27		2
Daines B.	32			Naylor T.	7	(1)	
Falco M.	9	(2)	2	Perryman S.	40		1
Galvin T.	10	(3)	4	Pratt J.	24	(5)	2
Gibson T.	1			Smith G.	14		
Hazard M.	3			Southey P.	1		
Hoddle G.	41		19	Taylor P.	9	(2)	
Hughton C.	39		1	Villa R.	22		3
Jones C.	37	(1)	9	Yorath T.	33		1
Kendall M.	2						

Final table for First Division

1	Liverpool	42	25	10	7	81:30	60
2	Manchester U.	42	24	10	8	65:35	58
3	Ipswich	42	22	9	11	68:39	53
4	Arsenal	42	18	16	8	52:36	52
5	Nottingham F.	42	20	8	14	63:43	48
6	Wolverhampton	42	19	9	14	58:47	47
7	Aston Villa	42	16	14	12	51:50	46
8	Southampton	42	18	9	15	65:53	45
9	Middlesbrough	42	16	12	14	50:44	44
10	West Bromwich	42	11	19	12	54:50	41
11	Leeds	42	13	14	15	46:50	40
12	Norwich	42	13	14	15	58:66	40
13	Crystal P.	42	12	16	14	41:50	40
14	TOTTENHAM	42	15	10	17	52:62	40
15	Coventry	42	16	7	19	56:66	39
16	Brighton	42	11	15	16	47:57	37
17	Manchester C.	42	12	13	17	43:66	37
18	Stoke	42	13	10	19	44:58	36
19	Everton	42	9	17	16	43:51	35
20	Bristol C.	42	9	13	20	37:66	31
21	Derby	42	11	8	23	47:67	30
22	Bolton	42	5	15	22	38:73	25

SEASON 1980/81

Date	Comp		Opponent	Res	Score		Date	Comp		Opponent	Res	Score
28 Jul	F	A	Southend	D	1-1		13 Dec	Lge	H	Man City	W	2-1
30 Jul	F	A	Portsmouth	W	2-1		17 Dec	Lge	H	Ipswich	W	5-3
2 Aug	F	A	PSV Eindhoven	L	2-4		20 Dec	Lge	A	Middlesbrough	L	1-4
4 Aug	F	A	Rangers	L	1-2		26 Dec	Lge	H	Southampton	D	4-4
5 Aug	F	A	Dundee Utd	L	1-4		27 Dec	Lge	A	Norwich	D	2-2
8 Aug	F	A	Swansea	L	0-1		3 Jan	FC	A	QPR	D	0-0
16 Aug	Lge	H	Nottm Forest	W	2-0		7 Jan	FCr	H	QPR	W	3-1
19 Aug	Lge	A	C. Palace	W	4-3		10 Jan	Lge	H	Birmingham	W	1-0
23 Aug	Lge	H	Brighton	D	2-2		17 Jan	Lge	H	Arsenal	W	2-0
27 Aug	FLC	A	Orient	W	1-0		24 Jan	FC	H	Hull City	W	2-0
30 Aug	Lge	A	Arsenal	L	0-2		31 Jan	Lge	A	Brighton	W	2-0
3 Sep	FLC	H	Orient	W	3-1		2 Feb	F	A	Jersey Sel XI	W	5-0
6 Sep	Lge	H	Man Utd	D	0-0		7 Feb	Lge	H	Leeds	D	1-1
13 Sep	Lge	A	Leeds	D	0-0		14 Feb	FC	H	Coventry	W	3-1
20 Sep	Lge	H	Sunderland	D	0-0		17 Feb	Lge	A	Man Utd	D	0-0
24 Sep	FLC	H	C. Palace	D	0-0		21 Feb	Lge	H	Leicester	L	1-2
27 Sep	Lge	A	Leicester	L	1-2		28 Feb	Lge	A	Sunderland	D	1-1
30 Sep	FLCr	A	C. Palace	W	3-1		7 Mar	FC	H	Exeter	W	2-0
4 Oct	Lge	A	Stoke	W	3-2		11 Mar	Lge	H	Stoke	D	2-2
11 Oct	Lge	H	Middlesbrough	W	3-2		14 Mar	Lge	A	Ipswich	L	0-3
18 Oct	Lge	A	Aston Villa	L	0-3		21 Mar	Lge	H	Aston Villa	W	2-0
22 Oct	Lge	A	Man City	L	1-3		28 Mar	Lge	A	Coventry	W	1-0
25 Oct	Lge	H	Coventry	W	4-1		4 Apr	Lge	H	Everton	D	2-2
1 Nov	Lge	A	Everton	D	2-2		11 Apr	FCsf	*	Wolves	D	2-2
4 Nov	FLC	H	Arsenal	W	1-0		15 Apr	FCsfr	*	Wolves	W	3-0
8 Nov	Lge	H	Wolves	D	2-2		18 Apr	Lge	H	Norwich	L	2-3
12 Nov	Lge	H	C. Palace	W	4-2		20 Apr	Lge	A	Southampton	D	1-1
15 Nov	Lge	A	Nottm Forest	W	3-0		25 Apr	Lge	H	Liverpool	D	1-1
17 Nov	F	A	Weymouth	W	6-1		30 Apr	Lge	A	Wolves	L	0-1
22 Nov	Lge	A	Birmingham	L	1-2		2 May	Lge	A	WBA	L	2-4
29 Nov	Lge	H	WBA	L	2-3		9 May	FCf	†	Man City	D	1-1
2 Dec	FLC	A	West Ham	L	0-1		11 May	‡	H	West Ham	D	0-0
6 Dec	Lge	A	Liverpool	L	1-2		14 May	FCfr	†	Man City	W	3-2

* First semi-final at Hillsborough, replay at Highbury
† Cup final and replay at Wembley   ‡ Testimonial for Barry Daines

Player	Lg App		Goals	Player	Lg App		Goals
Aleksic M.	10			Lacy J.	31		2
Archibald S.	41	(1)	20	Mazzon G.	2	(1)	
Ardiles O.	36		5	McAllister D.	18		
Armstrong G.	4	(4)		Miller P.	25	(1)	2
Brooke G.	18	(8)	3	O'Reilly G.	2	(1)	
Crooks G.	40		16	Perryman S.	42		2
Daines B.	28			Roberts G.	24	(3)	
Falco M.	3		1	Smith G.	20	(2)	1
Galvin T.	18	(1)	1	Taylor P.	8	(3)	1
Hazard M.	4	(2)		Villa R.	29	(1)	2
Hoddle G.	38		12	Yorath T.	15	(4)	
Hughton C.	34		1	Own Goal			1
Kendall M.	4						

Final table for First Division

1	Aston Villa	42	26	8	8	72:40	60
2	Ipswich	42	23	10	9	77:43	56
3	Arsenal	42	19	15	8	61:45	53
4	West Bromwich	42	20	12	10	60:42	52
5	Liverpool	42	17	17	8	62:46	51
6	Southampton	42	20	10	12	76:56	50
7	Nottingham F.	42	19	12	11	62:45	50
8	Manchester U.	42	15	18	9	51:36	48
9	Leeds	42	17	10	15	39:47	44
10	TOTTENHAM	42	14	15	13	70:68	43
11	Stoke	42	12	18	12	51:60	42
12	Manchester C.	42	14	11	17	56:59	39
13	Birmingham	42	13	12	17	50:61	38
14	Middlesbrough	42	16	5	21	53:61	37
15	Everton	42	13	10	19	55:58	36
16	Coventry	42	13	10	19	48:68	36
17	Sunderland	42	14	7	21	58:53	35
18	Wolverhampton	42	13	9	20	47:55	35
19	Brighton	42	14	7	21	54:67	35
20	Norwich	42	13	7	22	49:73	33
21	Leicester	42	13	6	23	40:67	32
22	C. Palace	42	6	7	29	47:83	19

SEASON 1981/82

Date	Comp		Opponent	Res	Score
8 Aug	F	A	Glentoran	D	3-3
10 Aug	F	A	Limerick	W	6-2
12 Aug	F	A	Norwich	D	2-2
16 Aug	F	A	Aberdeen	W	1-0
22 Aug	CS	*	Aston Villa	D	2-2
29 Aug	Lge	A	Middlesbrough	W	3-1
2 Sep	Lge	H	West Ham	L	0-4
5 Sep	Lge	H	Aston Villa	L	1-3
12 Sep	Lge	A	Wolves	W	1-0
16 Sep	ECWC	A	Ajax	W	3-1
19 Sep	Lge	H	Everton	W	3-0
22 Sep	Lge	A	Swansea	L	1-2
26 Sep	Lge	A	Man City	W	1-0
29 Sep	ECWC	H	Ajax	W	3-0
3 Oct	Lge	H	Nottm Forest	W	3-0
7 Oct	FLC	H	Man Utd	W	1-0
10 Oct	Lge	H	Stoke	W	2-0
12 Oct	F	A	Luton	D	2-2
17 Oct	Lge	A	Sunderland	W	2-0
21 Oct	ECWC	A	Dundalk	D	1-1
24 Oct	Lge	H	Brighton	L	0-1
28 Oct	FLC	A	Man Utd	W	1-0
31 Oct	Lge	A	Southampton	W	2-1
4 Nov	ECWC	H	Dundalk	W	1-0
7 Nov	Lge	H	WBA	L	1-2
11 Nov	FLC	H	Wrexham	W	2-0
14 Nov	F	A	Israeli Sel	W	3-2
21 Nov	Lge	H	Man Utd	W	3-1
28 Nov	Lge	A	Notts C	D	2-2
2 Dec	FLC	H	Fulham	W	1-0
5 Dec	Lge	H	Coventry	L	1-2
12 Dec	Lge	A	Leeds	D	0-0
22 Dec	F	A	Plymouth	D	1-1
29 Dec	F	A	Sp Lisbon	L	2-3
2 Jan	FC	H	Arsenal	W	1-0
18 Jan	FLC	H	Nottm Forest	W	1-0
23 Jan	FC	H	Leeds	W	1-0
27 Jan	Lge	H	Middlesbrough	W	1-0
3 Feb	FLCsf	A	WBA	D	0-0
6 Feb	Lge	H	Wolves	W	6-1
10 Feb	FLCsf	H	WBA	W	1-0
13 Feb	FC	H	Aston Villa	W	1-0
17 Feb	Lge	A	Aston Villa	D	1-1
20 Feb	Lge	H	Man City	W	2-0
22 Feb	F	A	Jersey Sel	W	8-3
27 Feb	Lge	A	Stoke	W	2-0
3 Mar	ECWC	H	Eintracht Fr.	W	2-0
6 Mar	FC	A	Chelsea	W	3-2
9 Mar	Lge	A	Brighton	W	3-1
13 Mar	FLCf	*	Liverpool	L	1-3
17 Mar	ECWC	A	Eintracht Fr.	L	1-2
20 Mar	Lge	H	Southampton	W	3-2
23 Mar	Lge	A	Birmingham	D	0-0
27 Mar	Lge	A	WBA	L	0-1
29 Mar	Lge	H	Arsenal	D	2-2
3 Apr	FCsf	†	Leicester	W	2-0
7 Apr	ECWCsf	A	Barcelona	D	1-1
10 Apr	Lge	H	Ipswich	W	1-0
12 Apr	Lge	A	Arsenal	W	3-1
14 Apr	Lge	H	Sunderland	D	2-2
17 Apr	Lge	A	Man Utd	L	0-2
21 Apr	ECWCsf	A	Barcelona	L	0-1
24 Apr	Lge	H	Notts C	W	3-1
28 Apr	Lge	H	Birmingham	D	1-1
1 May	Lge	A	Coventry	D	0-0
3 May	Lge	H	Liverpool	D	2-2
5 May	Lge	H	Swansea	W	2-1
8 May	Lge	H	Leeds	W	2-1
10 May	Lge	A	West Ham	D	2-2
12 May	Lge	A	Nottm Forest	L	0-2
15 May	Lge	A	Liverpool	L	1-3
17 May	Lge	A	Ipswich	L	1-2
22 May	FCf	*	QPR	D	1-1
27 May	FCfr	*	QPR	W	1-0

* at Wembley   † at Villa Park

Player	Lg App	Goals
Aleksic M.	2	
Archibald S.	27 (1)	6
Ardiles O.	26	2
Brooke G.	16 (4)	4
Clemence R.	38	
Corbett P.	4 (1)	1
Crook I.	4 (1)	
Crooks G.	27	13
Dick A.	1	
Falco M.	21	5
Galvin A.	32	3
Gibson T.	1	
Hazard M.	28 (2)	5
Hoddle G.	34	10
Hughton C.	37	2
Jones C.	7 (4)	
Lacy J.	12 (5)	
Miller P.	35	
O'Reilly G.	4	
Parks A.	2	
Perryman S.	42	1
Price P.	21 (3)	
Roberts G.	37 (2)	6
Smith G.	2 (1)	
Villa R.	27 (1)	8
Own Goal		1

Final table for First Division

1 Liverpool	42	26	9	7	80:32	87
2 Ipswich	42	26	5	11	75:53	83
3 Manchester U.	42	22	12	8	59:29	78
4 TOTTENHAM	42	20	11	11	67:48	71
5 Arsenal	42	20	11	11	48:37	71
6 Swansea	42	21	6	15	58:51	69
7 Southampton	42	19	9	14	72:67	66
8 Everton	42	17	13	12	56:50	64
9 West Ham	42	14	16	12	66:57	58
10 Manchester C.	42	15	13	14	49:50	58
11 Aston Villa	42	15	12	15	55:53	57
12 Nottm Forest	42	15	12	15	42:48	57
13 Brighton	42	13	13	16	43:52	52
14 Coventry	42	13	11	18	56:62	50
15 Notts Co.	42	13	8	21	61:69	47
16 Birmingham	42	10	14	18	53:61	44
17 WBA	42	11	11	20	46:57	44
18 Stoke	42	12	8	22	44:63	44
19 Sunderland	42	11	11	20	38:58	44
20 Leeds	42	10	12	20	39:61	42
21 Wolverhampton	42	10	10	22	32:63	40
22 Middlesbrough	42	8	15	19	34:52	39

SEASON 1982/83

Date	Comp		Opponent	Res	Score
3 Aug	F	A	Scunthorpe	W	5-0
6 Aug	F	A	Lausanne	L	0-3
8 Aug	F	A	Rangers	W	1-0
13 Aug	F	A	Ajax	L	2-3[1]
15 Aug	F	A	Cologne	D	0-0[1]
21 Aug	CS	*	Liverpool	L	0-1
28 Aug	Lge	H	Luton	D	2-2
31 Aug	Lge	A	Ipswich	W	2-1
4 Sep	Lge	A	Everton	L	1-3
8 Sep	Lge	H	Southampton	W	6-0
11 Sep	Lge	H	Man City	L	1-2
15 Sep	ECWC	A	Coleraine	W	3-0
18 Sep	Lge	A	Sunderland	W	1-0
20 Sep	F	A	Barnet	L	1-2[2]
25 Sep	Lge	H	Nottm Forest	W	4-1
29 Sep	ECWC	H	Coleraine	W	4-0
2 Oct	Lge	A	Swansea	L	0-2
6 Oct	FLC	H	Brighton	D	1-1
9 Oct	Lge	H	Coventry	W	4-0
16 Oct	Lge	A	Norwich	D	0-0
20 Oct	ECWC	H	Bayern Munich	D	1-1
23 Oct	Lge	H	Notts County	W	4-2
26 Oct	FLC	A	Brighton	W	1-0
30 Oct	Lge	A	Aston Villa	L	0-4
3 Nov	ECWC	A	Bayern Munich	L	1-4
6 Nov	Lge	H	Watford	L	0-1
9 Nov	FLC	A	Gillingham	W	4-2
13 Nov	Lge	A	Man Utd	L	0-1
20 Nov	Lge	H	West Ham	W	2-1
27 Nov	Lge	A	Liverpool	L	0-3
1 Dec	FLC	H	Luton	W	1-0
4 Dec	Lge	H	WBA	D	1-1
11 Dec	Lge	A	Stoke	L	0-2
18 Dec	Lge	H	Birmingham	W	2-1
20 Dec	F	A	Borussia Moen	L	0-2[3]
22 Dec	F	A	Israel Nat. Team	D	2-2[3]
27 Dec	Lge	A	Arsenal	L	0-2
28 Dec	Lge	H	Brighton	W	2-0
1 Jan	Lge	A	West Ham	L	0-3
3 Jan	Lge	H	Everton	W	2-1
8 Jan	FC	H	Southampton	W	1-0
15 Jan	Lge	A	Luton	D	1-1
19 Jan	FLC	H	Burnley	L	1-4
22 Jan	Lge	H	Sunderland	D	1-1
29 Jan	FC	H	WBA	W	2-1
5 Feb	Lge	A	Man City	D	2-2
12 Feb	Lge	H	Swansea	W	1-0
19 Feb	FC	A	Everton	L	0-2
26 Feb	Lge	H	Norwich	D	0-0
5 Mar	Lge	A	Notts County	L	0-3
12 Mar	Lge	A	Coventry	D	1-1
19 Mar	Lge	A	Watford	W	1-0
23 Mar	Lge	H	Aston Villa	W	2-0
25 Mar	F	A	Northerners (G.)	W	6-1
2 Apr	Lge	A	Brighton	L	1-2
4 Apr	Lge	H	Arsenal	W	5-0
9 Apr	Lge	A	Nottm Forest	D	2-2
16 Apr	Lge	H	Ipswich	W	3-1
19 Apr	F	A	Bristol Rovers	W	3-2[4]
23 Apr	Lge	A	WBA	W	1-0
30 Apr	Lge	A	Liverpool	W	2-0
3 May	Lge	A	Southampton	W	2-1
7 May	Lge	A	Birmingham	L	0-2
11 May	Lge	H	Man Utd	W	2-0
14 May	Lge	H	Stoke	W	4-1
17 May	F	A	Trinidad Nat. XI	D	2-2
20 May	F	A	A.S.L. Trinidad	W	2-1
23 May	F	A	Charlton	D	4-4[5]
30 May	F	A	Aaelsund	W	3-2
4 Jun	F	A	Man Utd	L	1-2[6]
11 Jun	F	A	Man Utd	W	2-0[6]

1. Amsterdam 707 tournament. 2. Brinkman testimonial. 3. In Tel Aviv. 4. Bristol Rovers centenary match. 5. Powell testimonial. 6. Sun international challenge trophy tournament in Swaziland. *at Wembley.

Player	Lg App	Goals
Archibald S.	31	11
Ardiles O.	2	
Brazil A.	12	6
Brooke G.	23 (4)	7
Clemence R.	41	
Corbett P.	1 (1)	
Crook I.	4 (3)	
Crooks G.	26	8
Dick A.	2	
Falco M.	16 (5)	5
Galvin A.	26	2
Gibson T.	16 (2)	4
Hazard M.	18 (3)	1
Hoddle G.	24 (2)	1
Hughton C.	38	3
Lacy J.	22	
Mabbutt G.	38	10
Mazzon G.	2	
Miller P.	23	1
O'Reilly G.	26 (1)	
Parks A.	1	
Perryman S.	33 (1)	1
Price P.	16	
Roberts G.	24 (4)	2
Villa R.	23 (1)	2
Webster S.	2 (1)	
Own Goal		1

Final table for First Division

1 Liverpool	42	24	10	8	87:37	82
2 Watford	42	22	5	15	74:57	71
3 Manchester U.	42	19	13	10	56:38	70
4 TOTTENHAM	42	20	9	13	65:50	69
5 Nottm Forest	42	20	9	13	62:50	69
6 Aston Villa	42	21	5	16	62:50	68
7 Everton	42	18	10	14	66:48	64
8 West Ham	42	20	4	18	68:62	64
9 Ipswich	42	15	13	14	64:50	58
10 Arsenal	42	16	10	16	58:56	58
11 W.B.A.	42	15	12	15	51:49	57
12 Southampton	42	15	12	15	54:58	57
13 Stoke	42	16	9	17	53:64	57
14 Norwich	42	14	12	16	52:58	54
15 Notts Co	42	15	7	20	55:71	52
16 Sunderland	42	12	14	16	48:61	50
17 Birmingham	42	12	14	16	40:55	50
18 Luton	42	12	13	17	65:84	49
19 Coventry	42	13	9	20	48:59	48
20 Manchester C.	42	13	8	21	47:70	47
21 Swansea	42	10	11	21	51:69	41
22 Brighton	42	9	13	20	38:68	40

SEASON 1983/84

Date	Comp	H/A	Opponent	Result	Score
2 Aug	F	A	Hertford Town	W	2-1
3 Aug	F	A	Southall	W	8-0
4 Aug	F	A	Enfield	W	4-1
6 Aug	F	A	Brentford	W	4-2[1]
6 Aug	F	A	Aylesbury	W	4-0[1]
9 Aug	F	A	Portsmouth	W	3-1
10 Aug	F	A	Aldershot	L	0-1
12 Aug	F	A	Brighton	D	0-0
13 Aug	F	A	Lewes	W	6-0
16 Aug	F	A	Celtic	D	1-1
17 Aug	F	A	Dundee Utd	D	1-1[2]
21 Aug	F	H	West Ham	D	1-1[3]
27 Aug	Lge	A	Ipswich	L	1-3
29 Aug	Lge	H	Coventry	D	1-1
3 Sep	Lge	H	West Ham	L	0-2
7 Sep	Lge	A	WBA	D	1-1
10 Sep	Lge	A	Leicester	W	3-0
14 Sep	UEFA	H	Drogheda	W	6-0
17 Sep	Lge	H	Everton	L	1-2
24 Sep	Lge	A	Watford	W	3-2
28 Sep	UEFA	H	Drogheda	W	8-0
2 Oct	Lge	H	Nottm Forest	W	2-1
5 Oct	FLC	H	Lincoln	W	3-1
8 Oct	F	A	Vale Recreation	W	7-2
15 Oct	Lge	A	Wolves	W	3-2
19 Oct	UEFA	H	Feijenoord	W	4-2
22 Oct	Lge	A	Birmingham	W	1-0
26 Oct	FLC	A	Lincoln	L	1-2
29 Oct	Lge	H	Notts County	W	1-0
2 Nov	UEFA	A	Feijenoord	W	2-0
5 Nov	Lge	A	Stoke	D	1-1
9 Nov	FLC	H	Arsenal	L	1-2
12 Nov	Lge	H	Liverpool	D	2-2
19 Nov	Lge	A	Luton	W	4-2
23 Nov	UEFA	A	Bayern Munich	L	0-1
26 Nov	Lge	H	Q.P.R.	W	3-2
3 Dec	Lge	A	Norwich	L	1-2
7 Dec	UEFA	H	Bayern Munich	W	2-0
10 Dec	Lge	H	Southampton	D	0-0
16 Dec	Lge	A	Man Utd	L	2-4
26 Dec	Lge	H	Arsenal	L	2-4
27 Dec	Lge	A	Aston Villa	D	0-0
31 Dec	Lge	A	West Ham	L	1-4
2 Jan	Lge	H	Watford	L	2-3
7 Jan	FC	A	Fulham	D	0-0
11 Jan	FCr	H	Fulham	W	2-0
14 Jan	Lge	H	Ipswich	W	2-0
21 Jan	Lge	A	Everton	L	1-2
28 Jan	FC	H	Norwich	D	0-0
1 Feb	FCr	A	Norwich	L	1-2
4 Feb	Lge	A	Nottm Forest	D	2-2
8 Feb	Lge	H	Sunderland	W	3-0
11 Feb	Lge	H	Leicester	W	3-2
21 Feb	Lge	A	Notts County	D	0-0
25 Feb	Lge	H	Birmingham	L	0-1
3 Mar	Lge	H	Stoke	W	1-0
7 Mar	UEFA	A	F.K. Austria	W	2-0
10 Mar	Lge	A	Liverpool	L	1-3
17 Mar	Lge	H	WBA	L	0-1
21 Mar	UEFA	H	F.K. Austria	D	2-2
24 Mar	Lge	A	Coventry	W	4-2
26 Mar	F	A	Wimbledon	W	5-0
31 Mar	Lge	H	Wolves	W	1-0
7 Apr	Lge	A	Sunderland	D	1-1
11 Apr	UEFAsf	A	Hajduk Split	L	1-2
14 Apr	Lge	H	Luton	W	2-1
18 Apr	Lge	H	Aston Villa	W	2-1
21 Apr	Lge	A	Arsenal	L	2-3
25 Apr	UEFAsf	H	Hajduk Split	W	1-0
28 Apr	Lge	A	Q.P.R.	L	1-2
5 May	Lge	H	Norwich	W	2-0
7 May	Lge	A	Southampton	L	0-5
9 May	UEFAf	A	Anderlecht	D	1-1
12 May	Lge	H	Man Utd	D	1-1
18 May	F	A	West Ham	L	1-4[5]
23 May	UEFAf	H	Anderlecht	D	1-1[6]
29 May	F	H	England XI	D	2-2[7]
2 Jun	F	A	Liverpool	L	2-5[8]
9 Jun	F	A	Liverpool	D	1-1[8]

SEASON 1984/85

Date	Comp	H/A	Opponent	Result	Score
25 Aug	Lge	A	Everton	W	4-1
27 Aug	Lge	H	Leicester	D	2-2
1 Sep	Lge	H	Norwich	W	3-1
4 Sep	Lge	A	Sunderland	L	0-1
8 Sep	Lge	A	Sheff Wed	L	1-2
15 Sep	Lge	H	QPR	W	5-0
19 Sep	UEFA	A	Sporting Braga	W	3-0
22 Sep	Lge	A	Aston Villa	W	1-0
26 Sep	Milk	A	Halifax	W	5-1
29 Sep	Lge	H	Luton	W	4-2
3 Oct	UEFA	H	Sporting Braga	W	6-0
6 Oct	Lge	A	Southampton	L	0-1
9 Oct	Milk	H	Halifax	W	4-0
12 Oct	Lge	H	Liverpool	W	1-0
20 Oct	Lge	A	Man Utd	L	0-1
24 Oct	UEFA	A	Brugge	L	1-2
27 Oct	Lge	H	Stoke	W	4-0
31 Oct	Milk	H	Liverpool	W	1-0
3 Nov	Lge	H	WBA	L	2-3
7 Nov	UEFA	H	Brugge	W	3-0
10 Nov	Lge	A	Nottm F.	W	2-1
17 Nov	Lge	A	Ipswich	W	3-0
21 Nov	Milk	A	Sunderland	D	0-0
24 Nov	Lge	H	Chelsea	D	1-1
28 Nov	UEFA	H	Boh. Prague	W	2-0
1 Dec	Lge	A	Coventry	D	1-1
5 Dec	Milk	A	Sunderland	L	1-2
8 Dec	Lge	H	Newcastle	W	3-1
12 Dec	UEFA	A	Boh. Prague	D	1-1
15 Dec	Lge	A	Watford	W	2-1
22 Dec	Lge	A	Norwich	W	2-1
26 Dec	Lge	H	West Ham	D	2-2
29 Dec	Lge	H	Sunderland	W	2-0
1 Jan	Lge	A	Arsenal	W	2-1
5 Jan	FC	H	Charlton	D	1-1
12 Jan	Lge	A	QPR	D	2-2
16 Jan	FC	A	Charlton	W	2-1
27 Jan	FC	A	Liverpool	L	0-1
2 Feb	Lge	A	Luton	D	2-2
23 Feb	Lge	A	WBA	W	1-0
2 Mar	Lge	A	Stoke	W	1-0
6 Mar	UEFA	H	Real Madrid	L	0-1
12 Mar	Lge	H	Man Utd	L	1-2
16 Mar	Lge	A	Liverpool	W	1-0
20 Mar	UEFA	A	Real Madrid	D	0-0
23 Mar	Lge	H	Southampton	W	2-0
30 Mar	Lge	A	Aston Villa	L	0-2
3 Apr	Lge	H	Everton	L	1-2
6 Apr	Lge	A	West Ham	D	1-1
13 Apr	Lge	A	Leicester	W	2-1
17 Apr	Lge	H	Arsenal	L	0-2
20 Apr	Lge	H	Ipswich	L	2-3
27 Apr	Lge	A	Chelsea	D	1-1
4 May	Lge	H	Coventry	W	4-2
6 May	Lge	A	Newcastle	W	3-2
11 May	Lge	H	Watford	L	1-5
14 May	Lge	A	Sheff Wed	W	2-0
17 May	Lge	H	Nottm Forest	W	1-0

1. Half the first team played in each match 2. McAlpine testimonial. 3. Nicholson testimonial 4. Bassett testimonial. 5. Holland testimonial. 6. Spurs won 4-3 on penalties. 7. Burkinshaw testimonial. 8. Sun international challenge trophy tournament in Swaziland.

SEASON 1983/84

Player	Lg App		Goals
Archibald S.	32	(1)	21
Ardiles O.	9	(1)	
Bowen M.	7	(1)	
Brace R.	1	(1)	
Brazil A.	19	(2)	3
Brooke G.	12	(5)	
Clemence R.	26		
Cockram A.	2		
Cooke R.	9		1
Crook I.	3		
Crooks G.	10	(4)	1
Culverhouse I.	2	(1)	
Dick A.	11	(1)	2
Falco M.	36	(4)	13
Galvin A.	30		1
Hazard M.	11	(2)	2
Hoddle G.	24		4
Hughton C.	34		3
Mabbutt G.	21		2
Miller P.	21	(1)	
O'Reilly G.	12	(3)	
Parks A.	16		
Perryman S.	41		1
Price P.	2	(1)	
Roberts G.	35		6
Stevens G.	40	(3)	4
Thomas D.	27	(1)	
Webster S.	1		

Final table for First Division

1	Liverpool	42	22	14	6	73:32	80
2	Southampton	42	22	11	9	66:38	77
3	Nottm Forest	42	22	8	12	76:45	74
4	Manchester U.	42	20	14	8	71:41	74
5	Q.P.R.	42	22	7	13	67:37	73
6	Arsenal	42	18	9	15	74:60	63
7	Everton	42	16	14	12	44:42	62
8	TOTTENHAM	42	17	10	15	64:65	61
9	West Ham	42	17	9	16	60:55	60
10	Aston Villa	42	17	9	16	59:61	60
11	Watford	42	16	9	17	68:77	57
12	Ipswich	42	15	8	19	55:57	53
13	Sunderland	42	13	13	16	42:53	52
14	Norwich	42	12	15	15	48:49	51
15	Leicester	42	13	12	17	65:68	51
16	Luton	42	14	9	19	53:66	51
17	W.B.A.	42	14	9	19	48:62	51
18	Stoke	42	13	11	18	44:63	50
19	Coventry	42	13	11	18	57:77	50
20	Birmingham	42	12	12	18	39:50	48
21	Notts Co	42	10	11	21	50:72	41
22	Wolverhampton	42	6	11	25	27:80	29

SEASON 1984/85

Player	Lg App		Goals
Allen C.	13	(1)	7
Ardiles O.	11	(1)	2
Bowen M.	6		
Brooke G.	4	(3)	1
Chiedozie J.	34	(3)	5
Clemence R.	42		
Crook I.	5	(3)	1
Crooks G.	22		10
Dick A.	2		
Falco M.	42		22
Galvin A.	38		4
Hazard M.	23	(8)	4
Hoddle G.	28	(2)	8
Hughton C.	31	(2)	1
Leworthy D.	6		3
Mabbutt G.	25	(10)	2
Miller P.	39		
Perryman S.	42		1
Roberts G.	40		7
Stevens G.	28		
Thomas D.	16	(2)	

Final table for First Division

1	Everton	42	28	6	8	88:43	90
2	Liverpool	42	22	11	9	66:35	77
3	TOTTENHAM	42	23	8	11	78:51	77
4	Man Utd	42	22	10	10	77:47	76
5	Southampton	42	19	11	12	56:47	68
6	Chelsea	42	18	12	12	63:48	66
7	Arsenal	42	19	9	14	61:49	66
8	Sheff Wed	42	17	14	11	58:45	65
9	Nottm Forest	42	19	7	16	56:48	64
10	Aston Villa	42	15	11	16	60:60	56
11	Watford	42	14	13	15	81:71	55
12	West Brom	42	16	7	19	58:62	55
13	Luton	42	15	9	18	57:61	54
14	Newcastle	42	13	13	16	55:70	52
15	Leicester	42	15	6	21	66:73	51
16	West Ham	42	13	12	17	51:68	51
17	Ipswich	42	13	11	18	46:57	50
18	Coventry	42	15	5	22	47:64	50
19	Q.P.R.	42	13	11	18	53:72	50
20	Norwich	42	13	10	19	46:64	49
21	Sunderland	42	10	10	22	40:62	40
22	Stoke	42	3	8	31	24:91	17

International Appearances by Tottenham Players

For England

Player	Caps won to 31 May 1985	Goals scored	International debut while at Tottenham		Opponents
Alsford W.J.	1	0	6 Apr	35	Scotland
Baily E.F.	9	5	2 Jul	50	Spain
Bliss H.	1	0	9 Apr	21	Scotland
Brooks J.	3	2	14 Nov	56	Denmark
Chivers M.	24	13	3 Feb	71	Malta
Clarke H.A.	1	0	3 Apr	54	Scotland
Clay T.	4	0	15 Mar	20	Wales
Clemence R.	5	0	9 Sep	81	Norway
Coates R.	2	0	12 May	71	Malta
Dimmock J.H.	3	0	9 Apr	21	Scotland
Ditchburn E.G.	6	0	2 Dec	48	Switzerland
Greaves J.	42	28	14 Apr	62	Scotland
Grimsdell A.	6	0	15 Mar	20	Wales
Hall G.W.	10	9	6 Dec	33	France
Henry R.P.	1	0	27 Feb	63	France
Hoddle G.	21	6	22 Nov	79	Bulgaria
Hunt G.S.	3	1	1 Apr	33	Scotland
Knowles C.	4	0	6 Dec	67	USSR
Mabbutt G.	9	0	13 Oct	82	West Germany
Medley L.D.	6	1	15 Nov	50	Wales
Mullery A.P.	35	1	9 Dec	64	Holland
Nicholson W.E.	1	1	19 May	51	Portugal
Norman M.	23	0	20 May	62	Peru
Osborne F.R.	2	3	8 Dec	24	Belgium
Perryman S.	1	0	2 Jun	82	Iceland
Peters M.	34	9	18 Apr	70	Wales
Ramsey A.E.	31	3	30 Nov	49	Italy
Robb G.	1	0	25 Nov	53	Hungary
Roberts G.	6	0	28 May	83	Northern Ireland
Rowe A.	1	0	6 Dec	33	France
Seed J.M.	5	1	21 May	21	Belgium
Smith B.	2	0	9 Apr	21	Scotland
Smith R.A.	15	13	8 Oct	60	Northern Ireland
Sproston B.	2	0	22 Oct	38	Wales
Stevens G.	3	0	17 Oct	84	Finland
Walden F.I.	2	0	4 Apr	14	Scotland
Willis A.	1	0	3 Oct	51	France
Woodward V.J.	21	27	14 Feb	03	Northern Ireland

Note: Chivers appearances total includes 2 as sub
Mullery appearances total includes 2 as sub
Peters appearances total includes 2 as sub
Hoddle appearances total includes 1 as sub
Mabbutt appearances total includes 1 as sub
Stevens appearances total includes 1 as sub
Perryman's one appearance was as a substitute

For Ireland/Northern Ireland

Player	Caps won to 31 May 1985	Goals scored	International debut while at Tottenham		Opponents
Armstrong G.	27	4	27 Apr	77	West Germany
Blanchflower R.D.	43	2	2 Oct	54	England
Jennings P.A.	66	0	3 Oct	64	England
Kirwan J.	12	2	24 Feb	00	Wales
McGrath R.C.	5	0	11 May	74	Scotland
O'Hagan C.	5	1	18 Mar	05	Scotland
Rowley R.W.M.	2	1	22 Apr	31	Wales

Note: Armstrong total includes 2 as substitute
McGrath total includes 1 as substitute

For Republic of Ireland

Player	Caps won to 31 May 1985	Goals scored	International debut while at Tottenham		Opponents
Galvin A.	11	0	22 Sep	82	Holland
Gavin G.T.	2	0	1 May	55	Holland
Holmes J.	12	0	30 Mar	77	France
Hughton C.	26	1	29 Oct	79	USA
Kinnear J.P.	24	0	22 Feb	67	Turkey

Note: Kinnear appearance total includes 1 as substitute
Hughton appearance total includes 1 as substitute
Galvin appearance total includes 2 as substitute

For Scotland

Player	Caps won to 31 May 1985	Goals scored	International debut while at Tottenham		Opponents
Archibald S.	22	4	16 May	80	Northern Ireland
Brazil A.	2	1	24 May	83	Wales
Brown W.D.F.	24	0	3 Oct	59	Northern Ireland
Conn A.	2	0	20 May	75	Northern Ireland
Gilzean A.J.	17	8	8 May	65	Spain
Mackay D.G.	18	4	11 Apr	59	England
Robertson J.G.	1	0	3 Oct	64	Wales
White J.A.	18	1	14 Nov	59	Wales

Note: Archibald appearances total includes 4 as sub
Conn appearances total includes 1 as sub
Gilzean appearances total includes 2 as sub

For Wales

Player	Caps won to 31 May 1985	Goals scored	International debut while at Tottenham		Opponents
Burgess W.A.R.	32	1	19 Oct	46	Scotland
Day A.	1	0	4 Nov	33	Northern Ireland
England H.M.	24	2	22 Oct	66	Scotland
Evans W.	6	1	7 Dec	32	Northern Ireland
Hopkins M.	34	0	11 Apr	56	Northern Ireland
Hughes E.	12	0	2 Mar	01	Scotland
Jones C.	41	12	16 Apr	58	Northern Ireland
Jones J.L.	12	0	19 Feb	98	Northern Ireland
Jones W.E.A.	2	0	23 Oct	48	Scotland
Medwin T.C.	27	6	20 Oct	56	Scotland
O'Callaghan E.	11	3	2 Feb	29	Northern Ireland
Price P.	14	0	18 Nov	81	USSR
Rees W.	1	0	8 Mar	50	Northern Ireland
Whatley W.J.	2	0	22 Oct	38	England
Yorath T.C.	8	0	11 Sep	79	Rep of Ireland

For Nigeria

Player	Caps won to 31 May 1985	Goals scored	International debut while at Tottenham		Opponents
Chiedozie J.	3	0	20 Oct	84	Liberia

For Argentina

Player	Caps won to 31 May 1985	Goals scored	International debut while at Tottenham		Opponents
Ardiles O.C.	8	1	1 Jan	81	West Germany

Note: These records only cover appearances while the player was registered with Tottenham. Many players have also made international appearances while with other clubs.

Football League Appearances September 1908–July 1984

Player	Total Apps	Came on as sub	Gls
Adams C.J.	6		1
Aleksic M.A.	25		
Alexander S.	9		1
Allen A.	1		1
Allen L.W.	119		47
Alsford W.J.	81		
Archibald J.	24		1
Archibald S.	131	3	58
Ardiles O.C.	151	1	14
Armstrong G.J.	84	19	10
Armstrong J.W.	28		7
Austin P.	1		
Baily E.F.	296		64
Baker P.R.B.	299		3
Banks J.A.	69		6
Bann W.E.	12		
Barnett F.W.	16		1
Barton K.R.	4		
Bauchop J.R.	10		6
Beal P.	333	3	1
Beavon S.M.	4	1	
Bell S.	15		6
Bellamy W.R.	70		9
Bennett L.D.	272		101
Bentley F.W.	36		
Bing T.E.	1		
Birnie E.L.	4		1
Blair J.G.	29		14
Blake H.E.	51		
Blanchflower R.D.	337		15
Bliss H.	194		93
Blyth J.	11		
Bolan L.A.	10		3
Bond D.J.T.	23	3	1
Boreham F.	20		
Bowen M.	7	1	
Bowering E.	7		
Bowler G.	3		
Brain J.	45		11
Brazil A.	31	2	9
Brittan C.	40		2
Brittan R.C.	40		
Britton J.	40		
Brooke G.	69	21	14
Brooks J.	166		46
Brooks S.	10		1
Brotherston N.	1		
Brough J.	1		
Brown D.C.	1		
Brown I.	12		
Brown J.	4		
Brown L.	62		3
Brown R.S.	37		
Brown R.E.	1		
Brown W.D.F.	222		
Buckingham V.F.	204		1
Bull W.	12		
Bulling E.	2		
Burgess W.A.R.	297		15
Burton A.	4		
Burton O.	37		
Cable T.H.	42		
Cantrell J.	160		74
Cartwright W.	13		
Castle S.R.	5		
Channell F.C.	95		1
Chipperfield J.	15		6
Chisholm J.R.	2		
Chivers M.H.	278	10	118
Clarke H.A.	295		4
Clarke R.	1	1	
Clay T.	318		23
Clayton E.	92	4	20
Clemence R.	105		
Coates R.	188	15	13
Cockram A.	2		
Collins Jim	2		
Collins John L	3		
Collins P.J.	83	6	4
Collins T.	113		1
Colquhoun D.M.	81		2
Conn A.J.	38	3	6
Cook G.W.	63		22
Cook R.	9		1
Coquet E.	77		
Corbett P.	5	2	1
Cox F.J.A.	98		15
Crompton A.	15		2
Crompton E.	8		
Crook I.	8	1	
Crooks G.	103		38
Crowl S.R.	1		
Culverhouse I.	2	1	
Curtis J.	82		5
Daines B.R.	146		
Darnell J.	150		3
Davies W.	109		19
Day A.	13		
Dick A.	14	1	2
Dicker L.R.	10		2
Dillon M.L.	24	3	1
Dimmock J.H.	400		99
Ditchburn E.G.	418		
Dix R.W.	36		5
Dodge W.C.	6		
Dowsett G.J.	1		1
Drabble F.	1		
Dulin M.C.	10		2
Duncan A.	93		22
Duncan J.P.	103	2	53
Dunmore D.G.	75		23
Duquemin L.	275		114
Dyson T.K.	184		41
Eadon J.	5		
Edrich W.J.	20		4
Elkes J.E.	190		49
Elkin R.H.	25		
Elliott J.E.	13		3
England M.H.	300		14
Evans A.A.	5		
Evans R.L.	136	4	2
Evans T.	94		4
Evans W.	178		77
Falco M.P.	86	11	27
Farley B.R.	1		
Felton W.	73		1
Fleming J.B.M.	19		3
Flint K.	5		1
Foreman G.A.	36		15
Forman T.	8		1
Forster M.	236		
Fullwood J.	34		1
Galloway R.	3		2
Galvin A.	116	3	11
Garwood L.F.	2		
Gavin J.T.	32		15
Gibbins E.	1		1
Gibbons A.H.	27		13
Gibson T.	18	2	4
Gilberg H.	2		
Gilzean A.J.	343	8	93
Goldsmith G.	1		
Goodman A.A.	16		1
Gorman J.	30		
Gosnell A.A.	5		
Greaves J.P.	321		220
Greenfield G.	31		11
Grice F.	47		1
Grimsdell A.	324		26
Groves V.G.	4		3
Grubb A.J.	2		
Hall A.E.	40		10
Hall A.G.	16		3
Hall B.A.C.	2		
Hall G.W.	202		27
Hall J.	53		
Hancock K.P.	3		
Handley C.H.J.	121		27
Hargreaves H.	35		7
Harmer T.C.	205		47
Harper E.C.	63		63
Harris W.	7		
Hartley F.	7		1
Hazard M.	64	9	8
Hedley F.	4		1
Helliwell S.	8		
Henry R.P.	247		1
Herod E.R.B.	57		
Hewitson R.	30		
Hills J.R.	29		
Hinton F.	57		
Hitchins A.W.	35		1
Hoddle G.	283	4	70
Hodgkinson H.	56		
Holder P.	13	4	1
Hollis R.W.	3		
Hollowbread J.F.	67		
Holmes J.A.	81		2
Hooper P.G.	97		
Hopkins M.	219		
Howe L.F.	165		26
Hoy R.E.	10		
Hughes W.A.	2		
Hughton C.W.	182		10
Humphreys P.	45		23
Hunt D.A.	17		6
Hunt G.S.	185		124
Hunter A.C.	23		
Hutchinson G.	5		1
Iley J.	53		1
Illingworth J.	10		
Ireland J.C.	3		
Jacques W.	122		
Jeffrey S.	1		1
Jenkins D.	14	3	2
Jennings P.A.	472		
Johnson N.J.	34	7	5
Jones Chas.	18		
Jones Chris H.	160	14	37
Jones Cliff	318	4	135
Jones E.W.A.	55		14
Jones G.	7		
Jordan J.W.	24		10
Joseph L.	1		
Joyce J.W.	73		1
Kaine W.E.	11		
Keeley A.	6	1	
Kendall M.	29		
Kennedy J.J.	13		1
Kerry A.H.G.	1		
King A.	19		
King D.A.	19		
King E.	1		
Kinnear J.P.	196	7	2
Knight J.G.	1		
Knowles C.B.	401	1	15
Lacy J.	104	5	2
Lane W.H.C.	26		7
Lee C.	62	5	18
Leese F.H.	1		
Leslie T.	10		
Levene D.	8		
Lightfoot E.J.	61		2
Lindsay A.F.	209		41
Lorimer H.H.	5		
Lowdell A.	86		
Low A.R.	8	2	1
Lowe H.	65		
Ludford G.A.	75		8
Lunn T.H.	86		
Lyle A.	1		
Lyman C.C.	46		10
Lyons A.	54		3
Mabbutt G.	59		12
MacFarlane D.	21		2
Mackay D.C.	268		42
Maddison G.	40		
Marchi A.V.	232		7
Marshall W.H.	1		
Mason T.L.	7		1
Massey F.	1		
Mazzon G.	4	1	
McAllister D.	172	4	9
McClellan S.B.	68		29
McCormick J.	137		26
McDonald R.J.	109		
McGrath C.	38	8	5
McNab N.	72	9	3
McTavish J.K.	37		3
McTavish R.	11		2
McWilkie R.	1		
Meads T.	184		6
Medley L.D.	150		45
Medwin T.C.	197		65
Meek J.	45		15
Messer A.T.	50		2
Middlemiss H.	244		53

Football League Appearances September 1908–July 1984

Player	Total Apps	Came on as sub	Gls
Miller L.	56		22
Miller P.R.	138	2	5
Minter W.J.	243		94
Moran J.	12		
Morgan R.E.	68	2	8
Moores I.R.	29	4	6
Morris T.	63		2
Morrison J.A.	133		87
Morton J.	2		
Mullery A.P.	312		25
Murphy P.	38		14
Naylor T.M.P.	243	6	
Neighbour J.E.	119	15	8
Newman E.	30		7
Nicholls J.H.	124		
Nicholson W.	314		6
Norman M.	357		16
O'Callaghan E.	252		93
Oliver W.	2		
O'Reilly G.	45	6	
Osborne F.R.	210		78
Osgood K.	113	1	13
Owen A.W.	1		
Page A.E.	55		
Parks T.	19		
Pearce J.J.	141	33	21
Pearson J.	47		
Perryman S.J.	590	1	29
Peters M.S.	189		46
Phypers E.	30		
Piper R.D.	1		
Pitt S.W.	1		
Possee D.J.	19		4
Poynton C.	152		3
Pratt J.A.	331	24	39
Price P.	42	4	
Ramsey A.E.	226		24
Rance C.S.	103		
Reddish J.	6		
Rees W.	11		3
Reynolds R.S.M.	86		
Richardson J.	38		
Ringrose A.	10		
Robb G.W.	182		53
Roberts G.	120	9	14
Roberts W.T.	4		2
Robertson J.G.	157	4	25
Robinson M.J.	6	1	2
Robshaw H.K.	1		
Roe T.W.	7		4
Ross J.	7		
Rowe A.S.	182		

Player	Total Apps	Came on as sub	Gls
Rowley R.W.M.	24		10
Rundle C.R.	28		12
Ryden J.J.	63		2
Sage W.	12		
Sanders A.W.	13		7
Sargent F.A.	93		24
Saul F.L.	116	4	37
Scarth J.W.	7		3
Scott J.	18		4
Seeburg M.	1		
Seed J.M.	229		64
Sharp B.	3		
Sharpe F.C.	2		1
Skinner G.	1		
Skinner J.F.	89		3
Skitt H.	212		
Smailes J.	16		3
Smith B.	291		9
Smith G.M.	40	3	1
Smith J.R.	2		
Smith J. (1919–39)	30		
Smith J. (1946–81)	21		1
Smith R.A.	271		176
Smy J.	17		6
Southey P.C.	1		
Sparrow H.	18		7
Spelman I.	28		2
Spiers C.H.	158		
Sproston B.	9		
Stead M.J.	15	1	
Steel A.	1		
Steel D.	129		3
Steel R.	226		40
Stevens G.	40	3	4
Stevens L.W.	54		5
Stokes A.F.	65		40
Tate J.A.	4		
Tattersall W.	44		3
Taylor A.	60		
Taylor P.J.	123	7	31
Thomas D.	27	1	
Thompson A.	153		20
Tickridge S.	95		
Tomkin A.H.	2		
Toulouse C.H.	2		
Townley J.C.	3		2
Trailor C.H.	11		
Tull W.D.	10		2
Uphill D.E.	6		1
Upton S.	2		

Player	Total Apps	Came on as sub	Gls
Venables T.	115	1	5
Villa J.R.	133	9	18
Walden F.	215		21
Walford S.J.	2	1	
Walley E.	5		
Walters C.	106		
Walters W.E.	209		66
Walton J.	24		2
Want A.G.	50	4	
Ward R.A.	115		10
Webster F.	82		
Webster S.		3	1
Weir F.	96		2
Weller K.	21	2	1
Wetton R.	45		
Whatley W.J.	226		2
Whitchurch C.H.	8		2
White J.A.	183		40
White S.E.	20		
Wilding H.T.	12		1
Wilkes F.	57		
Willis A.	144		1
Wilson C.	54		27
Withers C.F.	154		
Woodruff C.L.	10		1
Woods A.E.	6		
Woodward H.J.	63		1
Woodward V.	27		19
Woolcott R.A.	1		
Worley L.F.	1		
Wright A.	3		1
Yorath T.C.	48	4	1
Young A.	5		3
Young C.	4		
Young W.D.	54		3
Own goals			61

Notes: Appearances are for Football league games only and exclude the three games played at the beginning of the 1939–40 season. Also excluded are Southern League and all Wartime League appearances.

Goals are in Football League games only.

Figures are correct up to the end of the 1983–84 season.

Total appearances column includes **all** occasions when player came onto pitch i.e. includes occasions when player came on as sub. Came on as sub column is as stated i.e. it does **not** include occasions when player was sub but did not appear.

Bibliography

The best books written on Tottenham Hotspur were by Julian Holland – *Spurs* in 1954 and *Spurs – the Double* in 1961. The first of these, published before the era of Bill Nicholson, concentrates in great detail on the club's early years and the author was able to interview some of the founders. I can strongly recommend it to anyone who wishes to learn more about the pre-1951 period. The first real history of the club was put together in 1920 and 1921 by the *Tottenham Weekly Herald* and was later published as a pamphlet. It is also an invaluable source of reference, as is the first full history in book form, written in 1946 to celebrate the club's 75th season. This was called *History of Tottenham Hotspur 1882–1946* and was written by club director G. Wagstaffe-Simmons.

The Glory Game by Hunter Davies, published in 1972, is mentioned at length in the text of this history and is still regarded as the most entertaining and controversial look at any League club. I can recommend it to anyone interested in Tottenham, though many at the club retain a rather ambivalent attitude towards it. It was, nonetheless, a valuable insight and source of information for this history. There are two extremely good books on the double – Julian Holland's *Spurs – The Double*, which captures the mood of excitement perfectly, and Danny Blanchflower's *The Double and Before*, which gives a good insider's view of that season. There are numerous biographies and autobiographies of ex-Spurs players, many of which are still on sale. The most valuable of these, to me, have been Jimmy Seed's *The Jimmy Seed Story* and Stephen Studd's recent *Herbert Chapman: Football Emperor*. There are several histories published in recent years, of which I should mention Ralph Finn's *Tottenham Hotspur FC* (1972) and Anton Rippon's *The Tottenham Hotspur Story* (1981). Deryk Brown's *The Tottenham Hotspur Story*, published in 1971, is relatively short but is by far the most entertaining history I have read.

On the records side, most of the research by Ray Spiller, the late Morley Farror, A. Porter and A. Wilson is original, but the *Tottenham Weekly Herald* was obviously a primary source. Norman Lovett has produced an excellent softback detailing all of Spurs' League results over the years called *Tottenham Hotspur Records*, while, as ever, Ian Laschke's *Rothman's Football League Records* was essential.

Much of the pre-1939 information was drawn from the *Athletic News Yearbook* (annually since 1891). Spurs have also published their own yearbook annually since 1904 and this is another essential source for any biographer. Tottenham's expeditions into Europe are best covered in John Motson and John Rowlinson's *The European Cup 1955–1980*, published by Macdonald in 1980, and David Miller's *Cup Magic*, published by Sidgwick in 1981.

Index